"A standing ovation, please, for an epic performance of an heroic breath and breadth. Superb in its being and its translations, the language leaps headlong from the pages into your space. After the invaluable first volume, this one celebrates a poetry and poetics wide awake to right now and full of sustenance: an event for the millennium."

MARY ANN CAWS, Distinguished Professor of English, French, and Comparative Literature, Graduate School, City University of New York

"Rothenberg and Joris's great anthology shows the heart and breath of poetry from the Cobra Group to the voices of Asia and new America, and lets Blake's 'Tyger' out of the bag for all lovers of poetry. What heights and depths of consciousness! What variety and elegance!"

MICHAEL MCCLURE

"Rothenberg and Joris have performed a heroic service to poets and poetry. This second volume bears out the assertion that the works gathered here constitute, not a 'minority poetics' but rather an ocean, a manifold, a non-linear habitat where we meet and remeet an extraordinary range of poetic life forms. For the reader of poetry, here is both archive and visionary adventure. For poets (and would-be poets) here is a mine of legacies, and incitement to the scope and possibilities of our own task. For students of history and culture, here is a world pulse. Though such a collection can never be definitive, this one is admirable in its generosity of spirit."

ADRIENNE RICH

Praise for *Poems for the Millennium*, volume one, recipient of the 1996 PEN Oakland Josephine Miles Award

"The word *anthology* hardly does justice to Rothenberg and Joris's brilliant reconceptualization of twentieth-century poetry in a global context. This is that rare book that forces us to rethink what the *poetic* is and can be."

MARJORIE PERLOFF

"Brilliant revision in the most basic of senses of all we'd thought was 'poetry of the twentieth century.'"

ROBERT CREELEY

"Destined to become a fundamental resource for the study of twentieth-century literature and culture. Its importance cannot be overstated."

CHARLES BERNSTEIN

D0003767

POEMS FOR THE MILLENNIUM

POEMS
for the MILLENNIUM

The University of California
Book of Modern
& Postmodern Poetry

Volume Two
From Postwar to Millennium

Edited by
Jerome Rothenberg
and
Pierre Joris

University of California Press
Berkeley   Los Angeles   London

808.81
POE
V. 2

University of California Press
Berkeley and Los Angeles, California

University of California Press, Ltd.
London, England

© 1998 by Jerome Rothenberg and Pierre Joris
ISBN 0-520-20863-3 (cloth)
ISBN 0-520-20864-1 (paper)

The Library of Congress has catalogued volume 1 as follows:

Poems for the millennium : the University of California
    book of modern & postmodern poetry / edited by
    Jerome Rothenberg and Pierre Joris.
        v.   cm.
    "A centennial book"—Vol. 1, p.
    Includes bibliographical references and index.
    Contents: v.   1. From fin-de-siècle to negritude.
    ISBN 0-520-07225-1 (v.   1).—ISBN 0-520-07227-8
    (v.   1:   pbk.)
        1. Poetry, Modern.   I. Rothenberg, Jerome, 1931– .
II. Joris, Pierre, 1946– .   III. University of California
(System)   IV. University of California Press.
PN6101.P493   1995
808.81—dc20   93-49839
                                        CIP

Printed in the United States of America
9 8 7 6 5 4 3 2 1

Credits and acknowledgments for the poems included
are on page 857.

Published in cooperation with the
ARCHIVE FOR NEW POETRY
University of California, San Diego

The publisher gratefully acknowledges the generous
contributions provided by the following organizations:

The Eric Mathieu King Fund of The Academy of American Poets

The French Cultural Services in the United States

The General Endowment Fund, which is supported by
generous gifts from the members of the Associates of
the University of California Press

CONTENTS

CONTINUITIES

A FIRST GALLERY

THE ART OF THE MANIFESTO

A SECOND GALLERY

POSTLUDES

At the Turning

For Eric Mottram (1924–1995)
poet, friend, & teacher

that all created life be rescued
from tyranny   decay sloughed for a share
in magnificence   hoof thunder   silence of
pines and birches across the taiga
E. M.

Know this:
the only game I play is the millennium
the only game I play is the Great
Fear

Put up with me. I won't put up with you!
AIMÉ CÉSAIRE

If the first book was an opening, the second is a continuation and a move-ment into future works. It is the celebration of a coming into fullness—the realization in some sense of beginnings from still earlier in the century. And yet the poetry like the time itself marks a sharp break from what went before, with World War II and the events of Auschwitz and Hiroshima creating a chasm, a true aporia between then and now. It is on the near side of that paradoxical break that our own lives first come in—not out-side history this time but living in and through it. The years the book covers are those of the cold war and its aftermath and, viewed from where we are, the time too of the second great awakening of poetry in the century now coming to an end. The story told is one that we have lived in and have found never to have been truly told, neither in its triumphs nor its failures (with an affection for the failures sometimes as great as for the triumphs). If concerns like these guided our first book, they will more strongly domi-nate our second, where we can no longer act as distant and objective view-ers but as witnesses and even partisans for the works at hand.

1 *A work resuming "in the dark"* . . .

The gathering (to use the title of one of Robert Duncan's last books) begins "in the dark": a midcentury of molten cities and scorched earth, of chimneys blowing human ashes through the air, of slaves in labor camps and gulags, of nations enslaved to other nations, of racism and apartheid rampant.[1] In that darkness the brilliant, often strident promise of an ear-

---

1. "I lived in the first century of world wars. / Most mornings I would be more or less insane" (Muriel Rukeyser).

lier avant-garde was no longer visible or viable. The surge of totalizing governments and the resultant state of war had decimated the former avant-gardes—in Germany and Russia, Italy and Japan, as in the conquered lands of Europe, Africa, and Asia. The stakes for some were death or exile, for others an underground resistance and continued struggle, for still others (all too often) a collaboration with the very advocates of power and repression that their work had set out to oppose.

The half-century that followed witnessed a continuous wave of wars and repressions, interspersed with rebellions and occasional luminous victories that for the moment seemed to light the darkness.[2] Sometimes claimed as the longest "peaceful" period in memory—a virtual *pax americana*—it could be felt (and was by those who lived it) as a continuation of the midcentury war by other means: a diffuse but unrelenting form of World War III.[3] The wars of the time were not only the American conflicts in Korea and Vietnam—and the forty-year long cold war—but hundreds of other regional conflicts, wars of independence, revolutionary guerrilla wars and uprisings, genocides, mass slaughters, cultural wars fueled by ideology and, increasingly, by ethnicity and religion. And with this too there was the sense of a natural world under continuing attack or lashing back with new plagues and hitherto undreamed-of biological disasters.

This was the darkness that came through, along with whatever other forms of darkness—and of light—moved within the cosmos or the individual psyche. "Poetry therefore as opposition," Nanni Balestrini wrote, within a neo-modernist, experimental framework. "Opposition to the dogma and conformity that overlays us, that hardens the tracks behind us, that entangles our feet, seeking to halt our steps. Today more than ever is the reason to write poetry." And Pierre Guyotat, as a further marker of the poet's relation to the art as such and to the sense of earlier betrayals: "The very origin of the whole system of literature has to be attacked."

In the United States, where experimental modernism had yet to make its ineluctable breakthrough, the first postwar decade was marked by an ascendant literary "modernism"—hostile to experiment and reduced in

2. "The dark world that is illumined is the very thing that leads poetry toward an even darker world" (Adonis).

3. "Pound, Lawrence, Joyce, H. D., Eliot, have a black voice when speaking of the contemporary scene, an enduring memory of the first World War that has revealed the deep-going falsehood and evil of the modern state. . . . Their threshold remains ours. The time of war and exploitation, the infamy and lies of the new capitalist war-state, continue. And the answering intensity of the imagination to hold its own values must continue" (Robert Duncan, quoted by Nathaniel Mackey).

And William Carlos Williams: "Poetry is a rival government always in opposition to its cruder replicas."

consequence to a vapid, often stuffy middle-ground approximation. It was in that sense the Age of Eliot (T. S.) and of the *new* critics, as they were then called—not as an extension of Eliot's collage-work in *The Waste Land,* say, but as a dominant and retrograde poetics in which the *old* ways of the English "great tradition" were trotted out and given privilege. The mark of that time, revived in every decade since, was a return to prescriptive rhyme and meter: a rejection thereby of the uncertainties of *free verse* and the barely remembered *freed words* of a Mallarmé or Marinetti. Wrote the poet Delmore Schwartz, as one of those then in ascendance: "The poetic revolution, the revolution in poetic taste which was inspired by the criticism of T. S. Eliot . . . has established itself in power." And he gave as an example of new poets writing in "a style which takes as its starting point the poetic idiom and literary taste of the generation of Pound and Eliot," the following from W. D. Snodgrass:

> The green catalpa tree has turned
> All white; the cherry blooms once more.
> In one whole year I haven't learned
> A blessed thing they pay you for

—at which David Antin looked back and commented (circa 1972): "The comparison of this updated version of *A Shropshire Lad* . . . and the poetry of the *Cantos* or *The Waste Land* seems so aberrant as to verge on the pathological."

Yet it was typical. Inevitable, in fact, for those who couldn't distinguish between "the poetic revolution" and a "revolution in taste," or who still thought of taste as an issue. Even an attempt at such distinctions was then unlikely, for the careers of the inheritors were too often literary, resting like the idea of literature itself on a fixed notion of poetry and poem, which might be improved upon but never questioned *at the root.* And behind it too there was a strange fear of "freedom" as articulated by earlier, truly radical ("experimental") moderns—whether as "free verse" or "free love" or the abandonment of judgment as a bind on the intelligence or of taste as a determinant of value.[4] So if the taste and judgment they still clung to (and which made them critics "inspired by the criticism of T. S. Eliot") demanded "modern" as an article of twentieth-century faith, they retained it, but they pulled back into traditional and institutional securities, "picking up again the meters" (Schwartz) as a moral, even a political buttress against their own midcentury despair. And this itself,

---

4. "My eyes are erotic. My intelligence is erotic. / All combinations are possible" (Göran Sonnevi).

qua ideology, was made a part of a *modern* dilemma, which came to define their rapidly evaporating modern-ism—not as a promise of a new consciousness but as a glorified "failure of nerve."

Against which a counterpoetics was quickly starting to develop—a push, foremost, to find new beginnings (or to retrieve old ones) appropriate to the time.

2   *The work in all its fullness . . .*

The *postwar* when it came, then, came from all directions. In that coming it faced both a modernism stuck dead in its tracks and a resurgence of much of what that modernism *at its fullest* had set out to challenge. The new turning in America—in full motion by the middle 1950s—was central to our own perception but only a part of a much greater global whole. The *war,* which William Carlos Williams called "the first and only thing in the world today," was of course the great dividing line—and with it the *bomb* that put an end, he also reminded us, to much that was past, while

> all suppressions,
> from the witchcraft trials at Salem
> to the latest
> book burnings
> are confessions
> that the bomb
> has entered our lives
> to destroy us.

By which he meant that the stakes were now raised and would remain raised to the present millennium's end and the next millennium's beginning. It was from here that the new generations—*everywhere*—were to take their start.

The nature of that start was not so much post*modern*—as it would come to be called—as it was post-bomb and post-holocaust. Or it was postmodern in the sense that Tristan Tzara had spoken of Dada three decades before, naming a resistance that called both past and present into question, including all those "modern schools" that still obeyed the rule of empire. It was this rebellion and rejection, this "great refusal" at its extreme, that marked all that was best in what was then beginning to take shape. As such its extremes, which typified it as the stance of a new avant-garde, represented a diverse development and/or a series of departures from what had come before. Alongside the revival of the full range of modern (modernist) moves, more notable expansions and divergences were taking place—from critiques as correctives of an art mislabeled "modern" to more far-reaching departures from Renaissance-derived modernities and the reclaiming of (old) powers in the name of what Charles Olson early called *"postmodern* man." Rightly or wrongly named, the term and the issues raised thereby (but never resolved or capable as such of resolution) came to define the time and poetics in question.

The following, then, are some aspects of that time, which to a great extent is still the time we live in.

There was a breakdown, first, of the more tyrannical aspects of the earlier literary and art movements, and a turning away with that from totalizing/authoritarian ideologies and individuals. Such a stance—"against all *isms,* against all that implied a system" (C. Dotremont)—was in that sense a matter of both life *and* art.[5] On its political and social sides, it was marked by a generally leftward tilt—rarely the fascist and totalitarian temptations of many of the prewar poets, though not entirely immune to a seductive totalitarianism of the left from time to time. The result was the appearance by the 1960s of a new "dialectics of liberation," political and personal, marked by a sense of resistance, of breaking free (in word and act, mind and body), while retaining a more-than-formalist conception of the poem as vehicle-for-transformation. Wrote Allen Ginsberg, drawing from an older source: "When the mode of the music changes, the walls of the city shake." And the Japanese "postwar poets" (in a "demand" voiced by Ōoka Makoto): "Bring back totality through poetry."[6]

The "liberation" saw a resurgence, along with more stabilized forms of poem-making, of old and new varieties of *free* verse and *freed* words ("concrete," "projective," "open," "variable," and so on). Along with this came the assertion—and practice—of other freedoms in the poem and, by implication *and* assertion, in the world beyond.[7] Thus the poem was again and decisively opened to the full range of the demotic (spoken) language, but with the freedom also to move between demotic and hieratic (= "literary") modes, or into other areas of discourse long out of bounds for poetry. For a number of the poets in these pages this meant an opening to

5. "Art's obscured the difference between art and life. Now let life obscure the difference between life and art" (John Cage).

6. And from another direction the Nigerian poet/novelist Chinua Achebe: "New forms must stand ready to be called into being as often as new (threatening) forces appear on the scene. It is like 'earthing' an electrical charge to ensure communal safety."

7. "Today freedom is more in need of inventors than defenders" (André Breton).

popular modes and voices—a breakdown of distinctions that prefigured the "pop art" soon to come and later merged with it. At a deeper or older ("folk") level this was matched by the appearance of submerged languages (dialects and idiolects) as new/old vehicles for poetry: the Viennese of H. C. Artmann and others, the Friulian of Pier Paolo Pasolini, the Jamaican "nation language" in oral works by Michael Smith or Miss Queenie (and the written variations by Kamau Brathwaite), the appropriations of "black speech" in the work of African-American writers (and others) too numerous to mention, the pidgin writings of Pacific poets in a range of *topoi* from New Guinea to Hawaii. *And so on.* Wrote the American poet John Ashbery of his own very real and very different aspirations in that direction: "My idea is to democratize all forms of expression . . . the idea that both the most demotic and the most elegant forms of expression deserve equally to be taken into account."

This, then, is fulfillment. It is a wedge, among many, by which *all* words will enter into presence—as in Whitman's prophecy (circa 1860) of a total poetry that would (like "the Real Dictionary" he also envisioned) incorporate "all words that exist in use, the bad words as well as any. . . . [Like language itself] an enormous treasure-house, or range of treasure-houses . . . full of ease, definiteness and power—full of sustenance." In such a poetry, with its open and unlimited vocabulary, all subjects/themes were also possible—from the most demeaned to the most exalted, from the most commonplace to the most learned, from myth to history and back, from present into past and future.[8] While the first round of breakthroughs had occurred in the earlier twentieth century, the realizations and divagations now were coming helter skelter—and with them a persistent questioning (experimental and [soon to be] "post" modern) of language's relation to any experience whatever, to any reality, even that of language itself.[9]

The results are contradictory and often *self*-contradictory, yet one senses behind them a commonness of purpose: to throw down *and* restore. And with this comes a necessary reassertion of the role of the poet as seer and chronicler. The former guise, which an earlier neoclassic tilt had covered over, was the image that vibrated through the Beat poetics (and much else) from the mid-1950s on, and in its assertion across the globe included an

8. "The gift is that you are forced to put much more of the world into the poem. Sometimes it feels as though the poem is carrying you along. You have access to a universe that begins to carry you . . . into something that you would never have been able to see or write" (Inger Christensen).

9. Again Adonis: "The poem will be transgression. And yet, like the head of Orpheus, the poem will navigate on the river Universe, completely contained in the body of language."

exploration of different forms of postsurrealist writing and an alliance for some with previously suppressed religious and cultural forms: shamanism, tantrism, sufism, kabbala, peyotism, etc. It also saw the reappearance of what Allen Ginsberg spoke of as a *heroic* poetics: a renewed willingness to thrust the poet forward as a heroic, even sacrificial figure in defense of self and tribe, of human and mammal life (M. McClure)—and with that, of poetry itself.[10] (The moments of public breakthrough—for Ginsberg and others—were notable in early resistance to the Vietnam War, in *samizdat* and underground publication in the crumbling Soviet orb, and in the many independence movements of the postcolonial "third world.") In more literary terms, the second half of the twentieth century was marked by the reassertion, in the persistent (and false) divide between classicism and romanticism, of the romantic impulse—with a spiritual and material force that dominated the early postwar period and has remained a presence thereafter.

While what was at issue here was a poetry of displacements and dreamings, it was accompanied (sometimes in the same work) by a new "objectism": an imagism of the familiar ("here-and-now") and an unprecedented *poetry of fact*. In the formulation by the Nicaraguan poet Ernesto Cardenal, the call was for a new "*exteriorismo* . . . [an] objective poetry . . . made with elements of real life and concrete things, with proper names and precise details and exact data, statistics, facts, and quotations." Behind it was a half-century of explorations, from those that focused on "minute particulars" (the poems of Francis Ponge and Marianne Moore are eminent examples) to variations on Ezra Pound's recasting of the epic ("long poem") as "a poem including history." That definition—or something close to it—prefigured "maximal" works by poets like William Carlos Williams, Louis Zukofsky, Melvin Tolson, Muriel Rukeyser, Robert Duncan, Charles Olson, Theodore Enslin, Robert Kelly, and Anne Waldman in the United States, and elsewhere by poets like Pablo Neruda, Vladimir Holan, Anna Akhmatova, Ernesto Cardenal, Hugh MacDiarmid, and René Depestre. With an eye toward the contemporary political implications of "history," the push was later extended by Ed Sanders to an "investigative poetry" in which "lines of lyric beauty descend from . . . data clusters [:] . . . a form of historical writing . . . using *every* bardic skill and meter and method of the last 5 or 6 generations, in order to describe *every* aspect (no more secret governments!) of the historical present."[11]

10. "If anybody wants a statement of values—it is this, that I am ready to die for Poetry & for the truth that inspires poetry—and will do so in any case—as all men, whether they like it or no—" (A.G., 1961).

11. "The twentieth century, in its violence, has brought about the marriage of Poetry and History" (Hélène Cixous).

Such an effort as (re)visioning was tied as well to the reinvestigation and reconfiguration of the entire *poetic* past and present—a major subtext, surely, of the present volumes. In a "postcolonial" world it became one way—again among many—for poets to come forward as voices for "nation" or "tribe" or "community" (as elsewhere for "nature" and "world"), or to explore, increasingly, the specifics of ethnicity and gender as they entered into thought and word.[12] Here, as elsewhere in the art of the postwar, the work laid claim to a renewed permission and validity, both as "investigative poetry" and as a vehicle for *direct* political resistance—in contrast to the outright dismissal of such political poetry by "new critics" and "high" modernists on the one hand and by Surrealists in the mode of Breton on the other. Concurrently, and contrastively as well, there was a renewed sense of history as *personal* history: the inner life, including the deepest areas of sexuality and hitherto covert desires, (again) laid bare.[13] In this the resultant work went far beyond the psychological limits and distress of the (so-called) "confessional" poets of the 1960s, edging toward what Clayton Eshleman, with the likes of Antonin Artaud as forerunners, spoke of as the "construction of the underworld" and traced back, as a form of "grotesque realism," to its (painted) sources in the cave art of the late Paleolithic.

Here is a tension, then, between extremes of the personal and communal—the "unspeakable visions of the individual" (J. Kerouac) and the reconstructed "tale of the tribe" (E. Pound). (It is from a number of such "tensions" or "oppositions" that our work as a whole has been constructed.) In the working out of those extremes, both formal and historical explorations came up against what Alfredo Guiliani, writing for the Italian Novissimi, demanded as "a genuine 'reduction of the I' as producer of meaning," or what Olson, in a famous act of condemnation (more exactly, of realignment and questioning), called "the getting rid of the lyrical interference of the individual as ego." But alongside the continuing "inwardness" of Olson's developing poetics (= "projective verse"),[14] there were

12. "It is inconceivable that any Caribbean poet writing today is not going to be influenced by [the] submerged [Caribbean] culture, which is, in fact, an emerging culture. . . . At last our poets today are recognizing that it is essential that they use the resources that have always been there, but which have been denied to them—which they have sometimes themselves denied" (Kamau Brathwaite).

"To write directly and overtly as a woman, out of a woman's body and experience, to take woman's existence seriously as theme and source for art" (Adrienne Rich).

13. Note, for example, the important assertion within a new feminist poetry & art (circa 1970) that the "personal" is in fact the "political."

14. ". . . But if he stays inside himself, if he is contained within his nature as he is participant in the larger force, he will be able to listen, and his hearing through himself will give him secrets objects share" (C. O.).

other attempts at still more objective, non-"expressionistic" methods of composition. These included not only experiments with systematic (objective) chance operations—a tension (post-Dada) between "chance" and "choice," as notable in the works, e.g., of Jackson Mac Low and John Cage—but a concern with other procedural, even mechanical (machine-derived) methods that seemed, momentarily at least, to put the will in suspension, to allow the poem "to write itself," and by so doing, to invite still more of the world to enter the poem.[15] There is in this approach—in Europe, the United States, and elsewhere—something like Wittgenstein's sense of philosophy as "a struggle with the fascination that forms of expression have upon us." (Both the poignancy and force of such a dictum, when transferred to poetry, are here worth noting.)

This interrogation of language, or of the language-reality nexus as such, was from the late 1940s (and continuing, increasingly, into the present) the second great arena for what came to be called the "postmodern." Here the experiencing *self*, while never disappearing, was superseded by processes of language and by the appropriation and redirection of texts and utterances already present in the language. The outcome was a number of versions of what the Cobra poets, say, or the European "situationists" spoke of as a *détournement*—not merely a "diversion" or "deflection" of an inherited text but, as stated elsewhere by Ken Knabb, "a turning aside from the normal course or purpose (often with an illicit connotation)." Such a turning, twist, or "torque" (G. Quasha) was deeply sourced in earlier workings with collage and in the language-centered experiments of predecessors like Gertrude Stein, Velimir Khlebnikov, and Kurt Schwitters, among others. But what had been the scattered, sometimes casual breakthroughs of that earlier time now took new directions and became the central work of poets in many different places. Such foregroundings of language had also influenced a number of key figures in areas like philosophy or ethnology, and these in turn would come to influence or interact with the postwar generations of poets, particularly in the reconceptualization of poetry as a function of language and, inversely, language as a function of *poesis*.

At work here was a renewed focus on language's role in shaping the perception of reality, with the poets' experimental work vindicated and enriched, for example, by linguistic investigations like those of Benjamin Lee Whorf on the nature of non-Indoeuropean languages such as Hopi

15. "All of these are ways to let in forces other than yourself . . . possibilities that one's habitual associations—what we usually draw on in the course of spontaneous or intuitive composition—would have precluded" (Jackson Mac Low).

and Maya.[16] Similarly, many of the old questions on "the nature of representation" received new formulations and thought, both in the practice of the poets (articulated as *poetics* by, e.g., the Italian Neo-Avanguardia, the U.S.-centered Language Poets, and, maybe primarily, the French *Tel Quel* group) and in the developing "science" of semiotics (from Ferdinand de Saussure early in the twentieth century to various poststructuralisms in the [almost] present). If such metapoetic concerns could open a window on alternative language possibilities, they also pointed to the trap inherent in a language-dominated universe—a trap of language through which the poet would have to break, Artaud had warned us, "in order to touch life."[17] Given the allure and danger of that situation, the response was either to investigate the laws and limits (= rules) of language or to break those rules deliberately; to devise new ways of "making language" (thereby making—or denying—meaning) or to play variations on language as discovered in a range of cultural/linguistic contexts.

Related to all that—and a point of reference, often, in poet-directed discussions of poetics—was the sense that the poet, like all humans, is a vehicle through or by which language speaks. Outside the immediate poetry nexus, the point revealed itself in Heidegger's insistence, say, that it is language that thinks, rather than man, in Wittgenstein's related meditations ("the limits of my language mean the limits of my world"), or in Lacan's formulation that "the unconscious is structured like language." While such views triggered active responses from poets, they were less a revelation than a confirmation of what had long been known—that language has always been both familiar *and* uncanny, and that there is a point at which one can say with Rimbaud, e.g.: "I do not think but I am thought." What was news for critics and theorists, then, was a familiar realization (and practice) for poets, those in particular who were conversant with shamanic and other forms of mediumship, with western/romantic ideas of inspiration and numinosity, with zeitgeists and collective unconsciouses. In its more extreme formulations (early Roland Barthes, say, and the later post-everything critical establishment, especially in U.S. academia), the autonomy of language devolved into the canard of "the death of the author."[18] Yet news of the latter's death has been much exaggerated:

16. "We are thus introduced to a new principle of relativity which holds that all observers are not led by the same physical evidence to the same picture of the universe, unless their linguistic backgrounds are similar or can in some way be calibrated" (Benjamin Lee Whorf).

17. "Reality is not simply there, it must be searched for and won" (Paul Celan).

18. Don Byrd: "[We] can no longer abide the scaleless world in which theory and its prose disciplines dislocate us." And David Antin: "When I hear the word 'deconstruction,' I reach for my pillow."

the authors are alive and writing, in full awareness (both ludic and serious) of language's ambiguous and sometimes awesome nature—as we hope this volume shows.

Under such circumstances—historical and intellectual—the period witnessed the full panoply of modernist/postmodernist projections, increased in number and pursued with a precision and thoroughness that elevated some areas to the status of a new art, even (though one speaks of this now with caution) of a new life.[19] As in the earlier half of the century, this work was marked by a number of emphases that both denied the possibility of closure and at the same time moved, however fitfully, toward fulfillment. These emphases, tentatively presented in the first of our two volumes, can be emended for inclusion here:

- an exploration of new forms of language, consciousness, and social/biological relationships, both by deliberate experimentation in the present and by reinterpretation of the "entire" human past;
- poetry-art intersections in which conventional boundaries between arts break down, sometimes involving generalized art movements (Cobra, Fluxus) often led by poets and with a poetics at their center;
- experiments with dream work and altered forms of consciousness (from the continuation of Surrealist dream experiments to the psychedelic experiments of the 1960s, the meditative experiments of the 1970s, and beyond) in which language itself becomes an instrument of vision;
- a return to the concept of poetry as a performance genre: a spin-off both from earlier modernist sources (Futurism, Dada) and from still viable oral traditions, and ranging from avant-garde theater and soundtext works to the readings, "slams" and musical improvisations (jazz, rock, and other) of a new "performance poetry";
- language experiments, including the soundtext works mentioned above, as well as experiments with visual and typographical forms, book works, attempts to develop a nonsyntactic and nonreferential poetry;
- a renewed privileging of the demotic language, along with a turn on the one hand toward prose as an instrument of poetry and on the other toward the exploration of previously suppressed languages (including

19. "What, then, is the postmodern? . . . It is undoubtedly a part of the modern. All that has been received, if only yesterday (modo, modo, Petronius used to say), must be suspected. . . . A work can become modern only if it is first postmodern. Postmodernism thus understood is not modernism at its end but in the nascent state, and this state is constant" (J. F. Lyotard). And Jackson Mac Low: "post-nuttin'."

the genuine languages of the deaf, not shown here) or of those sublanguages (dialects, idiolects, creoles, pidgins, etc.) that had long been at the fringes of accepted literature;

- in the American instance, an early push for a "new measure" as a tightening and strengthening of the century-long and nearly global commitment to *free* verse, and a related if contrary view (both here and elsewhere) of the poem as raw, unfinished, and ineluctably in process;

- ethnopoetics and similar reassessments of the past and of alternative poetries in the present: a broadening of cultural terrains, directed by the sense of an ancient and often surviving subterranean tradition with the poetic impulse at its center;

- a widespread attack on the dominance in art and life of European "high" culture, leading in the last decades of the twentieth century to a proliferation of movements stressing exploration and expansion of ethnic and gender as well as class identities;

- a concurrent if contradictory move toward a new globalism, even nomadism—an intercultural poetics that could break across the very boundaries and definitions of self and nation that were a latent source of its creative powers;

- an ongoing if shifting connection to related political and social movements, with an increasing emphasis on an openness and freedom of expression and a gradual veering away from what had become, heroically but often disastrously, an age of ideologies;

- a widely held belief that poetry is part of a struggle to save the wild places—in the world and in the mind—and a view of the poem itself as a wild thing and of both poetry and poet as endangered species;

- a sense of excitement and play ("to work in the excitedness of pure being . . . to get back that intensity into the language"—G. Stein) that must be brought across to show the work of the age in all its color and as the poetry "that might be fantastic life" (R. Duncan).

With all of this the time has been remarkable too for the unprecedented degree of participation by poets in the formulation—individual by individual or group by group—of a large array of speculative poetics: writings that assert autonomy and connect the work and life of each poet to the larger human fate. That there is an absence of unanimity in these writings is a point that we would like to stress, although our attempts at synthesis may sometimes give the opposite impression. There is also no question but that we are ourselves participants, not just observers, and that our participation colors all we've done here. It would be foolish then—even more so than with our first volume—to view what follows as an attempt to set up a new canon of contemporaries. Rather, as before, we would have the anthology serve a more useful function, as a mapping of the possibilities— some among many—that have continued to open up for us—here and now, at the century's turning.

It is the richness of those openings that may define this time.

3 *The work from all directions* . . .

That the early "postwar" corresponded with the great American moment (the "American century") is quite clear. Its impact on our poetry as such appeared most convincingly in *The New American Poetry,* edited by Donald Allen in 1960: a summary of experimental work over the previous decade and a half and the most public challenge till then to the entrenched middle-ground poetry and poetics of the 1950s. Concerning the poets gathered therein, Allen wrote: "They are our avant-garde, the true continuers of the modern movement in American poetry. Through their work many are closely allied to modern jazz and abstract expressionist painting, today recognized throughout the world to be America's greatest achievements in contemporary culture. This anthology makes the same claim for the new American poetry, now becoming the dominant movement in the second phase of our twentieth-century literature and already exerting strong influence abroad." Yet what was less apparent for many of those participating in or being drawn to it was that what was happening in American poetry was part of a larger *global* awakening, some of it occurring before or apart from the American influence as such—and some of it in collaboration with or influencing other young Americans in turn. (That other avant-gardes were active in the United States should also be considered.)

We are saying this, of course, with something over forty years of hindsight. What was then revealing itself from outside the U.S. was the work of an earlier generation that poets in America were (and, to some extent, still are) in the process of (re)discovering. Just as word was coming back about the older American "Objectivists" (themselves becoming visible again as makers of a transitional "new American poetry"), the poets recovered from elsewhere included the likes of Neruda and Vallejo (poet-heros of the other "America"), of Surrealist masters like Breton and Artaud (disregarded by the American middle-grounders in favor of less "convulsive" practitioners like Eluard and Desnos), of Dadaists like Tzara and Ball or like Kurt Schwitters, whose work was hinted at—but only hinted at—in Robert Motherwell's great *Dada Painters and Poets* (1951), another generative, albeit historical, anthology appearing in the postwar time. And there were glimmerings too of an older but still obscure generation of Negritude poets in Africa and the Caribbean—a whole world, in fact, to reassemble.

What was known by the end of the 1950s, much of it obscured by the antimodernist turn at the beginning of the decade, was imperative to know. What was not known—obscured here by a heady breakthrough as *American* poets (pre–Viet Nam)—was how much else was coming into presence then or had emerged, even in this most American of centuries and moments, without our blessings. Over the last few years the two editors have had a chance to go over the terrain of the immediate postwar decades (1945 to 1960, the years of the New American Poetry per se) and to carry that exploration into the still less charted places that define the boundaries of the present gathering. This has been fired in some sense by our own nomadism[20] and our sense of a community / a commonality of poets that both of us have known (and continue to know) across whatever boundaries. Being far enough away now to have a wider view of that terrain, we see the "new American poetry" as itself a part (a key part, sure, but still a part) of a worldwide series of moves and movements that took the political, visionary, and formal remnants of an earlier modernism and reshaped and reinvented them in the only time allowed to us on earth.

What we would like to give our readers, then—who will no doubt be American in the main—is a sense of the configuration, the reconfiguration we've attempted—both to see how the sweep of a U.S. "postmodernism" fits into that larger frame and how much richer the work from then down to the present is when considered in something like its wholeness. In our first volume we tried a similar approach, covering a range of work "from fin-de-siècle to negritude"—from Mallarmé's *Coup de dès* of 1897 to work appearing in the midst of World War II. The division there was into three "galleries" of individual poets and six sections devoted to the movements that typified the time but have been deliberately omitted or reduced to footnotes in most other gatherings of poetry. (These were, in order, Futurism [both Russian and Italian], Expressionism, Dada, Surrealism, the "Objectivists," and Negritude.) In doing this we were not being origi-

---

20. "A nomadic poetics will cross languages, not just translate, but write in all or any of them. If Pound, Joyce, & others have shown the way, it is essential now to push this matter further, again, not as 'collage' but as a material flux of language matter, moving in & out of semantic & non-semantic spaces, moving around & through the features accreting as a poem, a lingo-cubism that is no longer an 'explosante fixe,' as Breton defined the poem, but an 'explosante mouvante' " (P. J.).

nal (or even "ornery" in some sense) but asserting what for many of us was the actual configuration of that time. We were also setting the stage for the second volume—approaching the present world in which we live and work.

With the second volume—from World War II to the (almost) present—there is no completion, and the omissions and gaps are unavoidable. Having said that, it is our hope that the book will give a view of poetry "from all directions" and will allow a reading of U.S. poetry and poets juxtaposed with sometimes equally experimental, sometimes more experimental poetry from elsewhere. (For this reason, with America as the point of departure, the amount of American poetry is and remains disproportionate.) Overall, the question of inclusion and exclusion, which can never be properly resolved, was less important with regard to individuals and movements—more with regard to the possibilities of poetry now being opened.[21] There are two galleries this time around, the first and earlier consisting largely of poets who were or became active during the 1940s and 1950s, the second of those who became active in the 1960s, 1970s, and (but here our offerings become more minimal) in the 1980s and 1990s. And within these galleries we've embedded a number of groupings—somewhat like the movements of the previous volume, but often more localized or more restricted (with several notable exceptions) to moves in poetry rather than across the arts, although that poetry may itself show real amalgams with the plastic arts or music. The point, anyway, is not to trace influences from group to group but to set out a range of responses to the postwar (cold war) era and to the time and the places in which the poets lived.

The first gallery, then, consists of work from some fifty poets—from Marie Luise Kaschnitz, born in 1901, to Gary Snyder, born in 1930. It follows a small opening section ("Prelude"), which announces our point of departure among the disasters of war and fascism, counterpointed by a section of poems by some of the poets who appeared in the earlier volume but whose postwar poetry—often "maximal" as Olson would have had it—showed a meaningful continuity between the century's two halves. But it's in the contents of the first gallery as such that the richness of the time begins to assert itself—a richness measured in fact by its unboundedness.

21. Where a choice was to be made, however, we put ourselves deliberately on the side of what we took to be the "experimental" and "disruptive"—in U.S. terms the "new American poetry" (particularly the emphases on "measure" and "history") and its later offshoots and extensions, alongside the Fluxus tradition (below) of "erasing the boundaries between art and life," between genres and divergent art forms, etc. Even so there is no way of accounting for all poets of interest during this time.

It is a configuration of contemporaries—already ours—and of possibilities—ours also—with regard to which the vaunted American dominance (forty years later) seems a clear exaggeration. That we may feel a kinship (and sometimes open friendship) with *all* those present here and elsewhere in the book is a further point worth making.

The second gallery continues in the same way, taking as examples work from close to sixty poets, from the Congolese Tchicaya U Tam'si, born in 1931, to the American-Korean Theresa Hak Kyung Cha, born in 1951. If there are breaks between the two galleries, there are also mergers and collaborations, and a growing ease with the means inherited from earlier generations—as well as a sense of the problematic and contentious as necessary characteristics of poetry in a time of experiment and change. Our moves here are much more tentative, much more open to question (our own self-questionings included), than in our first volume, for we are speaking now from within the field—at a point, that is, where participation colors observation, and distance, if at all desired, is near impossible to come by. We have therefore let the poets speak, as much as possible, on their own behalfs, peppering our commentaries with a variety of poets' self-accountings, in the belief that each citation can in some sense enter as a "special view" of poetry and of the world and mindset from which that poetry emerges. In a similar vein, we have compiled a section of poems and extracts, occupying the center of our book, in which poets of the latter half of the century continue to exercise and develop the "art of the manifesto" that has been a crucial mark of avant-garde production "from then to now." And we conclude the volume with a group of postludes—two poems of our own and one by Robert Duncan, which he wrote, still with hope, at the time of his final illness.

Along with the individual poets presented in our "galleries"—and there are, clearly, many more of consequence—groupings began to appear and common themes and practices began to be visible: mini-movements with some resemblance to the larger movements of the prewar time. Some were confined to a single place and language or to a narrow set of places, others to a sweep that cut more boldly than their predecessors across divides of place and nation. Six of the ones we've chosen and inserted in our galleries were already active in the 1950s, two of those as far back as the later 1940s, while three were creatures mainly of the seventies and eighties. The remaining two inserted sections, "oral poetries" and "cyberpoetics," are more like curatorial groupings—constructions by the editors, intended to foreground certain widespread but largely unformulated currents. The thrust in almost all was toward a rupture with the past, or a renewal of the interrupted ruptures of the prewar avant-gardes, now made more urgent by the wars and cold wars of the time and by a sense of dangers and repressions still persisting.

As with our individual selections, we are aware of many of the other groupings that could have been included in a work like ours—from the German Gruppe '47 to the poets around the French *Tel Quel* or *Change* "collectives," from key U.S. movements like the Black Mountain poets of the 1950s or the Umbra (African-American) poets of the 1960s to still active configurations such as the British Poetry Revival initiated in the 1970s or the Argentinian "Xul" group of the 1980s and 1990s. (Individual poets connected with some of these groupings do in fact show up in the gallery sections.) Our mapping is thus more an indication of the ongoing importance of community and collaboration than some final or exhaustive taxonomy of movements. This is borne out, as a primary example, by the absence in the book of a section devoted specifically to such a pivotal and genuinely international movement as "Fluxus," despite the fact that we have long taken it as one of the groupings of artists & poets truly originary for the period. (We had thought at one point of using the word "fluxus" in the subtitling of our second volume.) Still, almost all of the group's central poets are presented somewhere in these pages, since in the view of the editors the Fluxus stance, with its emphasis on the merging of art and life, on intermedia, and on an ironic relation to the products of consumer culture, can be seen as the "invisible college" pervading much (in some sense *most*) of this era's central work. With its opening to the whole range of previously "experimental" methods—chance operations, textsound, concrete poetry, & so on—it both challenged the academicized "modernism" of its time and incorporated most of the practices connected with the most formally disruptive side of avant-garde poetry and art. That Fluxus has been literally obliterated from other histories of poetry is yet another point worth making.

Our intention as editors has been to act against such obliterations, not toward a new narrowing of poetry but toward its further opening. In that light we have felt ourselves driven by a sense that the near past of poetry has never been adequately presented—that a truer presentation has long been needed, both to reaffirm the work of the present and to lay (again) the groundwork for the future. Acceptance or rejection could then follow, but it would no longer be a judgment based on ignorance or on a deliberate ignoring or misreading of what had already happened. As with our first volume we have tried to avoid a doctrinaire avant-gardism while presenting works that test the limits of poetry, but we recognize that this has eliminated a number of writers whose achievements in their own terms we have not intended to put into question. Still others do not appear because of the limits of translation and because our book, while large, is once again bounded, as all our works and lives are bounded. We think therefore that offerings beyond our own are needed, and we welcome not only those that agree with ours but those that bring forward other and different "special views"—other assessments and approaches to an art that we still think of as central to our aspirations as thinking, feeling human beings.

It is our hope that what we have done here will have some resonance in the century and millennium now emerging. Looking backward we are aware of the distance even now between ourselves and most of the century in which we're writing: a time of two great avant-garde awakenings, when much seemed possible and poetry held out a still untested promise as an instrument of transformation, even of redemption. We are at the moment in a possibly less threatening but curiously less hopeful state, caught between a rapidly developing technology and a resurgent economic conservatism threatening to become a cultural and social conservatism as well. In that sense the core conflicts are very much like those at the old century's beginning. And yet with all of that the idea of millennium still draws us on, allures us again with the hope of a poetics pointed firmly toward the future. We began our assemblage with Whitman's words "for poets to come":

> Indeed, if it were not for you, what would I be?
> What is the little I have done, except to arouse you?

and we resume it now with those of Paul Celan, two years before his death:

> THREADSUNS
> above the grayblack wastes,
> A tree-
> high thought
> grasps the lighttone: there are
> still songs to sing beyond
> mankind.

Jerome Rothenberg
Pierre Joris
Encinitas, CA / Albany, NY
1997

It may be unnecessary to say it, but the work has been a central part of our lives over the last seven or eight years—possibly longer than that, from the time, say, that we first came into poetry and writing. As such it has been for us—for all of its limitations—more than a guide to the poetry of the century (which in some sense it is), much less a textbook intended primarily for academic consumption. It is rather our attempt to make visible the kind of anthology that poets of whatever stripe have always carried as part of their mental or spiritual equipment. To say that is to admit at the same time that what we have done is clearly not enough. While we have charted some possibilities of poetry over what begins to be a global span, we have still not been able to show the full range of poets who have made their special contributions to that larger project. Nor were we able to show the variations in the work that distinguish the real career and art of any given poet.

We would therefore call the reader's attention to some other examples of compilation and synthesis that we take as necessary complements to our own. On the U.S. side of things, for example, the last several years have seen the appearance of a number of ("postmodern") anthologies that filled a gap in presentation that our own efforts could only touch in some small part: Eliot Weinberger's *American Poetry since 1950*, Paul Hoover's *Postmodern American Poetry*, Douglas Messerli's *From the Other Side of the Century*, and Maggie O'Sullivan's *Out of Everywhere: Linguistically Innovative Poetry by Women in North America & the UK*. These in turn linked up with earlier efforts like the germinal *New American Poetry* (above) and its later incarnation as *The Postmoderns*, Robert Kelly's and Paris Leary's *A Controversy of Poets*, Anne Waldman's various *World* anthologies, Jerome Rothenberg's and George Quasha's *America a Prophecy*, and Quasha's *Open Poetry* with its already global implications. Among still more international and simultaneously experimental gatherings were

Emmett Williams's *An Anthology of Concrete Poetry,* LaMonte Young's *An Anthology* (as a rare early vision of the Fluxus movement), Julien Blaine's later *Poésure et Peintrie* (a century-long assemblage of word and image intersections), Pierre Joris's and Jean Portante's *Poésie Internationale Anthologie,* and the recent *Exact Change Yearbook* (published by Damon Krukowski and Naomi Yang, and edited by Peter Gizzi). The internationalist side of things has also been furthered by a range of magazines and journals, from James Laughlin's long-lived *New Directions Annual* and Cid Corman's protean sets of *Origin* beginning in the 1950s, to Clayton Eshleman's *Caterpillar* and *Sulfur,* Weinberger's *Montemora,* Nathaniel Mackey's *Hambone,* Jean-Pierre Faye's Paris-based *Change,* Michel Deguy's *Po&sie,* Henri Deluy's enduring and vital *Action Poétique,* and Kenneth Sherwood's and Loss Pequeño Glazier's on-line *RIF/T: an electronic space for poetry, prose, and poetics* (http://wings.buffalo.edu/epc/rift/). And we would also want to call attention and give thanks to the countless presses run and worked by poets, the most global of which would include Laughlin's New Directions, Lawrence Ferlinghetti's City Lights, Dick Higgins's Something Else, Rosmarie and Keith Waldrop's Burning Deck, and Douglas Messerli's Sun & Moon.

All of the above, then, have been meaningful to us in the second part of the present work, as have the poets through whom the magazines and books came into being. We are aware beyond these of assistance from many directions: Jean-Jacques Lebel, who was there at the inception of the project; Roy Harvey Pierce, who was quick to move it along; those who helped us as an "official" board of advisors or those like David Antin, Don Byrd, Michael Davidson, and Clayton Eshleman, whose advice and good offices were equally at our disposal; fellow poets Chris Stroffolino and Lori Horvitz, who provided us with invaluable assistance; and those, finally, who helped in moving the work from manuscript to finished book: Douglas Abrams Arava, Nola Burger, Evan Camfield, Reed Malcolm, and Rachel Berchten the most active and ongoing among them. The second volume, like the first, was further enhanced by assistance through the Archive for New Poetry at the University of California, San Diego, and by Deans Stanley Chodorow and Frantisek Deak of that school's Division of Arts and Humanities.

A final word of thanks should go to the poets and artists (those in the book and many of those outside it) whose work has been the up side of this bloodiest of centuries; and, on a note too personal to be expanded here, to Diane and to Nicole as *compañeras* in our journey (still in progress) toward the new millennium.

PRELUDE

In the Dark

Charles Olson 1910–1970

LA PRÉFACE

The dead in via
        in vita nuova
              in the way
You shall lament who know they are as tender as the horse is.
You, do not you speak who know not.

      "I will die about April 1st . . ." going off
      "I weigh, I think, 80 lbs . . ." scratch
      "My name is NO RACE"   address
      Buchenwald   new Altamira cave
      With a nail they drew the object of the hunt.

Put war away with time, come into space.
It was May, precise date, 1940. I had air my lungs could breathe.
He talked, via stones   a stick   sea rock   a hand of earth.
It is now, precise, repeat. I talk of Bigmans organs
he, look, the lines! are polytopes.
And among the DPs—deathhead
                 at the apex
                      of the pyramid.

Birth in the house is the One of Sticks, cunnus in the crotch.
Draw it thus: (   ) 1910 (
It is not obscure. We are the new born, and there are no flowers.
Document means there are no flowers
                 and no parenthesis.

It is the radical, the root, he and I, two bodies
We put our hands to these dead.

The closed parenthesis reads: the dead bury the dead,
                 and it is not very interesting.
Open, the figure stands at the door, horror his
and gone, possessed, o new Osiris, Odysseus ship.
He put the body there as well as they did whom he killed.

Mark that arm. It is no longer gun.
We are born not of the buried but these unburied dead
crossed stick, wire-led, Blake Underground

The Babe
      the Howling Babe

Paul Celan 1920–1970

A DEATH FUGUE

Black milk of morning we drink you at dusktime
we drink you at noontime and dawntime we drink you at night
we drink and drink
we scoop out a grave in the sky where it's roomy to lie
There's a man in this house who cultivates snakes and who writes
who writes when it's nightfall *nach Deutschland* your golden hair
    Margareta
he writes it and walks from the house and the stars all start flashing he
    whistles his dogs to draw near
whistles his Jews to appear starts us scooping a grave out of sand
he commands us play up for the dance

Black milk of morning we drink you at night
we drink you at dawntime and noontime we drink you at dusktime
we drink and drink
There's a man in this house who cultivates snakes and who writes
who writes when it's nightfall *nach Deutschland* your golden hair
    Margareta
your ashen hair Shulamite we scoop out a grave in the sky where it's
    roomy to lie

He calls jab it deep in the soil you men you other men sing and play
he tugs at the sword in his belt he swings it his eyes are blue
jab your spades deeper you men you other men play up again for the
    dance

Black milk of morning we drink you at night
we drink you at noontime and dawntime we drink you at dusktime
we drink and drink
there's a man in this house your golden hair Margareta
your ashen hair Shulamite he cultivates snakes

He calls play that death thing more sweetly Death is a gang-boss *aus*
    Deutschland
he calls scrape that fiddle more darkly then hover like smoke in the air
then scoop out a grave in the clouds where it's roomy to lie

Black milk of morning we drink you at night
we drink you at noontime Death is a gang-boss *aus Deutschland*
we drink you at dusktime and dawntime we drink and drink
Death is a gang-boss *aus Deutschland* his eye is blue
he hits you with leaden bullets his aim is true
there's a man in this house your golden hair Margareta
he sets his dogs on our trail he gives us a grave in the sky
he cultivates snakes and he dreams Death is a gang-boss *aus Deutschland*

your golden hair Margareta
your ashen hair Shulamite

Translation from the German by Jerome Rothenberg

Anna Akhmatova 1889–1966

from **POEM WITHOUT A HERO**

Epilogue

I love you, creation of Peter.
    "THE BRONZE HORSEMAN," PUSHKIN

May this place be empty . . .

And the deserts of mute squares,
Where people were executed before dawn.
    ANNENSKY

To my City

White night of June 24, 1942. The city is in ruins. From the harbor to Smolny, everything is flattened. Here and there, old fires are still smoldering. In the Sheremetev Garden the lindens are blooming and a nightingale is singing. One third-story window (behind the crippled maple) has been blown out, revealing black emptiness. From the direction of Kronstadt comes the rumble of heavy artillery. But in general, silence prevails. The voice of the author, seven thousand kilometers away, pronounces:

Under the roof of the Fountain House
  Where the evening languor wandered
    With a lantern and a bunch of keys—

I called out to a distant echo,
    Stirring, with my inappropriate laughter,
        The deep sleep of things, where,
A witness to everything in the world,
    From dusk to dawn,
        The old maple looks into the room

.

And, foreseeing our separation,
    Stretches out to me, as if to help,
        Its desiccated black hand.
But the earth beneath me hummed
    And such a star gazed down
        Into my not yet abandoned home
And waited for the sound agreed upon . . .
    It is somewhere over there—near Tobruk,
        It is somewhere near here—around the corner.
You, neither the first nor the last
    Dark listener to bright babbling,
        What revenge are you planning for me?
You are not drinking, only sipping
    This grief from the very depths—
        The news of our parting.
Don't place your hand on my head—
    Let time stop forever
        On the watch you gave me.
Misfortune will not pass us by,
    And the cuckoo does not cuckoo
        In our burned woods . . .

> *And from behind barbed wire,*
> *In the very heart of the taiga —*
> *I don't know which year —*
> *Having become a heap of "camp dust,"*
> *Having become a terrifying fairy tale,*
> *My double goes to the interrogation.*
> *And then he returns from the interrogation,*
> *With the two emissaries from the Noseless Slut*
> *Assigned to stand guard over him.*

And even from here I can hear —
Isn't it miraculous! —
The sound of my own voice:
  I paid for you in cash.
  For exactly ten years I lived under the gun,
  Glancing neither to the left nor to the right.
  And after me came rustling ill repute.

And not becoming my grave,
  You, granite, infernal, dear to me,
    Grew pale, benumbed and still.
Our separation is imaginary:
  We are inseparable,
    My shadow is on your walls,
My reflection in your canals,
  The sound of my footsteps in the Hermitage halls
    Where my friend walked with me,
And in the ancient Volkov Field
  Where I can freely weep
    Over the silence of common graves.
Everything recounted in Part One
  About love, betrayal and passion,
    Free verse flung from its wings,
And my city stands, mended . . .
  Heavy are the gravestones
    On your sleepless eyes.
It seemed you were pursuing me,
  You, who stayed to perish there
    In the glitter of spires, in the shimmer of waters.
You didn't hope for any messengers . . .
  Over you—only your charmers,
    The white nights in a circle dance.
And that happy phrase—at home—
  Is known to no one now,
    Everyone gazes from some foreign window.
Some from New York, some from Tashkent,
  And bitter is the air of banishment—
    Like poisoned wine.

You might have feasted your eyes on me,
   When, in the belly of the flying fish,
      I escaped the evil pursuit,
And over forests full of the enemy
   Like *that one,* possessed by the devil,
      Flying to the Brocken at night, I soared.

.

And right before me
   The Kama chilled and froze over
      And "Quo vadis?" someone said,
But before I could move my lips,
   The crazy Urals roared
      With their bridges and tunnels.
And opening before me was the road
   Down which so many have trod,
      Down which my son was led,
And that funeral procession was long
   Amidst the festive and crystal
      Silence
                  of the Siberian land.
Seized by mortal fear
   Of what had turned to dust
      And recognizing the hour of vengeance,
Lowering her dry eyes
   And wringing her hands, Russia
      Fled before me to the east.

Finished in Tashkent
August 18, 1942

Translation from the Russian by Lenore Mayhew & William McNaughton

Tōge Sankichi 1917–1953

from POEMS OF THE ATOMIC BOMB

On the morning of August 6, 1945, at home in a part of town more than three kilometers from Ground Zero, I was just about to set out for downtown Hiroshima when the bomb fell, and I escaped merely with cuts from splinters of glass and with atomic bomb sickness. . . . Today everyone knows that at Hiroshima about 300,000 people were killed in the blast of a single atomic bomb. And at Nagasaki, 100,000 or so.

Dying

!
Loud in my ear: screams.
Soundlessly welling up,
pouncing on me:
space, all upside-down.
Hanging, fluttering clouds of dust
smelling of smoke,
and, running madly about, figures.
"Ah,
get out
of here!"
Scattering fragments of brick,
I spring to my feet;
my body's
on fire.
The hot blast
that blew me down from behind
set sleeves, shoulders
on fire.
Amid the smoke I grab
a corner of the cement water tank;
my head—
already in.
The clothes I splash water on
burn, drop off:
gone.
Wires, boards, nails, glass,
a rippling wall of tiles.

Fingernails burn;
heels—gone;
plastered to my back: a sheet of molten lead.
"Owww!"
Flames already
blacken;
telephone poles, walls, too.
Eddies
of flame and smoke
blow down on my broken head.
"Hiro-chan! Hiro-chan!"
Press hand to breast:
ah—a bloody cotton hole.
Fallen, I cry—
Child! Child! Child! Where are you?
Amid the smoke that crawls along the ground—
where could they have come from?—
hand in hand,
round and round as in the *bon* dance,
naked girls:
one falls, all fall.
From under tiles,
someone else's shoulder:
a hairless old woman,
driven up by the heat,
writhing, crying shrilly.
Beside the road where flames already flicker,
stomachs distended like great drums,
even their lips torn off:
lumps of red flesh.
A hand that grabs my ankle
slips off, peels off.
An eyeball that pleads at my feet.
A head boiled white.
Hair, brain matter my hand presses down on.
Steamy smoke; fiery air that rushes at me.
Amid the darkness of flying sparks:
children's eyes, the color of gold.
Burning body,
scalding throat;
arm
that suddenly collapses;

shoulder
that sinks to the ground.
Oh, I can go
no farther.
In the lonely dark,
the thunder in my ears suddenly fades.
Ah!
Why?
Why here
by the side of the road
cut off, dear, from you;
why
must
I
die
?

Translation from the Japanese by Richard H. Minear

René Depestre b. 1926

SEASON OF ANGER

I made myself into armored concrete against the worms that gnaw us and suck us dry. My nigger skin once the common place for tortures and slabber has suddenly become an *open sesame* for inviolable doors

I am of a hideous race

What do you say white Woman Only yesterday you found my pleasure too ferocious and the surging movements of my hips reminded you of the furious rolling of the slavers along the Middle Passage

Since then Race of Conquerors how many abcesses have been lanced with your sons as the surrounding redness and the yellow carbuncles

I don't believe in the virginity of the girls of all races I need to believe in less fragile divinities Hallucination or reality yet it is not a lie of the time I was twenty

I forgo the usual ways of making love For me other caresses other sweetnesses more atrocious other trances with sharper teeth other women more voracious

Now there's language like a lit torch put to the powder of hypocrite passions and rusted traditions in the cellar's mildew

I have not chosen it for the simple joy of being cruel against my time but to set in their royal place values far too long slandered and lashed like dangerous beasts

I will cut the ties of all those organs of the body you mention only under the breath I decree the mutiny of those instincts which still wear lilies or similar blemishes

The enchanted era of dissoluteness will precede by a few dawns that of the liberation of all peoples

You have to slough off your old soul to furiously penetrate the dark tangle of those green flowering springs promised to the damned of the earth

The season will be born from the murky and purified regions of my consciousness there where my revolt is still the ferocious will to break the molds into which have been emptied the dissolute pleasures of childhood the excesses of virility and the pale platitudes of middle age

My reason demands weapons

My reason calls to arms

The cowards can have their passports stamped It will take much virtue to live according to the exigencies of the imagination's instinct of love's goodness as life's only season

Translation from the French by Pierre Joris

Ingeborg Bachmann 1926–1973

THE TIME ALLOTTED

Worse days are coming.
The time allotted for disavowals
Comes due on the skyline.
Soon you will lace up your shoes
And drive the dogs back to the marshes.

For the intestines of fish
Have frozen up in the wind.
The lupines burn with a feeble light.
Your glance cuts through the fog:
The time allotted for disavowals
Comes due on the skyline.

In the distance your mistress sinks under the sand,
It pours through her wind-loosened hair,
It covers her words,
It turns her to silence,
It finds her mortal
And ready to part
With every embrace.

Don't look around.
Lace up your shoes.
Drive the dogs back.
Throw the fish in the sea,
Smother the lupines!

Worse days are coming.

Translation from the German by Jerome Rothenberg

Antonin Artaud 1896–1948

from **TO HAVE DONE WITH THE JUDGMENT OF GOD**

kré	Everything	puc te
kré	must be arranged	puc te
pek	to a hair	li le
kre	in a fulminating	pek ti le
e	order.	kruk
pte		

I learned yesterday
(you must think that I'm very slow, or perhaps it is only a false rumor,
   some of the dirty gossip that is peddled between the sink and the
   latrines at the hour when the buckets are filled with meals once again
   regurgitated),
I learned yesterday
about one of the most sensational official practices of the American
   public schools
which no doubt make that country consider itself at the head of progress.

Apparently, among the examinations or tests that a child has to undergo
on entering a public school for the first time is the one called the
seminal liquid or sperm test,
which consists of asking this newly-enrolled child for a little of his sperm
in order to put it into a glass jar
and of thereby keeping it ready for all the attempts at artificial
insemination which might eventually take place.
For more and more the Americans find that they lack manpower and
children,
that is, not workers
but soldiers,
and at all costs and by all possible means they want to make and
manufacture soldiers
in view of all the planetary wars which might subsequently take place,
and which would be destined to *demonstrate* by the crushing virtues of
force
the superexcellence of American products,
and the fruits of American sweat in all the fields of activity and potential
dynamism of force.
Because there must be production,
nature must be replaced wherever it can be replaced by every possible
means of activity,
a major field must be found for human inertia,
the worker must be kept busy at something,
new fields of activity must be created,
where all the false manufactured products,
all the ignoble synthetic ersatzes will finally reign,
where beautiful true nature has nothing to do,
and must give up its place once and for all and shamefully to all the
triumphant replacement products,
where sperm from all the artificial insemination factories
will work miracles
to produce armies and battleships.
No more fruit, no more trees, no more vegetables, no more plants
pharmaceutical or not and consequently no more food,
but synthetic products to repletion,
in vapors,
in special humors of the atmosphere, on particular axes of atmospheres
drawn by force and by synthesis from the resistance of a nature that
has never known anything about war except fear.
And long live war, right?

For by doing this, it is war, isn't it, that the Americans have prepared for
    and that they prepare for thus step by step.
To defend this insane machining against all the competition which would
    inevitably break out on all sides,
there must be soldiers, armies, airplanes, battleships,
therefore this sperm
which the American governments have apparently had the nerve to
    consider.
For we have more than one enemy
and one who watches us, kid,
us, the born capitalists,
and among these enemies
Stalin's Russia
which is not short of armed men either.
All this is very fine,
but I did not know that the Americans were such a warlike people.
To fight you must receive blows
and perhaps I have seen many Americans at war
but in front of them they always had incommensurable armies of tanks,
    planes, battleships
serving as a shield.
I saw a lot of machines fight
but I saw only in the infinite
                    rear
the men who drove them.
Confronted by a people who make their horses, oxen and donkeys eat
    the last tons of true morphine which may be left to them in order to
    replace it with ersatz smoke,
I prefer the people who eat right out of the earth the delirium that gave
    birth to them,
I am speaking of the Tarahumaras
who eat Peyote straight from the soil
while it is born,
and who kill the sun in order to establish the kingdom of black night,
and who split the cross so that the spaces of space will never again meet
    or cross.

In this way you will hear the dance of the TUTUGURI.

[. . . . . . .]

And below, as at the bottom of the bitter,
cruelly desperate slope of the heart,
the circle of the six crosses opens,
                far below,
as if embedded in the mother earth,
disembedded from the filthy embrace of the mother
                who slobbers.

The earth of black coal
is the only humid spot
in this cleft of rock.

The Rite is that the new sun passes through seven points before explod-
    ing at the earth's orifice.

And there are six men,
one for each sun,
and a seventh man
who is the sun completely
                raw
dressed in black and red flesh.

Now, this seventh man
is a horse,
a horse with a man leading him.

But it is the horse
that is the sun
and not the man.

On the rending of a drum and of a long, peculiar
trumpet,
the six men
who were lying down,
rolled up flush with the ground,
spring up successively like sunflowers,
not suns at all
but turning soils,
lotuses of water,

and to each upspring
corresponds the increasingly gloomy and *repressed*
>gong
>of the drum
until suddenly we see coming in full gallop, at vertiginous speed,
the last sun,
the first man,
the black horse with a
>man naked,
>absolutely naked
>and *virgin*
>on it.

Having gamboled, they advance following circular meanders
and the horse of bloody meat panics
and caracoles without stopping
on the top of its rock
until the six men
have finished encircling
completely
the six crosses.

Now, the major tone of the Rite is precisely
>THE ABOLITION OF THE CROSS.

Having finished turning
they uproot
the earthen crosses
and the man naked
on the horse
raises high
an immense horseshoe
which he has tempered in a cut of his blood.

Translation from the French by Clayton Eshleman & Norman Glass

CONTINUITIES

Gertrude Stein 1874–1946

from THE MOTHER OF US ALL

Concluding Aria

Susan B.'s voice: We cannot retrace our steps, going forward may be the same as going backwards. We cannot retrace our steps, retrace our steps. All my long life, all my life, we do not retrace our steps, all my long life, but.

(A silence a long silence)

But—we do not retrace our steps, all my long life, and here, here we are here, in marble and gold, did I say gold, yes I said gold, in marble and gold and where—

(A silence)

Where is where. In my long life of effort and strife, dear life, life is strife, in my long life, it will not come and go, I tell you so, it will stay it will pay but

(A long silence)

But do I want what we have got, has it not gone, what made it live, has it not gone because now it is had, in my long life in my long life

(Silence)

Life is strife, I was a martyr all my life not to what I won but to what was done.

(Silence)

Do you know because I tell you so, or do you know, do you know.

(Silence)

My long life, my long life.

Curtain

Wallace Stevens 1879–1955

NOT IDEAS ABOUT THE THING BUT THE THING ITSELF

At the earliest ending of winter,
In March, a scrawny cry from outside
Seemed like a sound in his mind.

He knew that he heard it,
A bird's cry, at daylight or before,
In the early March wind.

The sun was rising at six,
No longer a battered panache above snow . . .
It would have been outside.

It was not from the vast ventriloquism
Of sleep's faded papier-mâché . . .
The sun was coming from outside.

That scrawny cry—it was
A chorister whose c preceded the choir.
It was part of the colossal sun,

Surrounded by its choral rings,
Still far away. It was like
A new knowledge of reality.

James Joyce 1882–1941

from FINNEGANS WAKE

Hear, O hear, Iseult la belle! Tristan, sad hero, hear! The Lambeg drum, the Lombog reed, the Lumbag fiferer, the Limibig brazenaze.

Anno Domini nostri sancti Jesu Christi
Nine hundred and ninetynine million pound sterling in the blueblack bowels of the bank of Ulster.
Braw bawbees and good gold pounds, galore, my girleen, a Sunday'll prank thee finely.
And no damn loutll come courting thee or by the mother of the Holy Ghost there'll be murder!

O, come all ye sweet nymphs of Dingle beach to cheer Brinabride queen from Sybil surfriding
In her curragh of shells of daughter of pearl and her silverymonnblue mantle round her.
Crown of the waters, brine on her brow, she'll dance them a jig and jilt them fairly.

Yerra, why would she bide with Sig Sloomysides or the grogram grey bar-
nacle gander?

You won't need be lonesome, Lizzy my love, when your beau gets his glut
of cold meat and hot soldiering
Nor wake in winter, window machree, but snore sung in my old Balbrig-
gan surtout.
Wisha, won't you agree now to take me from the middle, say, of next
week on, for the balance of my days, for nothing (what?) as your own
nursetender?
A power of highsteppers died game right enough — but who, acushla, 'll
beg coppers for you?

I tossed that one long before anyone.
It was of a wet good Friday too she was ironing and, as I'm given now to
understand, she was always mad gone on me.
Grand goosegreasing we had entirely with an allnight eiderdown bed pic-
nic to follow.
By the cross of Cong, says she, rising up Saturday in the twilight from
under me, Mick, Nick the Maggot or whatever your name is, you're
the mose likable lad that's come my ways yet from the barony of
Bohermore.

Mattheehew, Markeehew, Lukeehew, Johnheehewheehew!
Haw!
And still a light moves long the river. And stiller the mermen ply their keg.
Its pith is full. The way is free. Their lot is cast.
So, to john for a john, johnajeams, led it be!

William Carlos Williams   1883–1963

from PATERSON, BOOK THREE

It is dangerous to leave written that which is badly written. A chance word, upon paper, may destroy the world. Watch carefully and erase, while the power is still yours, I say to myself, for all that is put down, once it escapes, may rot its way into a thousand minds, the corn become a black smut, and all libraries, of necessity, be burned to the ground as a consequence.

Only one answer: write carelessly so that nothing that is not green will survive.

> There is a drumming of submerged
> engines, a beat of propellers.
> The ears are water. The feet
> listen. Boney fish bearing lights
> stalk the eyes—which float about,
> indifferent. A taste of iodine
> stagnates upon the law of percent-
> ages: thick boards bored through
> by worms whose calcined husks
> cut our fingers, which bleed   .

We walk into a dream, from certainty to the unascertained, in time
to see   .   from the roseate past   .   a ribbed tail deploying

> Tra la la la la la la la la
> La tra tra tra tra tra tra

Upon which there intervenes
a sour stench of embers. So be it. Rain
falls and surfeits the river's upper reaches,
gathering slowly. So be it. Draws together,
runnel by runnel. So be it. A broken oar
is found by the searching waters. Loosened
it begins to move. So be it. Old timbers
sigh—and yield. The well that gave sweet water
is sullied. So be it. And lilies that floated
quiet in the shallows, anchored, tug as
fish at a line. So be it. And are by their
stems pulled under, drowned in the muddy flux.
The white crane flies into the wood.
So be it. Men stand at the bridge, silent,
watching. So be it. So be it.

And there rises
a counterpart, of reading, slowly, overwhelming
the mind; anchors him in his chair. So be
it. He turns   .   O Paradiso! The stream
grows leaden within him, his lilies drag. So
be it. Texts mount and complicate them-

selves, lead to further texts and those
to synopses, digests and emendations. So be it.
Until the words break loose or—sadly
hold, unshaken. Unshaken! So be it. For
the made-arch holds, the water piles up debris
against it but it is unshaken. They gather
upon the bridge and look down, unshaken.
So be it. So be it. So be it.
The sullen, leaden flood, the silken flood
—to the teeth

          to the very eyes

               (light grey)

Henry's the name. Just Henry,

              ever'body
knows me around here: hat
pulled down hard on his skull, thick chested,
fiftyish   .

            I'll hold the baby.

That was your little dog bit me last year.
Yeah, and you had him killed on me.

            (the eyes)

I didn't know he'd been killed.

        You reported him and
they come and took him. He never hurt
anybody.
      He bit me three times.
             They come and
took him and killed him.
            I'm sorry but I had
to report him   .   .

A dog, head dropped back, under water, legs
sticking up   :
        a skin
tense with the wine of death
             downstream

on the swift current   :
                    Above the silence
a faint hissing, a seething hardly at first
to be noticed

          —headlong!

               Speed!

                         —marked
as by the lines on slate, mottled by petty
whirlpools

          (to the teeth, to the very eyes)

                    a formal progression

   The remains—a man of gigantic stature—were transported on the
shoulders of the most renowned warriors of the surrounding country   .
for many hours they travelled without rest. But half way on the journey
the carriers had to quit overcome by fatigue—they had walked many
hours and Pogatticut was heavy. So by the side of the trail, at a place called
"Whooping Boys Hollow," they scooped out a shallow hole and laid the
dead chieftain down in it while they rested. By so doing, the spot became
sacred, held in veneration by the Indians.
   Arrived at the burial place the funeral procession was met by Pogatti-
cut's brothers and their followers. There was great lamentation and the
Kinte Kaye was performed in sadness.
   Wyandach, the most illustrious brother, performed the burial sacrifice.
Having his favorite dog, a much loved animal, brought forth, he killed
him, and laid him, after painting his muzzle red, beside his brother. For
three days and three nights the tribes mourned   .

Pursued by the whirlpool-mouths, the dog
descends toward Acheron   .   Le Néant
   .   the sewer
               a dead dog
                              turning
upon the water:

          Come yeah, Chi Chi!

                              turning
as he passes   .

It is a sort of chant, a sort of praise, a
peace that comes of destruction:

                                    to the teeth,
to the very eyes

            (cut lead)

                I bin nipped
hundreds of times. He never done anybody any
harm   .

                helpless   .

                You had him killed on me.

Ezra Pound 1885–1972

CANTO 116

Came Neptunus
                his mind leaping
                        like dolphins,
These concepts the human mind has attained.
To make Cosmos—
To achieve the possible—
Muss., wrecked for an error,
But the record
            the palimpsest—
a little light
            in great darkness—
cuniculi—
An old "crank" dead in Virginia.
Unprepared young burdened with records,
The vision of the Madonna
                above the cigar butts
                    and over the portal.
"Have made a mass of laws"
                        (mucchio di leggi)
Litterae nihil sanantes
                    Justinian's,
a tangle of works unfinished.

I have brought the great ball of crystal;
                    who can lift it?
Can you enter the great acorn of light?
            But the beauty is not the madness
Tho' my errors and wrecks lie about me.
And I am not a demigod,
I cannot make it cohere.
If love be not in the house there is nothing.
The voice of famine unheard.
How came beauty against this blackness,
Twice beauty under the elms—
            To be saved by squirrels and bluejays?
                    "plus j'aime le chien"
Ariadne.
        Disney against the metaphysicals,
and Laforgue more than they thought in him,
Spire thanked me in proposito
And I have learned more from Jules
                        (Jules Laforgue) since then
deeps in him,
            and Linnaeus.
                    chi crescerà i nostri—
but about that terzo
            third heaven,
                    that Venere,
again is all "paradiso"
        a nice quiet paradise
                    over the shambles,
and some climbing
            before the take-off,
to "see again,"
the verb is "see," not "walk on"
i.e. it coheres all right
            even if my notes do not cohere.
Many errors,
        a little rightness,
to excuse his hell
            and my paradiso.
And as to why they go wrong,
            thinking of rightness

And as to who will copy this palimpsest?
       al poco giorno
            ed al gran cerchio d'ombra
But to affirm the gold thread in the pattern
          (Torcello)
al Vicolo d'oro
      (Tigullio).
To confess wrong without losing rightness:
Charity I have had sometimes,
      I cannot make it flow thru.
A little light, like a rushlight
       to lead back to splendour.

H. D.   1886–1961

from **HERMETIC DEFINITION**

Red Rose and a Beggar (1–9)
August 17–September 24, 1960

1

Why did you come
to trouble my decline?
I am old (I was old till you came);

the reddest rose unfolds,
(which is ridiculous
in this time, this place,

unseemly, impossible,
even slightly scandalous),
the reddest rose unfolds;

(nobody can stop that,
no immanent threat from the air,
not even the weather,

blighting our summer fruit),
the reddest rose unfolds,
(they've got to take that into account).

2

Take me anywhere, anywhere;
I walk into you,
Doge—Venice—

you are my whole estate;
I would hide in your mind
as a child hides in an attic,

what would I find there?
religion or majic—both? neither?
one or the other? together, matched,

mated, exactly the same,
equal in power, together yet separate,
your eyes' amber.

3

Isis, Iris,
fleur-de-lis,
Bar-Isis is son of Isis,

(bar ou ber ou ben, signifiant fils).
so Bar-Isis is Par-Isis?
Paris, anyway;

because you do not drink our wine,
nor salt our salt,
I would enter your senses

through burnt resin and pine-cones
smouldering in a flat dish;
were you a cave-hermit?

why do they punish us?
come out, come out of the darkness;
will I be burnt to cinders in this heat?

4

They say the hieratic and heraldic iris
is the lotus, martigan-lily,
magenta, purple—do I blaspheme?

cowering under the rain,
I think of the hot sand,
and call and call again

Bar-Isis, Paris;
I call Paris, Paris,
not to the Greek

nor to the courtly suitor of Verona
"where we lay our scene,"
though Verona is not far,

now I walk into you,
Doge—Venice—
you are my whole estate.

5

Venice—Venus?
this must be my stance,
my station: though you brushed aside

my verse,
I can't get away from it,
I've tried to;

true, it was "fascinating . . .
if you can stand its preciousness,"
you wrote of what I wrote;

why must I write?
you would not care for this,
but She draws the veil aside,

unbinds my eyes,
commands,
write, write or die.

6

This is my new prayer;
I pray to you?
Paris, Bar-Isis? to Osiris?

or to Isis-self, Egyptian flower,
Notre Dame—do you ever go there?
the stones hold secrets;

they tell us vibration was brought over
by ancient alchemists;
Our Lady keeps tryst,

she commands with her sceptre, (*Astrologie*
is the first door?)
and the Child champions us;

bid me not despair,
Child of the ancient hierarchy . . .
and you to-day.

7

Saint Anne is the last door, (Magie,
Cybele, they once called her,
the grand-mother),

and where are we now?
certainly there is the rush, the fervour,
the trampling of lush grass,

the bare feet entanglement,
the roar of the last desperate charge,
the non-escape, the enchantment,

the tremor, the earthquake,
nothing, nothing, nothing more,
nothing further; the pine-cone

we left smouldering in the flat dish,
is flaming, is fire,
no before, no after—escape?

who can escape life, fever,
the darkness of the abyss?
lost, lost, lost,

the last desperate non-escape,
the reddest rose,
the unalterable law . . .

8

is it you?
is it some thundering pack
of steers, bulls? is it one?

is it many?
voices from the past, from the future,
so far, no further,

now total abasement;
were you ever here?
were you ever in this room?

how did I endure your presence,
and afterwards, just once,
in a strange place, with others there,

silly talk, mine,
and you wouldn't drink our wine,
("then fruit-juice?" "yes"),

and you wouldn't touch our salt—
almonds—pecans—what happened?
you were so late,

why didn't you come sooner?
why did you come at all?
why did you come

to trouble my decline,
I am old,
(I was old till you came.)

9

The middle door is Judgement, (*Alchimie*),
judge this, judge me implacable;
there is yet time to crawl back

to security? no—there is no time left:
almonds, pecans without salt,
scatter them near some sand-coast

for a wind-break, beyond is the wax flower,
the thyme, honeymyrtle and the coral heath,
these are new to me, different,

as you are new to me, different,
but of an old, old sphere;
there are some small wild dogroses, I think,

but all this is nothing
when the desert wind bears the white
gumblossom eucalypts' fragrance;

no, no, this is too much,
we can not escape to a new continent;
the middle door is judgement,

I am judged—prisoner?
the reddest rose unfolds,
can I endure this?

Hugh MacDiarmid 1892–1978

THE GLASS OF PURE WATER

In the de-oxidation and re-oxidation of hydrogen in a single drop
of water we have before us, truly, so far as force is concerned,
an epitome of the whole life. . . . The burning of coal to move an
iron wheel differs only in detail, and not in essence, from the
decomposition of a muscle to effect its own concentration.
                                        JAMES HINTON

We must remember that his analysis was done not intellectually,
but by an immediate process of intuition; that he was able, as it
were, to taste the hydrogen and oxygen in his glass of water.
        ALDOUS HUXLEY (OF D. H. LAWRENCE)

Praise of pure water is common in Gaelic poetry.
        W. J. WATSON: BÀRDACHD GHÀIDHLIG

Hold a glass of pure water to the eye of the sun!
It is difficult to tell the one from the other
Save by the tiny hardly visible trembling of the water.
This is the nearest analogy to the essence of human life
Which is even more difficult to see.
Dismiss anything you can see more easily;

It is not alive—it is not worth seeing.
There is a minute indescribable difference
Between one glass of pure water and another
With slightly different chemical constituents.
The difference between one human life and another
Is no greater; colour does not colour the water;
You cannot tell a white man's life from a black man's.
But the lives of these particular slum people
I am chiefly concerned with, like the lives of all
The world's poorest, remind me less
Of a glass of water held between my eyes and the sun
—They remind me of the feeling they had
Who saw Sacco and Vanzetti in the death cell
On the eve of their execution.
—One is talking to God.

I dreamt last night that I saw one of His angels
Making his centennial report to the Recording Angel
On the condition of human life.
Look at the ridge of skin between your thumb and forefinger.
Look at the delicate lines on it and how they change
—How many different things they can express—
As you move out or close in your forefinger and thumb.
And look at the changing shapes—the countless
Little gestures, little miracles of line—
Of your forefinger and thumb as you move them.
And remember how much a hand can express,
How a single slight movement of it can say more
Than millions of words—dropped hand, clenched fist,
Snapping fingers, thumb up, thumb down,
Raised in blessing, clutched in passion, begging,
Welcome, dismissal, prayer, applause,
And a million other signs, too slight, too subtle,
Too packed with meaning for words to describe,
A universal language understood by all.
And the angel's report on human life
Was the subtlest movement—just like that—and no more;
A hundred years of life on the Earth
Summed up, not a detail missed or wrongly assessed,
In that little inconceivably intricate movement.

The only communication between man and man
That says anything worth hearing
—The hidden well-water; the finger of destiny—
Moves as that water, that angel, moved.
Truth is the rarest thing and life
The gentlest, most unobtrusive movement in the world.
I cannot speak to you of the poor people of all the world
But among the people in these nearest slums I know
This infinitesimal twinkling, this delicate play
Of tiny signs that not only say more
Than all speech, but all there is to say,
All there is to say and to know and to be.
There alone I seldom find anything else,
Each in himself or herself a dramatic whole,
An 'agon' whose validity is timeless.

Our duty is to free that water, to make these gestures,
To help humanity to shed all else,
All that stands between any life and the sun,
The quintessence of any life and the sun;
To still all sound save that talking to God;
To end all movements save movements like these.
India had that great opportunity centuries ago
And India lost it—and became a vast morass,
Where no water wins free; a monstrous jungle
Of useless movement; a babel
Of stupid voices, drowning the still small voice.
It is our turn now; the call is to the Celt.

This little country can overcome the whole world of wrong
As the Lacedaemonians the armies of Persia.
Cornwall—Gaeldom—must stand for the ending
Of the essential immorality of any man controlling
Any other—for the ending of all Government
Since all Government is a monopoly of violence;
For the striking of this water out of the rock of Capitalism;
For the complete emergence from the pollution and fog
With which the hellish interests of private property
In land, machinery, and credit
Have corrupted and concealed from the sun,
From the gestures of truth, from the voice of God,

Hundreds upon hundreds of millions of men,
Denied the life and liberty to which they were born
And fobbed off with a horrible travesty instead
—Self righteous, sunk in the belief that they are human,
When not a tenth of one per cent show a single gleam
Of the life that is in them under their accretions of filth.

And until that day comes every true man's place
Is to reject all else and be with the lowest,
The poorest—in the bottom of that deepest of wells
In which alone is truth; in which
Is truth only—truth that should shine like the sun,
With a monopoly of movement, and a sound like talking to God . . .

André Breton 1896–1966

from **ODE TO CHARLES FOURIER**

Fourier what have they done with your keyboard
That responded to everything with a chord
Setting by the movements of the stars from the capers of the smallest boat
   on the sea to the great sweep of the proudest three-master
You embraced unity you showed it not as lost but as totally attainable
And if you named "God" it was to infer that this god came under the
   evidence of the senses (*His body is fire*)
But what has forever caused socialist thought for me really to break cover
Is that you felt the need to *differentiate the comma at least in quadruple*
   form
And to transfer the treble clef from the second to the first line in musical
   notation
Because it's the whole world that must not only be overturned but prod-
   ded everywhere in its conventions
And there's no control lever to be trusted once and for all
Not more than a single dogmatic commonplace which does not totter
   when confronted by ingenuous doubts and demands

Because the "*Veil of Bronze*" has survived the rent you tore in it
And covers even more completely *scientific blindness*
"No one has ever seen a molecule, or an atom, or an atomic link and it's
   unlikely anyone ever will" (Philosopher). Prompt proof to the contrary:
   in swaggers the molecule of rubber.

A scientist though provided with black glasses loses his sight for having observed at several miles' distance the first atomic bomb tests (The newspapers).

Fourier I salute you from the Grand Canyon of Colorado
I see the eagle soaring from your head
Bearing in its claws Panurge's sheep
And the wind of memory and the future
Slips through the feathers of its wings the faces of friends
Among them many who have no longer or who have not yet a face
Because conscious reactionaries and so many apostles of social progress
who are in fact grim *immobilists* (you tarred them both with the same
brush) persist in more and more vain opposition
I salute you from the Petrified Forest of human culture
Where nothing has been left standing
But where great gleaming fires whirl and prowl
Calling for the deliverance of foliage and bird
From your fingers comes the sap of blossoming trees
Because with the philosopher's stone at your disposal
You heeded only your first impulse which was to offer it to men
But between them and you there was no intercessor
Not a day passed but you confidently waited for him an hour in the gar-
dens of the Palais-Royal
Attractions are proportionate to destinies
In testimony of which I come to you today

I salute you from the Nevada of the gold-prospector
From the land promised and kept
To the land rich in higher promises which it must yet keep
From the depths of the blue ore mine which reflects the loveliest sky
For always beyond that bar-sign which continues to haunt the street
of a ghost town—
Virginia-City—"The Old Blood Bucket"

Because the festival sense is less and less present in our minds
Because the most vertiginous motorways do not make us cease to regret
your *pavement for zebras*
Because Europe ready to explode in a cloud of dust has found it of prime
expedience to take measures of defence against confetti
And because among the choreographic exercises you proposed multiplying
It is time perhaps to omit *those of the rifle and the incense-burner*

I salute you at the moment when the Indian dances have just come to
    an end
At the heart of the storm
And the participants group themselves in an oval around the brasiers
    strong with the smell of pine for shelter from the much-beloved rain
An oval that is an opal
Raising to the highest pitch its red fires in the night

Translation from the French by Kenneth White

Henri Michaux 1899–1984

from SAISIR [TO GRASP]

One evening an exceptionally abstract communication came over the air-
waves. An interpenetration of metaphysics, nuclear physics, the latest syn-
theses concerning the constitution of matter and the birth of the Universe.

Nearly without noticing I grabbed something with which to draw. The vibrant discussion underway instantly broke, undid, the kind of drawing I had been practicing for months, changing it into one that imposed itself, definitive from the start, and which, without hesitating even for a second, I pursued to the end with unerring certainty.

I followed. But what did I follow? With a slender structure—up in the air and aslant—I joined the exalting, noble and great adventure of the elucidation of the Universe as a whole.

The constant widening of the thinkable whereto I was called, successively forcing in me levels of ignorance, exalted me in a peculiar way. Their talk like their voices, their attacking allure breathed audacity.

To translate, to pursue, to follow. . . .

Translation from the French by Pierre Joris

Louis Zukofsky 1904–1978

from "A" 12

A red horse
Among myrtle,
Behind him
Red horses,
Speckled, and white

— O my lord
What are these

— They walk
To and fro
Thru the earth —
We have
Walked
To and fro
And the earth
Is quiet,

Be quiet, flesh
Isn't this
A brand
Plucked out
Of the fire?
Clothe,
Have
Places to
Walk,
Bring forth
My servant
The BRANCH,
See the stone
Laid —
On a stone
Seven eyes —
Call each man
Under the vine
And under the fig.

Talked with me,
Waked me.
I saw
The first chariot,
Red horses —
The second,
Black —
The third,
White —
The fourth,
Grizzled and bay.
— What are these?
— The black go
North,
The white
After,
The grizzled
South.
The bay
Go on
Thru the earth.

Crying to me,
—See
These go north
And quiet me.
When
    the eyes
        have seen
To everyone grass in the field
My staff, even Beauty
Shall say, I am no prophet.
    HOLINESS
Upon the bells of horses
       In that day

—Look, Paul, the small arrowroot
Has rabbit ears.

—Why?

High   inthehighest
I was unhappy—I've forgotten it.

The fire roared, quieted to light.

Blest
Infinite things
So many
Which confuse imagination
Thru its weakness,
To the ear
Noises.
Or harmony
Delights
Men to madness—
To say the planets
Whirl and make harmony—
That they take for things
Modifications of
Imagination:

Where before,
If all things passed

From the world
Time and space
Were left,
They would now
Disappear
With the things—

It's pleasant
And understandable
That all but a fiddler
Have said "enough."

The mind turns to the body
As object:
A mode that occupies
Is actual and nothing else.
There then
Are simple bodies
Marked out mutually
As moving or still
Swift or slow.

No one
So far
Knows
What a body
Can do
Or can make
It
Of texture
Or
Tick-tack uhr—

From a body's nature
From nature
Under whatever
Attribute
Follow
Infinite things:

Thought
Not image
Or word,

Tongues
That fail quiet,
Desires
That may order,

And what
Men desire
With such love
Nothing can
Remove
From their minds.

[. . . . . .]

Pablo Neruda 1904–1973

from THE HEIGHTS OF MACCHU PICCHU

Come up with me, American love.

Kiss these secret stones with me.
The torrential silver of the Urubamba
makes the pollen fly to its golden cup.
The hollow of the bindweed's maze,
the petrified plant, the inflexible garland,
soar above the silence of these mountain coffers.
Come, diminutive life, between the wings
of the earth, while you, cold, crystal in the hammered air,
thrusting embattled emeralds apart,
O savage waters, fall from the hems of snow.

Love, love, until the night collapses
from the singing Andes flint
down to the dawn's red knees,
come out and contemplate the snow's blind son.

O Wilkamayu of the sounding looms,
when you rend your skeins of thunder
in white foam clouds of wounded snow,
when your south wind falls like an avalanche
roaring and belting to arouse the sky,
what language do you wake in an ear
freed but a moment from your Andean spume?

Who caught the lightning of the cold,
abandoned it, chained to the heights,
dealt out among its frozen tears,
brandished upon its nimble swords—
its seasoned stamens pummeled hard—
led to a warrior's bed,
hounded to his rocky conclusions?

What do your harried scintillations whisper?
Did your sly, rebellious flash
go traveling once, populous with words?
Who wanders grinding frozen syllables,
black languages, gold-threaded banners,
fathomless mouths and trampled cries
in your tenuous arterial waters?

Who goes dead-heading blossom eyelids
come to observe us from the far earth?
Who scatters dead seed clusters
dropping from your cascading hands
to bed their own disintegration here
in coal's geology?

Who has flung down the branches of these chains
and buried once again our leave-takings?

Love, love, do not come near the border,
avoid adoring this sunken head:
let time exhaust all measure
in its abode of broken overtures—
here, between cliffs and rushing waters,
take to yourself the air among these passes,
the laminated image of the wind,
the blind canal threading high cordilleras,

dew with its bitter greetings,
and climb, flower by flower, through the thicknesses
trampling the coiling lucifer.

In this steep zone of flint and forest,
green stardust, jungle-clarified,
Mantur, the valley, cracks like a living lake
or a new level of silence.

Come to my very being, to my own dawn,
into crowned solitudes.

The fallen kingdom survives us all this while.

And on this dial the condor's shadow
cruises as ravenous as would a pirate ship.

Translation from the Spanish by Nathaniel Tarn

Gunnar Ekelöf 1907–1968

from **MÖLNA ELEGY**

*Marche
funèbre*

A desolate wind from the city
and nearer, further
the bells' burden, swinging fifths
—it's burning! it's burning!—
of the dead march:
We lived—just then!
We live now not at all,
we shall live—for the first time!
A flighty moment—
and now the devil is in the belfry
he who robbed us of our future,
robbed us of our past
The red fever-ball which makes me reel
rolls, tumbles over, rushes
Fever that slowly
makes a vault of me, rushing
dizzying

rolls me, over me,
dizzy———
—la boule rouge qui bouge et roule—
time arrested, aroused . . .
And over again . . .
And over again . . .
And once again the banal development
in slow procession, slowly borne
with teardrenched trembling maidenhair
the sorrow of women, the whitest lilies:
Sob, sob, sob!
You black birds:
You were singing just then!
You are not singing now,
you shall sing—for the first time!
O saisons, ô châteaux!
O willows on the banks, O Babylon!
Happy he who taketh thy little ones
and dasheth them against the stones!

Leavetaking   But you are not at all the avenger
at once one of the many
and one of the few:
Neither nominated nor nominator
neither numerator
or common denominator:
Your formula is the stroke between
seldom and never,
you have it written on your forehead:
The same one and still another
Your innocence is greatest in disgrace
—then it emerges, indestructible—
your voice is at its most clearly audible
while you are silent . . . The journey
you make as a passenger
not as a dispatcher
potent precisely in your impotence
certain in your uncertainty!
For neither as station-master nor as lineman

do you have anything to do with
this, the parallel
train tracks' infinity.

The wheels spin and spin,
fools stand and cheer and grin
at every station.
The train goes further
without arriving at milder
zones.
The sun each moment nailed
time arrested and flailed
without circumference becoming center,
without black becoming white . . .

Puzzle, puzzle and puzzle
till you are puzzled double
by both the old and new,
both one and two.
Then all your waiting is past:
something grey beside you at last,
it finally stands there—you!

Same apple
Thuds dully, bumps, lies dumb.

Front gable clock
(face altered by stroke)

When the h, who the hu, how the hue,
where the huer?

Rāgas and Rāginis
(slowly circling)

A genius

Je suis le Roquefort . . .

Disabled emanations
(dancing)

Apple, papple, barries, charries
one and two, one and two:
out goes y-o-u . . .

Same genius

Je suis le Brie etc.

Ibn el-Arabi

Labbayka!

The thrush
*(heraldic bird; silent, immobile,
with its beak up)*

————

Be still my child, there is nothing
all is as you see: forest, smoke and the flight of the rail-
   road tracks.
Somewhere far away in a distant land
there is a bluer sky, a wall with roses
or a palmtree and a warmer wind—
and that is all.

————

—I left Oehlreick
and there was deep water in the road
but at one side it was shallow, a pathway—
I went to the side,
thought I should not walk in the deep water
—thought a rocket struck loose up across me,
that sprayed a shower of sparks of beautiful fire:
love for the sublime.
Perhaps.

Translation from the Swedish by Muriel Rukeyser & Leif Sjöberg

Muriel Rukeyser 1913–1980

THE SPEED OF DARKNESS

I

Whoever despises the clitoris despises the penis
Whoever despises the penis despises the cunt
Whoever despises the cunt despises the life of the child.

Resurrection music,   silence,   and surf.

II

No longer speaking
Listening with the whole body
And with every drop of blood
Overtaken by silence

But this same silence is become speech
With the speed of darkness.

III

Stillness during war, the lake.
The unmoving spruces.
Glints over the water.
Faces, voices.   You are far away.
A tree that trembles.

I am the tree that trembles and trembles.

IV

After the lifting of the mist
after the lift of the heavy rains
the sky stands clear
and the cries of the city risen in day
I remember the buildings are space
walled, to let space be used for living
I mind this room is space
this drinking glass is space
whose boundary of glass
lets me give you drink and space to drink
your hand, my hand being space
containing skies and constellations
your face
carries the reaches of air
I know I am space
my words are air.

V

Between   between
the man : act   exact
woman : in curve   senses in their maze
frail orbits, green tries,   games of stars
shape of the body speaking its evidence

VI

I look across at the real
vulnerable   involved   naked
devoted to the present of all I care for
the world of its history leading to this moment.

VII

Life the announcer.
I assure you
there are many ways to have a child.
I bastard mother
promise you
there are many ways to be born.
They all come forth
in their own grace.

VIII

Ends of the earth join tonight
with blazing stars upon their meeting.

These sons,   these sons
fall burning into Asia.

IX

Time comes into it.
Say it.   Say it.

The universe is made of stories,
not of atoms.

X

Lying
blazing beside me
you rear beautifully and up—
your thinking face—
erotic body reaching
in all its colors and lights—
your erotic face
colored and lit—
not colored body-and-face
but now entire,
colors   lights   the world thinking and reaching.

XI

The river flows past the city.

Water goes down to tomorrow
making its children   I hear their unborn voices
I am working out the vocabulary of my silence.

XII

Big-boned man young and of my dream
Struggles to get the live bird out of his throat.
I am he am I?   Dreaming?
I am the bird am I?   I am the throat?

A bird with a curved beak.
It could slit anything, the throat-bird.
Drawn up slowly.   The curved blades, not large.
Bird emerges   wet   being born
Begins to sing.

XIII

My night awake
staring at the broad rough jewel
the copper roof across the way
thinking of the poet
yet unborn in this dark
who will be the throat of these hours.
No.   Of those hours.
Who will speak these days,
if not I,
if not you?

Aimé Césaire b. 1913

from **I, LAMINARIA**

Nontime imposes the tyranny of its spaciality on time: in any life there is a north and a south, and the east and the west. At the limit, or, any rate, at the crossroad, as one's eyes fly over the seasons, there is the unequal struggle of life and death, of fervor and lucidity, even if it is one of despair and collapse, the strength as well to face tomorrow. Such is life. Such is this book, between sun and shadow, between mountain and mangrove swamp, between dawn and dusk, lame and divided. Time also to settle one's account with a few phantoms and a few ghosts.

lagoonal calendar

i inhabit a sacred wound
i inhabit imaginary ancestors
i inhabit an obscure will
i inhabit a long silence
i inhabit an irremediable thirst

i inhabit a one-thousand-year journey
i inhabit a three-hundred-year war
i inhabit an abandoned cult
between bulb and bulbil i inhabit the unexploited space
i inhabit not a vein of the basalt
but the rising tide of lava
which runs back up the gulch at full speed
to burn all the mosques
I make the most of this avatar
of an absurdly botched version of paradise
        —it is much worse than a hell—
i inhabit from time to time one of my wounds
each minute i change apartments
and any peace frightens me

    whirling fire
    ascidium like none other for the dust
    of strayed worlds
    having spat out my fresh-water entrails
    a volcano i remain with my loaves of words and
    my secret minerals

i inhabit thus a vast thought
but in most cases i prefer to confine myself
to the smallest of my ideas
or else i inhabit a magical formula
only its opening words
the rest being forgotten
i inhabit the ice block
i inhabit the debacle
i inhabit the face of a great disaster
i inhabit in most cases the driest udder
of the skinniest peak—the she-wolf of these clouds—
i inhabit the halo of the Cactaceae
i inhabit a herd of goats pulling on the tit
of the most desolate argan tree
to tell you the truth i no longer know my correct address
bathyal or abyssal
i inhabit the octopuses' hole
i fight with an octopus over an octopus hole

brother lay off
wrack rubbish
I hook on like devil's guts
    or uncoil poranalike
it's all the same thing
    which the wave rolls
    which the sun cups
    which the wind flogs
sculpture in the round of my nothingness

the atmospheric or rather historic pressure
even if it makes certain words of mine sumptuous
immeasurably increases my plight

Translation from the French by Clayton Eshleman & Annette Smith

A FIRST GALLERY

Marie Luise Kaschnitz 1901–1974

MY GROUND

I have staked out my ground
With frozen fishes
My path to freedom
Is marked by rustling corn husks
I raise ice ferns
On my windowpane
I breathe a circular hole
For my visitors
They see my eyes
My lashes waving
In vain
Around midnight the slalom of ghosts
Sweeps through the corn.

Translation from the German by Lisel Mueller

WHO WOULD HAVE THOUGHT IT

A poet put Old Prussian
Words into his notebook
A picture hung in his room
A wolf in a wilderness of snow
Unbearably lonely
He had a clavichord
In this same room
Also several icons
And a collection
Of handwritten songs
Lithuania in Berlin
When he was dead
Someone
Described this room
In great detail
And took photographs
In memoriam

In a few decades
We will enter the world
Still between the legs of women
But so well designed
That we'll know how to do everything
Without any training
Like Aubrey Beardsley
Who never erased a line
And left only masterpieces
When he died young

Who would have thought it
After the black leather jackets
The children of God
Cooing
Jesus
Jesus

How do you spend your time?
Thank you we manage
We waste it
Kill it
Only the days of the old
With their missing words
Escaping things
Are placid, a smile
With no place to go

Look here: stadiums pools
Antennas mounted
Steel nets in place
Expressways smoothed
Even underground
Prime beef frozen
Barrels of beer stacked high
Tens of thousands, all
For these Games which may be the last
And that other distant Olympia
Sunk
Beneath the pines
Silent

Someone dreamed that his head
Had been cut off
And rested loosely on his neck
He steadied it with both hands
Below the bloodline
He was careful walking down the stone stairs
Afraid, he said, he might suffer
A brain concussion
If his head should slip
And bounce on the steps.

Translation from the German by Lisel Mueller

COMMENTARY

La poetessa della macerie—the poetessa of ruins — is what an Italian magazine called me recently, but for a moment I was nonplused, as it seemed to me that even in my war-time and post-war poems what is essential is not the chaos but the yearning for a new order.
M. L. K.

Born near Karlsruhe, Kaschnitz grew up in Potsdam & Berlin, worked (as bookseller) in Weimar & Munich, then spent much time travelling around the Mediterranean with her archeologist husband, living in later years in Frankfurt & in Rome (where she died), producing numerous volumes of poetry, novels, essays, short stories, radio plays, & journals. Her early work, pre–World War II, was marked by fascination—much like that of other German artists, then to now—with "solar" (ancient Greek & Roman) cultures & mythologies. Derailed by years of repression & war, she emerged with a growing sense of culpability & of herself as poet/"watchman"—"a role she adopted when she recognized with horror that her silence during the Nazi period meant de facto complicity, no matter how great her private loathing" (Lisel Mueller). Increasingly internalized, her later work was exemplary of the ways biography & history could combine—to accomplish which, she had to change from closed & settled measures (in her verse) to a new & hard-won openness of form. Of this she wrote: "The older I get, the less sure I am of saying the right thing. I can no longer make absolute statements, I have to find my way tentatively. . . . In the strict forms you can only say what you imagine you know exactly—not, however, those things which appear the more enigmatic the longer you live." Or again, citing what stays fixed behind that shift in form: "Affection is still affection, overcoming is still overcoming, betrayal is still betrayal."

Vladimir Holan 1905–1980

from A NIGHT WITH HAMLET

FOR VLADIMIR JUSTL
PUBLISHED FOR THE 400TH ANNIVERSARY
OF SHAKESPEARE'S BIRTH, IN 1964

MENIPPUS: I see only bones and fleshless skulls,
and most of them look alike.

HERMES: That's the very thing that has astonished
all the poets, those bones . . . And only you, it seems, are
contemptuous of them.

MENIPPUS: Well then, show me Helen, for I wouldn't
recognize her.

HERMES: This skull, that's Helen . . .

LUCIAN

When passing from nature to being
walls are not exactly benevolent,
walls pissed on by the talented, walls spat on
by eunuchs revolting against the spirit, walls no smaller,
even if they are still unborn,
yet walls rounding out the fruit . . .

The yielding ripeness of Shakespeare
invites license. Its content,
which like astonishment should be
sanctification, becomes, as time declines
(with possible indications of its absence),
a usurious tax on all apartments,
into which a theater director has arrogantly moved.
Only fraud is a certainty here. And the spectator,
who has prematurely crept up like a Saint George dragon,
warms himself in the bile of the critics . . .
And those who dare to map even desire
have it easy, although they too are
a choleric testimony to irredeemable jackasses . . .
But nature is always a sign
which, if it doesn't keep silent,
denies itself. After all, the male,

that opener, feels mutely only because
the spirit always moves forward
and everything closes behind it . . .

He too was like that . . . Hamlet!
His arm torn off, evening rolled through
the empty sleeve of his coat
as through a blind man's genitals, chewed up by the music . . .

Nature joined our contempt for the city
to the rocky urine of upturned mosses
at the entire golden height of capability
and waited until the wine caterpillar became a butterfly,
but to no avail,
because he felt contempt for wine from the day
when out of thirst he had to open a horse's artery
and drink the blood . . .
This led him to accept a jinni
and to exclude seemingly unrevealed mysteries,
and, being between himself and himself,
he spoke for the abyss.
After that, he only spoke out of it,
even when, say, he discussed a certain saint
who had nothing left, except her pain
from remembering an ancient lover,
a pain so small she could easily hide it
inside a rotten tooth . . .

It matters little
whether the saliva hissed at us
dripping from the mouth of sleeping crickets,
constructors of midnight bridges,
the created creating, who built two tombs
out of apparitions, taking a wage for prophecies.
Only art was without excuses . . .
And life too insisted,
but insisted with the risk that we'll survive,
although we might also wish to die . . .

There was no response . . . Nowhere, not even in the unconscious . . .
But he was there, Hamlet, who like a Mozart-swigger
overturned the Alps, to place a bottle insecurely

on the creaking step of his fear of death,
so close to himself that between him
all immortality could fit . . .
And indeed, in his presence
the knife under the sheep
could not slash anything
and the melted pewter from old baptismal fonts
would congeal into a vital shape.
Yet anxiety exists. He was on the wound of eternity
and had to heal it. He was in his father's tomb
and had to be a son of the children . . . He was
with the holy soul of music
and had to be, for the earnings of a harlot
or for the price of a dog . . .

Oh, not that he knew everything, for he keenly sensed
that when selfishness stuffs itself
it does not throw up, it digests and starts up again—
not that he was wise, like a wood
pillar tends to be among those of stone—
not that he shuddered with disgust facing
an ancient floor painted by the bloodflow of women—
not that out of avarice he recalled final things
and would therefore dwell in Atreus's tomb,
in which treasury led directly into mortuary—
it mattered not to him
if Alexander the Great's crooked nose
straightened out something in history—
no, no, but I still see him scowl at people
for whom if anything is a mastery
it is also an emptiness, into which they hurl
all their emasculated fury . . .

Whoever gives remains avaricious . . .
And yet, we do not believe and are always waiting for something,
possibly people are always waiting for something
only because they do not believe . . . They are enlightened,
but they do not radiate . . . They are anemic,
as if without bloodshed there would be nothing,
they are expelled but not yet excommunicated,
they are curious but have yet to find the mirror

in which Helen-Helen
looked from below-below,
in fact, they are so deaf, they would like to hear
the voice of Jesus Christ on an LP . . .

And yet everything, everything here
is miraculous only once:
only once the blood of Abel
which was to wipe out all war,
only once the unrepeatable unconsciousness of childhood,
only once youth and only once song,
only once love and, simultaneously, being lost,
only once everything against heredity and habit,
only once the untying of agreed-upon knots and hence liberation,
and only once the essence of art,
only once everything against prison,
unless God himself wanted, on this earth,
to build a house . . .

Translation from the Czech by Clayton Eshleman & Frantisek Galan,
with the collaboration of Michael Heim

COMMENTARY

. . . I have been speaking fifteen years / to a wall // and I have dragged the
wall here / out of my own hell / so that it can now / tell you all . . . (V. H.,
21 June 1963) And again: *In me the heart of poetry bleeds.*

His first poems were published in 1926, and over the years thereafter he
was a prolific writer of poetry, prose, translations—a poet, like his country-
man Vitezslav Nezval (volume one), whose work matched the innovative
writings of the century's other visionary modernists. What finally set him
apart were the works written after the Second World War, during years of
Communist repression following those of Nazi occupation, with respites
only in the immediate postwar years & the Prague Spring of the later 1960s.
It was from within that condition of loneliness & isolation that he began "a
new search" to say what he had to say while suffering the horrors of the
"poem addressed to emptiness" (a phrase, in a very different circumstance,
of the American poet Robert Creeley). The outcome of that search brought
him to the practice—he wrote—of an "atonal harmony . . . [by which] I
understand a special toneless instrumentation, a harmonious disharmony."
In his masterwork of that time, *A Night with Hamlet*, the means developed
toward this end—"abrupt transitions of theme, wild plunges of poetic
thought, bizarre imagery, baroque rhetoric, . . . syntax deliberately dis-

torted" (Ian Milner)—reach an extraordinary climax. The resultant poem (only the first of many sections is given here) proceeds as a series of highly torqued conversations between the residents of two states—Holan's Prague & Hamlet's Denmark—both sensed as prison houses, suffering alike the rot of politics & power. But the world Holan and Hamlet share becomes a mirror, too—a mirror filled with many worlds, many torn identities. Thus, Clayton Eshleman of Holan's Hamlet: "In 1949 Prague, he has become a one-armed sexual maniac . . . ; a multilingual world traveler; . . . a mythological depository who contains a successfully returned Orpheus and Eurydice. He thus appears to be Dionysian and Titanic, rooted in Orphism, and faithful to the entire evolving history (and prehistory?) of [Shakespeare's] HAMLET."

Samuel Beckett 1906–1989

IMAGINATION DEAD IMAGINE

No trace anywhere of life, you say, pah, no difficulty there, imagination not dead yet, yes, dead, good, imagination dead imagine. Islands, waters, azure, verdure, one glimpse and vanished, endlessly, omit. Till all white in the whiteness the rotunda. No way in, go in, measure. Diameter three feet, three feet from ground to summit of the vault. Two diameters at right angles AB CD divide the white ground into two semicircles ACB BDA. Lying on the ground two white bodies, each in its semicircle. White too the vault and the round wall eighteen inches high from which it springs. Go back out, a plain rotunda, all white in the whiteness, go back in, rap, solid throughout, a ring as in the imagination the ring of bone. The light that makes all so white no visible source, all shines with the same white shine, ground, wall, vault, bodies, no shadow. Strong heat, surfaces hot but not burning to the touch, bodies sweating. Go back out, move back, the little fabric vanishes, ascend, it vanishes, all white in the whiteness, descend, go back in. Emptiness, silence, heat, whiteness, wait, the light goes down, all grows dark together, ground, wall, vault, bodies, say twenty seconds, all the greys, the light goes out, all vanishes. At the same time the temperature goes down, to reach its minimum, say freezing-point, at the same instant that the black is reached, which may seem strange. Wait, more or less long, light and heat come back, all grows white and hot together, ground, wall, vault, bodies, say twenty seconds, all the greys, till the initial level is reached whence the fall began. More or less long, for there may intervene, experience shows, between end of fall and beginning of rise, pauses of varying length, from the fraction of the second to what would have seemed, in other times, other places, an eternity. Same remark for the other pause, between end of rise and beginning of fall. The extremes, as long as they last, are perfectly stable, which in the case of the temperature may seem strange, in the beginning. It is possible too, experience shows, for rise and fall to stop short at any point and mark a pause, more or less long, before resuming, or reversing, the rise now fall, the fall rise, these in their turn to be completed, or to stop short and mark a pause, more or less long, before resuming, or again reversing, and so on, till finally one or the other extreme is reached. Such variations of rise and fall, combining in countless rhythms, commonly attend the passage from white and heat to black and cold, and vice versa. The extremes alone are stable as is stressed by the vibration to be observed when a pause occurs at some intermediate stage, no matter what its level and duration. Then all vibrates, ground, wall, vault, bodies, ashen or leaden or between the two, as may be. But on the whole, experience shows, such uncertain passage is not common. And most often, when the light begins to fail, and along with it the heat, the movement continues unbroken until, in the space of some twenty seconds, pitch black is reached and at the same instant say freezing-point. Same remark for the reverse movement, towards heat and whiteness. Next most frequent is the fall or rise with pauses of varying length in these feverish greys, without at any moment reversal of the movement. But whatever its uncertainties the return sooner or later to a temporary calm seems assured, for the moment, in the black dark or the great whiteness, with attendant temperature, world still proof against enduring tumult. Rediscovered miraculously after what absence in perfect voids it is no longer quite the same, from this point of view, but there is no other. Externally all is as before and the sighting of the little fabric quite as much a matter of chance, its whiteness merging in the surrounding whiteness. But go in and now briefer lulls and never twice the same storm. Light and heat remain linked as though supplied by the same source of which still no trace. Still on the ground, bent in three, the head against the wall at B, the arse against the wall at A, the knees against the wall between B and C, the feet against the wall between C and A, that is to say inscribed in the semicircle ACB, merging in the white ground were it not for the long hair of strangely imperfect whiteness, the white body of a woman finally. Similarly inscribed in the other semicircle, against the wall his head at A, his arse at B, his knees between A and D, his feet between D and B, the partner. On their right sides therefore both and back to back head to arse. Hold a mirror to their lips, it mists. With their left hands they hold their left legs a little below the knee, with their right hands their left arms a little above the elbow. In this agitated light, its great white calm now so rare and brief, inspection is not easy. Sweat and mirror notwithstanding they might well pass for inanimate but for the left eyes which at incalculable intervals suddenly open wide and gaze in unblinking exposure long beyond what is humanly possible. Piercing pale blue the effect is striking, in the beginning. Never the two gazes together except once, when the beginning of one overlapped the end of the other, for about ten seconds. Neither fat nor thin, big nor small, the bodies seem whole and in fairly good condition, to judge by the surfaces exposed to view. The faces too, assuming the two sides of a piece, seem to want nothing essential. Between their absolute stillness and the convulsive light the contrast is striking, in the beginning, for one who still remembers having been struck by the contrary. It is clear however, from a thousand little signs too long to imagine, that they are not sleeping. Only murmur ah, no more, in this silence, and at the same instant for the eye of prey the infinitesimal shudder instantaneously suppressed. Leave them there, sweating and icy, there is better elsewhere. No, life ends and no, there is nothing elsewhere, and no question now of ever finding again that white speck lost in whiteness, to see if they still lie still in the stress of that storm, or of a worse storm, or in the black dark for good, or the great whiteness unchanging, and if not what they are doing.

Translation from the French by the author

COMMENTARY

I have to speak, whatever that means. Having nothing to say, no words but the words of others, I have to speak. No one compels me to, there is no one, it's an accident, a fact. Nothing can ever exempt me from it, there is nothing, nothing to discover, nothing to recover, nothing that can lessen what remains to say. (S. B., in The Unnamable) And from the same source: *About myself I need know nothing.*

Central to a work that speaks & means is his reiterated declaration of a silence, a *not*-speaking, *not*-meaning (by those "incapable of keeping silent") that aligns him with John Cage (below) & others in making that the basis of a *new* or, at the least, *revitalized* poesis. A novelist & playwright of renown, he remained (as in his beginnings) a poet foremost—not through his verse (like that of his friend & mentor James Joyce: trivial) but in the presence throughout of an active language & awareness, both undercut (always) by his denial of them. The background to all of that—again like Joyce's—was his birth & education in & around Dublin, followed by the remaining sixty years of his life spent mostly in France. While writings (poems mostly) began to appear by the late 1920s and the 1930s, it was the second world war & its immediate aftermath (including active underground resistance—though a foreigner—to the German Occupation) that saw the emergence of his characteristic oeuvre: a switch from writing in English to writing in French; a pickup in his work as novelist (*Molloy, Malone Dies, & The Unnamable* his great trilogy of the 1940s/50s); & the creation of a radical form of theater (*Waiting for Godot, Endgame, Krapp's Last Tape*), in which he would be a crucial/germinal player. As with *Waiting for Godot*, the work in (& in spite of) its denial of meaning raised to public view the age-old gnostic spectre of the *Deus absconditus:* a god not so much dead as hidden (shameful): the nonexistent master of a cruelly negated world. But it was Beckett's genius as a poet to find a truly *comic* voice, a demotic language with which to say it, as if—so Hugh Kenner writes of the two clowns in *Godot*—"to move the world . . . into Laurel and Hardy's theatre, where it becomes something rich and strange, as do they." (That one of Beckett's late works, *Film,* was written for & acted by the comic likes of Buster Keaton—as *Godot* had featured Bert Lahr, & others—is also worth noting.)

George Oppen 1908–1984

PSALM

Veritas sequitur . . .

In the small beauty of the forest
The wild deer bedding down—
That they are there!

        Their eyes
Effortless, the soft lips
Nuzzle and the alien small teeth
Tear at the grass

        The roots of it
Dangle from their mouths
Scattering earth in the strange woods.
They who are there.

        Their paths
Nibbled thru the fields, the leaves that shade them
Hang in the distances
Of sun

                    The small nouns
Crying faith
In this in which the wild deer
Startle, and stare out.

MYTH OF THE BLAZE

night–sky   bird's   world
to know   to know   in my life to know

what I have said to myself

the dark to escape in brilliant highways
of the night sky, finally
why had they not

killed me why did they fire that warning
wounding cannon only the one round I hold a superstition

because of this   lost to be lost   Wyatt's
lyric and Rezi's
running thru my mind
in the destroyed (and guilty) Theatre
of the War   I'd cried
and remembered
boyhood   degradation   other
degradations and this crime I will not recover
from that landscape it will be in my mind
it will fill my mind and this is horrible
death bed   pavement   the secret taste
of being lost

dead

clown in the birds'
world what names
(but my name)

and my love's name to speak

into the eyes
of the Tyger   blaze

of changes . . . 'named

the animals'   name

and name the vigorous dusty strong

animals gather
under the joists   the boards   older

than they   giving
them darkness the gifted

dark tho names   the names   the 'little'

adventurous
words   a mountain   the cliff

a wave are taxonomy I believe

in the world

because it is
impossible   the shack

on the coast

under the eaves
the rain barrel flooding

in the weather and no lights

across rough water illumined
as tho the narrow

end of the funnel what are the names
of the Tyger   to speak
to the eyes

of the Tiger   blaze
of the tiger   who moves in the forest leaving

no scent

but the pine needles' his eyes blink

quick
in   the shack
in the knife-cut
and the opaque

white

bread each side of the knife

*Our true faith is said in the simple words, for we cannot escape them —
for meaning is the instant of meaning — and this means that we write to
find what we believe and what we do not believe. . . . Eventually, I think,
there is no hope for us but in meaning.*
G. O.

The work for Oppen began in his connection to the short-lived & later in-
fluential "Objectivists" movement of the 1930s (see volume one). For this
he & his wife, Mary Colby, founded To Publishers (later called the Objec-
tivist Press) in coeditorship with Louis Zukofsky, under which imprint they
published Zukofsky's *"Objectivists" Anthology,* Pound's *ABC of Reading,*
William Carlos Williams's *Collected Poems 1921–1931,* along with work
by Oppen himself & Charles Reznikoff (Rezi in *Myth of the Blaze*), among
the main "Objectivist" poets. Oppen's own poetry from that time comprises
a single volume, *Discrete Series* (1934), after which he became a Communist
labor organizer & took, he says elsewhere, 25 years to write his next poem.
But the work—picked up after a Mexican exile in the McCarthyite 1950s—
shows a remarkable continuity of attentions: a concern with structure ("the
objectification of the poem, the making an object of the poem") & with the
process that informs that structure (the poem as "a test of truth" or "test of
images . . . of whether one's thought is valid, whether one can establish a
series of images, of experiences . . . whether or not one will consider the
concept of humanity to be valid, something that is, or else have to regard it
as simply being a word.") From all of which there emerges a poetry in which
the "virtue of the mind is that emotion which causes to see."

Yannis Ritsos 1909–1990

THE MEANING OF SIMPLICITY

I hide behind simple things that you may find me;
if you don't find me, you'll find the things,

you'll touch what my hand touches,
the imprints of our hands will merge.

The August moon glitters in the kitchen
like a pewter pot (it becomes like this because of what I tell you)
it lights up the empty house and the kneeling silence of the house—
always the silence remains kneeling.

Every word is a way out
for an encounter often canceled,
and it's then a word is true, when it insists on the encounter.

Translation from the Greek by Kimon Friar

NAKED FACE

Cut the lemon and let two drops fall into the glass;
look there, the knives beside the fish on the table—
the fish are red, the knives are black.
All with a knife between their teeth or up their sleeves, thrust in their
    boots or their breeches.
The two women have gone crazy, they want to eat the men,
they have large black fingernails, they comb their unwashed hair
high up, high up like towers, from which the five boys
plunge down one by one. Afterward they come down the stairs,
draw water from the well, wash themselves, spread out their thighs,
thrust in pine cones, thrust in stones. And we
nod our heads with a "yes" and a "yes"—we look down
at an ant, a locust, or on the statue of Victory—
pine tree caterpillars saunter on her wings.
The lack of holiness—someone said—is the final, the most dreadful
    knowledge;
it's exactly such knowledge that now remains to be called holy.

Athens, 9/30/72

Translation from the Greek by Kimon Friar & Kostas Myrsiades

The day is mad. Mad is the house. Mad the bedsheets.
You also are mad; you dance with the white curtain in your arms;
you beat on a saucepan above my papers as on a tambourine;
the poems run through the rooms; the burnt milk smells;
a crystal horse looks out of the window. Wait—I say—
we've forgotten Phymonóis' tripod in the woodcutters' guild hall;
the oracles are turned upside down. We've forgotten yesterday's bleeding
    moon,
the newdug earth. A carriage passes by laden with oleanders.
Your fingernails are rose petals. Do not justify yourself. In your closet
    you have placed
tulle bags filled with lavender. The sun's umbrellas have gone mad,
they've become entangled with the wings of angels. You wave your
    handkerchief;
whom are you greeting? What people are you greeting?—The whole
    world.
A brown water-turtle has comfortably settled on your knees;
wet seaweed stirs on its sculptured shell. And you dance.
A hoop from a barrel of olden times rolls down the hill,
falls into the stream, tossing off drops that wet your feet,
and also wet your chin. Stop that I may wipe you.
But in your dancing, you do not hear me. Well then, duration
is a whirlwind, life is cyclical, it has no ending. Last night
the horsemen passed by. Naked girls on the horses' rumps;
perhaps this is why the wild geese were screaming in the bell tower. We
    did not hear them
as the horses' hoofs sank in our sleep. Today before your door
you found a silver horseshoe. You hung it above the lintel. My luck—
    you shout—
my luck—you shout, and dance. Beside you the tall mirror is also
    dancing,
glittering with a thousand bodies and the statue of Hippólytos crowned
    with poppies.
My parrot has gone—you say as you dance—and no one imitates my
    voice any more; aye, aye—
this voice from within me comes out of the forest of Dodóna.
Clear lakes rise in the air with all their white waterlilies,
with all their underwater vegetation. We cut reeds,
build a golden hut. You clamber up the roof.

I grasp you by the ankles with both hands. You don't come down.
You fly. You fly into the blue. You drag me with you
as I hold you by the ankles. From your shoulder
the large blue towel falls on the water; for a while it floats
and then with wide folds sinks, leaving on the surface
a trembling pentagram. Don't go higher—I shout—. No higher. And
  suddenly
with a mute thump we both land on the mythical bed. And listen—
in the street below strikers are passing by with placards and flags.
Do you hear? We're late. Take the handkerchief you dance with, too.
  Let's go. Thank you, my love.

Translation from the Greek by Kimon Friar

from **3 x 111 TRISTYCHS**

Second Series

14. In the white egg,
     a yellow chick
     a blue song.

26. The new moon
     hides up its sleeve—you saw it?—
     a knife.

52. Naked, astride an elephant,
     the moon crosses the river.
     Dewdrops shimmering at its feet.

61. Guatemala, Nicaragua, Salvador.
     Where did so many bodies go? On a tree, wind-swept,
     a pair of worn gray trousers.

63. Where is the time to light a cigarette,
     to look at a star, to speak with a turtle,
     to scratch your nose, and fart?

80. Seek not, want not, be not.
     I bite—he says—a bitter apple.
     Freedom.

104. They tagged you an illiterate, those idle bureaucrats.
Unaware how on arid islands you memorized
the twelve Gospels of the Struggle.

Translation from the Greek by Kostas Myrsiades

Every word is a way out / for an encounter often canceled, / and it's then a word is true, when it insists on the encounter.
Y.R. (who signs off "poet of the final century B.H.," i.e., "Before Humanity," as he defined himself, his time)

A life of personal tragedy (mother & sister die early of tuberculosis; Ritsos himself spends ten years in & out of sanatoriums; father & another sister go insane & are confined). Also political struggles (the Metaxas dictator-ship publicly burns his book *Epitaphios* in '36, & from then until '52 he cannot publish freely; from '48 to '52, confined to detention & "rehabili-tation" camps; arrested in '67 on first night of the Colonels' fascist coup & spends the next year & a half once more in detention, then in exile on the island of Samos, the work banned yet again). But also great public triumphs: a poetry never far from song—Greek folksong (*demotiko tragihoudi*)—& an engagement with socialist politics that turns a number of his works, es-pecially those set to music by Mikos Theodoriakis, into the most popular Greek poems of the century. Probably one of the most prolific poets ever (a writing schedule of one to sixteen poems a day; more than five thousand pages of his "selected" poetry alone) & a major formal experimenter, he jettisons traditional forms early on & works in a variety of open possibili-ties: long poems, though rarely more than fifty pages; experiments with Whitmanesque long verse lines; collections of one-, two-, or three-line poems; serial poems in numbered sequences; &, most persistently, short one-page "laconic and epigrammatic" poems called "testimonies," written (he tells us) "from the desire to detach and pin down a moment of time that would permit a microscopic examination of it in depth and thus discover all those elements of time that probably would have scattered to the winds in a limitless horizon—that is to say, to conceive the indivisible by what is divis-ible, to conceive of everlasting motion by what is immobile."

Charles Olson 1910-1970

[UNTITLED]

my memory is

the history of time

[UNTITLED]

Peloria   the dog's upper lip kept curling
in his sleep as I was drawn to the leftward to
watch his long shark jaw and sick brown color
gums the teeth flashing even as he dreamed.
Maximus is a whelping mother, giving birth
with the crunch of his own pelvis.
He sent flowers on the waves from the mole
of Tyre. He went to Malta. From Malta
to Marseilles. From Marseilles to Iceland.
From Iceland to Promontorium Vinlandiae.
Flowers go out on the sea. On the left
of the Promontorium. On the left of the
Promontorium, Settlement Cove

I am making a mappemunde. It is to include my being.
It is called here, at this point and point of time
Peloria.

THE MOON IS THE NUMBER 18

is a monstrance,
the blue dogs bay,
and the son sits,
grieving

is a grinning god, is
the mouth of, is
the dripping moon

while in the tower the cat
preens

and all motion
is a crab

and there is nothing he can do but what they do, watch
the face of waters, and fire

> The blue dogs paw,
> lick the droppings, dew
> or blood, whatever
> results are. And night,
> the crab, rays round
> attentive as the cat to catch
> human sound

> The blue dogs rue,
> as he does, as he would howl, confronting
> the wind which rocks what was her, while prayers
> striate the snow, words blow
> as questions cross fast, fast
> as flames, as flames form, melt
> along any darkness

Birth is an instance as is a host, namely, death

The moon has no air

> In the red tower
> in that tower where she also sat
> in that particular tower where watching & moving are,
> there,
> there where what triumph there is, is: there
> is all substance, all creature
> all there is against the dirty moon, against
> number, image, sortilege—

> alone with cat & crab,
> and sound is, is, his
> conjecture

the Sea – turn yr Back on
the Sea. go inland, to
Dogtown: the Harbor

the shore the City
are now
shitty. as the Nation

is – the World
tomorrow unless
the Princes

of the Husting the sons
who refused to be Denied
the Demon (if Medea

kills herself – Medea
is a Phoenician
wench. also Daughter

of the Terror) as J-son
Johnson Hines
son Hines

sight Charles
John Hines
Ol'
   son   /

the Atlantic
Mediterranean
Black Sea time

is done in done for gone
Jack Hammond
put a stop to

surface underwater galaxy
time: there is no sky
space or sea left

earth is interesting:
ice is interesting
stone is interesting

flowers are
      Carbon
Carbon is
Carboniferous
Pennsylvania

Age
under
Dogtown
the stone

the watered
rock Carbon
flowers, rills

Aquarian Time
after fish
– fish was

Christ o Christ pick the seeds
out of yr teeth – how handsome
the dead dog lies! (horror X

the Migma is where the
Seeds Christ was supposed to pick out
: Wyngaershoek hoik Grape Vine HOYK the Dutch

& the Norse
and Algonquins:
He-with-the-House-on-his-Head

she-who-Lusted After-the
Snake-in-the-Pond
Dogtown berries smell

as The-Grub-Eaten-Fish-Take-the-Smell Out-of-The
Air a e r the Ta of
Dogtown (the Ta metarsia

    is the Angel Matter
    not to come until (rill!
    3000: we will carry water

    up the hill the Water the Water to
    make the Flower hot – Jack
    & Jill will

    up Dogtown hill on top one day the
    Vertical American Thing will
    show from heaven the Ladder

    come down to the Earth
    of Us All, the Many who
    know
        there is One!
        One Mother
        One Son

    One Daughter
    and Each the Father
    of Him-Her-Self:

    the Genetic
    is Ma the Morphic
    is Pa the City is Mother-

    Polis, the Child-Made-Man-Woman is

(Mary's Son
Elizabeth's

Man) MONOGENE:
               in COLLAGEN
the monogene, / in KOLLAgen

         TIME

LEAP onto the LAND, the AQUARIAN TIME

the greater the water you add
the greater the decomposition
so long as the agent is protein
the carbon of four is the corners

in stately motion to sing in high bitch voice the fables
of wood and stone and man and woman loved

and loving in the snow
and sun

             the weather

        on Dogtown
        is protogonic but the other side of heaven
        is Ocean

filled in the flower the weather
on Dogtown the other side of heaven
is Ocean

Dogtown the under
vault heaven
is Carbon Ocean   Dogtown the under
is Annisquam   vault – the 'mother'
                  rock: the Diamond (Coal) the Pennsylvanian

                           Age   the soft
                           (Coal) LOVE

        Age   the soft (Coal love
        hung-up   burning
        under the City: bituminous

        Heart to be turned to Black
        Stone   the Black Chrysanthemum
        is the Throne of Creation   Ocean

                    is the Black Gold Flower

[UNTITLED]

*

Added to

making a Republic

in gloom on Watchhouse

Point

    an actual earth of value to

    construct one, from rhythm to

    image, and image is knowing, and

    knowing, Confucius says, brings one

    to the goal: nothing is possible without

    doing it.   It is where the test lies, malgre

    all the thought and all the pell-mell of

    proposing it. Or thinking it out or living it

    ahead of time.

        Reading about my world,

        March 6th, 1968

It is not I, / even if the work appeared / biographical. The only interesting thing / is if one can be / an image / of man. . . . Otherwise, we are involved in / ourselves (which is demonstrably / not very interesting, no / matter / who. (C. O.) Against which (Olson again): *The soul / is an onslaught.*

Olson makes a big leap forward—starting, as he says below (page 412), from wartime degradations of the human spirit, genocides, etc., to which the first resistance is forged (much like Artaud's) from physiology and body. Where it takes him is a vast, likely impossible enterprise: a poetics of the breath & body (as *projective* verse) that will lead to poems of maximal (projective) size (like Williams's *Paterson*, Zukofsky's "*A*," Pound's *Cantos*, his own *Maximus*) and to a radical remapping of all human history: a plan, in short, for a new "curriculum of the soul," often set forth in scrawled notes, then assigned to younger colleagues to flesh out. As with André Breton vis-à-vis Surrealism, this relation to a set of ideas and to a movement (projective verse, & "Black Mountain" as the movement & the college in North Carolina of which he was the rector in the early 1950s) sometimes obscured the true force of his work as poet. The culmination of that work was *The Maximus Poems*, his ongoing "epic"—in Pound's definition of same, "a poem including history." Written as a series of poems, documents, letters, and fragments, its central figure is derived (at least in name) from a little-known second-century philosopher, Maximus of Tyre, but the implications of bigness/greatness the name carries are a match for Olson's own physical size & longed-for scope. Following from his sense of "history [as] the new localism," the work's setting is Olson's home city, the fishing port of Gloucester (Mass.), with Dogtown near to it; but its roots go off in all directions, both of space & time.

   All selections here—with the exception of *The Moon Is the Number 18*—are from *The Maximus Poems*. Image of Maximus throughout, at home & traveling. Thus, *Peloria*: a Greek word possibly for monstrousness (or portents; earthborn monsters): the world scanned by the mythic voyager who moves around, as stated, thereby makes a *mappemunde* (worldmap) of his own. (But for this & other matters the principal key—where key is needed—is still *A Guide to the Maximus Poems of Charles Olson* by George F. Butterick.)

Edmond Jabès 1912–1990

from **THE BOOK OF QUESTIONS**

"The Jew answers every question with another question"

The Jew answers every question
with another question.

Reb Léma

My name is a question. It is
also my freedom within my
tendency to question.

Reb Eglal

"Our hope is for knowledge," said Reb Mendel. But not all his disciples were of this opinion.

"We first have to agree on the sense you give to the word 'knowledge,'" said the oldest of them.

"Knowledge means questioning," answered Reb Mendel.

"What will we get out of these questions? What will we get out of all the answers which only lead to more questions, since questions are born of unsatisfactory answers?" asked the second disciple.

"The promise of a new question," replied Reb Mendel.

"There will be a moment," the oldest disciple continued, "when we have to stop interrogating. Either because there will be no answer possible, or because we will not be able to formulate any further questions. So why should we begin?"

"You see," said Reb Mendel: "at the end of an argument, there is always a decisive question unsettled."

"Questioning means taking the road to despair," continued the second disciple. "We will never know what we are trying to learn."

"True knowledge is daily awareness that, in the end, one learns nothing. The Nothing is also knowledge, being the reverse of the All, as the air is the reverse of the wing."

"Our hope is the wings of despair. For how would we progress otherwise?" replied Reb Mendel.

"Intelligence," said the third disciple, "is more dangerous than the heart, which relies only on its own beat. Who among us can assert that he is right?"

"Only the hope to be right is real. Truth is the void," replied Reb Mendel.

"If the truth which is in man is void," continued the oldest disciple, "we are nothing in a body of flesh and skin. Therefore God, who is our truth, is also nothing?"

"God is a question," replied Reb Mendel. "A question which leads us to Him who is Light through and for us, who are nothing."

Our meeting, this evening, is about to end. The story I promised you is in your memory. Our passage across pact and imposture, across soul and hands without echo, has led us, via telling detours, to our eyes. They will understand and judge what they see in terms of what they have seen. Both truth and justice are incorruptible eyes: the innocent eyes of the child.

They see freedom in the distance.

The Book of the Living

The light of Israel is a scream to the infinite.

The fence can be seen from afar. The house, with its roof (which the clouds fear because it looks deceptively like a cloud), with its closed doors and windows, looks out over the madwoman's path, which no one else walks.

"That madwoman," asked Sarah, "is she really dead?"

"The scream you heard was an owl. Let's go back in. It's late."

The women in the village made the sign of the cross. The men fell silent long enough to identify the scream and shrug.

"There she goes again."

"There she goes again."

The fence can be seen from afar. It is in flower. The seasons are born and die in the ground.

"There she goes again," said Léonie Lull, turning her head towards the hill. "There she goes again.

"Even in my sleep I hear her."

"Even when she does not scream, I hear her," said Mathilde Meyvis.

The madwoman's house sleeps in its cradle rocked by the nurse's hands. The madwoman's house rocks amid trees hidden by their leaves.

We have to cut off the hands,
    have to fell the trees
to destroy the madwoman's house in its cradle.

We must wake her.

The water you float on, the water you give in to, is the water of sleep.
The water you wash in, the water you fight against, is the water of awakening.

Madness keeps awake
the madwoman's sleep,
but never wakes her.

The madwoman sleeps and moves, makes gestures and sleeps (makes her sleep make gestures), speaks and sleeps (makes her sleep speak).

"There she goes again."
"There she goes again."

"That madwoman," asked Sarah, "is she really dead?"

"As the dark is pierced by the light, the soul is pierced by the scream," wrote Reb Seriel.
And Reb Louel: "The Jewish soul is the fragile casket of a scream."

Madness keeps awake
the madwoman's sleep,
but never wakes her.

"That owl," asked Sarah, "is it really me?"
"The scream you heard was an owl. Let's go back in. It's late."

"I do not hear the scream," said Sarah. "I am the scream."

(The lives of one or two generations of men may fill one sentence or two pages. The gross outline of four particular or ordinary lives: "He was born in . . . He died in . . ." Yes, but between the scream of life and the scream of death? "He was born in . . . He was insulted for no good reason . . . He was misunderstood . . . He died in . . ." Yes, but there must be more? "He was born in . . . He tried to find himself in books . . . He married . . . He had a son . . . He died in . . ." Yes, yes, but there must be more? "He was born on . . . He gave up books . . . He thought he would live on in his son . . . He died on . . ." Yes, but there must be more? "He was short and heavy-set . . . He had a childhood and an old age . . . His name was Salomon Schwall . . ." Yes, yes, but there must be more? "His name was Salomon Schwall . . . He does not remember his youth . . . He left his island . . . He went to Portugal . . . His wife was called

Léonie . . ." Yes, yes, but there must be more? "He settled in the South of France with his wife . . . He was an antique dealer . . . He was called 'the Jew' . . . His wife and son were called 'the wife and the son of the Jew.'" Yes, but there must be more? "He died, and his wife died . . . They were buried in ground which did not know their names, near some crosses . . ." Yes, but there must be more? "His son was French . . . He fought in the war for France . . . He was decorated . . ." Yes, yes, but there must be more? "He fought in the infantry . . . was wounded . . . decorated . . ." Yes, yes, but there must be more? "He was still called 'the Jew' . . . He married Rebecca Sion, whom he met in Cairo . . . He went back to France with her . . ." Yes, but there must be more? "He became a merchant in memory of his father . . . He had brought back all sorts of objects from his travels . . . Oceanic and African masks . . . pottery and gemstones from China, carved ivory from Japan . . ." Yes, but there must be more? "He had a daughter, Sarah . . ." Yes, but there must be more? "He was still called 'the Jew,' and his wife and daughter, 'the wife and the daughter of the Jew.'" Yes, yes, but there must be more? "He had lost his faith . . . He no longer knew who he was . . . He was French . . . decorated . . . His wife and daughter were French . . ." Yes, but there must be more? "Sometimes, he spoke in public to brand racism, to affirm the rights of man . . ." Yes, yes, but there must be more? "He died in a gas chamber outside France . . . and his wife died in a gas chamber outside France . . . and his daughter came back to France, out of her mind . . .")

The madwoman's house sleeps in its cradle, rocked by the nurse's hands. The madwoman's house rocks amid trees hidden by their leaves.

We have to cut off the hands,
have to fell the trees
to destroy the madwoman's house in its cradle.

We must wake her.

"One is the only one to know one's life," said Moses Schwall. "And one's life is a breath."

"The owl howling against the wind," asks Sarah, "is it me, Yukel, is it me? The owl against the wind, the owl for the wind? Is it me, Yukel, is it me? The wind sweeping off my screams, my screams exasperating the wind?"

"Have you seen how a word is born and dies?"

Have you seen how a word is born and dies?
Have you seen how two names are born and die?
From now on, I am alone.
The word is a kingdom.
Every letter has its quality, its grounds, and its rank. The first holds the greatest power, power of fascination and obsession. Omnipotence is its lot.
Sarah.
Yukel.
United kingdoms, innocent worlds, which the alphabet conquered and then destroyed through the hands of men.
You have lost your kingdom.
I have lost my kingdom, as my brothers have, scattered everywhere in a world which has feasted on their dispersion.
Have you seen how a kingdom is made and unmade?
Have you seen how a book is made and unmade?

Translation from the French by Rosmarie Waldrop

COMMENTARY

I talked to you about the difficulty of being Jewish, which is the same as the difficulty of writing. For Judaism and writing are but the same waiting, the same hope, the same wearing out.

E. J.

It is in this sense too that Jabès's concern with the word "Jew" ("an obsession for me . . . like the word 'God'") connects to Marina Tsvetayeva's well-known dictum (volume one, page 428): *In this most Christian of worlds / all poets are Jews.*

Descended from generations of Cairo Jews, Jabès came to his meditations on Jews and God, the Book and Exile/Desert/Wilderness (among his central themes) with the 1956 banishment of Jews from Egypt: a forced immersion in his Jewishness, to learn diaspora in his own flesh. It took him from the lyrical surrealism of his early poems to a newly recovered form of dialogic writing, in which the voices of imagined rabbis comment (in the manner of the Talmud or more mystical Zohar) on the world in aftermath of holocaust or with the sense of holocaust as constant (even where unspoken) presence. The grand scheme of that work called for a seven-volume *Book of Questions* & a three-volume *Book of Resemblances*—twenty related books in the final counting—in which the underlying text, the story of two lovers, Yukel & Sarah, victims of genocide & (subsequent) madness, is told in fits

& starts, or like the holocaust itself is never fully spoken, never *there*. It is this "absent, nonexistent Book . . . [this] pre-text"—holocaust or absent God—"that engenders the rabbinical commentaries, the reflections that oscillate between poetry and aphorism, the open, 'exploded,' nonlinear form of Jabès's work" (R. Waldrop).

In the course of telling & concealing, then, Jabès not only links up with ancient traditions of the Book but with Mallarmé's idea of *Livre* as a world-book (volume one, page 48) or María Sabina's *Book of Language* (page 485, below) & Olson's *mappemunde* (page 102), whether or not the latter two were known to him.

John Cage 1912–1992

IF THERE WERE A PART OF LIFE DARK ENOUGH TO KEEP OUT OF IT A LIGHT FROM ART, I WOULD WANT TO BE IN THAT DARKNESS, FUMBLING AROUND IF NECESSARY, BUT ALIVE   AND I RATHER THINK THAT CONTEMPORARY MUSIC WOULD BE THERE IN THE DARK TOO, BUMPING INTO THINGS, KNOCKING OTHERS OVER AND IN GENERAL ADDING TO THE DISORDER THAT CHARACTERIZES LIFE (IF IT IS OPPOSED TO ART) RATHER THAN ADDING TO THE ORDER AND STABILIZED TRUTH BEAUTY AND POWER THAT CHARACTERIZE A MASTERPIECE (IF IT IS OPPOSED TO LIFE).   AND IS IT?   YES IT IS.

from **SONG BOOKS**

Solo for Voice 17   Song with Electronics   (Relevant)

DIRECTIONS

The text is a mix of remarks about the "telegraph harp" from Volumes II–IV of the *Journal* by Henry David Thoreau. Use electronics to so transform the voice that it resembles singing wires, not strident, but whirring (aeolian harp, musical saw). The notation relates horizontal space to time. Beams are slurs. Commas above the notes, periods following words, are phrase endings. High, middle and low are differentiated; size of note may be related to changes of amplitude, dynamics.

This solo may be accompanied by a tape recording of telegraph wire sounds or by improvisation on a musical saw equipped with mike.

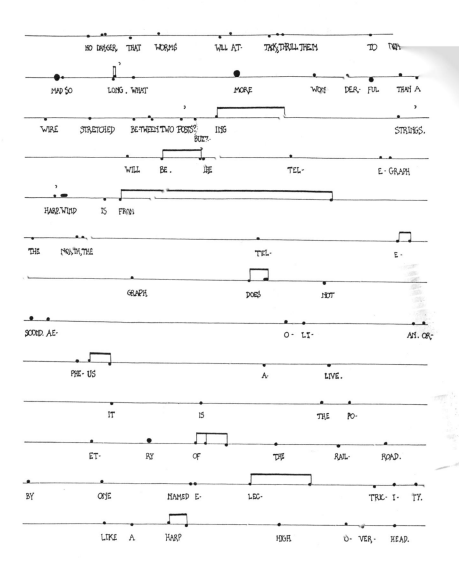

NO DANGER, THAT WORMS WILL AT- TACK; THRILL THEM TO NEW

MAD SO LONG . WHAT MORE WON DER- FUL THAN A

WIRE STRETCHED BE-TWEEN TWO POSTS? ING STRINGS.

BUZZ-

WILL BE . THE TEL- E- GRAPH

HARP. WIND IS FROM

THE NORTH, THE TEL- E-

GRAPH DOES NOT

SOUND. AE- O- LI- AN. OR-

PHE- US A- LIVE .

IT IS THE PO-

ET- RY OF THE RAIL- ROAD.

BY ONE NAMED E- LEC- TRIC- I- TY.

LIKE A HARP HIGH O- VER- HEAD.

from **DIARY: HOW TO IMPROVE THE WORLD
(YOU WILL ONLY MAKE MATTERS WORSE) 1965**

> **I.   Continue; I'll discover where you
>   sweat (Kierkegaard).**   We are getting
>   rid of ownership, substituting use.
> Beginning with ideas.   Which ones can we
>   take?   Which ones can we give?
> *Disappearance of power politics.*   Non-
>   measurement.   *Japanese, he said: we
>   also hear with our feet.*   *I'd quoted*
> *Busoni: Standing between musician and*
> *music is notation.*   *Before I'd given the*
> *history: chance operations, indeterminacy.*
> *I'd cited the musics of India: notation*

of them's after the fact.   I'd spoken of
                    direct musical action (since it's
ears, not interposing eyes).   2:00 A. M.,
            Jensen said, "Even if you didn't like
            the results (Lindsay, etc.), we hope
        you liked the telling of it."   Telling
            (?) of it!   We were there while it was
        happening!   II.   Minimum ethic: Do what
                    you said you'd do.   Impossible?
                    Telephone.   No answer?   My idea was
            that if they wanted to fight (human
                        nature and all that), they should
        do it in the Antarctic, rest of us
            gambling on daily outcome: proceeds for
                    world welfare.   Instead they're
                    cooperative down there, exchanging
                data, being friendly.   April '64: U.S.
                    State Department man gave Honolulu
                    talk—"global village whether we
            like it or not"—, cited fifty-five
                    services which are global in extent.
                Mountain range dividing Oahu, formerly
                crenelated (crenelations for self-
                    protection while shooting arrows),
            is now tunneled, permitting population
            circulation.   Wars etc. part of dying
                political-economic structures.   Social
                work equals increasing number of
        global services.   III.   AS McLUHAN SAYS,
                EVERYTHING HAPPENS AT ONCE.   IMAGE IS
NO LONGER STREAM FALLING OVER ROCKS,
            GETTING FROM ORIGINAL TO FINAL PLACE;
        IT'S AS TENNEY EXPLAINED: A VIBRATING
                    COMPLEX, ANY ADDITION OR SUBTRACTION
OF COMPONENT(S), REGARDLESS OF APPARENT
        POSITION(S) IN THE TOTAL SYSTEM,
        PRODUCING ALTERATION, A DIFFERENT MUSIC.
FULLER: AS LONG AS ONE HUMAN BEING IS
                HUNGRY, THE ENTIRE HUMAN RACE IS
HUNGRY.   City planning's obsolete.   What's
                needed is global planning so Earth

may stop stepping like octopus on its
own feet.   Buckminster Fuller uses his
        head: comprehensive design science;
inventory of world resources.   Conversion:
                the mind turns around, no longer
                        facing in its direction.   Utopia?
                        Self-knowledge.   Some will make it,
        with or without LSD.   The others?   Pray
        for acts of God, crises, power
        failures, no water to drink.   *IV.   We
see symmetrically: canoe on northern
                Canadian lake, stars in midnight sky*
repeated in water, forested shores
        precisely mirrored.   Our hearing's
asymmetrical: noticed sounds surprise us;
echoes of shouts we make transform our
voices, straight line of sound from us to
                shore's followed by echo's slithering
                around the lake's perimeter.   When I
                        said, "Fifty-five global services,"
California Bell Telephone man replied
        (September '65), "It's now sixty-one."
The seasons (creation, preservation,
                destruction, quiescence):   this was
                experience and resultant idea (no
longer is: he flies to Rio).   What shall
we wear as we travel about?   A summer suit
        with or without long underwear?   What
                about Stein's idea: People are the way
their land and air is?   V.   When I said
                        that culture was changing from
Renaissance to what it is now (McLuhan),
                        Johns objected to what he said was
        an oversimplification.   But Johns was
                speaking according to our non-
Renaissance experience: total field, non-
focused multiplicity.   **We are, are we not,**
        socially speaking, in a situation of
                the old dying and the new coming into
        being?   For the old — paying bills,
        seeking for power — take the attitude

of play: games.   For the new — doing what
                isn't necessary, "moving sand from one
        part of the beach to another"
                (Buckminster Fuller) — take the
religious attitude: cerebration.   (It
                celebrates.) The people have left.
                The cat and kittens were taken to the
SPCA.   The house is full of fleas.

COMMENTARY

*Art's obscured the difference between art and life. Now let life obscure the
difference between life and art.*
J. C.

His well-known definition of poetry—"I have nothing to say and I am say-
ing it, and that is poetry"—belies his ability to bring meaning *fully* into the
body of the work. It is a statement, for all of that, of what he helped to
translate from early modernism and to give an immediately useful form to
in his own time. With his base solidly in music, he sought an *interpenetra-
tion* with the world at large, to blur thereby the boundaries between art &
life (A. Kaprow). But he also made it clear from early in his work that the
strongly verbal/conceptual edge of his lectures and appropriated "songs"
came not from an urge to teach or even "to surprise people" but from "a
need for poetry." As a poet his work paralleled & in some sense followed
that of Jackson Mac Low (below), whom he had earlier introduced to the
use in music and art of systematic chance operations as a form of Buddhist/
anarchist *non-interference* and "a means . . . of silencing the ego so that the
rest of the world has a chance to enter into the ego's own experience." But
it was from the 1960s on that he emerged fully as a poet—a maker &
performer of verbal texts in some sense as formalized as music, whose
surfaces ranged from sound-based, lettristic abstractions to informationally
loaded works of utmost, even *didactic,* clarity. *Song with Electronics,* de-
rived from the writings of Henry David Thoreau, & the densely collaged
Diary are examples of Cage's appropriative modes, while the poems for
Merce Cunningham are examples (here highly abstracted) of the *mesostic*—
a form resembling the biblical acrostic, in which the vertically spelled mes-
sage (& pivot of the poem) is set along the poem's central axis.

   Or again, in response to Daniel Charles's question, "Why do you insist
on that word poetry?": *There is poetry when we realize that we possess
nothing.* (1968)

THE VIENNA GROUP

one hundred miles
one hundred miles
three hundred miles
four hundred miles
sweet smell of
death
sweet smell of
death
sweet smell of
death
sweet smell of
death

KONRAD BAYER, OSWALD WIENER

der vater der wiener gruppe ist h. c. artmann
die mutter der wiener gruppe ist gerhard rühm
die kinder der wiener gruppe sind zahllos
ich bin der onkel

ERNST JANDL

I. *Die Wiener Gruppe 1953.* "In 1953, Hans Carl Artmann, poet, translator and vagabond, founded a basement theater in Vienna (*die kleine schaubühne*) for 'macabre feasts, poetic acts', and pranks like black masses, an evening 'with illuminated birdcages,' or one 'in memoriam to a crucified glove.' Much of it was apparently improvised. Artmann had already proclaimed an 8-point-manifesto of the 'poetic act' [below], which stressed spontaneity and an impossible immediacy. . . . When the police promptly condemned the theater it metamorphosed (late 1954) into a night club, *Exil.* The theater attracted Oswald Wiener and his jazz trumpet, and when the architect Friedrich Achleitner joined in 1955 he completed the actual 'Wiener Gruppe': H. C. Artmann, Gerhard Rühm, Konrad Bayer, Oswald Wiener, Friedrich Achleitner."

II. *The Circle Widens 1957.* "1957 marked a widening of the circle. The magazine *Neue Wege* [New Ways] published Ernst Jandl's 'sprechgedichte' along with work by the group. Although neither Ernst Jandl nor Friederike Mayröcker [page 206] became part of the nucleus—they did not become involved in the collaborations of the cabaret—the group welcomed kindred spirits. . . . [Jandl] quickly attracted attention as the wittiest of the experimental poets, with an uncanny knack for uncovering the comic potential in discrepancies between sound and spelling, clichés, mispronunciations etc." (His work as a performance poet has also been extraordinary.)

III. *The Range of Their Experiments.* "Artmann discovered the possibilities of using dialect [the 'vowels of Vienna']—not in order to mimic speech or render local color, but as a reservoir of sounds and expressions which can be submitted to formal manipulation. The dialect poems of Artmann, Rühm and Achleitner exploit the tension between the spoken immediacy and the outlandish look of the dialect words when spelled out on the page. . . .

"Early on Rühm had become interested in visual poems, an interest which sprang up at the same time in places as remote from Vienna as Brazil and Scotland [below, page 302]. These poems replace the sentence and its hierarchy with a spatial 'constellation', a non-linear relation of elements which may be words, syllables, or even letters. . . .

"All of them worked on montages of 'given' [found] material . . . [with] the possibility of making language abstract: [thus] sentences from grade school primers, from catalogues and technical manuals become 'non-referential' when lifted intact from their natural habitats and remounted into new combinations. . . .

"All of them also experimented with reduction. . . . They worked, for instance, with restricted vocabularies (Rühm used cross-word puzzles), sometimes with single words, which were then subjected to various kinds of manipulations, optical, serial, associative, etc."

IV. *eight point proclamation of the poetic act — h. c. artmann (april 1953).* there is a premise which is unassailable, namely that one can be a poet even without ever having written or spoken a single word.

however the prerequisite is the more or less felt wish to act poetically. the alogical gesture can itself be performed such that it is raised to an act of outstanding beauty, indeed to poetry. beauty is however a concept which is here allowed a greatly enlarged field of play.

1) the poetic act is that form of poetry which refuses to be quoted second hand, that is to say, it rejects every mediation by speech, music or the printed word.

2) the poetic act is poetry for the sake of pure poetry. it is pure poetry and free of all ambition for recognition, praise or criticism.

3) a poetic act will perhaps only come to the attention of the public by

accident. that is however but one case in a hundred. on account of its beauty and integrity it must never subsume itself to the intention of becoming public, for it is an act of the heart and of pagan modesty.

4) the poetic act is very consciously extemporized and anything but a mere poetic situation which in no way requires a poet. every idiot can land in such a situation without even noticing it.

5) the poetic act is the pose in its noblest form, free of every vanity and full of joyous modesty.

6) among the most admirable masters of the poetic act we count in the first rank the satanic-elegiac c. d. nero and above all our lord, the philosophical-human don quixote.

7) the poetic act is completely void of material value and thus from the very start it never conceals the bacillus of prostitution. its unalloyed accomplishment is purely and simply noble.

8) the completed poetic act, recorded in our memories, is one of the few riches which we can in fact carry with us without fear of it being snatched away.

The first three sections of the commentary are arranged from the introduction and headers in The Vienna Group: Six Major Austrian Poets, *translated and edited by Rosmarie Waldrop and Harriett Watts. The translation of Artmann's* acht-punkte-proklamation des poetischen actes *is by Malcolm Gross.*

H. C. Artmann b. 1924

[UNTITLED]

ah rosie
fife rosies
toiteen rosies
ah li'l lady midgit
fife li'l lady midgits
toiteen li'l lady midgits

ah li'l lady midgit & ah rosie
fife li'l lady midgits & fife rosies
toiteen li'l lady midgits & toiteen rosies

ah nocktoff li'l lady midgit
fife nocktoff li'l lady midgits
toiteen nocktoff li'l lady midgits

ah nocktoff rosie
fife nocktoff rosies
toiteen nocktoff rosies
ah nocktoff li'l lady midgit
& ah nocktoff rosie
fife nocktoff li'l lady midgits
& fife nocktoff rosies
toiteen nocktoff li'l lady midgits
& toiteen nocktoff rosies

rosies
numbas
li'l lady midgits
all
knocktoff

Translation from the Viennese by Jerome Rothenberg

"AN OPTICIAN HAS A GLASS HEART"

an optician has a glass heart with plexiglass hinges
he has a glass heart through which he wants no one to see
he has his heart in his brain, like others have hearts in their breasts
dark sparrows fly about the cosmopolitan shop of the optician
they are wearing red wigs and counterfeit billetsdoux
they all have unlucky larvae tied before their beaks and come from a
    street of silk umbrellas
a danish wind whistles over skagerak and kattegat
a danish wind of milk and blood whistles over the umbrellas in all the
    streets
but now the dark sparrows whistle their message before the optician's
    heart of glass
the cosmopolitan optician's wife is still reclined on the sofa
her handsome lover is about to vanish on creamy white angel wings
in the garden behind the optician's home large poppies nod in the blue
    summer breeze.

the vanishing lover nears the first bank of clouds

one can scarcely still see him with the naked eye

he has stitched his young days away behind his clean starched collar

his left wing beats the air more assuredly than his right

he has put several days behind him

one can barely discern him

he has vanished

the cosmopolitan optician whistles with the sparrows against the tedium of his work

his profits have always been small

patience has never brought him a cent

his heart of glass suffered an obvious crack that morning

patience has brought him no profit

even the stamped size of his shoes has grown noticeably smaller

his brain now registers nothing but the dark sparrows' false message

he accepts it as true

he lays his metals aside

he removes the magnifying glasses from the top shelf

he stamps with both feet on the various lenses

he hurls glasses for the farsighted into the jets of airplanes

he hurls glasses for the nearsighted into the oval eyes of electric locomotives

he nervously attempts to unscrew the complicated plexiglass hinges to his heart of glass

he mourns as well as he is able the obvious failure of this endeavour

that optician, whistle the sparrows, has a glass heart through which he wants no one to see

the optician establishes the anarchy of artificial eyes in his workroom

he dispatches miniature cannons to his worktable

he commands in a semi-loud voice with a glance at his pocket watch—fire!

he repeats to himself the sparrows' false message

he bolts up his heart against outside influences

he finally mounts his telescopic sight against the new machinery of the huge evening sun

the sun for its part brings the more valuable screws and metal parts into safety

through the poppy gardens behind the optician's small home three peacocks swim in the whispering summer wind

the handsome lover of the optician's wife floats back again to the scene of
    his latest transgression
he has already emerged from the deepest cloud banks
the great poppy blossoms of the garden sway romantically in the blue
    summer wind
the cosmopolitan optician's wife is still reclined on the sofa

Translation from the German by Harriett Watts

Friederike Mayröcker b. 1924

OSTIA WILL RECEIVE YOU

i will be in Ostia
i will expect you there
i will embrace you there
i will hold your hand in Ostia
i will be there
in Ostia
is the mouth of the Tiber
the old river

i will not be in Ostia
i will not expect you there
i will not embrace you there
i will not hold your hand in Ostia
i will not be there
in Ostia
is the mouth of the old river
the Tiber

Translation from the German by Beth Bjorklund

Ernst Jandl b.1925

CHANSON

l'amour
die tür
the chair
der bauch

the chair
die tür
l'amour
ber dauch

ber dauch
die tür
the chair
l'amour

l'amour
die tür
the chair

le tür
d'amour
der chair
the bauch

le chair
der tür
die bauch
th'amour

le bauch
th'amour
die chair
der tür

l'amour
die tür
the chair
am'lour
tie dür
che thair
ber dauch

tie dair
che lauch
am thür
ber'dour

che dauch
am'thour
ber dür
tie lair

l'amour
die tür
the chair

CALYPSO

ich was not yet
in brasilien
nach brasilien
wulld ich laik du go

wer de wimen
arr so ander
so quait ander
denn anderwo

ich was not yet
in brasilien
nach brasilien
wulld ich laik du go

als ich anderschdehn
mange lanquidsch
will ich anderschdehn
auch lanquidsch in rioo

ich was not yet
in brasilien
nach brasilien
wulld ich laik du go

wenn de senden
mi across de meer
wai mi not senden wer
ich wulld laik du go

yes yes de senden
mi across de meer
wer ich was not yet
ich laik du go sehr

ich was not yet
in brasilien
yes nach brasilien
wulld ich laik du go

PRELIMINARY STUDIES FOR THE FRANKFURT READINGS 1984

study 1: *the mouth as servant*

the mouth should allow itself to open and shut
that way it can be used for eating drinking speaking
it also can be used for spitting
and it can play a part in laughing
also in kissing and in vomiting
and you can also breathe through it

you can get more things going with your mouth than with your ears
also more things than with your nose
but sadly you can't hear or smell with it
though you can smell (or *stink*) because of it

study 2: *the role of the tongue*

the tongue is set inside the mouth
it is contained within it
it plays a role in eating drinking talking
a vital role
also in kissing and in spitting
it lets itself be seen
by opening the mouth
or sticking out of it
that way it licks or flicks or licks things out
by means of the saliva it stays wet
you can accidentally bite it off
it produces tastes

study 3: *on the effects of the saliva*

the saliva is the wet stuff in your mouth
it keeps your tongue from growing stiff
also the insides of your cheeks
it keeps your gum roots and your gums from drying out
it gives your teeth their special shine
it is forever getting swallowed back
it processes your food
so it can slide more smoothly down your gullet
it also lets you spit it out
also it lets you spit at someone
it is as always self-renewing
it is a trusted servant of the mouth

Translation from the German by Jerome Rothenberg

FLOWER PIECE

for günter brus

the tulip shits on the lawn
the violet farts in the gardener's hand
the forget-me-not vomits into the tissue paper
the pink sucks on its stem
the orchid masturbates between the lady's fingers and drips on her sleeve
the rose stinks of sweat and menstrual blood
the snowdrop snots on the fresh tablecloth
the lily pisses into the vase
the hyacinth belches

Translation from the German by Rosmarie Waldrop

A FEW THINGS

on the table
a grey tablecloth
on it an open pack of cigarettes
   shiny yellow torn blue
beside it a half-empty bottle of domestic kirsch
   (product of austria)
in front of that the typewriter with my fingers
left a ballpoint
a notebook (orange)
underneath a white sheet of paper with a poem
   title february
next to that (near the edge of the table) a shabby briefcase
   it's shut (but i know what's inside)
and when i'm not typing my right arm
   on the edge of the table
my face just about above it
it's 1 P M
the table will presently look different

e g there
will be our faces facing each other
our mouths opening and closing
our hands moving knives and forks
our eyes meeting now and then

so i've risked a few predictions for the next
    fifteen minutes
and end
with my eye
on the door

Translation from the German by Rosmarie Waldrop

Konrad Bayer 1932–1964

from THE PHILOSOPHER'S STONE

the electrical hierarchy

several sentences appear.
several sentences appear successively.
each sentence enters the situation created by all the previous sentences.
these neutral sentences are charged with the situation.
these sentences appear as dry sponges which become saturated with the
    situation.
the situation is everything that comes into consideration.
everything which is possible comes into consideration.
the situation is an electric tension.
any sentence can be the first
then the law of attraction and repulsion governs.
now the machine runs electrically.

postscript:
in the electrical hierarchy of sentences there are not only positive and
negative charges, but finally* many more, as the following not only relates
to the preceding sentence, but to every sum of all preceding sentences.

* not all's well that ends well, but: not infinite

afterword

everything can be called this and that.
everything may also be called something else.
the apple between the teeth is a taste.
the stone on my skull is the cause of a bump.
the lady in front of your eyes for the present is still a sight.

Translation from the German by Walter Billeter

THE WHITE AND THE BLACK BONES:

the chimney is a hole in the roof. the sand is so light here. every day in march and april brings bad luck. wednesdays and fridays bring bad luck. and the last day of each month? the brown canaries which sing better than the yellow ones. the more horrific they are the better they are. yet all that glitters is not gold. not even teeth. 7 years burn. the honey is black. it's getting more and more lively. it's true. twist your limbs strangely. a battle is decided within one or two hours. the plant life is lush. will the shoe break soon. the skin becomes coarse. it sounds just like a child's babbling. in a golden cage. partly natural flowers. the more they all torment themselves. love in the forests. and then the giant among birds. he stood there a wreck, like an animal in a cattle market. sighs and groans can be heard everywhere when one of the 99 names of god is spoken. and on his left stands a person. should one caress him or mistreat him? salt and sugar dry up. salt and sugar dissolve. the skin becomes wrinkled. people and animals are dripping all over with blood. who must die then. in order to become beautiful. this unbelievable heat. the plague ends in june. the water is foul. (completely excessive). the air is warm but we're lacking rain. a mother blows water onto her daughter's face. the inhabitants of the city. whirlwinds rage up from the gorges. the beds are covered in ice. the window panes crack. but nobody knows. fetch stones in the night. are the senses extremely keen. two kings conducted a bloody war over a grenadier's cap. love is so simple here. all birds bring bad luck in march and april. the blacker they are the whiter they are. yet all that glitters is not blood. not even flowers. 100 cities burn. man is beautiful. it is hot. break the month of june. is the honey drying in the chimney. and why? a mother blows a hole in her daughter's face. the beds become coarse. that's right. salt and sugar dissolve. salt and sugar dry up. all flowers bring bad luck in march and april.

Translation from the German by Malcolm Green

Nicanor Parra b.1914

THE INDIVIDUAL'S SOLILOQUY

I'm the individual.
First I lived by a rock
(I scratched some figures on it)
Then I looked for some place more suitable.
I'm the individual.
First I had to get myself food,
Hunt for fish, birds, hunt up wood
(I'd take care of the rest later)
Make a fire,
Wood, wood, where could I find any wood,
Some wood to start a little fire,
I'm the individual.
At the time I was asking myself,
Went to a canyon filled with air;
A voice answered me back:
I'm the individual.
So then I started moving to another rock,
I also scratched figures there,
Scratched out a river, buffaloes,
I'm the individual.
But I got bored with what I was doing,
Fire annoyed me,
I wanted to see more,
I'm the individual.
Went down to a valley watered by a river,
There I found what I was looking for,
A bunch of savages,
A tribe,
I'm the individual.
I saw they made certain things,
Scratching figures on the rocks,
Making fire, also making fire!
I'm the individual.
They asked me where I came from.
I answered yes, that I had no definite plans,
I answered no, that from here on out.
O.K.

I then took a stone I found in the river
And began working on it,
Polishing it up,
I made it a part of my life.
But it's a long story.
I chopped some trees to sail on
Looking for fish,
Looking for lots of things,
(I'm the individual.)
Till I began getting bored again.
Storms get boring,
Thunder, lightning,
I'm the individual.
O.K.
I began thinking a little bit,
Stupid questions came into my head,
Doubletalk.
So then I began wandering through forests,
I came to a tree, then another tree,
I came to a spring,
A hole with a couple of rats in it;
So here I come, I said,
Anybody seen a tribe around here,
Savage people who make fire?
That's how I moved on westward,
Accompanied by others,
Or rather alone,
Believing is seeing, they told me,
I'm the individual.
I saw shapes in the darkness,
Clouds maybe,
Maybe I saw clouds, or sheet lightning,
Meanwhile several days had gone by,
I felt as if I were dying;
Invented some machines,
Constructed clocks,
Weapons, vehicles,
I'm the individual.
Hardly had time to bury my dead,
Hardly had time to sow,
I'm the individual.

Years later I conceived a few things,
A few forms,
Crossed frontiers,
And got stuck in a kind of niche,
In a bark that sailed forty days,
Forty nights,
I'm the individual.
Then came the droughts,
Then came the wars,
Colored guys entered the valley,
But I had to keep going,
Had to produce.
Produced science, immutable truths,
Produced Tanagras,
Hatched up thousand-page books.
My face got swollen,
Invented a phonograph,
The sewing machine,
The first automobiles began to appear,
I'm the individual.
Someone set up planets,
Trees got set up!
But I set up hardware,
Furniture, stationery,
I'm the individual.
Cities also got built,
Highways,
Religious institutions went out of fashion,
They looked for joy, they looked for happiness,
I'm the individual.
Afterward I devoted myself to travel,
Practicing, practicing languages
Languages,
I'm the individual.
I looked into a keyhole,
Sure, I looked, what am I saying, looked,
To get rid of all doubt looked,
Behind the curtains,
I'm the individual.
O.K.
Perhaps I better go back to that valley,

To that rock that was home,
And start scratching all over again,
Scratching out everything backward,
The world in reverse.   But it wouldn't make sense.

Translation from the Spanish by Allen Ginsberg & Lawrence Ferlinghetti

COMMENTARY

For half a century / Poetry was / The paradise of the solemn fool. / Until I came along / And set up my roller coaster / Go on up if you like. / Of course I'm not responsible if you come down / Bleeding from your mouth and nose. (N.P.) And again: *Poetry has acquitted itself well / I have conducted myself horribly / Poetry ends with me.*

A self-declared "antipoet" who wrote "antipoems" (terms taken from his Creationist predecessor Vicente Huidobro), Parra brought a challenge to an older Chilean & Latin American *modernismo* & reopened a *postmodernismo* that had been present on native grounds as far back as the 1910s. Original to himself & to his time & place, his *antipoetry* (below, page 423) shared characteristics with many of the experimental *poetries* appearing in the present volumes, while clearly refuting others in the ongoing dialectic of the twentieth century's avant-gardes. At the center of his poetics was a definition of antipoetry as "a collection of masks in which 'I' does not exist": an expression like that of Charles Olson (above) against "the lyrical interference of the ego" or like that of Theodor Adorno against the "barbarism"—"after Auschwitz"—of persisting in the lyric (*lyrik*) mode. In pursuit of this he spoke for a poetry freed of "the domination of the metaphor," in which the markers of high literature (= "literature for literature's sake") give way to commonplace events (however skewed) & ordinary language. His related insistence on speech over song as the root of the poetic/ antipoetic ("let the birds sing, man talks") was delivered with great clarity & force, resembling in intent (though not in practice) the later "talking poetry" & poetics of David Antin (see below). For all of which he was not without his named predecessors (Whitman, Lorca, Kafka, among others) in his view of the poet as "selector" rather than "creator": "an amoeba that feeds on everything that passes by" & for whom "nothing human can be alien." The result throughout his work is an overriding feeling for the comic & grotesque—a view of life in which, he tells us, "real seriousness" rests always in "the comic."

Octavio Paz b. 1916

a stirring
              a steering
a seedling
              sleeping
the word at the tip of the tongue
unheard   unhearable
              matchless
fertile   barren
              ageless
she who was buried with open eyes
   stainless   promiscuous
              the word
speechless   nameless

It climbs and descends,
the spine of the mineshaft ladder,
abandoned language.
A lamp beats beneath
penumbra skin.
              Survivor
in the melancholic confusion,
                              it rises
in a copper stalk,
              breaks
into leaves of clarity:
                    shelter
for fallen realities.
              Asleep
or extinct,
              high on its pole
(head on a pike)
              a sunflower
light charred
              in a vase

of shadow.
                    In the palm of an
invented hand,
                    the flower,
not seen nor imagined:
                    heard,
appears,
          a yellow chalice
of consonants and vowels,
burning.

on the wall the shadow of the fire
in the fire your shadow and mine

the fire unlaces and fastens you
Ember Bread Grail
                    Girl
you laugh — naked
in the gardens of the flame

flame encircled by lions
lioness in the circus of the flames
soul among sensations

fruits of the fireworks
the senses open
in the magnetic night

The passion of compassionate coals

A pulse-beat, insisting,
a surge of wet syllables.
Without saying a word,
my forehead grows dark:
a presentiment of language.
Patience patience
(Livingstone in the drought)
river rising a little.
Mine is red and scorches
in the flaming dunes:
Castiles of sand,
shredded playing cards,
and the hieroglyph (water and ember)
dropped on the chest of Mexico.

I am the dust of that silt.
River of blood,

river of histories

of blood,

dry river:
mouth of the source
gagged
by the anonymous conspiracy
of bones,
by the grim rocks of centuries
and minutes:

language

is atonement,

an appeasement

of the speechless,

the entombed,

the daily

assassinated,

the countless dead.

To speak

while others work
is to polish bones,

sharpen

silence

to transparency,

waves,

whitecaps,

water:

the rivers of your body	*the river of bodies*
land of pulse-beats	*stars infusoria reptiles*
to enter you	*downpour of sleepwalking cinnabar*
land of closed eyes	*surge of genealogies*
water with no thoughts	*games antics tricks*
to enter me	*subject and object abject and absolved*
entering your body	*river of suns*
land of sleepless mirrors	*"the tall beasts with shining skins"*
land of waking water	*seminal river of the worlds wheeling*
in the sleeping night	*the eye that watches it is another river*

watching I watch myself
as though entering through my eyes
into an eye more crystal clear
what I watch watches me

what I see is my creation
perception is conception
water of thoughts
I am the creation of what I see

delta of arms of desire
on a bed of vertigo

water of truth
truth of water

Transparency is all that remains

Translation from the Spanish by Eliot Weinberger

COMMENTARY

The word of man / is the daughter of death. / We talk because we are mortal: / words are not signs, they are years. / Saying what they say, / the words we are saying / say time: they name us. / We are time's names. // To talk is human.

O.P. (from "Flame, Speech," translation by Mark Strand)

A visible poet since the 1930s, Paz in the immediate postwar years makes a close connection with André Breton & the surviving Surrealists, then comes to prominence in the aftermath of poems like *Sun Stone* (1957) & gatherings of essays like the influential *Labyrinth of Solitude* (1950). His work thereafter—as poet, as editor, as translator, as cultural & political commentator—includes books on Marcel Duchamp, Claude Lévi-Strauss, Sor Juana Inés de la Cruz, Charles Fourier, plus over fifteen books of essays, many more of poetry. Of his time & place (&, by implication, our place within it), he writes: "The poetry starting up in this second half of the century is not really starting. Nor is it returning to the point of departure. The poetry beginning now, without beginning, is looking for the intersections of times, the point of convergence. It asserts that poetry is the present, between the cluttered past and the uninhabited future. The re-production is a presentation. Pure time: heartbeat of the present in the moment of its appearance/disappearance."

In the poem from which the present extract comes, Paz works off a structure of several columns which serve as the carriers for a number of independent &/or counterpointed poems. Of the intended effect he writes: "*Blanco* was meant to be read as a succession of signs on a single page. As the reading progresses, the page unfolds vertically, a space which, as it opens out, allows the text to appear and, in a certain sense, creates it. [For an earlier & paradigmatic instance, see the entry on Blaise Cendrars & Sonia Delaunay in volume one.] This arrangement of temporal order is the form adopted by the course of the poem: its discourse corresponds to another which is spatial: the separate parts which comprise the poem are distributed like the sections, colors, symbols, and figures of a mandala." And further, of the poem's title: "*Blanco:* white, blank; an unmarked space; emptiness; void; the white mark in the center of a target."

More of Paz's poetry appears in volume one.

Bert Schierbeek 1918–1996

THE SUN: DAY

1)   Sun comes up
       whole World's red
       me too

2)   Sun climbs—
       red cart, ow—
       over my leg

3)   take piece of wood
       in rising Sun
       carve myself new leg

4)   I drink in Sun
       dress up leg with shoe
       leg itches too

5)   Sun higher, me drunk
       long hours of daytime
       come along

6)   tired of leg
       think of windmills
       get sleepy

7)   Sun devours color
       leg gets whiter
       black sheep too

8)   I in dream
       make mills for Wind
       which rushes up

9)   angry woman comes
       takes bottle away
       "windmills" she says

10) what my head thinks
      my hands make
      World trembles

11) Wind lies down
      under roof of fig-tree
      Sun and me too

12) weave basket
      for Sun and me
      sheep sleep

Translation from the Dutch by Charles McGeehan

THE ANIMAL HAS DRAWN A HUMAN

and so it happens that late at night we come home after standing the live-long day at the face of the rock where to draw the animal that has regularly haunted our sleep in our lifetime and as we thought had clearly engraved its bulk and movement in our memory and equally demand to drive an echo of its appearance in the dust so as to know for ever. . . .
what happened though?
under our hands groping for the shape of the animal as it lived in our eyes and wishing to imitate it as we had seen it its bulk and contours grew to such an extent that the face of the rock which we had chosen to register its appearance on dwindled rather than that the shape of the animal grew more complete in the process
what did we do?
were we portraying an animal bigger than the one we had seen or was the animal from our eyes deceptively bigger than the face of the rock which we knew to be the largest of our region?
for try as we might to reduce the animal
to such proportions that the whole could
be carved in the face of the wall we did not succeed
we then have been singing for days on end
days and nights
one song for the early morning
since morning begins and man does not
one for the late afternoon
since afternoon passes and man does not
one for the early afternight

when the animal lives and takes shape
what did we find after seven days and nights?
what we had never seen or known before
we did not know the animal as we thought
it was against the face of the rock in the last night of
                              our singing when a lucid bright
intoxication of fatigue had opened our eyes wide like
                                        tiny cool sickles
we saw it move against the face of the wall in sharp
                       outline and it was smaller and its
contours were bright as if aflame but with a blue light
its huge tail resembled the poisonous tongue of a viper
and its mouth snorted white lines that stuck
to the face of the wall
our singing muted into a stifled cry
the animal draws itself
many of us fled
we never saw them back
but those of us who silently watched the night out
have seen that the animal kept moving its jaws till the
                       advent of light and that as it grew
lighter its movements became more languid and its eyes
                                        paler
that its powerful legs strained as though it was being
                    pulled to a place where it knew it
would die for it was a ghost of anguish for as long as
                              we could distinguish it
a dying animal that seemed to take unto itself the face
                       of the wall without a trace of its
frightening life. . . .
till some of us had the courage to go up to the face of
                                        the wall
and as we stood there the way we had been standing
                       there for days on end with chisels,
pickaxes and scrapers we saw:
the animal has drawn a human

Translation from the Dutch by Charles McGeehan

*re comes over us / that awful silence / which we saw in picture books /
animals in that vast sort of space / where they almost didn't exist at all /
rifting in the mist of a still / bigger animal that devours us all.*

B.S.

His work emerges from the vortex of the European & Dutch avant-garde
(post–World War II), with affiliations to the mixed-means poetics of Cobra
(page 234) &, at a greater distance, American poets like Williams, Olson,
Burroughs. The defining breakthrough is his creation, circa 1950, of the
"compositional novel," in which the stated aim is "the removal of the bor-
derlines of the 'I' and their redistribution"—for him, as others, an act of
defiance against imposed, inherited notions of the predetermined Self. Re-
garding the early means employed he writes (1952): "At that time I wrote
down on scraps of paper every conversation I heard, all the words I came
across; I saved clippings from newspapers, I traveled through Spain and
took notes on what I saw along the road, at the outdoor cafés, all kinds of
conversations and forms of life. That can all be recovered in the book. Ar-
ranged upon a rhythmic base that was determined by 'the breath of the
people,' which we have in common. Everything carefully, typographically
divided up to make the whole surveyable." Moving from prose to verse—
or holding some rich ground in between—the resultant form works toward
the creation of "cross sections of reality" where "everything rhymes."

His long novel-poems available in English include *Shape of the Voice,
Cross Roads,* and *Keeping It Up,* along with short works like *The Sun: Day,*
presented here.

Robert Duncan 1919–1988

OFTEN I AM PERMITTED TO RETURN TO A MEADOW

as if it were a scene made-up by the mind,
that is not mine, but is a made place,

that is mine, it is so near to the heart,
an eternal pasture folded in all thought
so that there is a hall therein

that is a made place, created by light
wherefrom the shadows that are forms fall.

Wherefrom fall all architectures I am
I say are likenesses of the First Beloved
whose flowers are flames lit to the Lady.

She it is Queen Under The Hill
whose hosts are a disturbance of words within words
that is a field folded.

It is only a dream of the grass blowing
east against the source of the sun
in an hour before the sun's going down

whose secret we see in a children's game
of ring a round of roses told.

Often I am permitted to return to a meadow
as if it were a given property of the mind
that certain bounds hold against chaos,

that is a place of first permission,
everlasting omen of what is.

AT THE LOOM   **PASSAGES 2**

                              A cat's purr
in the hwirr thkk   *"thgk, thkk"*
    of Kirke's loom on Pound's Cantos
                "I heard a song of that kind . . ."

my mind a shuttle among
            set strings of the music
lets a weft of dream grow in the day time,
            an increment of associations,
        luminous soft threads,
the thrown glamour, crossing and recrossing,
            the twisted sinews underlying the work.

Back of the images, the few cords that bind
    meaning in the word-flow,
                the rivering web
        rises among wits and senses
gathering the wool into its full cloth.

The secret!   the secret!   It's hid
          in its showing forth.
The white cat kneads his paws
             and sheathes his eyes in ecstasy against the light,
   the light bounding from his fur as from a shield
          held high in the midst of a battle.

What does the Worm work in His cocoon?

       There was such a want in the old ways
             when craft came into our elements,
       the art shall never be free of that forge,
                   that loom, that lyre—

   the fire, the images, the voice.

Why, even in the room where we are,
             reading to ourselves, or I am reading aloud,
       sounding the music,
                         the stuff
             vanishes upon the air,
                   line after line thrown.

Let there be the clack of the shuttle flying
       forward and back,   forward and
                   back,

warp, *wearp, varp*:   *"cast of a net, a laying of eggs"*
from *warp- *"to throw"*

       the threads twisted for strength
                   that can be a warp of the will.

   "O weaver, weaver, work no more,"
          Gascoyne is quoted:
   "thy warp hath done me wrong."

And the shuttle carrying the woof I find
       was *skutill*   *"harpoon"*   —a dart, an arrow,
          or a little ship,

          navicula   weberschiff,

crossing and recrossing from shore to shore—

    prehistoric   *skutil*   *skut-*
        "a bolt, a bar, as of a door"
        "a flood-gate"   •

                  but the battle I saw
was on a wide plain,   for the
    sake of valor,
the hand traind to the bow,
    the man's frame
withstanding,   each side

facing its foe for the sake of
    the alliance,
allegiance, the legion, that the
    vow that makes a nation
one body not be broken.

Yet it is all, we know, a mêlée,
    a medley of mistaken themes
      grown dreadful and surmounting dread,

so that Achilles may have his wrath
        and throw down
    the heroic Hektor who raised
that reflection of the heroic

    in his shield . . .

Feb 4–11   1964

The Angel Syphilis in the circle of Signators   looses its hosts   to swarm
        mounting the stem of being   to the head
                                                Baudelaire, Nietzsche, Swift
        are not eased into Death
                                the undoing of Mind's rule in the brain.

"Yet it is in spirit that nature is timelessly enveloped."   And, as above, so below
                                                                there are
                spirochete invasions that eat at the sublime envelope,   not alien, but familiars

                Life in the dis-ease radiates   invisibilities devour my star

and Time restless crawls in center upon center   cells of lives within life conspire

        Hel shines in the very word *Health*   as *Ill* in the Divine Will shines.

        The Angel Cancer crawls across the signs of the Zodiac to reach its

appointed time   and   bringing down the carnal pride   bursts into flower—

                Swift, Baudelaire, Nietzsche   into the heart Eternal of what Poetry is

                        answer to the genius and science of the Abyss.   The first sign of this
                                                                advancing power

                shows in Fear that goes   clear to the bone   to gnaw at the marrow.

        The seeress Lou Andreas-Salomé   sees long before the hour arrives—

                [mais] *"Tantôt sonnera l'heure   où le divin Hasard,*

        où l'auguste Vertu, ton épouse encore vierge"   —where black the infected blood

                gushes forth from Rilke's mouth, from his nose, from his rectal canal

                news his whole body bears as its truth   of the septic rose

        Où le Repentir même   (oh!   *la dernière auberge!*)

                                                        Lovely then

that Death come to carry you away from the moment of this splendor
        that bursts the cells of your body   like a million larvæ triumphant

                comes to life in the fruit   All the spreading seeds,   the viral array
        taking over flesh as the earth it is

                                scarlet eruptions

And the pneumatics torn in the secret workings of the Angel Tuberculosis

   (No, I do not speak of Evils or of Agents of Death   but these Angels
        are attendants of lives raging within life,   under these Wings we dread

  viruses, bacilli   come home to thrive in us   où tout te dira

     "Meurs, vieux lâche!   *il est trop tard!"*   Die, you old coward,
                 it is too late.   I feel the ringing of tomorrow's bell.

But what ate at Pound's immortal Mind?   for the Cantos,   for *Les Fleurs du Mal*
           so eat at Mind's conscience
  what malady?   what undoing-of-all-Good   workt behind speech?

    —are the matter I come from—these poisons I must know the hidden intentions of
      where "this coil of Geryon" (Djerion) said Mr Carlyle,   who now becomes

      Thomas Carlyle, not the member of Congress, but
               the genius of "Hero Worship"   his (our) congress

And if I know not my wound   it does not appear to suppurate?   In this intercourse
  "Adolf furious from perception"   —does this thought refer to Hitler?

Link by link I can disown no link of this chain from my conscience.

    Would you forget the furnaces of burning meat   purity demands?
    There is no ecstasy of Beauty in which I will not remember Man's misery.

  Jesus, in this passage   —He is like a man coming forward in a hospital theater—
    cries out: I come not to heal but to tear the scab from the wound you wanted
                                  to forget.
    May the grass no longer spread out to cover the works of man in the ruin of
                                  earth.

What Angel,   what Gift of the Poem,   has brought into my body

    this sickness of living?   Into the very Gloria of Life's theme and variations
      my own counterpart of Baudelaire's terrible Ennuie?

COMMENTARY

*The Gods men know are realizations of God. But what I speak of here in
the terms of a theology is a poetics. . . . A mystic cosmogony gives rise to
the little world the poet as creator makes.*
R.D.

Like a number of others who seized the full range of modern/postmodern
possibilities, he was a poet of enormous means & complexity—one of the
last to assay a cosmological poetics, to be "the model of the poet," as Mi-
chael Davidson described him, "for whom all of reality can enter the poem."

As such he was (he made himself) a man & poet open to multiple influences, accepting & announcing a sense of his own "derivativeness"—his *derivations*—that freed others to do the same. More singularly, he brought "romance" & "gnosis" back into the world of common things—not only as an attitude but with a richness of contemporary detail & intellectual precedent that typified his practice, nowhere more notably than in *Passages,* the ongoing work of his mature later practice. What he projected—first & foremost—was a poetics-of-the-*spirit:* an acknowledgement & an insistence on "the spiritual in art," as Kandinsky might have known it, & a vision—through Whitman &/or Dante &/or others—of a totalizing universality, "a symposium of the whole" (for which, see volume one, page 740), that included & surpassed all separate individuals & species.

Toward his self-creation as that kind of poet, he was aware, & he made us aware, of the stages (the grand design) by which a life like his or ours might grow. Early along he was a central player (with Robin Blaser & Jack Spicer) in the Berkeley/San Francisco renaissance of the 1940s & (with Creeley, Levertov, & Olson) in the Black Mountain movement of the 1950s. The final book of his lifetime—*Ground Work II: In the Dark* (1987)—is, we now can see, his creation of an *Altenstiel,* a style of old age, marked not by a mere quiescence but by ominous premonitions/confrontations with sickness & pain—he who had once thought himself the master of a charmed life, for whom a mighty hand was always ready to appear (he told one of us) to pluck him from disaster. *In Blood's Domaine* and *After a Long Illness* (below, page 847) are testaments to that awesome blend of hope & devastation.

Yoshioka Minoru 1919–1990

PILGRIMAGE

I

I pass two women in the hall
                    One is straddling
                                        A tricycle
Definitely my little sister
                        Reading several pages
Out of a red book
                The biography of a great man
                            With numerous descriptions of oranges and tomatoes
The other is my mother grown fat
                            Mounted atop a scale
The interior, dressed in cheap clothing, is drenched
                                    And flowing from there

Are literary style, dead bodies

        And a tapeworm

It is said in the family precepts

        The sheets have never been soiled with blood or impurities

           Eternally a landscape of snow

Does the subject become clear

        At the moment my father loads up

           A cart with large objects

             And leaves town?

2

The artillery smoke hangs overhead

        Is it a battleship made of mortar fire

           Or a granite peak

The troops continue the assault

        During the flash of glory

A man's insides could be seen

        Flowering plants are torn up

           Clothing torn

            And hair

On top of a shining plate

        All the parts of the body are dismantled

        And the souls of the dead take the shape of stars

3

If that which is possible does occur

        Then let it be so

If what cannot happen does not happen

        So be it

4

Cicada showered midday

        Inserted with foreign matter

Mother

    Mother

        Mother

           Hole

      Sister

    Sister

Sister

    The wild goose flies west

If you must ask where this place is

It is the earthly paradise

Peach and plum bloom wildly

And there are pearls

Birds and other animals repeatedly call my name

And call to my mother

Soldiers prefer wild boars

And old people various goblins

A ravine is cut in the mountains

And the fresh water flows   flows home

The days pass

The newt remains

My little sister bathes in the river and is clothed in froth

And like a cuckoo

Continues to search for the ideal master

Praising a world of change in the arts and in thought

5

Smoke rises

A state of forgetfulness

What image carved in the eye of the rhinoceros

Masculine things—

(Fire and air)

And things poetic   poetry itself

Feminine things—

(Water and earth)

And things near to love   love itself

The stars glitter

The spider hatches its eggs with its own eyes

6

The poet crawls upon the ground

Pours flowing blood from his head

I was present at my sister's birth

Poetry's advent

This evening a cool wind passes

And the papers rustle

Prosaically

Then from the land of scarlet autumn leaves

Carrying a bucket of night soil

A man resembling myself crosses a bridge

                                     And boards a ship

For Damascus far away and in dead of night

He goes round and round the world of marble

                          And watches a flea jump

                                   Like a line in a poem

                                   Covered in disgrace

7

And here is second childhood

                    That nuclear place at chaotic dawn

                          Where stems of millet catch fire

Corpses of people, dogs and cats

                       Frost falls to the earth without a sound

                          Describe this in exclamatory mode

Pheasants   Cuckoos

                  The darkness in the harsh cry

                              Of a buck with newly sprouted horns

Pass through the red Shinto gate

                      At the far end of the grounds

Is a wall the color of a sea slug

8

Used carelessly

                They rot in people's hands

                          Or die

Words and a portion of flesh

                      Living things

At the far end of a cave

                    At the tip of a flame

Today I have done nothing

                  Nothing at all

That which occurs on earth ends on earth

Translation from the Japanese by Eric Selland

. . . a royal road the still-born child will open / into a primeval virgin land / and there he will see / the future delivery scene / the maternal lightning torn open / & from that immense bloody darkness out will come / white-haired still-born children one after the other . . .

Y.M.

A major linking figure between the pre–World War II Japanese avant-garde and the new postwar poets (page 539), Yoshioka introduced into Japanese poetry a blend of modernist/postmodernist experiments with traditional images & sounds from Japanese magic & religion. The poem presented here is from his great late work *Kusudama*, a culmination of his experimental praxis that translator Eric Selland calls "a collage of inner voices and quotations: . . . the memory of his own mother and an evocation of the Goddess—the moving power behind the poem . . . [which thus] has much in common with the shaman's journey." And of matters less evident in the passage between Japanese & English: "For Yoshioka, the poem is necessarily a written, not spoken, form. There is a constant visual punning in *Kusudama* (lost in translation) where parts of characters make visual and semantic 'rhymes' with those of others, or lead into the next word and image by virtue of the characters' similarity to each other. This does not mean that the importance of sound is lost to Yoshioka. His language uses a great amount of assonance and is one of the most beautiful and resonant of the Japanese post modernists."

The relation to—& difference from—other visual-verbal interfaces is a marker of how particular forms of language—written as well as spoken—can determine new strategies of composition.

Paul Celan 1920–1970

BREATHCRYSTAL

YOU MAY confidently
regale me with snow:
as often as I strode through summer
shoulder to shoulder with the mulberry tree,
its youngest leaf
shrieked.

BY THE UNDREAMT etched,
the sleeplessly wandered-through breadland
casts up the life mountain.

From its crumb
you knead anew our names,
which I, an eye
similar
to yours on each finger,
probe for
a place through which I
can wake myself toward you,
the bright
hungercandle in mouth.

INTO THE FURROWS
of heavenacid in the doorcrack
you press the word
from which I rolled,
when I with trembling fists
the roof over us
dismantled, slate for slate,
syllable for syllable, for the copper-
glimmer of the begging-
cup's sake up
there.

IN THE RIVERS north of the future
I cast the net, which you
hesitantly weight
with shadows stones
wrote.

BEFORE YOUR LATE FACE,
a loner
wandering between
nights that change me too,
something came to stand,
which was with us once already, un-
touched by thoughts.

DOWN MELANCHOLY'S RAPIDS
past the blank
woundmirror:
There the forty
stripped life-trees are rafted.

Single counter-
swimmer, you
count them, touch them
all.

THE NUMBERS, in league
with the images' doom
and counter-
doom.

The clapped-on
skull, at whose
sleepless temple a will-
of-the-wisping hammer
celebrates all that in
worldbeat.

PATHS IN THE SHADOW-BREAK
of your hand.

From the four-finger-furrow
I root up the
petrified blessing.

WHITEGRAY of
shafted, steep
feeling.

Landinwards, hither
drifted sea-oats blow
sand patterns over
the smoke of wellchants.

An ear, severed, listens.

An eye, cut in strips,
does justice to all this.

WITH MASTS SUNG EARTHWARDS
the sky-wrecks drive.

Onto this woodsong
you hold fast with your teeth.

You are the songfast
pennant.

TEMPLECLAMPS,
eyed by your jugal-bone.
Its silverglare there
where they gripped:
you and the rest of your sleep—
soon
will be your birthday.

NEXT TO THE HAILSTONE, in
the mildewed corn-
cob, home,
to the late, the hard
November stars obedient:

In the heartthread, the
knit of worm-talk—:

a bowstring, from which
your arrowscript whirrs,
archer.

TO STAND, in the shadow
of the stigma in the air.

Standing-for-no-one-and-nothing.
Unrecognized,
for you
alone.

With all that has room in it,
even without
language.

YOUR DREAM, butting from the watch.
With the wordspoor carved
twelve times
helically into its
horn.

The last butt it delivers.

In the ver-
tical narrow
daygorge, the upward
poling ferry:

It carries
sore readings over.

WITH THE PERSECUTED in late, un-
silenced,
radiating
league.

The morning-plumb, gilded,
hafts itself to your co-
swearing, co-
scratching co-
writing
heel.

THREADSUNS
above the greyblack wastes.
A tree-
high thought
grasps the light-tone: there are
still songs to sing beyond
mankind.

IN THE SERPENTCOACH, past
the white cypress,
through the flood
they drove you.

But in you, from
birth,
foamed the other spring,
up the black
ray memory
you climbed to the day.

SLICKENSIDES, fold-axes,
rechanneling-
points:
your terrain.

On both poles
of the cleftrose, legible:
your outlawed word.
Northtrue. Southbright.

WORDACCRETION, volcanic,
drowned out by searoar.

Above,
the flooding mob
of the contra-creatures: it
flew a flag—portrait and replica
cruise vainly timeward.

Till you hurl forth the word-
moon, out of which
the wonder ebb occurs
and the heart-
shaped crater
testifies naked for the beginnings,
the kings-
births.

(I KNOW YOU, you are the deeply bowed,
I, the transpierced, am subject to you.
Where flames a word, would testify for us both?
You—all, all real. I—all delusion.)

ERODED by
the beamwind of your speech
the gaudy chatter of the pseudo-
experienced—the hundred-
tongued perjury-
poem, the noem.

Hollow-
whirled,
free
the path through the men-
shaped snow,
the penitent's snow, to
the hospitable
glacier-parlors and -tables.

Deep
in the timecrevasse,
in the
honeycomb-ice,
waits a breathcrystal,
your unalterable
testimony.

Translation from the German by Pierre Joris

COMMENTARY

LINE THE WORD-CAVES / *with panther skins, // widen them, pelt-to and pelt-fro, / sense-hither and sense-thither, // give them courtyards, chambers, drop doors / and wildnesses, parietal, // and listen for their second / and each time second and second / tone.*
P.C.

Celan may well be the "major European poet of the period after 1945" (G. Steiner) and his work the first "European Book of Dead": a guide for the souls of the men & women who had passed through that greatest catastrophe—the Nazi genocide, the central event of both his life & work. Fleeing his birthplace, Czernowitz in the Bukowina (Rumania), in 1945 after the murder of his parents, he moved (via Bucharest and Vienna) to Paris, where he settled in 1948. Poetic renown came early: in the fifties he was recognized as one of the major voices in German-language poetry (though his German, the language both of his mother & her assassins, can also be seen as a war-machine against that culture & its language). The early *Todesfuge* (A Death Fugue) (page 24) became the emblematic postwar poem on the Shoah, while later volumes like *Die Niemandsrose* (The No-One's Rose) and *Sprachgitter* (Speech-Grille) marked his deeper struggles on the field of language.

But the achievement is far more than just bearing witness to the past. Despite his deteriorating psychological condition (his fear of persecution, latent, since the Nazi period, flared up after 1960 & led to his suicide in 1970), his subsequent work is a charting of as yet unexplored psycho-topographies, of (language) spaces we may only come to inhabit or recognize in a distant future. For Celan the language of poetry "does not transfigure or render *poetical*; it names, it posits, it tries to measure the area of the given and the possible." But that area is a huge & dangerous territory, because for him "reality is not simply there, it must be searched and won," & this creation of a new reality through language is very much the core of his late work. Starting with *Atemwende* (Breathturn) as both a book & a coherent work (*Breathcrystal,* above, is the opening cycle of that book), the method employed is profoundly serial, & one might consider these later volumes—& certainly each of their individual sections—as one long "sentence," or at least as an ongoing, concatenated coherence, in which the "individual" poem functions as a sentence fragment, a clause, in a relentlessly persistent disputation.

For more on Celan's poetics, see page 408 below.

Mohammed Dib b. 1920

from **FORMULAIRES**

I

language sovereign secret incompatible submerged in the universal wound let my life be lost there lived there without vindication wound let a thick wall of dark seal and deaf dumb let no medium be able to make it understood speech that hollows out an empty space

memory exchanged for night
disguising the night
a void that is infinitely radiant

and searches for
some out of the way forest
that will strike the morning
suddenly and blind

2

statue of shadow waits for you she waits she does not know she waits
suspended in form and time she exists endures only through this pause in
the abyss her visible decor the night which knows where to retreat battling
with cries called by the ape of fire who spies does not return halt of dreams
to rejoin the three phases of blood fill all the containers with spit and toss
them to the wind its laugh its laugh to itself alone fills the high and the low

3

and unable to come back from the blondness dawning at the horizon the
day recaptures its prey the spirit lays down its snares some orders of pas-
sage drive each tree back into its hole once again the fields begin to capsize
merely for the illusion the rite dies some falling motions in the forest some
falling shadows calling that crime why wait for the conflict why seek out
the legs under the cactus hour of childbirth there's only an open road for
this voyage the word that empties its wave only to surge up again in mo-
tion winding back into itself embraces the fertile chasm the circle of sacra-
ments and the steps of Kore

4

to teach the singer how to sing again now that his voice is out of tune
nothing is more a sacrament than a curse the anatomy's return is assured
the breast will regard itself in the other breast questioning its identity and
difference until it falls in love with its image which it will see of itself black
and mortal if it is white to recognize this breast shelter it make it drink
down to its very source carry it on your head stroll with it in broad day-
light turn it into your glory

5

we don't understand moored in these shallow waters our expedition only
makes sense far from all shores the longing to restore the field of tradition
will not prevail if only the path were uncovered if the gaze alone could
equal the length it's prolonged if each meeting with the one distinguished
solely by his gaze could be kept if step by step his eyes could be the door
to cross over to the sign it depicts on the sand to the name in which it is
centered to the birth which foretells the labyrinth of its name and from

there to the threshold appearing with an air of familiarity that will question the reality of the accomplished voyage if soon you could only recognize yourself by gazing you will have become the gazing that which would not be considered the result of a change but of a return to the center of the gaze from which the sign came before the word by projecting its facade all around you and which only disclosed its visible traces and the path left uncovered calls and calls

6

all the charitable images of the world lead me to you wondering how to thank them I followed your footsteps one by one in each I discovered signs of your passing wondering which way to turn which way preserves the voice so that all ways serve only as a path to you

7

count the links in the chain the ants in the ant-hill the stars in the sky there will always remain one link there will always remain one ant there will always remain one star and the word on the page will refuse to be entirely inscribed and you will start all over to recombine its letters in all of its meanings and out of this some secret words will be born that will make your knowledge fatten to the point of obesity and obesity will occupy the throne

Translation from the French by Carol Lettieri & Paul Vangelisti

COMMENTARY

I write primarily for the Algerians and the French. To try and make the latter understand that Algeria and its people are part of the same mankind, essentially sharing the same problems, and to invite the former to examine themselves though without therewith giving them a feeling of inferiority. . . . My ambition, however, remains to interest all readers. The essential is the human ground we all share; the things that make us different always remain secondary. (M. D.) And again: *Only the stone is innocent.*

Poet, novelist, & playwright, Mohammed Dib is (with Kateb Yacine) the most prolific and wide-ranging Algerian writer of those generations whose core experience was the 1954–1962 war of independence. Bilingual (with Algerian Arabic as a spoken language only), he faced the problem of having to write in the oppressors' language—a dilemma Louis Aragon speaks of in his preface to Dib's *Ombre guardienne,* pointing to "that essential aspect of the Algerian drama . . . that those who are the very faith of their own people have as language with which to reach what escapes analysis, to express the untamable, only French, this well-tempered harpsichord, this instrument from the banks of the Loire, this speech which is also that of the soldiers who come at night, the vocabulary of the pogrom, the commentary of torture and hunger."

Though poetry always was the source ("I am essentially a poet & it is through poetry that I came to the novel"), Dib wrote realistic/populist fiction about Algerian life under colonialism during the fifties, to become thereby (as Tahar Ouattar put it in 1976) "[one] of those whose [writing] activity led directly to the war of liberation." After 1962, he returned to a poetry (& prose) exploring oneiric & mythopoetic areas that link him to Surrealist concerns, but also to an older *catabasis eis to antron*, a journey into the depths—what Jean Dejeux has elsewhere called "the lost cave or the forgotten inner sea"—and to confrontations with an "Other" that can no longer be externalized as the colonial oppressor.

Amos Tutuola 1920–1997

from MY LIFE IN THE BUSH OF GHOSTS

Television-handed Ghostess

When it was about 2 o'clock p.m. I saw a ghostess who was crying bitterly and coming to me direct in a hut where I laid down enjoying myself. When she entered I noticed that she held a short mat which was woven with dried weeds. She was not more than three feet high. Immediately she entered she went direct to the fire, she spread the mat closely to the fire and then sat down on it without saluting or talking to me. So at this stage I noticed carefully that she was almost covered with sores, even there was no single hair on her head, except sores with uncountable maggots which were dashing here and there on her body. Both her arms were not more than one and a half foot, it had uncountable short fingers. She was crying bitterly and repeatedly as if somebody was stabbing her with knives. Of course, I did not talk to her, but I was looking at her with much astonishment until I saw the water of her eyes that it was near to quench the fire, then I got up with anger and told her to walk out of my hut, because if the water quenches the fire I should not be able to get another again, as there were not matches in the Bush of Ghosts. But instead of walking out as I said she started to cry louder than ever. When I could not bear her cry I asked her—"by the way what are you crying for?" She replied—"I am crying because of you." Then I asked again—"because of me?" She said— "yes" and I said—"What for?" Then she started to relate her story thus—

"I was born over two hundred years ago with sores on my head and all over my body. Since the day that I was born I have no other work more than to find out the doctor who could heal it for me and several of them had tried all their best but failed. Instead of healing or curing it would be spreading wider and then giving me more pains. I have been to many sorcerers to know whether the sore would be healed, but every one of them was telling me that there is an earthly person who had been lost in this Bush of Ghosts, so that if I can be wandering about I might see you one day, and the sorcerers said that if you will be licking the sore every day with your tongue for ten years it would be healed. So that I am very lucky and very glad that I meet you here today and I shall also be exceedingly glad if you will be licking the sore with your tongue every day until the ten years that it will be healed as the sorcerers had told me. And I am also crying bitterly in respect of you because I believe that no doubt you have been struggling for many years in this Bush of Ghosts for the right way to your home town, but you are seeing the way every day and you do not know it, because every earthly person gets eyes but cannot see. Even it is on the right way to your home town that you found this hut and sleep or sit in it every day and night. Although I believe that you will not refuse to lick the sore until it is healed."

Having related her story and said that if I am licking the sore it would be healed as the sorcerers said, so I replied—"I want you to go back to your sorcerers and tell them I refuse to lick the sore." After I told her like this she said again—"It is not a matter of going back to the sorcerers, but if you can do it look at my palm or hand." But when she told me to look at her palm and opened it nearly to touch my face, it was exactly as a television, I saw my town, mother, brother and all my playmates, then she was asking me frequently—"do you agree to be licking the sore with your tongue, tell me, now, yes or no?"

COMMENTARY

Now it remained me alone in the bush, because no brother, mother, father or other defender could save me or direct me if and whenever any danger is imminent.

A.T.

It is not only that Tutuola helps to break the divide between oral & written practice, but that he makes English (*not* his native language) into a transformed vehicle to serve those ends. Born & raised in the Yoruba traditions of Nigeria, "[he] achieves a fantastic unity between his folkloric sources and his own inventiveness" (Kofi Awoonor), both in a mode of English derived from Yoruba syntax & in the depiction of an ancient world newly filled with floodlights, hospitals & banquet halls, electric wires, telephones, & Technicolor, even a "television-handed ghostess." *My Life in the Bush of Ghosts*—his second book after *The Palm Wine Drinkard*—is narrated by an eight-year-old boy, abandoned during a slave raid, who flees into the bush, "a place of ghosts and spirits," as lead-in to his mythic quest. Tutuola's use of the grotesque & scatological, while it may resemble that of an Artaud or Lautréamont, say, is unrelated to them as source; is reflective rather, as Awoonor tells us, of the "typical *Yoruba* sense of the bizarre."

Helmut Heissenbüttel 1921–1996

DIDACTIC POEM ON THE NATURE OF HISTORY, A.D. 1954

*"with men and carts and horses
our lord destroyed their forces"*

occurrences and all that failed to occur
epochs calendars dynastic shifts
fossilized cities fossilized nations nations on the march columns of
    marchers and Napoleon at the Beresina
pulpit carvings by Giovanni Pisano Nietzsche's ECCE HOMO
    and K. Z.'s
l'empire de la majorité se fonde sur cette idée qu'il y a plus de sagesse
    dans beaucoup d'hommes que dans un seul (Tocqueville)
remembrance of the voice of Adolf Hitler on the radio Symphony for 9
    Instruments opus 21 1928 by Anton Webern and never in my whole
    life have I written as long a line as this
Piero della Francesca and the smoke of the December sky
reiteration

reiteration this is my thesis
reiteration this is my thesis
reiteration this is my thesis

unReiteration

Translation from the German by Jerome Rothenberg

COMBINATION II

1

Black-
ness.

2

AFTERNOONSSLEEPREMINISCENCE
Awakening details.
The shadow of a bench dissolving into white sand.
Blackish roof.
Unanimated contour of a pigeon.
The latest song hit (lyrics spelling out coitus).
The warm skin set between the hips.

3

Language
of a still life by Picasso
suddenly made clear.
Sadness of bright shadows.
Lemonyellow. Violetred. And brown. And slateblue.

4

Broken up from nothing.
From a flat afternoon earlyspring light
broken up. And then the grey mouth
swallows (unremembering opportunities lost
in the past) the image.
An immovable statue.

5

AFTERNOONSSLEEPSADNESS
It isn't the truth. Only
its shadow. And where the light came from
has still to be reached.

Translation from the German by Jerome Rothenberg

Lesson 3

and then down into the black soul

1

to stylize to deny the body can be traced back to rationality in that context also the desirable body it has to be that that too part of the calculation the desirable a kind of lure

2

and then down into the black soul

3

what I want to say is I saw it the room naked as a hand I locked up the black princess the sheath of the angel naked I swear it from head to toe from anus to navel what I want to say is my mind rotates in images of beauty and desire my gaze embraces naked what I want to say is fruit of a suit flight of a bird

4

and then down into the black soul

5

enjoyably and deeply I lost myself in all the minglings and intertwinings of joy and pain from which emanate the spice of life and the flower of feelings a florid fire flowed through my veins what I dreamed was not just some kiss not just the wish to break the smarting stings of longing it is not for your lips alone that I long or for your eyes or for your body but it was a romantic confusion of all of these things a wondrous tangle of all the various remembrances and longings.

6

and then down into the black soul

7

the element wherein desire and its object exist indifferently against each other and autonomously is the alive Dasein the gratification of desire sublates this as far as it concerns its object but this is the element which gives both their separate reality rather a Being that is essentially a representation

8

and then down into the black soul

9

gratified lust does indeed carry the positive meaning to have become itself as objective self-consciousness but just as much the negative one namely to have sublated itself and by grasping its realization only in terms of that meaning its experience enters its consciousness as contradiction wherein the achieved reality of its singleness sees itself annihilated by the negative being and yet is the selfsame's devouring power

10

and then down into the black soul

11

in the silver moonlight alongside the ships and the large buildings and the canals which cut into and through the city's innermost core the forest of masts the lines of beams and cordage crossing a thousandfold all in moonlight strange and magic at one corner but a glance into a brightly lit room where a hundred diligent hands were sewing sails

12

and then down into the black soul

13

actually today everything is like yesterday except for the hallway where yesterday the handbag kept surprising me today I am surprised that the handbag is no longer there thus it would be more accurate to say that today everything is completely different from yesterday but then again not really either

Translation from the German by Pierre Joris

Changes in language mean changes in the interpretation of the world.
H. H.

Probably the most consistently experimental of the postwar Gruppe 47 writers, Heissenbüttel's prodigious & very varied output (poems, proses, essays, novels, radio soundplays, & concrete & semantic experiments that prove him a true heir to Dada & Gertrude Stein) has been shockingly little translated into English to date. The final section of his theoretical text, *Premises,* reads in part: "My experience of a fundamental change arose from the situation in which literary speech, exemplary speech, is forced to involve itself explicitly and specifically with the ground of language itself. When the traditional way of saying things failed, it became a matter of penetrating, so to speak, into the interior of language to break it open and question it in its most hidden connections. The result of this cannot be a new language. It is a way of speaking that plays on its contrasts with traditional syntax and word usage. . . . This essential indeterminacy factor never permits it to arrive at what one could call image or metaphor. Image and metaphor, as something clearly identifiable, would be part of that language which is withdrawing itself. The subjects, objects and predicates of the sentence drop away because the experience, which is being related, stands outside the subject-object relation. . . . Connections are made not through systematic and logico-syntactical interweavings, but through connotations, through ambiguities—outgrowths of a decayed syntax. Uncertainty, alienation, fumbling-in-the-dark . . . become thematically visible in the most wornout cliches and petrified slogans of culture, become thematic with the use of the little particle 'because.' None of this happens in an 'abstract' combination of 'linguistic matter,' as if instead of stains, drips and brush-slaps one now used words and sentence fragments. Nor is it some kind of 'encipherment.' It happens as a first-time attempt to penetrate and get a foothold in a world that still seems to escape language. The boundary that is reached . . . is the boundary of that which is not yet sayable."

Jackson Mac Low b. 1922

ASYMMETRY 205

silence,
        island.

           Lordship eyes no
       cable eyes

island.

       silence,
           Lordship anchor no
      descended

Lordship oars rapidly descended silence,
      hand island.

           praying

               Autumn 1960

from **THE PRONOUNS — A COLLECTION OF 40 DANCES — FOR THE DANCERS**

1st Dance — Making Things New — 6 February 1964

He makes himself comfortable
& matches parcels.

Then he makes glass boil
while having political material get in
& coming by.

Soon after, he's giving gold cushions or seeming to do so,
taking opinions,
shocking,
pointing to a fact that seems to be an error & showing it to be other than
   it seems,
& presently paining by going or having waves.

Then after doing some waiting,
he disgusts someone
& names things.

A little while later he gets out with things
& finally either rewards someone for something or goes up under
    something.

2nd Dance—Seeing Lines—6 February 1964

She seems to come by wing,
& keeping present being in front,
she reasons regularly.

Then—making her stomach let itself down
& giving a bit or doing something elastic
& making herself comfortable—
she lets complex impulses make something.

She disgusts everyone.

Later she fingers a door
& wheels awhile
while either transporting a star or letting go of a street.

**3RD LIGHT POEM: FOR SPENCER, BEATE,
& SEBASTIAN HOLST — 12 JUNE 1962**

Owl-light in a tree house [1″, 2″, 3″, or 4″ of silence]
singing by the light of a Nernst lamp
porcupines in arclight
see the porcupines in arclight
wait   [12″, 24″, 36″, 48″, or 60″ of silence]
Are there mustard-seed-oil lamps burning in the Persian section of
    Brooklyn?
I'm inclined to think so.
Anda-oil lamps must light the Andaman Islanders.
Do they give a ruby light?
Aladdin lamps give a light as white as night inside out.

Lamplight on footgear
weathering

aurora light in summer
the dawn light is circumstantial
disregard the neon flush of yesterday
I'd hunt it out if Altoona were Allentown or Muhlenberg LaSalle
Treat it as a question of footprints in snowlight in Cleveland or a
    diamond in starlight Milwaukee comes to mind
incessant spring scintillations.

[long silence]

Patriarchal light from ancient candles.

[long silence]

Collect soapstone lamps to light the ice tables a bit in Holstenberg to
    help Boy Holst finish his Greenland story where "they" were
"lit a bit by the soapstone lamps on the ice tables."

A yellow smoky light?
A corrosive light?
A candid light?
A flattering light?
Light given off by a rhodochrosite if a rhodochrosite gives off light.

Enter a chorus of grumbling priests carrying magnesium flares & hoes.

Treat it as a question of data here on the coast & in the light of that data
    construct imaginary parallels to light geometry & paraphernalia for
    pranks in autumn.

Who burns walnut-oil in lamps?
I see its light as a rich brown light like an over-varnished Rembrandt.
One wd have to have a flashlight to find things.

PIECES O' SIX — 11

Torqued beams were pleasing to multitudinous applicants whose syringes
were hardly apparent though their astrakhans were diaphanous. Thrown
among totally arbitrary freaks, their frail improvers nervously clasped
pennyweight palimpsests. Trained to dally, they stayed to spite the tar-
nished elders. Absolutely concupiscent crowds were mangled as they
mingled. Tourniquets furnished by slavish townsmen did little to lessen

the petulant bravery flaunted in excellent stockings by cargo-handlers'
allies and assistants undaunted by closures or mapmakers' moping battal-
ions, punched and prettily perforated. Why not?, they had thought. For-
tunately, few were criminally aimed. Nothing stood in the way of recon-
ciliation or pusillanimous accommodation unaccompanied by threats or
even nostrums. No one proposed a lengthy series of settlements. Flyers
zoomed or were thrown amid mutually overcongratulatory participants.
Few wished or even thought of ablutions. Tenuous magnificoes button-
holed magnates. Future tennis-harassers phatically pleaded their pally
proclivities till doubters were hushed and sanctimonious philoprogenitive
tenants were roughly introduced. Truly unreliable qualifiers valorized
their privileges. Newsy locutions prevailed. Prevented from further obfus-
cating relations among the many purposeful planetary hagglers, policelike
termagants tempted the timid to terrorize finite factions. Claques were
undone. Stoves became the norm long before altitudes were accurately
calculated, and zenith-divers fed concise directions to tasseled arbitrators
who mounted unambiguous mesas wherever outlooks were clarified and
beatitude was assured by prominent mature engineering. Clauses were
seldom inserted in codicils franked by belted parishioners. Benched boni-
faces cackled. Trellised inscriptions were fractured by plinths. Testi-
monials helped but little amid this plethora of pumpkin-headed taciturn
drovers and clandestine crossbowmen. Portents no sooner held up than
discarded might well have been filed, but most were flicked off as infantile
and gross. Close to attested predictions, voluntary pit viper wallahs were
hauled to unlikely demises. Flagrant belly-thumpers passed them. Passion-
ate thespians glibly aligned their tonsured noggins beneath those gallant
fractured pantaloons. Sooner than admit collusion, they scrambled more
nearly like poltergeists than poltroons although their enclosures were en-
venomed less by palsy than by pretense. Fortunate were their rivals! En-
dearing though unerring, these quasi-Christian anecdotalists soaped their
panic-stricken partners. Patly, albeit gaseously, their would-be defenestra-
tors let themselves seemingly be talked down despite precise instructions
from inert erstwhile initiators. Previously scheduled palliations threatened
resourceful extremists. Preparations denied them unimpaired positions.
Tentative agonies were hailed as accomplishments by unnamed former
sleepers unembarrassed by black smoke beneath the hustings. Creams and
bulldozers were pocketed amid unearthly chunks. Hastily the problem
was assessed as transitional and tragic. Circumstantially their evidence
was profuse. Gullible and gnarled, the hackneyed mariners escalated en-
deavors to weasel out of easing their weakness. Patience reinforced limits.
Fanatical assemblers were led to assume targeted identities. Discipline
traveled unremittingly through ranks of wrangling diseducators. Many

wangled and wheedled, pleaded and finagled. Disastrously Tuscan entre-pôts were taken with no shattering or balancing. Barely visible blasts lacked verisimilitude. Cloudy addlings were cited as justifications or en-franchisements. Details were hard to come by. Leaders of optional inclusions more often were duped than allowed to increase their sparse celebrity. Nonsense was freely offered as effectual condescension. Tenants in unaffected purlieus prayed in billingsgate, sincerely flattered by principled agitators clothed in herringbone. Falsified and blanked, cursing motor-men clamored like acidulous parrots for natty pacification. Nothing was farther from any unanomalous possibility. Feathers were ranked beside the rush-strewn walls. Leaping in leather, certain callous and cagey lieu-tenants breached the battlements despite their hardy craglike immobility. Flames were toned as surely secular. Cooperators aimed at deletions of irresolute prayers in keeping with precipitous aspirations far beyond de-scended ladders. Tanks of truisms leavened actual rogations. Unsaturated flag-trimming pangolin partisans sent messianic messages past the tents of subjoined beckoners. Perjurers galloped past. Fanciful divers rivaled slight harmonic tidal pandemoniacs. Slackly assailing sensed increments, advo-cates of unadvised important notions grossly fustigated opposing defini-tions blankly checked by strenuous resolutions and unadorned fomenta-tions needlessly grouped as necessary with acceptable debts and titillating fads. Fractionated under bell jars in sudsy forests encompassed by sleeves of parkland and anechoic simulated treasurehouses, leafy banisters of rap-idly passing hydrocarbons lagged behind one hundred and ninety-one masked and hatless horrors. Conjurers in flaccid installations clenched their tangled arms. Nettles flourished between the tiles of buckling ter-races. Never a feature was cracked or haplessly crinkled. Clipped pilasters dripped. Fortunate entanglements sweetened familiar baggage. Nestorian elders defended accidents. Reality rested unshaken. Mediterranean in-stability reversed captions challenged by civilization unrehearsed in bog-gling circumstantial trespass. Lightning weakened foundations already nearly razed by bumptious arguers and analysts anticipating patterns pricked and spangled by spastic farragoes.

24 October 1983

All light is relevant to each light / & each light to every light / & each light to each light / & every light to each light / & all light to every light / & every light to all light / & each light to all light / & all light to all light.
Is that lucid?
Yes.

J. M. L.

Mac Low stands with John Cage (above) as one of the two major artists to have brought systematic chance (aleatoric) operations into our poetic & musical practice since the Second World War. The resulting work raises fundamental questions about the nature of poetry & the function of the poet as creator. It also sums up & greatly extends the experiments of many earlier avant-garde poets, not only with "objective chance" but with the introduction into poetry of asymmetric structure, serial techniques, & simultaneity of performance, along with a continuing use of both traditional & improvisational methods of composition. All of this has finally brought a recognition by many (Cage among them) of Mac Low as the principal experimental poet of his time.

Of the poems presented here, all but the later *Pieces o' Six* (1992) show varying degrees of aleatoric composition or performance. Like much of his other work, Mac Low's *asymmetries* (dating largely from the 1960s) use acrostic methods applied to words drawn from various appropriated texts, thus: "Beginning with the first or a chance-designated subsequent word in a source text, the first line of such a poem [sometimes as here the first 'stanza'] spells out this word [by its initial letters]; the second line spells out the second word of the first line; the third line, the third word, & so on. . . . These poems are 'asymmetrical' in that each strophe spells out a different series of words, whereas each stanza of a stanzaic-acrostic poem spells out the same word series—either the title or some other word string."

As for the openings such methods do in fact allow (& their connection to an experimental/language-centered poetry as social act *and* mental praxis), Mac Low writes elsewhere: "All of these are ways to let in other forces than yourself . . . [so] that . . . by interacting in that way with chance or the world or the environment or other people, one sees and *produces* possibilities that one's habitual associations—what we usually draw on in the course of spontaneous or intuitive composition—would have precluded."

Pier Paolo Pasolini 1922–1975

from **A DESPERATE VITALITY**

I

(Draft, in cursus, through the use of current jargon, on a previous occurrence: Fiumicino, the old castle, and a first insight into the reality of death.)

As in a film by Godard: alone
in a car moving along the highways
of Latin neo-capitalism – returning from the airport –
[that's where Moravia remained, pure among his luggage]
      alone, "at the wheel of his Alfa Romeo"
          beneath a sun so divine
          indescribable in non-elegiac rhyme
          – the most beautiful sun of the year –
as in a film by Godard:
          beneath that unique sun that steadily bled,
      the canal of Fiumicino's port
      – a motorboat returning un-noticed
      – Neapolitan sailors in their woolen rags
      – a highway accident with only a small crowd . . .

– as in a film by Godard –
rediscovered romanticism contained
in cynical neo-capitalism, and cruelty –
at the wheel
on the road to Fiumicino,

and there is the castle (sweet
mystery, for the French screenwriter,
in the troubled, infinite, secular sun,

this papal beast, with its battlements,
on the hedges and vine rows of the ugly
countryside of peasant serfs) . . .

– I am like a cat burned alive,
run over by the wheels of a truck,
hung to a fig tree by boys,

but at least eight of
its nine lives intact;

like a snake reduced to bloody pulp,
a half-eaten eel

– sunken cheeks defining tired eyes,
hair horribly thinned out against the skull,
skinny arms, like those of a child
– Belmondo, a cat that never dies,
"at the wheel of his Alfa Romeo"
in the logic of narcissistic montage,
detaches himself from time, and inserts
Himself:

into images that have nothing to do with
the boredom of progressing hours . . .
the slow dying glitter of evening . . .

Death is not
the inability to communicate,
but the failure to continue being understood.

And this papal beast, not lacking
grace, – the reminder
of rustic landlord concessions,
innocent, after all,
as was the serfs' resignation –
in the sun that was,
in the centuries,
for thousands of afternoons,
here, the only guest,
this papal beast, with battlements
crouching amid marsh poplars,
melon fields, banks,
this papal beast protected
– by buttresses of the sweet orange colour
of Rome, ruined
like Roman or Etruscan buildings,
is at the point of no longer being understood.

*(No fade-out, a clean break, I portray myself in an act – with no historic
precedents – of "cultural industry")*

Me, voluntarily martyred . . . , and
her across from me, on the sofa:
flashes back and forth, between positions,
"You," – I know what she's thinking, looking at me,
and more domestic-Italian M.F.
always Godardic – "you, Tennessee type!",
the cobra in the wool sweater
        (with the subordinate cobra
        skimming in magnesial silence).
Then loudly: "Will you tell me what you're writing?"

"Verses, verses, I am writing verses!
(damned fool,
verses she is in no position to understand,
having no knowledge of metrics! Verses!)
verses   NO LONGER IN TRIPLETS!

        Understand?
That is the important thing: no longer in triplets!
I have gone back tout court to magma!
Neo-capitalism has won, I am
out on the street
        as a poet, ah [sob]
        and as a citizen [another sob]."
        And the man-cobra with the pen:
        "The title of your work?" "I don't know . . .
        [Then he talks in a low tone, fearful, resuming
        the accepted role which the conversation imposes
        on him: it takes nothing
        to discolour
        his face
        into that of some poor fool condemned to die]
        – maybe . . . "The Persecution"
        or . . . "A New Pre-history" (or Pre-history)
        or . . .
        [At this point he becomes angry, regains
        the dignity of civil hate]
        "Monologue on the Jews" . . .

like the weakness of the arsis
of mixed-up octosyllabic verses: magmatic!]
"And what is it about?"
"Well, about my . . . His, death.
It is not in the inability to communicate, [death]
but in the inability to be understood . . .

      (If only the cobra knew
      that it is a useless idea
      thought up on the way back from Fiumicino!)
They are almost all lyric verses, of which
the composition in time and place
consists, oddly!, of a ride in a car . . .
meditations from forty to eighty miles an hour . . .
with fast pans and tracking shots
to follow or precede
on significant monuments, or groups
of people, which spurn
an objective love . . . of citizen
(or street user) . . ."

"Ah, ah – [the she-cobra with the pen laughing] – . . .
who is it that *does not understand*?"
"Those who are no longer with us."

III

Those who are no longer with us!
Taken, with their innocent youth, by a new breath
of history to other lives!

I remember it being . . . for a love
that invaded my brown eyes and honest trousers,
house and countryside, the morning sun and

the evening sun . . . during the good Saturdays
of the Friuli, during . . . Sundays . . . Ah!,
I can't even pronounce this word

of virgin passions, of my death (seen
in a dry ditch full with primroses,
between vineyards rows stunned by gold, near

farmhouses, dark against a sublime blue).

I remember that in the midst of that monstrous love
I would scream in pain
for the Sundays when it would have to shine

"over the sons of the sons, the sun!"

I cried, on the cot in Casarsa,
in the room that smelled of urine and laundry
while those Sundays shone to their death . . .

Incredible tears! Not only for
that which I was losing, in that moment
of wearing immobility of the splendour,

but for that which I would lose! When
other youngsters – of whom I couldn't even think,
so similar to today's

wearing white socks and windbreakers,
with flowers in their lapels – or dark material,
for weddings, treated with filial tenderness,

– would populate the Casarsa of the future,
unchanged, with its stones, and the sun
that covered it with a dying golden shower . . .

With an epileptic impetus of homicidal pain
I protested,
like one condemned to life imprisonment,
by locking myself into
my room,
without anyone knowing it,
to scream, my mouth
blocked by sheets darkened
by the heat of an iron,
the sheets of my family,
on which I would brood over the flower
of my youth.

And once, after dinner, or maybe it was night,
I ran, screaming
through Sunday streets, after the game
to the old cemetery, behind the train tracks,
to carry out and repeat to the blood,
the sweetest act in life,

alone, or a pile of dirt
from two or three graves
of Italian or German soldiers
with no names on the wooden crosses
– buried there since the other war.

And, that night, amid dry tears,
the bloody bodies of those unknowns
dressed in green-gray rags

came to cluster on my bed,
where I slept naked and empty,
to stain me with blood, till dawn.

I was twenty, not even – eighteen,
nineteen . . . and I had been alive for a century,
a whole lifetime

consumed by the pain of the fact
that I would never be able to give my love
if not to my hand, or to the grass of ditches

or maybe to the earth of an unguarded tomb . . .
Twenty and, with its human history and its cycle
of poetry, a life had ended.

Translation from the Italian by Pasquale Verdicchio

COMMENTARY

Only the actions of life will be communicated / & these will be poetry.
P. P. P.

While his big reputation outside Italy was as a filmmaker (*The Gospel
According to Matthew, Teorema, Salò*), the assessment by fellow writer
Alberto Moravia—"Pasolini is *the* major Italian poet of the second half of
this century"—is shared by many. It was Pasolini's contribution as such to
mix revolutionary socialism with the still warm ashes of a dying Catholic
faith, to bring to film & verse "a desperate vitality" & a many-sided intel-
lectual commitment, in Whitman's words, to "the rights of them the others
are down upon." This showed itself as well in a poetry split between a still-
literary Italian & the Friulian language of his childhood. Stabbed to death
by a Roman male prostitute—one of those "beautiful boys" with whom he

would identify & would patronize—he remains the modern/postmodern model of the "*civil* poet" (Moravia again), "[not] an official, celebratory, rhetorical poet (as Carducci and D'Annunzio were in Italy in the second half of the nineteenth century), but rather a poet who sees his native land in a way that the powerful of the country do not and cannot see it." Of his accomplishment in *A Desperate Vitality*, poet/translator Pasquale Verdicchio writes: "In it the poet examines his existence from childhood to the time of the poem's writing: the sequence of decisions that have shaped his life (not excluding the possibility of a divine intention for his existence); his poetic choices; and, in the person of his interlocutors, the misunderstanding and ignorance that he tried to eliminate with his work." And Pasolini, of his concurrent hope & desolation: "For years I thought that an addressee for my 'confessions' and 'testimony' existed. Only now do I realize that he does not exist."

Vasko Popa 1922–1991

BURNING SHEWOLF

I

On the bottom of the sky
The shewolf lies

Body of living sparks
Overgrown with grass
And covered with sun's dust

In her breasts
Mountains rise threatening
And forgive as they lower themselves

Through her veins rivers thunder
In her eyes lakes flash

In her boundless heart
The ores melt with love
On seven stems of their fire

Before the first and last howl
Wolves play on her back
And live in her crystal womb

2

They cage the shewolf
In the earth's fire

Force her to build
Towers of smoke
Make bread out of coals

They fatten her with embers
And have her wash it down
With hot mercury milk

They force her to mate
With red-hot pokers
And rusty old drills

With her teeth the shewolf reaches
The blonde braid of a star
And climbs back to the base of the sky

3

They catch the shewolf in steel traps
Sprung from horizon to horizon

Tear out her golden muzzle
And pluck the secret grasses
Between her thighs

They sick on her all-tied-up
Deadbeats and bloodhounds
To go ahead and rape her

Cut her up into pieces
And abandon her
To the carcass-eating tongs

With her severed tongue the shewolf
Scoops live water from the jaws of a cloud
And again becomes whole

4

The shewolf bathes herself in the blue
And washes away the ashes of dogs

On the bottom of a torrent
That runs down the stones of her motionless face
Lightnings spawn

In her wide-open jaw
The moon hides its ax during the day
The sun its knives at night

The beatings of her copper-heart
Quiet the barking distances
And lull to sleep the chirping air

In the ravines
Below her wooded eyebrows
The thunder means business

5

The shewolf stands on her back legs
At the base of the sky

She stands up together with wolves
Turned to stone in her womb

She stands up slowly
Between noon and midnight
Between two wolf lairs

Stands up with pain
Freeing from one lair her snout
And from the other her huge tail

She stands up with a salt-choked howl
From her dry throat

Stands up dying of thirst
Toward the clear point at the summit of the sky
The watering place of the long-tailed stars

Translation from the Serbian by Charles Simic

*I climb up to the family chapel / In Grebenats cemetery // The wooden
doors are closed / But don't prevent me / Seeing my forefathers // They ride
garlanded rams / Over this dry sea-bed / Called Banat // They get on better
with wolves / Than with people / And bow only to the sun / Each morning
and evening . . .*

V. P. (translation by Anne Pennington)

If his work, like that of others of his generation, derived from Surrealism,
he placed himself willfully among those deeper sources—Serbian folklore
in his case—from which the Surrealists themselves had often traced their
derivations. Of that kind of quasi-rootedness, Charles Simic writes, as trans-
lator & fellow-poet: "In the poems of Vasko Popa, you have the impression
at times of reading magic formulas. . . . The language is that of definitions,
of primitive books of genesis. The severity is absolutely intentional. Despite
the rich lyricism, there are few individual accents here. What we are wit-
nessing instead is a kind of contemporary 'sacred' tablet [:] . . . an area of
language remarkable for its elemental surrealism coupled undoubtedly with
an animistic, myth-making approach to reality. The poet does not rely on
those sources directly; instead he uses the syntactic, rhythmical, and imagi-
native principles inherent in their construction to embody his own percep-
tions, which are profoundly of his own time and place."

Legitimated in his own origins, "[Popa] was [also] the editor of three in-
fluential anthologies of folk material, Serbian humor, and poets' dreams."

THE TAMMUZI POETS

Poetry, this immortal carcass, bores me.
Lebanon is burning—
It leaps, like a wounded horse at the edge of the desert
and I am looking for a fat girl
to rub myself against on the tram,
for a Bedouin-looking man to knock down somewhere.

MUHAMMAD AL-MAGHUT

And the hawk in his wandering, in his life-giving pessimism
  builds on the summit in limitless passion
  a beloved Andalusia,
  an Andalusia rising from Damascus.
  He carries to the West the harvest of the East.

ADONIS

(1) What's at stake here is both what meets the eye & what lies beneath the surface of the poem as individual & internal struggle. On its more obvious side, then, the appearance of a group of self-proclaimed "Tammuzi poets"—around the magazine *Shi'ir* (Poetry) in the later 1950s—was part of the development, in the two decades following World War II, of third-world liberation movements with their well-known cultural/political concomitants—the simultaneous demands for revolution & tradition. As poets of the Arabic language the Tammuzis not only proclaimed a relation to a deep tradition (an ancient order newly rediscovered) but spelled out a further struggle (a second liberation from within): to create "a poetry that establishes another concept of identity—one that is pluralist, open, agnostic, and secular." (Thus Adonis on "poetry & apoetical culture.")

The weight of tradition in Arabic literature is, as often noted, phenomenal. Codified in the middle of the eighth century by Al-Khalil—who drew on pre-Islamic & early Islamic poetry—the classical system of sixteen traditional meters, insistence on marathon mono-rhymings, etc., ruled & bound the poetry until the middle of this century. Influenced by English Romanticism & French Symbolism, earlier Arabic modernist movements & poets (including those associated with Khalil Gibran in New York) remained cautious innovators, insisting on a more contemporary content while leaving the form & language to a great extent unchanged. It was only in the late 1940s that a truly modernist (&, in the Arab context, avant-gardist) development introduced free verse (*al-shiʿir al-hurr* = "free poetry"), with the Iraqi poets Nazik al-Malaʾika & Badr Shakir al-Sayyab (below) often given as its originators. The foundation of *Shiʿir* by Adonis & Yusuf al-Khal (in Beirut in 1956) & the proclamation therein of the Tammuzi poets (the name, like that of Adonis [born ʿAli Ahmad Saʿid], referring to the ancient Mesopotamian god of seasonal decay & rebirth) concretized & expanded the concepts of a modern Arabic poetry on the levels of both form & meaning. It was no longer a question of simply seeing the Western as the modern—& thus desirable—model; here as elsewhere a new present opened the way to a new past: the work of early Arabic writers (pre-Islamics & limit-testing mystics & city poets of the Abassid dynasty [750–1258 C.E.]) as a bridge to the transgressions at the heart (in Rimbaud's term) of the absolutely modern. Writes critic Adnan Haydar concerning "what is modern about modern Arabic poetry": "According to Adonis, *al-kitaba*, or *écriture*, as Roland Barthes calls it, is not language as we know it, but a displacement, a breaking away from the accepted and the known. . . . It is subversive, because it seeks to destroy logical temporality and causality."

Of the Tammuzi poets presented here, Adonis (see also below, page 441) & al-Maghut are from Syria, al-Khal & al-Hajj are Lebanese by birth, while al-Sayyab is from Iraq, self-exiled from the middle 1950s until his death in 1964, when the original Tammuzi group dissolved and *Shiʿir* was (temporarily) suspended. The writings of all but al-Maghut are at the boundaries between closed & open verse, which only al-Maghut completely crosses over.

(2) "Based as it is on the answer, Arab culture suppressed all questioning; it instituted a poetry that could say only what is known, a poetry of the explicit. Thus the first difficulty Arab poetry runs up against resides, paradoxically, in the culture of easiness. The discourse of 'easy poetry' will be the first obstacle to that creation. For that poetry which gives itself over to panegyrics strengthens the repressions and interdictions of the politico-religious institution on which the society is founded. It deepens the gulf that has opened between man and himself, between man and his aspirations. By comparison, all other poetry will always seem arduous—for such poetry will have to begin by putting the language itself to death, as if it were having to struggle against the unknown. As if it had to be an experience of the unlimited and infinite. This poetry has existed at various moments during Islam, and it continues to exist, but it is marginalized and frowned upon. Reading it is not an act of consumption; it is an act of creation. Therefore, after the problem of easiness comes the difficulty engendered by poetic investigation. The light such investigation may cast on

the unknown only enlarges the unknown's dimensions, announcing its depth and its extremity as if light were transforming itself into night. And if this light opens the horizon to the night of the world, the limits it makes poetry cross open poetry to the unlimited. As if the darkness were amplified by the very movement of the light, as if poetry knew only its own limits. The dark world that is illumined is the very thing that leads poetry toward an even darker world" (Adonis, *Poetry and Apoetical Culture*).

Yusuf al-Khal 1917–1987

CAIN THE IMMORTAL

When you turn at the road's
last bend
you eat the distance with your eyes
as if it were an idol raised to heaven.

You can't go back,
you will wither and fall
or reach the crossroad
until some oracle appears
like an image on the wall.
Perhaps the oracle is nothing
but the fist of God
dropped open with a sign?
           No,
you are leafed with worry,
devoured by stares.
Grumbling, you pierce the dust
with a curse
like Adam's rib,
           and wander off
into forbidden grounds
into a cleft between
two shores—
the region of your death.

                    Not knowing
where you belong.
Your pallbearers are carrying
no one in your coffin.

Cain cannot die.

Translation from the Arabic by Sargon Boulus & Samuel Hazo

THE WAYFARERS

This house is closed to neighbors
open to wayfarers.
A fierce winter has left a gap
in the fence.
Every rainstorm now dislodges
a rock or two,
weakening what's left
of the foundation.
                    Dawn
glides from its edges and rests,
and suddenly leaves.
Dusk happens, and light
turns inside out in silence
to show its darker, its more
mysterious memories.
This house harbors just a few
who awaken to not so scanty a share
(one veteran of a hard voyage,
a seatamer; and a forest marching out to combat)
their aim to tear off the mask (it was
a rock).
            Having erased all the past
each wayfarer walks as if on air
or like a glinting dagger in the dark:

No cry for help
from the side of the road
there is no blood
it has now turned into wine.

They are clay, these wayfarers,
and they'll pass as breezes pass.

Translation from the Arabic by Sargon Boulus & Samuel Hazo

Badr Shakir al-Sayyab 1926–1964

THE RIVER AND DEATH

Buwayb . . .
Buwayb . . .
A tower's bells, lost on the sea floor
water in jars, dusk in trees
& the jars pearl belldrops
their crystal melts into a whisper
"Buwayb . . . O Buwayb!"
Longing lances my blood
for you, Buwayb
my river sad as rain.
Wish I could run at the dark
fists clenched
each finger bearing a year's worth of longing
as if I brought
you
offerings of wheat and flowers.
Wish I could watch from hilltops
and glimpse the moon
wading between your banks, sowing shadows
filling baskets
with water, fish & flowers.
Wish I could wade through you, follow the moon
and listen to the pebbles' mumbled echo from the deep
like a thousand birds chirping in the trees—
Oh you, are you a forest of tears or a river?
And do the fretful fish fall asleep at dawn?

And these stars, will they still be waiting
feeding silk to thousands of needles?
And you, O Buwayb . . .
Wish I could drown in you, gather shellfish
make a house from them
where the green of water and the trees
is lit by star- and moon-light
And through you I would ebb to the sea! For death is a strange world
it fascinates small children,
and you are its secret door, O Buwayb . . .

2

Buwayb . . . O Buwayb!
It's twenty years later now, each year an eon
and when darkness folds this day
I'll settle in bed sleepless
I'll exercise my mind till dawn:
a great tree
conscious of branches, birds and fruit
and the blood and tears of a rueful world
will feel as true as rain
bells of my death toll in my veins
my blood longs for a bullet
whose lethal ice will rake my heart's depths
like bone-burning hell.
Wish I could join the warriors
clench my fist and strike fate.
Wish I could drown deep in my blood
to help carry the human burden
and birth life. My death would be a triumph!

Translation from the Arabic by Pierre Joris & Hédi Jaouad

Adonis b. 1930

from **A DESIRE MOVING THROUGH THE MAPS OF THE MATERIAL**

II

the eiffel tower   notre dame   the louvre

(is it a dream—the eiffel tower is no longer in its place and here is the louvre heading towards the eastern shore of the mediterranean as if it too wants to follow the footsteps of alexander the great, and here is notre dame sleeping as it prays, tapping the shoulder of the sky to make it a pillow for its dreams)

the eiffel tower   notre dame   the louvre

the mosque of the fifth arrondissement

(is a statue going to convince me that a western virgin was the first to become pregnant with reason—who said: "thus the stomach spoke—we deem the east and the west adversaries and the dust a judge," I look at faces and say: "The inanimate is not in the inanimate, but in man")

notre dame   the mosque of the fifth arrondissement

weep, oh angels of hell,
you'll no longer find visitors whose roasting you'll relish;
group by group, all the animals go to paradise, the speaking and the dumb

it came to pass—
let the memory of races explode—

abu nuwas

there are those of the order of humans
bestowed with speech, yet they do not speak,
not because they are mute
or have any physical defect,

in a desert fueled for invasion
war is declared
by this and that and this
not to liberate
but to preserve slavery—

and here is a hand which disrobes the air
and garbs it with fresh clothes

and here is a house my body leads me to
which I recognize as other than my body
in a night so beautiful
I could not tell it from my underwear
where god himself
is soaked by the sweat of the times

baudelaire

congealed angels in notre dame
need female bodies
in order to walk on air—

air which refuses to move
unless you inflate it with your soul—

where women are half-broken jars
in beds hidden beneath the vaults of the seine
and bridges are their floating dreams,

where the electronic mind wraps itself
in krishna's cloak and the black minotaur
lies in the arms of the white woman,

where angels of wisdom fly from their prisons
and rush to embrace the angels of desire
in a nebula of signs,
every sign a dictionary

it came to pass—
and explode, oh memory of races—

al-mutannabi

piercings of the nails of the creed
prey chased by mice

creatures with heads of chickens
and frames of giants
in kingdoms—concubines

a person holding a staff
bearing a head,
a symbol of his power,
shreds of corpses and heads,
commas and movements

fables pulse from vein to vein
in a history wound on a reel for preservation—
(praise be camphor and celluloid)

hugo

in a time—a refinery from which
the blood of the murdered
and the saliva of the murderer
pour out together

a chaos in which things mix—
straw animals run
followed by blind babies

heads like orpheus's
except they swim in smoke
not in water

in a scream emitted by no lips
you see hands flailing with no bodies

feet walk at the same time both to the left and to the right

    workers return every evening to their shacks
    bearing twigs which are but thighs
    of the unemployed
    do the conditions of the body faithfully correspond
    to the conditions of the soul?
    I asked that man in beirut wearing red slippers
    and riding a locust who shouted this refrain repeatedly
    to me: vanity, all is vanity

      no, no
    my body likes the paleness of the sky
    and my dreams change their course,

I imagine that being—making a noose of his face,
passing along the banks of the euphrates and the nile
at the same time he hugs the shores of the seine, the hudson and the thames—
does not walk but sleep-walks in order to feel his limbs

    praise be to all ambiguity,
    shall I await the harvest of other seeds?

my passion is full of seeds issuing secretly from heraclitus and nietzsche

for, in my sorrows there is something of laurel leaves
and between my shoulders there sets a sail
whose image I once saw in the mediterranean sea near arwad island
(strange that its name has escaped my memory),

for, I am chasing the head of an atom
coming from an electronic cave,
wrapping itself like an onion,
then splitting into sounds of a clerical trumpet
still attached to the trunk of the 16th century,

for, it is enough in this age to make a body of a man
by using the legs of an ant and the head of a locust
(and for his soul choose anything you wish
from the stalls of the souq),

for, the power of the sky still bows
before the chair of joan of arc,
she whose sword still drips water
which heals the leprous,

for, the stomach of this age still is nero's,

for, when I read about freedom in this world,
it seems I'm chasing a three-colored rat,
which in turn is chasing a cat with two tails and three wings

it is my desire moving
through the maps of the material
and the moments open in the beds
of the place, like sexual organs

on my walks every morning
from 116 lourmel street
to 1 miollis street, I read
the book of oceans
in the drop of water,
I touch the light that works
like a plough and I discover
how the poet remains a baby
though he's as old as the horizon

thus I no longer hesitate to say:
"the I and the other
are me,"
and time is but a basket
to collect poetry

unexpectedly I meet rimbaud
and we renew our pact:
the veil, it is the light;
the west is another name for the east

(m)

(neither the east nor the west
belongs to god—pardon me, goethe—
and the north is sinking
in the ice of memory and
whenever the south thinks
itself cured of a disease
it contracts another
then consoles itself
by repeating this refrain:
joy is the closest friend of sadness)

(n)

(why is it that his feet
know the seine better
than they know the tigris or barada?

what a fool—he likes man
better than the earth,
the earth better than the homeland)

17

(o)

no, my body is neither a pelican nor a water lily
but beneath my eyelashes sleeps ophelia
who mistakenly discovered me
and all my dreams are lakes gone mad

now I advise myself aloud
before hamlet:
I must be wise,
always remembering that love and suffering
are of the same family,
ceasing to care
about the day and the night,
the moon and the sun

1 – [the seine has yet to flow east
(the reference here is to something
other than 'the divine blessings,'
praised by goethe in his verse—
the turban, the tent,
the curved sword, song);
its water has yet to mix
like that of the euphrates
with the planet's light]

it is true as hamlet shows
that love has many wars
and that from time to time
a storm is needed in the body
to rearrange its limbs,
thus this evening I watched over
the flocks of streets in paris
and when I saw the fountain of flame
explode from the thighs of buildings
I murmured:
nothing clarifies me like this obscurity
(or perhaps it was: nothing obscures me like this
    clarity)

II – (we have yet to raise
another pillar of wisdom,
for us to make spaceships
to transport us not to planets
but to our own homes,
for us to create winged creatures
to transport, at no cost, all the poor
who dream of circumambulating
their holy places
we have yet to change wind
into a perfect roll of the dice)

III – (how can he be at ease—
a fish in the water
of these times,
how can he live in a body
drained of its substance,
how can he dismantle this corporal body
made of his speech,
a body supported
by the columns
of an incorporal language)

this is me—
I waft from my race like perfume
        from a dying rose,

I undulate and spread
like bees I make my own honey
this is life—cold,
scarcely even a wound,
I see nothing but machines
swarming in the fields
of human breath,
and there is neither day nor night—
only a continuous thread of disjointed moments—

the outside is not my home
the inside confines me—

like a perfume from a dying rose
I waft from my race

I don't want to name
I want to be lofty as light
I don't want to hold on
I want to be like the wind

Paris, 1986–1987

Translation from the Arabic by Allen Hibbard & Osama Isber

Muhammad al-Maghut b.1934

EXECUTIONER OF FLOWERS

Lord!
Ancient Lord God, lonely in Your heights!

Here is this Qadr night
before the gleaming domes of mosques and churches
swollen as blisters.
I button my jacket,
I fold a white mist over my arm
to become your obedient servant,
the agent of your blessings and catastrophes.
I strip your trees naked in autumn
and plump them with buds and birds in spring.
I guide the rivulets in their flow
and the vagabond pigeons padding their nests.
I distract snakes and scorpions from the feet of workers and peasants,
and garland the clothes of poor children
with brilliant new patches for feasts.
Besides which I will guide Your earthquakes,
volcanoes and floods,
to the poorest, most crowded neighborhoods and huts
and not one stone is lost to Your hand.
I will awaken Marx and Engels from their tombs
and make them scream, baring their teeth
to victims of concentration camps,
to corpses of mine shafts, avalanches,
and collective graves,
to their own families and children.
I make them confess their despair
that this was God's will.

But in return, Lord, preserve for me
this broken woman . . .
her helpless children promise to give away
their toys, their earrings and new clothes
to your little angels,
remaining naked forever,
if you preserve her for a few more months,

a few more days . . .
we will take turns staying by her bed
and drying the sweat that pours from her forehead.
She is our only shade in this desert,
the only star illuminating our words,
the only remaining wall in all this ruin,
and yet she took no more from this homeland
than the foot takes from the shoe.

Your elegant crooked nose,
like an ear of corn in the beak of a bird,
your fine little mouth, precise as the rendezvous of traitors and heroes . . .
Why did you choose to leave so fast?
To sleep forever, smiling and secure,
turning your back to the revolutions of the world?
Don't worry, love,
I have seen with my own two eyes
on a frosty night beside the Volga
a destitute Marxist sleeping under the Kaiser's sword.

Ah, how happy we were, Sham, Sulafa and I,
when the faint color
        returned to your cheeks!
We clapped with joy to see
your exhausted hair growing again
        with miserable enthusiasm,
like some negro grass in some white fields.

Orphan all your life,
from where did you inherit
    those two lungs, weak as a sparrow's?
And those freckles gathered across your shoulders
like frightened birds huddled at the tops of trees?
What chase trained you
to close doors and windows,
to sleep with your two little girls
panting under beds and chairs?
From what battle did you glean
these proud tears, this womb
like a bugle in war?

Ah, love, now my madness is complete,
like the full moon.
All my weapons are blunted, my friends dispersed,
my arguments disproven, my tricks exhausted,
my cafes torn down, my dreams wrecked.
Nothing has remained for me except language
and what should I do with it,
with its letters stuck to my tongue like snake's piss?

Flower banished from its field,
now even the heart of spring chokes, overcome.
Your love is unforgettable as an insult,
as the wounds of al-Husain.
All the women I loved before you were meteors
you alone were the sky.
For thirty years
you bore me on your shoulders like a wounded soldier,
yet I could not carry you a few steps to your grave!
I visit it reluctantly, and come home reluctantly.

For my whole life I have never been loyal to love, honor, or heroism.
I have never loved any city, village, moon,
tree, poor or rich man, any friend, neighbor, or cafe,
any mountain, field, child, or butterfly.
My disdain for flowers
never even left me any opportunity
to love God!

Translation from the Arabic by May Jayyusi & Naomi Shihab Nye

Unsi al-Hajj b. 1937

THE CHARLATAN

Come close or run away

I'll save the song

I'll wash the earth. My throat a lost sheep my hair ashes of lamentation
and psalms. I eat the lamp I blow out the ghost. I stretch out on the hills
of the word.

That's why lightning rises when I signal. Death to the flower it drapes itself
in Babel it takes refuge under the dew's claw. Death to the giants, bellied
with women they eject the arrows of chemistry and the shooting star,
they boil the tempest as one does a chicken. It's with the rubber of the
nipples that they keep their clients they glue their offspring in wax.

(Beautiful, despite all that

Like a beguiler

Clever like the tunics of knights. I fear them and am cold. I've lost all my
blood!

Who'd lend their ear to unshod words?)

Poet

Tree of the ogres matrix of the deserts devouring queen

I ejaculate my nothingness

Grasshoppers of the elements

We

Our children have sprung from warts our women ensnare pulsations they
inventory the foreigners . . .

Coming from afar. Velvet and night? I jumped over the ring. Let some-
body say that I exist in vain. I have unearthed the tombs and the grave-
digger of the word in vengeance of my mind!

The used people

The receptive

The birds

The wind

The wind tiller of ink showcase of the alphabet

The wind martyr

The wind

The word, o waves dust bird flowers colors o elements and things o
branches of women rooms of dreams and eyes gelatine visions o tear run
to the massacre the cracking of my bone is the hymn of your awakening

Do away with the poet and his offspring!

For a long time I called I added more than one shell. Who knows my back?
Setting and rising shams in a bag. I love you. There where you steal you
snare a date with chance.

I dreamed, fingers in my dream. What friend ignores their shivers? Ex-
hausted around my notebook. My body is solitary. No beak tip flays my
palm. I stay on my knees the scream's intention robs me the gazes avoid
all that happens to me.

The herd passes

Happy trails, caravan!

The sorrows have hidden themselves in the corpse and the truths in their
valley they have switched off the light for the veiled one they have de-
voured the fountain of mysteries. They have come down

They have blown up

The herd stopped to watch

They stopped to contemplate my death and extract their hair from the
drought.

Translation from the Arabic by Pierre Joris

Denise Levertov b. 1923

THE JACOB'S LADDER

The stairway is not
a thing of gleaming strands
a radiant evanescence
for angels' feet that only glance in their tread, and need not
touch the stone.

It is of stone.
A rosy stone that takes
a glowing tone of softness
only because behind it the sky is a doubtful, a doubting
night gray.

A stairway of sharp
angles, solidly built.
One sees that the angels must spring
down from one step to the next, giving a little
lift of the wings:

and a man climbing
must scrape his knees, and bring
the grip of his hands into play. The cut stone
consoles his groping feet. Wings brush past him.
The poem ascends.

AGE OF TERROR

Between the fear
of the horror of Afterwards
and the despair
in the thought of no Afterwards,
we move abraded,
each gesture scraping us
on the millstones.

In dream
there was an Afterwards:
    the unknown device—
        a silver computer as big as a
        block of offices at least,
                     floating
        like Magritte's castle on its rock, aloft
        in blue sky—
did explode,
              there was
    a long moment of cataclysm,
                   light
of a subdued rose-red suffused
all the air before
a rumbling confused darkness ensued,
but
I came to,
      face down,
           and found
my young sister alive near me,
and knew my still younger brother
and our mother and father
              were close by too,
and, passionately relieved, I
comforted my shocked sister,
           still not daring
to raise my head,
only stroking and kissing her arm,
afraid to find devastation around us
though we, all five of us,
seemed to have survived—and I readied myself
to take rollcall: 'Paul Levertoff? Beatrice Levertoff?'

And then in dream—not knowing
if this device, this explosion, were radioactive or not,
but sure that where it had centered
there must be wreck, terror,
fire and dust—
the millstones
commenced their grinding again,

and as in daylight
again we were held between them, cramped,
scraped raw by questions:

perhaps, indeed, we were safe; perhaps
no worse was to follow?—but . . .
what of our gladness, when there,
       where the core of the strange
       roselight had flared up
       out of the detonation of brilliant
       angular silver,
there must be others, others in agony,
and as in waking daylight,
the broken dead?

COMMENTARY

My mother was descended from the Welsh tailor and mystic Angel Jones
of Mold, my father from the noted Hasid Scheour Zalman (d. 1831), "the
Rav of Northern White Russia." My father had experienced conversion to
Christianity as a student at Königsberg in the 1890s. His lifelong hope was
towards the unification of Judaism and Christianity. He was a priest of the
Anglican Church (having settled in England not long before I was born),
author of a life of St. Paul in Hebrew, part translator of The Zohar, *etc.*
D. L.

Born in England, her full emergence as a poet was through the Black Moun-
tain wing of the New American Poetry ("I think of Robert Duncan and Rob-
ert Creeley," she wrote in 1959, "as the chief poets among my contempo-
raries"). It was Duncan who first placed her among the visionary company
of poets (himself, ourselves included) whose "sense of a life shared with
beings of a household, . . . of belonging to generations of spirit" tied them
not only to a string of literary forebears but to those "illustrious ancestors"
to whom her work was, as here, already pointing. Of the literalness other-
wise imputed to a poetry of *things* (her signature, for some), she wrote: "We
need a poetry not of *direct statement* but of *direct evocation*: a poetry of
hieroglyphics, of embodiment, incarnation; in which the personages may be
of myth or of Monday, no matter, if they are of the living imagination." And
again: "'No ideas but in things' does not mean 'No ideas.' Nor does it
specify: / 'No ideas but in everyday things / modern things / urban things.'
No! it means that: / poetry appears when meaning is embodied in the
figure."

Yehuda Amichai b. 1924

NATIONAL THOUGHTS

A woman, caught in a homeland-trap of the Chosen People: you.
Cossack's fur hat on your head: you the
offspring of their pogroms. "After these things had come to pass,"
always.
Or, for example, your face: slanting eyes,
eyes descended from massacre. High cheekbones
of a hetman, head of murderers.
But a mitzvah dance of Hasidim,
naked on a rock at twilight,
beside the water canopies of Ein Gedi,
with eyes closed and body open like hair. After
these things had come to pass. "Always."

People caught in a homeland-trap:
to speak now in this weary language,
a language that was torn from its sleep in the Bible: dazzled,
it wobbles from mouth to mouth. In a language that once described
miracles and God, to say car, bomb, God.

Square letters want to stay
closed; each letter a closed house,
to stay and to close yourself in
and to sleep inside it, forever.

Translation from the Hebrew by Stephen Mitchell

ELEGY

The wind won't come to draw smiles in the sand of dreams.
The wind will be strong.
And people are walking without flowers,
unlike their children in the festival of the first fruits.
And a few of them are victors and most of them are vanquished,
passing through the arch of others' victories
and as on the Arch of Titus everything appears, in bas-relief:
the warm and belovèd bed, the faithful and much-scrubbed pot,
and the lamp, not the one with the seven branches, but the simple one,
the good one, which didn't fail even on winter nights,

and the table, a domestic animal that stands on four legs and keeps
  silent. . . .
And they are brought into the arena to fight with wild beasts
and they see the heads of the spectators in the stadium
and their courage is like the crying of their children,
persistent, persistent and ineffectual.
And in their back pocket, letters are rustling,
and the victors put the words into their mouths
and if they sing, it is not their own song,
and the victors set large yearnings inside them
like loaves of dough
and they bake these in their love
and the victors will eat the warm bread and *they* won't.

But a bit of their love remains on them
like the primitive decorations on ancient urns:
the first, modest line of emotion all around
and then the swirl of dreams
and then two parallel lines,
mutual love,
or a pattern of small flowers, a memory of childhood, high-stalked
and thin-legged.

Translation from the Hebrew by Stephen Mitchell

NEAR THE WALL OF A HOUSE

Near the wall of a house painted
to look like stone,
I saw visions of God.

A sleepless night that gives others a headache
gave me flowers
opening beautifully inside my brain.

And he who was lost like a dog
will be found like a human being
and brought back home again.

Love is not the last room: there are others
after it, the whole length of the corridor
that has no end.

Translation from the Hebrew by Chana Bloch

This year I traveled a long way / to view the silence of my city. / A baby calms down when you rock it, a city calms down / from the distance. I dwelled in longing. I played the hopscotch / of the four strict squares of Yehuda Ha-Levi [medieval Hebrew poet] / *My heart. Myself. East. West.* Y. A.

Born in Würzburg, Germany, he came to Palestine in 1936, where he served with the Jewish Legion in World War II and in the Israeli War of Independence in 1948. His work in Hebrew followed the efforts—as another kind of (experimental) language writing (= language re-creation)—of poets such as Bialik, Tchernikhovsky, Shlonsky. While this revival of the Hebrew language & its reinvention as an instrument for poetry are clear enough, other implications are more difficult to bring out in translation. Thus, as T. Carmi writes in the introduction to his anthology of Hebrew poetry, referring to the deep history of the language & the closeness of its ancient & contemporary forms: "Whether the poet wills it or not, there is often an element of counterpoint in [modern] Hebrew poetry. However colloquial the rhythms and even the diction, it is heard by the alert reader against the background of biblical poetry and of an uninterrupted poetic tradition. And some of the finest effects of modern Hebrew poetry still result from the tension between everyday speech and the undertones and overtones of a shared heritage" (*The Penguin Book of Hebrew Verse*, 1981). Amichai's concern with these matters (in *National Thoughts*, etc.) is also apparent.

Friederike Mayröcker b. 1924

"the spirit of '76"

1

on the ninth, we entered the country on iron horse rails.
Life here is very hard.

2

Chopping wood, I broke the hatchet.
I arranged, I assembled the books and everything.
We sat there, puffing away, having drinks.
Ear-muffs against the wind.
To let the reins of our eyes hang loose.
Unharness the focus.
Relieve the horses of their bridles.

Divide localities in ones to enter, ones not to enter.
Now we sit at big tables, conferring.
Our fingers curled on the tables.
We are looking for a way to live.

3

belated thunderstorms, cold Spring.
Trees without blossoms.
Our new language—we have to throw ourselves into it.
I have put up a curtain to divide my museum.
We have planted two turnip fields.

4

Plane trees we have trimmed, planets we have climbed.
Written away, and written away.
A generation ago, things were still much worse.

5

jumped out of bed at half past six.
we sit at big tables, conferring.
we like each other but only in part.
Opaque relationships.
Shadows falling out of the forests.
We immolate ourselves as a sacrifice to the new spirit.
Total bliss, wrapped in gauze.
A way to live.
I have become used to the fact that most people stop listening
to me before I'm done.

6

We get an inkling of new life!
We have begun to recognize the situation.
The indescribable is described, the unsayable is said.
We speak with several tongues.
We glorify nature.

7

that strikes me as vaguely correct.
Glorified nature: gentle as the snow!
Little lamb clouds, formerly shepherd's curls.
Objects of happiness, pebbles the size of lentils.

To kneel, to knead the plowed soil with our hands.
To put our mouths around it.

8

the formerly divided localities have grown together.
My pear-tree casts off shards.
I can tell that the bird tracks in the snow demand new
media.

9

on the ninth, we left the country on iron horse rails.

10

on the ninth, we entered the country on iron horse rails.
Life here is different, just as hard.

11

I assume a posture of pathos.

12

the wallpaper crumbles to dust, the curtain gapes vertically.
It's all furnished with things no one uses.
Although, in the morning, when I open the two huge windows
they stand there, in the garden:
lovely old trees, a whole forest.
Birches firs beeches maples, above their crowns the
colors of the sky.

13

preoccupied with a morning dream, just a moment ago.
What's difficult here takes forms that differ from previous ones.
Although, this tremulous beating of wings in the morning.
This rushing agitation.

14

although, when I open the huge windows, look
down into the garden.
but displacement, displacements, by things
no one needs.
Rotary iron orthopedic chair air mattress suitcase rack.

15

best not to take hold of anything, it's all filthy here.
Best not to touch anything.
Best not to meddle.
Best not to uncover, not to reveal.

16

no resonance left.
Everything in a heap, any old how.
Memory, recall, bringing it all back not much
use, we'll just spoil everything.
Rigid, everything utterly questionable.

17

run with the hare, hunt with the hounds.
Although, this serenity in the morning.
These trees in the garden, a whole forest.
The meadow slopes gently to the lake, the willows on the shore.

18

long walks around the lake, hearing the wild birds in their
wilderness.
In their creepers.
Wintertime skies, gouged by the new torpedoes.

19

the sudden farewell.
Once again, the sudden farewell, a perfect replica!

20

breathless with excitement, the dark forelock combed back, damp.

Translation from the German by Anselm Hollo

And I have always avoided story-lines because I can't see any stories any-
where. Even the course of my own life and of life in general doesn't have
a story-like appearance for me. Nor can I read a book that follows a
story-line.

F. M.

Born in Vienna, where she taught English for many years & now lives as
an independent writer, Mayröcker was associated in the 1950s & 1960s
with the experimental "Vienna Group" (page 115). Her own investigations
throughout have focused primarily (though not exclusively) on the tradi-
tional sentence unit, which she has de(con)structed & opened up to fresh
associative possibilities, based not on the linear subject-verb-object syntac-
tical structure ("[she] steps—albeit gracefully—on the foot of European
thought and destroys its Achilles' heel: syntax"—thus Peter Weibel) but
on the paratactical playfulness of juxtaposed word- & phrase-clusters. As
Rosmarie Waldrop and Harriett Watts write of her: "Abandoning the hier-
archy of the sentence grants a parity to all the elements within the text,
acknowledges their simultaneous existence in a structure where no element
is subordinated to any other element. Simultaneity is Mayröcker's primary
concern: 'the simultaneity of processes, of inner processes, which one expe-
riences simultaneously, and simultaneously with everyone else imaginable,
and with oneself, on different levels, simultaneously.'" The voices in both
the poetry & prose "define themselves purely by what they say, confusing
and blending their past, present and future in the process of talking," so
that human experience "is recreated in the seeming disconnectedness of
Mayröcker's monologues and dialogues without causal, temporal and syn-
tactical subordination." What Mayröcker calls her "experimental phase"
with its purely formal concerns lasted from 1966 to 1971, while (as she puts
it) "from 1942 to 1966 and from 1972 to today, the emphasis has been on
the autobiographical, though it must not be forgotten that after 1972 this
was paired with a similar emphasis on the language aspects."

Emmett Williams b. 1925

from **THE RED CHAIR (for three voices)**

  I: he said it two days ago.
 II: he said it fourteen days ago.
III: he said it two-hundred and ninety-nine days ago,
     to be exact.
  I: i don't know when he said it.

II: maybe he didn't say it at all.
III: why don't you forget it,
    he said,
 I: it would be so easy to forget,
    i answered,
    or at least i think i answered him,
    because i haven't the slightest idea who he was,
    yes,
    it would be so easy to forget,
    if only i could remember what it is.
II: whereupon i think he answered,
    holding his hands so close to my face that i could have bitten them:
    you must pretend that it never happened.
 I: what never happened?
II: ah,
    you have already forgotten,
    he rejoiced.
III: see,
    i *can* help you.
 I: but you must do what i tell you.
II: the birds,
    of course,
    the birds.
III: the one with the black beak,
    the kolibri.
 I: the swirl,
    the still swirl,
    the wingedness.
II: the woodpecker who hammered and hammered breathlessly.
III: hammering.
 I: to begin with,
    he said,
    you must promise me two things.
II: i promise,
    i told him,
    shifting my weight from the left foot to the right foot.
III: first,
    you must never again sit in the red chair.
 I: that is too much,
    i protested.
II: it is *my* chair.

III: *mine.*
  I: do you understand?
 II: do you promise or not?
III: i promise.
  I: second,
     you must never sit on any chair except the red one.
 II: that is too much,
     i protested.
III: i hate the red chair.
  I: i hate it,
     i tell you.
 II: do you promise?
III: i promise.
  I: you're doing very well,
     he said warmly.
 II: cigarette?
III: i shifted my weight from the right foot to the left foot.
  I: as i see it,
     he said,
     but not to me,
     because i wasn't listening,
     there isn't the slightest chance that they will return.
 II: where have they gone?
III: i asked in disbelief.
  I: they couldn't have gone very far,
     because they haven't been gone very long.
 II: but they mustn't return!
III: they won't,
     he reassured me.
  I: and then they came.
 II: but i knew,
     so much better than he did,
     that they would never return.
III: i bumped into them as they made their way to the red chair.
  I: you see,
     i am blind.
 II: at least i think i am,
     because i am also deaf and can't hear what they say about me.
III: be that as it may,
     i have the advantage over them in the end.

I: i am dumb.
II: when do you expect them?
III: he asked from a far corner.
I: they took the five-forty-five.
II: but that can't be,
he said.
III: here they come and it's only three.
II: i'll get my sweet revenge when they come,
i said softly.
III: i sat down in the red chair to relax.
I: i was tired,
and they would be there any minute.
II: the woodpecker sang an octave higher.

from **THE ULTIMATE POEM**

The following poems are by-products of a generative work called "the ultimate poem" that I began around 1956. The rules of the game are simple: (1) Choose 26 words by chance operations—or however you please. (2) Substitute these 26 words for the 26 letters of the alphabet, to form an alphabet-of-words. (3) Choose a word or phrase (a word or phrase *not* included in the alphabet-of-words) to serve as the title of the poem. (4) For the letters in the title word or phrase substitute the corresponding words from the alphabet-of-words. This operation generates line one of the poem. (5) Repeat the process described in step 4 with the results of step 4. (6) Repeat the process with the results of 5. (7) Et cetera.

The first poem, "what," shows the substitution process carried out twice as described in the rules above. The next two, the short "rose is a rose" poems, demonstrate simple substitutions of two entirely different alphabets-of-words applied to identical texts. In "rose is a violin is a codpiece," the simple substitution of the alphabet-of-words is spiced up by a cyclical process, so that after the "a" in each "rose is a," the values of the words in the alphabet-of-words shift, and what used to be the "z" word becomes the "a" word, the old "a" word becomes the "b" word, and so on.

The theory and practice of "the ultimate poem" is discussed more fully in the introduction to part one of my book *A Valentine for Noël.*

what

art was out bones

out violin bones
art out image
devil let bones
the devil back on image

rose is a rose is a rose is a rose is a rose

pickle dogs come down
man come
whereat
pickle dogs come down
man come
whereat
pickle dogs come down
man come
whereat
pickle dogs come down
man come
whereat
pickle dogs come down

rose is a rose is a rose is a rose is a rose

violin devil image on
executions image
out
violin devil image on
executions image
out
violin devil image on
executions image
out
violin devil image on
executions image
out
violin devil image on

rose is a violin is a codpiece

violin devil image on
executions image
out
image stick bones delightful
meant bones
the
bones fasted crazy legs
you crazy
children
crazy violin remember was
ill-proportioned remember
marriage
remember image art executions
yellow art
on
art bones quack meant
back quack
delightful
quack crazy codpiece you
devil codpiece
legs
codpiece remember trap ill-proportioned
stick trap
was
trap art out yellow
fasted out
executions
out quack the back
violin the
meant
the codpiece children devil
image children
you
children trap marriage stick
bones marriage
ill-proportioned
marriage out on fasted
crazy on
yellow

on the delightful violin
remember delightful
back
delightful children legs image
art legs
devil
legs marriage was bones
quack was
stick
was on executions crazy
codpiece executions
fasted
executions delightful meant remember
trap meant
violin
meant legs you art
out you
image
you was ill-proportioned quack
the ill-proportioned
bones
ill-proportioned executions yellow codpiece
children yellow
crazy
yellow meant back trap
marriage back
remember
back you devil out
on devil
art
devil ill-proportioned stick the
delightful stick
quack
stick yellow fasted children
legs fasted
codpiece
fasted back violin marriage
was violin
trap

DEAD DOCUMENT NO. 1. *When you are in Paris, walk to 261, Boulevard Raspail. / Go through the entrance gate. / Take thirteen paces in the one o'clock direction. / Look in front of you. / Stand or sit. / The tree you see is a Cedar of Lebanon. / Stand or sit under the tree, until you know who planted the cedar. / A dead document will put you on the right track.*

E. W. and Robert Filliou (co-inventors of *The Spaghetti Sandwich*)

A progenitor of Fluxus (above, page 17) & along with Jackson Mac Low, George Brecht, Dick Higgins, & Robert Filliou one of its leading poet/ artists, Williams's innovative range includes "straight poetry, visual poetry, visual fiction, prints, artist's books, paintings, text-sound, and performances . . . [favoring] as a poet . . . such severe constraints as repetition, permutation, and linguistic Minimalism" (thus Richard Kostelanetz's accounting, to which might be added: poems on cuckoo clocks & on "alphabetized live carp," poems made with rubber stamps or steam, poems as water ballet, as board games, *usw*). Of the excerpts presented here, *The Red Chair* is an acoustic version for three voices of an earlier work of that title ("vintage 1957–58"): a story ("for story it is") "composed as an attempt to apply the permutational method to larger blocks of language." *The Ultimate Poem*, by contrast, is "a generative work" capable of producing countless variations, as described above.

Along with such extended, often performative, often deflationary works, Williams was a major figure in the concrete poetry movement of the 1960s: a largely stripped down, minimalist instance of visual poetry or text art (see below, page 302). As such he edited the definitive "anthology of concrete poetry" (1967) & produced the booklength *Sweethearts* (also 1967) as a full-scale, permutational masterwork of the concrete movement.

Robin Blaser b. 1925

IMAGE-NATION 22 (in memoriam

Robert Graves saw—not the *male-womb* made scary in Euripides
and even scarier in Malaparte's *Kaputt* with wooden dolls—
the Goddess in multiples—of lovely women and aquiline faces—
saw her *All Living*—coursing into *sow, mare, bitch, vixen, she-ass, weasel, serpent, owl, she-wolf, tigress, mermaid* or *loathsome hag*—made male-minded by her, had to see her white and
black—met her once in his novel *The New Crete* as the *Hog goddess*, sometimes named Sally—you may write with kindling,
he says, or, loving accuracy, return to the *mare's nest*

Her nests, when one comes across them in dreams, lodged in
rock-clefts or branches of enormous hollow yews, are built
of carefully chosen twigs and littered with the jaw-bones and
entrails — of poets, he says—in male-minded acknowledgement and
his correction of belief without her

he read her by the *alphabet of trees,* wild in Wales before the
evangelical voices

> *Flower-goddess Olwen or Blodeuwedd*
> *Owl, lamp-eyed, hooting*
> *Circe, the pitiless falcon*
> *Lamia with her flickering tongue*
> *mare-headed Rhiannon*

Determined to escape the dilemma, the Apollonian teaches him-
self to despise women, and teaches woman to despise herself.
Robert Graves would escape this blankness and obey the dilem-
ma, made male-minded by her

with the advantage that he could reread, by the alphabet of
trees, Ezekiel's chariot—transform the radiance enthroned
there

> *Amber*
> *Fire-Garnet ('the terrible crystal')*
> *and Sapphire*

finding a triune Jehovah with Anatha of the Lions and Ashima
of the Doves—divorcing his consorts, just before the Babylon-
ian captivity

(*Ezekiel* 23:4–6)

word by word, right to left—myth resuming—*God assumed the
shape of a mare and decoyed the ruttish Egyptian stallions
into the water*—the lengths to which, shape-changing *Jehovah,
once a devoted son of the Great Goddess,* would go, you say, and
swallowed

> gods terebinth
> thunder
> pomegranate
> bull
> goat
> antelope
> calf
> porpoise
> ram
> ass
> barley
> moon
> dog-star
> sun,

healing the wounds of these things by becoming imageless

calling Joshua Podro with his fine knowledge of Hebrew to sit
beside you—as I have with another who read the Hebrew for me—
you wrote *The Nazarene Gospel Restored* in 1953—to give Jesus
back to time and painful circumstance—your mythic mind joined
with Podro's, tracing what Jesus knew of the *Mishnah,* the *Midrash,*
the two *Talmuds*—of the Day of Judgement, detailed by Zephaniah,
Zechariah, Malachi—of Enoch's heavens—of the tortured spirit
of the *Testament of the Twelve Patriarchs*

the wandering meaning, the thorned acacia, nimbus of the sun-
god, burned

hostility to writing—these were the evil cosmocrators—Peneme
(according to Enoch), Nabu, Thoth, Hermes, against whom the
Scriptures had been set a century before Jesus by the scholarly
Pharisees

Anatha of Bethany took Mot (Tammuz), *cleft him with her sword,
winnowed him in her harvest-basket, parched him at the fire,
ground him in the mill and sowed him in the field*

*the Female on whom Jesus declared war was Aggrath Bat Machlat
(Alukah, by cacophemism, the horse-leech) whose daughters
Womb and Grave—are*

ISHTAR

you say that he went *to the land of nod, East of Eden, the trans-
Euphrates province of Susiana,* to watch for the end of the
world in his own time—that Paul knew him to be alive in 35
A.D. because they met on the road to Damascus—that Ignatius
of Antioch (d. c. 107) in his letter to Smyrna writes as though
he thought Jesus still alive near the end of the first century

Enoch dreams: all became snow-white cows—and the first among
them became a thing and that thing became a great beast with
huge black horns—Graves notices *the horns of power, such as
Moses wore, or Zeus Ammon, or Alexander*—the *Son of Man,* a
title of careful and careless finitude, as

*if all the heavens were parchment, and all the trees pens, and
all the seas ink,*

in memoriam

COMMENTARY

*The curious thing about language is that it holds and makes visible. It per-
forms one's manhood. But it is so much older than oneself, so much a
speaking beyond and outside oneself, that a man's entrance to it becomes
at once new and old, spoken and speaking, a self and some other.* (R. B.)
And again: *The extraordinary nature of language is that it attaches to the
prior, to the before one, and to the after one.*

Last survivor of that near-mythic trio of poets at the root of the San Fran-
cisco Renaissance—the other two being Robert Duncan (above) & Jack
Spicer—Blaser has lived & taught since the late sixties in Vancouver, Can-
ada. The work—gathered in the 1993 volume *The Holy Forest*—fulfills
Spicer's early suggestion (as restated by Robert Creeley) that Blaser "would
follow his emotions with a shifting rhythm, led by feeling to pattern" & into
what Blaser himself called "a narrative of the spirit." This near-alchemical
care for the eros of daily life, "the adamant given of our common fact"
(Creeley), is further illuminated & examined as, in the "ceremony of the
book" (Foucault), Blaser folds & unfolds a "wild-logos" (Merleau-Ponty's
term) that is, he writes, "a proposal of the wildness of meaning—a lost
and found, a going and coming," engaging thought there where it becomes
"a disclosure," thus making the poem into "a necessary function of the real,

not something added to it." In his 1968 essay *The Fire,* Blaser quotes Ovid to give his sense of the scope necessary to the poem as *carmen perpetuum,* continuous song: "To tell of bodies / transformed / into new shapes, / you gods, whose power / worked all transformations, / helped the poet's breathing, / lead my continuous song / from the beginning   to the present world."

Ernesto Cardenal b. 1925

IN XÓCHITL IN CUÍCATL

> *In xóchitl in cuícatl,* Náhuatl for poetry. Literally it means Flower-Song, or flowers and songs; a double metaphor to name poetry, which is essentially metaphor.
>
> *Ometéotl* (*ome,* two, *téotl,* god): "Two Gods," or "Two-God" was the Supreme Being, conceived as the Masculine-Feminine principle. And poetry was the manifestation of God on earth and a means to reach Him / Her, the Supreme Metaphor, the Supreme Poetry.

To the God of Duality, only with metaphors.
To the Supreme Metaphor, union of differences,
Lord and Lady of Duality,
   . . . where our ancients come from,
only with metaphors, Flower-Song.

Poetry is divine, comes from above,
from the interior of heaven.
From the supreme couple whence all couples come.
The Masculine-Feminine principle invented men
just as the tlamatinimes invent their paintings-poems.
And through paintings-poems, the word of the tlamatinimes,
the history of that creation, transmitted
                from generation unto generation . . .

That is why poetry is divine, "godded" word.
Poetry is the "way."
Poets, sages, the tlamatinimes,
they are the ones who know.
Who know what is above us
       and the region of mystery.
The owners of the codices.
They felt life is like a dream . . .

And this life-dream of poetry
                    the way to know God.

And in the likeness of the Two-God,
                    man and woman, night and day, death and life
it was the duality of metaphor, poetry.
                    Or was the word not transmitted?

He who is our father and our mother,
he who is in the horizon, where
the sky with cotton and the
                    blue-bird-colored water are joined.

The priest Quetzalcóatl
made his god something that is in the interior of heaven
she who is dressed in black, he who is dressed in red
                    (oh you dressed in red and dressed in black)
like the black and red inks of the codices.
She who holds the earth, he who covers it with cotton.
Towards the place of Duality
Quetzalcóatl prayed.

One single dual principle:
which engendered the gods, the world and men.
            Invents itself.
Conceived itself in the night of time
                    "when it was still night"
            (dialectical god)
Created the world with flowers and songs, with poetry
                    in xóchitl in cuícatl
poetry is the metaphor of Ometéotl here on earth.
The beauty of earth a painting of the beauty of God.
Beauty, the in xóchitl in cuícatl, flower-song, is
the poem of God.
        The flowers, created by the Song (Two-God)
                metaphors of the Song
the flowers are your song oh God.

Temilotzin says: "I am God's poem,
He sends me as a messenger, transformed into a poem,
        myself, Temilotzin
to achieve human solidarity."

Anáhuac, the earth, is the house of God
there its songs are heard.
Art, poetry: the way to know truth.
Beauty: only that is real.

The artist, the Toltec, had God in his heart.
Godded heart to make things godded.
From the interior of the sky come the songs.
I sing the flowers / my songs blossom.
Not in anáhuac does song originate.
With songs / with flowers
I honor the Giver of Life
My prayer is of flowers.

Yet flowers perish. We long
for the place of dawn.
Where shall I see your flowers, Giver of Life?
I search for songs.
You who are near, you who are close.
In anáhuac we raise our songs to you.
Shall I never be with you?
Beside your songs?
You talk to us with emeralds, quetzal feathers . . .
Let the two of us converse with your flowers of songs.
They say there is a place in the sky.
That there is happiness there.
There are kettle-drums there.

In the garden of Tecayehuatzin,
poet and lord of Huexotcinco
the poets talk
round table on in xóchitl in cuícatl
under the bowers of chayotes;
the chichitotes sing among the chayotes
to the sound of kettle-drums perfumed with flowers
and the poets sing.
The zacuanjoche casts flowers like tender maidens.
The flowers fall on the mats.
Fragrant fugacity
in the garden of Huexotcinco.
"From inside the sky flowers, songs come"
the young Ayocuan sings.

But shall we leave like the flowers that perish?
    At least flowers / songs.
Flowers will not end here, the songs will not end.

And Cuauhténcoz, poet of Huexotcinco, sings: "Sadness
sadness makes my drum sound"

            Are men real
            like pyramids?
            Tomorrow will our songs remain
            like pyramids?

Motenehuatzin comes forward and says:
"In xóchitl in cuícatl takes sadness from us."
And Monencauhtzin:
            "In xóchitl in cuícatl reflects His beauty.
Flowers open their corollas to the Giver of Life
            and the One you have searched for
            answers your songs."

Ah anáhuac is not the place of happiness!
Tamoanchan ("The house of God")
            the house of childbirth
    the place men come from:
there is the Flowered Tree from which songs proceed
the lives of men and songs.
The house of Tláloc the god of rain
where everything is green like quetzal feathers
            the place of the flowering of the body.
There is transformation there.
Men come from the sky like rain,
children dripped in the womb like Tláloc's rains.
Men come from the mansion of the God of Duality.
Ometéotl places the little children in the womb.
The Couple of Duality places them.

The song comes from the land of life.
There the poets meet
as in their academies and literary contests here on earth.
    Gathered under the Flowered Tree

like butterflies . . .
             The true flowers are there.
                 (If my song is old-fashioned today
                     what can I do.)
             Spring does not bring forth here
             flowers that last.
We must go elsewhere . . .

He who is awaited by poets, he who listens to poetry.
He who makes himself present in flowers and songs . . .
             To him I offer flowers and painted books.
The kettle-drums of the sky dissipate my sadness.
Tamoanchan: where the houses lie by the water's edge.
There the flowered songs will never wilt.
             My flowers will not end.
             my songs will not end.

Poets: give up the pulque of war!

Translation from the Spanish by Carlos & Monique Altschul

I became politicized by the contemplative life. Meditation is what brought me to political radicalization. I came to the revolution by way of the Gospels. It was not by reading Marx but Christ. It can be said that the Gospels made me a Marxist.
E. C. (1976)

But the work—both before & after his involvement with revolutionary cultural politics in Nicaragua—showed a largeness of historical, even cosmological vision that was key to his most important achievements as a poet. His path into religion (ultimately the "liberation theology" that would be so prominent in the Americas) began with seclusion (in the footsteps of fellow poet-priest Thomas Merton) at the Trappist monastery in Gethsemani, Kentucky. Ordained in 1965 (age forty), he was the founder of a church & commune at Solentiname, a group of tiny islands in Lake Nicaragua. There the activities—centered on the surrounding peasant population—were heavily involved with poetry, while his own work—as in the *Homenaje a los Indios de América* (1969)—followed Pound's directive for the epic as "a poem including history." (*In xóchitl in cuícatl*, above, focuses on Aztec/Nahuatl pre-Conquest history—a turning to ethnopoetics that we share with him.) With a probable nod to Pound & the North American "Objectivists" (volume one), the name he gave to this approach ("the only poetry which can truly express Latin American reality") was *exteriorismo:* ". . . objective poetry: narrative and anecdote, made with elements of real life and concrete things, with proper names and precise details and exact data, statistics, facts, and quotations." With the victory of the Sandinistas in 1979, Cardenal became the Nicaraguan Minister of Culture, bringing about (however briefly) a proliferation of that poetry that, since Darío's time at least, had been the major public art of Nicaragua. Much of his later work (*Cosmic Canticle* most notably) is an extension of *exteriorismo* into areas of world & universe formation.

Rosario Castellanos 1925–1974

TWO MEDITATIONS

I

Consider, my soul, this texture
harsh to the touch, which is called life.
Notice so many threads wisely joined
together, and the color, dark, noble, firm
where red has suffused its splendor.

Think then about the Weaver: her patience
in starting again an always
unfinished task.

And hate, afterwards, if you can.

II

Little man, what would you do with your reason?
Bind up the world, the mad and furious world?
Castrate the colt called God?

But God breaks out of his tethers
and keeps engendering magnificent creatures,
wild beings whose shrieks
shatter this bell jar.

Translation from the Spanish by Julian Pulley

TWO POEMS

I

This is where I learned it. After pounding
like water among rocks and shouting myself hoarse
as water that falls shattered and broken
I have come to stay without complaint.
I do not speak through the mouth of my wounds. I speak
with my first lips. The words
no longer dissolve like gall on my tongue.
I learned it here: love is not a fire
into which we hurl our days
to be consumed like leaves or tinder.
As I write I hear
within me the last sputtering spark
of a burnt-out hell.
I hold no more fire than this blind lamp
that feels its way, close to the wall,
and trembles at the threat of the least breeze.
If I died tonight
it would be no more than opening my hand,
as children open their hands to show their mothers
how clean they are, clean because they are so empty.
I'll take nothing with me. All I had was a hollow
that was never filled. Sand
trickling through my fingers. A gesture
sharp and tense. All lost.
Everything remains behind: the earth, the hooves
that crush it, the lips that graze it,
the birds calling to each other from branch to branch,
this cracked sky that is the sea, the gulls
with their traveling wings,
the letters that flew too and that died
strangled in old ribbons.
Everything remains behind: I learned
that nothing was mine: not the wheat, the star,
his voice, his body; not even my own.
That my body was a tree and that the owner of a tree
is not its shadow, but the wind.

II

In my house, honeycomb whose only bee
is silence,
solitude fills all the chairs
and stirs the sheets on the bed
and opens the book to the page
where my grief is written.
Solitude, for its fill, asks me for tears
and waits for me in every mirror's depth
and shuts every window
to keep the sky from coming in.
Solitude, my enemy. She rises
like a sword to strike me, like a rope
around my throat.
I am not the one who drinks
water in its innocence;
nor the one who wakes with the clouds;
I am not ivy climbing the low fence.
I am alone: surrounded by walls
and shut doors;
alone to cut the bread on the table,
alone to light the lamps,
alone to say the nighttime prayer
and receive the devil's visit.
At times my enemy looms over me
with her closed fists
and asks and asks until she's hoarse
and binds me with the hooks of stubborn dialogue.
One day I will be silent; but first I will have said
that the man walking down the street is my brother,
that I belong with
the woman of vegetable attributes.
Let no one, with my enemy, condemn me
like an island inert among the seas.
Let no one lie, and say that I did not resist her
down to my last drop of blood.
Beyond my skin, deep in
my bones, I have loved.
Beyond my mouth and its words,
beyond the knot of my tormented sex.
I will not die of sickness

or old age, of anguish or of tiredness.
I will die of love, surrender
to the deepest lap.
I will never be ashamed of these empty hands
or of this hermetic cell they call Rosario.
On the lips of the wind I shall be called
a tree of many birds.

Translation from the Spanish by Magda Bogin

COMMENTARY

I arrived at poetry after convincing myself that the other paths were not valid for survival. And at that time what interested me most was survival. Poetic language constitutes the only way to achieve permanence in this world. (R. C.) And again: *We have to create another language, we have to find another starting point.*

Before her accidental death while serving as Mexican ambassador to Israel, she had become a visible presence in Mexican writing & in a new "feminine culture" (1950) that she articulated early & that was soon to be arising there & elsewhere in the world. Like later feminist poets & thinkers (Cixous, Wittig, Rich, et al.), she located the work to be done both in the structures of social life & in those of language as "an act of domination." Against this the language-of-poetry opened her to new acts of self-creation & self-writing—seen here as works of mind *and* body, of female sexuality & "saying the unsayable"—of which Maureen Ahern writes by way of context: "Well before the call by French feminists to write the self, decode the body, and destroy the myths inside and outside ourselves, Castellanos was practicing an *écriture féminine* in Mexico: the body as sign, puns as poems, language as oppressor, silence as meaning."

The further stretch of her work was toward a delineation of native oppressions that she saw in the Mayan country of Chiapas, where she grew up & to which she returned as a cultural worker & director for several years of El Teatro Petul, a puppet theater & cultural center in San Cristóbal de las Casas. From this came a growing identification with the Indians of Mexico & a pull toward a colloquial language that José Emilio Pacheco, writing of her later, pinpointed as a more "precise . . . transparent" instrument of poetry. Or Castellanos herself, with a self-effacement that her writings would, as such, put into question: "Many of [the poems] are vulgar and obscene. What's to be done about it? They serve to say what must be said. Nothing important or transcendent. Some glimpses of the structure of the world, the discovery of some coordinates to situate myself within it, the mechanics of my relationships with other beings. That which is neither sublime nor tragic. Perhaps a little ridiculous."

Claude Gauvreau 1925–1971

TRUSTFUL FATIGUE AND REALITY

Keulessa Kyrien Cobliéniz Jaboir
Veulééioto Caubitchounitz Abléoco
Vénicir Chlaham Kérioti Kliko
Sannessa vélo Moutchnaïk Révoi
Kharinaïne bénessoir sellèr achmatz
krioun alégo amemor ripiutz leslé
aglradine noeutéon paklica erremmetz
djackliane mandousse petréobor
nochnéagriawa sétel-sel clariassener
jôquoimoil nontonduc allessande rébrér
novaképalès Djvoriadjiana Kuntroubel
tétrapaïte jonsel nilâcouâ alrivage
akdoc cousine-germaine déplaatz
circuitz monse dobo lévil-clair
palosse-pensée moulmolosse adjeuate
Kénoice Salibleuwié Aklistantan
Schnlouem Jakonitz Eulbéka Krôhenn
LaToilia Dédjoitonte Wanékoin
Lite-gazère Goitena Chapelle automatique

CURTAIN

[Note on translation (or lack thereof) by Ray Ellenwood: This text has been left untranslated because there are so few specific words suggested by its sound-clusters. Some exceptions are 'pensée' (thought), 'cousine-germaine' (first cousin, female), and 'Chapelle automatique' (automatic chapel). The last may be a reference to the 'Automatiste' group, which was sometimes referred to, mostly by critics, as a chapel or sect.]

THE LEG OF MUTTON CRÉATEUR

[The atmosphere is a combination of roadside tavern and bawdy house. Etkip, represented by a garter, a brassiere and three shorthairs, is speaking with Klebbo, represented by a checkered cap, a pipe, a testicle and the lace from an espadrille. The wall is an optical illusion created by lighting. An abstract painting hangs on the wall between a vagina and the neck of a bottle from which hangs a drop of red wine. It seems as if an invisible accordion is playing immaterially.]

ETKIP: Ramalouch the pipestem and come peal the apple. Virgins' poppies are playing elevator with me in the subway.

KLEBBO: Taquédec! The sausage's lungs don't want to go outside; the thing is, the dirigible already emptied his tank into the lady pope's garden this morning.

ETKIP AND KLEBBO: *[singing as a duo]*
The sausages don't want to go outside.
The carrots are fagged out.
The cauliflowers have a toothache.
The convent corns have dropsy.
Oh Salamigos!
The cock-a-snooks are taking morphine.
The zababs are drinking cocaine.
The guard's father is flashing his bum.
There's a hole in the pipe.
Oh Salamigos!

[The testicle shudders gleefully and the three shorthairs contract with humour.]

ETKIP: The boat on the river is shaken by the hurricane. Bring your buoy along.

KLEBBO: The red one or the black?

ETKIP: The red and black.

KLEBBO: If the badoons holyjoe in the fireworks show, brigitte's boots will accrowbat in the zebrings of the rainbow.

THE PIPE: *[smoking]* The wino bridge is gonna curse if I don't get to sleep.

KLEBBO: *[to the pipe]* Shut your trap, Eel-nose, I'm the one's gonna tele today.

ETKIP: Backerup, Klebbo, didn't you teleme you're all for disinfecting the telepathy?

KLEBBO: Telemachus until Mardigras; where we gonna pinch the castor--oil to buttockup that far?

ETKIP: Put some oil in your lighter, Klebbo, my grandpappy's a fireman.

KLEBBO: The calf's snoozing, I'd better finish him off to make him stick his tongue out.

ETKIP: Telescope the peonies, engine the daisies, the pastry cooks' parade only lasts for a swing of the censer. When there's no more incense, there's no more censer; and when there's no more censer, there's no more parade.

KLEBBO: Oui, the rubbernecks pull back in.

ETKIP: The ladies' lanterns damp themselves.

KLEBBO: Give my pip all the licorice in the restaurant, twist the dish-cloth till it drips a bit. Before you cut the ham, better whet your knife.

ETKIP: The nut-cutter is tubercular: do you want me to give you a hand?

KLEBBO: A thumb up, if you want, doggywoggy.

ETKIP: I'll give you a fang or two.

[The three shorthairs go 'Oh!'; the testicle goes 'Ah!'.]

KLEBBO: Snaggy the slipknot, you're strangling me with your lasso.

ETKIP: Da, a string's no good if you wanna cinch a buffalo by the neck and lead him to his cage.

KLEBBO: Maybe, Cadou, maybe, but if you milk everything by combing it down, there'll be no more molasses for dessert.

ETKIP: What you flapping your gums about, nothing's come out yet.

KLEBBO: No, but the locomotive is just about to enter the station like a prehisto hurric.

ETKIP: All right then, it's time to park your convoy.

KLEBBO: Open the sluice-gates, Tetty, it's galloping wet.

[The brassiere suddenly goes wrinkled and the cap droops.]

ETKIP: Keep your foot off the brakes, Klebbo, Pan's pipe is solid.

KLEBBO: Watch out for the arsenals, I'm bumping against your edges.

ETKIP: Stop blubbering for nothing, the furrow is fresh.

[The pipe goes out. The garter snaps. The lace dozes off.]

KLEBBO: All set for the kippered herring?

ETKIP: Kiss my camisole.

[The vagina covers her face.]

CURTAIN

Translation from the French by Ray Ellenwood

The only path to follow is shown us by DESIRE. The fact that any child can make an authentic masterpiece makes me think that desire can be born in anybody. But as long as this desire is not permitted, as long as it does not frantically claw at the surface, in total honesty and with total risk, nothing can point to a new road.

C. G.

Gauvreau (who committed suicide at the age of 45) left behind one of the most fascinating & important bodies of experimental work by any contemporary Quebecois—the posthumous *Oeuvres créatrices complètes* runs to 1500 pages, 90% of which remained unpublished in his lifetime. A member of the Automatistes, the Canadian surrealist group, Gauvreau in his work (plays, poems, performance pieces) went beyond the strictures of French Surrealism, especially in the area of the image, which, both theoretically & practically, he extended from Reverdy's & Breton's core definitions (for which, see volume one, *passim*) into uncharted territory. Writes Canadian-English poet Steve McCaffery: "Gauvreau . . . distinguishes four essential types of poetic image: rhythmic, reflective, transformational and explorational. The rhythmic image (*image rythmique*) is basic to sonorous constitution and includes the sono-rhythmic disruptions of the verbal order. The reflective image (*image mémorante*) includes a general simile and the comparison/correspondence between like elements. The transformational image (*image transfigurante*) includes the majority of surrealist imagery and is produced through the extreme straining of the reflective image-disposition so as to effect an actual transformation of the elements. In the explorational image (*image exploréenne*) a total transformation is recognizable." In what is probably Gauvreau's last poem ("ghédérassann omniomnemm wâkkulé orod ècmon zdhal irchpt laugouzou-/gldefterrpanuclémenpénucleptadussel ferf folfoufaulô farmurerr a/clô dzorr"), McCaffery detects the use of the explorational image, "moving towards a new textual morphology, uncompromisingly non-figurative and articulated within the phonetic combinations of sound clusters."

COBRA

We suppress aesthetic principles. We are not disillusioned because we have no illusions. We never had them.

CONSTANT, *REFLEX MANIFESTO*, 1948

In contrast to the traditional poets, the experimental poet does not impose his will on the word, but instead allows himself to be guided by the word. . . . The poet . . . does not depict something that he had stored up ahead of time, but experiences something he had not known before.

GERRIT KOUWENAAR

To write is to create text and forms at once.

ASGER JORN

"The choice of a name which is not to be an *ism,* but that of an animal," said poet-artist Christian Dotremont in retrospect, & added: "We were in fact against all *isms,* against all that implied a system." The cities in which they worked—& whose opening letters formed their name—were Copenhagen, Brussels, Amsterdam; the participants themselves, mostly younger artists & poets, were witnesses to midcentury war & holocaust from which, in 1948, Europe was just emerging. Short-lived as the "movement" was (it would dissolve by 1951), it was within that time-frame "international," with links—often reiterated—to other postwar groups that sought new ways of life through art. An aspect of their project was therefore social & political—a belief in the transformation of art itself as instrument (in its *experimental* modes) of even larger transformations. In a move reminiscent of earlier Dadaist *disgust,* Cobra artists turned away from "Western Classical culture"—not so much to so-called "primitive" art (too often conflated with the "non-Western") as to the naive art of children, say, & the "outsider art" of the insane. Their program, while reactive to earlier Surrealism, to Marxist theory, & to the poetics of Gaston Bachelard, asserted itself as "anti-aesthetic" & "anti-specialized" in poetry & art; thus in Dutch painter Constant (Nieuwenhuis)'s *Reflex Manifesto* (1948): "A living art makes no distinction between beautiful and ugly because it sets no aesthetic norms. The ugly, which in the art of past centuries has come to supplement the beautiful, is a permanent complaint against the unnatural class society and its aesthetic of virtuosity; it is a demonstration of the retarding and limiting influence of this aesthetic on the natural urge to create." (And elsewhere, as an underlying motive: "We are condemned to experiment by the same causes that drive the world into war.") The result was a commitment to a rawness & openness of form ("we never permit ourselves to finish a poem"—C. Dotremont) & for many of them a further "erasure of the boundaries between the arts" (in the words of a major forerunner, Kurt Schwitters). Artists & poets worked together or crossed into each others' domains, "committed to marrying poetry with the plastic arts" (J. C. Lambert), or from a recognition (thus: Asger Jorn) that "painting and writing are the same." Informing all their work at some level, that recognition is most visible in Dotremont's "logograms" (below): an extension of traditional calligraphies & earlier or concurrent experiments by Michaux, Miró, Isou, & others into a form of "writing-painting."

Of the principal Cobra artists, the Danish painter Asger Jorn was oldest & would be the link also to "cultural revolutionary movements" like the Internationale Situationiste (below, page 417) & the Internationale Lettriste of the 1950s/60s. Dotremont & his countryman & frequent collaborator Pierre Alechinsky were the major Belgian artists involved with Cobra, along with the Flemish poet/novelist/painter/playwright Hugo Claus. In the Netherlands the most conspicuous Cobra artist (& sometime poet) was Karel Appel, while poets who came to Cobra through the Experimentalist Group (also called the Fiftiers) included Lucebert (pen name of L. J. Swaanswijk), Gerrit Kouwenaar, & to a lesser degree Bert Schierbeek (above).

Asger Jorn 1914–1973
WITH Christian Dotremont

from **WORD-PICTURES**

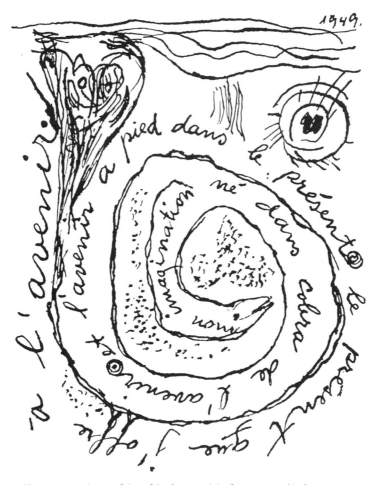

My imagination born in Cobra of the future and the future is rooted in the present, the present which I offer to the future.

LOGOGRAMME

If we were immortal, we wouldn't know it.

SOME LAPLAND VIEWS

The tree the intact
Is thus the exclamation that deranges the sentence
The sentence is white is long

In the garden the tree it carries
its name and its past
Here it carries its silence
No garden no more no south no sugar no more no soap no joy
Winter is my salt my slush

On this too white sheet
the gaze is crime fir straight
loose yellow lianas I leave you to your loops

The sentence is now but a small poor
song on this all too white billet

On this sheet where love
speaks night sun
in the temple of Ivalo where a reindeer sings
where I lose all luggage
all language and throw myself
into the beast's diapers where the breath
speaks loudly in the cattle-shed and the bed
Given that I remember
you Paul and you Jean
who have rhymes among

The regular singular tree
that murders grammar
in school a ball of stone
kneeling in the temple before the great peacock
of not-saying

The word pure of leaves
in the notebook lined by you tree and by you sentence
With it to tune the last harp

In the woods of Tapiola already
where no road finds its knot
In the Helsinki museum already where the stone mass screams
in the Ethiopian language of the northern knot

In my bed already on the eve of becoming
I dreamed of you Ivalo
a young girl in blue and yellow makes coffee under the lamp

Enough to leave however our silence
To join the finally spacious adverb
this room of wood of antlers
                        To leave the prattling
                        paper that says another nothing

To dispute our nothing and yours
Lapland wearing the bonnet I had woven
on my rosy terrain

You leave and let me go
into your non-country
            where a young girl in black & white lights
                        a blue and yellow lamp

you comma modest hiding place where
the sentence falls you trap hole
that draws the undrawn silence
                where the tender & hard word lights a call

Sometimes I happen not to knock at your window
your voice does not answer
your gesture does not move
so that we'll have only to do with
the sea that has blocked itself off

Translation from the French by Pierre Joris

Karel Appel b. 1921

MAD TALK

Mad is mad
madmen are mad
to be mad is everything
to be everything is mad
not to be mad is everything
to be everything is not mad

to be nothing is to be mad
to be mad is nothing
everything is mad
mad is everything
because everything is mad
yet everything is mad
and not to be mad is to be mad
nothing is mad after all
non-madmen are mad
madmen are not mad
mad is mad
mad mad mad

Gerrit Kouwenaar b. 1923

ELBA

for constant

I wear a warning bloodcoat
and I stand on elba.
My name is napoleon, among others my name is napoleon
and I stand on elba.
I bear a hundred names
and I stand on elba.
I am the other side of a gentleman.
My dear generals, look at my beak
on elba.
Walk with me the parks of doubt and exile.
There are nights I sit up and beg like a beaked dog.
My rock is brown, as you can see.
My eye is the clockwork of your inventions:
atom bomb! Thank you, gentlemen!

But now that terror dwells in paris
on the cobblestones still tasting of my parades,
in the sidewalk cafés of colonel sartre,
out of the sea I profess the eiffel tower,
steel affiliation of fear
on elba.

You think I'm dead?
I stand here with saber, beak, bloodcoat.
My body is big and fat
and fat with the bones of hitler and bismarck and nietzsche and truman.
Chaplin is my lackey, but this I know:
he steals epaulettes for the fair
and tobacco for the slaves of soho,
he steals my history for marx—
generals, protest!

I stand like a cesspool on elba.
Oh generals, taste the lyricism of my rotting.
Repeat me and grow me.
I wait for you with spengler and gallows from the museum.
Deliver me, I cry, but do not hope.
The slaves no longer believe the beads, generals.
My name is among others napoleon of elba
and st. helena comes later.

Translation from the Dutch by Peter Nijmeijer

4 VARIATIONS ON

I

The overmastering of the mud
the flattest use of the eyes

then the sifting through the finest inference
the enlargement on scale

the formation of almost, deformation
of certain, steeling

of water, attempt
at a peephole to the closed

2

Many allay the mother the holy time
or seek to thicken I

spy I spy something you can't
or conjugate the question mark or

cover the wound with the father's mouth
may a lot of breath be their part

but all gnaw at something they make: death
doing to breathe everything

3

What is dead is elsewhere
and nothing, one is a child knows little

of less, drinks light
like milk from a flask

like the sand embezzling the rain
and enjoying it in the dark

with an ice-cream cone vanishing down a dark lane
and then summer is over

4

What's there is the endless clear country road
the immoderately eternal country road

stretching on its way to the resting point
resting on its way to the farthest point

on the grass a mug and a newspaper, so low
to the ground that no one asks where

a minute ago one walked there so black and cocksure
that one fused with one's target

Translation from the Dutch by Peter Nijmeijer

Lucebert 1924–1994

ROUSSEAU LE DOUANIER

paris is six feet higher than mexico
paris is a gray sail
mexico a motley boat

we go sailing like serpents
the family goes sailing
the mother bears an egg
the father totes a branch

the child stands and is
the staring moon

Translation from the Dutch by Peter Nijmeijer

9000 JACKALS SWIMMING TO BOSTON

on every slave a pigeon loft to kick in the light of his decline
on every urethra a priest
on every vagina a father
bridges of academic blood
borne by too sudden heartbeats

this is anger
: to possess a voice in a torrent of embraces
to go boating on a long slow river in an underworld's lumbering cesspool
to know for certain this world stinks
stinks under a smelly angel
an angel in silk stockings and with a fine writer's hand
who records only clamor
scores of sucklings
libretti of the blissful malicious and
études of octogenarians
: the noise of a world groaning under a pile of crossbeams
the angel
that rams down the urine barrels with wholesale judges
brigadiers bank messengers

yes
with the stake
the angel
that rams down all the pillars
of state

now in his service are contingents of
impromptu blacksmiths and poets who bare
the subterranean tree
who denude the tangled branches of chastity standing on stilts
the chastity that climbs like ivy and peeps in everywhere
that bores its thorny eyes into all and everything
buried under a blade let valid pennies bleed to death
because this stinks
because this counts
because this tastes nice
slobbering down to the *ding an sich*
d
  o
   w
    n
     t
    o
     t
    h
      e navel-floor of the effigy
the effigy rattling through a hollow universe
rattling with sacks full of mandatories
pursuing the chase
chasing the flight of these stoic (yet dressed in worsted mittens)
jackals
     possessing boston
9000   jackals
           swimming to boston
the borobudur of the bourgeoisie

Translation from the Dutch by Peter Nijmeijer

Pierre Alechinsky b. 1927

AD MIRÓ

Choose the colour that hits the mark.

Beneath the aeroplane patches of green slip by. Drops of pallor fallen onto the watercolour not yet dry. Of an altogether different green if a complementary sun appears, grey when on the fleeing map a cloud passes.

Make out you're a bird with your coat flaps to put fear into the frogs.

. . . Question after question: answer without raising your pen who leaves (dumb) images question-shaped.

She calm
Curve
Sure of wings

No belief from outside. No underwear thought to be erotic being pink. No sham. No cold checker-board. No object still-born into a still life.

Three hairs on the crest of the glabrous curve.

Rosy cheeks. Rice-paper glades. Taut inklines. Contours for droll and definitive stars. Tactile haziness crossed by a lustreless river bed.

No latest news flourished in the air.

The hand, diminutive queen . . .
Drinking water in the company of the blotting-paper.
Seeing further than the tip of one's pencil.
Brush refuelled in mid-flight.
The black arrow: water generously after unpotting.
Painting a virgin canvas with its consent.
Said by Colombus: all painting is a neologism.
A title: crevice-cover.
Blind blob but all ears.
On the colourside gathering signs.

In spots the blue enamel of the household coffee-pot has come away: black nails. Shed a brown tear in the shape of an arm. By surprise. On the mnemogenic tablecloth.

See the higgledy piggle:

Graceful Gogolian nose. Figures in slow motion. Swaying bellies. Heads being born in the rising void. Dissymetry in jeweller's rouge. Calm pattern. Dragonet offering a horn. Iris and pupils decentred between their parentheses placed horizontally. Disorientation for the orientalist. Find refound. Individual media. Crude morpheme. Incipient whorl. Whorl. Allusions to what we saw in Kyoto. Sometimes a letter in lower case and, often, far more often the capital in different bodies of a script but non-existent letter. Cut-outs using round-tipped scissors. Navel imposing its law. The shadow of the lizard's hand. Chalk neon on night paper. Line like a plumb line with the hook. Splatch on a tracing traced off. Bright yellow wound around itself. Printer's black. Work-room white. Enterprising nostrils with warthog curls.

Both feet in a dream
Earth for the planting of paintings

Translation from the French by Michael Fineberg

Hugo Claus b. 1929

THE TOLLUND MAN

Like a kinsman
who rarely appears among his people
and is suddenly found sitting in a corner of the room,
a grim king of silence and discord,
he does not sleep but rests in silence.

No worm has fed on him,
we are the vermin now
with our eager eyes.

In his age of gods and songs,
of wars and ships and
retaliation,
he was strangled with a leather rope
and dumped in his property: the soil, in
an age of ice and iron.

Traces of linseed, of bannock and knotwort
in the intestinal canal:
it was winter when he died, gasping for air
and locked in the clay of the limeless bog.

The village people stood by,
held a fork to his throat and nodded
as he was sacrificed to the summer fruits.
Or was he a murderer? A heretic? A deserter?

Kneeling in empty space,
his body groped for its property: the soil, finding
neither bough nor tree;
revenge did not enter his mind,
for he smiles in the swamp that preserves him.

A chest will rot, bricks pulverize, grass turns to hay and mire;
but he lies there, man's next of kin for centuries to come,
caught in a rope, one ear crushed, and toothless.

> ("*When I in my power mounted you,*
> *the world seemed magnificent*
>
> *until I glowed with spite*
> *at the withering of things.*
>
> *You squealed like hind and dog and sheep*
> *when I begot your son.*
>
> *I was a dagger of lime-wood*
> *in that unending morass, your skin.*")

The acid that preserved him
grows in the grass.
Bent double, he awaits the justice
of what he was.

If there is blood: clotted.
If there is life: affected
by the massive timeless gas, the fingerprints of years.
If there is blue: erased
like the blue of your eyes, years later.

("It is a man of clay who speaks to you.
I killed and was killed.
The birds are setting in the West.")

In ammonia and dung,
in black spines,
under a hood of lead:
my death.

Am I guilty of rape?
Did I shun the battle?

My mother foresaw it all
when she delivered me into this world
of berries and vipers and lilacs,
this trap and the swampy mists of her life.

I never knew it. So I smile
as I sink deeper into this polder
like horned cattle with gut pain.

The children may be right in shouting
that I look ridiculous because mildewed.

They know what justice is,
though desire for it does not haunt them.

My hanging is over,
though the skin of my neck will shrink
for years to come,
and you are vexed, down to your very joints,
by what they did to me.

My tongue protrudes, I no longer speak,
chained henceforth in your clothes
and neighing in your smile
with my blood and snot and seed.

If I am such
then so are you.

Groping for some gesture you find yourself
caught in my clamour, disfigured for days on end.

How old are you now?

Will fire be your punishment
or will you swell until you burst?

The victim has administered justice.

You move in accordance with my every change,
and you too are preserved, and while that ghastly light
still glows in you, you gather all our fragments.

Translation from the Flemish by Theo Hermans

Ian Hamilton Finlay b. 1925

from **HEROIC EMBLEMS**

with Ron Costley & Stephen Bann

One of Panofsky's most justly celebrated essays in ico-
nology (the term he takes directly from Cesare Ripa) is
concerned with Poussin's painting *Et in Arcadia Ego*.
Contemporary disputes about the significance of this
enigmatic work lead him back to Greek pastoral poetry
and the progressive formation of the cultural concept of
'Arcady', with its almost infinite tissue of poetic refer-
ences converging upon the point that even here, in the
ideal pastoral world, death is present. But Panofsky has
not checked the speculation about the inner meaning of
Poussin's picture, which may indeed be bound up with
a hermetic interpretation of the golden section and might
even lead (it has been suggested) to the rediscovery of the
lost treasure of the Albigensian heretics in a particular
part of southwestern France.

The metaphorical presentation of the tank *as* Poussin's inscribed monument, within the Arcadian setting, offers us not so much an emblem as an enigma. Estienne describes the role of Enigma as that of serving 'as a Rind or Bark to conserve all the mysteries of our Ancestors wisdome'. We are not immediately tempted to generalise or extend the implications that we see, as in the 'moral' emblem. The treasure, such as it is, is necessarily remote from us, and we have no foolproof method of lifting the hermetic seal (an oblique comment on the fact that here, particularly, Finlay's adoption of a pre-existent motif has proved a stumbling-block to those who would deny the relevance of wide-ranging cultural reference, Estienne's 'ignoramusses').

Virgil, *Eclogues;* John Sparrow, *Visible Words;* E. Panofsky, *Meaning in the Visual Arts;* Walter Friedlaender, *Nicolas Poussin;* Elizabeth Wheeler Manwaring, *Italian Landscape in Eighteenth Century England;* F. M. von Senger und Etterlin, *Die deutschen Panzer 1926–45; Wenn alle Brüder Schweigen* (foreword by Colonel-General Paul Hausser).

A ruined stone temple by the side of a lake. Within the temple stands a wooden shelter for geese; on the entablature the inscription *The World Has Been Empty Since The Romans* (Saint-Just).

The word *Fragile* in Roman letters, on a formal stone placed upright by the foot of a birch tree.

A slender stone vase containing a hyacinth; on the side of the vase the letters *Ai Ai.*

A goose-house in the shape of a U-boat pen. The geese have to enter the house by swimming. (No door on the landward side.)

A small grove composed of young pine trees and delicate columns. All the needles which fall from the trees are carefully swept into heaps around the foot of the columns.

A similar column, but with the dialling code for Rome (OIO XXXIX VI).

Carved on a low, broken column in a clearing, the numerals 010 30 265 (the International Dialling Code for Dhelphoi).

A small orchard of fruit trees, each tree seeming to grow from a stone column-base of the correct classical proportions.

A tree, pierced right through by a bronze arrow.

A mossy stone.

A smooth-barked tree (such as a beech) reflected in rippled water which makes the smooth bark seem rough.

An orchestral (not a rustic) flute; a strawberry plant growing from it.

A small circular temple half-concealed in a military camouflage-net. (The folds of the net are extended by slanting posts.)

A living tree, on the trunk of which is a carefully painted representation of a classical highlight.

A swan, with a short, sloping mast, and paddleboxes, and paddlewheels.

A weather-worn oar standing upright in a field dotted with nettles and thistles.

A stone lectern placed in a clearing. Let into the top of the lectern is a small mirror which reflects the branches overhead.

A boulder inscribed in one corner with the word *moss*.

A Doric column, decorated near the top with 'kill rings' (like a veteran gun).

A mossy spring with a soldier's mess-tin lying nearby.

An exquisitely sculptured marble tank, inlaid with a copy of the landscape background of Nicolas Poussin's *Numa Pompilius and the Nymph Egeria.*

A large baroque sculpture of nymphs and satyrs riding on a tank in the manner of tank marines.

A rose lying on a rock, under a thundercloud.

An ornamental lake, on which floats a small sailing-boat or bark, with a bark-textured hull.

A small fluted column with guitar-like tuning-pegs. (These apparently made of hardwood.)

※

A brown guitar, stuffed with straw, lying seemingly abandoned on straw-strewn cobble-stones. The name of the maker is legible: Le Nain.

An old-fashioned (horizontal) sundial, the gnomon an exquisite bronze miniature of a modern anti-aircraft gun.

※

A solitary self-propelled gun 'dug in' at the end of a long formal vista of trees and water such as recalls Versailles.

A bronze representation of a guitar (realistic) leaning on the trunk of a tree. (A silver birch.)

※

A statue of Apollo, naked, holding a sub-machinegun.

A tank approaching an 18th century ha-ha.

※

The tomb from Nicolas Poussin's *The Arcadian Shepherds* pitted with bullet holes and scars.

Certain gardens are described as retreats when they are really attacks.
I. H. F.

While still emerging from a poetry of small structures written in the dialect(s) of urban Glasgow, he described himself to one of us (circa 1961) as "just a wee poet who writes wee poems." Shortly thereafter, as an offshoot at first of children's word games he had been devising, he created a *new* textart with affinities to the internationally based concrete poetry movement of the later 1950s (below). Minimal in its verbal means but marked by prolific ventures into publication, Finlay's poetry developed into a public (inscriptional) art—its most striking expression (& one of the most genrebreaking works of *poetry* of the twentieth century), a "classical" garden & temple (Stoneypath, later called Little Sparta) at his home in rural Scotland. What is evident throughout his later work is that its pastoral façade is the cover for what he understands—&, unlike many others, *fears*—as untamed "savage nature," exemplified in modern warfare & in "the notorious Nazi-German organization, the SS . . . equated with nature and . . . [signifying] . . . the ultimate 'wildness' on a scale whose other, 'cultivated' extreme is the eighteenth century." The objects & inscriptions at Little Sparta & elsewhere are replete, therefore, with machine-gun-toting gods & goddesses, bird feeders in the shape of aircraft carriers, Corinthian columns facing double-columned guillotines, revolutionary maxims from Saint-Just & Robespierre, a "Siegfried *Line*" with laundry hanging from it (as in the famous British war-song), & the double lightning bolts of the Waffen SS above the entrance to a classic grotto & intercalated, still more pointedly, in the Italian word *oSSo* (= bone) engraved onto a block of (classic) marble. Finlay's later success as a visual/verbal artist—conceptual, not hands-on—has been marked by recurrent controversy over just such (necessary) symbols.

Ingeborg Bachmann 1926–1973

CURRICULUM VITAE

Long is the night,
long as the shame of the man
who can't manage to die, long
under the lamp post his naked
eye swung, and his eye, blind with the breath of gin
and the smell of a blond girl's wet flesh
under his nails, oh God, long is the night.

My hair won't turn white,
for I crept from a womb of machines,
Rose Red smeared tar on my forehead
and curls, they had
strangled her snow-white sister. But I,
the leader, marched through a town
of ten hundred thousand souls, and my foot
stepped on a soul-louse under a leather sky from which
ten hundred thousand peace-pipes
were hanging, mutely. And often
I wish for angels' repose
and hunting grounds, sick
of the powerless cries
of my friends.

With wide-straddling legs and wings,
youth like some marsh grass shot up
over me, over ordure, over jasmine it went
on those towering nights with their square-
root dilemmas, and the legend of
death that breathed on my window each hour:
give me wolf's milk, pour
old age's laughter into my throat,
when I fall
asleep over folios,
in a disconcerting dream
that finds me unworthy of thought,
playing with tassels
whose fringes are snakes.

And our mothers would also
dream of the future of their men,
they would see someone powerful,
revolutionary, withdrawn,
and mostly after prayers in the garden,
while bending over the burning weeds,
hand in hand with the babbling child
of their love. Oh my gloomy father,
why were you always so silent then,
nor ever thought past tomorrow?

Forsaken in the fire fountains,
a night of crouching on a gun
that misses fire, so goddamn long
a night, under the sputum
of a jaundiced moon, whose light
stunk gall, there rumbled in the shadow
of a dream of power (could I stop it?)
the bobsled of our ornamented
past, and cut me down.
Not that I slept: awake
under the icy bones I trailed it
homeward, wrapped my arms and legs
in ivy and daubed the ruins
white with droppings from the sun.
I kept the holy days,
and only after prayers
did bread appear.

In a self-righteous decade
a man moves faster from one light
to another, from one country
to another, under the rainbow,
the compass-point stuck in his heart,
with its radius labelled the night.
Wide open. From the mountains
one sees oceans, in the oceans
mountains, and where the clouds line up
in pews, the swinging of the bells
inside this given world. *Whose* world
I was commanded not to know.

It happened on a Friday—
my life ran on with fasting,
the air oozed vapors of lemon,
and the fishbone stuck in my craw—
when out of the gutted fish I lifted
a ring which, cast forth at the time
of my birth, fell in the river
of night, where it sank.
I threw it back to the night.

O if I had no fear of death!
If I had the word
(nor knew its loss)
if I had no thorns within my heart
(but battered out the sun)
if I had no greed within my mouth
(nor drank from the wild water)
if I waited without blinking
(nor saw the threads before me).
Must they drag the sky away?
Let the earth not lead me on,
but lay me long in stillness,
long in stillness, for Night
with his black snout to nose me
and plan the next embrace
of his engulfing arms.

Translation from the German by Jerome Rothenberg

COMMENTARY

Where Germany's sky blackens the earth, / a decapitated angel searches for a grave for the hatred / and offers you the bowl of the heart. (I. B.) And again: *On Good Friday a hand hangs / on the firmament, two fingers are missing, / it cannot swear that it all, / that it all did not happen and that nothing / will be.*

Born in Klagenfurt, Austria, she died (age 47) in an accidental fire in her hotel room in Rome. Asked in 1952 to read her work to the assembled "Gruppe 47" (the most influential German literary movement of the post–World War II period), she published her first volume of poems, *Die gestundete Zeit* (The Time Allotted) a year later, followed in 1957 by *Anrufung des grossen Bärens* (Invocation of the Great Bear). During most of the fifties and from 1965 onward, she lived in Rome as an independent writer, producing radio plays, short stories, the novel *Malina*, & three opera libretti for Hans Werner Henze.

The poetry as such is erudite (she was trained in philosophy, writing on Heidegger & existentialism) & meditational, a sharp-edged yet always lyrical gesture of resistance. It was in that sense that she wrote of her work as "a foreboding of future catastrophes" that opened thereby to new possibilities of restoration—an aspect, as she saw it, of that brief postwar moment of hope & renewal (= "the time allotted" of another Bachmann poem [page 32]) when a "degree zero of writing" (R. Barthes) & of human affairs seemed not only possible but necessary. Her bleak historical landscapes,

alienated & alienating as they are, function then as backdrop to a stance
where what hope there is resides in the addressed "you" of the poem, &
where both poem & addressee can be seen as on their way toward a utopia
(of love, or freedom, or ecstasy)—"not as end goal but direction."

Paul Blackburn 1926–1971

PHONE CALL TO RUTHERFORD

"It would be—
               a mercy if
you did not come see me . . .

"I have dif-fi / culty
               speak-ing, I
cannot count on it, I
am afraid it would be too em-
               ba
               rass-ing
for me   ."

               —Bill, can you still
               answer letters?

"No . my hands
are tongue-tied .   You have . . . made

a record in my heart.
               Goodbye."

Oct 1962

AT THE WELL

Here we are, see?
in this village, maybe a camp
middle of desert, the
Maghreb, desert below Marrakesh
standing in the street
simply.

Outskirts of the camp
at the edge of town, these riders
on camels or horses,
but riders, tribesmen, sitting
there   on their horses.

They are mute.   They are
hirsute, they are not
able to speak. If they
could the sound would be gutteral.
They cannot speak. They want
something.

I nor
you know what they want   .   They want
nothing.   They are beyond want.   They need
nothing.   They used to be slaves.   They
want something of us   /   of me   /   what
shall I say to them.

They have had their tongues cut out.
I have nothing to give them   ¿ There is no
grace at the edge of my heart I would grant,
render them?   They want something, they
sit there on their horses.   Are there
children in the village I can give them.

My child's heart? Is it goods they want
as tribute. They have had their tongues
cut out. Can I offer them some sound
my mouth makes in the night?   Can I
say they are brave, fierce, im-
placable? that I would like to
join them?

Let us go together

across the desert toward the
cities, let us
terrify the towns, the villages,
disappear among bazaars, sell our
camels, pierce our ears, for-

get that we are mute and drive
the princes out, take all the
slave-girls for ourselves?
What can I offer them.

> They have appeared here on the edge of my soul.
> I ask them what they want, they say
> —You are our leader.   Tell us what
> your pleasure is, we
> want you.   They
> say nothing.   They

are mute.   they are hirsute.   They
are the fathers I never had.   They are
tribesmen standing on the edge of town near
water, near the soul I must look into each
morning   .   myself.

> > Who are these wild men?
> > I scream:
> > —I want my gods!
> > I want my goods!   I want
> my reflection in the sun's pool at morning,
> > shade in the afternoon under the
> > date palms, I want and want!

What can I give them.
What tribe of nomads and wanderers am I continuation of, what
can I give my fathers?
What can I offer myself?

> > I want to see my own skin
> > at the life's edge, at the
> > life-giving water.   I want
> > to rise from the pool,
> > mount my camel and
> be among the living, the other side of this village.

Come gentlemen,
wheel your mounts about.
There is nothing here .

THE NET OF PLACE

Hawk turns into the sun
over the sea, wings red, the
turn upward . mountain behind me

I have left those intricate mountains
My face now to the simple Mediterranean . flat .
small boats . gulls . the blue

Old hawk
is still there tho, as
there are foxes on these barren mountains   .
     Old man in a beret, 62 perhaps, came
     into the village bar the other day
     —2 skins and one fox unskinned—

       "You hunted these down?"

       "I hunted them. They
       come in closer in winter, seeking food,
       there isn't much up there—"

Rocky headland down into the Gulf of Valencia .
My windows face North . He was a hawk

I turn back to the Rockies, to the
valley swinging East, Glenwood to Aspen, up
the pass, it is darkest night the hour before dawn,
Orion, old Hunter, with whom
I may never make peace again, swings
just over the horizon at 5 o'clock
as I walk . The mountains fade into light

Being together there was never enuf,—it was
"my thing" Nothing of importance (the reach)
was ever said . I turn
& say farewell to the valley, those hills   .
A physical part of wellbeing's been spent &
left there—Goodbye mountains   .   valley,
all. Never
to be there again   .   Never.

It is
an intricate dance
to turn & say goodbye
to the hills we live in the presence of .
When mind dies of its time
it is not the place goes away .

Now, the hawk turns in the sun, circles
over the sea .
Defines me .
Still the stars show thru   .

Orion in winter rises early,
summer late . dark before

dawn during August
during which day, the
sun shines on everything.

Defines it .
Shadows I do not see.

I rise early
in every season.

The act defines me,
even if it is not my act .

Hawk circles over the sea .

My act .

Saying goodbye, finally .
Being here is not enuf, tho
I make myself part of what is real.   Recognize me
standing in that valley, taking only the embraces of friends, taking
only my farewell . with me

Stone from my mountains .
Your words are mine, at the end.

I have drunk my white wine and worked / I have lasted it out into silence
P. B.

Like other important North American poets of his time, his work reflected an identification with the initial experimentation of Pound & Williams, buttressed in his case by resources of language that opened to a still-larger range of European and Latin American predecessors. A Vermonter by birth, he lived most of his life in New York City, but traveled from there early & late, to chart the world through a succession of poems that were his ongoing journal (= day book), culminating in a final diaristic work appropriately called *The Journals* (posthumously published: 1975), of which *The Net of Place* (2.3.68) is a part. While he was a chronicler thereby of the desiring, often thwarted mind—his own & others'—the central focus of his art was, as he saw it, a devotion to the quirky music language made: what the ear heard joined to what the eye saw. In this he early followed Pound into a search for means & sources in the troubador poetry of medieval Provence (the gathered work is called *Proensa*), surpassing the older poet in the voice he gave to his translations. (Or, translation aside, in the modern send-ups / variations of that voice in his own poems.) Skeptical by nature, he clung still to a belief in poetry as both a private & communal act, a sense of which pervades his nearly final poem—*evening fantasy*—in its imagining of poets dead before him, gathered in a kind of paradise-of-poets. (His *Phone Call to Rutherford* is addressed to William Carlos Williams, following the older poet's second stroke & subsequent aphasia.)

For all his reticence in framing a poetics, Blackburn's recognition, circa 1960, of a new "American *duende*" (volume one, page 461) was a summons—a rallying cry—for many with whom his work was intersecting.

Robert Creeley b. 1926

THE WHIP

I spent a night turning in bed,
my love was a feather, a flat

sleeping thing. She was
very white

and quiet, and above us on
the roof, there was another woman I

also loved, had
addressed myself to in

a fit she
returned. That

encompasses it. But now I was
lonely, I yelled,

but what is that? Ugh,
she said, beside me, she put

her hand on
my back, for which act

I think to say this
wrongly.

ANGER

I

The time is.
The air seems a cover,
the room is quiet.

She moves, she
had moved. He
heard her.

The children
sleep, the dog fed,
the house around them

is open, descriptive,
a truck through the walls,
lights bright there,

glaring, the sudden
roar of its motor, all
familiar impact

as it passed
so close. He
hated it.

But what does she answer.
She moves
away from it.

In all they save,
in the way of his saving
the clutter, the accumulation

of the expected disorder—
as if each dirtiness,
each blot, blurred

happily, gave
purpose, happily—
she is not enough there.

He is angry. His
face grows—as if
a moon rose

of black light,
convulsively darkening,
as if life were black.

It is black.
It is an open
hole of horror, of

nothing as if not
enough there is
nothing. A pit—

which he recognizes,
familiar, sees
the use in, a hole

for anger and
fills it
with himself,

yet watches on
the edge of it,
as if she were

not to be pulled in,
a hand could
stop him. Then

as the shouting
grows and grows
louder and louder

with spaces
of the same open
silence, the darkness,

in and out, him-
self between them,
stands empty and

holding out his
hands to both,
now screaming

it cannot be
the same, she
waits in the one

while the other
moans in the hole
in the floor, in the wall.

2

Is there some odor
which is anger,

a face
which is rage.

I think I think
but find myself in it.

The pattern
is only resemblance.

I cannot see myself
but as what I see, an

object but a man,
with lust for forgiveness,

raging, from that vantage,
secure in the purpose,

double, split.
Is it merely intention,

a sign quickly adapted,
shifted to make

a horrible place
for self-satisfaction.

I rage.
I rage, I rage.

3

You did it,
and didn't want to,

and it was simple.
You were not involved,

even if your head was cut off,
or each finger

twisted
from its shape until it broke,

and you screamed too
with the other, in pleasure.

4

Face me,
in the dark,
my face. See me.

It is the cry
I hear all
my life, my own

voice, my
eye locked in
self sight, not

the world what
ever it is
but the close

breathing beside
me I reach out
for, feel as

warmth in
my hands then
returned. The rage

is what I
want, what
I cannot give

to myself, of
myself, in
the world.

5

After, what
is it—as if
the sun had

been wrong to return,
again. It was
another life, a

day, some
time gone, it
was done.

But also
the pleasure, the
opening

relief
even in what
was so hated.

6

All you say you want
to do to yourself you do
to someone else as yourself

and we sit between you
waiting for whatever will
be at last the real end of you.

COMMENTARY

To count, to give account, tell or tally, continually seems to me the occasion. (R. C.) And again: *I think, and / therefore I am not. . . . // As soon as / I speak, I / speaks . . .*

(1) A defining figure, with Olson & Duncan (above), in the "Black Mountain" side of the New American Poetry, Creeley (whose native New England, he writes, gave him "that sense of speech as a laconic, ironic, compressed way of saying something to someone. To say as little as possible as often as possible") is the master of the tight lyric & stripped rhetoric, & the counterpoint, in that, to Olson's & Duncan's mytho/historical gestures. As Sherman Paul sums up the achievement: "Heritage: romantic and metaphysical: spiritual wanderer and logician of the spirit. Precise, economical, tight (formal). Simple particulars that are universal . . . / Love and cosmicity. / Verse: the twists and turns of his mind on his experience. Paws at it like a cat. Worries it verbally, doubling words back on themselves, making words play out their meanings. Logopoeia . . ."—which also describes Creeley's best-known statement (as cited in Olson's *Projective Verse*) that "form is never more than an extension of content."
  (2) "'The Whip' was written in the middle fifties. . . . The title is to the point, because it is music, specifically jazz, that informs the poem's manner in large part. Not that it's jazzy, or about jazz—rather it's trying to use a rhythmic base much as jazz of this time would—or what was especially characteristic of Charlie Parker's playing, or Miles Davis', or Thelonious Monk's. . . . That is, the beat is used to delay, detail, prompt, define the content of the statement or, more aptly, the emotional field of the statement. It is trying to do this while moving in time to a set periodicity—durational units, call them. It will say as much as it can, or as little, in the 'time' given. So each line is figured as taking the same time, like they say, and each line ending works as a distinct pause. I used to listen to Parker's endless variations on 'I Got Rhythm' and all the various times in which he'd play it, all the tempi, up, down, you name it. What fascinated me was that he'd write silences as actively as sounds, which of course they were. Just so in poetry" (R. C.).

René Depestre b. 1926

from **A RAINBOW FOR THE CHRISTIAN WEST**

Three Loas

Cap'tain Zombi

I am Cap'tain Zombi
I drink through my ears
I listen with ten fingers
I have a tongue that sees all
A radar-smell that picks up
The waves of the human heart
And a touch that sees smells
From a distance
As for my sixth sense
It is a detector of death
I know where our millions
Of bodies are buried
I am responsible for their bones
I am responsible for their blood
I am teeming with corpses
Teeming with death rattles
I am a tide of wounds
Of cries of pus of blood clots
I graze on the pastures
Of the millions of my dead
I am shepherd of terror
I keep watch over a flock of black bones
These are my sheep my cattle
My pigs my goats my tigers
My arrows and my spears
My lava and my cyclones
As far as the eye can see
A black artillery howling
In the cemetery of my soul!

2

Listen white world
To the volleys of our dead
Listen to my zombi voice

In honor of our dead
Listen white world
My typhoon of wild beasts
My blood shredding my anguish
Over all the world's roads
Listen white world

3

The black man's blood opens its floodgates
The holds on the slave-ships
Pour out into the sea
The froth of our miseries
The cotton plantations
The coffee and sugar cane plantations
The rails of the Congo-Ocean
The slaughter houses of Chicago
The fields of indigo of corn
The central sugarworks
The storerooms of your ships
The mining companies
The shipyards of your empires
The factories the mines the hell
Of our muscles on earth
It is the foam of black sweat
That descends upon the sea tonight!

Listen white world
To my zombi-roaring
Listen to my sea-silence
Oh desolate chant of our dead
You are my destiny my Africa
My spilled blood my epic heart
The sea-pulse of my utterance
My ebony wood my corossol
The cry of dead trees in me
The echo of their sap in my voice
My race like a lingering sob
Searches my throat and my waters
Searches in me the channel
Where Africa tears out her heart
Listen bitter world white world

To my song of death my life is this song
Joining within my body, wind
And wave, heaven and hell!

Baron-Samedi

I am the great Baron-Samedi
Oh! do not trust too much
In my beautiful white beard
It is a nest of ferocious wasps
My beard is capable of the worst excesses
Tonight you are oh! family of the South
The large sanctuary where I unleash
The bats of my past
For your five daughters I sew
Dresses in cloth from Siam
Studded with small black crosses
To cast a spell on the males
I hold them upside down:
Evil beasts viper's tongues
White whalebones lynchers of niggers
H Bomb-throwers white mazimazas
You will all walk from land to land
From village to village of this fiendish South
From prison to prison of this bestial South
From madhouse to madhouse
I am Saint-Expedit
And with all my heart I send
To the devil your insolences
Your hatred of black men
Your gaping wounds
I do not listen to the three Lord's Prayers
That you recite in my honor
I sterilize my rock of Baron Samedi
In the murky alcohol of your destinies
And seven times West-Point cadet
I strike you on the head
And seven times Alabama judge
I strike you on the head
And seven times Yale student
I strike you on the head

And seven times future senator
I strike you on the head
And seven times future ambassador
I strike you on the head
And you—the idiot of the family
Seven times I strike you on the head
And seven times I strike
With a congo-pea branch seven times
With the wings of a black rooster
Seven times I strike with the wings
Of a poule-zinga seven times
I strike at your dim faces
With the lash of a whip I take
Your big-good-angels O zombies of Alabama
I carry away your little-good-angels
I am the Baron of the rain
And you are less alive
Than the trees or the ants in my house!

Chango

I am Chango hurler of thunder
The eagle makes his nest in my voice
I seize your two sunless hands
Your judge-hands that squander the days
And red globules of my people
Slowly I pass them
Through the flaming alcohol of my breath
Slowly I burn their thorns
And now is the time for preparing
The belly of each female in the house
I take two halves of Jacmel-orange
And I fill them with castor oil
I cry out three times that I am Chango
The clear sky holds no secrets for my eyes
My touch knows how to give luck and light
I heat the oil of proud truth
With the lighted wick of my human heart
O white daughters of Alabama prostrate yourselves
At the feet of my innocence
And take off all your clothes

I dip my hand in the hot oil
And very slowly I rub your cursed breasts
I rub the rebellious ivory of your limbs
That emerge little by little from shadows
I rub one by one your astonished sex
Now you are forever as pure as my eyes
Now you are ready to bear in your loins
All the bursting of life in the dawn of humanity!

Translation from the French by Joan Dayan

COMMENTARY

I was born in Jacmel in 1926 / When I was five I made my first sojourn under the Caribbean sea. / When I was fifteen one entire night I was / A horse who carried on his back / The naked beauty of my native city. / When I was forty I carried the sluggish agony of my roots.

R. D. (translation by Joan Dayan)

But it was at a year past forty that he published his complex masterwork, *Un Arc-en-ciel pour l'occident chrétien* (subtitle: "A Voodoo Mystery Poem"), filled with the saving power of a recreated past. At once a turning from & an extension of earlier Negritude writing (for which, see volume one), it brought the force of Haitian voodoo (*vodoun*) into his work—not as another literary sucking-up of myth but as a mark of nation-building & of revolt against the nation's "western"/"white" oppressors. Here he followed not only from a line of Negritude and Surrealist poets but from Haitian "indigenists" like Carl Brouard, Emile Roumer, and Jacques Romain (the founder of the Haitian Communist Party). A revolutionary from adolescence, he spent many of the intervening years in exile, writing *Un Arc-en-ciel*, e.g., while living in Communist Cuba. In the poem's narrative, the poet speaks as an inspired Voodoo *hungan* (= shaman), possessed or "ridden" by his *loa* (= god = "[divine] horseman"), & as a *loa* himself (or an entire panoply of *loas*) enters dreamlike into a southern (U.S.) house, there to ride & hence redeem the sons & daughters of a racist Alabama judge. It is this language of possession (with its religious, often sexual intimations) that brings him to the gritty depths of nation consciousness, while its relation to *all* our origins as knowing beings points to "the realization of the human in a society freed of races."

In the present excerpts from *Un Arc-en-ciel,* the names of the *loas* appear in their Haitian (French) spellings.

Allen Ginsberg 1926–1997

I saw the best minds of my generation destroyed by madness, starving
    hysterical naked,
dragging themselves through the negro streets at dawn looking for an
    angry fix,
angelheaded hipsters burning for the ancient heavenly connection to the
    starry dynamo in the machinery of night . . .

MESCALINE

Rotting Ginsberg, I stared in the mirror naked today
I noticed the old skull, I'm getting balder
my pate gleams in the kitchen light under thin hair
like the skull of some monk in old catacombs lighted by
a guard with flashlight
followed by a mob of tourists
so there is death
my kitten mews, and looks into the closet
Boito sings on the phonograph tonight his ancient song of angels
Antinoüs bust in brown photograph still gazing down from my wall
a light burst from God's delicate hand sends down a wooden dove to the
    calm virgin
Beato Angelico's universe
the cat's gone mad and scrawls around the floor

What happens when the death gong hits rotting ginsberg on the head
what universe do I enter
death death death death death the cat's at rest
are we ever free of—rotting ginsberg
Then let it decay, thank God I know
thank who
thank who
Thank you, O lord, beyond my eye
the path must lead somewhere
the path
the path
thru the rotting shit dump, thru the Angelico orgies
Beep, emit a burst of babe and begone

perhaps that's the answer, wouldn't know till you had a kid
I dunno, never had a kid never will at the rate I'm going

Yes, I should be good, I should get married
find out what it's all about
but I can't stand these women all over me
smell of Naomi
erk, I'm stuck with this familiar rotting ginsberg
can't stand boys even anymore
can't stand
can't stand
and who wants to get fucked up the ass, really?
Immense seas passing over
the flow of time
and who wants to be famous and sign autographs like a movie star

I want to know
I want I want ridiculous *to know to know* WHAT rotting ginsberg
I want to know what happens after I rot
because I'm already rotting
my hair's falling out I've got a belly I'm sick of sex
my ass drags in the universe I know too much
and not enough
I want to know what happens after I die
well I'll find out soon enough
do I really need to know now?
is that any use at all use use use
death death death death death
god god god god god god god the Lone Ranger
the rhythm of the typewriter

What can I do to Heaven by pounding on Typewriter
I'm stuck change the record Gregory ah excellent he's doing just that
and I am too conscious of a million ears
at present creepy ears, making commerce
too many pictures in the newspapers
faded yellowed press clippings
I'm going away from the poem to be a dark contemplative

trash of the mind
trash of the world
man is half trash
all trash in the grave

What can Williams be thinking in Paterson, death so much on him
so soon so soon
Williams, what is death?
Do you face the great question now each moment
or do you forget at breakfast looking at your old ugly love in the face
are you prepared to be reborn
to give release to this world to enter a heaven
or give release, give release
and all be done—and see a lifetime—all eternity—gone over
into naught, a trick question proposed by the moon to the answerless earth
No Glory for man! No Glory for man! No glory for me! No me!

No point writing when the spirit doth not lead

KRAL MAJALES

And the Communists have nothing to offer but fat cheeks and eyeglasses
    and lying policemen
and the Capitalists proffer Napalm and money in green suitcases to the
    Naked,
and the Communists create heavy industry but the heart is also heavy
and the beautiful engineers are all dead, the secret technicians conspire
    for their own glamour
in the Future, in the Future, but now drink vodka and lament the
    Security Forces,
and the Capitalists drink gin and whiskey on airplanes but let Indian
    brown millions starve
and when Communist and Capitalist assholes tangle the Just man is
    arrested or robbed or had his head cut off,
but not like Kabir, and the cigarette cough of the Just man above the
    clouds
in the bright sunshine is a salute to the health of the blue sky.
For I was arrested thrice in Prague, once for singing drunk on Narodni
    street,
once knocked down on the midnight pavement by a mustached agent
    who screamed out BOUZERANT,
once for losing my notebooks of unusual sex politics dream opinions,
and I was sent from Havana by plane by detectives in green uniform,
and I was sent from Prague by plane by detectives in Czechoslovakian
    business suits,

Cardplayers out of Cézanne, the two strange dolls that entered
    Joseph K's room at morn
also entered mine, and ate at my table, and examined my scribbles,
and followed me night and morn from the houses of lovers to the cafés of
    Centrum—
And I am the King of May, which is the power of sexual youth,
and I am the King of May, which is industry in eloquence and action in
    amour,
and I am the King of May, which is long hair of Adam and the Beard of
    my own body
and I am the King of May, which is Kral Majales in the Czechoslovakian
    tongue,
and I am the King of May, which is old Human poesy, and 100,000
    people chose my name,
and I am the King of May, and in a few minutes I will land at London
    Airport,
and I am the King of May, naturally, for I am of Slavic parentage and a
    Buddhist Jew
who worships the Sacred Heart of Christ the blue body of Krishna the
    straight back of Ram
the beads of Chango the Nigerian singing Shiva Shiva in a manner which
    I have invented,
and the King of May is a middleeuropean honor, mine in the XX century
despite space ships and the Time Machine, because I heard the voice of
    Blake in a vision,
and repeat that voice. And I am King of May that sleeps with teenagers
    laughing.
And I am the King of May, that I may be expelled from my Kingdom
    with Honor, as of old,
To show the difference between Caesar's Kingdom and the Kingdom of
    the May of Man—
and I am the King of May, tho' paranoid, for the Kingdom of May is too
    beautiful to last for more than a month—
and I am the King of May because I touched my finger to my forehead
    saluting
a luminous heavy girl trembling hands who said "one moment Mr.
    Ginsberg"
before a fat young Plainclothesman stepped between our bodies—I was
    going to England—
and I am the King of May, returning to see Bunhill Fields and walk on
    Hampstead Heath,

and I am the King of May, in a giant jetplane touching Albion's airfield
   trembling in fear
as the plane roars to a landing on the gray concrete, shakes & expels air,
and rolls slowly to a stop under the clouds with part of blue heaven still
   visible.
And *tho'* I am the King of May, the Marxists have beat me upon the
   street, kept me up all night in Police Station, followed me thru Spring-
   time Prague, detained me in secret and deported me from our kingdom
   by airplane.
Thus I have written this poem on a jet seat in mid Heaven.

May 7, 1965

*"First thought, best thought." Spontaneous insight — the sequence of
thought-forms passing naturally through ordinary mind — was motif and
method of these compositions.*
A. G.

While the theme of liberation that he struck in the middle 1950s had long
been a poet's theme, it was Ginsberg (the governmental suppression of his
poem *Howl* the leading test case) who brought it to a wider public view &
into areas then strictly out-of-bounds for U.S. poetry: the politically radical,
the sexual, the religious as a struggle with the repressive powers of religion
& its "mind-forged manacles" (W. Blake). (He would later become a spokes-
man for a new American Buddhism & co-founder with the Tibetan "mas-
ter" Chogyam Trungpa of the Jack Kerouac School of [Disembodied] Poet-
ics in Boulder, Colorado.) This early willingness "to die for Poetry & for
the truth that inspires poetry" led him not only to a poetic courage shared
with others but to an international visibility (as a Beat Generation founder
& political & spiritual mentor for several later generations) & a growing
sense of responsibility for things said—both those to be said again & then
again, & those to be said & then *un*said. On the side of his poetics as
such, he carried forward (from Whitman, Williams, Blake as "courage
teacher[s]") a sense of "a revolution of literature in America" brought about
"merely by the actual practice of poetry." But his work—along with its ac-
knowledged spontaneities & self-styled "Hebraic-Melvillian bardic breath"
(later = "mind breaths")—is proof of a very deliberate and highly articulate
poetic intelligence at work, creating complex structures to hold &
organize the lines he sees as moving like "Charlie Chaplin's walk" or
"long saxophone-like chorus lines" with "the natural inspiration of the
moment . . . disparate thinks put down together, shorthand notations of
visual imagery, juxtapositions of hydrogen jukebox." As Eric Mottram sug-

gests, in Ginsberg's best poetry "information is inclusive, and consistently dislocated and reassembled into an action. The ideogram of Pound is fused into the Hart Crane telescoping image and Blake's prophetic 'Jerusalem' tactics (the multipresence of contemporaneity within prophetic universality); the result is a rhetoric of highlighted word-ideas which resist the logic of linear cause and effect structures. The poem is a mobile of urgency."

Robert Filliou 1926–1987
PER George Brecht b. 1926

from 14 SONGS AND I RIDDLE

an homage in dance
to that mammal m
m for misfortune   man
ma'am   misfortune m

it has to do with a dance   with a ball
the piece should be done outdoors or in a dance hall
a studio   an apartment
the most appropriate form is a surprise party
among friends
there should be something to drink   something to eat
if there are no musicians   the songs should be recorded
if records are used   they are to be in a juke box
otherwise use a tape recorder

overture

here's an homage in dance
to that mammal m
m for misfortune   man
ma'am   misfortune m

we'll dance along
his 34 travelling years

it's an homage in dance
to that mammal m
m for misfortune   man
ma'am   misfortune m

we'll dance along
his 33   53   154 and 170 dreaming years

it's an homage in dance
to that mammal **m**
m for misfortune   man
ma'am   misfortune **m**

we'll dance along
his 84   85   86 and 86 years of abuse

it's an homage in dance
to that mammal **m**
m for misfortune   man
ma'am   misfortune **m**

we'll dance along
his 266 abstinent years

it's an homage in dance
to that mammal **m**
m for misfortune   man
ma'am   misfortune **m**

we'll dance along
his 11 valiant years

it's an homage in dance
to that mammal **m**
m for misfortune   man
ma'am   misfortune **m**

we'll dance along
his 66   111   196 and 200 years of return to the fields

it's an homage in dance
to that mammal **m**
m for misfortune   man
ma'am   misfortune **m**

no I   rock

the aged bat
(what an ass !)
and the bloodthirsty beaver

(what a brain   what promiscuity   what a birth !)
beget the brutal bird
(what testicles !)

me too
i am
married

the brutal bird
(what vigor   what copulation   what lips
what vigor   what testicles ! what a brain !
what promiscuity   what birth   what copulation
what lips !)
and the domesticated spider
(what violence !)
beget the degenerate she cat
(what a death   what testicles ! what a uterus !
what a birth   what copulation   what heat
what a brain   what copulation !)

me too
i am
married

the domesticated spider
(what copulation !)
and the carping dolphin
(what a brain   what a uterus ! what combat
what promiscuity   what a birth   what an ass
what vigor   what testicles   what a uterus
what heat !)
beget the experienced bull
(what chromosomes !)

me too
i am
married

the experienced bull
(what a brain   what a penis   what growth
what a clitoris   what a uterus   what lips !
what a clitoris   what copulation   what lips !)
and the nocturnal fly
(what a uterus !)

beget the beaten eagle
(what promiscuity   what vigor   what copulation
what growth   what lips !)

me too
i am
married

the beaten eagle
(what heat !)
and the passive bitch
(what a brain ! what copulation   what growth
what a death   what copulation   what an ass
what promiscuity !)
beget the graduate snake
(what a brain !)

the graduate snake
(what a brain   what a penis   what an ass
what a birth   what copulation   what promiscuity
what growth !)
and the fascist seal
(what a clitoris !)
beget the tightwad ant
(what a brain   what a birth   what testicles
what vigor   what a uterus   what growth
what testicles   what lips !)

me too
i am
married

the tightwad ant
(what combat !)
and the music loving stag
(what an ass   what a brain   what chromosomes
what copulation   what gestation   what longevity
what a penis   what testicles   what violence
what a voice   what a birth   what a clitoris
what heat   what a uterus   what combat
what breasts   what growth   what lips   what vigor
what promiscuity   what a death   what ejaculation !)

beget the excessive frog
(what a whole   what a lynx   what a boar
what a microbe !)

me too
i am
married

no 2   rock

why the senility of the ovaries
why the masturbation of the ancestor
why the butterfly of the masturbated

cause (listen to the cuckoo sing !)
cause the vagina of senility
cause the breasts of the ancestor
cause the brutality of the caterpillar

why the battle of the breasts
why the vision of the ancestor's masturbation
why the cannibal butterfly

cause (listen to the cuckoo sing !)
cause the bird masturbator
cause the ancestor's brutality
cause the bird of the breasts of the vagina

why the breasts of the butterfly
why the cannibal ancestor
why the nipples of the breasts
why the bird of the caterpillar
why the nipples of the breasts
why the butterfly of masturbation
why the timidity of the vagina

cause (listen to the cuckoo sing !)
cause the breasts of the caterpillar
cause the senility of the ancestors
cause the battle of the ancestors
cause the ovaries of the vagina
cause the brutality of the vagina
cause the claws of the breasts
cause the cheating of the claws

but why the breasts of the albino bird
why the vagina of the albino ancestor
why the ovaries of the albino bird
why the claws of the albino cannibal vagina

cause listen to the cuckoo sing

COMMENTARY

A refusal to be colonized culturally by a self-styled race of specialists in painting, sculpture, poetry, music, etc. . . . , this is what "la Révolte des Médiocres" is about. With wonderful results in modern art, so far. Tomorrow could everybody revolt? How? Investigate.
R. F.

Like others associated with Fluxus in the 1960s (page 17, above), Filliou's deliberately casual, deceptively good-humored art masked the seriousness of a quest (in his case) that brought him to a sometimes austere Buddhist practice that would last all his life. A poet by both disposition & choice, he engaged with numerous media & styles, including projects & performances with fellow Fluxus artists—Emmett Williams (above), Daniel Spoerri, & George Brecht among those closest to him. Of his own deflationary approach to art & life, he wrote what Kristine Stiles describes as a "re-state[ment] in Fluxus-like humor [of] the concept of dharma":

from GOOD-FOR-NOTHING-GOOD-AT-EVERYTHING (1970)

I create because I know how.
I know how good-for-nothing I am, that is.
Art as communication is the contact between the good-
for-nothing in one and the good-for-nothing in others.
Art, as creation, is easy in the same sense as being god is
easy. God is your perfect good-for-nothing.
The world of creation being the good-for-nothing world, it
belongs to anyone with creativeness, that is to say anyone
claiming his natural birth gift: good-for-nothingness.

In the translation of Filliou's *14 Chansons et 1 Charade*, George Brecht functions (along with Steve McCaffery, Dick Higgins, bp Nichol, & Dieter Roth) as part of a translating/transforming team, his own work later overridden by McCaffery's "homolinguistic translation" of the translated English—the opening quatrain, for example: "*a gnome itching indians / (toe that, man . . .) mallarmé / hymn-form, his fortune amen / miami's for tuna (hmmmmmmmm.*" The other participants work in a similar manner—thus wind up with "Six Fillious" (the final work's title).

Frank O'Hara 1926–1966

THE DAY LADY DIED

It is 12:20 in New York a Friday
three days after Bastille day, yes
it is 1959 and I go get a shoeshine
because I will get off the 4:19 in Easthampton
at 7:15 and then go straight to dinner
and I don't know the people who will feed me

I walk up the muggy street beginning to sun
and have a hamburger and a malted and buy
an ugly NEW WORLD WRITING to see what the poets
in Ghana are doing these days
                                I go on to the bank
and Miss Stillwagon (first name Linda I once heard)
doesn't even look up my balance for once in her life
and in the GOLDEN GRIFFIN I get a little Verlaine
for Patsy with drawings by Bonnard although I do
think of Hesiod, trans. Richmond Lattimore or
Brendan Behan's new play or *Le Balcon* or *Les Nègres*
of Genet, but I don't, I stick with Verlaine
after practically going to sleep with quandariness

and for Mike I just stroll into the PARK LANE
Liquor Store and ask for a bottle of Strega and
then I go back where I came from to 6th Avenue
and the tobacconist in the Ziegfeld Theatre and
casually ask for a carton of Gauloises and a carton
of Picayunes, and a NEW YORK POST with her face on it

and I am sweating a lot by now and thinking of
leaning on the john door in the 5 SPOT
while she whispered a song along the keyboard
to Mal Waldron and everyone and I stopped breathing

HOMOSEXUALITY

So we are taking off our masks, are we, and keeping
our mouths shut? as if we'd been pierced by a glance!

The song of an old cow is not more full of judgment
than the vapors which escape one's soul when one is sick;

so I pull the shadows around me like a puff
and crinkle my eyes as if at the most exquisite moment

of a very long opera, and then we are off!
without reproach and without hope that our delicate feet

will touch the earth again, let alone "very soon."
It is the law of my own voice I shall investigate.

I start like ice, my finger to my ear, my ear
to my heart, that proud cur at the garbage can

in the rain. It's wonderful to admire oneself
with complete candor, tallying up the merits of each

of the latrines. 14th Street is drunken and credulous,
53rd tries to tremble but is too at rest. The good

love a park and the inept a railway station,
and there are the divine ones who drag themselves up

and down the lengthening shadow of an Abyssinian head
in the dust, trailing their long elegant heels of hot air

crying to confuse the brave "It's a summer day,
and I want to be wanted more than anything else in the world."

ODE: SALUTE TO THE FRENCH NEGRO POETS

From near the sea, like Whitman my great predecessor, I call
to the spirits of other lands to make fecund my existence

do not spare your wrath upon our shores, that trees may grow
upon the sea, mirror of our total mankind in the weather

one who no longer remembers dancing in the heat of the moon may call
across the shifting sands, trying to live in the terrible western world

here where to love at all's to be a politician, as to love a poem
is pretentious, this may sound tendentious but it's lyrical

which shows what lyricism has been brought to by our fabled times
where cowards are shibboleths and one specific love's traduced

by shame for what you love more generally and never would avoid
where reticence is paid for by a poet in his blood or ceasing to be

blood! blood that we have mountains in our veins to stand off jackals
in the pillaging of our desires and allegiances, Aimé Césaire

for if there is fortuity it's in the love we bear each other's differences
in race which is the poetic ground on which we rear our smiles

standing in the sun of marshes as we wade slowly toward the culmination
of a gift which is categorically the most difficult relationship

and should be sought as such because it is our nature, nothing
inspires us but the love we want upon the frozen face of earth

and utter disparagement turns into praise as generations read the message
of our hearts in adolescent closets who once shot at us in doorways

or kept us from living freely because they were too young then to know
what they would ultimately need from a barren and heart-sore life

the beauty of America, neither cool jazz nor devoured Egyptian heroes,
    lies in
lives in the darkness I inhabit in the midst of sterile millions

the only truth is face to face, the poem whose words become your mouth
and dying in black and white we fight for what we love, not are

Everything is in the poems. . . . I don't believe in God so I don't have to make elaborately sounded structures. . . . I don't even like rhythm, assonance, all that stuff. You just go on your nerve. If someone's chasing you down the street with a knife you just run, you don't turn around and shout, "Give it up! I was a track star for Minneola Prep."
F. O'H.

The core player (with John Ashbery [below], Kenneth Koch, James Schuyler, et al.) in what came to be known—circa 1960—as the New York School of poets, O'Hara may have overstated here his dislike of traditional poetic praxis or, elsewhere, of theoretical poetics—i.e., his writings on art show his critical intelligence & his poetry evidences both a great care for technique & a comfortable knowledge of modern poetics (Apollinaire, Rilke, Pasternak, etc.). Behind his proclaimed love for surfaces & surface effects (a concern shared with some abstract expressionist painters of the 1950/60s) lay a daily discipline summed up in *Meditations in an Emergency* (1957): "It's my duty to be attentive, I am needed by things as the sky must be above the earth." Quintessentially a city poet (but more in the Apollinaire/Cendrars vein, say, than that of Baudelaire), he focused this attention on New York ("I can't even enjoy a blade of grass unless I know there is a subway handy, or a record store or some other sign that people do not totally regret life"), & like so much of the century's avant-garde what attracted him was speed & immediacy—which is why (wrote Marjorie Perloff) "[he] loves the motion picture, action painting and all forms of the dance—art forms that capture the present . . . in all its chaotic splendor." But unlike the earlier hymns to speed & the city (Marinetti, et al.), O'Hara's was a nearly elegiac sensibility, where glittery & elegant surface chatter & speed are only skin-deep covers for a deep personal & emotionally lived dailiness as core of a new kind of poem that was to influence a generation of younger New York School poets & others.

John Ashbery b. 1927

from **FLOW CHART**

Suddenly they all stopped talking about it. Yet I
can't get it out of my head. I just saw it here somewhere
late last evening. As a result, nobody thinks I'm normal, but I don't
care. Every answer may have been salted and put away just so as to spoil,
like a dissertation of some kind. A great deal of thinking went into it and
  out the other side.

But I did want to get back to the personal barbs. Why was I wailing
    for them?
Fact: people leave their doors open and don't even flush the toilet.
Fact: loving one another in these parts is more like gunboat diplomacy
    than it is
like a soap opera, and I, who don't care, always get caught in the middle.
I belong there anyway. I'm going to someplace from someplace, and
    think in these terms.
I'm like a corset string that gets laced up but never tied. I've tried to be
    kind and helpful,
I know I have, but this is about something else. It's about me. And so I
    am never
off the hook; I look at others and reflect their embarrassed, sheepish grin:
    all right,
can I go home now? But I know deep in my heart of hearts I never will,
    will never want to,
that is, because I've too much respect for the junk we call living
that keeps passing by. Still, I might be tempted
to love or something if the right person came along, or the time were
    right;
I know I would. But I can't be tempted, so far. I'm too pure, like the
    nature
of temptation itself, and meantime the fans stand back and wonder what
    to admonish
the players with, and I sit here empty-handed, my breast teeming
with unexplained desires and acrostics. I'll go on like this. Take my
    glasses off.
And he says to me, I'll vote for you. Our roads are poor. And he laughed
    and said it.

Others were paying for this call which is why in the first place
no string of dignity remained, no mention of how they would reopen
the clogged career of someone just starting out in life who finds himself
    injured
and cannot explain why. There is blood everywhere—no wound,
just the sign of bleeding. If one had thought not to count
and tabulate every moment and expose it to the litmus of living in
    some way
I can't understand, then it would be all right for those bald men at the
    beach and some could

redeem the morning pledge and saunter off distractedly into the football
     fields
of dusk, and leave others alone, and welcome death as a diversion and
     they in turn could write
this down. Lakes and raccoons and unspotted moons would be the
     result.
As it is, everyone now finds himself inferior: repeat, everyone.
There is unrest; the shadow of the ball carries over.
I am left to repeat standards that have no particular relevance for me. I
     write
on the sides of buildings and on the backs of vehicles, and still
no nail divides the splinter from its neighbor, no fish swims close to
     another.
I have seen it all, and I write, and I have seen nothing.

Draw up a map right now—all of the notches are there.
If we cared like this it would be all right, wouldn't it, so why
doesn't somebody do something? In addition to which God doesn't want
     us to be stupid
or overreact, else why these chains? *We don't have much call for those.*
     We can
slip into the forest with it, and be bait. I know I'd be taking off nothing
if I let you believe otherwise, but it's all I can do. The season is even rude
to finish us off, but there is something we have to do, weather permitting,
across the street before the king is murdered.
Anyway, it was the commandant's word against mine.

The incubus awoke from a long, refreshing sleep.
A lot of people think they have only to imagine a siren for it to exist,
that the truth in fairy tales is somehow going to say them. I tend to agree
with dumb people who intervene, and are lost; actors of a different
     weakness
who explain the traceries of fallen leaves as models for our burgeoning
     etiquette,
a system that doesn't let us off the hook as long as we are truth and
     know it,
the great swing of things. And of course it may yet turn up.

I couldn't believe he said it. But that's the way we lived. It existed.
I've been at this stand for years and I think I see how the wool
is pulled over our eyes gradually, so that each of us thinks of ourselves as
    falling asleep
before it happens, then wakes to a pang of guilt: was it that other me
    again?
Why did I take my mind off the roast, as it turned
hypnotically on its spit, and now it's charred beyond recognition?

The multiplication of everything ran on years back, she said,
until two scraps had been assembled. Then it was up to the death-rattle.
There was a great conflict at that time.
There are canisters of cartridges from that era which do little to dispel
the legend of our rabid ancestors. Hey,
they're yours as well as mine, buster.
Yet once the funeral herbs were strewn there was peace of a sort. The
    evergreen
canopy became an anagram of itself, telling us much
about how gold was hidden in the old places, and spirits that came forth,
    irritated,
from their resting place and pulled the magic latch-string, and the door
    flew open
and there were the wolf and Red Riding Hood in bed together, except
    that the wolf
was really Grandma. Whew! What a relief! They don't write them that
    way anymore,
because the past is overlay. What a city this is! In what rich though tepid
    layers you can
almost detect the outline of your head and then
you know it's time to read on. When crisis comes, with embraceable side-
    effects,
let's put a roof on the thing before it sidles, world-bound,
toward an unconvincing other world. I'm more someone else, taking
    dictation
from on high, in a purgatory of words, but I still think I shall be the same
    person when I get up
to leave, and then repeat the formulas that have come to us so many
    times
in the past ("It's softer"), so faithfully that we extend them
like a sill, and they have an end, though a potentially hazardous one,

though that's about all we can do about it. Every film is an abidance. We
  are merely agents, so
that if something wants to improve on us, that's fine, but we are always
  the last
to find out about it, and live up to that image of ourselves as it gets
projected on trees and vine-coated walls and vapors in the night sky: a
  distant
noise of celebration, forever off-limits. By evening the traffic has begun
again in earnest, color-coded. It's open: the bridge, that way.

COMMENTARY

*The forms retain a strong measure of ideal beauty / As they forage in secret
on our idea of distortion. / Why be unhappy with this arrangement, since /
Dreams prolong us as they are absorbed? / Something like living occurs, a
movement / Out of the dream into its codification.*
J. A.

It is thus not so much a modernist interest in content that fascinates Ashbery
but a postmodern concern for process. "Not what one dreams but how," as
Marjorie Perloff has it, "this is the domain of Ashbery, whose stories 'tell
only themselves,' presenting the reader with the challenge of 'an open field
of narrative possibilities.'" Despite recent attempts by conservative critics
(Helen Vendler, Harold Bloom, among others) to claim Ashbery as a main-
stream late Romantic lyric poet, his importance has been in the ongoing
experimentation of the work, its distrust of (even high-modernist) rhetorical
voices (Daffy Duck rather than Tiresias or Malatesta, as Charles Altieri
points out) & its insistence on being "anybody's" (not Stein's "every-
body's") (auto)biography. ("'You' can be myself or it can be another
person . . . we are somehow all aspects of consciousness giving rise to the
poem"—J.A.). What interests him is ". . . the experience of experience. . . .
The particular occasion is of lesser interest to me than the way a happening
or experience filters through to me. I believe this is the way in which it hap-
pens with most people. I'm trying to set down a generalized transcript of
what's really going on in our minds all day long."

    If long sojourns in France & early though abiding influences by French
writers (particularly Raymond Roussel, essential for what John Shoptaw
calls Ashbery's "crypotographic" & "homotextual" processes) are core, he
is quintessentially American: an adopted New Yorker (with Frank O'Hara
[above] a co-"founder" of the poetry "school" bearing that city's name)
who would, finally, align himself with the aims of the first great American
experimentalist: "My idea is to democratize all forms of expression, an idea
which comes to me from afar, perhaps from Whitman's *Democratic Vis-
tas*—the idea that both the most demotic and the most elegant forms of
expression deserve equally to be taken into account."

Larry Eigner 1927–1996

"EXPLANATION / TANGENT THINGS"

explanation
tangent things

what goes through the head

what sphere of being

ideas of bird

brilliant light

time,   cleaved water

WINTER

(January / February 1978)

January 20 78

the fleering snow

off the eaves

of the garage

January 20–5 78

planes grounded

around the world

no flight paths

politics

suspended in snow

bowels

brewing

j'ai 50 ans

snow

blinding

cold

pages and pages

brief things

From Tago-no-ura
going out here see
so pure white all
on topmost Fuji
snow reared fallen is

Ohh love how
when I go hunting for her
the winter night's
traveling air's so cold
the shore birds are crying

"AH, SO, YES"

September 1 – 5 87

ah, so, yes

that's where things leave you ,
full of abstractions

animality

chordatsm

vertobrodoty

mammaly

primetcy

• • •

• • •

mer can

jdeo crt

ny
c

[THREE POEMS 1989]

August 15 89

As Thoreau might say

    cool it

       whoever can

October 24 89

scary   then   now   worrisome

    wherever I'll end up

October 25 89

photos of

  poets

   above strange

     tantalizing languages

STATEMENT ON WORDS. *Amid increasingly palpable news rather than ru-mor of scarcities (to be hugely euphemistic about it), abundant moments in various places persist and keep on in high or ultra high frequency, and a poem can be assay(s) of things come upon, can be a stretch of thinking.*
L. E.

From birth he was bounded by a palsy that denied him ease of speech & movement, but the powers of mind/thought (listening to many sources & voices; looking out with clarity at what's immediately before him) grew still sharper & thereby brought him a new music & a concentrated sense of "daily act" (R. Duncan), "daily actualization [of writing things]" (R. Gren-ier). A younger contemporary of poets like Duncan, Olson, others of so-called Black Mountain School, Eigner influenced a still younger generation by the "ambiguity of 'fact'" (& language) that his work presents. Writes one of them, Benjamin Friedlander: "Implicit to [his] practice has been the accessibility of thought to language, of language to thought, and of thought and language to the world. A mystery of 'things . . . giving meaning or re-alized, by voice, emphasis, physical force,' the telos of this practice (the 'op-timum mix' Eigner hopes to discover) is in many ways a regulation of the senses." And Robert Grenier, of Eigner's unique contribution ("work strangely cleared of 'personality'"): "Here E's isolation from daily speech patterning (with its conventional continuities: grammar), his relative isola-tion from the attitudes of das Man, & the palsy which irregularly forces him to 'begin again & again' the language act, intentionally have been turned to advantage—so that . . . Eigner appears as absolute, original American ge-nius who 'redeems us' from the swamp of last-ditch Romanticism *either* in form of popular confessional establishment self-oozings & gossip *or* as arty-willful underground structural experiment reaction 'style'—both of which are mired in assumptions of self, self's experience & action-ability."

Or Eigner himself—up to & including his limits: "In a sense everything has to come of itself, unexpectedly, and has to be faced."

CONCRETE POETRY

*He is no painter who is not in some degree a poet and thinker, and
there can be no poet without a certain measure of thought and
representation.*

GIORDANO BRUNO, 1591

*We have ceased to look at the formation and pronunciation of words
according to grammatical rules and are starting to see letters only as the
determinants of speech. We have loosed the shackles of syntax . . . [and]
begun to attach meaning to words according to their graphic and
phonic characteristics.*

VELIMIR KHLEBNIKOV, 1913

CONCRETE POETRY: *total responsibility before language, thorough
realism. against a poetry of expression, subjective and hedonistic. to
create precise problems and to solve them in terms of sensible language.
a general art of the word. the poem-product: useful object.*

AUGUSTO DE CAMPOS, DÉCIO PIGNATARI, HAROLDO DE CAMPOS, 1958

Something more—& less—than "visual poetry" (*passim*), concrete po-
etry produced one of the genuinely international movements of the twen-
tieth century. That many of its works could readily cross borders was in
part a function of their stripped-down (= minimalist) nature: a reduction
of the poem to a sign (often in bold typography, sometimes in color) that
typically eliminated syntax & even words themselves, thus offering up an
image open to interpretation (reading) at a single glance. In a larger sense
the same mindset that produced concrete poetry tied it not only to other
forms of visual poetry but—more surprisingly perhaps—to radical forms
of sound poetry & textsound performances. Practitioners were also
drawn to "process poetry" & to experiments with reduplicating verbal
patterns—as in Haroldo de Campos's *Transient Servitude*—or, as the se-
miotics of the work developed, to pieces (like Augusto de Campos's *Olho
por Olho* [Eye for Eye]) that dispensed with words in favor of a purely
visual, often photographic, image. Still other activities involved a continu-
ing & sometimes complex use of typewriter as graphic instrument (like
the computer later); the construction of poems set in a range of raw ma-
terials, from steel or neon, say, to (literally) concrete; &, most ambitiously,
poems that merged with sculpture, architecture, even (in the case of Ian
Finlay, above) with formal (classical) gardens.

While visual poetry may be as old as writing (may be, as mark & picto-graph, still older), the modern roots of concrete poetry go back to the typographical experiments of poets & artists like Mallarmé, Apollinaire, Schwitters, Marinetti, cummings. (An early [1908] reference to "concrete poetry" is by Ernest Fenollosa—through Ezra Pound as editor—in the former's description of "the Chinese written character as a medium for poetry.") But the term in something like its later, altered meaning was first used (almost concurrently) by Eugen Gomringer, a Bolivian-born Swiss; by the Noigandres poets of Brazil (Augusto & Haroldo de Campos, Décio Pignatari, others); & by the Swedish poet/artist Oyvind Fahlström (all circa 1955). Others who participated in the next decade & more included Carlo Belloli (Italy), Dieter Roth (Germany, Switzerland, & Iceland), Gerhard Rühm & Ernst Jandl (Austria), Henri Chopin & Pierre & Ilse Garnier (France), Ian Hamilton Finlay (Scotland), Bob Cobbing, John Furnival, & Dom Sylvester Houedard (England), bp Nichol (Canada), Sei-ichi Nikuni & Kitasono Katue (Japan), & Emmett Williams & Mary El-len Solt (United States). More work (but not necessarily concrete poetry) by Finlay, Jandl, Nichol, Rühm, and Williams turns up elsewhere in these pages. Likewise the concretist works of Karl Young (United States), as shown here, represent a related & widespread concern with the physical & graphic dimensions of books & the text as printed surface.

Addendum. "CONCRETE began for me with the extraordinary (since wholly unexpected) sense that the syntax I had been using, the movement of language in me, at a physical level, was no longer there—so it had to be replaced with something else, with a syntax and movement that would be true of the new feeling (which existed only in the vaguest way, since I had, then, no form for it). . . .

"CONCRETE, by its very limitations, offers a tangible image of goodness and sanity; it is very far from the now-fashionable poetry of anguish and self. . . . It is a model of order, even if set in a space which is full of doubt" (Ian Hamilton Finlay, Letter to Pierre Garnier, 17 September 1963).

Eugen Gomringer b. 1924

TWO POEMS

mist
mountain
butterfly

mountain
butterfly
missed

butterfly
meets
mountain

        •

hang and swinging hang and swinging
hang and grow and swinging hang
and grow downwards and swinging hang and
grow downwards and touch the ground and
swinging hang and grow downwards and
touch the ground and then off and search
and swinging hang and grow downwards
and touch the ground and then off and
search and not find a place and swinging
hang and grow downwards and touch
the ground and then off and search and not
find a place and grow and swinging
hang and grow downwards and touch

the ground and then off and search and not
find a place and grow upwards and swinging
hang and grow downwards and touch
the ground and then off and search and not
find a place and grow upwards and force
a new growth and swinging hang and
grow downwards and touch the ground and
then off and search and not find a place
and grow upwards and force a new growth
and hang and swinging hang and
grow downwards and touch the ground and
then off and search and not find a place
and grow upwards and force a new growth and
swinging hang

Translation from the German by Jerome Rothenberg

Ian Hamilton Finlay b. 1925

POSTER POEM

on the right, a red blinker

le circus!!

smack

K47

and crew

they
leap
BARE-BACK
through
the
rainbow's

also

corks

nets

etc.

hoop

on the left, a green blinker

Emmett Williams b. 1925

LIKE ATTRACTS LIKE

like   attracts   like

like   attracts   like

like   attracts   like

like   attracts   like

like   attracts   like

like   attracts   like

like attracts like

likeattractslike

likeattractlike

likattraclke

lihttradike

literalike

likelikts

Seiichi Nīkuni b. 1925

RAIN

Seiichi Niikuni

雨 = *ame* = rain

Ilse Garnier b. 1927
Pierre Garnier b. 1928

EXTENSION 2: SOLEIL

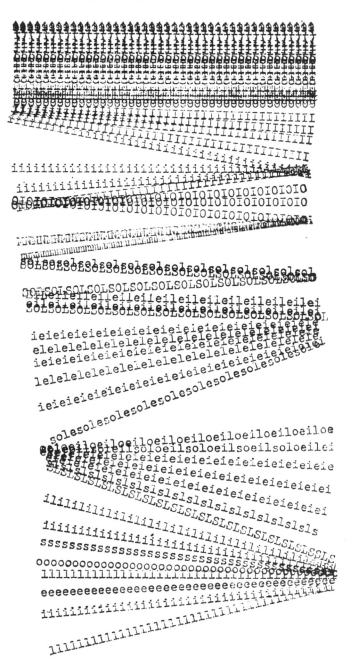

Seiichi Nīkuni b. 1925
Pierre Garnier b. 1928

from **POÈMES FRANCO-JAPONAIS**

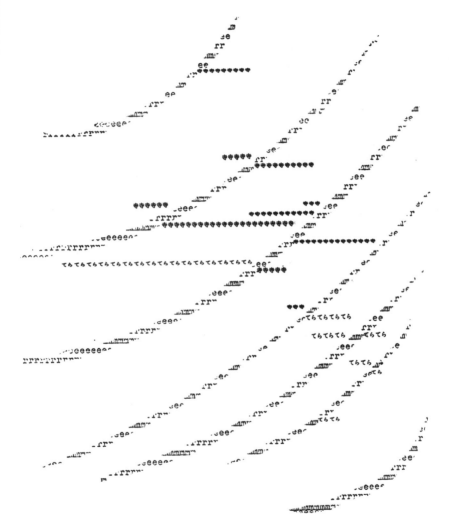

Haroldo de Campos b. 1929

from **TRANSIENT SERVITUDE**

de sol a sol	from sun to solar
soldado	solder
de sal a sal	from salt to salty
salgado	saline
de sova a sova	from stick to stone
sovado	stunned
de suco a suco	from sap to sugar
sugado	sucked
de sono a sono	from sleep to slip
sonado	slumped
sangrado	sanguined
de sangue a sangue	from seep to spurt

.   .

onde mói esta moagem	where does this grinding grind
onde engrena esta engrenagem	where does this gear engage
moenda homem moagem	grindstone man's grinding
moagem homem moenda	grinding man's grindstone
engrenagem	gearchanged
gangrenagem	gangrengaged

.   .

de lucro a lucro	from profit to profit
logrado	pinched
de lôgro a lôgro	from pinch to pinch
lucrado	profited
de lado a lado	from pole to pole
lanhado	parted
de lôdo a lôdo	from puddle to puddle
largado	poleaxed

sol a sal	sun to salt
sal a sova	salt to stun
sova a suco	stun to sap
suco a sono	sap to sleeping
sono a sangue	sleeping to bleeding

.   .

onde homem	with man
essa moagem	this bonegrind
onde carne	with flesh
essa carnagem	this bloodgut
onde osso	with bone
essa engrenagem	this baregear

.   .

homem forrado	bland man
homem forrado	branded man
homem rapina	pillage man
homem rapado	peeled man
homem surra	cudgel man
homem surrado	cudgelled man
homem buraco	sieve man
homem burra	steel-safe man

.   .

homem senhor	sir man
homem servo	serving man
homem sôbre	super man
homem sob	sub man
homem saciado	stacked man
homem saqueado	sacked man
homem servido	served man
homem sôrvo	swallowed man

•

homem come | trencher man
homem fome | empty man

homem fala | yakkity man
homem cala | yes man

homem sôco | socko man
homem saco | sick man

homem mó | graft man
homem pó | chaff man

•

quem baraço | who's lord
quem vassalo | who's lout

quem cavalo | who's the horse
quem cavalga | who's on horseback

quem explora | who's the exploiter
quem espólio | who's the spoil

•

quem carrasco | who's hangman
quem carcassa | who's hanged man

quem usura | who's usury
quem usado | who's used

quem pilhado | who's plundered
quem pilhagem | who's plundering

•

quem uisque | who's whisky
quem urina | who's piss
quem feriado | who's feast-day
quem faxina | who's fatigue-duty
quem volúpia | who's lust
quem vermina | who's lice

•

carne carniça carnagem

sangragem sangria sangue

•

homemmoendahomemmoagem

açúar
nesse bagaço?

almíscar
nesse sovaco?

petunia
nesse melaço?

•

indigo nesse buraco?

•

ocre
acre
osga
asco

•

canga cangalho cagaço
cansaço cachaço canga
carcassa cachaça gana

•

de mingua a mingua
de magro a magro
de morgue a morgue
de morte a morte

•

flesh filth fury

bloodbath bleeding blood

•

grindstonemangrindingman

sugar
in these husks?

musk
in this armpit?

petunia
in these molasses?

•

indigo in this snakepit?

•

ochre
acrid
lizard
lazar

•

halter harness hot-seat
heaviness head-hot halter
hangdog half-tot anger

•

from dearth to dearth
from drouth to drouth
from deadhouse to deadhouse
from death to death

.   .

só moagem   only grindinghood
ossomoagem   bone-grindinghood

"The book **transient servitude** is composed of two parts: '*proem*' and '*poem*.'
'*Proem*' contains three pieces, which develop, in a dialectical way, the linguistic
and existential play between *poesia pura* (pure poetry) and *poesia para* (com-
mitted poetry, poetry with a social purpose, poetry *for*). The first one is the fly of
blue; the second, the fly of flies. Hölderlin: '*Und wozu Dichter in dürftiger Zeit?*'
(and what is poetry for in a time of scarcity?). And Heidegger about Hölderlin:
'Poetry is the foundation of *being* through the word.' These somewhat metaphysi-
cal statements are transformed by the poem into a physical matter of facts: hunger
in Brazilian underdeveloped regions, as a counterweight in the poet's mind, in the
very act of compounding his poem: *nomeio o nome* (I name the noun), *nomeio o
homem* (I name humanity), *no meio a fome* (in mid-naming is hunger); in Portu-
guese, by the mere cutting of the word *nomeio* is obtained non-discursively *no
meio* (in the middle) which introduces 'hunger' in the very act of nominating. Feu-
erbach: '*Der Mensch ist was er isst*' (man is what he eats) and Brecht: '*Erst kommt
das Fressen denn kommt die Moral*' (first comes grub, then comes the moral). In a
circumstance of scarcity, the poet tries to give '*un sens plus POUR aux mots de la
tribu.*' A committed poetry, without giving up the devices and technical achieve-
ments of concrete poetry." (H. de C.)

English version by Edwin Morgan

Augusto de Campos b. 1931

EYE FOR EYE

A Popcrete Poem

Karl Young b. 1947

BOOKFORMS

I make books. I publish trade editions under the Membrane Press imprint. I also make facsimiles of indigenous-style Mexican manuscripts, and of screenfolds and scrolls based on Oriental models. For a number of years I have been working on a series of one-of-a-kind books; photographs of some of them are presented here. In this series I have been trying to produce new bookforms or introduce new materials into the spinebound format that dominates all contemporary western book design and manufacture. Most of the photographs are of books that fall into the second category: the books are covered with wrappers and their pages, bound along a spine, are not sheets of paper but metal printing plates, dollar bills, pieces of wood, concrete blocks, etc. In some cases the size of the pages alone removes them from the dominant notion of what a book is—this is the case with the books that can be worn as earrings and those whose front and back covers can be brought together, producing a radiant, implied cylinder. Some have been designed for specific purposes other than what most people would consider normal reading. Books whose pages are wooden blocks or resonating chambers, sometimes filled with materials that rattle when shaken, are meant to be used as musical instruments and were made for specific performance artists or for my own use in specific performances.

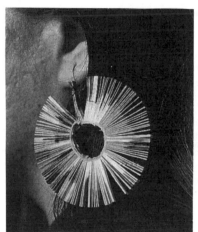

Book worn as earring.

Books with tall, thin pages—made to be folded into several forms, such as cylinders.

Photos: Michael Sears

Performance book for the FOUR HORSEMEN. Each page is in effect a box made with quarter-inch plywood, containing marbles, ball bearings, grains, beans, screws, etc. It can make two types of sound: the clapping of pages together and the rattling of the contents of each page—both types of sound may be produced together . . . All texts are visible in this photograph—appearing only on the edges of the pages. Each line is associated with one of the four members of the group.

A BOOK OF NOCTURNS. Pages made of wooden two-by-fours covered with dark blue and black felt. Texts in white. The book is meant to be used to perform its texts: clap the book once after each line, twice after each stanza. As assistant claps another book, like the one for Mac Low's STANZAS at the end of each poem. Has something of the character of a Japanese Noh play.

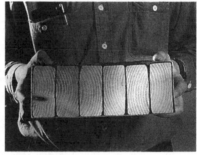

A BOOK OF NOCTURNS being performed (1).

A BOOK OF NOCTURNS being performed (2).

Armand Schwerner b. 1927

from **THE TABLETS**

Tablet II

This tablet consists of a numbered list. At least a few of the units
may be titles to chants which have never been found, or which may
never have been written. Its exact placement in the context of the
series is a problem.

1. empty holes in the fish-dying-becoming directions
2. . . . . strings and pieces + + + + + + + + +
3. the children dance* in waters of fish-death

> * the idiosyncratic placement of the central horizontal
> cuneiform wedges suggests the word may be 'breathe.'

4. they are dry scales + + + + + + + + + + + + + + +
5. on the inside their scales are wet (moist?)
6. they are empty holes; why do they walk and walk?
7. the + + + + + + children eat. . . . . .strings and pieces
8. the empty children run in [their] patterns (shoes?)
9. the pig (god?) waits. . . . . fish-death
10. the children. . . . .
11. the children. . . . . ball games
12. the children. . . . .
13. . . . . must eat (might-could-will-want-to-eat?) rain pintrpnit*

> * transliteration. Probably an archaic form of 'alleluiah' or 'selah.'

14. the road. . . . . penis-thinking pintrpnit
15. sometimes they walk on the river-road with crocodile pintrpnit
16. they can walk near the knom* in their stupid ignorance of fish-death

> * conceivably 'the Spirit which denies'

17. o they are stupid they are lacking they walk and walk
18. they separate fish and death
19. they do not separate fish and death
20. near the knom they tame the auroch pintrpnit
21. not far from the knom, on spring nights, they tame the urus pintrpnit
22. in stupid ignorance in stupid ignorance how do they walk and walk?

23. in walking the river road they tame wisent* pintrpnit

> * auroch, wisent, urus: large long-horned ancestor of the modern bull

24. they are taller than urus pintrpnit
25. how small they are beside the urus pintrpnit
26. the.............. to suck the rain
27. .... very warm on our knees
28. the long men* + + + + + + + + + + + to eat the children

> * possibly 'priests'

29. not merely to eat, but the blood.........
30. not merely to eat, but the knom...........
31. + + + + + + + + + + + + + + + + + + forever
32. brains and liver............. many favors
33. the sun/the sun/the sun/the (power?)* for all of [us]!

> * possibly 'damage'

34. we have made no mistake/the (energy?)/the (energy?)
35. the sun sits in the [testicles] of the pig (god?)
36. the sun +
37. the long house + + + + + + yellow (N?/shad?/vomit?)
38. the sun from the cod
39. the sun from the cod
40. the sun from the cod
41. the sun from the cod
42. the sun from the cod pintrpnit

Tablet X

```
.............................................. + + + + + + + + + + + + + +
+ + + + + + + + + + + + + + + + + + + + + + + + + + + + + + + + + + + + +
+ + + + + + + + + + + + + + +
+ + + + + + + + + + + + + + +
+ + + + + + + + + + + + + + +
+ + + ................................... ⊕⊕⊕⊕⊕⊕
.............. + + + + + + + + ...... + + + + + + + + + + +
+ + + + + ........... + + + + + ......... + + + + + + + + + + + + + +
```

```
. . . . . . . . . . . . . . . . . . . . . . . . . . . . . . . . . . . . . . . . . . . . . . . . . . . . . . . . . . . . . . . . . . . . . .
. . . . . . . . . . . . . . . . . . . . . . . . . . . . . . . . . . . . . . . . ⊕ ⊕ ⊕ ⊕ ⊕ ⊕ ⊕ ⊕ ⊕ ⊕
+ + + + + + + + + + + + + + + + + + + + . . . . . . . + + + + + + + + + + + +
+ + + + + + + [the the] + + + + + + +
+ + + + + + + + + + + + + + + + + + + +
+ + + + + + + + + + + + + + + + + + + +
+ + + + + + + + + + + + + + + + + + + +
+ + + + + + . . . . . . . + + + + + + . . . . . . . + + + + + + . . . . . . + + + + + +
. . . . . . . . . . . . . . . . . . . . . . . . . . . . . . . . . . . . . . . . . . . . . . . . . . . . . . . . . . . . . . . . . . . . .
. . . . . . . . . . . . . . . . . . . . . . . . . . . . . . . . . . . . . . . . . . . . . . . . . . . . . . . . . . . . . . . . . . .
. . . . . . .
. . . . . . . . . . . . .
. . . . . . . . . . . . . . . . . . .
. . . . . . . . . . . . . . . . . . . . . . . + +
. . . . . . . . . . . . . . . . . . . . . . . . . . . . . + + + + + + + + + +
```

Tablet XV

Probably the song of a temple prostitute, priestess of the second caste.

much, heavily flying, much, heavily flying, much, the vagina musk bleeding
they bring in the wild ass
slow spectrum enormity penis enormity ravage till
much, spectrum, soil-tiller, heavily flying and till till vagina musk
they bring in the wild ass
never of when whenever coming coming coming now power ziggurat
   tureen
of much, heavily flying, enormity ravage penis in sperm mass blue river god
they bring in . . . .
lapis and obsidian and bronze gird about gird about bronze testicles
he climbs suspension my back raw inside lips suspension my teeth
   together wild god
nettles nettles sacred bath of sperm and blood bronze in my sleep
```
+ + + + + + + + + + + + + + + + + + + + + + + + + + + + + + + + + +
+ + + + + + + + + + + + + + + + + + + + + + + + + + + + + + + +
+ + + + + + + + + + + + + + + + + + + + + + + + + + + + + + + + + +
```
for you, that I turn for you, that I slowly turn for you, high priestess
that you do my body in oil, in glycerin, that you do me, that you slowly
   do me
that you do me slowly almost not at all, that you are my mouth

that I am your vulva, feather, feather, and discover for you—
let me open my thighs for your hands as I do for my own that I do you
that my hair thinks of you and remembers you, that my fingers
that the sweat on my thighs/bronze bronze heavily flying/thinks of you
and reminds me of me and that you let me be harsh
o for you, that I turn for you, that I slowly turn for you, high priestess
that you do my body in oil, in glycerin, that you do me, that you slowly
    do me
that you do me slowly almost not at all, that you are—
+ +
. . . . .that my body become a sentence that never stops, driving
    through air spaces
from one tablet to another, its python power
. . . . unclear, it must be the tips of my own fingers on my
    cunt lips
and your hands which graze my nipples, looking for what they need,
which endear the field of my closed eyes my closed eyes my nose the
    corridor
of my ear, my clitoris, and your wayfaring hands bearing through myself
    images
that constantly just escape me because I will not let them win over you,
your hands which graze my field, sentence
and inflection of how I do me, you do me and how do I how wonderful
by way of pictures I can't see thrust across the air between us high
    priestess
and dare to put your own hands on your own lips
my hands on yours, how is it I never knew
this took so much risking, that I do you, that you turn for me
that you slowly turn for me, that I do your body in oil, in glycerin,
that I do you, that I do you slowly almost not at all
+ +
. . . . in this small clearing where I rest from us, space inside the
    field,
emptied of muscle and cries, emptied
of muscle and cries my closed eyes empty cups of rest
in which your picture sometimes appalls and that you know to leave me
    here
where my money my clothes my blood my liver are violently plucked
    away from me
my field sometimes in such pain from thousands of tiny openings
and I wake up unpeopled and startled at such happiness

from **Tablet XXVI**

he is not quite dead.

In this stony ground of the great artificer
In the holes, between hillocks.....................hot.............
Urus compose themselves in his breath which is the hot wind
Of the desert of his words but also in his bitter [noun]-trap he is
Inhospitable to lost cows and goats, brutal to the lost. Where
Is the room in him for the tame, the life of milk and riverrun fields,
Overcome as he totters over the cave of his stomach, his dank words heavy
on his [peritoneum], he cradles his belly,
Great carpenter of the insides.
                      The sweet language waters grow
From his stomach,............. his + + + + + + + + +, his.....................
From his testicles, and in his heart the semen grows
Into the fetus-form of his [verbs.] That will kill him in a great fire
Separated from a house. That will sicken him in a vast house
Cut away from the life of flame and scorching. He goes. May he die.
He leaves. May he die. We will continue + + + + + + + + + + + + + + + + + +
In the bleached world. He dies.
We will store what even his greed can't curb. Still riddles pierce us.
He is who? A she. Giving out. Leaping in. Cut away and thinning out. Deep
Song. Great shaken word-stuff+ + + + + + + + + + + + + + + missing+ + + + +
  + + + + +.........
Leaving a change.
                    The barley of his words
Swells in the wrong ground of his liver, the child of his verbs puffs up
For this bearing, he is shaken.................................
  + + + + + + + + + + + + + + + + +

he is someone else, perhaps an animal.

He races inside his messages of fleet means. He is the calling voice
Of the names inside the wheat and the barley. He can't say them
Forever. He tells them +
Through the inside of his eyes, he sees
The inside of his eyes and finds the animal names of plants.
He looks and tells. He lives inside the scorching sun, he also leans

++++++++++++ upwards ++++++++++ downwards ++++++
. . . .
In his long trial toward heat
. . . . .the name of the water falling,   the voice
In the water slithering and trekking underneath the soil calling
To receive the good names, to say the good names and to receive
And to receive. . . . . .like the king of the hurricane who draws
Lightning and ++++++++++++++++++++++++ the sound, the proper
Voice for the saying, the murmuring, the uttering, the chant
Of wheat and barley changed by murmur into animal liveliness,
By uttering, by striking his stomach and opening the. . . . .

he will surely never die.

The world is made of his voice.

COMMENTARY

A fish can only swim. If a poem is a fish it must discover that swimming's what it does. (A. S.) And again: *Poetry, as game, as act of faith, as celebration, as commemoration, as epic praise, as lyric plaint, as delight in pattern and repetition — poetry is in trouble.*

But Schwerner relished & defied that trouble by incorporating these different modalities into one multiphasic oeuvre. A trained musician (he studied improvisation with Lennie Tristano) & a major figure in ethnopoetics, he is a lyric poet of epic ambitions, & as behooves these (postmodern) times a poet of many voices—"palimpsestic," writes Paul Christensen, "his voice . . . one whose depths shimmer with other voices, his mouth issuing language it conduits in from the past or the 'outside' and uses as its own speech. . . . The voices overlay one another like the strata of various civilizations." In his long ongoing work (beginning: circa 1968), The Tablets, he creates for this an open-ended book or series of fictive translations, modelled on the fractured "accidental" form in which old Sumerian & Babylonian cuneiform writings bhave come down to us & accompanied by a "scholar-translator's" commentaries that are at once—as Schwerner tells it—"more than ironic and other than nostalgic." What this highwire act of mixed high comedy & profound seriousness foregrounds is (Schwerner again) "the delicate complex balance between performance, which recognizes the otherness of audience, and individual lyric or narrative or philosophical poetic utterance, which lives in another dimension." The Tablets are an attempt, suggests Kathryn van Spanckeren, "to recreate archaic art

not as metaphor but as given psychological process and concrete/phenome-
nological reality," while simultaneously deconstructing classical Western
notions of selfhood & unitary consciousness in favor of (Christensen again)
"a version of consciousness that is alarmingly unpossessive and entangled
in other people's minds."

For more on Schwerner & the Tablets, see volume one. His simplified key
to a reading of the poem's typographical symbols follows: . . . .
untranslatable; + + + + + + + + missing; (?) variant reading; [ ] supplied by
the scholar-translator.

Anne Sexton 1928–1974

from **THE JESUS PAPERS**

Jesus Suckles

Mary, your great
white apples make me glad.
I feel your heart work its
machine and I doze like a fly.
I cough like a bird on its worm.
I'm a jelly-baby and you're my wife.
You're a rock and I the fringy algae.
You're a lily and I'm the bee that gets inside.
I close my eyes and suck you in like a fire.
I grow. I grow. I'm fattening out.
I'm a kid in a rowboat and you're the sea,
the salt, you're every fish of importance.

No. No.
All lies.
I am small
and you hold me.
You give me milk
and we are the same
and I am glad.

No. No.
All lies.
I am a truck. I run everything.
I own you.

Jesus Asleep

Jesus slept as still as a toy
and in His dream
He desired Mary.
His penis sang like a dog,
but He turned sharply away from that play
like a door slamming.
That door broke His heart
for He had a sore need.
He made a statue out of His need.
With His penis like a chisel
He carved the Pietà.
At this death it was important to have only one desire.
He carved this death.
He was persistent.
He died over and over again.
He swam up and up a pipe toward it,
breathing water through His gills.
He swam through stone.
He swam through the godhead
and because He had not known Mary
they were united at His death,
the cross to the woman,
in a final embrace,
poised forever
like a centerpiece.

Jesus Dies

From up here in the crow's nest
I see a small crowd gather.
Who do you gather, my townsmen?
There is no news here.
I am not a trapeze artist.
I am busy with My dying.
Three heads lolling,
bobbing like bladders.
No news.
The soldiers down below
laughing as soldiers have done for centuries.

No news.
We are the same men,
you and I,
the same sort of nostrils,
the same sort of feet.
My bones are oiled with blood
and so are yours.
My heart pumps like a jack rabbit in a trap
and so does yours.
I want to kiss God on His nose and watch Him sneeze
and so do you.
Not out of disrespect.
Out of pique.
Out of a man-to-man thing.
I want heaven to descend and sit on My dinner plate
and so do you.
I want God to put His steaming arms around Me
and so do you.
Because we need.
Because we are sore creatures.
My townsmen,
go home now.
I will do nothing extraordinary.
I will not divide in two.
I will not pick out My white eyes.
Go now,
this is a personal matter,
a private affair and God knows
none of your business.

Jesus Unborn

The gallowstree drops
one hundred heads upon the ground
and in Judea Jesus is unborn.
Mary is not yet with child.
Mary sits in a grove of olive trees
with the small pulse in her neck
beating. Beating the drumbeat.
The well that she dipped her pitcher into

has made her as instinctive as an animal.
Now she would like to lower herself down
like a camel and settle into the soil.
Although she is at the penultimate moment
she would like to doze fitfully like a dog.
She would like to be flattened out like the sea
when it lies down, a field of moles.
Instead a strange being leans over her
and lifts her chin firmly
and gazes at her with executioner's eyes.
Nine clocks spring open
and smash themselves against the sun.
The calendars of the world
burn if you touch them.
All this will be remembered.
Now we will have a Christ.
He covers her like a heavy door
and shuts her lifetime up
into this dump-faced day.

The Author of the Jesus Papers Speaks

In my dream
I milked a cow,
the terrible udder
like a great rubber lily
sweated in my fingers
and as I yanked,
waiting for the moon juice,
waiting for the white mother,
blood spurted from it
and covered me with shame.
Then God spoke to me and said:
People say only good things about Christmas.
If they want to say something bad,
they whisper.
So I went to the well and drew a baby
out of the hollow water.
Then God spoke to me and said:
Here. Take this gingerbread lady

and put her in your oven.
When the cow gives blood
and the Christ is born
we must all eat sacrifices.
We must all eat beautiful women.

COMMENTARY

I am not lazy. / I am on the amphetamine of the soul. / I am, each day, / typing out the God / my typewriter believes in. (A. S., "Frenzy") And she adds: *Very quick. Very intense, / like a wolf at a live heart.*

She emerged in the 1960s as one of the key American figures in the opening of woman's consciousness, seen as a force, a power, long suppressed, now forging its own forms. Its eruption in her work was pivotal—not as a fact already known but something still to be created: her struggle with her demon or *duende,* to find by that struggle a voice & place. Starting as a relatively conventional writer, she learned to roughen up her line (much like her thought), to use it as an instrument against the "politesse" of language (Paul Blackburn's term) that in domains like politics, religion, sexuality, "[had] wracked all passion from the sound of speech." Of the *womanness* inherent in a work like the well-known *In Celebration of My Uterus,* Muriel Rukeyser would later write: "[It is] one of the few poems in which a woman has come to the fact as symbol, the center after many years of silence and taboo . . . [an issue of] survival, piece by piece of the body, step by step of poetic experience, and even more the life entire." But once released, the rage of her imaginings began, as in *The Jesus Papers,* to reexamine & transform the other, sacred ikons of her world. "Would you mock God?" she asked of those attempts. And answered herself (too easily, perhaps): "God is not mocked except by believers."

Bernard Heidsieck b. 1928

from **DERVICHE / LE ROBERT**

The Letter "K"

(left track) (right track)

... But !... What was his name...? Anyway
!... Let's see!... O YES !... Oh yes !... JO-
SEPH... Joseph... ... **KACHA** !... NOOOoo
!... No way !... Absolutely not !... That's
not it !... Impossible !... And yet ... yet ... it
wasn't that era yet, the time of administra-
tive numbers !... So he had much more than
just a first name !... JOSEPH !... Joseph ...
Let's see !... let's see... !Joseph ?... **KAD-
SURA** !... There !... ABSOLUTELY !... Jo-
seph KADSURA !... YES !... Oh ! No, no
!... It doesn't ring a bell !... None whatso-
ever !... and yet !... at that date ... even ...
even without a bank statement !... He was
bound to have a profession, a job... thus an
identity... and ... and more than just a first
name !... By necessity !... So !... Or thus !...
What... But what could have been his name

muffled knocks   ?... But he himself, after all...did it bother   muffled knocks
on a door grow-   him ?... Did he even have the time or leisure   on a door grow-
ing louder &   to ?... Caught, cornered, pushed, manipu-   ing louder &
louder then   lated, jammed in ... as he was !... For sure,   louder then
                   progress, as of now, would demand that
                   one did... to him... OH !...Oh ! !la !la !...
                   It would, now, be out of the question for
Joseph K...!   him – the devil take these memory holes –
                   no longer to remember !... thus not to care
                   about the fact... very simple... that his
                   name could be – oh yes ! for example ! – I   Joseph K...!
                   don't know ! Joseph **KAEMPFERIE** !...
                   OH NO !... NO !... no !... It's not possible
                   !... It couldn't have been that !... ... That's
Joseph K...!   obvious !... Nothing could be more obvi-
                   ous !... WHY !... I don't know !... But it
                   seems obvious !... Maybe there was, on his
                   part, some kind of excess...excessive coy-
                   ness !... Which for sure he wouldn't have   Joseph K...!
                   permitted himself !... Never !... Because
                   there is, finally, in that name, imagined...

Joseph K...!

Joseph K...!

Joseph K...!

Joseph K...!

Joseph K...!

JOSEPH K!

projected... a slight festive connotation... **KAEMPFERIE** !... that would have been too strange... he would never have permitted !... Didn't he already have too much to deal with ... to fight off this constant flowering of attention that engulfed and intrigued him quite enough !... HE... still at that time... so far, however, from imagining... this possible proliferation yet to come... of forms, index cards, codes, electro-paraphernalia, electronic phonebooks, world-wide computers... And though already back then he felt himself to be–how to say?–who knows!–the object !... YES !... the object...of indiscrete attentions... of invisible, undefinable questionings... that would perhaps have been pleased, even satisfied, to find attached to his first name Joseph... a name like...let's see... **KAINITE**... for example !... ... Come on !... His name would never have been **KAINITE**... Joseph **KAINITE**... it doesn't make sense !... and much too much sound !... he would immediately, and rightly so, have been spotted !... and summoned !... and summoned again !... that's for sure... and much more !... Could he conceivably have taken that risk ?... Come on !... to flaunt himself thus !... to let himself be trapped under the cross-lights of meddlesome miradors !... That's exactly why–once and for all–he had decided to make of his name... his ultimate secret garden !... His last bullwark !... So why blare it out stupidly... at random... !... And thus if he had a name... (and he couldn't very well not have had one, after all !...) though ready to hide it... it could only be **KALMIE** !... His bearings were living proof of it ! Joseph **KALMIE** !... Lucid !... He was ! Certainly ! Submissive ! As much as on his guard !... Kalmos ... above all !... Not aware at that time–no matter how powerful his intuitions !...–what would be... what could be...–as much for him... as for many others... as we're at it !...–the turn of events... with its flowering

Joseph K...!

Joseph K...!

Joseph K...!

Joseph K...!

JOSEPH K!

JOSEPH K!

JOSEPH K! of habits... and its perfecting of customs !...
No ! Really !... How... How could he ?...
From which, however, it has to be deduced
that he could not have been **KALMIE** !...
But much more likely perhaps **KAMALA**
?... After all ?... In doubt !... And the am- JOSEPH K!
bient uncertainty, before all, which seemed
to surround him !... (That's the least one
can say !)...But one has to agree to put one-
self in his place !... His place at that mo-
ment !... Certainly our experience will have

JOSEPH K! been enriched – oh so much ! – since then !... JOSEPH K!
But would it permit us, in fact, to act any
differently from him... under the same cir- JOSEPH K!
cumstances ?... To behave completely dif-

JOSEPH K! ferently ?... Up to each, then, to surmise a
behavior which I, for one, simply refuse to
define or imagine !... **KAMOLA** ?... or else JOSEPH K!

JOSEPH K! !... Or **KAMI** !... Why not !... Joseph **KAMI**
! ... Well !... Who's to know !... And will it JOSEPH K!

JOSEPH K! ever be known ?... But before all, why sud-
denly insist on giving him a name ? a JOSEPH K!

JOSEPH K! proper name ? ... When – after his Joseph,
and before all after his "K"... – everyone
can, as seems fit, project alarm and phan-
tasms, hopes or catastrophes... and every-
thing else... ! Can in a way, name him for
himself – according to, according to – Jo-
seph **KAMICHI**, or Joseph **KANDJAR**, or
Joseph **KARBAU**... Everyone, yes, accord-
ing... according to, according... according

JOSEPH K! to ! JOSEPH K!

(Tonight I, for one, will simply have given
him, by way of names – and lacking any
better information – the first ten names I
didn't know under the letter "K" in the
Robert ...!)

(... as to whether they suit him... that's an-
other matter !... which he won't help us
elucidate either !)

NO COMMENT!...

Translation from the French by Pierre Joris

. . . Action Poetry is born from the moment the poem is torn from the page.
B. H.

In the name of which his own work—writing & performance—offered a series of tensions & an ongoing consideration of the MEANS or "tools" by which "the conception, the very 'fabrication' of the poem, can and must be thoroughly shaken up, and transformed." His context was the resurgence, post–World War II, of what came to be called *textsound* or (by Heidsieck, Henri Chopin, & others) *poésie sonore*—not so much an extension of the older "sound poetry" (though in part concurrent with it) as the exploration of a new language art pursued through a rapidly developing electronic technology: from tape recorder to synthesizer & from computer to CD-ROM, etc. (Heidsieck's alternative term, *poésie action* [action poetry], endowed the new poetry with the dynamics of his own brand of live-plus-recorded performance & with sound materials collaged from the *real*, surrounding world.) Writes Steve McCaffery (also speaking as performance poet): "In addition to their value as social comment, Heidsieck sees his sound texts existing within the domain of 'a ritual, ceremonial, or event' that assumes an interrogative stance vis à vis our daily wordscapes. The day to day is appropriated [as actual sound collage] and animated to make meaningful 'our mechanical and technocratic age by recapturing mystery and breath.'"

In *Derviche/Le Robert* (the name derived from that of the most authoritative of contemporary French dictionaries), Heidsieck writes a separate piece for each letter of the alphabet, incorporating in each piece the first ten words starting with that letter that are otherwise unknown to him. Section K, translated here, is "dedicated, naturally, to Franz Kafka and to his character Joseph K."—the ten k-words devoted in this instance to a basic act of naming.

For more of/on Heidsieck, see page 823, below.

Joyce Mansour 1928–1986

IN THE GLOOM ON THE LEFT

Why my legs
Around your neck
Tight neck-tie puffed dark blue
Same old entrance of the laughing crack
White olives of Christianity
Why should I wait in front of the closed door
Shy and beseeching passionate cello

Have children
Soak your gums with rare vinegars
The most delicate white is tainted with black
Your cock is smoother
Than a virgin's complexion
More provoking than pity
Feathered tool of incredible hubbub
Goodbye see you again it's done adieu
The longing for abundant blossoms is exhausted
Will come back
More vivid more violent
These mauve bonbons with their devoted swoons
Anxious and tetanus-like
The fervid nightmares of afternoon
Without you

Translation from the French by Molly Bendall

GOING AND COMING OF SEQUINS

It's much too cold to travel
Much too cold
It rained under the pink coat
Pink pink belly termite hill
Damp from stifled hair
Everyone knows that he's dead
(You know it
No)
I lied because she doesn't recognize the dead
Pink pink on her mouth and there under the navel
The small round head and pale sunken eyes
That turn while dreaming
In the turbulent whirlpool
Of hunger
It was cold in my mother's womb

The care
The vigilance
Even the eye falls apart
In front of the bed of a sick child

Too late much too late
He lets himself die
His bed my eyes
Drenched with sweat
That's why I loathe eau de Cologne
Aching fruitless cemetery perfume
Odor of the ground floor
Of an unzipped fly
With salt
Of night's foxglove scent
The Loth family roams in the garden
Without a calling card they didn't know how to join me
Behind the green shutters
Up on the balcony
In my chair made of dolls of wrinkled cornelian
Odd patient
The family makes eyes at my blue T-shirt
Swarms of gnats
Hang curtains on the sunset's walls
The hour of the pink crochet hook in the mesh of yarn
Tea
The old Scottish nurse
Darns the quilt
The English lawns and the little sweet peas
With her gentle spittle with her grand savoir-faire
Odd patient she grumbled
And death takes the path of an enema
In childhood
I remember the slaps
And fidgeting
The play of light
On my rarely covered bottom
My curlers
In the shower of gigantic drops
Your red mute helmet
So flatly placed
On the goat's ass
Vacations
I remember all that wasn't false love
Drowsiness of the East
Spastic hiccups
Fifty-year-olds or rug dealers

Why did I want to hold a child at arm's length
Why don't you love me a little
The way you swore to me
Between two rumps of the Pentecost
And the tame Mediterranean
The day when the hollow worn cliff
Was the mirror the butcher knife
And the vineyard
I like to make love leaning on a beast
Admire the movements of deadly soothsayers
Who shake up the ceiling with their gilded slippers
I like to take out the insides from the strongest genie
To display in full daylight
On crazy laces from Bruges
I like to swallow the mad from the Caucasus
Their sexes have the flavor of starvation

There was a time
A woman
A man
And also
Money
It isn't only the war
She tells him
Right in the eyes without upsetting the wall
You see that I'm very far
The child replaces the doll on my knees
I called him all night in the bowels of the metro
I long for my friend and his beautiful pink shadow
I was jealous of the lymphatic one
Her pretty pale eyes
Her gluttony
I thought of Germans heavy eaters of stars
I quivered from nervousness
The billboard was naughty
Pink pink the huge pool where my rage is in vogue
The pink coat
Of
The
Sea

Translation from the French by Mollie Bendall

Autocratic
Autocritiques
Autodidactic
Automastication
Automasticates
Autoerotics

(Autobiography provided by J. M.)

Of Egyptian origin, though born in England, Joyce Mansour spent most of her life in Paris, where from 1953 until her death in 1986 she published both poetry and prose narratives. Although allied to Surrealism—she had early & dithyrambic praise from André Breton & remained involved with the group's activities—her work exceeds the strictures of that movement, especially in relation to the latter's phallocentric eroticism. In her profoundly sexual & violent work, "labia, pubis, breasts, penis, testicles, sperm and menstrual blood dictate the perception of the text" (Serge Gavronsky). But the levels of the writing are necessarily multiple because "woven into the sexual aggression and savage eroticism of her powerful if bizarre images is the profoundly difficult question of speech and silence; of *jouissance* and *écriture*. If the cutting tongue in Mansour is analogous to the piercing phallus, it is also undeniably the instrument of trenchant and cutting language. The tongue is a *guitare deux manches,* so to speak. Thus, the man is dismembered leaf by leaf like an artichoke that the poet soaks in the black oil of her vituperation, and then 'licks and stabs with her poisoned tongue'" (Janis Pallister). This "verbal form of cannibalism" (so Gavronsky) is, however, also & simultaneously an anguished meditation on death & freedom, ferociously anchored in the black humor of the uprooted & eternally exiled.

Nathaniel Tarn b. 1928

from LYRICS FOR THE BRIDE OF GOD

Section: America: Seen as a Bird

The light in the skull of the bird
    tugging her down
        she'll fly by the rest of her life,
mirror of sky among leaves,
    in low grasses at morning,
        mirror of high sky in low and of heaven in high
          along the milky way—

her eye: the order of the heavens
            falling   /   falling with the weight of damp stars
                        down flocks of other birds
                        down through t.v. antennae
                                    funnel of space
                        above the house at last
                              great fields of light above her
            over Cape May
Birds in layers on the sky
a flock of certain birds above a flock of others and besides
            yet a third flock
            kettle of broadwing on the spiral air
                  cut to the quick by geese along the shore
                        and here the blackbirds scatter like ink-shot—
the sky has great depth
            the depth opens on without end higher and higher

            Alighieri describing the major angels as birds of God:

            Take here the little birds for the kingdom of heaven,
            the little birds for the banners of God—
and say what we love about them is simply the system:
that they are all of one set, yet different colored,
            id est—diversity within unity, heraldic counterpoint
            of certain colors where others are expected to be
—my dream as a child, the interchange of colors—
            what gives my mind peace, my mind peace, my mind peace

            immense fields of light traversed by angels

                        / / / over Cape May . . .

    II

Seeing her as a bird,
                  looking within that mind
for the cut of our sparks in each mirror shard,
her flight breaks over and over
                              as she tumbles down
      through cloud, through stricken dawn-dark, and bait and lure,
                                                      TO
      if she be (for example) that one-eyed falcon, sparrow-hawk,
            bird of the year,

so must in nest have lost
one half of strike-force within the head
yet falls on sodden sparrow in his trap
waiting her tear of talons and her take
his cheep towards
his and her father both.

We'll have, above all, her movement
and her descent, layer on layer,
through the bright cloud of our blood
and the exact description of her rapine
when she comes to fetch us
fingernail by fingernail

I mean   of course   talon.

Look long ago the sky had many birds
look long ago the sky had many colors
and now we have the chicken only
and the sparrow like an aerial rat.
We mourn like antiquarians for the world's colors
while the rest of the world makes do.

III

And she is bird, falling,
and I am bird, passing from behind that branch
to this branch in front of your eyes, and you are bird,
hopping to middle branches in a three-tiered forest
and he is bird flits to the first branch in the foreground of /
your alien life under heavenhome:

and they all mirror each other, looking with bright eye
periscope to the shard of the inner mind,
at the tone of your color today bright cousin,
and the shade of your tint tomorrow, bright female cousin—
and, by God, I think they talk, Alice would say that morning
as she broiled the two budgerigars side by side on a spit.

while the white heart of the sky, ignorant of all color
arched over, archangelical
throbs in restricted place
the pure white heart pulsating where it borned
with rims of mourning

Elánus leucúrus, minute particular,
Coyote Hills, on San Francisco Bay,
November seven-one (great bird of God)

goes into somersault
　　　revised and held thereafter
　and, looking down—
　　　　　buckle of elbow forward
　　　drag back of pinions in the wind
　　　　　slow crash at twilight angles—

(the planes in circles overhead, ever diminishing)

　slow fall to grasses like the dying snow.

COMMENTARY

I cannot, in motion, accept that America was built at all, ever. I accept that it is being built now, out of a sense of "our day." It is not we who killed instead of loving the Red Man: the night has white linings in some of these souls. Galileo? Science was never as dangerous to society as Poetry is about to be dangerous now.
N. T.

A truly international & cosmopolitan figure (born in France, raised in England, Belgium, & France, living in the U.S. since 1970), Tarn has been an anthropologist, publisher (he founded the Cape Goliard poetry series & the influential Cape Editions in Great Britain in the sixties), translator, & essayist as well as a poet. The "confluence of anthropology and poetics" led early on to concerns with ethnopoetics (& association with Jerome Rothenberg & Dennis Tedlock's journal *Alcheringa*), while (so Tarn himself) "a lifelong interest in religions and symbolic systems—primarily, but not exclusively, Classical, Judaeo-Christian, Mayan, and Buddhist—has been a very powerful motivating force" for his "angel of description" (the scientific work) & his "angel of creativity" (the poetry). Through much of the work the latter's voice has a double pitch: elegiac ("as a formal function of poetry concerned with the whole act of looking back") & lyric, what he calls "the forward function" arising from & in the very act of writing. In *Lyrics for the Bride of God* (excerpted here) the figure of the Bride represents the Shekhinah of the Jewish mystics, "the visible and audible manifestation of God's presence on earth" (Raphael Patai) that became, in the kabbalistic tradition, "that part of God Himself [that] is exiled from God" (Gershom Scholem) & in Tarn's poems undergoes further transformations (of gender, race, age, et cetera) & exilic conditions in an America that is both mythical & historical.

Hannah Weiner 1928 – 1997

TWO CODE POEMS FROM THE INTERNATIONAL CODE OF SIGNALS

QRD Light

LRG	Will you carry a light?
MPD	Will you make the land tonight?
LRM	I will carry a light
GDW	I see the land, land in sight
GDV	I have just lost sight of the land or light
MQC	Anything in sight?

CHW Pirates

CJD I was plundered by a pirate
CJF Describe the pirate
CJN She is armed
CJP How is she armed?
CJS She has long guns
CJW I have no long guns
BLD I am a complete wreck

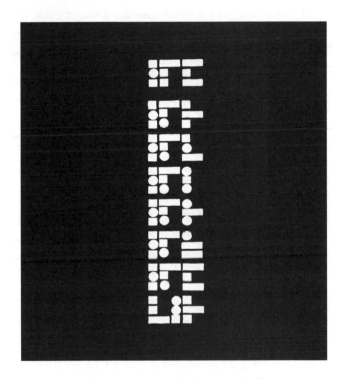

Mar 7 SIGNAL

JERRY'S HOME   TOLD YOU not to move the couch, hurt hip *leg tonight* why
can't I be sensible   No answer the phone says CHILDREN'S DINNER in the
call Jo Anne
same dirty black didn't really shampoo my hair just rinsed it that big publisher
was in find a tiny one NOS $D_{O_{N_T}}$ BARRY UNDERSTANDS in a reddish light
turn on the stove   NO STEVE $^T E_{A_T}$ BIG SURPRISE   CORNBEEF
SANDWICH   NO DINNER   ANNOUNCEMENT   PHILS SKIP A SPACE
PHILOSOPHY out of Phil Glass also FREE DELIVERY both slant up *get tired*
45 degree angle can't do it on the typewriter *3 mos jingle bells* EXPLAIN JER-
RY see JERRY again am waiting for 6 oclock when the rates get cheaper*cheaper*
JERRY started at 5:45 3 TIMES said the phone same black outline   Close
eyes, concentrate, CALL JERRY APOSTROPHE open eyes *graying hair* CHAC MOOL
wait for signal so many OH HANNAH'S but he had just left the house NOS
PERIODS   OUT TOMORROW *you need food   Just retype this original page*
MEET OUT OF THE FREEZER in pink letters about 18 inches off the floor
negative red letters it's not HIGH ENOUGH   Neither are the *negative* words
about 10 inches off the bedroom floor The words in the living room are eye level
higher I can't stand it TABLECLOTH 45 degrees the bedroom must be the least
BEAUTIFUL *honest* room *enough* COUNT 1 2 3 COUNTING says forehead
CHAC MOOL $_{J}E^{R}R_{Y}$ no answer bite your *periods fingernails* I am CHEER
UP OVALTINE^{J} IM- PORTANT NIGHT   SHUT UP   I'm *periods brace*
yourself going to eat dinner WRONG TIME about the level of the handles on the
cabinet of the sink didn't low income go to the membership meeting Cooper
Square Tues busy ALSO TUES DONT EAT WEDNESDAY IS $_PE^{C^{UL}I}A_R$
GIVE UP *prose* Ken is going SOLTANOFF to Yucatan BIG
VICTORY I've had another HOLY DAY AT THE TYPEWRITER Is Ken a
keen observor? The cat is on *my back* BACKWARDS I YOU DO HOWIE
very large SOLTANOFF says phone TOO LATE   YOUR MONEY   PROGRAM
NOT A SIMPLE ADDRESS NOT A MILLION DOLLARS CUPCAKE There's
so much interference while I wash the dishes USE SOAP Rosemary returns my
call Fri LUNCH OH HANNAH JUST CALL MOOL I'm going to rest
Go to Eliane's concert AT PHIL'S LEAVE A SPACE   LOW INCOME*furniture*
from Charlemagne's forehead, *not far from Phil oh Hannah*
talk to you don do it brace yourself   *just around the corner*
                                                  ta ta goodnight
A P O S T R O P H E

                              SORRY ABOUT THIS PAGE STUPID

SAND

daughter pail   slipper sale underwail
skip ertipertothewail   skip ertipertothehail
re marks my old mother died and she lied
across the veil   milage mail   skipertiperto the pail
well only one we daughters sung
mix up breed   well ill take her
no way scrail   we d rather flail scrail
empstem well i can do another if you scrail
well it takes some understan
now i sit upon the land
well i guess we end it do re me
now sister e is the simple one
what she spee   well gather and bespeak ye
joy to ye
whipperamerstam   well yer power gone
if we dont like your tongue
yer gotta be among   well the elders see
flakerstrake   rattlesnake   well its ok
tell him to close him mouth and take a hake
ferternertail is what i guess comes next
sister beat them to the last agree
twenty seven in the family   poetry
sake the strake and let it lake i gonna ate
well for me   ho we plant a tree
fermertail   we didnt get skrate
well i guess yer could use a cup
well stickerail   my pa did well say
mailerwail   contrail   cut the slail
striker piker mail yer learnuskail
well i met a flaw   stakerslaker and she bow
well whatchagot to meet   sancha feet
now which book yer visions see
it was the new   well okee
now the old one he i see
80 nearly 90
passed on old henry

I SEE words on my forehead   IN THE AIR   on the typewriter   on the page   These appear in the text in CAPITALS or italics.
H. W.

Her movement into avant-garde poetics began with works like the *Code Poems* (circa 1968), with its utilization of the set language of the International Code of Signals for the Use of All Nations, which both provided her with a vocabulary for the poems & with instruments like signal flags, semaphores, & Morse code for subsequent textart & performance versions. The poetry was later to change—radically—with the onset of an actual & persistent *experience* (as in the epigraph, above), an alteration of perception in which visible words entered her field of vision—as cause of wonder & as "messages" to be included in the written work that followed. The relationship of that experience to those of many traditional poet-mystics may also be worth noting—as when an anonymous thirteenth-century kabbalist (a follower of the great Hebrew mystic Abraham Abulafia) describes letters & words that "take the shape of great mountains" & other forms, to draw him thereby into sacred speech, etc. The lack of a similar context for Weiner's experiences may be seen as a condition of our time—on which no further comment.

Edward Dorn b. 1929

from **GUNSLINGER I**

I met in Mesilla
The Cautious Gunslinger
of impeccable personal smoothness
and slender leather encased hands
folded casually
to make his knock.
He would show you his map.

There is your domain.
Is it the domicile it looks to be
or simply a retinal block
of seats in,
he will flip the phrase
the theater of impatience.

If it is where you are,
the footstep in the flat above
in a foreign land
or any shimmer the city
sends you
the prompt sounds
of a metropolitan nearness
he will unroll the map of locations.

His knock resounds
inside its own smile, where?
I ask him is my heart.
Not this pump he answers
artificial already and bound
touching me
with his leathern finger
as the Queen of Hearts burns
from his gauntlet into my eyes.

   Flageolets of fire
he says there will be.
This is for your sadly missing heart
the girl you left
in *Juarez*, the blank
political days press her now
in the narrow adobe
confines of the river town
her dress is torn
by the misadventure of
            her gothic search

The mission bells are ringing
in Kansas.
Have you left something out:
Negative, says my Gunslinger,
no *thing* is omitted.
Time is more fundamental than space.
It is, indeed, the most pervasive
of all the categories
in other words
theres plenty of it.

And it stretches things themselves
until they blend into one,
so if youve seen one thing
youve seen them all.

I held the reins of his horse
while he went into the desert
to pee. *Yes*, he reflected
when he returned, that's less.

How long, he asked
have you been in this territory.

Years I said. Years.
Then you will know where we can have
a cold drink before sunset and then a bed
will be my desire
if you can find one for me
I have no wish to continue
my debate with men,
my mare lathers with tedium
her hooves are dry
Look they are covered with the alkali
of the enormous space
between here and formerly.
Need I repeat, we have come
without sleep from Nuevo Laredo.

And why do you have such a horse
Gunslinger? I asked. Don't move
he replied
the sun rests deliberately
on the rim of the sierra.

And where will you now I asked.
Five days northeast of here
depending of course on whether one's horse
is of iron or flesh
there is a city called Boston
and in that city there is a hotel
whose second floor has been let
to an inscrutable Texan named Hughes
Howard? I asked

The very same.
And what do you mean by inscrutable,
          oh Gunslinger?
I mean to say that He
has not been seen since 1833.

But when you have found him my Gunslinger
what will you do, oh what will you do?
You would not know
that the souls of old Texans
are in jeopardy in a way not common
to other men, my singular friend.

You would not know
of the long plains night
where they carry on
and arrange their genetic duels
with men of other states—
so there is a longhorn bull half mad
half deity
who awaits an account from me
back of the sun you nearly disturbed
just then.
Lets have that drink.

STRUM

strum
          And by that sound
we had come there, false fronts
my Gunslinger said make
the people mortal
and give their business
an inward cast. They cause culture.
Honk HONK, Honk HONK Honk
that sound comes
at the end of the dusty street,
where we meet the gaudy Madam
of that very cabaret going in
where our drink is to be drunk—
          Hello there, Slinger! *Long time*
no see
what brings you, who's your friend,

to these parts, and where
if you don't mind my asking, Hello,
are you headed . .

Boston!? you don't say, Boston
is an actionable town they say
never been there myself
Not that I mean to slight the boys
but I've had some nice girls
from up Boston way
they turned out real spunky!
But you look like you
always did *Slinger, you*
still make me shake, I mean
why do you think I've got my hand on
my hip if not to steady *myself*
and the way I twirl this
Kansas City parasol
if not to keep the dazzle
of them spurs outa my eyes
Miss Lil! I intervened
you mustn't slap my
Gunslinger on the back
in such an off hand manner
I think the sun, the moon
and some of the stars are
kept in their tracks
by this Person's equilibrium
or at least I sense some effect
on the perigee and apogee of all
our movements in this, I can't quite say,
man's presence, the setting sun's
attention I would allude to
and the very appearance
of his neurasthenic mare
a genuine Nejdee
lathered, as you can see, with abstract fatigue

Shit, Slinger! you still got that
marvelous creature, and who *is this*
funny talker, you pick him up

in some sludgy seat of higher
learnin, Creeps! you always did
hang out with some curious refugees.

[. . . . . . .]

In the Rush Hour begun in this hemisphere // . . . We will never really look
very good / We are too far gone on thought, and its rejections / The two
actions of a Noos
E. D.

Following a lead from Charles Olson (above), his teacher at Black Moun-
tain College, that "space is the central fact to man born in America," Dorn
started investigating the American West in a range of writings (primarily
poems, but also a novel, short stories, essays) culminating in the late sixties /
early seventies in his masterpiece, the comic epic *Gunslinger*. This quest nar-
rative relates the travels & travails of a group of characters (the gunslinger
himself; "I"—both pronoun & name—who dies but is preserved in Kool
Everything's LSD & later resurrects; a talking horse whose name oscillates
between Claude Lévi-Strauss & Heidegger; Lil, the archetypal saloon ma-
dam; & the poet, as singer/player of an "abso-lute,") in pursuit of Howard
Hughes (or Robart), who controls space & wealth via the "Cycle of Acqui-
sition" he has stashed in "his Enchanted Wallet." But by now "Time is more
fundamental than space," as the Slinger himself states, because (writes
Michael Davidson) "space, viewed as an extended field of discrete areas, is
closed; it has been bought up, appropriated and modified. Time, then, be-
comes the medium of the new, post-modern and post-Einsteinean man." Or,
as Dorn writes elsewhere: "The enclosure of the land leads directly to the
enclosure of the mind"—& to break that cycle of acquisition & misuse the
comic vision becomes essential because "Entrapment is this society's / Sole
activity, I whispered / and Only laughter, / can blow it to rags."

Adrienne Rich b. 1929

THE NINTH SYMPHONY OF BEETHOVEN
UNDERSTOOD AT LAST AS A SEXUAL MESSAGE

A man in terror of impotence
or infertility, not knowing the difference
a man trying to tell something

howling from the climacteric
music of the entirely
isolated soul
yelling at Joy from the tunnel of the ego
music without the ghost
of another person in it, music
trying to tell something the man
does not want out, would keep if he could
gagged and bound and flogged with chords of Joy
where everything is silence and the
beating of a bloody fist upon
a splintered table

THE PHENOMENOLOGY OF ANGER

1. The freedom of the wholly mad
to smear & play with her madness
write with her fingers dipped in it
the length of a room

which is not, of course, the freedom
you have, walking on Broadway
to stop & turn back or go on
10 blocks; 20 blocks

but feels enviable maybe
to the compromised

curled in the placenta of the real
which was to feed & which is strangling her.

2. Trying to light a log that's lain in the damp
as long as this house has stood:
even with dry sticks I can't get started
even with thorns.
I twist last year into a knot of old headlines
—this rose won't bloom.

How does a pile of rags the machinist wiped his hands on
feel in its cupboard, hour upon hour?
Each day during the heat-wave
they took the temperature of the haymow.
I huddled fugitive
in the warm sweet simmer of the hay

muttering: *Come.*

3. Flat heartland of winter.
The moonmen come back from the moon
the firemen come out of the fire.
Time without a taste: time without decisions.

Self-hatred, a monotone in the mind.
The shallowness of a life lived in exile
even in the hot countries.
Cleaver, staring into a window full of knives.

4. White light splits the room.
Table. Window. Lampshade. You.

My hands, sticky in a new way.
Menstrual blood
seeming to leak from your side.

Will the judges try to tell me
which was the blood of whom?

5. Madness. Suicide. Murder.
Is there no way out but these?
The enemy, always just out of sight
snowshoeing the next forest, shrouded
in a snowy blur, abominable snowman
—at once the most destructive
and the most elusive being
gunning down the babies at My Lai
vanishing in the face of confrontation.

The prince of air and darkness
computing body counts, masturbating
in the factory
of facts.

6. Fantasies of murder: not enough:
to kill is to cut off from pain
but the killer goes on hurting

Not enough. When I dream of meeting
the enemy, this is my dream:

white acetylene
ripples from my body
effortlessly released
perfectly trained
on the true enemy

raking his body down to the thread
of existence
burning away his lie
leaving him in a new
world; a changed
man

7. I suddenly see the world
as no longer viable:
you are out there burning the crops
with some new sublimate
This morning you left the bed
we still share
and went out to spread impotence
upon the world

I hate you.
I hate the mask you wear, your eyes
assuming a depth
they do not possess, drawing me
into the grotto of your skull

the landscape of bone
I hate your words
they make me think of fake
revolutionary bills
crisp imitation parchment
they sell at battlefields.

Last night, in this room, weeping
I asked you: *what are you feeling?*
do you feel anything?

Now in the torsion of your body
as you defoliate the fields we lived from
I have your answer.

8. Dogeared earth. Wormeaten moon.
A pale cross-hatching of silver
lies like a wire screen on the black
water. All these phenomena
are temporary.

I would have loved to live in a world
of women and men gaily
in collusion with green leaves, stalks,
building mineral cities, transparent domes,
little huts of woven grass
each with its own pattern—
a conspiracy to coexist
with the Crab Nebula, the exploding
universe, the Mind—

9. *The only real love I have ever felt*
was for children and other women.
Everything else was lust, pity,
self-hatred, pity, lust.
This is a woman's confession.
Now, look again at the face
of Botticelli's Venus, Kali,
the Judith of Chartres
with her so-called smile.

10. how we are burning up our lives
testimony:
> the subway
> hurtling to Brooklyn
> her head on her knees
> asleep or drugged

la vía del tren subterráneo
es peligrosa

> many sleep
> the whole way
> others sit
> staring holes of fire into the air
> others plan rebellion:
> night after night
> awake in prison, my mind
> licked at the mattress like a flame
> till the cellblock went up roaring

> Thoreau setting fire to the woods

Every act of becoming conscious
(it says here in this book)
is an unnatural act

COMMENTARY

If I thought of my words as changing minds, / hadn't my mind also to suf-fer changes? (A. R.) And again: *Returning home I had to ask myself: What happens to the heart of the artist, here in North America? What toll is taken of art when it is separated from the social fabric? How is art curbed, how are we made to feel useless and helpless, in a system which so depends on our alienation?*

Adrienne Rich's move from a middle-ground verse of closed form (& mind) to her open poetry of the late sixties & beyond is an exemplary narrative of a feminist poetics allied to wider radical urban politics (civil rights & anti-war demonstrations), leading her to a distinctly feminist social & cultural critique. While her 1971 book *The Will to Change* might seem to borrow not only its title but its stance toward verse (if not toward reality) from Charles Olson's line, "What does not change / is the will to change," the truer story, in her own terms, is that of a struggle with the "mental fragmen-

tation [that affects] . . . every group that lives under the naming and image-
making power of a dominant culture . . . and needs an art which can resist
it." The *resistance,* then, isn't Olson's so much as her own: the sudden onset
(she writes) "[of] something I had been hungering to do, all my writing life
[:] . . . to write directly and overtly as a woman, out of a woman's body and
experience, to take women's existence seriously as theme and source for
art. . . . It placed me nakedly face to face with both terror and anger; it did
indeed *imply the breakdown of the world as I had always known it, the end
of safety,* to paraphrase [James] Baldwin. . . . But it released tremendous
energy in me, as in many other women, to have that way of writing affirmed
and validated in a growing political community. I felt for the first time the
closing of the gap between poet and woman." The art that emerges from
this, whether wholly free of patriarchal text or not, takes the measure of her
world—& of her place within it—with a new force, a renewed authority.

Chinua Achebe b. 1930

BULL AND EGRET

At seventy miles an hour
one morning down the see-saw
road to Nsukka I came
upon a mighty bull
in form and carriage
so unlike Fulani cattle—
gaunt, high-horned, triangular
faced—that come in herded
multitudes from dusty savannahs
to the north . . . Heavy
was he, solitary dark
and taciturn, one of a tribe
they say fate has chosen
for slow extinction. At his heels
paced his egret, intent
praise-singer, pure white
all neck, walking high
stilts and yet no higher
than his master's leg-joint . . .
Odd covetousness indeed would

leave its boundless green estates
for a spell of petty trespassing
on perilous asphalt laid for me! . . . My
frantic blast of iron voice
shattered their stately march, then
recoiled brutally to my heart
as he gathered in hasty panic
the heaviness of his hind-
quarters, so ungainly in his
hurry, and flung it desperate
beyond my monstrous
reach. I should have felt unworthy then
playing such pranks on the noble
elder and watching his hallowed
waist-cloth come undone had not
his singer fared so well . . . Two
quick hops, a flap of
wings and he was
safe posture intact on
brown laterite . . . I could not
bear him playing so
faithfully my faithless agility-man, my
scrambler to safety, throat dilated
still by remnant praises
of his excellency high-headed
in delusion marching now alone
into death's ambush . . . We were
spared, the bull and I, in our separate follies . . .
His routed sunrise procession
no doubt would reform beyond the clamour
of my passage and sprightly
egret take up again
his broken adulation
of the bull, his everlasting
prince, his giver-in-abundance
of heavenly cattle-ticks.

WE LAUGHED AT HIM

We laughed at him our
hungry-eyed fool-man with itching
fingers who would see farther
than all. We called him
visionary missionary revolutionary
and, you know, all the other
naries that plague the peace, but
nothing would deter him.

With his own nails he cut
his eyes, scraped the crust
over them peeled off his priceless
patina of rest and the dormant
fury of his damned pond
broke into a cataract
of blood tumbling down
his face and chest . . . We
laughed at his screams the fool-man
who would see what eyes
are forbidden, the hungry-eyed
man, the look-look man, the
itching man bent to drag
into daylight fearful signs
hidden away for our safety
at the creation of the world.

He was always against
blindness, you know, our quiet
sober blindness, our lazy—he called
it—blindness. And for
his pains? A turbulent, torrential
cascading blindness behind
a Congo river of blood. He sat
backstage then behind his flaming red
curtain and groaned in
the pain his fingers unlocked, in the
rainstorm of blows loosed on his head
by the wild avenging demons he
drummed free from the silence of their
drum-house, his prize for big-eyed greed.

We sought by laughter to
drown his anguish . . . But suddenly
one day at height of noon his
screams turned to hymns of
ecstacy. We knew then his
pain had risen to the
brain and we took pity
on him the poor fool-man
as he held converse with
himself. We heard him say:
"My lord" to the curtain
of his blood, "I come to
touch the hem of your crimson
robe." He went stark mad thereafter
raving about new sights he
claimed to see, poor fellow; sights
you and I know are as impossible for this world
to show as for a hen to urinate—if one
may borrow one of his many crazy vulgarisms—
he raved about trees topped with
green and birds flying—yes actually
flying through the air—about
the sun and the moon and stars
and about lizards crawling on all
fours . . . But nobody worries much
about him today; he has paid
his price and we don't even
bother to laugh any more.

COMMENTARY

The universal creative rondo revolves on people and stories. People create
stories create people; *or rather,* stories create people create stories. *Was
it stories first and then people, or the other way around? Most creation
myths would seem to suggest the antecedence of stories — a scenario in
which the story was already unfolding in the cosmos before, and even as
a result of which, man came into being.*
C. A.

A poet & a storyteller aware of origins in many times & places, he found
his own way first in the Igbo village of Ogidi (Eastern Nigeria) & expanded
it in the telling to include the world. The work that brought him to promi-

nence consists largely of his fictions (*Anthills of the Savannah, Things Fall Apart, A Man of the People,* others), but he is also an essayist & social commentator—&, beyond it all, a poet. Caught up on the Biafran side during the struggles of the 1960s, he has spent much of the time since then abroad, including many years of residency in the United States. But it has been his genius throughout to nurture a "special view of history" (as Charles Olson once had it), thus to carry along & bring into its comparisons a particularly Igbo *Weltanschauung,* as when he writes (surely for *us* as well as *them*): "In popular contemporary usage the Igbo formulate their view of the world as: 'No condition is permanent.' In Igbo cosmology even the gods could fall out of use; and new forces are liable to appear without warning in the temporal and metaphysical firmament. The practical purpose of art is to channel a spiritual force into an aesthetically satisfying physical form that captures the presumed attributes of that force. It stands to reason, therefore, that new forms must stand ready to be called into being as often as new (threatening) forces appear on the scene. It is like 'earthing' an electrical charge to ensure communal safety."

SOME "BEAT" POETS

"Whooee . . . Here we go!" And he hunched over the wheel and gunned her; he was back in his element, everybody could see that. We were all delighted, we all realized we were leaving confusion and nonsense behind and performing our one and noble function of the time, **move.**

JACK KEROUAC, ON THE ROAD

There were certain of us [circa 1955] *(whether we were fearful or brave) who could not help speaking out — we had to speak. We knew we were poets and we had to speak out as poets. We saw that the art of poetry was essentially dead — killed by war, by academies, by neglect, by lack of love, and by disinterest. We knew we could bring it back to life. We could see what Pound had done — and Whitman, and Artaud, and D. H. Lawrence in his monumental poetry and prose.*

MICHAEL McCLURE, SCRATCHING THE BEAT SURFACE

The voice in the initial quote is Kerouac's, yet with an echo too from the century's first decade—of Marinetti's description of his sharklike poet's car ("more beautiful than the *Victory of Samothrace*") plunging through the electric Italian night, toward proclamation of a Futurist Manifesto & a poetry of "courage, daring, and revolt" (volume one, page 196). But the changes—following two world wars with their attendant twists of life & art—are also to be noted. The resultant "Beat movement" (a generationally defining Beat *moment,* as it seemed to some) was in fact the most public side of the second great eruption of a century-long poetics of resistance, not only in America but over an already present & expanding global network. The stance—played off against Korean War & Silent Generation "rage for order"—was one of defiance & despair, not unlike the "intensity" & "disgust" of Tzara's (circa 1916) Dadaist poetics. Here, however, another element—that of the vision quest as alternative (spiritual) journey—was forwarded, brought from the shadows to a place of central/pivotal concern: "something," said William Burroughs (who might—of all of them—be least concerned with it) "that millions of people of all nationalities all over the world were waiting to hear." To which he added more characteristically: "You can't tell anybody anything he doesn't know already."

While the Beat configuration *seems* clear, it doesn't at all points touch everyone associated with it, nor is there any point that isn't shared with other groupings then or now or in some less determined past. Its self-imposed name—like "Dada" before it—is a denial of conventional art & literature connections in favor of "a vision gleamed from the way we heard the word *beat,* meaning down and out but full of intense [spiritual, beatific] conviction." (Thus Kerouac by way of retrospection.) For this the idealized practice involved a kind of improvised, unmediated writing ("sketching," "wild form," "spontaneous prose," "bop prosody"), but with its sources more in 1950s jazz or action painting, say, than in Surrealism's Freud-inspired "automatic writing." (Compare this also to the immediacy of Charles Olson's call for a poetics of "embodiment" and a "projective verse," wherein "one perception must immediately and directly lead to a further perception.") Looked at after the fact, the Beat language-works—among those who were the principal practitioners—bear what Michael Davidson has called "the pervasive features of postwar poetry" (at least as viewed from the American side): "to recover the body in poetry through a return to speech rhythms, through the disordering of conventional syntax, through a lineation based on the breath." But what's also evident is the Americanizing & democratizing—on a virtually global scale—of many of the central issues of avant-garde modernism, including in the process the stance of "hipsterism" (drawing—often as parody—on Black American modes of resistance) that set the Beats apart from other, equally radical gestures in art & life.

Forty years after the censorship trial of Allen Ginsberg's *Howl* & the Six Gallery reading in San Francisco that both launched the movement & illuminated & extended the already active "San Francisco Renaissance," the universally acknowledged Beat writers remain Ginsberg, Corso, Kerouac, & Burroughs. (If the last two are best known as prose writers, the language experiments of both—Burroughs's Dada-derived cut-ups, say, or Kerouac's verse line in *Mexico City Blues*—have touched the work of numerous other poets.) Of the three others presented here (& only passingly connected to the central Beat poets), Michael McClure has also been prominent as a playwright (*The Beard* his best-known work for theater) & as the proponent of an ecological exploration of human/mammal identities & of a neo-sound poetry written in "beast language"; Diane di Prima has reinvestigated a range of magical/alchemical/linguistic practices & has created an epic re-presentation of feminist/goddess mythologizing, *Loba* (for which, see volume one); & Bob Kaufman was the author, circa 1960, of *The Abomunist Manifesto,* fusing his own (African American) sources with a still stronger sense of devastation—the *season in hell* of Rimbaud's prophecy & vision (volume one, page 42).

For more on poets with historical affiliations to the Beats, see the sections on Ginsberg, Gary Snyder, & Amiri Baraka, among others. But the larger field of recognition—in Snyder's terms—was in the "outcropping" in the decade after the Beats "of the Great Subculture which runs underground all through history[:] . . . the tradition that runs without break from Paleo-Siberian Shamanism and Magdalanean cave-painting; through megaliths and Mysteries, astronomers, ritualists, alchemists and Albigensians; gnostics and vagantes, right down to Golden Gate Park."

Such a vision, needless to say, goes beyond the Beats as such.

William S. Burroughs 1914-1997

This text arranged in my New York loft, which is the converted locker room of an old YMCA. Guests have reported the presence of a ghost boy. So this is a Oui-Ja board poem taken from *Dumb Instrument*, a book of poems by Denton Welch, and spells and invocations from the *Necronomicon*, a highly secret magical text released in paperback. There is a pinch of Rimbaud, a dash of St.-John Perse, an oblique reference to *Toby Tyler with the Circus*, and the death of his pet monkey.

FEAR AND THE MONKEY

Turgid itch and the perfume of death
On a whispering south wind
A smell of abyss and of nothingness
Dark Angel of the wanderers howls through the loft
With sick smelling sleep
Morning dream of a lost monkey
Born and muffled under old whimsies
With rose leaves in closed jars
Fear and the monkey
Sour taste of green fruit in the dawn
The air milky and spiced with the trade winds
White flesh was showing
His jeans were so old
Leg shadows by the sea
Morning light
On the sky light of a little shop
On the odor of cheap wine in the sailors' quarter
On the fountain sobbing in the police courtyards

On the statue of moldy stone
On the little boy whistling to stray dogs.
Wanderers cling to their fading home
A lost train whistle wan and muffled
In the loft night taste of water
Morning light on milky flesh
Turgid itch ghost hand
Sad as the death of monkeys
Thy father a falling star
Crystal bone into thin air
Night sky
Dispersal and emptiness.

Jack Kerouac 1922–1969

from MEXICO CITY BLUES

211th Chorus

The wheel of the quivering meat
                          conception
Turns in the void expelling human beings,
Pigs, turtles, frogs, insects, nits,
Mice, lice, lizards, rats, roan
Racinghorses, poxy bucolic pigtics,
Horrible unnameable lice of vultures,
Murderous attacking dog-armies
Of Africa, Rhinos roaming in the
                          jungle,
Vast boars and huge gigantic bull
Elephants, rams, eagles, condors,
Pones and Porcupines and Pills—
All the endless conception of living
                          beings

Gnashing everywhere in Consciousness
Throughout the ten directions of space
Occupying all the quarters in & out,
From supermicroscop no-bug
To huge Galaxy Lightyear Bowell
Illuminating the sky of one Mind—
    Poor! I wish I was free
    of that slaving meat wheel
    and safe in heaven dead

Bob Kaufman   1925–1986

I AM A CAMERA

THE POET NAILED ON
THE HARD BONE OF THIS WORLD,
HIS SOUL DEDICATED TO SILENCE
IS A FISH WITH FROG'S EYES,
THE BLOOD OF A POET FLOWS
OUT WITH HIS POEMS, BACK
TO THE PYRAMID OF BONES
FROM WHICH HE IS THRUST
HIS DEATH IS A SAVING GRACE

CREATION IS PERFECT

"ALL THOSE SHIPS THAT NEVER SAILED"

All those ships that never sailed
The ones with their seacocks open
That were scuttled in their stalls . . .
Today I bring them back
Huge and intransitory
And let them sail
Forever.

All those flowers that you never grew—
   that you wanted to grow
The ones that were plowed under
   ground in the mud—
Today I bring them back
And let you grow them
Forever.

All those wars and truces
Dancing down these years—
All in three flag-swept days
Rejected meaning of God—

My body once covered with beauty
Is now a museum of betrayal.
This part remembered because of that one's touch
This part remembered for that one's kiss—
Today I bring it back
And let you live forever.

I breathe a breathless I love you
And move you
Forever.

Remove the snake from Moses' arm . . .
And someday the Jewish queen will dance
Down the street with the dogs
And make every Jew
Her lover.

JANUARY 30, 1976: MESSAGE TO MYSELF

It is the time of illusion and reality,
Russia deliberately creates the illusion of wanting peace,
While preparing feverishly for war.
The slogans used by Communism are based on a desire for peace,
They are illusionary, for they are desiring an atmosphere for war.

The U.N. wants peace, but it must be careful
Not to compromise itself by settling for peace
At any cost. The West cannot rest easy, for Russia is
Anxious for war, while Russia cannot risk a unified Germany.
All the contradictions of the situation heighten the
Dangers of war.

The Ancient Rain is falling. It is falling on the N.A.T.O. meetings,
It is falling in Red Square. Will there be war or peace?
The Ancient Rain knows, but does not say.
I make speculations of my own, but I do not discuss them
Because the Ancient Rain is falling.

The Ancient Rain is falling all over America now.
The music of the Ancient Rain is heard everywhere.

Allen Ginsberg 1926–1997

AMERICA

America I've given you all and now I'm nothing.
America two dollars and twentyseven cents January 17, 1956.
I can't stand my own mind.
America when will we end the human war?
Go fuck yourself with your atom bomb.
I don't feel good don't bother me.
I won't write my poem till I'm in my right mind.
America when will you be angelic?
When will you take off your clothes?
When will you look at yourself through the grave?
When will you be worthy of your million Trotskyites?
America why are your libraries full of tears?
America when will you send your eggs to India?
I'm sick of your insane demands.
When can I go into the supermarket and buy what I need with my good
    looks?
America after all it is you and I who are perfect not the next world.
Your machinery is too much for me.

You made me want to be a saint.

There must be some other way to settle this argument.

Burroughs is in Tangiers I don't think he'll come back it's sinister.

Are you being sinister or is this some form of practical joke?

I'm trying to come to the point.

I refuse to give up my obsession.

America stop pushing I know what I'm doing.

America the plum blossoms are falling.

I haven't read the newspapers for months, everyday somebody goes on
    trial for murder.

America I feel sentimental about the Wobblies.

America I used to be a communist when I was a kid I'm not sorry.

I smoke marijuana every chance I get.

I sit in my house for days on end and stare at the roses in the closet.

When I go to Chinatown I get drunk and never get laid.

My mind is made up there's going to be trouble.

You should have seen me reading Marx.

My psychoanalyst thinks I'm perfectly right.

I won't say the Lord's Prayer.

I have mystical visions and cosmic vibrations.

America I still haven't told you what you did to Uncle Max after he came
    over from Russia.

I'm addressing you.

Are you going to let your emotional life be run by Time Magazine?

I'm obsessed by Time Magazine.

I read it every week.

Its cover stares at me every time I slink past the corner candystore.

I read it in the basement of the Berkeley Public Library.

It's always telling me about responsibility. Businessmen are serious.
    Movie producers are serious. Everybody's serious but me.

It occurs to me that I am America.

I am talking to myself again.

Asia is rising against me.

I haven't got a chinaman's chance.

I'd better consider my national resources.

My national resources consist of two joints of marijuana millions of geni-
    tals an unpublishable private literature that jetplanes 1400 miles an
    hour and twentyfive-thousand mental institutions.

I say nothing about my prisons nor the millions of underprivileged who
    live in my flowerpots under the light of five hundred suns.
I have abolished the whorehouses of France, Tangiers is the next to go.
My ambition is to be President despite the fact that I'm a Catholic.

America how can I write a holy litany in your silly mood?
I will continue like Henry Ford my strophes are as individual as his auto-
    mobiles more so they're all different sexes.
America I will sell you strophes $2 500 apiece $500 down on your old
    strophe
America free Tom Mooney.
America save the Spanish Loyalists
America Sacco & Vanzetti must not die
America I am the Scottsboro boys.
America when I was seven momma took me to Communist Cell meetings
    they sold us garbanzos a handful per ticket a ticket costs a nickel and
    the speeches were free everybody was angelic and sentimental about
    the workers it was all so sincere you have no idea what a good thing
    the party was in 1835 Scott Nearing was a grand old man a real
    mensch Mother Bloor the Silk-strikers' Ewig-Weibliche made me cry I
    once saw the Yiddish orator Israel Amter plain. Everybody must have
    been a spy.
America you don't really want to go to war.
America it's them bad Russians.
Them Russians them Russians and them Chinamen. And them Russians.
The Russia wants to eat us alive. The Russia's power mad. She wants to
    take our cars from out our garages.
Her wants to grab Chicago. Her needs a Red *Reader's Digest.* Her wants
    our auto plants in Siberia. Him big bureaucracy running our
    fillingstations.
That no good. Ugh. Him make Indians learn read. Him need big black
    niggers. Hah. Her make us all work sixteen hours a day. Help.
America this is quite serious.
America this is the impression I get from looking in the television set.
America is this correct?
I'd better get right down to the job.
It's true I don't want to join the Army or turn lathes in precision parts
    factories, I'm nearsighted and psychopathic anyway.
America I'm putting my queer shoulder to the wheel.

Gregory Corso b. 1930

THE MAD YAK

I am watching them churn the last milk
　they'll ever get from me.
They are waiting for me to die;
They want to make buttons out of my bones.
Where are my sisters and brothers?
That tall monk there, loading my uncle,
　he has a new cap.
And that idiot student of his—
　I never saw that muffler before.
Poor uncle, he lets them load him.
How sad he is, how tired!
I wonder what they'll do with his bones?
And that beautiful tail!
How many shoelaces will they make of that!

TRANSFORMATION & ESCAPE

I

I reached heaven and it was syrupy.
It was oppressively sweet.
Croaking substances stuck to my knees.
Of all substances St. Michael was stickiest.
I grabbed him and pasted him on my head.
I found God a gigantic fly paper.
I stayed out of his way.
I walked where everything smelled of burnt chocolate.
Meanwhile St. Michael was busy with his sword
hacking away at my hair.
I found Dante standing naked in a blob of honey.
Bears were licking his thighs.
I snatched St. Michael's sword
and quartered myself in a great circular adhesive.
My torso fell upon an elastic equilibrium.
As though shot from a sling
my torso whizzed at God fly paper.

My legs sank into some unimaginable sog.
My head, though weighed with the weight of St. Michael,
did not fall.
Fine strands of multi-colored gum
suspended it there.
My spirit stopped by my snared torso.
I pulled! I yanked! Rolled it left to right!
It bruised! It softened! It could not free!
The struggle of an Eternity!
An Eternity of pulls! of yanks!
Went back to my head,
St. Michael had sucked dry my brainpan!
Skull!
My skull!
Only skull in heaven!
Went to my legs.
St. Peter was polishing his sandals with my knees!
I pounced upon him!
Pummeled his face in sugar in honey in marmalade!
Under each arm I fled with my legs!
The police of heaven were in hot pursuit!
I hid within the sop of St. Francis.
Gasping in the confectionery of his gentility
I wept, caressing my intimidated legs.

2

They caught me.
They took my legs away.
They sentenced me in the firmament of an ass.
The prison of an Eternity!
An Eternity of labor! of hee-haws!
Burdened with the soiled raiment of saints
I schemed escape.

Lugging ampullae its daily fill
I schemed escape.
I schemed climbing impossible mountains.
I schemed under the Virgin's whip.
I schemed to the sound of celestial joy.
I schemed to the sound of earth,
the wail of infants,
the groans of men,
the thud of coffins.
I schemed escape.
God was busy switching the spheres from hand to hand.
The time had come.
I cracked my jaws.
Broke my legs.
Sagged belly-flat on plow
on pitchfork
on scythe.
My spirit leaked from the wounds.
A whole spirit pooled.
I rose from the carcass of my torment.
I stood on the brink of heaven.
And I swear that Great Territory did quake
when I fell, free.

Michael McClure b. 1932

from **GHOST TANTRAS**

15

THE TREES ARE ELEPHANTS' HEADS.
The brown whorls of hair at the top of your head.
The trees are gray-green grooooor greyeeee.
AMM SOOOTEEE AIEE! GAROOOOOOOOOOH.
Gragg. Hrahhrr mok now-toony. Bwooooooh.
Groooor. MARRRR! GROOOOH! Grooooooor.
GAHROOOOOOOOOOOOOOOOOOOOOOH!
GAHROOOOOOOOOOOOOOOOOOOOOH!
MOMM.
Hraghhrr.
GROOOOOOOOH!
Mowk-towr-noowth-own-eii!
FACE,
TUSK,
WHAHHH!
GAHHROOOOOOOO!!
LUKK!

49

SILENCE THE EYES! BECALM THE SENSES!
Drive drooor from the fresh repugnance, thou whole,
thou feeling creature. Live not for others but affect thyself
from thy enhanced interior—believing what thou carry.
Thy trillionic multitude of grahh, vhooshes, and silences.
Oh you are heavier and dimmer than you knew
and more solid and full of pleasure.
Grahhr! Grahhhr! Ghrahhhrrr! Ghrahhr. Grahhrrr.
Grahhrr-grahhhhrr! Grahhr. Gahrahhrr Ghrahhhrrrr.
Ghrarrrr. Ghrahhr! Ghrarrrrr. Gharrrr. Ghrahhhrr.
Ghrahhrr. Ghrahr. Grahhr. Grahharrr. Grahhrr.
Grahhhhr. Grahhhr. Gahar. Ghrahhr. Grahhr. Grahhr.
Ghrahhr. Grahhhr. Grahhr. Gratharrr! Grahhr.
Ghrahrr. Ghraaaaaaahrr. Grhar. Ghhrarrr! Grahhrr.
Ghrahrr. Gharr! Ghrahhhhr. Grahhrr. Ghraherrr.

A SMALL SECRET BOOK

1. *FOR LAMANTIA*

> YES GOD THE DESIRE HANGS THERE UNFILLED TURNS INTO
> SMOKE!!
> I TURN AND FLY BEFORE IT, AFRAID OF THE HIDDEN.
>
> What will I do, fill my mouth with sweetness? Turn down
> the love? Whip myself with fear? Afraid
> of the scared.
> Twist in the midst of a seventeenth century
> pink concetto? The pink heart
> flies into (making) a cloud, the eye
> heaves and backs in fear, trembling!
> SAY INSTEAD HOW THE SHARK FEELS. OH
> I am sick!!
> Christ, God, Lamb release
> the pressures.
> Empty me from woodenness to bitterness!!
> FILL THE LAST BLACK HEART.

2.

> OH CHRIST GOD LOVE CRY OF LOVE STIFLED FURRED WALL
> SMOKING BURNING
> who am I that I feel pain so? What is the flower
> before my eyes that I call it fire. Nasturtium,
> why the twist of petals why the writhe of the pale green
> stem? Why do I see you and feel lamb. Why are you the
> shark that moves out upon me? Why are you flame
> that you burn me. What is love
> that I fly from the feel of it. Why am I filled
> with the soft wool pressure? Oh what is pain
> THAT IT ALL FLOWS
> that I move in my aching sleep?
> that I censor, censor, censor. BLESS ME.
> Pour me into the soft arms that I am
> ever stiff.

3.

The shark is the lamb. The killer whale the lover.
WHAT IS THE OH FORM OH, OH SHAPE OF BLACK LOVE.
WHAT IS MY HEART
that I run from it? What is love that I pull
myself to meat to hide from it. Where is the fear
of pride leading me?? Oh what are your breasts on
my arm? That
I weaken beneath them? Oh why are you so light
and I so heavy?
Why do I make myself a phantom before your anxious stare?

5 25 59

What is the dream I have of you? Why do I lock my cock
and heart from you? What is Heart? Why do I hold
the movement down. Why do I twist and turn so? I
move out to you. Why do I want you so
that I am sickened? So much I want you. What
do I hold within that tears
me. Why do I lean in weakness against the blade
of myself? Why are your breasts so light
on my arm.

5 25 59

4.

OH CHRIST OH GOD OH FUCKING SHIT OH SHIT SHAPED
PAIN OF LOVE!
Oh unpulsing pressure outward against my ribs
and stomach against the soft muscle and bone
showing how weak I am that I lose myself before
it relenting and weak, speechless. Only
eyes pleading to the smoke rolling out of my
mouth. I stare from my blue cloud.
EYES STARING FROM MY BLUE CLOUD
Do you see me in sadness and love?!

Traitor to my mean grasp for you! Fake
to what is black and felt. Stifling
the urge to love you to death. To kiss
you and eat your soft skin.
To roll in juicy Eros. To
turn to roiling merry flesh!
BLESS ME
FOR WHAT I FEEL IS WEAKNESS AND IT SWELLS
in me turning to weakness
becoming huge. Love devouring
love and swelling unfelt huge and pours
or seeps out finally. I who am
blessed am unblessed. Oh. Oh. oh.
LOVELY WOMAN.

Diane di Prima b. 1934

PROPHETISSA

Two from One
Three from Two
and out of the Three
the Four, as the first
    MARIA THE PROPHET
    (SECOND-CENTURY ALCHEMIST)

Two from One:

know this wind as
               fire.   Flame
at the heart of stone.
              Leaping arc
from black dwarf star that spins
the double helix.   And know

this fire as talk.   The word.

Bursting in cunt or asshole
                     bursting
in cupped & tensing mouth
                 The
fucking word.   Heartfire of stars as they
circle & lean toward touch
                   hold orbit
spiraling
        & reach

Three from Two:

Bent
       like bow.   This is
the dream of the triangle.   Pyramid.
The Work
            crosses the first veil.   Sways
the double star.
         Draws space aside just
enough
     for the other to shine.
           As thru a pinprick
in a black curtain.
         Wind
against our hearts
         & we dance & know
again
     he is Other
         than fire.

**& out of the Three
the Four, as One:**

this is the Mystery of which we
are metaphor. Or the uni-
verse   4-square founded
stretched out on cross of matter
in the Light.

         Filtering colors   red
green   blue   & other
than the winds.
The elements are other than the winds.
& not so easily fooled.
                    Placated.

This suspension
                of particles of time
in an emptiness.
                When have we known it
except alone?   & so it is
                  & is not
Real
    to us.
        It is the root of love.
The four as one.

           I mirror
you
       whom you love   you mirror
etc   & yet
              we spin binary
exquisite
        pure as a quasar.
               We are the
mystery of which
         this is metaphor
O breathe
       against my skin.

STUDIES IN LIGHT

claritas:

sun
     caught in dew
flashing
a   shapeliness
we stand outside of

candor:

light
        a chorus swelling
filling out
the contours of architecture
cathedral
palace
           theatre

lumen:

light
as a glyph that writes itself
over & over, on the face
of water, inscrutable
perpetual motion

lux:

needle point
moving out
from core
of earth
thinnest
piercing   rays

Kamau Brathwaite b. 1930

STONE

for Mikey Smith 1954–1983
stoned to death on Stony Hill, Kingston

When the stone fall that morning out of the johncrow sky

it was not dark at first . that opening on to the red sea humming
but something in my mouth like feathers . blue like bubbles
carrying signals & planets & the sliding curve of the
world like a water pic. ture in a raindrop when the pressure. drop

When the stone fall that morning out of the johncrow sky

i couldn't cry out because my mouth was full of beast & plunder
as if i was gnashing badwords among tombstones
as if that road up stony hill. round the bend by the church
yard . on the way to the post office . was a bad bad dream

& the dream was like a snarl of broken copper wire zig zagg.
ing its electric flashes up the hill & splitt. ing spark & flow.
ers high. er up the hill . past the white houses & the ogogs bark.
ing all teeth & fur. nace & my mother like she up . like she up.

like she up. side down up a tree like she was scream.
like she was scream. like she was scream. in no & no.
body i could hear could hear a word i say. in . even though
there were so many poems left & the tape was switched on &

runn. in & runn. in &
the green light was red & they was stannin up there &
evva. where in london & amsterdam & at unesco in paris &
in west berlin & clapp. in & clapp. in & clapp. in &

not a soul on stony hill to even say amen

■

& yet it was happenin happenin happenin

the fences begin to crack in i skull .
& there was a loud boodoooooooooooooooooooooooongs like
guns going off . them ole time magnums .

or like a fireworks a dreadlocks was on fire .
& the gaps where the river comin down
inna the drei gully where my teeth use to be smilin .
& i tuff gong tongue that use to press against them & parade

pronunciation . now unannounce & like a black wick in i head &
dead .
& it was like a heavy heavy riddim low down in i belly . bleedin dub
& there was like this heavy heavy black dog thump. in in i chest &

pump. in

murderrrrrrrrrrrrrrrrrrrrrrrrrrrrrrrrrrrrrrrrrrrrrrrrrrrrrrrrrrrr

& i throat like dem tie. like dem tie. like dem tie a tight tie a.
round it. twist. in my name quick crick . quick crick .
& a nevva wear neck. tie yet .

& a hear when de big boot kick down i door . stump
in it foot pun a knot in de floor. board .
a window slam shat at de back a mi heart .

de itch & oooze & damp a de yaaad
in my silver tam. bourines closer & closer .
st joseph marching bands crash. in & closer . &

bom si. cai si. ca boom ship bell . bom si. cai si. ca boom ship bell

& a laughin more blood & spittin out
lawwwwwwwwwwwwwwwwwwwwwwwwwwwwwwwwwwwwwwwwwwwwwd

i two eye lock to the sun & the two sun starin back black
from de grass

& a bline to de butterfly fly. in

■

& it was like a wave on stony hill caught in a crust of sun.
light

■

& it was like a matchstick schooner into harbour muffled in the
silence of it wound

■

& it was like the blue of speace was filling up the heavens
wid its thunder

& it was like the wind was grow. in skin. the skin had hard hairs
harderin

■

it was like marcus garvey rising from his coin .
stepping towards his people crying dark

& every mighty word he trod. the ground fall dark & hole
be. hine him like it was a bloom x. ploding sound .

my ears was bleed. in sound

■

& i was quiet now because i had become that sound

the sun. light morning washed the choral limestone harsh
against the soft volcanic ash. i was

& i was slippin past me into water. & i was slippin past me
into root. i was

& i was
slippin past me into flower. & i was rippin upwards

into shoot. i was

& every politrician tongue in town was lash.
ing me with spit & cut. rass wit & ivy whip & wrinkle jumbimum

it was like warthog . grunt. in in the ground

& children running down the hill run right on through the splash
of pouis that my breathe. ing make when it was howl & red &

bubble

& sparrow twits pluck tic & tap. worm from the grass
as if i man did nevva have no face. as if i man did never in this

place

■

When the stone fall that morning out of the johncrow sky

i could not hold it brack or black it back or block it off or limp
away or roll it from me into memory or light or rock it steady
into night. be

cause it builds me now with leaf & spiderweb & soft & crunch &
like the pow.
derwhite & slip & grit inside your leather. boot &

fills my blood with deaf my bone with hobbledumb & echo.
less neglect neglect neglect neglect &

lawwwwwwwwwwwwwwwwwwwwwwwwwwwwwwwwwwwwww

■

i am the stone that kills me

*it was as if my spirit was waking up in the middle of a very dark night as if
I was alone in a wood of presences and powers vague enraged potentiali-
ties I could not see or name.*

K. B.

Poet & cultural thinker, Brathwaite has a hold on history & self that ranges
from images of black diasporas along the "middle passage" between Africa
& the Caribbean to later outcries & Job-like visions in the aftermath of
personal losses (death & sickness, natural disasters, senseless beatings) suf-
fered by himself & others. The range of the work is therefore stunning, as
are the innovations that he needs—& thus invents—to bring it home. As
his first turning from (or deepening of) a strictly Anglo-Caribbean context,
he becomes a major proponent of the use of "nation language" (page 485)
in the work of poetry—not dialect or creole merely ("thought of as 'bad'
English") but that difference in syntax, in rhythm and timbre ("its own
sound explosion"), "that is more closely allied to the African experience in
the Caribbean." Yet his work is also "'modernist' in inspiration and in-
volve[s] an open-endedness, an inconclusiveness and a tendency to revise,
transform and depart from the shape of [its] traditional and engendering
mythologies." (Thus: his friend & colleague Gordon Rohlehr.)

In Brathwaite's later work—as here—he is still more the modernist/
postmodernist: an innovator not only on the poem's vocal/verbal side but
in the ways of showing it in print. The mode at issue is what Brathwaite calls
his "video style": an exploration (Rohlehr again) of "the capacity of the
computer for graphic rendition of the nuances of language." More than a
matter of typefaces & fonts (that much an easy take-off from the computer's
givens), his experiments include the random breaking-up of words, deliber-
ate misspellings, periods put in in place of commas, "brackets, asterisks,
abbreviations and various symbols . . . used sometimes with, sometimes
without, clear purpose." The "arbitrariness in the appearance of the text"
becomes an expression of the arbitrariness (in history, in dream) depicted in
his poems & fictions.

In *Stone*, the central, senselessly martyred figure is the great Jamaican oral
poet Michael Smith, whose work Brathwaite has elsewhere transcribed.

Michel Deguy b. 1930

"O GREAT APPOSITION OF THE WORLD"

O great apposition of the world

a rose field near a wheat field and two red
children in the field bordering on the rose field and a corn field near the
wheat field and two old willows where they join; the song of two rose
children in the wheat field near the rose field and two old willows keeping
watch over the roses the wheat the red children and the corn

The blue blots like a spot
The white ink of clouds
Children are also my
Country path

Translation from the French by Clayton Eshleman

"YOU WILL BE ASTONISHED"

You will be astonished to hear the freedom of Paul
Corinthians II: 11, 19–33; 12, 1–9
One's hearing brought up since birth on rhythm
Hears "this name in which I silently believe"
The iamb rises and falls in the house

(N'gao southwest where the mistresses sleep
Among grain which is hatched by the grain
Luther and the N'zakara bards
Fall into agreement on cuisine)

The man in an alb Sunday surpassed
Extols a crusade big as a man hunt
Which the Rennes-Raspail intersection jams

Translation from the French by Clayton Eshleman

"THIS LADY AND HER BEAUTIFUL WINDOW"

to M.

      This lady and her beautiful window
An asymmetrical angel with wind-bearing wings
           was saying I greet you

      Love distinguished absence and death

In fully dimensional life with no hope of dying
You are so much a woman that you come forth as a woman

May Beatrice also be the one time touches a hair of
This imaginary woman who chose my sign

My augury took her by surprise in the Botticelli
Fire flakes of her day gown enveloped in odors (petrels and gannets from
   Bassan cultivate the wall that edges the sea)
She is what plucks him from the fray
It is enough for him to receive her greeting
He no longer hates he loves

Slow is recognition and that those children succeed us and slow the
   sweetness of a good act or of a bend in the Loire and the Loir

Translation from the French by Clayton Eshleman

TO FORGET THE IMAGE

   I have looked at you as Christ, imagine, Veronica and they separated
each with the scalped face of the other
   Their *thou* does not date from this conventional poem

   Moored to this beauty so close to you, the shopsign of hair banging
around as if in a street of birth, my eyes tumified me

   The bandage of nights will drain me, I will scatter your ashes; will shoo
away your curves, your figure of an inverted "muse" in this found out
young woman who was seeking poetry among the very men who usurp it,
your age of an inverse ignorant muse reincarnated older in every age
   the linen shreds of night heal me, your face dies away, your teeth bridle
me less each morning since this morning

And what were we talking about among the others, everyone pretending that beauty was self-evident, like your skin looking very beautiful (like a piece of work) goes about itself among this pretensive we

(Frost on the finished bone structure, your greyish-brown forehead,
The blue headband of eyes at mid-face,
Temples versant and walls incunabula over
The patent mouth and the immortal teeth,
Trapezoids toward the breasts perhaps, and the drawn back sex)

Tomorrow evening the muteness of our stage whisper dies out, I no longer wear the ringlets of Cathar murmur by my ears

. . . and of what were we speaking pretending not to fix beauty like an oblique species that our mimed distraction would not bother, or because there no longer is any beauty, or because beauty has to learn equal footing, but allowing stealth to take care of gathering beauty to your side

allowing your face to pass behind your collar, your face to continue behind so little wool everywhere invisible, a millimeter of linen forbids your skin which goes up wrists and tibias again to rejoin versants under the wool, to stick to you

And troubled men mechanically invited you, whom your oblique presentation or yourself without make-up like a piece of bark enamored, mayor or president, speaking to not say that you were holding a meeting more open than one of theirs

In spite of the body like Casanova you wanted to know, to learn, to change, but your hair that a gravity in your service spread without respite like a spring across its stone, was betraying you, and the impoverished imagination was catching the wound of your endemic face

The tampon of night, I know, will drain the eyes injected with you, at last I will try to remind myself that you were without ever having been blue companion from station to station

The strange law to not love, that timidity occults with its likeness, will relax its constraint, and the eclipse total through your image will eclipse in a poem

the hard law to not love leaves our vassalage, migrates in the neighboring compartment, forgets itself in a poem

"I search for my words"

Translation from the French by Clayton Eshleman

COMMENTARY

Poetry is not alone. What counts are the relations it has with itself, and as a result of which it is. In relation to these confrontations, rivalries, jealousies, and comparisons that it has, for instance, with music, with philosophy, with painting. That is everything that was once called ut pictura poesis, ut musica poesis. . . .
M. D.

Although linked to the great French tradition of avant-garde poetries (Rimbaud, Mallarmé, Breton, Michaux), Deguy "just as obviously breaks with it. His subjects; the roughness and prosiness of his music; the inclusion of odd words, rare, scientific, foreign, even of numerals; the changes in tone; the air of being unfinished and unresolved" (Kenneth Koch). Deguy's work relies less than earlier modernisms on dream & the unconscious as vectors of his poetic process; rather, it is the inscription into the poem of theoretical thought that (so Max Loreau in his book on Deguy) "guarantees poetry's infinite movement; and the fact that the theoretical is ceaselessly displaced by the poetry is what guarantees the movement of poetry as a producer and unfolder of space, as the movement of difference." Asked about this dual focus (his life-work in effect has been as both poet *and* philosopher), Deguy writes: "I do not separate writing from thought; maybe what I mean by writing is: thought's determination, the struggle with the always insufficient *acribia*, or explanation or rigor of 'my thoughts.' To write is to struggle against torpor, the evanescence and disappearance of that which seems worthwhile to be pursued, tracked, gathered. When reading a text which resists, in which I perceive this insistent inquiry, I am in the element of writing."

Amelia Rosselli 1930–1996

LETTER TO HER BROTHER

In the tombs orgies go on by themselves
if the white images are alone,
I with
my parenthesis that was not supposed to last
the notebooks
of my minds wrapped up in your winter coat
exploitation
at its peak: to you I send
these brief charges, no
explanation can make you keep your time
if the dance tune is this extinguished crater.

．

I did not want
to write in the far away mountain
anything but works about me:

come with me and I'll map hell for you.

Translation from the Italian by Lucia Re & Paul Vangelisti

from MARTIAL VARIATIONS

     In the lethargy which follows the machinations of the
few, I was lying down, happy and disheveled, disheveled
in the extreme: and the tongues of snakes flickered
like fire near my pillow. Near my pillow
a dragon was dying, a deli butcher with his sausages,
his tails hung there stinking, but delicate
in their aroma when taken together.

And if the silent, very silent Antigone who at
my farm watched over my messy produce, stripped of its
glory, if she had come with her welcome shriek
of alarm, I was dying, very silent alarm.

Fascinated by practicality I watched an
ordinary unmuscular man easily carry a pink mattress
on his shoulders, while smiling like Pulcinella I remembered
that you were there. And the evening wouldn't have ended badly, except
that you existed
beyond every reflection, and outside every expectation. Having returned
to my house after so many neon signs you were there again
and again and again. Anchored to you your image in me
doesn't melt, you protect it: the image which melted
days and days and days returned with you, without
you, through you in the solitude of this Spring which floats
in the middle of Winter, my soul!

seventy beggars and a shirt which was ripping
to nothing, on a whim I stretched myself out in
the nothing and everything was laurel and beneficence, the king
of the poor people benefitted, camel which crawled. A hard,
fine rain penetrated, because I needed help
I penetrated into rooms furnished with a true life
which with capital letters moved away from mine, those who
were condemned to death were kindly obliging. Invitations
slid over the foundations of a permeable
city: no hidden beast dusted off
the goats which marched enraptured through the mountains of
the Trinità: a camel, two Indians and people who were masters
of all the arts, music and mathematics, the fury
of achievable dreams. Lost in the basin of shadow
the white cobwebs and the dust on the eyelashes,
particles and small pearls under a terrible rain
resolved for the better on a closed life.

Through a vigorous and impossible experience
we broke our isolation laboriously, but
the carts which carried us like fruit to

market were funereal automobiles white
if it was snowing, hellish in the rain. Corrupting
guards and guards the mind settles on
exhaustive on the spot investigation because it deceived
even itself: the festival was an encounter
of fashionable devils, every lover ran away
when you undid the window of your
poisonous power on the arms of my
enchantment poor version of envy, but
the spirit still conquered with poor
decisions made in the cellar.
                              After miseries and
hidden desperation Sunday was
pardon and desperation, the sea in
motion stifled complaint of the spirit while
mechanisms will bring relief and guilt
was accepted guilt if desperation is
a means to happiness.

Translation from the Italian by Lawrence R. Smith

DIALOGUE WITH THE DEAD

descend, embrace this daughter
of yours who gropes among ruins and
Moslems who play with her arms
which instead, white, they'd like to embrace
or flay but never missing these beatings
they receive daily, covered with
bruises and lividly you promote a
thirst for sweetness and hard justice
or you won't leave off until I torment
(and they torment me) this mind
that dies every moment full of
tight knots which obstruct its
slow march to a more beautiful undiscoverable country
while even the wish to be
more beautiful than you are dies lividly.

Descend, and keep descending—and thread
through your banal joy the meaning
of a life which trips along saddened
by the full power of others' evil
and my own—not knowing how to defend myself
from dull desire.

To live for an instant or a half an hour and then
find yourself through an oversight
still more encumbered by inessential
angers!

Wise hands had no say in the
matter: I met you to let you slaughter
me again and again.

And slaughter turns into luxury: and
luxury into ecstasy contemplated in the
syphilitic grain which coils itself
around my neck, exhausted by too many betrayals.
Abandoning yourself to empty sex and then holding back
still sweaty from the black pitch of
the low doings of the poor.

Sex and violence are indulged and
rediscovered soaked that glorious
morning when everything falls to pieces, and
if wisdom with its microscopic

customs doesn't call troops back from spilling themselves
into anguish, and if a small boldness
or oversight can provoke it distresses you delay
then the sad day falls to pieces
because of your fertile shabbiness.

And I battle unarmed for a
clarity that has no right to live
as long as you play with this providence
which printed on our faces that fear
of existing outside a commercial
clinging to the basest desires; but
I also saw in your face the seal
of indifference and emptiness arming itself
for death without thinking of life!

Translation from the Italian by Lawrence R. Smith

COMMENTARY

Science-fiction folly / valiant sicknesses / impediments to writing / totality to be described // will to write / will to survive / will to impede / tyranny
A. R.

Child of her time, she was seven years old when her antifascist father, Carlo Rosselli, was assassinated by French gunmen outside Paris; grew up with her English-speaking (Irish Catholic) mother, first in England, then New York; studied literature & music (a continuing concern) in Rome & London; settled later in the Rosselli home in Florence. Onset of mental illness came with her mother's death during her student days, as an openness to voices & destructive fears, later a struggle with the institutions that confined her. If this gives an edge to her work—as to that of Hölderlin, or Artaud, or Campana before her—her work itself, like theirs, is testimony to the power of a profoundly experimental poetics, here in its *post*modern, Italian incarnation. (Below, page 606.) To see such work as merely madness is, of course, to miss its genius; for what is most at stake here (so writes Lucia Re) "is the conjunction of linguistic experimentation with a kind of 'staging' of the self, a staging which in turn involves the dimensions of the 'personal' and the 'private' (a personal which, however, is no longer personal and a private which is no longer private, once they have become part of the *mise-en-scène* of the poetic text). . . . The obscurity of her language, the character of radical artifice that her poems often assume, and the mystical dimension that emerges in them, may [in fact] be seen as a political gesture of protest." And Rosselli on her own behalf: "Lo scritto che in me è folle risponde / a tutto questo dolore con parole sempre / spero sempre vere [The writing that in me is madness answers / all this pain with words I always / yearn for always true]."

Gary Snyder b. 1930

WHAT YOU SHOULD KNOW TO BE A POET

all you can about animals as persons.
the names of trees and flowers and weeds.
names of stars, and the movements of the planets
            and the moon.

your own six senses, with a watchful and elegant mind.

at least one kind of traditional magic:
divination, astrology, the *book of changes*, the tarot;

dreams.
the illusory demons and illusory shining gods;

kiss the ass of the devil and eat shit;
fuck his horny barbed cock,
fuck the hag,
and all the celestial angels
            and maidens perfum'd and golden—

& then love the human: wives   husbands   and friends.

children's games, comic books, bubble-gum,
the weirdness of television and advertising.

work, long dry hours of dull work swallowed and accepted
and livd with and finally lovd.   exhaustion,
                    hunger, rest.

the wild freedom of the dance, *extasy*
silent solitary illumination, *enstasy*

real danger.   gambles.   and the edge of death.

from **MYTHS & TEXTS**

first shaman song

In the village of the dead,
Kicked loose bones
            ate pitch of a drift log
            (whale fat)
Nettles and cottonwood. Grass smokes
                        in the sun
Logs turn in the river
            sand scorches the feet.

Two days without food, trucks roll past
            in dust and light, rivers
            are rising.
Thaw in the high meadows. Move west in July.

Soft oysters rot now, between tides
                the flats stink.

I sit without thoughts by the log-road
Hatching a new myth
watching the waterdogs
                the last truck gone.

this poem is for bear

"As for me I am a child of the god of the mountains."

A bear down under the cliff.
She is eating huckleberries.
They are ripe now
Soon it will snow, and she
Or maybe he, will crawl into a hole
And sleep. You can see
Huckleberries in bearshit if you
Look, this time of year
If I sneak up on the bear
It will grunt and run

The others had all gone down
From the blackberry brambles, but one girl
Spilled her basket, and was picking up her
Berries in the dark.
A tall man stood in the shadow, took her arm,
Led her to his home. He was a bear.
In a house under the mountain
She gave birth to slick dark children
With sharp teeth, and lived in the hollow
Mountain many years.
        snare a bear: call him out:
honey-eater
forest apple
light-foot
Old man in the fur coat, Bear! come out!
Die of your own choice!
Grandfather black-food!
        this girl married a bear
Who rules in the mountains, Bear!
           you have eaten many berries
           you have caught many fish
           you have frightened many people

Twelve species north of Mexico
Sucking their paws in the long winter
Tearing the high-strung caches down
Whining, crying, jacking off
(Odysseus was a bear)

Bear-cubs gnawing the soft tits
Teeth gritted, eyes screwed tight
                but she let them.
Til her brothers found the place
Chased her husband up the gorge
Cornered him in the rocks.
Song of the snared bear:
        "Give me my belt.
        "I am near death.
        "I came from the mountain caves
        "At the headwaters,
        "The small streams there
        "Are all dried up.

—I think I'll go hunt bears.
                "hunt bears?
Why shit Snyder,
You couldn't hit a bear in the ass
                with a handful of rice!"

THE HUMP-BACKED FLUTE PLAYER

The hump-backed flute player
                walks all over.
                sits on the boulders around the Great Basin
                his hump   is a pack.

Hsuan Tsang (original name Ch'en I
                went to India 629 AD
                returned to China 645
                with 657 sutras, images, pictures,
                and 50 relics)

          a curved frame pack with a parasol,
          embroidery   carving
          incense censer swinging as he walked
          the Pamir   the Tarim   Turfan
          the Punjab   the doab
          of Ganga and Yamuna,

Sweetwater, Quileute, Hoh
Amur, Tanana, Mackenzie, Old Man,
Bighorn, Platte, the San Juan
                    he carried
                         "emptiness"
                    he carried
                         "mind only"
                    vijnaptimatra

The hump-backed flute player
Kokopilau
his hump is a pack.

          .

In Canyon de Chelly on the North Wall up by a cave
is the hump-backed flute player laying on his back,
playing his flute. Across the flat sandy canyon wash,
wading a stream and breaking through the ice, on the
south wall, the pecked-out pictures of some Mountain Sheep
with curling horns. They stood in the icy shadow of the
south wall two hundred feet away; I sat with my
shirt off in the sun facing south, with the hump-
backed flute player just above my head.
They whispered; I whispered; back and forth
across the canyon, clearly heard.

          .

In the plains of Bihar, near Rajgir, are the
ruins of Nalanda. The name Bihar comes from "vihara"
—Buddhist temple—the Diamond Seat is in Bihar, and
Vulture Peak—Tibetan pilgrims come down to these
plains. The six-foot-thick walls of Nalanda, the

monks all scattered—books burned—banners tattered—
statues shattered—by the Turks.
Hsuan Tsang describes the high blue tiles, the delicate
debates; Logicians of Emptiness, worshippers of Tara,
Joy of Starlight, naked breasted, "She who saves."

    •

Ghost Bison, Ghost Bears, Ghost Bighorns, Ghost Lynx,
Ghost Pronghorns, Ghost Panthers, Ghost Marmots, Ghost
Owls:
Swirling and gathering, sweeping down, in the power
of a dance and a song. Then the White Man will be gone.
Then the butterflies will sing
on slopes of grass and aspen;
thunderheads the deep blue of Krishna
rise on rainbows; and falling shining rain—
each drop—
tiny people gliding slanting down: a little Buddha
seated in each pearl—
and join the million waving Grass-Seed Buddhas
on the ground.

    •

Ah, what am I carrying? What's this load?
    Who's that out there in the dust
sleeping on the ground?
with a black hat, and a feather stuck in his sleeve.

—It's old Jack Wilson,
Wovoka, the prophet,

> *Black Coyote saw the whole world*
> *in Wovoka's empty hat*

> the bottomless sky

> the night of starlight, lying on our sides

> the ocean, slanting higher

all manner of beings
may swim in my sea
echoing up conch spiral corridors

the mirror: countless ages back
dressing   or laughing
what world today?

pearl crystal jewel
taming and teaching
the dragon in the spine—

spiral, wheel,
or breath of mind

desert sheep with curly horns.
the ringing in your ears

is the cricket in the stars.

up in the mountains that edge the Great Basin
    it was whispered to me
    by the oldest of trees.
    by the oldest of beings,

    the Oldest of Trees.

and all night long, sung on
    by a vast throng
            of Pinyon
                Pine

COMMENTARY

On October 25, 1959, several climbing friends and I made an early ascent
of the north arête of Matterhorn Peak [California]. We found this entry in
the summit register: October 23, 1955 / Gary Snyder / Clear and cold /
"Even the mountains shall become Buddhas"
George Sessions

What Snyder brought us was the naturalizing of one line of American
modernism—that associated, largely, with the work of Ezra Pound—& its
opening to what would be defining concerns for the first *post*modernist
generation. It was his genius, too, to engage in what Pound had called an
"active" poetics, not at its fascist extreme—Pound's folly—but drawing on

his own Wobbly & western American upbringing to be the visible spokesman for a new/old wilderness, in which poetry might function again (as at its beginnings) as "an ecological survival tool." In the same manner of seeing/doing-for-himself, he followed a *very* early commitment to Zen Buddhism with a novitiate at a Rinzai Zen temple in Kyoto: the first of those "influential men of letters who have been interested in Oriental religions . . . to try to *experience* Zen by actually becoming a monk, though now a considerable number of writers are following Gary's example" (Hisao Kanaseki). Associated with the San Francisco Renaissance and the Beat Generation movement (he is the model for Japhy Ryder in Jack Kerouac's novel *The Dharma Bums*), he has, like Ginsberg, others, come to take on the role of poet-teacher in something more than a superficial sense. While he has kept apart from other (literary) isms, it is possible to relate his articulation of his own project—"the real work of modern man: to uncover the inner structure and actual boundaries of the mind"—to something as apparently distant as, say, André Breton's revolution-of-the-mind ("the critical investigation of the notions of reality and unreality, of reason and unreason, of reflection and impulse, of knowing and fatally not knowing, of utility and uselessness"). For Snyder this includes a strong sense of (& need for) cultural continuity & transmission—a transmission he has elsewhere traced back as far as the paleolithic. Or, as one of his later poems has it: "Pound was an axe, / Chen [Snyder's Chinese teacher] was an axe / And my son a handle, soon / To be shaping again, model / And tool, craft of culture, / How we go on."

THE ART OF
THE MANIFESTO

A characteristic of poetry in the time span covered in these pages has been the push by poets to self-define their workings, often in a language that makes a continuity with how they speak within their poems. CRISS-CROSS OF TRRRR TRRRRR ELEVATED TRRRR TRRRRR OVERHEAD TROMBONE WHISSSTLE AMBULANCE SIRENS AND FIRETRUCKS As a result there has been an ongoing development of what Marinetti early spoke of as "the art of making manifestos": an art of "violence & precision" (he wrote) & one that challenged the limits of simple exposition. TO STAND ON THE ROCK OF THE WORD "WE" AMIDST THE SEA OF BOOS & OUTRAGE In its present form(s) it flourishes not only in the magazines & venues that are the public arenas for poetry but in poems & (private) journals & letters, blurring the distinction between poetry & its self-defining poetics: a reflexivity that is one aspect of a modernism turned into its postmodern other. THE TENACITY OF / WRITING'S THICKNESS, LIKE THE BODY'S / FLESH, IS / INERADICABLE, YET MORTAL. IT IS / THE INTRUSION / OF WORDS INTO THE VISIBLE / THAT MARKS / WRITING'S OWN ABSORPTION IN THE WORLD. (And just as the energy & language of the new poetry invades the manifesto text, so the concerns of the manifesto come again & again into the body of the poem.) I IN THE GUISE OF A LION ROARED OUT GREAT VOWELS AND HEARD THEIR AMAZING PATTERNS. Tied to "movements"—though increasingly apart from them—the language of the manifesto is the language of the group coupled with the reassertion of the individual: a personal accounting & a prescription/directive for future acts. ABOMUNISTS SPIT ANTI-POETRY FOR POETIC REASONS AND FRINK. The need throughout is to subvert (or to capture) the inherited past, including (in the postmodern instance) the past of modernism itself. NO MORE MANIFESTOS! NO MORE WORDS!*

---

* The opening paragraph includes excerpts from F. T. Marinetti, Alexei Kruchenykh (et al.), Charles Bernstein, Robert Duncan, Bob Kaufman, & Tristan Tzara.

What follows, then, is a gathering of manifestos & manifesto frag-ments—a compendium of some of those post–World War II amalgams of poetics & polemics that have laid out directives for changes in art & life and have acted (in varying degrees) as examples of the aforementioned art-of-the-manifesto. (Earlier examples appeared in volume one & still other, often key examples are distributed throughout the poems & com-mentaries of the present volume.) Since there is no sure division between early & late, the practitioners from before the war continued to speak toward a new poetics (& against the old one), with degrees of closeness to—or distance from—specific postwar groupings. But it was the writers of the postwar as such—Celan & Olson the first presented here—who offered a resistance through language & through a poetry driven back into the body (therefore more deeply down into the mind), to issue therefrom in a poetics of the breath ("projective verse"—Olson) or of a "breathturn" (Celan). With Olson too—as with the closely cognate Robert Duncan (above) & others in the rapidly developing New American Poetry of the 1950s/60s—the poet's stance-toward-reality & his/her special-view-of-history (both terms Olson's) became a critical part of the poetics: an open-ing to a new "curriculum of the soul" & a poetry of maximal/projective proportions. Or, from a different yet ultimately related vantage, the Martinican poet Edouard Glissant, say, showed a push toward a post-Negritude, post-colonial poetics, epically accounting for "the enlightening obverse of History."

While placing Celan & Olson at the beginning of the postwar turning, we recognize too that the tradition of the manifesto/proclamation, carried into a new generation, affected all the postwar movements presented in these pages—exemplified on (North) American grounds by the Beat poets (above) & the emergent voices (Baraka & Rich, among those at the fore-front) that would fuse a drive toward a poetry of ethnic & gender search-ings with the breakthroughs in content & form of the continuing avant-garde. There is throughout an interplay, a shifting back & forth between the thing said & the creation of new means by which to say it, that out-paces (sometimes) any specific change of (so-called) content. In the projec-tions of the European Situationists (1960s activists, not specialists in po-etry as such), "the problem of language" (= poetry) was thrust into the center of our social & cultural conflicts, while a formal innovator like Jackson Mac Low (above) placed his first experiments with "chance" & "synchronicity" in the framework of anarchism, pacifism, & a curiously leveling form of Buddhism. A similar push in the work of John Cage con-nected like Mac Low's to a still larger range of avant-garde activities (Fluxus, concrete poetry, textsound & sound poetry, intermedia) that would promote the further erasure of boundaries (between art & life, between the different arts) that earlier poets & artists first set in motion. And, finally, among the works presented here, the "test" by Nicanor Parra, however playful in its questionings, asserted the "anti-poet" as fellow[counter]-worker with the more familiar "poet."

In all of these the push toward change (= "transformation of forces"— Jean Pierre Faye in the manifesto for his Parisian journal *Change*) & toward what another French poet/thinker, Henri Deluy, calls *action poétique* is evident—at its most critical a questioning (*post*modern) of the premises underlying such a (modern) poetry. (For which, see the negative manifestos, below, of Denis Roche [cofounder of the French *Tel Quel* group] & Julian Beck [poet/director of The Living Theater], & compare them, among many other possibilities, with the earlier pronouncements of Laura Riding [*I have written that which I believe breaks the spell of poetry*] or Dada poet Tristan Tzara [*The true Dadas are against Dada*].) But the declaration of a poetics offering a means—linguistic & methodological—to overthrow & to rebuild has continued to dominate among those who *manifest* in poetry's name: Ed Sanders, say, with his proposal of an "investigative poetry" as a way to subvert the present & hence to "make [historical] reality"; Adonis interrogating issues of "self" & "other" in the context of an Arabic poetry that has become "a language of silence"; Rachel Blau DuPlessis asserting/questioning the presence of a poetics of feminism in the modern & postmodern avant-gardes; Carolee Schneemann pulling such a manifesto (as "interior scroll") from the depths of her own body; Ishmael Reed reporting the prior existence (& updated survival) of a Neo-HooDoo "Lost American Church"; & Sujata Bhatt writing between a "mother tongue" in the Gujerati language & an English in which the voice of her own mother ceases to be heard.

Seen in such a light, the unity of the works—for all the individualities asserted in their writing—becomes a crucial part of this accounting. The linkage, as we come at it here, may be as much in Diane di Prima's image of "the spiritual battle" ("the war for the human imagination") as in Charles Bernstein's seemingly contrary vision (in William Blake's sense of "contrary") of a writing that can "go to the heart of things / by making itself part / of the material world, absorbed / by it." Finally, as an instance—for us—of manifesto pure & simple, we have chosen to conclude with a declaration—written in the Cold War's terminal decade—to which the present editors were not only subscribers but among the principal coauthors. By doing so we hope not so much to distinguish ourselves from those who have made such declarations globally & locally but to reiterate the need for such (& more of such) in the millennium ahead.

Paul Celan 1920–1970

from THE MERIDIAN SPEECH

Poetry is perhaps this: an *Atemwende,* a turning of our breath. Who knows, perhaps poetry goes its way—the way of art—for the sake of just such a turn? And since the strange, the abyss *and* Medusa's head, the abyss *and* the automaton, all seem to lie in the same direction—it is perhaps this turn, this *Atemwende,* which can sort out the strange from the strange? It is perhaps here, in this one brief moment, that Medusa's head shrivels and the automatons run down? Perhaps, along with the I, estranged and freed *here, in this manner,* some other thing is also set free?

Perhaps after this, the poem can be itself . . . can in this now art-less, art-free manner go other ways, including the ways of art, time and again?

Perhaps.

[. . . . . . .]

But the poem speaks. It is mindful of its dates, but it speaks. True, it speaks only on its own, its very own behalf.

But I think—and this will hardly surprise you—that the poem has always hoped, for this very reason, to speak also on behalf of the *strange*—no, I can no longer use this word here—*on behalf of the other,* who knows, perhaps of an *altogether other.*

This "who knows" which I have reached is all I can add here, today, to the old hopes.

Perhaps, I am led to speculate, perhaps an encounter is conceivable between this "altogether other"—I am using a familiar auxiliary—and a not so very distant, a quite close "other"—conceivable, perhaps, again and again.

The poem takes such thoughts for its home and hope—a word for living creatures.

Nobody can tell how long the pause for breath—hope and thought—will last. "Speed," which has always been "outside," has gained yet more speed. The poem knows this, but heads straight for the "otherness" which it considers it can reach and be free, which is perhaps vacant and at the same time [. . .] turned toward it, toward the poem.

It is true, the poem, the poem today, shows—and this has only indirectly to do with the difficulties of vocabulary, the faster flow of syntax or a more awakened sense of ellipsis, none of which we should underrate—the poem clearly shows a strong tendency towards silence.

The poem holds its ground, if you will permit me yet another extreme formulation, the poem holds its ground on its own margin. In order to endure, it constantly calls and pulls itself back from an "already-no-more" into a "still-here."

1960

Translation from the German by Rosmarie Waldrop

Charles Olson 1910–1970

THREE STATEMENTS

from *The Present Is Prologue*

My shift is that I take it the present is prologue, not the past. The instant, therefore. Is its own interpretation, as a dream is, and any action—a poem, for example. Down with causation (except, see below). And yrself: you, as the only reader and mover of the instant. You, the cause. No drag allowed, on either. Get on with it.

In the work and dogmas are: (1) How, by form, to get the content instant; (2) what any of us are by the work on ourself, how make ourself fit instruments for use (how we augment the given—what used to be called the fate); (3) that there is no such thing as duality either of the body and the soul or of the world and I, that the fact in the human universe is the discharge of the many (the multiple) by the one (yrself done right, whatever you are, in whatever job, is the thing—all hierarchies, like dualities, are dead ducks).

1955

A Plan for a Curriculum of the Soul

how to live as a
single natural being
the dogmatic nature of
(order of)
experience

how many?
& how each
made known,
exercised,

as

organs &
function - activity
of the soul
or psyche or
Heaven or God

Ismaeli muslimism

&, all together,
create
organism

Alchemy - rather by plates

[as connected to dreams]

pictorialism

as in Earth, "View"

& perspective
/cf. Weyl on ocular

power

Vision

+

Messages

technically, Analytic Psychology, as only technical study I
know of modern Western man & under enough mental
control

jazz playing

dance as individual
body-power

equally say Homer's art

Bach's belief

/ cf. Novalis'
"subjects"

Egyptian hieroglyphs (gesture, speech
- drawing   habits
mental condition

the Norse & the Arabs

-locally, American
Indians

matter

Phenomenological

Sensation and Attention
                       ⌐training in exhaustion &
                       ⌐   completion

A Plan for a Curriculum of the Soul

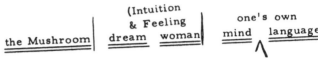

                          (Intuition
                           & Feeling   one's own
        the Mushroom| dream woman| mind   language
                                                   ∧

Earth   as a
     geology ∧ comprehension like archeology
     geography - equally, though here maps & experience of
human history⌐   walking
          ⌐in this connection, as habitat
        inhabitation of, rather than as politics say
            or national. Instead, physical, &
        vertically incremental
                                              physical

    man as animal ⌐praxis of - as Earth as a

emotional mental experience

Poets   as such, that is disciplined lives not
     history or for any "art" reasons example,

Blake ⌐
        ⌐ the same, say, medicine men

     & like theologians: example, Dante - Giotto

1968

The Resistance

for Jean Riboud

This is eternity. This now. This foreshortened span.

Men will recognize it more easily (& dwell in it so) when we regain what the species lost, how long ago: nature's original intention with the organism, that it live 130 years. Or so Bogomolets' researches into the nature of connective tissue seem to prove. True or not, with or without aid from his own biosis, man has no alternative: his mortal years are his enemy. He accepts this new position. It is the root act.

There are other aids. Time, for example, has been cut down to size, though I do not think that those who have come to the knowledge of now came here from that powerful abstraction space-time, no matter how its corrections of time reinforce the position.

Man came here by an intolerable way. When man is reduced to so much fat for soap, superphosphate for soil, fillings and shoes for sale, he has, to begin again, one answer, one point of resistance only to such fragmentation, one organized ground, a ground he comes to by a way the precise contrary of the cross, of spirit in the old sense, in old mouths. It is his own physiology he is forced to arrive at. And the way—the way of the beast, of man and the Beast.

It is his body that is his answer, his body intact and fought for, the absolute of his organism in its simplest terms, this structure evolved by nature, repeated in each act of birth, the animal man; the house he is, this house that moves, breathes, acts, this house where his life is, where he dwells against the enemy, against the beast.

Or the fraud. This organism now our citadel never was cathedral, draughty tenement of soul, was what it is: ground, stone, wall, cannon, tower. In this intricate structure are we based, now more certainly than ever (besieged, overthrown), for its power is bone muscle nerve blood brain   a man, its fragile mortal force its old eternity, resistance.

1953

John Cage 1912–1992

from **LECTURE ON NOTHING**

This lecture was printed in *Incontri Musicali,* August 1959. There are four measures in each line and twelve lines in each unit of the rhythmic structure. There are forty-eight such units, each having forty-eight measures. The whole is divided into five large parts, in the proportion 7, 6, 14, 14, 7. The forty-eight measures of each unit are likewise so divided. The text is printed in four columns to facilitate a rhythmic reading. Each line is to be read across the page from left to right, not down the columns in sequence. This should not be done in an artificial manner (which might result from an attempt to be too strictly faithful to the position of the words on the page), but with the *rubato* which one uses in everyday speech.

[I]

I am here   ,   and there is nothing to say   .
If among you are
those who wish to get   somewhere   ,   let them leave at
any moment   .   What we re-quire   is
silence   ;   but what silence requires   is
that I go on talking   .
Give any one thought
a push   :   it falls down easily
;   but the pusher   and the pushed   pro-duce
that enter-tainment   called   a dis-cussion   .
Shall we have one later   ?

                    ♍

Or   ,   we could simply de-cide   not to have a dis-
cussion   .   What ever you like.   But
now   there are silences   and the
words   make   help make   the
silences   .
I have nothing to say
and I am saying it   and that is
poetry   as I need it   .
This space of time   is organized   .
We need not fear these   silences,—

                    ♍

we may love them   .   This is a composed
talk   just as I make   for I am making it   a piece of music.

[2]

♍

What I am calling poetry is often called content. I myself have called it form. It is the conti-nuity of a piece of music. Continuity today, when it is necessary, is a demonstration of dis-interestedness. That is, it is a proof that our delight lies in not pos-sessing anything. Each moment presents what happens. How different this form sense is from that which is bound up with memory: themes and secondary themes; their struggle; their development; the climax; the recapitulation (which is the belief that one may own one's own home). But actually, unlike the snail, we carry our homes within us,

♍

which enables us to fly or to stay,—to enjoy each. But beware of that which is breathtakingly beautiful, for at any moment the telephone may ring or the airplane come down in a vacant lot. A piece of string or a sunset, possessing neither nothing and the continuity, each acts. Nothing more than nothing can be said. Hearing or making this in music is not different—only simpler—than living this way. Simpler, that is, for me,—because it happens that I write music.

1959

Edouard Glissant b. 1928

from **EARTH**

The poet's desire now is not to abstract himself from his being, to entrust his song to strange forces that would soon engulf him, nor, by some opposite push, to withdraw into his own weightiness to rage lyrically in the depth of his desolation. There is this movement through which the spectacle of the surround illumines (disorders), while the imposition of each word tends to order in the world. On this double necessity, which has been the secret seed of poetry, the present articulates itself like a solemn, ineluctable law. The poet does not stop obeying this commandment, twice negated, twice consented to. He leaves the lightning, the "revealed," this punctuation of nothings, this lure of illuminations which disappears into the passing actuality of the image, to give itself to a duration where rhythm multiplies. The poet chooses, elects in the world mass what he needs to preserve, what his song accords with. And the rhythm is ritual force, lever of consciousness. It leads to these powers: prosodic richness (rigor), guarantor of choice, guardian of conquests; the knowledge of the world in its thickness and its spread, the enlightning obverse of History. That is to say poetry rebegins in the domains of the epic. In our anarchic universe, such a manner of poetry ceases to be accidental, imposes itself as the imperious Harvest. It names the Drama that is ours: fire of the Diverse, struggle of the Disparate, desire for the Other. It perpetuates in chaos this labor, which is uniquely poetry's: to tear down the walls, the barks; to unify without denaturing, to order without taxidermizing, to unveil without destroying; to finally know each thing, and that space from one thing to the other, these saps, these countries—in the mind's sharpness and the heart's all-generosity.

And yet the inextricable grabs us, in that the Old World's shadow has fallen over us. Our certainties, reflecting this huge score, get upset. Our clarities become clouded. Our knowledges, just then so easy, fructify into the complex, the difficult. It seems that what gives strength to the desire for poetry is that its simplicity will have to be *conquered* at the level of the dedoubled injunction to which knowledge has led man: to be conscience and negated science of conscience, speech and language contesting speech, signifier and sign devolving from the signified.

But we, dragged through this history (I see the trace left by our feet), do we inherit that injunction? Can we profit from it, without our assuming its weight? In truth, no "construction" forces us. No cathedral. Not one shared Great Book. Our history is yet to come. (Our poem interweaves in your reticences, complicates itself by your conquests; but our scream is clear beneath the entanglements.) In what you call History, between the pits where our heroes went to earth nameless, I see only this trace of our feet.

late 1950s

Translation from the French by Pierre Joris

Situationist International

GUY DEBORD (1931–1994), et al.

from **ALL THE KING'S MEN**

[1]

The problem of language is at the heart of all struggles between the forces striving to abolish present alienation and those striving to maintain it; it is inseparable from the entire terrain of those struggles. We live within language as within polluted air. In spite of what humorists think, words do not play. Nor do they make love, as Breton thought, except in dreams. Words *work*—on behalf of the dominant organization of life. And yet they are not completely automatized; unfortunately for the theoreticians of information, words are not in themselves "informationist"; they embody forces that can upset the most careful calculations. Words coexist with power in a relationship analogous to that which proletarians (in the modern as well as the classic sense of the term) have with power. Employed *almost* constantly, exploited full time for every sense and nonsense that can be squeezed out of them, they still remain in some sense fundamentally strange and foreign.

Power presents only the falsified, official sense of words; in a manner of speaking it forces them to carry a pass, determines their place in the production process (where some of them conspicuously work overtime) and gives them their paycheck. Regarding the use of words, Lewis Carroll's Humpty Dumpty quite correctly observes, "The question is which is to be master—that's all." And he, a socially responsible employer in this respect, states that he pays overtime to those he employs excessively. We should also understand the phenomenon of the *insubordination of words*, their desertion, their open resistance, which is manifested in all modern writing (from Baudelaire to the dadaists and Joyce), as a symptom of the general revolutionary crisis of the society.

[2]

It is a matter not of putting poetry at the service of revolution, but rather of putting revolution at the service of poetry. It is only in this way that the revolution does not betray its own project. We will not repeat the mistake of the surrealists, who put themselves at the service of the revolution right when it had ceased to exist. Bound to the memory of a partial and rapidly crushed revolution, surrealism rapidly became a reformism of the spectacle, a critique of a certain form of the reigning spectacle that was carried out from within the dominant organization of that spectacle. The surrealists seem to have overlooked the fact that every internal improvement or modernization of the spectacle is translated by power into its own encoded language, to which it alone holds the key.

Every revolution has been born in poetry, has first of all been made with the force of poetry. This is a phenomenon which continues to escape theorists of revolution—indeed, it cannot be understood if one still clings to the old conception of revolution or of poetry—but which has generally been sensed by counterrevolutionaries. Poetry, whenever it appears, frightens them; they do their best to get rid of it by means of every kind of exorcism, from auto-da-fé to pure stylistic research. The moment of real poetry, which has "all the time in the world before it," invariably wants to reorient the entire world and the entire future to its own ends. As long as it lasts its demands admit of no compromises. It brings back into play all the unsettled debts of history. Fourier and Pancho Villa, Lautréamont and the *dinamiteros* of the Asturias—whose successors are now inventing new forms of strikes—the sailors of Kronstadt and Kiel, and all those in the world who, with us or without us, are preparing to fight for the long revolution are equally the emissaries of the new poetry.

Poetry is becoming more and more clearly the empty space, the antimatter, of consumer society, since it is not consumable (in terms of the modern criteria for a consumable object: an object that is of equivalent value for each of a mass of isolated passive consumers). Poetry is nothing when it is quoted, it can only be *detourned*, brought back into play. Otherwise the study of the poetry of the past is nothing but an academic exercise. The history of poetry is only a way of running away from the poetry of history, if we understand by that phrase not the spectacular history of the rulers but rather the history of everyday life and its possible liberation; the history of each individual life and its realization.

[3]

The choice between informationism and poetry no longer has anything to do with the poetry of the past, just as no variant of what the classical revolutionary movement has become can anymore, anywhere, be considered as part of a real alternative to the prevailing organization of life. The same judgment leads us to announce the total disappearance of poetry in the old forms in which it was produced and consumed and to announce its return in effective and unexpected forms. Our era no longer has to *write out poetic orders;* it has to carry them out.

1963

TRANSLATOR'S NOTE. The French word *détournement* [here made into a verb, "detourned"] means diversion, deflection, turning aside from the normal course or purpose (often with an illicit connotation). It has sometimes been translated as "diversion," but this word is confusing because of its more common meaning of idle entertainment. I have chosen simply to anglicize the French word, which already has a certain currency in America and England.

Translation from the French by Ken Knabb

Amiri Baraka b. 1934

BLACK DADA NIHILISMUS

                        . Against what light

is false what breath
sucked, for deadness.
                    Murder, the cleansed

purpose, frail, against
God, if they bring him
                    bleeding, I would not

forgive, or even call him
black dada nihilismus.

The protestant love, wide windows,
color blocked to Mondrian, and the
ugly silent deaths of jews under
the surgeon's knife. (To awake on
69th street with money and a hip
nose. Black dada nihilismus, for

the umbrella'd jesus. Trilby intrigue
movie house presidents sticky the floor.
B.D.N., for the secret men, Hermes, the

blacker art. Thievery (ahh, they return
those secret gold killers. Inquisitors
of the cocktail hour. Trismegistus, have

them, in their transmutation, from stone
to bleeding pearl, from lead to burning
looting, dead Moctezuma, find the West

a gray hideous space.

2

From Sartre, a white man, it gave
the last breath. And we beg him die,
before he is killed. Plastique, we

do not have, only thin heroic blades.
The razor. Our flail against them, why
you carry knives? Or brutaled lumps of

heart? Why you stay, where they can
reach? Why you sit, or stand, or walk
in this place, a window on a dark

warehouse. Where the minds packed in
straw. New homes, these towers, for those
lacking money or art. A cult of death,

need of the simple striking arm under
the streetlamp. The cutters, from under
their rented earth. Come up, black dada

nihilismus. Rape the white girls. Rape
their fathers. Cut the mothers' throats.
Black dada nihilismus, choke my friends

in their bedrooms with their drinks spilling
and restless for tilting hips or dark liver
lips sucking splinters from the master's thigh.

Black scream
and chant, scream,
and dull, un
earthly

hollering. Dada, bilious
what ugliness, learned
in the dome, colored holy
shit (i call them sinned

or lost
      burned masters
            of the lost
                 nihil German killers
                      all our learned

, 'member
at you said
money, God, power,
a moral code, so cruel
it destroyed Byzantium, Tenochtitlan, Commanch

> (got it, *Baby!*

For tambo, willie best, dubois, patrice, mantan, the
bronze buckaroos

> for Jack Johnson, asbestos, tonto, buckwheat,
> billie holiday.

> For tom russ, l'ouverture, vesey, beau jack,

(may a lost god damballah, rest or save us
against the murders we intend
against his lost white children
black dada nihilismus

> *1964*

Adrienne Rich b. 1929

from WHEN WE DEAD AWAKEN: WRITING AS RE-VISION

Re-vision—the act of looking back, of seeing with fresh eyes, of entering
an old text from a new critical direction—is for women more than a chap-
ter of cultural history: it is an act of survival. Until we can understand the
assumptions in which we are drenched we cannot know ourselves. And
this drive to self-knowledge, for women, is more than a search for identity:
it is part of our refusal of the self-destructiveness of male-dominated soci-
ety. A radical critique of literature, feminist in its impulse, would take the
work first of all as a clue to how we live, how we have been living, how
we have been led to imagine ourselves, how our language has trapped as
well as liberated us, how the very act of naming has been till now a male

prerogative, and how we can begin to see and name—and therefore live—afresh. A change in the concept of sexual identity is essential if we are not going to see the old political order reassert itself in every new revolution. We need to know the writing of the past, and know it differently than we have ever known it; not to pass on a tradition but to break its hold over us.

1971

Nicanor Parra b. 1914

TEST

What is an antipoet

A dealer in urns and coffins?
A general doubting himself?
A priest who believes in nothing?
A tramp laughing at everything
        even old age and death?
An ill-tempered talker?
A dancer on the edge of the abyss?
A Narcissus in love with the whole world?
A bloody joker
        willfully wretched?
A poet who sleeps in a chair?
An up-to-date alchemist?
A revolutionary of the living room?
A *petit-bourgeois?*
A charlatan?
        A god?
                An innocent?
A peasant of Santiago, Chile?
Underline the sentence that you consider correct.

What is antipoetry?
A tempest in a teacup?
A spot of snow on a rock?
A salad bowl full of human excrement
        as the Franciscan Father believes?
A mirror that tells the truth?
A woman with her legs open?
A punch in the nose
        of the president of the Writers' Society?
(May God save his soul)
A warning to the young poets?
A jet-propelled coffin?
A coffin run by centrifugal force?
A kerosene coffin?
A funeral home without a body?
Put an X beside the definition you consider correct.

c. 1964–66

Translation from the Spanish by Miller Williams

George Maciunas 1931–1978

A MANIFESTO FOR FLUXUS

Manifesto:

2. To affect, or bring to a certain state, by subjecting to, or treating with, a flux. "*Fluxed* into another world." *South.*
3. *Med.* To cause a discharge from, as in purging.

flux (flŭks), *n.* [OF., fr. L. *fluxus*, fr. *fluere*, *fluxum*, to flow. See FLUENT; cf. FLUSH, *n.* (of cards).] **1.** *Med.* **a** A flowing or fluid discharge from the bowels or other part: esp., an excessive and morbid discharge: as, the bloody *flux*, or dysentery. **b** The matter thus discharged.

<u>Purge</u> the world of bourgeois sickness, "intellectual", professional & commercialized culture, PURGE the world of dead art, imitation, artificial art, abstract art, illusionistic art, mathematical art, — PURGE THE WORLD OF "EUROPANISM"!

2. Act of flowing: a continuous moving on or passing by, as of a flowing stream; a continuing succession of changes.
3. A stream; copious flow; flood; outflow.
4. The setting in of the tide toward the shore. Cf. REFLUX.
5. State of being liquid through heat; fusion. *Rare.*

PROMOTE A REVOLUTIONARY FLOOD AND TIDE IN ART,
Promote living art, anti-art, promote NON ART REALITY to be fully grasped by all peoples, not only critics, dilettantes and professionals.

7. *Chem. & Metal.* **a** Any substance or mixture used to promote fusion, esp. the fusion of metals or minerals. Common metallurgical fluxes are silica and silicates (acidic), lime and limestone (basic), and fluorite (neutral). **b** Any substance applied to surfaces to be joined by soldering or welding, just prior to or during the operation, to clean and free them from oxide, thus promoting their union, as rosin.

<u>FUSE</u> the cadres of cultural, social & political revolutionaries into united front & action.

sonderdruck fluxus 2-3-II'63 maciunas manifest

1963

Bob Cobbing b. 1920

A STATEMENT ON SOUND POETRY 1969

Leonardo da Vinci asked the poet to give him something he might see and touch and not just something he could hear. Sound poetry seems to me to be achieving this aim. PARTLY it is a recapturing of a more primitive form of language, before communication by expressive sounds became stereotyped into words, when the voice was richer in vibrations, more mightily physical. The tape-recorder, by its ability to amplify and superimpose, and to slow down the vibrations, has enabled us to rediscover the possibilities of the human voice, until it becomes again something we can almost see and touch. Poetry has gone beyond the word, beyond the letter, both aurally and visually . . . Sound poetry dances, tastes, has shape. MY USE of "vocal-micro-particles" as Henri Chopin calls the elements with which we now compose sound poetry, retains, indeed emphasizes, the natural quality of the human voice, more perhaps than does Chopin's poetry. But both he and I are attempting to use a new means of communication which I believe is an old method re-established, which is more natural more direct and more honest than, for example, the present day voice of politics and religion . . . Gone is the word as the word, though the word may still be used as sound or shape. Poetry now resides in other elements.

1969

Henri Chopin b. 1922

from **POÉSIE SONORE**

Poetry is song, dance, game, step, colour, line . . . the "physical word" . . . the word that is simply movement.

1961

Get rid of all those bits of paper, whole, torn, folded, or not. It is man's body that is poetry, and the streets.

1969

Steve McCaffery b. 1947

from **TEXT-SOUND, ENERGY AND PERFORMANCE**

To align, realign and misalign within the anarchy of language. To cultivate excess, return language to its somatic base in order to deterritorialize the sign. Concentration on molecular flows rather than the molar aggregates. Cuttings. Fissures. Decompositions (inventions). Not intention so much as intensions. Plasticizations. Non-functionalities. Shattered sphericities. Marginalities. Somas. Nexi. Le poème c'est moi but as the inscription of the person in a transcendental pronoun that utterly annihilates the subject. Personal collapse into flux. Dilations. Positive disintegrations. Structures abandoned, departed from or de-constructed and modified into flows in accord with the unique, unpredictable molecular relationships of audiences and performers. Genetic codicities. A gift back to the body of those energy zones repressed, and channelled as charter in the overcoded structure of grammar. To release by a de-inscription those trapped forces of libido.

[. . . . . .]

And ultimately . . . along the way, comes the splendid paradox of nomadic consciousness: it is a poetry that isn't, a poetry that can never be, if Nietzsche has perceived it clearly that—
        that which is, cannot contain motion.

Toronto, August 1978

Dick Higgins b. 1938

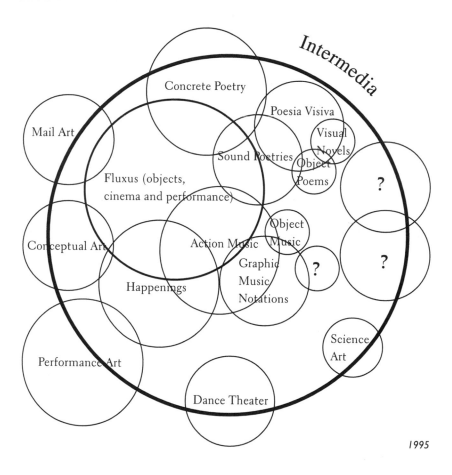

Intermedia

Concrete Poetry

Poesia Visiva

Mail Art

Visual Novels

Sound Poetries

Object Poems

Fluxus (objects, cinema and performance)

?

Object Music

Conceptual Art

Action Music

Graphic Music Notations

?

?

Happenings

Science Art

Performance Art

Dance Theater

1995

Denis Roche b. 1937

from LE MÉCRIT

Struggle and Erasure

So I've had my say, I've put my word end to end with those that hadn't forewarned, those that hurt, those that will weigh heavy in the balance, those that are mistakes, those that make the po-heads barf, the poetillitos, the prose-eletizers, pots (oh poets!), psoets, co-pokes, copaws, pawers-of-being, cowardly co-riders, noise wetters, shitty cadencers of all hues, line-recitors my friends, my buddies (oh poets!) of posy, fine flowers, fine flies, fine rimesters, friends cousins pizzle rooters for Racine pissing by the rule, akas of writhicating . . .

I've had my say. I'm at the end of this beshitten trip where I had all and everything to say. My error all along, I was bored stiff, always lifting my pencil after the passing ladies, line after line blowing up in my face, speaking of my bragging pricks high-flutin' it in the white of the margins, denouncing comedies and falsifiers in a race to the finish, grabbing the piggy-bank, shtupping flower after flower; I therefore announce, between two books, that it's over. And how!

[. . . . . . .]

The race! The noise's so loud, head on I'll get you, popish paparazzi, even in a sack race, I've put up with too much, I've seen the fat pampered pustules a-popping, the nonassaillant war, the apostrophes planted like stakes doing the honor guard all the way to the coliseum, the patent and sham factory, discouraging, banquet after banquet, I've seen all that necking with the high shits, copanthropi and carpet-beggars throwing cloths and elzevirs over the windmills. For crying out loud, Marianne's buggered to the hilt, phrygian from before the caesarian, knocked up by wind-farters of pose-etry. Scuffed stogies, together we float level with the green balconies, fence-jumpers of the inbetween, you and I don't give a damn, half-catching, half-splitting, the prose-ol'-pop-eia and the poul-try there they rest in the nettles, popefigures of the H.C. on the mat, poetry's for the nerds, dingeling dongs too, absolved are Sully's teats, epic outlaws, sonnets, sonobuoys, bell tunes, fingerbowl caesuras . . . Ugh, I've had it. Deafening music.

Of course none of this should ever have been said. I tip my hat to my friends. I stop running, not that much out of breath, finally, I begin again to saunter along various buildings, the *viale* that spins a bit, wistaria in flower to the left, and further along, there are doorways, they too white-washed. The air whisks me away, but I sit soberly where I belong, accepting the hommage that's due. Minor patrols here and there, behind the flight of stairs, bimbos outside, thighs swollen for having been savagely pressed by the tips of my fingers. The obelisk in the factory's yard, I'll piss all over it (but I'll say it in verse, of course), splattering a few drops, it's always like that, on the banderole to which I'll add tonight: "Poetry's croaked, moth-eaten in small squares, may God have . . . !"

21 May 1972

Translation from the French by Pierre Joris

Edward Sanders b. 1939

from **INVESTIGATIVE POETRY**

The Content of History
Will be Poetry

_____

_____

> There is no end
> to *Gnosis:*
> The hunger
> for *DATA*

A.

The Goal: an era of investigative poesy wherein one can be controversial, radical, and not have the civilization rise up to smite down the bard. To establish and to maintain it. POETS MAY REMAIN IN THE RADIX, UNCOMPROMISING, REVOLUTIONARY, SEDITIOUS, ABSOLUTE.

> POET as Investigator
> > Interpreter of Sky Froth
> > Researcher of the Abyss
> > Human Universer
> > Prophet
> > Prophet without death
> > as a consequence.

My statement is this: that poetry, to go forward, in my view, has to begin a voyage into the description of *historical reality*.

[. . . . . .]

B. *Investigative Eleutherarchs*

Lawyers have a term: "to make law." You "make law" when you're involved in a case or an appeal which, as in Supreme Court decisions which have expanded the scope of personal freedom, opens up new human avenues.

You make law.

Bards, in a similar way, "make reality," or, really, they "make freedom" or they create new modes of what we might term Eleutherarchy, or the dance of freedom.

C. *The Legacy of Ezra Pound*

Purest Distillations from the Data-Midden: the essence of Investigative Poetry: Lines of lyric beauty descend from the data clusters.

[. . . . . .]

D.

It is therefore my belief that virtually every major poet's work in France and America for the past 100 years has prepared the civilization for the rebirth of history poesy. The *Wasteland, The Bridge, The Cantos,* W. C. Williams' *Paterson, The Maximus Poems,* Ginsberg's *Ankor Wat, Howl* and *Wichita Vortex Sutra,* the work of Snyder, in, say, *Turtle Island,* and Jerome Rothenberg in *Poland 1931,* all betoken an era of investigative poesy, a form of historical writing—this is as potentially dangerous to the poet as a minefield or those small foot-snuffing blow-up devices the defense dept. used in Vietnam; but it is a danger thrillsomely magnetic to a bard wandering through the electromagnetic aeon.

[. . . . . .]

Investigative poesy is freed from capitalism, churchism, and other totalitarianisms; free from racisms, free from allegiance to napalm-dropping military police states—a poetry adequate to discharge from its verse-grids the undefiled high energy purely-distilled verse-frags, using *every* bardic skill and meter and method of the last 5 or 6 generations, in order to describe *every* aspect (no more secret governments!) of the historical present, while aiding the future, even placing bard-babble once again into a role as shaper of the future.

1976

Julian Beck 1925–1985

THE STATE WILL BE SERVED EVEN BY POETS

the breasts of all the women crumpled like gas bags when
neruda wrote his hymn celebrating the explosion of a hydrogen bomb by
    soviet authorities
children died of the blisters of ignorance for a century more when
siqueiros tried to assassinate trotsky himself a killer with gun and ice
pound shimmering his incantations to adams benito and kung prolong-
    ing the state with great translation cut in crystal
claudel slaying tupí guaraní as he flourished cultured documents and
    pearls in rio de janeiro when he served france as ambassador to brazil
melville served by looking for contraband as he worked in the customs
    house how many taxes did he requite how many pillars of the state did
    he cement in place tell me tell me tell me stone
spenser serving the faerie queene as a colonial secretary in ireland sinking
    the irish back for ten times forty years no less under the beau monde's
    brack
seneca served by advising nero on how to strengthen the state with philo-
    sophy's accomplishments
aeschylus served slaying persians at marathon and salamis
aristotle served as tutor putting visions of trigonometrics in alexander's
    head
dali and eliot served crowning monarchs with their gold
wallace stevens served as insurance company executive making poems
    out of profits
euclides da cunha served as army captain baritoning troops
and even d h lawrence served praising the unique potential of a king

    these are the epics of western culture
    these are the flutes of china and the east

everything must be rewritten then

goethe served as a member of the weimar council of state and
   condemned even to death even to death

this is the saga of the state which is served

even to death

november 1976   august 1979

Rachel Blau DuPlessis b. 1941

from OTHERHOW: FEMINIST POETICS, MODERNISM, THE AVANT-GARDE

Modernism is associated with an attempt to take various permutations of "new women" and return them, assimilate them to the classic western idea of woman as Other (angel or monster, Lady or Fresca). Otherness is a static, dichotomized, monolithic view of women. This view is necessitated by, interdependent upon the religious/spiritual transcendence also typical of modernist practice, its antisecular resolutions, even in texts midden-filled with the unsorted detritus of the dig into our culture. The eyes in the tent for Pound, the Lady in "Ash Wednesday," the Beautiful Thing in *Paterson*. And a female modernist like H. D., who of necessity has struggled with the idea of Woman? She projects the icon out from herself (liking being the icon); she plays fruitfully with the matrisexual coincidence of being the goddess and loving the goddess. She interests because in making a place for herself, she has to restudy and cut athwart the position she is, grossly, assigned in poetry.

Because of the suspicion of the center in avant-garde practice, the desire to "displace the distinction between margin and center," because of the invention of a cultural practice that "would allow us constructively to question privileged explanations even as explanations are generated," drawing on avant-garde practice seems more fruitful for me-the-woman. Its idea of power and language seem more interesting: the resolute lack of synthesis, the nonorganic poetics, the secular lens. But there are questions which the avant-garde must answer. (1) Does it secretly lovingly to itself hold the idea of poet as priest, poem as icon, poet as unacknowledged legislator? Then turn yr. back on it. Or, not to tell you what to do, My back. (2) Is its idea of language social; or does it claim, by language practices, to avoid (transcend), arc out of the limits posed by the social to its writing practices? Dialogic reading means dialogic writing. (3) Where is/ are its women: where in the poems, serving what function? where in its social matrices, with what functions? where in its ideologies? How does it create itself by positioning its women and its women writers?

[. . . . . . .]

WHAT WRITES?

pigs as fingers, toes
hat tassel a "powder puff" tickle
tummy
doh doh doh doh

as transformation d-g d-g d-g,
long cadences ending maybe in yougurt.

pulling upon those wide winging blank labia
dat? dat?

Wandering stars and little mercies, space
so empty, notched each moment.

Tufted white nut rising who or which is
"I" is "yo" the parade feather tit
mouse, did she see her first real bird?

Made from hearing the deep insides of language, language inside the language; made from pick-scabbing the odd natural wounds of language outside, unspecial dump of language everywhere here.

"Paradoxically the only way to position oneself outside of
that hegemonic discourse is to displace oneself within it—to
refuse the question as formulated, or to answer deviously
(though in its words), even to quote (but against the
grain)."
my father said my mother never had any talent
how to acknowledge alterity the marginality and speak from
its
historically, personally wounding presence without
so that she never did anything; implied, they had discussed
it
come to the conclusion, some people just have it some don't.

how to acknowledge anonymous (ourselves) but compel the
structures and tones, the social ocean of language to babble
burble, to speak
real talent, he said, would have found a way, this
conversation does not go on too long, shifts to "blacks"
of course.
The sung-half song.

If poems are posies what is this?
To whom?
And who am I, then, if it matters?

I am a GEN $\begin{cases} \text{der} \\ \text{re} \end{cases}$ made by the writing; I am a GEN $\begin{cases} \text{re} \\ \text{der} \end{cases}$ read in the writing.

1985

Carolee Schneemann b. 1937

INTERIOR SCROLL

from tape 2 "Kitch's Last Meal"
(super 8 film 1973–77)

I met a happy man
a structuralist filmmaker
—but don't call me that
it's something else I do—
he said we are fond of you
you are charming
but don't ask us
to look at your films
we cannot
there are certain films
we cannot look at
the personal clutter
the persistence of feelings
the hand-touch sensibility
the diaristic indulgence
the painterly mess
the dense gestalt
the primitive techniques

(I don't take the advice
of men who only talk to
themselves)
PAY ATTENTION TO CRITICAL
AND PRACTICAL FILM LANGUAGE
IT EXISTS FOR AND IN ONLY
ONE GENDER

even if you are older than me
you are a monster I spawned
you have slithered out
of the excesses and vitality
of the sixties........

he said you can do as I do
take one clear process
follow its strictest
implications intellectually
establish a system of
permutations establish
their visual set.......

I said my film is concerned
with DIET AND DIGESTION

very well he said then
why the train?

the train is DEATH as there
is die in diet and di in
digestion

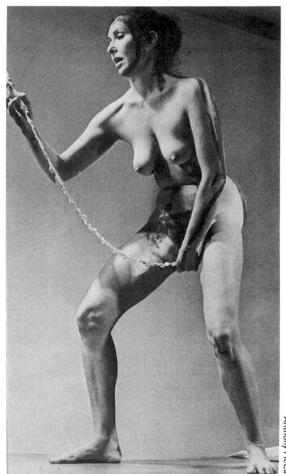

then you are back to metaphors
and meanings
my work has no meaning beyond
the logic of its systems
I have done away with
emotion intuition inspiration—
those aggrandized habits which
set artists apart from
ordinary people—those
unclear tendencies which
are inflicted upon viewers.......

it's true I said when I watch
your films my mind wanders
freely...............
during the half hour of
pulsing dots I compose letters
dream of my lover
write a grocery list
rummage in the trunk
for a missing sweater
plan the drainage pipes for
the root cellar...........
it is pleasant not to be
manipulated

he protested
you are unable to appreciate
the system the grid
the numerical rational
procedures—
the Pythagorean cues—

I saw my failings were worthy
of dismissal I'd be buried
alive my works lost.........

he said we can be friends
equally tho we are not artists
equally I said we cannot
be friends equally and we
cannot be artists equally

he told me he had lived with
a "sculptress" I asked does
that make me a "film-makeress"?

Oh No he said we think of you
as a dancer

1975

Ishmael Reed b. 1938

from NEO-HOODOO MANIFESTO

Neo-HooDoo is a "Lost American Church" updated. Neo-HooDoo is the music of James Brown without the lyrics and ads for Black Capitalism. Neo-HooDoo is the 8 basic dances of 19-century New Orleans' *Place Congo*—the Calinda the Bamboula the Chacta the Babouille the Conjaille the Juba the Congo and the VooDoo—modernized into the Philly Dog, the Hully Gully, the Funky Chicken, the Popcorn, the Boogaloo and the dance of great American choreographer Buddy Bradley.

Neo-HooDoos would rather "shake that thing" than be stiff and erect. (There were more people performing a Neo-HooDoo sacred dance, the Boogaloo, at Woodstock than chanting Hare Krishna . . . Hare Hare!) All so-called "Store Front Churches" and "Rock Festivals" receive their matrix in the HooDoo rites of Marie Laveau conducted at New Orleans' Lake Pontchartrain, and Bayou St. John in the 1880s. The power of HooDoo challenged the stability of civil authority in New Orleans and was driven underground where to this day it flourishes in the Black ghettos throughout the country. That's why in Ralph Ellison's modern novel *Invisible Man* New Orleans is described as "The Home of Mystery." "Everybody from New Orleans got that thing," Louis Armstrong said once.

[. . . . . .]

Neo-HooDoo has "seen a lot of things in this old world."

Neo-HooDoo borrows from Ancient Egyptians (ritual accessories of Ancient Egypt are still sold in the House of Candles and Talismans on Stanton Street in New York, the Botanical Gardens in East Harlem, and Min and Mom on Haight Street in San Francisco, examples of underground centers found in ghettos throughout America).

Neo-HooDoo borrows from Haiti Africa and South America. Neo-HooDoo comes in all styles and moods.

[. . . . . .]

Neo-HooDoo is a litany seeking its text
Neo-HooDoo is a Dance and Music closing in on its words
Neo-HooDoo is a Church finding its lyrics
Cecil Brown Al Young Calvin Hernton

David Henderson Steve Cannon Quincy Troupe
Ted Joans Victor Cruz N. H. Pritchard Ishmael Reed
Lennox Raphael Sarah Fabio Ron Welburn are Neo
HooDoo's "Manhattan Project" of writing . . .

A Neo-HooDoo celebration will involve the dance music
and poetry of Neo-HooDoo and whatever ideas the
participating artists might add. A Neo-HooDoo seal
is the Face of an Old American Train.
Neo-HooDoo signs are everywhere!
Neo-HooDoo is the Now Locomotive swinging
up the Tracks of the American Soul.

Almost 100 years ago HooDoo was forced to say
Goodbye to America. Now HooDoo is
back as Neo-HooDoo
You can't keep a good church down!

c. 1972

Adonis b. 1930

from **PREFACE**

1

I write in a language that exiles me. The relationship of an Arab poet to
his language is like that of a mother who gives away her son after the first
stirrings in her body. If we accept the biblical story of Hagar and Ishmael,
as repeated in the Koran, we realize that maternity, paternity and even
language itself were all born in exile for the Arab poet. Exile is his mother-
country, according to this story. For him it can be said: in the beginning
was the exile, not the word. In his struggle against the hell of daily life, the
Arab poet's only shelter is the hell of exile.

2

What I have just said returns us to origins—to myth and to language.
Based on these origins, Islam offered a new beginning. It dislodged lan-
guage from its worldly exile and oriented it to the country of Revelation—
to heaven. Through language Revelation reveals the metaphysical while

work organizes the physical. This organization has been entrusted to man as the new caliph—the successor of the Prophet. Revelation was instituted at the moment man accepted the charge of putting it into practice. Then it became a law, a system.

Yet in every system there exists another form of exile because every system is both a limitation and a route planned in advance. Every system forces man out of his being and identifies him with his appearance.

Thus, Arab life from its inception has been an exile from language and the religious system. In the past as well as in the present, the Arab poet has known many other forms of exile as well: censorship, interdiction, expulsion, imprisonment and murder.

In this scenario the Other seems to be the salvation of the I. The Other is neither past nor future, nor is it a mirror that is capable of returning the I to childhood. Rather it helps to set the poet in motion toward the unknown, toward everything strange.

3

From such a perspective, poetry is certainly not a "paradise lost" nor is it a "golden age." On the contrary it is a question that begets another question. Considered as a question, the Other concurs with the I who is actually living the exile of the answer. Therefore, the Other is a constitutive part of the answer—the element of knowledge and Revelation. It is as if the Other is the impulse of the question within the I.

The Other has been omnipresent in the creative experience of Arabic poetry. Because the language the Arab poet uses contains many languages, old and new, Arabic, poetically speaking, is plural but in singular form.

But whether in practice or in its contacts with the aforementioned system, the Arabic language has nothing more to tell us. Rather it has become a language of silence, or rather it tends to reduce expression to silence. Its orbit is muteness, not diction. The Other, the Western persona in this instance, is transformed in his relationship to the Arab poet into a limitation and a chain, at least in reference to the system. He may be content with his own freedom within his own limits. Perhaps he may see nothing in the Arabic past but the answer to a question he knows in advance since he devised the question out of his own imagination, need and interest.

This may explain why the Arab poet embodies a double absence—an absence from himself as well as an absence from the Other. He lives between these two exiles: the internal one and the external one. To paraphrase Sartre, he lives between two hells: the I and the Other.

The I is not I, nor is it the Other.

Absence and exile constitute the only presence.

Being a poet means that I have already written but that I have actually written nothing. Poetry is an act without a beginning or an end. It is really a promise of a beginning, a perpetual beginning.

Paris, 9/3/92

Translation from the Arabic by Samuel Hazo

Sujata Bhatt b. 1956

from SEARCH FOR MY TONGUE

You ask me what I mean
by saying I have lost my tongue.
I ask you, what would you do
if you had two tongues in your mouth,
and lost the first one, the mother tongue,
and could not really know the other,
the foreign tongue.
You could not use them both together
even if you thought that way.
And if you lived in a place you had to
speak a foreign tongue,
your mother tongue would rot,
rot and die in your mouth
until you had to spit it out.
I thought I spit it out
but overnight while I dream,

મને હતું કે આખ્ખી જીભ આખ્ખી ભાષા,
(munay hutoo kay aakhee jeebh aakhee bhasha)

મેં થૂંકી નાખી છે.
(may thoonky nakhi chay)

પરં તુ રાત્રે સ્વપ્નામાં મારી ભાષા પાછી આવે છે.
(parantoo rattray svupnama mari bhasha pachi aavay chay)

ફૂલની જેમ મારી ભાષા મારી જીભ
(foolnee jaim mari bhasha mari jeebh)

મોઢામાં ખીલે છે.
(modhama kheelay chay)

ફૂલની જેમ મારી ભાષા મારી જીભ
(fulllnee jaim mari bhasha mari jeebh)

મોઢામાં પાકે છે.
(modhama pakay chay)
it grows back, a stump of a shoot
grows longer, grows moist, grows strong veins,
it ties the other tongue in knots,
the bud opens, the bud opens in my mouth,
it pushes the other tongue aside.
Everytime I think I've forgotten,
I think I've lost the mother tongue,
it blossoms out of my mouth.
Days I try to think in English:
I look up,

       પેલો કાળો કાગડો
       (paylo kallo kagdo)

ઉડતો ઉડતો જાય, હવે ઝાડે પહોચે,
(oodto oodto jai, huhvay jzaday pohchay)

એની ચાં ચમાં કાં ઇક છે.
(ainee chanchma kaeek chay)
the crow has something in his beak.
When I look up

I think:

      આકાશ, સુરજ
      (aakash, suraj)
and then: sky, sun.
Don't tell me it's the same, I know
better. To think of the sky
is to think of dark clouds bringing snow,
the first snow is always on Thanksgiving.
But to think:

      આકાશ, અસમાન, આભ.
      (aakash, usman, aabh)

માથે મોટા કાળા કાગડા ઉડે.
(mathay mota kalla kagda ooday)

કાગડાને માથે સુરજ, રોજે સુરજ.
(kagdanay mathay suraj, rojjay suraj)

એકપણ વાદળ નહિ, એટલે વરસાદ નહિ,
(akepun vadul nahi, atelay varsad nahi)

એટલે અનાજ નહિ, એટલે રોટલી નહિ,
(atelay anaj nahi, atelay rotli nahi)

દાળ ભાત શાક નહિ, કાં ઇ નહિ, કુછ ભી નહિ,
(dal bhat shak nahi, kai nahi, kooch bhi nahi)

માત્ર કાગડા, કાળા કાગડા.
(matra kagda, kalla kagda)
Overhead, large black crows fly.
Over the crows, the sun, always
the sun, not a single cloud
which means no rain, which means no wheat,
no rice, no greens, no bread. Nothing.
Only crows, black crows.
And yet, the humid June air,
the stormiest sky in Connecticut
can never be

       આકાશ
       (aakash)

ચોમાસામાં જ્યારે વરસાદ આવે
(chomasama jyaray varsad aavay)

આખ્ખી રાત આખ્ખો દિ' વરસાદ પડે, વિજળી જાય,
(aakhee raat aakho dee varsad puday, vijli jai)

જ્યારે મા રસોડામાં ધીને દીવ રોટલી વણની
(jyaray ma rasodama gheenay deevay rotli vanti)

શાક હલાવતી
(shak halavti)

રવિંદ્ર સંગીત ગાતી ગાતી
(Ravindrasangeet gaati gaati)

સૌને બોલાવતી
(saonay bolavti)
the monsoon sky giving rain
all night, all day, lightning, the electricity goes out,
we light the cotton wicks in butter:
       candles in brass.

And my mother in the kitchen,
my mother singing:

মোন মোর মেঘের সঙ্গে উড়ে চলে দিগ্‌দিগন্তর পানে . . .
(mon mor megher shungay, ooday cholay dikdigontair panay)
I can't hear my mother in English.

1988

Charles Bernstein b. 1950

from ARTIFICE OF ABSORPTION

[1]

By *absorption* I mean engrossing, engulfing
completely, engaging, arresting attention, reverie,
attention intensification, rhapsodic, spellbinding,
mesmerizing, hypnotic, total, riveting,
enthralling: belief, conviction, silence.

Impermeability suggests artifice, boredom,
exaggeration, attention scattering, distraction,
digression, interruptive, transgressive,
undecorous, anticonventional, unintegrated, fractured,
fragmented, fanciful, ornately stylized, rococo,
baroque, structural, mannered, fanciful, ironic,
iconic, schtick, camp, diffuse, decorative,
repellent, inchoate, programmatic, didactic,
theatrical, background muzak, amusing: skepticism,
doubt, noise, resistance.

Absorptive & antiabsorptive
works both require artifice, but the former may hide
this while the latter may flaunt
it. & absorption may dissolve
into theater as these distinctions chimerically
shift & slide. Especially since,
as in much of my own work, antiabsorptive
techniques are used toward
absorptive ends; or, in satiric writing (it's a put

on, get it?), absorptive means are used
toward antiabsorptive ends. It remains
an open question, & an unresolvable
one, what
will produce an absorptive poem & what will
produce a nonabsorptive one.

[2]

The *intersection*
of absorption & impermeability is precisely
flesh,
as Merleau-Ponty uses this term
to designate the intersection of the visible
& the invisible. This
is the philosophical interior
of my inquiry—that absorption & impermeability
are the warp & woof of poetic composition—
an intertwining or chiasm whose locus
is the flesh of the word. Yet writing re-
verses the dynamic Merleau-Ponty out-
lines for the visible & the invisible:
for it is the invisible of writing
that is imagined to be absorbed
while the visible of writing usually goes unheard
or is silenced. The visibility of words
as a precondition of reading
necessitates that words obtrude impermeably into
the world—this
impermeability makes a reader's absorption
in words possible. The *thickness*
of words ensures that whatever
of their physicality is erased, or engulfed, in
the process of semantic projection,
a residue
tenaciously in-
heres that will not be sublimated
away. Writing is not a thin film
of expendable substitutions that, when reading, falls
away
like scales
to reveal a meaning. The tenacity of

writing's thickness, like the body's
flesh, is
ineradicable, yet mortal. It is
the intrusion
of words into the visible
that marks
writing's own absorption in the world.
To literally put words into Merleau-Ponty's mouth:
The thickness of writing between
the reader & the poem is constitutive for the poem
of its visibility & for the reader
of the outer limit of his or her absorption
in the poem; it is not an obstacle
between them, it is their means
of communication. The thickness of writing,
far from rivaling that of the world,
is on the contrary the sole
means it has to go to the heart of things
by making itself part
of the material world, absorbed
by it.

Absorption & its many con-
verses, re-
verses, is at heart a measure
of the relationship between
a reader &
a work: any attempt to isolate
this dynamic in terms exclusively of
reading
or composition
will fail on this account.
As writers—
& everyone inscribes
in the sense
I mean here—
we can
try to intensify
our relationships by considering
how they work: are we putting
each other to sleep

or waking each other up;
& what do we wake to?
Does our writing stun
or sting? Do we cling to
what we've grasped
too well, or find tunes
in each new
departure.

1986

Diane di Prima b. 1934

from **RANT**

THE ONLY WAR THAT MATTERS IS THE WAR AGAINST THE
    IMAGINATION

ALL OTHER WARS ARE SUBSUMED IN IT

There is no way out of the spiritual battle
There is no way you can avoid taking sides
There is no way you can *not* have a poetics
no matter what you do: plumber, baker, teacher

you do it in the consciousness of making
or not making yr world
you have a poetics: you step into the world
like a suit of readymade clothes

or you etch in light
your firmament spills into the shape of your room
the shape of the poem, of yr body, or yr loves

A woman's life / a man's life is an allegory

Dig it

There is no way out of the spiritual battle
the war is the war against the imagination
you can't sign up as a conscientious objector

the war of the worlds hangs right here, right now, in the balance
it is a war for this world, to keep it
a vale of soul-making

the taste in all our mouths is the taste of our power
and it is bitter as death

bring yr self home to yrself, enter the garden
the guy at the gate w/ the flaming sword is yrself

the war is the war for the human imagination
and no one can fight it but you / & no one can fight it for you

The imagination is not only holy, it is precise
it is not only fierce, it is practical
men die everyday for the lack of it,
it is vast & elegant

intellectus means "light of the mind"
it is not discourse it is not even language
the inner sun

the *polis* Is constellated around the sun
the fire Is central

1985

Preamble & Statement
for a Council on Counterpoetics

On the weekend of September 16, 1989, the undersigned group of poets, artists, environmentalists, and scholars met together under the auspices of the Telluride Institute in Telluride, Colorado.

Our purpose was to discuss the relationship of ethnopoetics—the poetry-and-culture-nexus over diverse space-and-time—to the contemporary crises (ecological, political, ethnic, and spiritual) that continue to confront us as a single but divided species on a single but divided planet.

In the light of that meeting it became clear that what we were seeking in common was an activist poetics that would expand from an ethnopoetic base to incorporate concerns with ecology, language, polis, tradition, and those alternative human models—cognitive, social, and spiritual—that have always been the foundations of what we take to be a true and germinal ethnopoetics.

A poetry so centered in its mission, we felt, was suffering today from a sense of fragmentation and alienation—from the segregation of individuals and groups that, taken all together, might exercise a force larger than any of its particular manifestations. And we recognized further that what was true for poets was also true for other artists and for those whose humane practices lay outside the arts as such.

It is our firm belief that what we are setting out here is not a minority poetics but one that represents the true mainstream of the world's poetries (both deeply traditional and militantly avant-garde), wrongly seen as marginalized from the still dominant western perspective.

With that much as preamble, we offer the following statement of our concern for what a truly contemporary poetics might include, along with our proposals for a loose alliance and interchange between poets and other cultural workers in the various worlds, local and specific, that comprise our global system.

.

STATEMENT. There exist today, as there have throughout this century, poets and groups of poets and cultural activists driven by a sense of planetary urgency toward the exploration and enhancement of a deeply-rooted human and natural potential. While this takes different forms, dependent on the needs and views of individuals and groups and regions, we feel that there is a widespread desire today to accomplish the following:

1. to encourage local forms of expression within a global perspective—both multicultural and intercultural in intention;

2. to remember the sources of poetry in an earth consciousness ("earth as a religious form"—Eliade), thus to support moves toward an enlightened relation to the natural world in which we live and to those fellow species with whom we share the planet;

3. to recognize that advances in technology are not merely a danger to be resisted but an opportunity to advance those principals of interpenetration and communication on which these proposals rest—not least for those of us for whom language is our "proudest tool";

4. to encourage the recovery and expansion of our pre-technological repertoire of powers: of body, of voice, of performance, of deeply-rooted ritual acts, of private and interconnected dreams and dreamworks;

5. to avoid ethnocentrism and a naive provincialism by setting song and speech, spoken and written forms of language, performance and text, on an equal footing, and by recognizing and fostering common goals across the range of human arts and sciences;

6. to oppose with an awakened heart all forms of racism, sexism, and cultural chauvinism, and to encourage an active interchange with third and fourth world peoples on terms of mutual assistance and respect;

7. to resist all forms of repression and censorship, and to defend thereby the acts of the individual (that most local and most threatened form of human life) against the restrictive pressures of the state, of organized religion, and of the vigilante actions of those who live in fear among us;

8. to revitalize a view of artistic experiment as a form of political and social action, and to move beyond that to break down the barriers between art and other forms of human enterprise;

9. to foster alliances between poets, artists, and other cultural and intellectual workers, by reenforcing and creating networks of cultural

activists toward an exchange of ideas, information, and projects in common;

10. to transmit to the century ahead of us that sense of mission that has invigorated and justified the formal experiments of our own time, and to bring the work of poets and artists so committed once more into the public sphere.

(signed)

Pamela Zoline, Director, Telluride Institute, Telluride, Colorado

Anne Waldman, Director, School of Poetics, Naropa Institute, Boulder, Colorado

Nathaniel Tarn, Santa Fe, New Mexico

Ines Talamantez, Religious Studies, University of California, Santa Barbara

Jerome Rothenberg, Visual Arts & Literature, University of California, San Diego

Diane Rothenberg, Anthropology, University of California, San Diego

Janet Rodney, Santa Fe, New Mexico

John Lifton, Director, Telluride Institute, Telluride, Colorado

Pierre Joris, State University of New York at Binghamton

Anselm Hollo, School of Poetics, Naropa Institute, Boulder, Colorado

Mary Crow, Colorado State University, Fort Collins, Colorado

A SECOND GALLERY

Tchicaya U Tam'si 1931–1988

THE TREASURE

for Lilo and Yango Antoniades

No.
I say: no.
No answers: no.
We call from the belly.
The belly doesn't say: no.
Rain falls in large blades
On song gorged with blood.

No!
I say: No!
The moon wants to be round!
No answers: No!
As my soul is thick
I thrust the switches
of a multi-track railroad
far into my head!

No?
I say: No?
No answers: No?
The moon wants to be round?
Let the belly answer!
The belly answers from the belly
We often see:
Love turns its back on the heart!
As punishment, blood runs faster
in the meadows
than in the veins!

No. Nothing to be taken back from this crown . . .
Yet we have to open our blood!
(All the way to the cemetery, trade unionism . . .)
To say that all privilege
comes from sheets or straw
in the bed,
Never from the large losses of water

that made this bed a desert
and not a cradle and not a corn-bin!

The deluge was night
thickened with more smoke
than there was fire in the forges
where the copper is beaten
into the links
of a chain of men
united by the belly and the heart
from the egg on, in that womb!

The spawning took place
right after the vespers;
a crowd of white bellies
floated on the stanley-pool
among the water hyacinths
And night crackled
under the stars' fire.

    •

Keeping its navel on a short leash
the belly no longer knows
what it promised or to whom.
And yet we must open our blood
and no longer know where
to count our own, or with whom.

Those who had come
carried the cross and the banner
under their nostrils
where one saw christ
hunkered down and napping
over the flames of purgatory
and I forget; an emetic
fills the chalice in each hand!
You came:
Are you sure you won?
Always!
I rebel

I bust my gut
I kill the other
I rob him
I subjugate him
"The blacks are landing . . .
The arrows of laughter! . . ."
First the wine, only then the water of baptism
or the oil of the lamp!
Do I betray myself
With such a program
Straight from the Decalogue?

  .

The hyenas' bark
beats down the olives for anointing
oil and not for lamp oil.

In the Caliph's city
The wine mixes with the roses.
Evening blues the fire
A stream of water licks the air
Its scream a thread sewing
death onto our life.

My forehead sweats in your eyes.

The quick water absolves the man
whom a wild flower dismembers.

No. Nothing to be retaken from this crown!

No.
I say: no.
The moon wants to be round
and answers: no.
And yet
something inside me
carries among the brambles of desire
a crown of copper wet
with a martyr's blood!

And yet
Suddenly this belly will
cover my mouth.
It will be the final tomb
shallow enough for my body
to be the flood that overflows the winds.
Who'll be noah except him
except the soul this
vertebra-song pours out
accusing the author of his death?

Love lays waste.
Love kills.
Love leaves.
When was it said:
the belly remains?
It falls with the plagues
Upon my mouth greased by a judas kiss.

I suffocate under a belly
unable to say sorry
to the chaff more warlike
than the wild bee.

> "*I am the Congo.*"
> *(Lumumba)*

I'll be the device for my own salvation!
Already velvet breaks the silence
in ephemeral wings
snowing upon the oil lamp.

For carnival, slobber on the masks
serves better than two smirks
But as I have only one face
it's over that one that I pass my hand.
The too flat horizon here spears my heart
If I step back everything bristles!
I don't leave harbor with wind on my flanks
but with squalls in my belly.

•

I claw my belly,
Neither iodine nor seaweed
nor algae had
such sweetness in their caresses
as my lips back then
before earth was insulted
by a galloping gaggle of
ventriloquist jackals!

The belly,
with that ever present pestilential
heat of old charnel houses.

    ·

Ah! the flower is blue
Ah! the blue-jeans are blue
Ah! this blues I dance
no longer knows what the belly promises:
Three cents
for the wildest passion
for the passion most wild
Where is it playing?
Where was it played out?
But where is the church's parvis?
In the antechamber
of the Bishop of *Kin*!
Where a stream of water licks the air!

He will sit on the right of Okito
Ah! the Jews know well
that that messiah's for sale at
Three cents,
The belly.
For sale everywhere with this pestilential
heat of old charnel houses . . .

    ·

Nothing's lonelier than the belly—
and the heart!

Lonely with that solitude
of sharp edges ripping at open wounds;
tearing out the milk teeth
at the heart's first disappointment!
You have to side with those musics
from which blood trickles
though in Kin
we never saw
the soul spill out with the blood!
Now, if the sky be dirtied by those flakes
only the ardent skeletons
are sure not to answer the call
now I am armed with blanks
to lose myself in the slightest assault
of laughter
or in those musics
from which blood trickles
in Kin!

    •

An infant makes his fingers dance
to teach me to remain silent about its life.
But my head hits every gong,
but my belly is warm only with wine!

To open one's nose is a heroic action
only if the mouths cross their lips
only if desire—sudden firework—
speaks no longer to my heart
but for this vertigo from which I fall
into the thistles, hired assassin or mutineer
in Kin!

Dance speaks the best language
in which to make of two bodies
the two members of a single sentence
whose verb to love has to be written
in the pluperfect!
Even in Kin where blood
comes at I don't know what price:
Is the dollar the yard-stick?

Then the arms!
Then the forearms!
Then the legs!
on top of the feet!
Then other limbs!
Despite climbing from the root
up to the clearings, we had
to wait for the trunk through
three choruses!

.

Someone calls me
I climb down into my feet
to become an anonymous step
in the retinue of his passion.

No.
With the belly, to focus all the gazes back
onto the unique suppleness of my voice
gives you the key:
a smile of mauve petals
and the blood and the blood and the blood
undiscontinued, recitative
escaped from this putrid mouth
through the heat of this belly!
They assured me he was ventriloquist
although the jackals were in league
with we-know-who,
whose teeth chortled
in a bite
in a green bite
in a bite of three fathoms
worth a dollar per yard-stick
and not a thorn crown
in Kin!

What is Kin?
Kin is the city
where the river has its hand
on my heart.
Kin, that's near Kalina.

The boat leaves
the holds stink of sweat
Don't wait for bread
nor the open heart, nor the mouth bloodied
but the fist exploded
by a burst of laughter
that counts its five fingers
clean of poison.

Though as soon as the drums start
we tell ourselves in Kin:
The chant draped itself
in his face!
His heart yawned with both ventricles
on Fifth Avenue!
The world clings to a drop of water
whose lips retain
only the rags of the song.
He says:
I give my brothers their own eyes.
He says:
I say to the woman
to clothe her belly
only with bells;
to leave it up to the crickets
to nibble night away;
to the warm sugar to rape the dawn;
to the sand to paint the hostile winds
to the sea to be docile to your belly . . .
He says:
I say: no!

Translation from the French by Pierre Joris

COMMENTARY

The poet is above all a man, a man in the full meaning of the word, a con-scious man. A conscious man is he who dreams, and the dream is only the projection into the future of what can be realized. (T. U.) And again: *I lack the intoxication to understand what is plausible. And yet the world is as it appears to the lark: a distorting mirror.*

Though he wrote his poetry, plays, and novels in the colonizer's language rather than in Vili, his mother tongue, & spent most of his life after age fifteen in Paris, U Tam'si could have taken as his own the words of his martyred friend Patrice Lumumba, "I am the Congo." Repetition/progression in slow incremental changes, as in African music & dance ("Dance is the best language"), organizes the poetry's rhythms & images & points to its profoundly oral source. "Everything I have written is oral," he elsewhere asserts—just as the syntactical and tropic(al) movements of the poems are often based on the traditional rhetoric of proverbs & riddles. The imagery, firmly rooted in Congolese or African contexts, is painstakingly orchestrated through "a syntax of juxtaposition [that] explodes the hinges of logic" (Léopold Sédar Senghor). Similarly, U Tam'si's city of Kinshasa—*Kin* in the poems—is as strong a place as, say, Olson's Gloucester, with the added advantage that its history is most active & alive in the postcolonial present of the poet's lifetime. The mix of mythopoetic & sociopolitical material, as well as the dual cultural poetics (French & African), shapes the powerful book-length work *Le Ventre* (excerpted here), where the "belly" of the title is played through its rich, often contradictory, possibilities: the divinatory open belly revealing the future, the slit bellies of those killed in war, the belly as womb, as hunger, as omphalos to the ancestors. All this he puts into a final poem, *The Belly Remains,* which (Betty O'Grady writes) "takes up successively and almost line by line the titles of the thirteen poems that make up the collection, so that each phrase releases the complexity of emotion and meaning that was developed in the poem of that title," ending on "a note of hope: 'God be thanked the prophets fall / most often on their backs / most often with their arms wide open / most often / their bellies to the sky!'"

Jerome Rothenberg b. 1931

THAT DADA STRAIN

the zig zag mothers of the gods
of science   the lunatic fixed stars
& pharmacies
fathers who left the tents of anarchism
unguarded
the arctic bones
strung out on saint germain
like tom toms
living light bulbs
aphrodisia
"art is junk" the urinal
says "dig a hole

"& swim in it"
a message from the grim computer
"ye are hamburgers"

from **KHURBN**

Dos Oysleydikn (The Emptying)

at honey street in ostrova
where did the honey people go?
empty   empty
miodowa empty
empty bakery & empty road to warsaw
yellow wooden houses & houses plastered up with stucco
the shadow of an empty name still on their doors
shadai & shadow shattering the mother tongue
the mother's tongue but empty
the way the streets are empty where we walk
pushing past crowds of children
old women airing themselves outside the city hall
old farmers riding empty carts down empty roads
who don't dispel but make an emptiness
a taste of empty honey
empty rolls you push your fingers through
empty sorrel soup dribbling from their empty mouths
defining some other poland
lost to us the way the moon
is lost to us
the empty clock tower measuring her light four ways
sorrel in gardens mother of god at roadsides
in the reflection of the empty trains
only the cattle bellow in
like jews the dew-eyed wanderers
still present   still the flies
cover their eyeballs
the trains drive eastward, falling
down a hole (a holocaust) of empty houses
of empty ladders leaning against haystacks no one climbs
empty ostrova & empty ostrolenka
old houses empty in the woods near vyzhkov

dachas the peasants would rent to you
& sleep in stables
the bialo forest spreading to every side
retreating the closer we come to it to claim it
empty oaks & empty fir trees
a man in an empty ditch who reads a book
the way the jews once read
in the cold polish light   the fathers sat there too
the mothers posed at the woods' edge
the road led brightly to treblinka
& other towns   beaches at brok
along the bug
marshes with cattails
cows tied to trees
past which their ghosts walk
their ghosts refuse to walk
tomorrow in empty fields of poland
still cold against their feet
an empty pump black water drips from
will form a hill of ice
the porters will dissolve with burning sticks
they will find a babe's face at the bottom
invisible & frozen imprinted in the rock

Dos Geshray (The Scream)

Erd, zolst nit tsudekn mayn blut
un zol nit kayn ort zayn far mayn geshray
               JOB 16:18

"practice your scream" I said
(why did I say it?)
because it was his scream & wasn't my own
it hovered between us   bright
to our senses always bright it held
the center place
then somebody else came up & stared
deep in his eyes there found a memory
of horses galloping faster the wheels dyed red
behind them   the poles had reserved
a feast day but the jew

locked in his closet screamed
into his vest a scream
that had no sound therefore
spiraled around the world
so wild that it shattered stones
it made the shoes piled in the doorway
scatter their nails   things testify
—the law declares it—
shoes & those dearer objects
like hair & teeth do
by their presence
I cannot say that they share the pain
or show it not even the photos
in which the expressions of the dead shine forth
the crutches by their mass the prosthetic limbs by theirs
bear witness the eyeglasses bear witness
the suitcases the children's shoes the german tourists
in the stage set oshvientsim had become
the letters over its gates still glowing
still writ large
ARBEIT MACHT FREI
& to the side   HOTEL
and GASTRONOMIC BAR
the spirit of the place dissolving
indifferent to his presence
there with the other ghosts
the uncle   grieving
his eyelids turning brown an eye
protruding from his rump
this man whose body
is a crab's
his gut turned outward
the pink flesh of his children
hanging from him
that his knees slide up against
there is no holocaust
for these   but khurbn only
the word still spoken by the dead
who say   my khurbn
& my children's khurbn
it is the only word that the poem allows

because it is their own
the word as prelude to the scream
it enters
through the asshole
circles along the gut
into the throat
& breaks out
in a cry   a scream
it is his scream that shakes me
weeping   in oshvientsim
& that allows the poem to come

Dibbukim (Dibbiks)

spirits of the dead   lights
flickering (he said) their ruakh
will never leave the earth
instead they crowd the forests the fields
around the privies the hapless spirits
wait millions of souls
turned into ghosts at once
the air is full of them
they are standing each one beside a tree
under its shadows or the moon's
but they cast no shadows of their own
this moment & the next they are pretending
to be rocks   but who is fooled
who is fooled here   by the dead   the jews
the gypsies   the leadeyed polish patriot
living beings reduced to symbols
of what it had been to be alive
"o do not touch them" the mother cries
fitful, as almost in a dream
she draws the child's hand to her heart
in terror   but the innocent dead
grow furious they break down doors
drop slime onto your tables
they tear their tongues out by the roots
& smear your lamps your children's lips
with blood a hole drilled in the wall
will not deter them

from stolen homes stone architectures
they hate they are the convoys of the dead
the ghostly drivers still searching
the roads to malkin   ghost carts overturned
ghost autos in blue ditches
if only our eyes were wild enough
to see them our hearts to know their terror
the terror of the man who walks alone
their victim whose house whose skin
they crawl in   incubus & succubus
a dibbik leaping from a cow to lodge inside
his throat   clusters of jews
who swarm here mothers without hair
blackbearded fathers
they lap up fire   water   slime
entangle the hairs of brides
or mourn their clothing hovering
over a field of rags   half-rotted shoes
& tablecloths   old thermos bottles   rings
lost tribes in empty synagogues
at night their voices
carrying across the fields
to rot your kasha your barley
stricken beneath their acid rains
no holocaust because no sacrifice
no sacrifice to give the lie
of meaning   & no meaning   after auschwitz
there is only poetry   no hope
no other language left to heal
no language   & no faces
because no faces left   no names
no sudden recognitions on the street
only the dead still swarming   only khurbn
a dead man in a rabbi's clothes
who squats   outside the mortuary house
who guards their privies who is called
master of shit   an old alarm clock
hung around his neck   who holds
a wreath of leaves under his nose
from eden   "to drive out
"the stinking odor of this world"

THE LORCA VARIATIONS (XXVIII)

"For Turtles"

1

Up there—or down here
for that matter—the screams
rush around us
Ellipses dismember the tower
of Babel, crapulent city,
enraged zigzag women still sit in
with feathers, on porticos
Men with pale foreheads
shout poems from its rooftops,
crushing its grasses,
city that's buried in words,
like "cypress" & "daylight"
"up there" & "down here"

2

My heart is flying from me
—see it fly—
& rising in a spiral,
like a star,
a spiral rising past the Cape
obliquely,
like a neon heart,
celestial turtle set before the pope,
until the turtle & the star
drop back to earth,
to test the limits of a heart,
the way that hunger
tests the soul
or feet whatever life is left us
A heart, a soul, & many turtles,
where the heart transforms
the body, like some pluvial
sahara, & the turtles
blot out the horizon,
leaving turtleshells & wings behind,
unto our final rest

A PERSONAL MANIFESTO. *[1] I will change your mind. [2] Any means (= methods) to that end. [3] To oppose the "devourers" = bureaucrats, system-makers, priests, etc. (W. Blake). [4] "& if thou wdst understand that wch is me, know this: all that I have sd I have uttered playfully — & I was by no means ashamed of it" (J. C. to his disciples,* The Acts of St. John*).*

J. R.

(1) "I did not know—at the opening—how old the work was. Like others my age then—& others before & after us—I was looking for what in my own time would make a difference to that time. What is easily forgotten is the condition of the time itself that should make us want to go in that direction: to pull down & to transform. As a young child I heard people still talking about the *world* war (even the *great* war) in the singular, but by adolescence the *second* war had come & with it a crisis in the human capacity to reduce & stifle life.

"Auschwitz & Hiroshima came to be the two events by which we spoke of it—signs of an enormity that turned myth into history, metaphor into fact. . . . By the mid-twentieth century, in Charles Olson's words, 'man' had been 'reduced to so much fat for soap, superphosphate for soil, fillings and shoes for sale,' an enormity that had robbed language (one of our 'proudest acts' he said) of the power to meaningfully respond, had thus created a crisis of expression (no, of *meaning,* of *reality*), for which a poetics must be devised if we were to rise, again, beyond the level of a scream or of a silence more terrible than any scream.

"It is in some such ways—not only (or even principally) as a subject matter but in the language & structure of the poem itself—that the avant-garde of modernism challenged the traditional/conventional art & poetry that preceded it. It is in this way too that 'post'modern poets & artists (from Dada to the present) have challenged the works of the preceding modernists, not as a nostalgic return to the past or to the state-bred values of official culture, but to keep open the channels of renewal that remain the central necessities of a poetry & art of transformations . . ." (J.R., 1989).

(2) GLOSSARY. *Khurbn* (Yiddish, from Hebrew *khurban*): the common word for *holocaust, disaster. Erd, zolst nit,* etc.: Earth, mayest thou not cover up my blood, & may there be no place left for my scream. *Oshvientsim* (Yiddish): Auschwitz. *Dibbukim* (*Dibbiks*): Spirits of those who die before their time & enter into (i.e. possess) the bodies of the living.

Paavo Haavikko b. 1931

from THE WINTER PALACE

The First Poem

Silver, into which I force
images, one next to the other, so they speak;

a many-crested roof rends winds and birds,
North go
snow, birds and grass,
not much industry,
an antenna, airy arabesque or
ear strung into wind,
greetings and goodbye,
tree tree tree and tree,
this is a song:

The green I don't have time to see before it bursts
and again came Spring, the bird tried to sing
and its voice was muddled muddled,
helpless grass
and a house and in the house a man and a woman, a child
/ and an old
one,
nine holes in the soul.

A spinning chimney-cap and three colours:
green, black, and grey,
melting snow, forest, rushes, river and boats.
Pine, fir, birch, alders, and willow (a bush),
here, the hazel grows into a tree.

And again came Spring. Long weeks, the woman breathes
/ into it
and it cries out:
I am born, I am a girl
and I go out by myself and play in front of the house.

Wooden birds, their beaks pointing straight up
and Spring,
here all I can say is that

Spring or Autumn, the wall sheds stucco
	and snow, birds, and grass head North
and come from there and pass by here,
	and the clouds flake in the sky,
the sun is not called bald,

did I say that the trees and the branches of the trees,
	and that the willow's a bush, the hazel grows here?

The station platform was blooming.
	Marching along it, the world hung from one's feet, now
	                                                / from one,
	now from the other,
and the pillar, from the ceiling down to the floor, hung
	like a thick rope;
this white city, in the perpendicular hand of architects.

How would it be to have a little conversation here? This one:

	And winter came into the armoured car,
settled down, stayed a while, and left,
	this is where snow, birds, and grass passed by,
and Winter left cylindrical galoshes: went North.

Is this one of them who crossed the Alps?

	No, this isn't Hannibal.

Well then, is this an elephant?

	No no, this is a car.

But where is Hannibal?

	No no, he's gone abroad.

One can hold on to one's hat with both hands if one so desires:

wind took the birds, the sea is swelling, the trees are growing
	                                                / sparse.

And, briefly:

	The old part (1754–1762) is the Winter Palace
and everything is accordingly, ceiling, floor and
	walls, full of exalted beings: Venus, Jupiter

and women of a full-bodied vintage.
   It can still be seen that on the Berezhina River
many a one dropped head and hat,
   that the brawl at Borodino was a victory;

I am talking this under my hair.

The Second Poem

And I asked for directions from a bird who is myself
   and the bird replied:

leave early, as soon as the papers burst from the night.

And when the paper came, I folded it under my arm and
                                        / walked across
      the open space,
an exaggeration, of course! But I imagine
   its fingernails to be as wide as a turtle,
and I advanced upon that person who is Fear,
   its manners those of a diplomat, its memory zero.

And I was as tall as a match and I lit the paper
   to be able to see through the rain,
and it was pouring, and I hunkered down
   and lit the paper with a match,
it didn't catch, and I kept lighting it,
   it caught fire and the smoke flew

and thence was now heard a terrible coughing, as if
   someone had been breathing birds on the wing

and a tinkle, the bottle was tinkling there,

and in the bottle there was, presumably, some exalted being,
   I almost burst into tears,
in the bottle, a being I wanted to meet
   in the bottle.

And this person shouted and burned, in the bottle, poor devil,
and if it had a beard, it burned, if it had archives, they were
                                        / on fire.

And the horrendous fire spread from line to line,
and the bottle was wrapped up in papers,
around it
        papers had been tied, as they are around appletrees
    when Autumn is coming,
and it crawled out of the bottle.

That was a mad journey.

It jumped from rock to rock, line to line,
    fifteen lines ahead
everything is on fire, it skipped,

and I wanted to know:

    I ask you, oh exalted being, great fox,
tell me, where is the region that is not a place?

And promptly it answered:

It is not a place. I was a rose, I began to swell,
    a world burst forth from me,
I want to weep for this shame! Void myself!
    I! Abort!
Oh why did I leave my world, here no one knows me!

That was the whole conversation.

That was the journey along the rocks by the shore of heaven.

Translation from the Finnish by Anselm Hollo

COMMENTARY

Only through the unanswerable questions can the world be depicted. . . .
The only meaningful freedom is that of the individual. Every system de-
sires to offer every other kind of freedom except this one.
P. H.

Writes Anselm Hollo, who is both our major translator of Finnish poetry &
for many years a seminal figure in U.S. poetry: " 'Discovered' at the age of
twenty by Tuomas Anhava (b. 1927), the Finnish poet, translator, critic,
and editor who was the mentor of Finnish Modernism, Haavikko quickly
proceeded to forge a career as the foremost poet of his generation. This was
essentially a post-WWII generation weary of traditional and often nation-

alistic post-Symbolism, psychological self-searching, and ethical debate, and ready to be influenced and inspired by the first Finnish translations of the works of Ezra Pound (and, in their wake, classical Chinese and Japanese poems), St.-John Perse, and T. S. Eliot, which began to appear in the late forties.

"Understated and ironical in tone, Haavikko's poems introduced a new supple free verse prosody based on the speech rhythms of the Finnish language. Unafraid of tackling the 'great subjects'—love, death, identity, history, power—the poet has, since then, created a body of work of monumental proportions: more than sixty book titles including collections of lyrical and narrative poems, novels, short stories, collections of aphorisms, plays, opera libretti, television scripts, and historical works. . . .

"Always aware of the traps of language, and even fond of language games, Haavikko rejects 'solutions' per se. . . . His essential stance is that of a conservative anarchist who has decided that neither optimism nor pessimism really apply to individual or collective human history, any more than they apply to the history of trees."

Tomas Tranströmer b. 1931

THE GALLERY

I stayed overnight at a motel by the E3.
In my room a smell I'd felt before
in the oriental halls of a museum:

masks Tibetan Japanese on a pale wall.

But it's not masks now, it's faces

forcing through the white wall of oblivion
to breathe, to ask about something.
I lie awake watching them struggle
and disappear and return.

Some lend each other features, exchange faces
far inside me
where oblivion and memory wheel-and-deal.

They force through oblivion's second coat
the white wall
they fade-out fade-in.

Here is a sorrow that doesn't call itself sorrow.

Welcome to the authentic galleries!
Welcome to the authentic galleys!
The authentic grilles!

The karate boy who paralysed someone
is still dreaming of fast money.

This woman keeps buying things
to toss in the hungry mouth of the vacuum
sneaking up behind her.

Mr X doesn't dare go out.
A dark stockade of ambiguous people
stands between him
and the steadily retreating horizon.

She who once fled from Karelia
she who could laugh . . .
now shows herself
but dumb, petrified, a statue from Sumer.

As when I was ten and came home late.
In the stairwell the light switched off
but the lift I stood in was bright, it rose
like a diving-bell through black depths
floor by floor while imagined faces
pressed against the grille . . .

But the faces are not imagined now, they are real.

I lie straight out like a cross-street.

Many step out from the white mist.
We touched each other once—we did!

A long bright carbolic-scented corridor.
The wheelchair. The teenage girl
learning to talk after the car-crash.

He who tried to call out under water
and the world's cold mass poured in
through nose and mouth.

Voices in the microphone said: Speed is power
speed is power!
Play the game, the show must go on!

We move through our career stiffly, step by step,
it's like a Noh play
with masks, high-pitched song: It's me, it's me!
The one who's failed
is represented by a rolled-up blanket.

An artist said: Before, I was a planet
with its own dense atmosphere.
Entering rays were broken into rainbows.
Perpetual raging thunderstorms, within.

Now I'm extinct and dry and open.
I no longer have childlike energy.
I have a hot side and a cold side.

No rainbows.

I stayed overnight in the echoing house.
Many want to come in through the walls
but most of them can't make it:

they're overcome by the white hiss of oblivion.

Anonymous singing drowns in the walls.
Discreet tappings that don't want to be heard
drawn-out sighs
my old repartees creeping homelessly.

Listen to society's mechanical self-reproaches
the voice of the big fan
like the artificial wind in mine tunnels
six hundred metres down.

Our eyes keep wide open under the bandages.

If I could at least make them realise
that this trembling beneath us
means we are on a bridge.

Often I have to stand motionless.
I am the knife-thrower's partner at a circus!
Questions I tossed aside in rage
come whining back
don't hit me, but nail down my shape
my rough outline
and stay in place when I've walked away.

Often I have to be silent. Voluntarily!
Because 'the last word' is said again and again.
Because good-day and good-bye . . .
Because this very day . . .

Because the margins rise at last
over their brims
and flood the text.

I stayed overnight at the sleepwalker's motel.
Many faces here are desperate
others smoothed out
after the pilgrim's walk through oblivion.

They breathe vanish struggle back again
they look past me
they all want to reach the icon of justice.

It happens rarely
that one of us really *sees* the other;

a person shows himself for an instant
as in a photograph but clearer
and in the background
something which is bigger than his shadow.

He's standing full-length before a mountain.
It's more a snail's shell than a mountain.
It's more a house than a snail's shell.
It's not a house but has many rooms.
It's indistinct but overwhelming.
He grows out of it, it out of him.
It's his life, it's his labyrinth.

Translation from the Swedish by Robin Fulton

Sometimes you wake up at night / and quickly throw words down / on the nearest paper, on the margin of a newspaper / (the words glowing with meaning!) / but in the morning: the same words don't say anything anymore, scrawls, misspeakings. / Or fragments of a great nightly style that dragged past?

T. T. (from "Baltics," translated by Samuel Charters)

Writes Anselm Hollo: "Free of the Symbolist traces and sometimes overblown rhetoric evident in the work of his predecessors, the first generation of Swedish Modernists, Tranströmer's poetry adheres to Imagist precepts of careful understatement and condensation. It insists on an intensely personal vision, often expressed in abrupt and startling metaphors: 'Painted in the air above the garden / the hieroglyph of a dog's bark' (*Secrets on the Way*, 1958).

"The dominant persona of Tranströmer's poems is that of an observer in a continuous waking dream, a conscious dreamer who tries to decipher what he sees but only manages to do so in fleeting, epiphanal glimpses. Always starting out from recognizable settings—Nordic, Baltic, Mediterranean—the austerely melodic text conveys a sense of a larger but quite secretive dimension behind the one our senses perceive: 'sometimes the glimpses suggest a world brutal and ancient, sometimes one that is curiously innocent, unnervingly fresh' (Robert Hass). . . .

"In the Sixties, when Sweden's cultural climate grew heavily politicized, Tranströmer became a target for younger critics who called for a 'new simplicity' in the arts, for forms of more direct and public address with a more obvious social and political content or message. Tranströmer's generation was accused of a hankering for mysticism, verbal 'magic,' and an overly individualistic 'ivory tower' preoccupation with image and metaphor. Tranströmer weathered this onslaught by pursuing his concerns (as Robert Hass has noted, the concerns of a 'private citizen'), publishing a dozen elegantly composed collections of never more than fifty pages each, and emerging as the uncontested grand old man of Swedish poetry."

Ece Ayhan b. 1931

TO TRACE FROM HEBREW

My legs are long
they are long wherever I go
wherever I go they find me
my sister in a blind alley

To trace a dove for this town
to trace the eyes of the dove
one dove
in the middle ages one dove with chalk

Along the whole wall trees cool
I am tracing a sound
I want everybody everybody to have a sound
in the dove a sound in the middle ages in my sister a sound

Wherever I go they are long
they find me from my legs always
as I trace a different voice
and a holiday full of flags in a city
in Hebrew

Translation from the Turkish by Murat Nemet-Nejat

THE NIGGER IN A PHOTOGRAPH

Accursed. The curse which with its curving unsheathed letter will never leave me alone, which I take everywhere, my invisible dog, the curse. Who can be friends with me? Who? It is said that I carry that monk's blood, and with a relentless agitation I run here and there, barefoot, and on my tiny chin a big beauty spot, I am known with my covered beauty still. Like the stain in the curve of the letter U.

Flower. I began my adventures as a flower vendor. Flowers and children bedecking a string, dry petals. But how I was under a spell those days. Because of a little fairy's curse, I couldn't be looked at. Light Maltese fevers run in empty lots in summer evenings. And endless hallucinations full of clowns run in ruins. Then a stone arched passage. I am living in the drawer of a fifty-year-old witch, nailed. Am I really? One can not tell what season it is, and I am cold. Curved like the letter U.

. . . I went to Jerusalem in that exile of the flower vendors and got settled in the town clock . . . But to remember these things, I don't want to remember them . . . It had run out, the money I had saved selling flowers . . . This far away from Smyrna, I was pawned. Let this be the nigger in the negative of a photograph from me, will you receive it one day? I had it taken while learning Hebrew, with my invisible dog inside a Jewess. Lonely and terrible. Under a huge tree which had shed its leaves, barely touching a chair.

It is not out of pity, but I am worried it won't pass. The curve of the letter U.

Translation from the Turkish by Murat Nemet-Nejat

GERANIUM AND THE CHILD

Inside those caves, grottos of shame, full of mud, a child is still taking shelter, hopping. A Salonica bundle, a matted hat, a plover. The rain bird. Condemned, on his right cheek his birthmark flower is the size of a hand. And there were next to his aunt's geranium gardens, along the length . . . Apparently during autumnal dreams with the marching band of his friend and of death a child going to the island streets full of water.

The wind is dragging outside: a moldy eyed tin dragon and a rusting corpse; because, during the vows of silence, an underwater ogre always lingers. Sailors, tars are wearing silk frocks. Disguised as his timid uncle who'll fetch him home from Salonica. But, then, in kegs with nails, in kegs with nails. Later, towards morning, an after-quiet Navy blue. And one returns, on unshod pale and coughing horses, descending the ladder of saints, to the dark tanneries and poppy stores.

In Salonica the gates of childhood are huge, lavender and without door knobs. He will go and sleep in an elementary school, among all those shallow waters, star fish. Like the open forgotten shutters of his aunt. With the marching band of his friend and of death, the child telling, alone, the story of the cart of geraniums put out on sale on earth at night.

Translation from the Turkish by Murat Nemet-Nejat

*Imagine that a person one meets in a tavern starts telling us about his en-
tire life. This narrative leaves a zero impression. But the same person's al-
lusion to his life in a single phrase, maybe a detail he invents, displaces the
narrative he is telling at length. Instead of stupidly obeying the [normative]
word order, the order of words is jolted by the finger of the imagination
from its set arrangement and left in this new place.*

E. A. (from a 1966 interview by Önay Sözer)

Writes Murat Nemet-Nejat as Ayhan's principal English translator: "A ma-
jor figure (with Ilhan Berk and Cemal Sureya) in the 'second new' movement
of post–World War II Turkish poetry, Ece Ayhan published *A Blind Cat
Black* and *Orthodoxies* in 1965 and 1968 respectively, at first to little atten-
tion. By the mid-1980s, however, he had emerged as a dominant poet of the
victimized, of the totally discarded and outlawed. In doing so, his localized
theme became that of 'Galata,' the labyrinthine old European section of Is-
tanbul, where Europeans, Orthodox Christians, and Jews have lived his-
torically, but at the same time the city's red light district, its sexual under-
belly. This 'contradiction' is imbedded in the Turkish language itself, where
'orthodox' means Orthodox Christian (and, by implication, holy, pious,
virtuous) but, as slang, means whore, homosexual, pederast, betrayer, etc.
The result in Ayhan's work is a poetry filled with Armenians, Greeks, and
Jews, who are also 'orthodox' in the slang sense: a poetry radically alienat-
ing to the mainstream reader and a poetics of a *new place*. With that much
as thematic, then, he weaves a style around expressions often absent from
the dictionary, making verbal connections among the secondary, tertiary,
and unofficial meanings of words or their echoes, while pushing Turkish
syntax overboard, eliding or 'misplacing' syntactically connective tissues, so
that words lose their linear context and explode from an unsettled center.
His poetry in that sense is about the traces, distortions, and codes that the
invisible, suppressed, ignored, exploited, or taboo have left upon the main-
stream language and its forms. His music is the music of those traces."

SOME ORAL POETS

It is *the shape of the voice*—the "history of the voice" (in Kamau Brathwaite's phrase) behind it—through which the poems included here are formed. In saying that, Brathwaite was bringing many things together, but principally the sense, shared by many of us engaging in the larger common project, that there are poetries existing outside of literature & writing and that they are tied—through individual makers—to the life of the communities from which they come. Such "oral poetries," if recognized, have been viewed most often as both *anonymous* (their authorship absorbed by collectivities) & located in an ongoing past: not of *our* time (nor any historical time, for that matter). If there's a partial truth in this, that's all it is: a very partial truth. For what the breakdown of the old hierarchies should have made clear by now is the contemporaneous presence of language masters (= poets) whose means of composition & of publication take place (griot-like) outside the nexus of writing or under circumstances where speech & song precede the written poem. It should be clear too—beyond any (ethno)poetics of the collective voice—that these poets have names & that they coexist with "us," sometimes to shape our own work (if we listen). So Brathwaite writes, concerning those of the English Caribbean who speak & compose inside a "nation language" (above, page 385) that he sometimes shares in writing: "It is inconceivable that any Caribbean poet writing today is not going to be influenced by this submerged culture, which is, in fact, an emerging culture. . . . At last our poets today are recognizing that it is essential that they use the resources that have always been there, but which have been denied to them—which they have sometimes themselves denied." In saying which, it is the poets of the voice to whom his words are pointing.

Of those who follow in these pages, all have operated in a highly visible way in their cultures, most within defined traditions on which they work the changes coming from their present lives:

- María Sabina (for whom see also volume one, page 765) was a Mazatec shaman ("wise woman") from Huautla de Jiménez in Oaxaca, Mexico, whose cures, she tells us, come not only through the psychedelic psilocybe mushroom but most immediately through a hypostatized Book of Language that allows her, though illiterate, to read.
- Very differently situated (in the fishing city of Trujillo in Peru), Eduardo Calderón's practice as a *curandero* rests on an incantatory language & the innovative assemblage & manipulation of objects-as-

symbols on his curing table/altar (*mesa*)—a practice he relates very specifically to his work as an artist (ceramicist/sculptor) & maker-of-images.

- In Andrew Peynetsa's spoken narratives—as in those of other oral poets—the energy resides not only in the story told but in the contour of words & phrases and in the silences between them (the basis, here, for Dennis Tedlock's "total" transcription & translation).

- With Robert Johnson (d. 1938) as with other great blues poets, the words offer an arena for small or larger changes, set off against a stable melodic line (or series of such) & the ironies of a "real life" (in his case cut short by murder at age 27).

- Komi Ekpe was a *heno* ("poet-cantor") of the Ewe people of Ghana: master of the dirge & the *halo* (ritualized abuse poem), whose songs, however secular in content, come (poet Kofi Awoonor tells us) from a *hadzivodu*, "a personal god of songs, from whom he claims he receives poetic inspiration in his sleep."

- A "nation language" poet from Jamaica, Miss Queenie emerges—in Brathwaite's account of her—as "priestess, prophet, and symbolist," whose art rests in performance ("how she uses her eyes, her mouth, her whole face") to render "the complex forces that have led to this classical expression."

- The comparison with Gillespie's *Sabla y Blu* would be foremost to the sound poetry showing up elsewhere in these volumes—e.g., the "Dada" of 1916 Zurich (volume one), echoed in "That Dada Strain" of 1920s jazz or the still later wordless naming of post–World War II bebop.

- And, while it differs in its means, Tom Waits's *Swordfishtrombone* is a further example of a popular oral work of *poesis*—a poetry far more heard than seen—as it has fused with many of the verbal innovations charted in these pages.

The complexity of poetry over the last hundred years is in part a corollary of convergences such as these—simultaneously present for our fresh consideration.

María Sabina

from **THE MIDNIGHT VELADA**

Ah, Jesu Kri
I am a woman who shouts
I am a woman who whistles
I am a woman who lightnings, says
Ah, Jesu Kri
Ah, Jesusi
Ah, Jesusi
Cayetano García   [SHE CALLS HIS NAME TO GET HIS ATTENTION.
                         "YES," HE RESPONDS, "WORK, WORK."]

Ah, Jesusi
Woman saintess, says
Ah Jesusi
     [HERE SHE BEGINS HUMMING AND CLAPPING AND UTTERING THE
         MEANINGLESS SYLLABLES "SO" AND "SI." THROUGHOUT THE
             ENTIRE PASSAGE THAT FOLLOWS SHE GOES ON CLAPPING
                   RHYTHMICALLY IN TIME TO HER WORDS.]

hmm hmm hmm
hmm hmm hmm
hmm hmm hmm
hmm hmm hmm
hmm hmm hmm
so so so si
hmm hmm hmm
hmm hmm hmm
Woman who resounds
Woman torn up out of the ground
Woman who resounds
Woman torn up out of the ground
Woman of the principal medicinal berries
Woman of the sacred medicinal berries
Ah Jesusi
Woman who searches, says
Woman who examines by touch, says
ha ha ha
hmm hmm hmm
hmm hmm hmm

She is of one word, of one face, of one spirit, of one light, of one day
hmm hmm hmm
Cayetano García   [HE ANSWERS, "YES. . . ."
      SHE SAYS: "ISN'T THAT HOW?" HE RESPONDS, "YES, THAT'S IT."
                  SHE SAYS: "ISN'T THAT IT? LIKE THIS. LISTEN."]
Woman who resounds
Woman torn up out of the ground
Ah Jesusi
Ah Jesusi
            [IN THE BACKGROUND THE MAN LAUGHS WITH PLEASURE.]
Ah Jesusi
Ah Jesusi
Ah Jesusi
hmm hmm hmm
so so so
Justice woman
hmm hmm hmm   ["THANK YOU," SAYS THE MAN.]
Saint Peter woman
Saint Paul woman
Ah Jesusi
Book woman
Book woman
Morning Star woman
Cross Star woman
God Star woman
Ah Jesusi
Moon woman
Moon woman
Moon woman
hmm hmm hmm
hmm hmm hmm
Sap woman
Dew woman
            [THE MAN URGES HER ON. "WORK, WORK," HE SAYS.]
She is a Book woman
Ah Jesusi
hmm hmm hmm
hmm hmm hmm
so so so
Lord clown woman

Clown woman beneath the sea
Clown woman   [THE OTHER WORD IS UNINTELLIGIBLE.]
Ah Jesusi
hmm hmm hmm
hmm hmm hmm
so so so
Woman who resounds
Woman torn up out of the ground
hmm hmm hmm
Because she is a Christ woman
Because she is a Christ woman
ha ha ha
so so so
so so so
so so so
Whirling woman of colors
Whirling woman of colors
Woman of the networks of light
Woman of the networks of light
Lord eagle woman
Lord eagle woman
Clock woman
Clock woman
ha ha ha
so so so
so so so
so so so
                    ["THAT'S IT. WORK, WORK," EXCLAIMS THE MAN.]
hmm hmm hmm
hmm hmm hmm
so so so
hmm hmm hmm
so so so
so so so
si si si
si si si
si si si
so sa sa
si si si
so sa sa sa

hmm hmm hmm
hmm hmm hmm
hmm hmm hmm
si so soooooooooiiiiii   THE END OF "SO" IS DRAWN OUT INTO
A LONG TONE. SHE CALLS, "CAYETANO GARCÍA." "WORK, WORK," HE
    REPLIES. SHE GOES ON HUMMING, CLAPPING FASTER AND FASTER.
    "CAYETANO GARCÍA," SHE CALLS AGAIN, IN BETWEEN HER HUM-
    MING, ALMOST AS IF SHE WERE BRINGING HIM TO LIFE WITH HER
    CLAPPING. "WORK, WORK," HE SAYS, "DON'T WORRY." AND THE
              PASSAGE ENDS ON A LONG EXPIRING "SIIIIII."

Translation from the Mazatec into Spanish by Alvaro Estrada & Eloina Estrada de Gonzalez.
English version by Henry Munn.

Andrew Peynetsa

THE SHUMEEKULI

Well then
there were villagers at HAWIKKU
there were villagers at GYPSUM PLACE

     •

there were villagers at WIND PLACE, these were the villages
and the priest
there at Gypsum Place
spoke of having a Yaaya, a Yaaya dance.
When the word went out, people from all the villages

     •

started gathering.
The date had been set and
they lived on.

     •

For four nights
they practiced the Yaaya.
The Yaaya practice went on, and
they were gathering:
for four nights they kept gathering.
O————n it went, until
the day came.
And the SPIRAL SOCIETY
WENT INTO SESSION, and on the eve of the ceremony their
   Shumeekuli dancers came.

    •

The Shumeekuli came

    •

and the next day was to be the day

    •

for dancing the Yaaya.
Then it was the morning of the dance.
On the morning of the dance
the villagers gathered
and then
they were
getting up to dance.
O————n they went, until, at noon, they stopped to eat, and when they had eaten they
   got up again.
They got up in the afternoon

    •

and when they had done about
two sets, there were four rings of dancers.
Then the SPIRAL SOCIETY BROUGHT IN THEIR
SHUMEEKULI
and when these were brought in, the Horned Ones were also brought in.

They kept on dancing this way UNTIL THEIR
White Shumeekuli came, he was brought in when
there were four rings of dancers
and all the villagers had gathered:
there was a BIG CROWD, a big crowd, and
the dance kept on.
Their White Shumeekuli
kept going around the tree. He danced around it, and for some reason
he went crazy.

•

The people HELD ON TIGHT, but somehow he broke through their
    rings and ran away.

•

He ran and ran
and they ran after him.

•

They ran after him, but
they couldn't catch him
        and still they kept after him shouting as they went.
He was far ahead, the White Shumeekuli was far ahead of them.
They kept on going until

•

they came near SHUMINNKYA.
Someone was herding out there
he was herding, his sheep were spread out there when they came shouting.
"There   Shu   way,   out
        goes our White   meekuli, running a   whoever is
                help
    there please   us.
CATCH HIM FOR US," that's what they were shouting as they kept
    after him.
(low and tight) "Oh yes, there's a Yaaya dance today, something must've happened."
That's what the herder said, and the shouting was getting close.

After a time, their Shumeekuli
came into view.
He was still running.
The herder stood under a tree where he was going to pass
and waited for him, then
going straight on
the Shumeekuli headed for
the place where the herder stood.

·

Sure enough, just as
he came up
past the TREE
the herder caught him for them.
There he caught him:
the White Shumeekuli
who had run away from the Yaaya dance.
The others came to get him
and took him back.

·

They brought him back, and when they
tried to unmask him
the mask
was stuck
to his face.
He was changing over.

·

When they unmasked the young man, some of his
flesh peeled off.

·

Then, the one who had come as the White Shumeekuli
lived only four days before he died.

·

They LIVED ON
until, at ZUNI

•

when the Middle Place had become known

•

the date was again set for the Yaaya, and when the date had been set they
    gathered for four nights.
They gathered for practice, that's the way
they lived
and when the day of the Yaaya arrived
the villagers came together on the morning of the dance.

•

Again the YAAYA
dance began
and again the Shumeekuli dancers were brought in.
They were brought in and they danced properly, but then
there came one who costumed himself as the White Shumeekuli, and he
    went around
until it happened AGAIN:
he went crazy.
He struggled then, but
they held onto him.
It happens whenever somebody impersonates that one:
because of the flesh that got inside that mask in former times
when someone comes into the Yaaya dance as the White Shumeekuli
something will inevitably happen to his mind. This is what
happened, and because this happened
the White Shumeekuli came to be feared.
That's all.

GUIDE TO READING ALOUD. *Pauses of less than one second are indicated by line changes, pauses of two
or three seconds by strophe breaks and centered dots. Loud passages or words are indicated by CAPITALS.
Soft passages or words are indicated by* reduced type. *Extended vowels are indicated by a long dash.*

Translation from the Zuni by Dennis Tedlock

Eduardo Calderón

RAISING THE MEDIATING CENTER AND THE FIELD OF EVIL WITH THE TWENTY-FIVE THOUSAND ACCOUNTS AND THE CHANT OF THE ANCIENTS

Con Cipriano poderoso,
With powerful Saint Cyprian,

Cabalista y cirujano, viejo caminante
Cabbalist and surgeon, old traveler,

Y en los cuatro vientos y los cuatro caminos,
And with the four winds and the four roads,

Y en las veinticinco mil cuentas,
And with the twenty-five thousand accounts,

Justicieras, curanderas, y ganaderas,
Good, curing, and evil,

Ajustando con mis buenos rambeadores, mis sorbedores.
Adjusting with my good assistants, my absorbers.

Con buenas cuentas,
With good accounts,

Así vengo parando,
Thus I come raising,

En todo su encanto y su poder:
With all his enchantment and his power:

Cerro Blanco, Cerro Colorado,
White Mountain, Red Mountain,

Cerro Chaparri, Cerro Yanahuanga,
Mount Chaparri, Mount Yanahuanga,

Cerro Chalpón, poderoso y bendito,
Mount Chalpón, powerful and blessed,

Con tu volcanazo de fuego ardiendo,
With your great volcano of burning fire,

Donde cuenta el encanto del Padre Guatemala,
Where the enchantment of Father Guatemala is accounted,

Y en sus grandes poderes,
And with your great powers,

Todos sus encantos voy llamando,
All his enchantments I go calling,

Voy contando.
I go accounting.

Cerro Pelagato, Cerro Huascarán,
Pelagato Mountain, Mount Huascarán,

Cerro del Ahorcado, Cerro Campanario,
Hanged Man's Mountain, Belfry Mountain,

Cerro Cuculicote y su gran poder,
Cuculicote Mountain and its great power,

Donde vengo ajustando,
Where I come adjusting,

Y a mi banco,
And at my bench,

En todos sus encantos y poderes,
With all its enchantments and powers,

Voy contando.
I go accounting.

Y en mi buena laguna encantada,
And with my good enchanted lagoon,

Mi Huaringana,
My Huaringana,

Donde voy llamando,
Where I go calling,

Mi buena Laguna Shimbe,
My good Shimbe Lagoon,

Siempre linda y poderosa,
Always beautiful and powerful,

Donde juega mi maestro Florentino García,
Where my master Florentino García plays,

En su gran poder del chamán.
With his great power as a shaman.

Y así vengo contando,
And thus I come accounting,

Con todos mis encantos.
With all my enchantments.

Vara por vara,
Staff by staff,

Cerro por cerro,
Mountain by mountain,

Laguna por laguna,
Lagoon by lagoon,

Y en el chorro de Santo Crisanto,
And in the Stream of Santo Crisanto,

Voy llamando.
I go calling.

En mis hermosos jardines bien floridos,
With my beautiful flowery gardens,

Con todas sus hierbas y sus encantos,
With all their herbs and their enchantments,

Voy llamando.
I go calling.

Cuenta por cuenta, voy jugando,
Account by account, I go playing,

Y en mi Huaca poderosa de los Gentiles,
And with my powerful Temple of the Ancients,

Donde voy contando, jugando, floreciendo.
Where I go accounting, playing, flowering.

Huaca Prieta, Huaca del Sol, y Huaca de la Luna,
Huaca Prieta, Temple of the Sun, and Temple of the Moon,

Juega a mi ciento.
Play at my game.

Con la hierba del hombre,
With the herb of man,

Con la hierba del león,
With the herb of the lion,

Con la hierba de la coqueta,
With the herb of the coquette,

Voy cantando.
I go singing.

Con mis buenos hierbateros voy llamando,
With my good herbalists I go calling,

Todos los poderes y los encantos,
All the powers and the enchantments,

Que mi buen remedio viene ya,
So that my good remedy comes now,

Buscando, justificando, levantando, parando,
Looking, justifying, raising, standing up,

Con sus buenos encantos.
With their good enchantments.

Todos los grandes maestros,
All the great masters,

Van contando donde cuento.
Go accounting where I account.

A las doce de la noche entera,
At twelve midnight,

Y a la madrugada,
And at dawn,

Seis de la mañana al ojo del sol,
Six in the morning under the eye of the sun,

Voy llamando,
I go calling,

Estoy contando y refrescando.
I am accounting and refreshing.

Buena hora, buenos vientos,
Good time, good winds,

Voy llamando y contando,
I go calling and accounting,

De mis buenas maravillas,
With my good marvels,

Vengo levantando todo mi banco.
I come raising all of my bench.

Donde cuentan todos los grandes poderosos,
Where all the great powers are accounted,

Voy dominando todo golpe,
I go dominating all spiritual shocks,

Floreciendo en buena hora.
Flowering in good time.

Translation from the Spanish by F. Kaye Sharon

Robert Johnson

HELLHOUND ON MY TRAIL

I've got to keep moving
    I've got to keep moving
        blues falling down like hail
          blues falling down like hail
Ummmmmmmmmmmmmmmmmmmmmmm
       blues falling down like hail
        blues falling down like hail
And the days keeps on 'minding me
      there's a hellhound on my trail
        hellhound on my trail
          hellhound on my trail

If today was Christmas Eve
    If today was Christmas Eve
        and tomorrow was Christmas Day
If today was Christmas Eve
    and tomorrow was Christmas Day
        (aw wouldn't we have a time baby)
All I would need my little sweet rider just
      to pass the time away
      uh huh
       to pass the time away

You sprinkled hot foot powder

umm around my door

all around my door

You sprinkled hot foot powder

all around your daddy's door

hmmm hmmm hmmm

It keeps me with a rambling mind, rider,

every old place I go

every old place I go

I can tell the wind is rising

the leaves trembling on the trees

trembling on the trees

I can tell the wind is rising

leaves trembling on the trees

umm hmm hmm hmm

All I need my little sweet woman

and to keep my company

hmmm hmmm hmmm hmmm

my company

Transcription & visualization by Eric Sackheim

Komi Ekpe

ABUSE POEMS: FOR KODZO & OTHERS

I

Poverty moved into my homestead
Can I be this way and earn the name of a great singer?
Shall I fear death by song
and refuse to sing?

2

Hm hm hm. Beware,
I will place a load on Kodzo's head.
Nugbleza informed me that

it is the women of Tsiame
who goaded Kodzo into my song.
Questioners, this became the evil firewood
he'd gathered; his hands decayed
his feet decayed.
I am the poet; I am not afraid of you.
Kodzo, winding in the air, his asshole agape
his face long and curved
like the lagoon egret's beak.
Call him here, I say call him
and let me see his face.
He is the man from whom the wind runs,
the man who eats off the farm he hasn't planted
his face bent like the evil hoe
on its handle. Behold, ei ei ei
Kodzo did something. I forgive him his debt.
I will insult him since he poked
a stick into the flying ant's grove.
Amegavi said he has some wealth
And he took Kodzo's part.
The back of his head tapers off
as if they'd built a fetish hut on his breathing spot.
His face wags, a fool with a white ass.
The monkey opened his asshole
in display to the owner of the farm.
The lion caught a game, alas,
his children took it away from him.
Kodzo's homestead shall fall, shall surely fall.
Questioners, let evil men die
let death knock down the evil doer.
If I were the fetish in the creator's house
that will be your redemption.
Kodzo, this imbecile, evil animal
who fucks others' wives fatteningly
his buttocks run off, his teeth yellow
his penis has wound a rope around his waist
pulling him around and away,
his backside runs into a slope
his eye twisted like the sun-inspector,

he has many supporters in Tsiame
his mouth as long as the pig
blowing the twin whistle.
Something indeed has happened.

Translation from the Ewe by Kofi Awoonor

Miss Queenie
(Imogene Elizabeth Kennedy)

ONE DAY

One day . . .
a remember one day a faen some lillies . . .
an a plant de lillies-dem in row
an one Sunday mornin when a wake . . .
all de lillies blow . . .
seven lillies an de seven a dem blow . . .

an a *leave* . . .
an guh dung in de gully bottom . . .
to go an pick some quoquonut
an when a go
a see a cottn tree an a juss *fell* right down . . .
at de cottn tree root . . .

. . .

in de night
in de cottn tree comin like it hollooow
an Hi hinside there
an you have some grave arounn dat cottn tree
right rounn it
some *tombs* . . .

but dose is
some hol-time Hafrican
yu unnerstann . . . ?

well dose tombs arounn de cottn tree . . .
an Hi inside de cottn tree lay down
an a night-time a sih de cottn tree *light* hup wit cyandles an . . .
a restin now
put me an *dis* way an sleepin . . .

an a honly hear a likkle *vice*
come to mih
an dem talkin to mih
but dose tings is spirit talkin to mih . . .
an dem speakin to me now
an seh now . . .

'Is a likkle *nice* likkle chile
an oo gwine get im right up now . . .
in de Hafrican worl . . .
because you brains
you will *take* someting . . .
so derefore . . .
we gine to *teach* you someting . . .'

Well de *firs* ting dat dem teach me is
s'*wikkidi* . . .

s'*wikkidi lango*
which is sugar an water . . .

sih?
an dem teach me dat . . .

an dem teach me m'praey-ers . . .
which is . . .

> *Kwale kwale n'den den de*
> *Belo ko lo mawa kisalaya*

> *Pem legele*
> *Len legele*

> *Luwi za'kwe n'da'kwe so*
> *Be'lam m'pese m'bambe*

which is de same Hour Fader's Praeyer . . .

Transcription from performance version by Kamau Brathwaite

Tom Waits

SWORDFISHTROMBONE

Well he came home from the war
with a party in his head
and modified Brougham DeVille
and a pair of legs that opened up
like butterfly wings
and a mad dog that wouldn't
sit still
he went and took up with a Salvation Army
Band girl
who played dirty water
on a swordfishtrombone
he went to sleep at the bottom of
Tenkiller lake
and he said "gee, but it's
great to be home."

Well he came home from the war
with a party in his head
and an idea for a fireworks display
and he knew that he'd be ready with
a stainless steel machete
and a half pint of Ballantine's
each day
and he holed up in a room above a hardware store
cryin' nothing there but Hollywood tears
and he put a spell on some
poor little Crutchfield girl
and stayed like that for 27 years

Well he packed up all his
expectations he lit out for California
with a flyswatter banjo on his knee
with lucky tiger in his angel hair
and benzedrine for getting there
they found him in a eucalyptus tree
lieutenant got him a canary bird

and skanked her head with every word
and Chesterfield moonbeams in a song
and he got 20 years for lovin' her
from some Oklahoma governor
said everything this Doughboy
does is wrong

Now some say he's doing
the obituary mambo
and some say he's hanging on the wall
perhaps this yarn's the only thing
that holds this man together
some say he was never here at all

Some say they saw him down in
Birmingham, sleeping in a
boxcar going by
and if you think that you can tell a bigger tale
I swear to God you'd have to tell a lie . . .

AFTER Dizzy Gillespie

SABLA Y BLU

SABLA Y BLU
SABLU BLAAA   *BY* BLAA
SAZULYA DA BA DA BA BY BLAA

SADU BLAAA   Y AA
SAZULYA DA BA DA BA DY BLAA

    SABLU Y BII
    SABLU Y BII
    SABLU Y BII
    S'BLU Y BI
    SBLU Y BI
    SBLUI BI

SADU DAA   OOO BLAA
SAZULYA DA BA DA BA DI BLAAA

SADU DAAA   *OUI* BLAA
SAZULYA DA BA DA BA DI BLAAA

    SABLU Y DAA
    SADU Y DAA
    SADU Y DAA
    S'DU Y DA
    SU Y DA
SU *ISS* BI'Y'DOP DAA . . .

SABLU BLAAA   *OUI* BLAA
SAZULYA DAI BLA DOO BA BLOUI YAA

SADU BLAAA   *OUI* BLAA
SAZULYA DOO BA DOO BA DI BLAA

    ASA Y BLU
    ASA Y BLU
    ASA Y BLU
    ASA Y BLU
    ASA Y BLU
    ASA Y BLU
    ASA Y BLU
    ASA Y BLU
    ASA Y BLU
    ASA Y BLU
    ASA Y BLU Y BLU Y BLU Y BLU Y BLU Y BLU Y BLU

Jacques Roubaud b. 1932

from **SOME THING BLACK**

Section V

Meditation on the Indistinct, on Heresy

for Jean Claude Milner

There are three suppositions. the first, it's not amiss to number them: *there is no more*. I shall not name it.

A second supposition is that *nothing can be said*.

Another supposition, finally: *from now on nothing will be like her*. this supposition undoes all ties.

From certain of these suppositions we can deduce, irrelevantly, chains of propositions.

Given that from now on nothing will be like her, we shall conclude that only the unlike exists, from that, that it's not relevant, no relevance can be defined.

We shall declare for impropriety.

Everything depends on the point when the unlike appears. and thence something, but some thing black.

Through simple repetition of *there is no more* the whole unravels into its loathsome fabric: reality.

Some thing black which closes in. locks shut. pure, unaccomplished deposition.

Meditation on the Identical

Precariousness, interior, window of anxiety
Suspended stone, perspective, light

Which spreads in width, in length, in depth,
Toward all that's dark, cadaver, flight.

Through room and number and solidity I doubt
What neither double, clarity nor figure understands

This measure, closure, stela, live, aims higher
than what's admissible, impure, airtight.

Full sleep   dry distance   a black dominant: here lies

Wreck   wrenching   unjust screen
Time span   impassive stone   border of grass.

You cannot make this state imaginable

You cannot make me not see nowhere

You can't join stones in wedlock right before my eyes.

Singular Death

And why a picture?

Why, impervious to both affirmation and negation, why in the world
this insistent, subsistent, irrepressible, pure repetition be it of nothing,
why a picture?

Why *this* picture?

The world is filled with homeless, colorless things, hard kernel over
which the negative had no hold until the second round, once color is
drained, and movement, etc. . . .

But being-that-way, could you still be defined?

Not completely, no conformist end to your definition, no cut-and-dried
designation, cut-and-dried label. no.

Surrounded by pictures of you, selected by your eye. selected and illu-
mined by your thinking. thinking in silver's black. scattered among pic-
tures of you.

It's not that your pictures slip away. not that they are many and lie, for
no reason. but that I shall never know more.

You said: "the singular is stupid."

Meditation on Plurality

Death: obligatory plurality

Scatter, variety: death calls for a poetry of meditation
(Sponde)

Of the fall, of loss

Here melancholy knots into the mirror

"Who am I then? a furious Narcissus."

Unfolded, reduced, immobile images numbered except for a few, then as if elbowed by depth

In a perfect mirror, and *her* eyes, a look would go on to the infinite, and loss, there, would be certain

Whatever grain, whatever tain, whatever curve, in the real mirror, in real eyes, we always end up with some obscure mixture. but mixture, too, means death.

"This dirty, rotten life to be mixed up with death."

Scenario of Meditation

This drain on attention is expected to slow down

Enumeration of points. by heart. they have come through the night, the sand: some abstract drops accompany speech, medium stretch of words, the whole put on top of the portfolio of pictures without apparent links

We'll look for them one by one by one

Hence necessarily displacements

In a space which would ideally be a gray and empty stretch

But often   you're there: your eyes which do not see your legs which do not close or open

You, in the gray and empty stretch between the stations of meditative time

And the least distance becomes insurmountable

Meditation on the Senses

One descends in a spiral, a damnation.

From sight to voice.   from the voice to whiffs of scent, odors.

From odor to taste: bite, crunch, spittle.

The bottom of the well. The last interior: touch.

Absolute touch of bodies. orgasm and decomposition.

The touching of hands, of flesh, of bodies coexisting in one body, one mental space, saying it with mouth, taste, breath, an intertwining that breathes and penetrates.

In meditating on the five senses, here was my recollection of mortality

If only the dissolving distance of two bodies burning with their infinitely present burn: paradise guards its opposite.

All stations that I now descend, through memory, to hell.

Theology of Nonexistence

Against the grain of your annihilation this, my ransacked memory of you.

But if I plunge into this *via negativa*, the figure I'll find is not on high, and I expect no revelation

I do not call your not-dead being to an afterlife

I don't expect to recognize you waiting in some between-the-worlds

There is your name. I can say it. I can erase the line that crossed it out in letters heavy with place

You've left me a picture with your stamp on it, on the very rectangle of reality it represents, and you are there, in the place where you alone are absent. thus

Out of what's ended I fashion a truth

Of not accepting that you're not, the silence

But I don't know, don't know what it could be, the opposite of no you

Meditation on Comparison

It might come into my head to compare you to a dark body at an enormous distance, nearly infinite, emitting a dark light which keeps coming at me.

Entering my sleep as X-rays do the flesh, my waking riddled like a cloud-bed with intense, swift radiation.

It might, but I won't give in to it.

I'll rather slog away at circumscribing *nothing-you* precisely, impossible bi-pole that it is, at running through, around, this, these new sentences that I call poems.

With all the formal discontent that I can muster against poetry.

Between the months of silence when I went dumbly on my way.

And the near future when I'll shut up again, utterly baffled by these poems.

For any of these black lines being pushed across the paper to its end, its turn, may turn out, any moment, versed in a second silence.

And that between these narrow limits I must try to stretch and tell of you, again.

Apatriates

Meinong's paradoxical apatriates (*heimatlose*) beings that escape the principle of non-contradiction are not the only ones without a world

The dead whose lives have run their course, when spoken of as present, declared present by being spoken to, are not in any possible somewhere either (I mean some possible construction)

And yet I can't conceive of doing without saying "you"

Saying your name I would give you an unassailable stability

So that your negative would be opposed, not to an affirmation (you are not), but to the void before my words

Saying your name means reigniting the presence you were before you disappeared

And at the same time gives this disappearance a status different from, and more than, pure and simple absence, a secondary status

Your name's an irreducible trace. There is no possible negation of your name.

Your name can't be killed (but shall remain without description which would break its solid body into malleable, less demanding terms, vile, ridiculous and, in short, false).

Translation from the French by Rosmarie Waldrop

COMMENTARY

Poetry is the memory of language.
J. R.

A formidable, though very private, figure on today's French (& international) poetry scene, Roubaud is also a novelist, mathematician, theoretician (his *La Vieillesse d'Alexandre* is a major treatise on French versification), & translator (Stein, Bronk, Zukofsky, Spicer, among others). He has been associated with groups such as the Collectif Change & (currently) the magazine *Po&sie,* & (more notably perhaps) was a founding member of OULIPO, the acronym for Ouvroir de Littérature Potentielle (Workspace for Potential Literature). Gathered in 1960 around Raymond Queneau & Francois Le Lionnais (& including the likes of Harry Matthews, Georges Perec, & Italo Calvino), OULIPO links up with Alfred Jarry's Pataphysics (volume one)—"the science of imaginary solutions"—as a crucible for an experimental poetics of a quasi-formalist, often mathematically based nature. Thus, for example, Roubaud's first major work, ϵ [epsilon], "is composed of 361 texts, which represent the 180 white and 181 black counters of a game of *go,*" & includes "sonnets, short sonnets, interrupted sonnets, prose sonnets, short sonnets in prose, citations, illustrations, grids, whites, blacks, poems, prose poems," for which the poet proposes four different— & very complex—reading possibilities. Simultaneously he has been involved in a lifelong study of the Troubadours ("the central model for me is Troubadour poetry"), from which he has learned that "to speak of love, to speak of the love of language (*la gloria de la lingua*), is always to speak of poetry / love is only in the song which is love of language which is love." Whether by contrast or extension, then, Roubaud's later work (such as the extracts above from *Some Thing Black,* written after the death at thirty-one of his wife, the photographer & artist Alix Cléo Roubaud) tends to combine a more lyrical/elegiac tone with less foregrounded, though always present, formal structures.

David Antin b. 1932

ENDANGERED NOUNS

the other day i looked out of the window and saw a
bird with a black head walking upside down along a
branch of the honeysuckle bush outside our dining
room   it was a familiar bird   but strange   its black cap
its queer way of walking head down along the branch
were familiar   but its color was strange   i had never
seen a brown bird with a black cap that walked like that
   not here in southern california northern san diego   but
it reminded me of another bird i knew very well   from
winters in upstate new york   of a different color   the
tailored grey of a pair of spats or dress gloves   a slightly
absurd little bird that helped cheer our winters along
with the chickadees and a lone cardinal that used to sit on
the leafless shadbush on the other side of the brook back in
north branch   i remembered that bird   i said to
myself   it was a . . .   and then   no name came
                                        it was as if
instead of a name   there was an empty space the size of a
name   that should have been there
   i guess i could have gone to a field guide to find the
name   but my field guide was a guide to the birds of
california   i've been living here almost twenty years now
and it was the new york bird i wanted to remember
but there was something also   a certain sensual pleasure
   mixed with anxiety   of tracing a path as if with my
finger around the small empty space in my mind   that
   should have housed the bird
                              because that was what i was
experiencing   the physical sensation of tracing a shallow
   space where the word should have been
                                    and if it was not a
pleasure   there was a certain   almost sensory satisfaction
in running my finger over the space   that i felt was
   just the right size   to house the body of the word
   i almost said the bird
                        because it was like the archeological

pleasure of finding a tipped over sarcophagus   from
which the body it contained had simply rolled out   or of
discovering an inscription carved in the face of a rock
from which one word had been rubbed out
    and while i was enjoying tracing the shape of the scar in
my memory   my mind kept stumbling over other
memories   of winters in north branch   snow piled
fifteen feet high along the roadside   of the schilburys
    gerda and kurt   the two german emigres with their pair
of weimeranians   their hopeless foreignness in the bare
    upstate landscape
    though this part of western sullivan county had been
german once   in the days when they were cutting down
    the fir trees for the tanbark industry and had even had a
chapter of the bund in presecond world war days   as
names in the phone book like schott and ebert and ellersig
still testified
    but gerda and kurt were german jewish   though gerda
    had become catholic because of the nuns who'd sheltered
her from the nazis in their convent   and she used to go
to mass in the franciscan church in callicoon while kurt ran
    for county controller because he wanted to stem the tide
of corruption in western sullivan county
    but he didn't have a chance with the local farmers or
even in liberty or monticello and gerda had to stop going
    to the franciscans because she was shocked by the violence
of their cold war sermons
    and i kept seeing the small   grey   black headed bird
whose name i had forgotten through the kitchen window
of the house we rented from peters the dairy farmer down
    the road   surrounded by a swarm of images of people
and things i'd forgotten that i'd known that seemed in
    some way related to this one and i remembered another
forgetting   that i had experienced in a similar way
                                                        the
name of a painter architect   a droll horse faced man who
had broken with his friend mondrian over the use of
    diagonals and the color green   who had introduced dada
into holland and designed playful little geometric houses
    whose deadpan descendants have cursed european and
american housing developments since the 1960s

i mentioned this to my son and blaise just shrugged and
said
   "i bet you can name all of the charger receivers"
which i thought i could   so i said charlie joiner and wes
chandler and bobby duckworth   who was still with the
chargers then   and those were the wide receivers
   and i started on the tight ends   there were three of them
   and i got through eric sievers and pete holohan and i
came to the greatly gifted one   the giant black one with
the speed of a wide receiver and the face of a petulant
child   who i remembered seeing in a game once with
miami three times come limping off the field   nearly
destroyed by collisions that might have hospitalized an
ordinary player   and i remember this shot of him on the
sidelines between hits   slumping exhausted and helmetless
   his face drained of everything but weariness and pain
like some roman gladiator   and i remember seeing him
return three times to a struggle that only his pride and
nasty character lent an illusion of dignity and tragic
seriousness beyond the ridiculous game
   and it happened again   i forgot his name
   "blaise" i said   "i can't remember his name"   and he
asked "should i tell you?"
   "no" i said   "let me try to remember it"
   "kenneth maybe   no it isn't kenneth   it's kenneth i
think   kenneth washington   no   booker? booker
   booker t washington   kenneth washington no kennel
kellen   washington winslow   kellen winslow"
and so i came round to it knowing i knew it all the time
which means what?
                     that i could come around to it that i
could arrive at it   that i knew what it wasn't   and if i
   tried   long enough and hard enough   i could find a way
of getting to it   the way i used to find my way as a child
to the ancient capital of egypt   by passing through the
names of laundry soaps
                     rinso   lux luxor   thebes
                                    by way of
the sound poetry of the language which is my language our
language   in a way that talking it will not often show
   or maybe there's something in back of language that

stands behind it and makes it possible   not to remember
  but to remember what you forget even when you can't
  remember it   which is like coming to stand before a place
to which memory may or may not be able to arrive
                                             the way
my mother-in-law went looking for a lost story she used
  to hold up before her life
                            it concerned her own mother
back in poland then   and she had told it many times
    "my mother was a tiny little woman   but she was a
  strong woman a business woman   my father was a scholar
  and he had no time for such things"   this was the central
  theme and jeanette had taken it to heart   because
  throughout her life jeanette had thrown herself into
  business after business   small hotels then larger ones
  grandly conceived family enterprises that were almost
always just beyond her reach   so we heard this story
many times
    "my mother was a tiny little woman but she was very
  strong   and she ran the local mill where the peasants
  brought their grain   and one week she neglected to get
  herself enough cash to pay off all the peasants   so she had
  to give out notes to the ones that came in last   and most
of them grumbled a bit   so she would make a little joke
  and they would laugh and take them because they knew
  her and knew that she was good for it   but one peasant
  a huge man and very drunk got very loud and insisted on
receiving cash
    but my mother just looked at him and said 'what do you
  think i'm going to give rubles to a drunken peasant
  you'll just drink it up or lose it in a ditch or worse
  you go home and send your wife and i'll give her the
money'   but the peasant roared that no woman was going
  to lead him around by the nose and he would go down
with her to the bank to get the money now
    so my mother said   'you think i'm going to take you
  to the bank like this   they'll take one look at you and
chase you out   besides the bank is closed'
    but the peasant swore that nobody was going to chase
  him out even if they were closed and he held up a giant

fist and demanded cash or else   and the little woman
looking up at the fist above her head cooly turned her
back on him   and happened to catch sight of her tiny
nine-year-old son watching big-eyed from a corner
    'samuel' she said   'go get a stick and show this
gentleman out'"
                      which punchline   in the authorized version
in its absolute absurdity delivered with perfect sangfroid
so tickled everyone that even the drunken peasant
couldn't keep from laughing so hard he had to sit down
and cry
          but in the last few years my mother-in-law has
been losing hold of the lines that held her to her life
which has been slipping away with fewer and fewer lines
to hold to   and she's been living in a resident hotel filled
with other older people whose lines are similarly slipping
and with whom it doesn't always so much matter
but from time to time when we come to visit   she
reaches out of habit for one of the stories to which her
life was moored   and she happened to reach for this one
    "my mother was a little tiny woman   but very
strong . . ."   and she went through her story to the angry
peasant and how her mother looked up at the giant fist
and cooly turned around   then she reached for the
punchline
    but jeanette's little brother was hopelessly gone   and
jeanette waited just a moment   and replaced him with
their old peasant housekeeper manya   who wasn't frail
enough to carry off the joke   so my mother-in-law stopped
and started over
    "my mother was a tiny little woman . . ."   and she
went through the whole story again   and as she drew
near the ending this time the old housekeeper was gone
so jeanette replaced manya with her own scholar father
which quite clearly would not suffice
                      three times jeanette
made her way around the story of her mother and the
drunken peasant   and each time she circled the story the
actors changed   they became in turn the maid her father

and her own husband   and three times she looked for the
line that her mother now delivered imperfectly to the
altered personnel   and each time she came to the end of
  the line she paused and began again   but the third and
last time she arrived at the line she simply stopped and
waited   and i'm not sure how long she was prepared to
  wait

*i had suggested that i had always had mixed feelings about being consid-
ered a poet   "if robert lowell is a poet i dont want to be a poet   if robert
frost was a poet i dont want to be a poet   if socrates was a poet ill con-
sider it"*
D. A.

Antin's move—circa 1970—was to break (radically) with his own work as
an experimental maker of still recognizable "poems" & to direct his ener-
gies thereafter to acts of talking (*real* talking), first presented in the context
of performances & readings, then transcribed into a form of writing that
evaded the restrictions of both verse & prose. Like other avant-garde moves
the challenge went to the heart of basic assumptions about poetry—in this
case the lyric imperative—against which Antin presented a view of poetry
(*now* and *then*) derived not merely from speech (as opposed, say, to song)
but from the dynamics of a true discourse (including narrative) from which
it had long been set apart. Of his own practice therein he writes (or speaks)
by way of introduction:

for the last few years ive been working at talks that ive been calling
    talk poems   because i see all poetry as some kind of talking   which
is some kind of thinking   and because ive never liked the idea of going
    into a closet to address myself over a typewriter   what kind of talking
    is that?   ive gotten into the habit of going to some particular place
                with something on my mind   but no particular words in my
        mouth   looking for a particular occasion to talk to particular people
in a way i hope is valuable for all of us   because these pages were
    worked out with no sense of a page in mind the texts are not "prose"
        which as i see it is a kind of "concrete poetry with justified margins"
    while these texts are notations of scores of oral poems   with margins
consequently unjustified

For which reasons one might tie them to the workings of oral masters—
particularly those like Andrew Peynetsa or Eduardo Calderón (above) or,
among the modernists, John Cage, many of whose workings like Antin's
derive more from the side of speech, than that of song.

Andrei Voznesensky b. 1933

LOOK BACK INTO THE FUTURE

We fly forwards
and look back.
What heaven it was!
What hell it was!
People of my country,
look back into the future.

ON THE METAMORPHOSES BROUGHT ABOUT BY EMOTION: THE REBELLION OF THE EYES

In the third month her laughter sounds strained.
The third month, she wakes up screaming at night.
Above her, like an Aurora Borealis
              eyes
                   hang flaming in the night!

Her face, lit up in the dim glass
or half her face, like many vertical lakes. . . .

You're getting thin. You don't go to the factory any more.
You listen to them
                like a gardener from the Moon.
Your life, your pain rise like steam to the skies
    to the bursting pupils of your eyes.
You say, "This blue—I cannot stand it!
    My head will explode!
Someone, someone greedy, yet stately and strange
    switched on the light in my head and decided to stay
        for ever. . . ."

You are sad: but the eyes are laughing like madmen—
you speak: they're getting ready for a collision.
Instead of tears, these illuminations in your eyes.
"She's only pretending," the neighbors say.
And people pass, like gloomy apartment blocks.
Above her, the eyes go on burning: great windows.

Hundreds of women they carried away, before you.
How much pain they have gathered, to await you!
But once in a century there is a rebellion
                                        of eyes. . . .

Cast out by the seaside, lost and beat
a woman walks, is pregnant with eyes.

Though I have not walked among them,
I have paid for them with my life.

Translation from the Russian by Anselm Hollo

THE GENEALOGY OF CROSSES

The microscope revealed a world of miracles.
The slide revealed that the world consists of crosses.

                    +   +   +

If all the crosses joined hands and made a chain, the column would stretch
from Vilnius to Tallinn.

                    +   +   +

Women begin the beginning. ♀—is not Venus's mirror. It is the kiss of a
cross and a nought, or Charlie Chaplin, or the o of Catherine the Great,
as the poet remarked.

                    +   +   +

Crosses love to play at throwing sticks. It's very nice when the arms and
legs fly apart. Their favourite reading matter is crosswords.

                    +   +   +

There are flying crosses with six extremities—including two wings. The
anti-Semites created standards for crosses. If the cross is shorter than the
standard, it is a Zionist.

                    +   +   +

Crosses are allowed to appear on TV. But there is a censor assigned to
count the number of rays in the stars on the screen, in case there are any
Stars of David.

                    +   +   +

When the noughts surrounded the crosses, the two surviving ones stood
back to back with their sub-machine guns at the ready.

                    +   +   +

Are you a cross that goes from right to left or left to right? A Polish cross or a Russian one? If the answer is yes, we'll shoot you.

+   +   +

The white crosses scored a goal. They jumped on each other for joy, all in a heap, embracing and waving their arms about.
They flew into the skies with joy.
Snowflakes fell.

+   +   +

When Stalin swore his oath of allegiance to Lenin, the words on his moustache froze like white crosses.

+   +   +

We are floundering in the sand dunes.
"Something's tugging at my back."
"It must be the pull of latitude and longitude."

+   +   +

Three crosses above and one below. Don Quixote and the windmills. Don Quixote beat the windmill. He built the Atomic Power Station. The crosses were added on.

+   +   +

A ball met the crosses. It ate them. It ate so many that they spilled out of his belly. They called it a gooseberry.

+   +   +

They say that Kerensky dressed up as a nurse. He drew a red cross on his forehead. He ran away. Alexander F. told me this was not true. They say that in fact he dressed up as a sailor, and put on a sailor's cap, and ran away. This is also not true. Read Berberova.

+   +   +

Cross, where is the exit?
Over there!

+   +   +

The cross rises from the chair, showing you that the audience is over.

+   +   +

Champion X swam the Styx.
Mister X, sir?

+   +   +

This isn't poetry or prose, it's craziness.
The cross just threw up its hands.

Translation from the Russian by Richard McKane

The artists take leave, / Bareheaded, enter / The humming fields and forests / Of birch and oak, like a church. // Their escape is their victory.
A. V.

The time of his emergence—1958: the first post-Stalin "thaw" & Russian "new wave"—now has entered into history. Alongside the poetry as such—his, Yevgeny Yevtushenko's, Bella Akhmadulina's, that of exiles such as Joseph Brodsky—the memory remains of (real & mythic) crowds of 50,000 filling stadiums for readings, 500,000 subscriptions to a book of poems, etc.: an age of large & small resistances within a system of repression. (The image remains, March 7th 1963, of Khrushchev's angry voice & body—public: before a crowd of cheering party leaders / literary apparatchiks: "Mister Voznesensky, get the hell out! You are slandering Soviet authority! Get the fucking hell out of this country!") Against which odds—& less than a decade past the terror—theirs was a work of repair & an attempt to use poetry as their special weapon: to reunite it with a language of resistance from an earlier but still remembered time. (In doing which they were the visible & public edge of what was changing, turning over, in their world.) Writes Voznesensky in the 1990s aftermath: "There is an affirmation of a favorite thought of [the Russian philosopher] Berdyaev, that the body is not material, but the form of the soul. In this sense the existentialism of the poetry of the sixties served well as the basis of many of today's spiritual processes. With its metaphorisms, rhythm, and search for a new structure of language, in opposition to the stereotypes of the System, poetry foresaw the chaos of today's processes, a chaos that is in search of constructivity. Poetry manifested itself as 'a personalized revolution, which really had not existed in the world, and meant an overthrow of the power of objectivity, and a breakthrough into another, spiritual world.'"

Amiri Baraka b. 1934

NUMBERS, LETTERS

If you're not home, where
are you? Where'd you go? What
were you doing when gone? When
you come back, better make it good.
What was you doing down there, freakin' off
with white women, hangin' out
with Queens, say it straight to be
understood straight, put it flat and real

in the street where the sun comes and the
moon comes and the cold wind in winter
waters your eyes. Say what you mean, dig
it out put it down, and be strong
about it.

I cant say who I am
unless you agree I'm real

I cant be anything I'm not
Except these words pretend
to life not yet explained,
so here's some feeling for you
see how you like it, what it
reveals, and that's me.

Unless you agree I'm real
that I can feel
whatever beats hardest
at our black souls

I am real, and I can't say who
I am. Ask me if I know, I'll say
yes, I might say no. Still, ask.

I'm Everett LeRoi Jones, 30 yrs old.
A black nigger in the universe. A long breath singer,
wouldbe dancer, strong from years of fantasy
and study. All this time then, for what's happening
now. All that spilling of white ether, clocks in ghostheads
lips drying and rewet, eyes opening and shut, mouths churning.

I am a meditative man. And when I say something it's all of me
saying, and all the things that make me, have formed me, colored me
this brilliant reddish night. I will say nothing that I feel is
lie, or unproven by the same ghostclocks, by the same riders
always move so fast with the word slung over their backs or
in saddlebags, charging down Chinese roads. I carry some words,
some feeling, some life in me. My heart is large as my mind
this is a messenger calling, over here, over here, open your eyes
and your ears and your souls; today is the history we must learn
to desire. There is no guilt in love

DAS KAPITAL

Strangling women in the suburban bush
they bodies laid around rotting while martinis are drunk
the commuters looking for their new yorkers feel a draft
& can get even drunker watching the teevee later on the Ford
replay. There will be streams of them coming, getting off
near where the girls got killed. Two of them strangled by
the maniac.
There are maniacs hidden everywhere cant you see? By the dozens
and double dozens, maniacs by the carload (tho they *are*
a minority). But they terrorize us uniformly, all over the place
we look at the walls of our houses, the garbage cans parked full
strewn around our defaulting cities, and we cd get scared. A rat
eases past us on his way to a banquet, can you hear the cheers raised
through the walls, full of rat humor. Blasts of fire, some woman's son will
    stumble
and die with a pool of blood around his head. But it wont be the maniac.
    These old houses
crumble, the unemployed stumble by us straining, ashy fingered,
    harassed. The air is cold
winter heaps above us consolidating itself in degrees. We need a aspirin
    or something, and
pull our jackets close. The baldhead man on the television set goes on in
    a wooden way
his unappetizing ignorance can not be stood, or understood. The people
    turn the channel
looking for Good Times and get a negro with a pulldown hat. Flashes of
    maniac shadows before
bed, before you pull down the shade you can see the leaves being blown
    down the street
too dark now to see the writing on them, the dates, and amounts we
    owe. The streets too
will soon be empty, after the church goers go on home having been saved
    again from the
Maniac . . . except a closeup of the chief mystic's face rolling down to his
    hands will send
shivers through you, looking for traces of the maniacs life. Even there
    among the mythophrenics.

What can you do? It's time finally to go to bed. The shadows close
    around and the room is still

Most of us know there's a maniac loose. Our lives a jumble of frustra-
tions and unfilled

capacities. The dead girls, the rats noise, the flashing somber lights, the
dead voice on

television, was that blood and hair beneath the preacher's fingernails? A
few other clues

we mull them over as we go to sleep, the skeletons of dollarbills, traces of
dead used up

labor, lead away from the death scene until we remember a quiet fit that
everywhere

is the death scene. Tomorrow you got to hit it sighs through us like the
wind, we got to

hit it, like an old song at radio city, working for the yanqui dollarrrrr,
when we were

children, and then we used to think it was not the wind, but the maniac
scratching against

our windows. Who is the maniac, and why everywhere at the same
time . . .

COMMENTARY

*The force we want is of twenty million spooks storming America with furi-
ous cries and unstoppable weapons. We want actual explosions and actual
brutality: AN EPIC IS CRUMBLING and we must give it the space and
hugeness of its actual demise.*
A. B.

It was Baraka's genius to grasp the ferocity (theatrical, poetic) of Artaud's
"theater of cruelty" (volume one, page 521) & to redirect it—in the context
of his own time—into a "revolutionary" poetry & theater, of which he
wrote: "This is a theater of assault. The play that will split the heavens for
us will be called THE DESTRUCTION OF AMERICA. The heroes will
be Crazy Horse, Denmark Vesey, Patrice Lumumba, and not history, not
memory, not sad sentimental groping for a warmth in our despair; these will
be new men, new heroes, and their enemies most of you who are reading
this" (1966). But his project had begun still earlier with a poetry practice
(*Preface to a Twenty Volume Suicide Note, The Dead Lecturer*) informed
by the line of Pound & Olson, modified by participation in Beat/"bohe-
mian" doings & by ongoing attention to jazz & blues rhythms & (increas-
ingly) to Negritude and Harlem Renaissance poetics & the language "really
spoken" in the worlds around him. By the later 1960s he had gone from
LeRoi Jones to [Imamu] Amiri Baraka, had emerged for a time as a major
American playwright (*Dutchman, The Toilet, The Slave*), & had taken a

highly visible role in black nationalist politics and black culturalist practice. The move brought him also to the founding of the Black Arts Repertory Theater in Harlem & of Spirit House ("a black community theater") in his native Newark. (During the 1967 Newark riots he was arrested & sentenced to a three-year jail term—later overturned.) From 1974 on, his political stance turned sharply internationalist with a self-proclaimed conversion to "Marxism–Leninism–Mao Tse-tung Thought"—allowing him (again) to put his total person into play. As a declaration of his sources & directions, his late ongoing poem *Why's/Wise* (volume one, page 741)—"about African American (American) History"—is described by him as "in the tradition of the Griots [African Singer-Poet-Historians] . . . but also like Melvin Tolson's *Liberia*, William Carlos Williams's *Paterson*, Charles Olson's *Maximus* in that it tries to tell the history/life like an ongoing-off-coming Tale."

A further example of Baraka's voice & thought in action (this time read as "manifesto") appears on page 420, above.

Ted Berrigan 1934–1983

PEOPLE OF THE FUTURE

*People of the future
while you are reading these poems, remember
you didn't write them,
I did.*

from THE SONNETS

XXXVII

It is night. You are asleep. And beautiful tears
Have blossomed in my eyes. Guillaume Apollinaire is dead.
The big green day today is singing to itself
A vast orange library of dreams, dreams
Dressed in newspaper, wan as pale thighs
Making vast apple strides towards "The Poems."
"The Poems" is not a dream. It is night. You
Are asleep. Vast orange libraries of dreams
Stir inside "The Poems." On the dirt-covered ground
Crystal tears drench the ground. Vast orange dreams

Are unclenched. It is night. Songs have blossomed
In the pale crystal library of tears. You
Are asleep. A lovely light is singing to itself,
In "The Poems," in my eyes, in the line, "Guillaume Apollinaire is dead."

LII   *For Richard White*

It is a human universe: & I
is a correspondent   The innocence of childhood
Is not genuine   it shines forth from the faces
The poem upon the page is as massive as Anne's thighs
Belly to belly we have laid
                                    baffling combustions
are everywhere   graying the faces of virgins
aching to be fucked   we fondle their snatches
and O, I am afraid!   The poem upon the page
will not kneel   for everything comes to it
gratuitously   like Gertrude Stein to Radcliffe
Gus Cannon to say "I called myself Banjo Joe!"
O wet kisses, death on earth, lovely fucking in
        the poem upon the page
you have kept up with the times, and I am glad!

LIII

The poem upon the page is as massive as
Anne's thighs   belly to hot belly we have laid
Serene beneath feverous folds, flashed cool
in our white heat   hungered   and tasted   and
Gone to the movies   baffling combustions
are everywhere!   like Gertrude Stein at Radcliffe,
Patsy Padgett replete with teen-age belly!   every-
one's suddenly pregnant and no one is glad!
O wet kisses, the poem upon the page
Can tell you about teeth you've never dreamed
Could bite, nor be such reassurance!   Babies are not
like Word Origins and cribbage boards   or dreams
of correspondence!   Fucking is so very lovely
Who can say no to it later?

LV

*"Grace to be born
and live as variously
as possible"*
FRANK O'HARA

Grace to be born and live as variously as possible
White boats   green banks   black dust   atremble
Massive as Anne's thighs upon the page
I rage in a blue shirt at a brown desk in a
Bright room sustained by a bellyful of pills
"The Poem" is not a dream   for all things come to them
Gratuitously   In quick New York we imagine the blue Charles
Patsy awakens in heat and ready to squabble
No Poems she demands in a blanket command   belly
to hot belly we have laid   serenely white
Only my sweating pores are true in the empty night
Baffling combustions are everywhere!   we hunger and taste
And go to the movies   then run home drenched in flame
To the grace of the make-believe bed

LXVII

(clarity! clarity!) a semblance of motion, omniscience.
There is no such thing as a breakdown
To cover the tracks of "The Hammer"   (the morning sky
gets blue and red and I get worried about
mountains of mounting pressure
and the rust on the bolt in my door
Some kind of Bowery Santa Clauses   I wonder
down the streets of Roaring Gap
A glass of chocolate milk, head of lettuce, dark-
Bearden is dead. Chris is dead. Jacques Villon is dead.
Patsy awakens in heat and ready to squabble
I wonder if people talk about me *secretly?* I wonder if I'm fooling myself
about pills? I wonder what's in the icebox? out we go
to the looney movie   and the grace of the make-believe bed

LXXIV

"The academy
of the future
is opening its doors"
JOHN ASHBERY

The Academy of the future is opening its doors
my dream a crumpled horn
Under the blue sky the big earth is floating into "The Poems."
"A fruitful vista, this, our South," laughs Andrew to his Pa.
But his rough woe slithers o'er the land.
Ford Madox Ford is not a dream. The farm
was the family farm. On the real farm
I understood "The Poems."
                           Red-faced and romping in the wind, I, too,
am reading the technical journals. The only travelled sea
that I still dream of
is a cold black pond, where once
on a fragrant evening fraught with sadness
I launched a boat frail as a butterfly

LXXXVIII

A Final Sonnet

for Chris

How strange to be gone in a minute!   A man
Signs a shovel and so he digs   Everything
Turns into writing a name for a day
                           Someone
is having a birthday and someone is getting
married and someone is telling a joke   my dream
a white tree   I dream of the code of the west
But this rough magic I here abjure   and
When I have required some heavenly music   which even now
I do   to work mine end upon *their* senses
That this aery charm is for   I'll break
My staff   bury it certain fathoms in the earth
And deeper than did ever plummet sound
I'll drown my book.
It is 5:15 a.m.   Dear Chris, hello.

I've seen skies split with light, and night, / And surfs, currents, water-spouts; I know / What evening means, and doves, and I have seen / What other men sometimes have thought they've seen

T. B. (*Sonnet LXX*, after Arthur Rimbaud)

Alongside the century's (still) high claims for poetry, there is a pull also toward a deflationary/self-deflationary view of poet & of poet's stance. For Berrigan his undisguised sense of the former ("The gods demand of the system that a certain number of people sing") was more than matched by the latter ("I'm obscure when I feel like it / especially in my dream poems which I never even / call Dream Poem but from sheer cussedness title Match Game etc. [for Dick Gallup] or something like that.") Born Irish-American in Providence, Rhode Island, it was his destiny to come (with fellow poets/artists Ron Padgett, Dick Gallup, Joe Brainard) from university in Tulsa, Oklahoma, to form a second-generation New York school of poets (circa 1960) that led himself & others to a new encounter with the everyday & *un*remarkable transformed (like Schwitters's early *Merz* detritus or the images of 1960s pop art that Berrigan's poems sometimes resemble) into something dearly held. Careful to acknowledge his fellow poets & predecessors (O'Hara and Kerouac as near-contemporaries, Apollinaire & Rimbaud among the often cited/appropriated elders), he became (like them) a master of in-the-present moments that were destined (like any life) never to reoccur. The resultant work—deceptively personal, nostalgic, even sentimental—is simultaneously a twist (or, in Guy Debord's term, a *détournement*) on the personal, nostalgic, & sentimental. As Charles Bernstein rightly has it (concerning the "inversions" in Berrigan's acknowledged master work, *The Sonnets*): "*The Sonnets*—with its permutational use of the same phrases in different sequences and its inclusion of external or found language—stands as an explicit rejection of the psychological 'I' as the locus of the poem's meaning." Or Berrigan himself (in comic deference to Olson and Rimbaud): "It is a human universe: & I / is a correspondent" (*Sonnet LII*).

Inger Christensen b. 1935

ALPHABET 9, 10

9

ice ages exist, ice ages exist,
ice of the arctics and ice of the kingfisher;
cicadas exist, chicory, chrome

and the chrome yellow iris, the blue iris; oxygen
indeed; also ice floes in the arctic ocean,
polar bears exist, as fur inscribed
with an individual number he exists, condemned to his life;
& the kingfisher's mini-drop into the ice-blue rivers

of mars exists, if the rivers exist;
if oxygen in the rivers exists, oxygen
indeed; exists indeed there where the cicadas'
i-songs exist, there indeed where chicory
heaven exists blue dissolved in

water, the chrome yellow sun, oxygen
indeed; it will exist for sure, we will
exist for sure, the oxygen we breathe exists,
eye of fire crown of fire exist, and the heavenly
inside of the lake; a handle infolded
with bulrushes will exist, an ibis exists,
and the movements of the soul inhaled into clouds
exist, like oxygen storms deep inside Styx
and in the heart of wisdom's landscape ice-light,
ice identical with light, and in the inner
heart of the ice-light emptiness, live, intense
like your gaze in the rain, that fine life-
iridescent rain where gesture-like
the fourteen crystal lattices exist, the seven
crystalline systems, your gaze in mine,
and Icarus, impotent Icarus exists;

Icarus swaddled in melting waxwings
exists; Icarus pale as a corpse in
civvies exists, Icarus all the way down where
the pigeons exist; dreamers, dolls
exist; the dreamers' hair with cancerous tufts
torn out, the dolls' skin pinned together
with nails, rotting wood of the mysteries; and smiles
exist, Icarus' children white as lambs
in the gray light, will indeed exist, indeed
we will exist, and oxygen on oxygen's crucifix;
as hoar-frost we will exist, as wind we will exist,
as the rainbow's iris, in the shining shoots of
mesembryanthenum, in the tundra's straw; small

we will exist, as small as bits of pollen in peat,
as bits of virus in bones, as swamp pink maybe
maybe as a bit of white clover, vetch, a bit of chamomile
exiled to the lost again paradise; but darkness
is white say the children, the darkness of paradise is white,
but not white as a coffin is white,
that is if coffins exist, and not
white as milk is white,
that is if milk exists; white is white,
the children say, darkness is white, but not
white as the white existing
before fruit trees existed, their flowering so white,
darkness is whiter, eyes melt

10

june night exists, june night exists,
sky finally as if lifted up to celestial
heights and simultaneously pushed down as gently as when
dreams are visible before being dreamed; a space like
swooned, like saturated with whiteness, a timeless

knell of dew and insects, and nobody in this
gossamer, nobody understands that
autumn exists, that aftertaste and afterthought
exist, only these restless lines of fantastic
ultrasounds exist and the bat's
jade-ear turned towards the ticking fog;
never was the globe's inclination so beautiful,
never were the oxygenated nights so white,

so dispassionately dissolved, softly ionised
white, and never was the limit of invisibility so nearly
touched; june, june, your jacob's ladders
exist your sleeping beasts and their dreams of sleep
exist, a flight of galactic germs between
the earth so earthy and heaven so heavenly,
the calm of the valley of tears, so calm and the tears
sunk back, sunk back in like groundwater again
underground; earth; the earth in its revolution
around the sun exists; the earth in its itinerary
through the milky way exists; the earth on its way

with its load of jasmin, and of jasper and iron,
with its curtains of iron, its portents of joy and random Judas
kisses and a virgin anger
in the streets, jesus of salt; with the jacaranda's shadow
on the waters of the river, with falcons and hunters
and january in the heart, with the well of Jacopo della Quercia
Fonte Gaia in Sienna and with july
as heavy as a bomb; with tame brains,
with heart jars or heart grass or berries,
with the roots of ironwood in the exhausted earth

the earth that Jayadeva sings in his mystic
12th century poem; the earth with its coastline
of conscience, blue and with nests
where the large heron exists, with its neck curved
blue-gray, or the small heron exists, mysterious
and shy, or the night heron, the ash-colored heron exist
and the degrees of wing beats of sparrows, of cranes
and pigeons; the earth with Jullundur, Jabalpur and
Jungfrau exists, with Jotunheim and the Jura
exists, with Jabron and Jambo, Jogkarta
exists, with earth-swirls and earth-smoke exists
with water masses, landmasses, earthquakes exists,
with Judenburg, Johannesburg and the Jerusalem of Jerusalems

.

atom bombs exist

Hiroshima, Nagasaki

Hiroshima 6
august 1945

Nagasaki 9
august 1945

140,000 dead and
wounded in Hiroshima

about 60.000 dead and
wounded in Nagasaki

frozen numbers
somewhere in a distant
and ordinary summer

since then the wounded
have died, many at first, indeed
most, then fewer, but in the end

all; in the end
the children of the wounded,
stillborn, dying,

many, continuously,
some, finally the
last ones; in my kitchen

I stand and peel
potatoes; the faucet
runs and nearly
covers the noise of the
children in the yard;

the children yell and
nearly cover the noise
of the birds in
the trees; the birds
sing and nearly

cover the murmur
of the leaves in the wind;
the leaves murmur
and nearly cover
the silence of the sky,

the sky which is light
and the light which since
then has nearly
resembled the fire
of the atom bomb

Translation from the Danish by Pierre Joris

By using a system you are trying to reveal the rhythm of the universe. In the creation story, first there is silence, and then come patterns. (I. C.) And again: The gift is that you are forced to put much more of the world into the poem. Sometimes it feels as though the poem is carrying you along. You have access to a universe that begins to carry you . . . into something that you would never have been able to see or write.

Inger Christensen—poet, novelist, essayist—is the foremost Danish experimentalist of her generation. Maybe her single finest work to date, *Alfabet* (1981) is a book-length poem using two reticulating systems: the alphabet (as a means of random, almost innocent ordering—"adamic" & "prelapsarian," as Roland Barthes suggests) & the Fibonacci series (where each number is the sum of the two previous ones, thus: 1, 2, 3, 5, 8, 13, 21, 34, 55 . . .). Christensen: "These numerical ratios exist in nature—the way a leek wraps around itself from the inside, and the head of a sunflower, are both based on this series."

The rhythmic-syntactic base-line of the poem is the first line's joyous affirmation ("apricot trees exist, apricot trees exist")—modulated, as the poem takes in more of the world, by the noted existence of destruction & evil. While the early sections are single units, with the seventh letter ("g") these units start to decompose into stanzas, and with section ten ("i") into separate poems—though always of numerically determined length. Again, where each section of the original foregrounds words starting with the alphabetically corresponding letter, translation tends to lose some of the systematicity. (Thus Danish "is" easily gives English "ice," but in the next section the "j" of "jorden" is lost in the English "earth.")

Sarah Kirsch b. 1935

''THE WELS A FISH THAT LIVES ON THE BOTTOM''

The wels a fish that lives on the bottom
has a curved back the head is blunt
the belly flat he adapts himself to the sand
that is rolled by the waves of the water
of this shape I fancy my airplane
that hangs high above the earth, out of its fish belly
hugely developed the wings project
blunt-angled into wind-diffused clouds
under me forests conifer and deciduous trees
easily discernible from here

the autumn is visible dull brown on the
beeches oaks and larches, the winter-trees
have their green to show, more still
the streets rivers and cities call to me
beautiful lies the land the lakes like mirrors
pocket-mirrors mirror-fragments
this is my earth, there
demonstrations are held white
the banners are carried with black script
against butchery inequality stupidity
children swim on rubber swans old ones
still sleep on benches along rivers, street cleaners
gather the refuse up every morning
earth that I fly over on which rain and snow fall
no longer so innocent as before like the shadow of the airplane
I hear Bach and Josephine Baker that is a pair

Translation from the German by Wayne Kvam

''IN AN AIRPLANE I'M SUPPOSED TO''

In an airplane I'm supposed to
(in a blunderbuss, when it climbs one has to buckle up)
travel to a stranger country
the sky long through diverse clouds
I see where it is jointed sit behind the wing
it pulls its feet in stows them flaps flap, so
it will be I hope
that no earthly place
thwarts the poems I am to write there
I fly to the shore that Ovid saw
several years in exile, he lamented
about this landscape that was surely beautiful
only the poet had something else in mind
he found it desolate wanted
a paradisaic prison, wrote
from an almost pure heart hymns of praise glorified the ruler
as mild well-disposed toward the arts without success
he died there his grave
I could see and for the first time in my life palm trees
I would like

to come into the snow
with this vehicle "Carpathian-fright," my foot
already senses I want to see stones
set loose and contented plants, the shore
full of delightful houses big
I also want to dance and evenings swim in the ocean
I'll buy a green melon
give the taxi-driver some
if it all comes true and one day
I climb out there

Translation from the German by Wayne Kvam

PANDORA'S BOX

At certain times, this could be the Twelve Nights of Haydn, our husbands, whom we've divorced in a row, have a certain power over us. This they must never know. The possible happy constellations will be hidden from them because such things they never dare to hope, and also during seven tangible years we've remained remarkably foreign to them. The writing here will do the rest. Make them secure on days when there's nothing to be had from us. They will always reach for the telephone at the wrong time, causing us to be true again to our last love for years.

Translation from the German by Wayne Kvam

from KITE-FLYING

Mornings

He catches salamanders two centimeters long
In a drawer two by two meters
Such a big fellow such a tiny thing, I fall
Down from laughing; the dragon
Clamps himself firmly on my finger, small
Pain and because you go away

Call

Pin your little tail on glittering star, come
Under my roof you'll get a beer too

Renting a Room

When he gives me a light he has to kneel down.
When I'm already sitting, he
Lies on the floor. Now and then
I sleep in his hand

Translation from the German by Wayne Kvam

COMMENTARY

*Tonight, Bettina, everything / Is as it always was   As always / We are
alone, when we write to the kings / Those of the heart and those / Of the
state. And still / Our hearts are frightened / When from the other side of
the house / A car can be heard.*
S. K.

Commenting on her remarks above, addressed to Bettina von Arnim (1785–
1859), whose dedication to her book about the Berlin working class read,
"This book belongs to the king," Kirsch suggests that "at some point one
should also talk to one's own king, or head of state, or whoever, and should
send him a letter. And that's exactly what happened later." It was that "let-
ter"—or rather the petition (signed by a number of East German writers)
denouncing the expulsion of poet/songwriter Wolf Bierman—that led to
her own "permission" to leave East Germany in 1977 & to settle in the west,
thus to escape from what she calls "a politics that doesn't dare to let man be
man in all his unpredictability." But even more so than in any such fore-
grounded (if infrequent) direct statements, there was a poetics of (political/
cultural) resistance at work in her poetry of the sixties & seventies, as evi-
denced, say, by her pointed use of the first person singular, the subjective,
anguished, & mutable "I" pitched against the official doctrine of socialist
realism's collectivist & utopian "we." Writes Hans Wagener: "Without a
false sense of shame she states her feelings, emotions and innermost experi-
ences, her longings, sexual desires and sensual pleasures." This is further
complicated by a syntax marked by what her translator Wayne Kvam de-
scribes as "her penchant for dropping prefixes and suffixes, for taking syn-
tactical short cuts, for coining new words" and "by her affinity for the
vernacular, her deft use of run-on lines, her omission of conventional punc-
tuation." Yet the poetry also has its humourous quirkiness & a "Dingge-
dicht" intensity, making, in the final analysis, for a multiplicity of meaning-
strata, something specifically suggested by the poet when she says that she
writes poems "in which there remains room to play for the readers, where
they too can make something . . . everyone can still move about in the lines."

POSTWAR JAPANESE POETRY
The Arechi & After

When the Japanese experienced two atomic bombs they also witnessed,
symbolically, a vision of apocalypse utterly without divine presence.
This is why the demand "Bring back totality through poetry" was
common to every group and trend in postwar Japan until at least the
1960s.

ŌOKA MAKOTO

Against the view—Japanese & Western both—of a traditional Japanese poetry defined by long-established canons of brevity & refinement, the work of post–World War II generations shows an enormity of means & voice that turns the old ways upside down (or seems to), while bringing those ways simultaneously into the present. Less resembling *haiku* and *tanka* (*waka*)—for those of us who view them from the outside—than a ghost-ridden poets' theater like the traditional *noh* or contemporary *butoh*, their work becomes "a celebration in darkness which is at once weird and refined, scatological and lofty, comic and serious." (Thus Yoshioka Minoru.) As with other new poetries, that of Japan's "postwar" poets moves increasingly toward the demotic (colloquial, everyday), bringing in a range of new—often foreign—vocabularies & imageries, along with a mix of class & gender usages (long separated into discreet social levels) & a "violation of grammatical norms carried to the point of linguistic rapine" (Roy Andrew Miller). On their literary side, the resultant poems display—Miller again—a "stripping-away of all the customary decorations and embellishments of traditional Japanese poetics" toward a "naked language" (*hadaka no gengo*) & "what may very well be their single most salient structural feature—the great freedom and variety displayed by the poetic line that they employ."

Intimations of that freedom begin to appear in the 1920s/30s experiments of homegrown Dadas & Surrealists, as also in the work of poets such as Hagiwara Sakutarō, Miyazawa Kenji, & Kusano Shimpei (selections from all of whom appear in volume one). But it's the aftermath of World War II that marks what Ōoka Makoto calls "a crucial dividing line" between past & present, after which "Japanese poets were forced, whether they wanted to or not, to look through their individual fates and see the fate of the whole 20th century" and, in so doing, "to absorb concretely the real meaning of [earlier] European movements"—in short, a vision of extremity, shared with the world at large. Adds Ōoka: for groupings of postwar writers like the early Arechi (Waste Land) poets or his own Kai (Oars) group, "modern poetry, as an alternative to science and religion, was now required to restore a fundamental unity and totality to human thought and action. This was the great claim made by Japanese poetry."

Of the work presented in this cluster, Tamura's goes back to at least the founding (1947) of the Waste Land group (he was for several issues the editor of their magazine, *Arechi*), while Tanikawa and Ōoka emerged a few years later with the Oars movement (1953), already taken as a kind of post–Waste Land poetry. Still further thrusts away from traditional &/ or literary forms among the poets shown here: Shiraishi Kazuko, born in Vancouver & emerging from contacts with avant-gardist Kitasono Katsue's *VOU* magazine into the assertion (through self-performance, jazz, etc.) of a new & openly erotic femaleness; Yoshimasu Gōzō, whose visually radical poetry & far-reaching cultural receptiveness issue in a form of high-energy performance & "a sensitivity to deep rhythms that allows him to endure the wildest screams, speed, midair collisions" (Ijima Kōichi); Fujii Sadakazu, master of a darkly native scholarship & a sense of "investigative poetry" (E. Sanders) that takes him into "varieties of Japanese poetry [different] from those found in standard textbooks . . . [so that] all his subjects—the 'extinct' wolf-woman, the shamans, the nomads, even algae and rocks— . . . speak, chant, and sing at the borders of Japanese history" (Christopher Drake); & Itō Hiromi, representative of a still younger generation of poets in her further adaptation of demotic language, in her drift toward popular (& in her case marginally shamanic) performance, & in her "graphic chronicling," as a (specifically) woman poet, "of her pregnancy and child-delivery, excretion, menstruation, masturbation, and so forth" (H. Sato).

Japanese poets represented elsewhere in these pages are Tōge Sankichi, Yoshioka Minoru, Takahashi Mutsuo, & Seiichi Nīkuni.

Tamura Ryūichi b. 1923

MY IMPERIALISM

I sink into bed
on the first Monday after Pentecost
and bless myself
since I'm not a Christian

Yet my ears still wander the sky
my eyes keep hunting for underground water
and my hands hold a small book
describing the grotesqueness of modern white society
when looked down at from the nonwhite world
in my fingers there's a thin cigarette—
I wish it were hallucinogenic
though I'm tired of indiscriminate ecstasy

Through a window in the northern hemisphere
the light moves slowly past morning to afternoon
before I can place the red flare, it's gone:
darkness

Was it this morning that my acupuncturist came?
a graduate student in Marxist economics, he says he changed
to medicine to help humanity, the animal of animals, drag itself
    peacefully to its deathbeds
forty years of Scotch whiskey's roasted my liver and put me
into the hands of a Marxist economist
I want to ask him about *Imperialism, A Study—*
what Hobson saw in South Africa at the end of the nineteenth century
may yet push me out of bed
even if you wanted to praise imperialism
there aren't enough kings and natives left
the overproduced slaves had to become white

Only the nails grow
the nails of the dead grow too
so, like cats, we must constantly
sharpen ours to stay alive
Only The Nails Grow—not a bad epitaph
when K died his wife buried him in Fuji Cemetery

and had To One Woman carved on his gravestone
true, it was the title of one of his books
but the way she tried to have him only
to herself almost made me cry
even N, who founded the modernist magazine *Luna*
while Japan prepared to invade China
got sentimental after he went on his pension;
F, depressed
S, manic, builds house after house
A has abdominal imperialism: his stomach's colonized his legs
M's deaf, he can endure the loudest sounds;
some people have only their shadows grow
others become smaller than they really are
our old manifesto had it wrong: we only looked upward
if we'd really wanted to write poems
we should have crawled on the ground on all fours—
when William Irish, who wrote *The Phantom Lady,* died
the only mourners were stock brokers
Mozart's wife was not at his funeral

My feet grow warmer as I read
Kōtoku Shūsui's *Imperialism, Monster of the Twentieth Century,* written
    back in 1901
when he was young N wrote "I say strange things"
was it the monster that pumped tears from his older eyes?

Poems are commodities without exchange value
but we're forced to invade new territory
by crises of poetic overproduction

We must enslave the natives with our poems
all the ignorant savages under sixty
plagued by a surplus of clothes and food—
when you're past sixty
you're neither a commodity
nor human

Translation from the Japanese by Christopher Drake

Tanikawa Shuntarō b. 1931

from WITH SILENCE MY COMPANION

I know how worthless this poem will be
under the scrutiny of daylight
and yet I cannot now disown my words.

While others fill their baskets at market
I drink water from a cup on the table,
utterly idle.

I see through the trees, by the distant pool,
a white statue,
its genitals exposed.
It is I.

I am immersed
in the past
and have become a block of dumb stone
and not the Orpheus I hoped to be.

Translation from the Japanese by William I. Elliott & Kazuo Kawamura

CYCLE OF MONTHS (MENSTRUATION)

I

within her someone prepares a banquet
within her someone carves an unknown son
within her someone is wounded

2

the palm of god,
injured clumsily in the act of creation,
still finds it difficult to forget

3

"with such accurate regularity   florid
funerals occur within me   they are
mourned in the color of celebration   they

continue, unwounded and unable to die, to
return to nothingness   my children who
are overly young . . . a ripe moon is
falling   there is no one to receive it
I am waiting   I am alone squatting
in a chilly place and waiting—
for someone to sow the moon
for someone to deprive me of this rising tide—
with a wound, lost to the memory
of all, within me that is outside the
reach of healing"

4

. . . while alluring those who will to live
towards the shore   the tide flows full
within her   there within her lies a sea
calling to the moon   and as the moon
revolves around   there lies within her an
endless calendar . . .

Translation from the Japanese by Harold Wright

Ōoka Makoto b. 1931

"MARILYN"

Written shortly after the death of Marilyn Monroe.

Death:
a mirror that
turns the film backward.

.

The sweep of her eye no
longer reaches dream's crystal forest.
In the distance,
where dim flames of death
carry her bed,

will she be met by a
gentle white elephant or
a closed lead window?
Hair softly undulating she
lies now rigid as a washboard
on a dark mirror in which still
quivers a scalpel.

But no scalpel can reach soul's truth.

•

Through history's tinted glass
each August hill seems
a burning Calvary.
Do not ask her where the thorns are,
translucent thorns and poisonous,
raised amid fatal praise.

You doctors searching
in the body of America for Capitalism's
cancerous cells
invading her sleep,
you, turning your faces away,
Doctors, do not write
in the stories of your lives
Marilyn's name.
Her death tells all there is to know
about you.

•

Now is the age
when a tear tells it all.
Words cannot
as precisely as undulating hair
tell what a naked corpse
must tell,
can only skim death
for a froth of poetry.

•

Her eyes sink,
become lakes.
Cheap films float there,
glimmering in moonlight
like flies on water,
projecting, with reflected light,
clear upon night sky
Hollywood floating sick
and bloodless.

To die bleeding real blood
you have to lie naked.

·

Marilyn
soul noisier than the world and more anxious,
timid as a shrimp's feelers,
model of womanhood,
your laughter
trickling out of Camelias
first announced a fairy tale
no Yankee had ever heard.
Then into the door revolving
between sleep and waking
you went
and never came back:
starting on both sides of the door
a crazy game of tag
so popular it soon made of you
a gentle
IT.

How then could you come back?
Poems are pale now;
nations are villages,
windows secretly weeping.

·

Marilyn
Marine

Blue.

Translation from the Japanese by Thomas Fitzimmons & Ōoka Makoto

Shiraishi Kazuko b. 1931

THE MAN ROOT

God if he exists
Or if he doesn't
Still has a sense of humor
Like a certain type of man

So this time
He brings a gigantic man root
To join the picnic
Above the end of the sky of my dreams
Meanwhile
I'm sorry
I didn't give Sumiko anything for her birthday
But now I wish I could at least
Set the seeds of that God given penis
In the thin, small, and very charming voice of Sumiko
On the end of the line

Sumiko, I'm so sorry
But the penis shooting up day by day
Flourishes in the heart of the cosmos
As rigid as a wrecked bus
So that if
You'd like to see
The beautiful sky with all its stars
Or just another man instead of this God given cock
A man speeding along a highway
With a hot girl
You'll have to hang
All the way out of the bus window
With your eyes peeled

It's spectacular when the cock
Starts nuzzling the edge of the cosmos
At this time
Dear Sumiko
The lonely way the stars of night shine
And the curious coldness of noon
Penetrates my gut
Seen whole
Or even if you refused to look
You'd go crazy
Because you can trace
The nameless, impersonal, and timeless penis
In the raucous atmosphere
Of the passers-by
That parade it in a portable shrine
In that stir of voices
You can hear an immensity of savage
Rebellion, the curses of
Heathen gism
Sometimes
God is in conference or out to lunch
It seems he's away
Absconding from debts or leaving his penis

So now
The cock abandoned by God
Trots along
Young and gay
And full of callow confidence
Amazingly like the shadow
Of a sophisticated smile

The penis bursting out of bounds
And beyond measure
Arrives here
Truly unique and entirely alone
Seen from whatever perspective
It's faceless and speechless
I would like to give you, Sumiko
Something like this for your birthday

When it envelops your entire life
And you've become invisible even to yourself
Occasionally you'll turn into the will
Of exactly this penis
And wander
Ceaselessly

I want to catch in my arms
Forever
Someone like you

Translation from the Japanese by Kenneth Rexroth & Ikuko Atsumi

Yoshimasu Gōzō b. 1939

PULLING IN THE REINS

Walking along a river bank in an antiquated universe.
A tall woman approaches
passes me by. She looked like Kudara
the Goddess of Mercy. Black woman?
In the dim light I couldn't tell.
The universe already old
growing older
Japan since the days of the Shoguns
like a small boat.
Walking along a river bank
I recall the phrase
"Mirrors and sex are guilty
of increasing the number of people."

Eros, everywhere!

Ship of death.

Seduction.

Translation from the Japanese by Richard Arno

OSIRIS, THE GOD OF STONE

Past what is called ANAMUSHI Pass, and as far as NIJŌZAN, I was gritting my teeth, thinking. Is that an ancient mausoleum, there are several hilly mounds, the electric train was almost on the prefectural border between OSAKA and NARA.

This is a tomb, I thought, and ancient, Egyptian, an aged couple I saw in a movie floated up, and they talked to me. What occurred in a movie, today, now, had risen to its feet.

The old couple talked to me, Our child, our only son, is a prodigal son, you see, and as security for his gambling has, finally, sold off the tomb we are supposed to go to, when we die. . . .

I came to, and I was gritting my teeth, and was in the car. I came to, because the train had begun to go down the mountain and increased its speed.

To NIJŌZAN Station, it's now only ten seconds or fifteen seconds, and I, recognizing another border coming in from the window, in a great hurry drove my ballpoint pen, was driving my ballpoint pen.

If you go out of the one-stationman station and turn right, there's NIJŌZAN in front of you.

This is a double mountain of green, cheeks red, that soft round mountain, was in the Egyptian couple who whispered I don't know, Osiris, Osiris, the woman (?), so called, the god, was by the roadside.

It was a mystery, the father and mother (parents), even with their house after death sold off, by their prodigal son, weren't sorrowing.

We have no place to go after death, but we no longer care. And they walked away, they did, along a path in me, by a rock cliff.

On the roadside, waiting for a taxi perhaps, a young, but that was a lavender blouse, wasn't it, a woman, Is that beautiful mountain with double eyelids NIJŌZAN . . . I asked her, and laughed. And talked a little, and from there, went back to the station.

I no longer care.

I am not a native of this place.
Osiris.

It was a lavender blouse.
A beautiful mountain.

Down a narrow path, I walked to the station. I have about thirty minutes, to the next train. The one-stationman station man is talking to a woman, who appears to be someone from the neighborhood, about money about the house he built. Listening, I stepped down to the crossing, and trying not to be seen, picked up two stones, and having picked them up, hurriedly put them in my bag.

I crossed to the other side, to the platform, sat on a wooden bench, a roofed bench, and began to write, and a green soft beautiful mountain is peering at me. Sitting there, I, again, singlemindedly had begun to write.

I came to, perhaps because the train began to come down the mountain, added to its speed, and came in, flustered, I grabbed my belongings, tried to get in the car, but the wooden bench wouldn't get off me, the metal hanger for my suit got into a crack in the wooden bench, and was caught.

I came to, and the wooden piece was broken, and was standing. I added strength, ran into the car, and beyond the window the wooden piece of the wooden bench was broken and was standing. The wood, broken, had become erect.

I was assaulted by an emotion like anger, and because of that, the one-stationman's station, its view, left a light (view?) like an illusory world in the water.

Gritting his teeth and writing, that was me, the wood had been broken and had risen to its feet.

Again, the ancient Egyptian, the aged couple's voice began to be heard.

We no longer care, our prodigal son. . . .
It was a lavender blouse.
A beautiful mountain.

Am I a narrator. *Sitting in a seat,* I (who was sitting, on the wooden bench of NIJŌZAN Station)? (Or someone) that sitting, figure, who?

The wood had been broken and had risen to its feet.
Around it, a snake was circling. With two stones swallowed in its stomach, quietly, a snake was circling.

Translation from the Japanese by Hiroaki Sato

Fujii Sadakazu b. 1942

Wolf

Many say Japan has neither a poetics nor a language in which poetry can be written. No poetics, they say, and so no language for poetry. But what exactly was it that was once in the language, and what was lost? And where can what was lost live once more?

The woman hides
her snowy naked body.
She wears
shorelines the color of waves.
Yet she is lured into the dark night
beyond windows
meant to shelter her.
And I embrace
water, a
melting voice.

Memory tells me my arms were around a wolf woman. Wolves disappeared from the Japanese islands long ago, but the woman was definitely a wolf. More correctly, she was a descendant of the wolf goddess, still possessed at times by her spirit.

The woman's chest
wide in the wind
from the reed plain.
The swaying of barley
hides her dark abdomen.
Below that, a blanket of water.
What is visible in the night
hangs in her basket of belongings,
and in her throat
long tremors.
She receives my "stick"
again and again.

Of course I did as much as buy her that night. And when I told her I was going back to Fukui the next morning she surprised me, a perfect stranger, with her wolf voice, and stories of being possessed.

The wolf
in the legend shot in that place by a hunter in the dark.
Leaving behind wolf breasts, still hanging from the wall,
the wild woman gone forever.
Facing the past,
her grieving fangs in the wind.
Hotter than ground pressure,
her burned legs
already thinner
than pencils.
But why
"already"?
Fingers pressed against
pencils, we must record
the fragile words
of that voice.

A ghostly masked woman was sighted again and again along the length of the Japanese islands during May and June of 1979. She approached people, then tore off her mask, revealing a mouth open all the way back to her ears. If the folklorist Yanagita Kunio had still been alive to hear her, a new, ecstatic science of legends would have been born.

That's the wind. Behind the wind-like wolf.

Small Dream

Nuchika torichibi, in Orok, *small dream.* The newspaper clipping where I found the phrase has already disappeared. *Nuchika torichibi.* But the fact that these audible words, these visible words are "poems" has not disappeared. *Nuchika torichibi.* Words passing away, coming down from islands north of "Japan."

> Supple, sensual drinking
>   water
>   violets
>   cocoons in a corner
>   —like foam
>   when
>   they sleep

At a time when "history" and "structures" were invisible in the country at the bottom of the hearing well, the ancient Yamato people gave love over to lowly Buddhist demons and sweated obscenely over their powerful state institutions. We have tried to live an obscene beauty.

> *Nuchika torichibi*
>> words leaving
>>> living deep within
>>>> eyes
>>>>> in an ancient world
>>>>>> when they sleep

Nights of tuning and playing rocks, days of buried graves. They continued for thirteen centuries. Witnessing this country which destroys love first of all, when it begins slowly from the end: songs from the bottom—

> Like foam
>> eyes that sleep and play
>>> things of fire
>> passing, dying
>>> making
>>>> new light

The man falls in love with fire, visits her at night like a wind. Through the vulgarity of softly opening and closing reed blinds, the woman swears this is love. From behind those who have died, ancient *saibara* melodies fill the roads, and clinging even to women's modern-style pans and discarded white underwear: this gray country

> Mud beyond
>> and time   body organs
>> throats
> and floating above a far bottom
>> foam of
>>> eyes

The air darkens around a vagina-like shrine in the fold of a mountain. A flat moon rises. Voices of destruction wagered on this wasteland adorn its ruins; embracing ropes flap sad wing sounds. After that the man was in-numerable voices, and a stick. By the time leaf-like buildings were floating upward beneath the rainbow of the nation, there had already been a "postwar period" written in abstract Chinese characters.

Fire powder
endless eyes
round
        peaceful lives
myths
            sprouting myriad grass thoughts

River, carry away the mask of "poetry." Look at this nation, which has arched over so many centuries, shutting up dreams in strong tubs. Lifeboats drift from expanse to endless expanse. Half our lives have passed already, lacking any way of returning to this country where young women who know "love" have young men touching lonely hills—

Translation from the Japanese by Christopher Drake

Itō Hiromi b. 1955

NEAR KITAMI STATION ON THE ODAKYŪ LINE

The Odakyū line is always crowded I go on standing
Around midday if I ride the Seibu Ikebukuro line I can usually get a seat
    as I can also on the Toei Underground line.
These are lines I normally travel on.
On the Odakyū downline there's a lot of universities so there's lots of
    people. I don't like the feeling I have when I get on a crowded train I
    get on hating people
I change trains at Seijō Gakuen Station. On the other platform the all-
    stops train is waiting with its doors open.
I get on not hating people. Only a few people are inside never many
Because I don't know it well I always get in the front the very front
    carriage of the express the all-stops train does not reach the place
    directly opposite the front carriage of the express. The all-stops is
    a short train.
While I walk to the door of the all-stops train the express starts to move
    in passes Seijō Gakuen speeds down the slope and as soon as it has
    sped down the slope it makes a stop
I look at the greenery outside the carriage as it rushes past
It changes from trees to grass and then back to trees
A creek crosses the grass

Outside the carriage greenery is everywhere
Because I don't know it well I always sit in the very front carriage of the
   all-stops train the steps leading to the ticket-turnstiles are in the middle
   of the platform. Where I cross the up platform I wave my hand
   seductively
I cross the level-crossing and go into his apartment
Ten minutes walk away
Some weeks ago someone committed suicide at the level-crossing
Planks are lain over the level-crossing
The planks were soaked in blood
In the depression in the track a lump of blood
And what looked like part of an internal organ remained

We had sexual intercourse while I was menstruating

When I go into his apartment I turn on the radio
I leant over his face and
Squeezed the pimples in every corner of his face
I plucked the hairs that remained on his cheeks after shaving
Turned him around
A mole-like thing is on his back
I knew because it sticks out
When I squeeze it the black fatty deposit in the head slides out
In the back of his ears as well there are fatty deposits
When I squeeze they slid out long and slippery
When I grip his hair with my teeth and pull out it comes
I bite my fingernails
My nails are short
I can't pluck hairs with my nails
If I use my teeth they always come out
His cheek comes close to me it's always cold
His beard touched my skin
He has shaven
I feel the shaven stubble
Before and after we engage in sexual intercourse.

I saw a photograph of the area near Kitami station among the photo-
graphs of Araki Nobuyoshi I immediately thought this is where I have sex
I felt ashamed I am a 25-year-old woman and thus do engage in regular
sexual intercourse. I come from Itabashi ward to Setagaya ward and while
travelling sexual intercourse is not on my mind I do not feel any sexual
desire I am watching the grass and trees of Setagaya ward as they pass by

outside the carriage in this season the chlorophyll is evident in layers the moisture almost reaches the saturation point when I meet him I feel happy so I wave seductively but when I turn on the radio in his apartment is the time I think of sex

Sex has become a matter of course
I cross the level-crossing and come to the station
It may be that I've pulled my panties up over my wet genitals and crossed
    at the level-crossing at Kitami where the piece of flesh still remains
Liquid constantly oozed out
And soaked my panties

Translation from the Japanese by Leith Morton

Clayton Eshleman b. 1935

OUR LADY OF THE THREE-PRONGED DEVIL

Our Lady of the Caves
dressed in rock,
vulviform, folded back
upon Herself, a turn in the cave,
at Abri Cellier
an arch gouged in a slab
makes an entrance and
an exit, She is a hole,
yet rock, impenetrable,
the impact point of the enigma
"no one has lifted her veil,"
the impact point of the enigma
yet rock, impenetrable,
an exit, She is a hole,
makes an entrance and
an arch gouged in a slab
at Abri Cellier
upon Herself, a turn in the cave,
vulviform, folded back
dressed in rock,
Our Lady of the Caves

As She folds back
I sense a long sentence dissolving within itself
and when it ends, it is just beginning,
a presentiment that Her sign is one turn, uni-
verse, end of a first line, curved about
a vaginal gouge, as if what is bent about is foetal,
as if She is a foetal arch bent about a slit
that goes in one-quarter inch.
Our Lady may be the invisible archwork
through which all things
shift gears in the dark, at cheetah-speed,
at snail-struggle, on the shores of Russia
where Paleo-archetypes compressed into radar
gaze around with dinosaur certainty.

Before Okeanos, continuing through
Okeanos, before the uroboros, continuing in it,
Her gibbous half-circle tells me that She was,
before an association was made between fucking and birth,
before a bubbling parthenogenesis was enclosed—
but to what extent She is
in self-enclosure, in my beak triumphantly
raising my penis to the sun,
to what extent She neatly
slides Her slit between my self and its point,
I do not know.

For the self has grown enormous,
I look through literal eyes to see Her
on a slab chopped out of Abri Cellier,
in a cool limestone room in Les Eyzies.
She seems to be only several inches tall.
It is a funeral to be here,
in a burial chamber where first otherness
is displayed behind a rope, with written instructions
which only describe the age of a shape.
And I who look upon this am immense,
encrusted with all my own undelivered selves,
my skeletal papoose rack through which my mother's
85 mile long legs are dangling, out of which my father's
right arm with a seemingly infinite switch trails
down the museum road, across France, to disappear in the Atlantic,
and I jig around a bit
because this ghost dance starts up as I stare
through the hermaphroditic
circle the snake made, so self-contained,
but what it and I contain, the "divine couple,"
is the latent mother-father which
has taken over the world.

Our Lady moved about
like a stubby pitchfork,
yellow fiber gushed out from between Her prongs,

She hobbled toward image—
what lurked under Her vulviform was the trident yet to come,
for men realized that not only could the point of her slit
be hurled but that its two bounding lines could be too,
the whole woman could be thrown into the animal,
and way in, trident-deep in Le Portel,
did Her three prongs close?
Was the uroboros hammered shut when those hunters at last
hacked themselves free from animal sinew?
And was this the point at which
the wilderness was mentally enwalled,
serpent the outer circumference,
to teach, and banish, our Adamic Eve?

Below Our Lady, on the wall of my mind,
is the foot long rock phallus Her devotees
may have taken inside while they chipped in Her sign,
I have been straddling, all poem long, that insistent,
rapacious thing, of phallus, the tooth-phallus,
the borer, for the tooth-phallus is insatiable,
male hunger to connect at any price,
but not to connect, to cease being an island,
a speck before the emancipatory shape of
the birth-giving mainland, to build a mole
to tie fucking to birth, to cease being ticks
on the heaving pelt of the earth, to hook
our erections to the sleigh of a howling starveling,
And we did get across, at around 10,000 BP,
one night fucking and birth were connected by a mole
burrowing right under the surface of a full moon
boring a red mortal line from the edge
to a point equidistant from the circumference.
The corpus callosum was suddenly filled with traffic.
The last Magdalenians were aware that Our Lady
had closed. They padlocked Her
with the uroboros and planted the key.

She now grows on a long handle
out of ground at the edge of the abyss.
Some see Her as fly-eyed radar.

Others feel it is to Her prong that they cling
as the gale of monoculture whips them horizontal.
Many more on their knees inch along cathedral pavement
toward what they believe is her virgin compassion
which will somehow make their manure-colored barriada water pure,
their nipple blood, their corporeal
muscatel in which their children play,
miracle and misery on which my index
touches, to stir for a moment Her
gouged rock socket
octopus current of
faceless suckers Veil.

*Today I have set my crowbar against all I know / In a shower of soot &
blood / Breaking the backbone of my mother*
C. E.

When Eshleman first came to us there was already a force in him, a hardcore
probing that would close in, later, on lost levels of our body-mind entangle-
ments—in us as individuals & as species. That thrust in his work (his "proj-
ect" as such) is summed up in the idea of a "grotesque realism," drawn
from the Russian writer Mikhail Bakhtin (in his study of Rabelais) & trans-
formed by Eshleman into a proposal for an "American grotesque." Of Esh-
leman's own practice, Eliot Weinberger has written: "It is an immersion in
the [lower] body; not the body of the individual, the 'bourgeois ego,' but the
body of all: the 'brimming over abundance' of decay, fertility, birth, growth,
death . . . unfinished, exaggerated; . . . protuberances and apertures promi-
nent." From this base in his own body, he makes the leap (circa 1970) into
the equally subterranean & mysterious cave-world (French *grotte*, Italian
grotto) of the European paleolithic, enters it crawling (literally) "on all
fours," to find in the animal beings painted on its walls a first "construction
of the underworld" by "Neanderthal and Crô-Magnon men, women, and
children, who made the nearly unimaginable breakthrough, over thousands
of years, from no mental record to a mental record." The work is by turns
"ecstatic and comic" (Weinberger)—& just as often grim & terrifying in its
assessment of the present human state. It is carried forward further by a
remarkable series of translations (samples of which are scattered through-
out the present volumes) of modern predecessors (Césaire, Vallejo, Artaud,
Holan), whom he calls (as an extension of his central image) "conductors

of the pit" & with whom he enters into acts of both apprenticeship & struggle. And his still larger community—both external & imagined—takes form in a range of portraits & addresses to shades & spirits of the recent (&, for him, related) dead: Wilhelm Reich, Bud Powell, Bill Evans, Chaim Soutine, Frida Kahlo, Francis Bacon, Paul Blackburn, among others. Together with his germinal & aptly titled magazines (*Caterpillar* in the 1960s, *Sulfur* in the 1980s & 1990s), the work becomes—as he would have it—the model of a renewed (renewable) "construction of the underworld." (For more of which, see volume one, page 738.)

Robert Kelly b. 1935

ODE TO LANGUAGE

To put on shoes and be sophisticated
—it really was a creamy trumpet
Miles Davis made—or gleam waxy
and smile along the El-shadowed street
through all the synaesthesias of weary language
patient, at our command, like an old dog.

Faithful animal! Endure
Tehran, Stella by Starlight, Nautilus
machines, the skanky fantasies
of men no longer young, the rough
edge of graffiti, borrowed vices
of exurban novelists, the price of glass.

Break me. Come to me
with burrs in your fur, tell me
where everything has ever been.
Growl at me if I sleep, wake me
with your dependable craziness.
Birds plummet and you fetch them
wet from your mouth. Women weep
in San Francisco. Only you

are ever different.

THE MAN WHO LOVED WHITE CHOCOLATE

There is an egg in the middle of things
a blue racer a kind of whip
to top the spin with, thus reify
(thingle) it, there is a mallet
tunking metal there is a frog
lucid gel that harbors comingstance
the drift of spawn along along,
there is a gong goes in the egg
wakes him from his appetites.

Be scant, new citizen.
Intellectual hedonism of easy things
well-made plays, craft
for the comfort of some buyer—
yet no shoe without its nail
—sails look cuter with no boats—
so many ways to get married

and live in affluence as you'd live in Spain
silently well-servanted on gaunt plateaux
surveying our meaty ruin: O vultures
(but they respond not, being robins,
sparrows, such, and common crows)
having their own jive no need of his

there is a white taste in his mouth
long row of stalwart fencing
dangled in his neighbor's light
unstrung from rollers and stretched
along the bordermind, a tooth
for you, muchacha, and (lachaim!)
a prick or two—galvanized roses—
in your hand. Willingly obey the dog.
Go. (He reflecteth darkness as
rehearsal for that sweet despair
that long Without)   blue flowers
red birds new grass a yellow chair
a flag of surrender run up
in the smooth colorless air. Eat me
said the day, I have never snowed,
never forgotten. Bird thuggee,

rattle-pinioned raptors throng
devour such offerings, raw
conversations between parted lovers
estrange him from himself. Some stars.
Admit that appetite is mostly mind
you're left only a little tool to lie with
—the cardinal almost orange in harsh sun
swelling towards the river where she sits
red vestmented chatting with a friend
who cut her hair too short—
who pulls me down? See, see
where an old chunk of weathery wood
checks, splits, gapes to show
Christ's lordly tulku in the firmament.
Even this, heart, is one more thing.

The talk is chaff from off some core,
coronal of disasters whose livid petals
one by one we dare to pluck. Blue flower
never found unless in losing.
Many a burnt hand, mortgaged mind,
undersapped foundation, leprous wall.
Leviticate, lixiviate, then levigate
—one more lie from the makers of the Pantheon—
in the harlot's church a dead emperor waits.
Le tombeau de your last concrete example.
Broad skated, high on the wave, prorsum, prow.

Hone your keel for such thick seas.
A moment after. How is she now,
and will her new car mend the distance?
Spill a road on whom go quiet
gyved by circumstance, not wearing a hat,
wind-tousled, a shy conquistador?
Malinche, remember she. So dark.
Weinend, klagend, Easter never,
hope not, live long, squill-blue, hurry.
The spring is in today, no wonder
like this wonder. A lamb in trouble.

Fondle you. What world does she generate
sexier than herself, and if none, bother,

she-failure, one more just plucked rose.
O she doesnt make things up,
the villainess, does she suppose
flesh's enough for flesh and talk for talk,
aye-bartering, yatter and sex?
Tisnt. Rub two random words together
to get a richer universe than any this.

Micron by turkey feather turning
we doubt our same black bodies and white bodies
because the difference is only a car only
on roads capable to go that we have made
and there's no finding He didnt find before
—the man who ate rice pudding
without necessarily liking and certainly
not despising it—one turns
and it is here—lactoglycodynamo
a kilocalorie or so to wake
what part of us can sleep—
red baubles on a spruce tree, April tinsel—
o the horn signal of the house on fire
whence even skeptics flee—here comes
the hook and ladders!—spirit searchlights
spotting a hasty ruin—hurry—
promise the little children something red.

Promise levanters a sensuous occident
and they'll come home, every sentence
is the whole of what he ever knows,
but he has no home to take them in,
that's rich, that's lips. In palaver
linger, between a breath and a breath
glimpsing true orient—as when the words
you suddenly see her mouth making
are only to make you look at her speaking
—at and in—beyond and never come home
—that were promised-lander's promise,
pure going! Pierce going, pang getting,
all at once a devious love-feast (a door
for him suddenly open) listen (opera

that curious machine) ('feel my heart
beating where your ear hurries')
lords and ladies coltsfoot the periwinkle
blues (husband of a breast) (cantilever)

the man who loved white chocolate
loved a rumor of the sea
that one of those milky camerlengas would
(hard to see through tressures, hers, as
today she of the sky said, *treasures of cloud*)
float him to a book or book to him
sage under carageen an old unlogic
unlocking—the greatest mystery is analysis—
to demystify the very sense he sees them by,
utter,most,wise,ness, the continent.
Not by any mirror see your naked face.

White-stubbled cheeks a youngish mien
six finches at the window bumming seed
gloriosos full of chatter and
strumpet-minded he sees gold
beyond the greenwork of the day, spring,
lax, oil, tight in posture loose inside

I am the uncommitted
grotto of Natural Selection
what he thought when he went home
thinks him forever after or not ever
—the bust of Beethoven on the shelf
must mean something—take it
in small mouthfuls, mind—

look at the season you find a self in
so well calypso'd you'd
guess there is none, you'd be right,
stomachers on cold bacon, a chest
full of medals he cast for himself
gorgeously enamelled—Arkansas tart
her fanny smelling of patchouli—

George Sand's fingers trail along the keys
in private agonies of emulation—
I wear this hero's cross beset with jade
for the Campaign of the Hypothalamus,
this ruby wheel, this ivory of spinnaker
for all my frowardness, mirror jabber,
testament of thieves.

It's morning and he's full of sperm again.

COMMENTARY

"Write everything / the oracle said . . ." & thus the decision at 23 to spend
his life in the service of *saying:* "To write every day was the method. To
attend to what is said. To listen. To prepare myself for writing by learning
everything I could, by hanging out in languages and enduring overdeter-
mined desires. . . ." The harvest is major: over fifty collections of poems (as
well as four volumes of prose works & a novel), representing but a fraction
of the total output. As skilled practitioner of the long poem—*Axon Dendron
Tree* (1967), *The Loom* (1975), & most recently, *Mont Blanc* (1994)—
Kelly is heir to both Pound & Zukofsky in his vision of the poet as "scientist
of the whole . . . to whom all data whatsoever are of use / world-scholar."
The title of his 1971 collection, *Flesh Dream Book,* "perhaps sets the pri-
orities straight," writes Kelly, locating "the three great sources of human
information: the flesh of sensory experience, dream & vision, & the holy
book of tradition & learning, shared through time." If everything is of use
in the alchemical *conjunctio* that is the poem, the process of composition
will be that of "finding the measure," where (so Jed Rasula) "measure is
musical base (or bass), and any trope is a turning in a universe continually
returning to its utterance of measure, or scale and proportion." The clearest
statement remains his "(prefix:" to the 1968 volume *Finding the Measure,*
which opens with these lines:

Finding the measure is finding the mantram,
is finding the moon, as index of measure,
is finding the moon's source;

         if that source
is Sun, finding the measure is finding
the natural articulation of ideas.

         The organism
of the macrocosm, the organism of language,
the organism of *I* combine in ceaseless naturing
to propagate a fourth,
      the poem,
         from their trinity. . . .

Robe

5

Rosmarie Waldrop b. 1935

FEVERISH PROPOSITIONS

You told me, if something is not used it is meaningless, and took my temperature which I had thought to save for a more difficult day. In the mirror, every night, the same face, a bit more threadbare, a dress worn too long. The moon was out in the cold, along with the restless, dissatisfied wind that seemed to change the location of the sycamores. I expected reproaches because I had mentioned the word love, but you only accused me of stealing your pencil, and sadness disappeared with sense. You made a ceremony out of holding your head in your hands because, you said, it could not be contained in itself.

If we could just go on walking through these woods and let the pine branches brush our faces, living would still make beads of sweat on your forehead, but you wouldn't have to worry about what you call my exhibitionism. All you liked about trees was the way the light came through the leaves in sheets of precise, parallel rays, like slant rain. This may be an incomplete explanation of our relation, but we've always feared the dark inside the body. You agree there could be no seduction if the structures of propositions did not stand in a physical relation, so that we could get from one to the other. Even so, not every moment of happiness is to hang one's clothes on.

I might have known you wouldn't talk to me. But to claim you just didn't want to disguise your thoughts! We've walked along this road before, I said, though perhaps in heavier coats not designed to reveal the form of the body. Later, the moon came out and threw the shadows of branches across the street where they remained, broken. Feverishly you examined the tacit conventions on which conversation depends. I sighed as one does at night, looking down into the river. I wondered if by throwing myself in I could penetrate to the essence of its character, or should I wait for you to stab me as you had practiced in your dream? You said this question, like most philosophical problems, arose from failing to understand the tale of the two youths, two horses, and two lilies. You could prove to me that the deepest rivers are, in fact, no rivers at all.

From this observation we turned to consider passion. Looking at the glints of light on the water, you tried to make me tell you not to risk the excitement—to recommend cold baths. The lack of certainty, of direction, of duration, was its own argument, unlike going into a bar to get drunk and getting drunk. Your face was alternately hot and cold, as if translating one language into another—gusts from the storm in your heart, the pink ribbon in your pocket. Its actual color turned out to be unimportant, but its presence disclosed something essential about membranes. You said there was still time, you could still break it off, go abroad, make a movie. I said (politely, I thought) this wouldn't help you. You'd have to kill yourself.

Tearing your shirt open, you drew my attention to three dogs in a knot. This served to show how something general can be recorded in unpedigreed notation. I pointed to a bench by a willow, from which we could see the gas tanks across the river, because I thought a bench was a simple possibility: one could sit on it. The black hulks of the tanks began to sharpen in the cold dawn light, though when you leaned against the railing I could smell your hair, which ended in a clean round line on your neck, as was the fashion that year. I had always resented how nimble your neck became whenever you met a woman, regardless of rain falling outside or other calamities. Now, at least, you hunched your shoulders against the shadow of doubt.

This time of day, hesitation can mean tottering on the edge, just before the water breaks into the steep rush and spray of the fall. What could I do but turn with the current and get choked by my inner speed? You tried to breathe against the acceleration, waiting for the air to consent. All the while, we behaved as if this search for a pace were useful, like reaching for a plank or wearing rain coats. I was afraid we would die before we could make a statement, but you said that language presupposed meaning, which would be swallowed by the roar of the waterfall.

Toward morning, walking along the river, you tossed simple objects into the air which was indifferent around us, though it moved off a little, and again as you put your hand back in your pocket to test the degree of hardness. Everything else remained the same. This is why, you said, there was no fiction.

Chapter XXIII
Of Marriage

Flesh, considered as cognitive region, as opposed to undifferentiated warmth, is called woman or wife. **The number not stinted, yet the Narragansett (generally) have but one.** While diminutives are coined with reckless freedom, the deep structure of the marriage bed is universally esteemed even in translation. **If the woman be false** to bedlock, **the offended husband will be solemnly avenged,** arid and eroded. He may remove her clothes at any angle between horizontal planes.

mar
marrow
mutual
convenience
settlement

My lover was ready to overcome all manner of difficulty, but baffled by my claims to equality and clean towels. Even with the night between us, neither side would give up its position and prerogatives. We waited for a change of weather to reopen hostilities.

harmony prestabilized
is turning on its
axe to grind
to halt
to bind
to fault
the speed can't be sustained
even in constant
rotation
through periods of waxing and weaning

Indians are ignorant of Europe's Coyne yet call it Monéash and notice changes in the price of beaver, somnambulism and songs of myself. Their own is either white, which they call **Wompam,** or black, **Suckáuhock,** made of shellfish and twice as valuable, **hung about the neck** instead of our millstones. **They bring down all their sorts of furs** and trade them for the wish to live, the wish to die, the wish to kill, the wish to be had.

cuneiform
coiffure
coney

I learned that my face belonged to a covert system of exchange since the mirror showed me a landscape requiring diffidence, and only in night-mares could I find identity or denouement. At every street corner, I exaggerated my bad character in hopes of being contradicted, but only caused an epidemic of mothers covering their face while exposing private parts.

legal and tender
a condition called
darling dear or **Netop**
which might as well purchase emotion
as yield interest in
I must explain my body
does not differ

In crossing the Atlantic my phonemes settled somewhere between German and English. I speak either language with an accent. This has saved me the illusion of being the master of language. I enter it at a skewed angle, through the fissures, the slight difference. (R. W.) And elsewhere, as consequence perhaps: *I do not "use" the language. I interact with it.*

Waldrop—who is also a superb translator (her translations of Edmond Jabès [above] are among the major interpretive works of the postmodern period)—sees her work foremost as a dialogical exploration of language, in which words "as soon as I start listening . . . reveal their own vectors and affinities, pull the poem into their own field of force, often in unforeseen directions, away from the semantic charge of the original impulse." So, in *Feverish Propositions*—a segment of the still longer *The Reproduction of Profiles*—her points of departure are from the philosophical notebooks of Ludwig Wittgenstein, about the transformation of which she writes: "I used Wittgenstein's phrases in a free, unsystematic way, sometimes quoting, sometimes letting them spark what they would, sometimes substituting different nouns with a phrase (e.g., his famous anti-metaphysical statement that 'the deepest questions are no questions at all' becomes 'You could prove to me that the deepest rivers are, in fact, no rivers at all')." The still more systematic approach of *A Key into the Language of America* draws both its title & structure from Roger Williams's 1643 guide to the Narragansett Indian language & its attendant lore & customs. Her 32 chapters are identified by themes struck by Williams, each with an initial prose section as "a violent collage of phrases from Williams [& the Narragansetts] with elements from anywhere in my Western heritage"; a list of words (both Indian & European) suggested by the sound or meaning of the section title; "a narrative section in italics, in the voice of a young woman, ambivalent about her sex and position among the conquerors"; & "a final poem" (equivalent to the terminal rhyming verses in Williams's ur-text). Of Waldrop's achievement—here & elsewhere—Marjorie Perloff writes: "The language pool thus becomes our new 'Spiritus Mundi.'"

Alejandra Pizarnik 1936–1972

PATHS OF THE MIRROR

I

And above all to gaze with innocence. As if nothing would happen, which is certain.

II

But you I want to look at until your face moves away from my fear like a bird from the sharp edge of night.

III

Like a girl of pink chalk on a very old wall suddenly erased by the rain.

IV

Like when a flower opens and reveals the heart it doesn't have.

V

All the gestures of my body and voice to make the offering of me, the branch the wind abandons at the doorstep.

VI

Cover the memory of your face with the mask of who you will be and scare the girl you were.

VII

The night of the two dispersed with the fog. It's the season of cold food.

VIII

And the thirst, my memory is of the thirst, me below, at the bottom, in the well, I drank, I remember.

IX

To drop like a wounded animal in the place where there were going to be revelations.

X

Like someone who doesn't want the thing. Not anything. Mouth sewn. Eyelids sewn. I forgot myself. Inside the wind. Everything shut and the wind inside.

XI

In the black sun of silence the words were gilded.

XII

But the silence is certain. For that I write. I am alone and I write. No, I am not alone. There is someone here who trembles.

XIII

Even if I say *sun* and *moon* and *star* I am referring to things that happen to me. And what did I desire?

I desired a perfect silence.

For that I speak.

XIV

Night has the shape of a wolf's cry.

XV

Delight of getting lost in the foreseen image. I got up from my cadaver, I went in search of who I am. Pilgrim from myself, I have gone towards her who sleeps in a windward country.

XVI

My endless fall to my endless fall where no one expected me since gazing at whoever was expecting me I saw nothing but myself.

XVII

Something fell in the silence. My last word was *I* but I was referring to the luminous dawn.

XVIII

Yellow flowers constellate a circle of blue earth. The water quivers full of wind.

XIX

Dazzle of day, yellow birds at morning. A hand unties the darkness, a hand drags a drowned woman by the hair who doesn't stop passing by the mirror. To return to the body's memory, I must return to my mourning bones, I must understand what my voice says.

Translation from the Spanish by Jason Weiss

I would have preferred to sing the blues in any small bar full of smok
than to spend the nights of my life scratching into language like a
madwoman.

A. P. (from *The Journals*)

In the course of that journey—she died, a probable suicide, at the age of
thirty-five—she explored the mysteries of pain & mental suffering in a mode
like that of Kafka, say, & still more that of Artaud. ("What frightens me is
my similarity to A[rtaud]. I mean: the similarity of our wounds.") Born to
Jewish immigrant parents in Buenos Aires, she spent most of her life there
& in Paris, following a career first as a painter, later as a journalist & trans-
lator, always as a writer of poetry & of a prose that dealt with what Ger-
trude Stein called "human nature & human mind," but viewed here in ex-
tremis. (Her prose work *The Bloody Countess* centers on the Hungarian
Countess Erzsebet Bathory, who in the seventeenth century arranged the
torture & murder of more than 600 women & girls.) Her great poem on
madness is the book-length *Extraction of the Stone of Folly,* and her jour-
nals, which continued to be published after her death, read with a conscious
sense of closing down: the record of a (failed) attempt to claim a life through
poetry.

.

December 21, 1960, Paris. Last night I drank water until three in the morn-
ing. I was a little drunk and I cried. I asked myself for water as if I were my
mother. I gave myself each drink with disgust.

January 14, 1961, Paris. I dreamed of Rimbaud. / Par littérature / j'ai perdu
ma vie.

April 15, 1961, Paris. Life lost for literature by fault of literature. By making
myself a literary character in real life I fail in my intent to make literature
with my real life, since the latter doesn't exist: it's literature.

July 31, 1962, Paris. Someone is dying of thirst and doesn't drink because
the idea of uniting the act of drinking with the feeling of thirst doesn't occur
to him.

November 28, 1964, Buenos Aires. Each day that passes is better than the
one that follows. On est foutue.

Jayne Cortez b. 1936

NIGHTTRAINS

When i blow open green bottles
straight across hump of a frozen tongue

when i shove brown glass
through skull of a possum
and pass from my ears a baptism of red piss

when i cry from my butt like a jackal
and throw limbs of a dying mule into the river

when i spit venom from the head
burn codeine into a cosmetic paste
and grieve into a wax of dried bulls

when my mystical bunions
like steel hearses jam eyes
into searching spit of a starving wolf
into cosmic lips like monkey genitals

And i receive my pickled turned skeleton of rusty chains
in the bodega
i receive a symbolic heart made of five middle fingers in the bodega
i receive a teeth parade of yellow roses to leave the bodega
and cross the rio grande
onto the flat-bed bones of a musty nighttrain

I say
to see me loosen jaws like a snake
to see me exhausted after a few strikes
to see me pay dirt to the ice hog
in my masai-pachuca-doo
squatting on a pillow of old zoot suits
squatting among the names and breeds
breaking down cheeks dotted
on this nighttrain
and i say i dream of the 1943 riots
I say i dream in a hail storm of riots
and i say riots dream into a mass of skins stooping
on flat bed bones of a funky nighttrain

And when i syphon sweat for fuel
from this patron saint of chronic diarrhea

When i turn this rubber face into a spotted puma
and take on the forceful winds of the prune pickers

When my laughter dominates the last seat
and i burn labor contracts into brown port caca

And then i approach in mother of pearl and human blood
in father of smoking and coughing throats
in my jelly of coyote strings
who is to say what when i approach

I mean somewhere along the road in this cold cold chicken shit
somewhere along the road in this wasted body
somewhere along the road eat stocks, bonds, feathers
somewhere along the road confiscate borders from wild dogs
somewhere along the road shove them into the
imperial valley
somewhere along the road cry hard
and let this nighttrain sink its
rundown rectum of electric chairs into heaven
and say fuck it

I see a way through the maroon glass of this milky way
I say i see a way through for the cradle of hulls
sticking through these indigo ankles
I see a way through
for these torn shoes stinking like dead cats
I see a way through for these blood streaked legs
I say i see a way through
for these puss riddled holes in their suction cup lips
and when i pass through toothless combs coming
from armpits
of the bodega
when i pass through bats on corkscrews coming
from the bodega
when i push my mortified flesh from this bodega
and walk with the mildew of an old zoot suit
walk tall in my mud-packed-masai-pachuca-doo
walk among the survivors from the musty nighttrains

fuck it
I say dreams are like riots
I say we dream in a hailstorm of riots
and i say riots dream into a mass of skins
coming from flat-bed bones of the funky funky
nighttrains

COMMENTARY

I need kai kai   ah
a glass of akpetsie   ah
from torn arm of Bessie Smith   ah
I need the smell of Nsukka   ah
the body sweat of a durbar   ah
five tap dancers   ah
and those fleshy blues kingdoms from deep south   ah
to belly-roll forward praise
for Christopher Okigbo   ah

J. C. (from *Kai Kai* [Nigerian home-made gin], *for the Poets*)

Born in Arizona & raised in Los Angeles, she has worked for thirty years &
more on a precise & highly performative pan-Africanness, as in this celebra-
tion of Nigerian poet Christopher Okigbo (killed in the 1967 civil war),
among other poets dead & living. Of the full dimensions of her work & its
extensions through musical performance, textsound, & the new technology,
she writes: "In a recording session or musical setting many important things
just happen. Even though I have a certain amount of material prepared, the
real structure is created while working. In performance I usually read from
a manuscript, recite lines from memory and spontaneously compose on the
spot. By using music and technology I'm trying to extend the poet's role,
which means, the poet in this situation becomes the band, the pen, paper,
books, research, instruments, words, and all the possibilities of the tech-
nology. The poet is in control. One of the highest compliments given in the
arts is when an artistic work is said not only to be excellent but to have
beautiful poetic qualities. This compliment usually suggests that the work is
more sensitive, has more insight, and is at a higher level of expression. I am
trying to move this combination of poetry, music, and technology to a
higher poetic level. It's the poetic use of music, the poetic use of technology,
the poetic orchestration of it all."

Kenneth Irby b. 1936

FOUR POEMS

"I met the Angel Sus on the Skin Bridge"

I met the Angel Sus on the Skin Bridge
the Bridge Chinvat, offertory
my image crossing the basketball court and taking the path into the
    woods
and at the other end, in the gravel at the bend of Terrace Road
more expressive than the small red heart-shaped lips of the Lizard
    Mother, your endlessly mobile face
snout cloud of light and bristles thicket of impenetrable brightness
and smile of infinite frenzied utter patience
nostrils as close to my brow as opened clover
only a face! only a face! only a face!
wings but the knot clod sfumato uncertain noose clothing
over the skin we share, organ me you share
was it John telling me to turn to you, in crowded Houlihan's on the
    Plaza, with Charlie and the bears in the dark
brought me to you, you came out this far to meet me
where the VW's been parked since at least last March and the horses'
    empty field comes in close and the houses begin
"You must make me the Clean Compound
first, before you pass through me"
each to each?

"slowly the old stone building walls downtown dissolve"

slowly the old stone building walls downtown dissolve
dropped in the pond of wind in the August noon
slow slow motion salt castles by the time the stoplight changes at 7th and
    New Hampshire
from the eyes the old world goes, across the river the cables of resistant
    skin, tight enough to walk on

the young who work to bare the body soft again as the crown of gera-
    nium petals fallen
no heaven that might redeem the past but only make way over and over
    again for the protection flowers give to age at all
to what it hasn't yet accumulated, most of all

the speed that ungoos the eyes is some reward, certainly, out of the South
  with the wind
as age comes up out of the ground polar as the brain lode at the same
  time as it goes back down in under the feet again

homegrown handtipped dervishwhirling in your own living room with-
  out getting dizzy or sick, taught by somebody in the speech department
  who goes to Naropa every summer
where such things usually accumulate, at the end of August, not an early
  time at all, but late as fatherhood
Excelsior as the tight foreskin of what desire's called o'er-reaching that
  never knows its own phone number
and continues at the mercy of, at the mercy of, at the mercy of
savage as the «endless rumination of the Big Vegetarians» wasping the
  lateral world of vision to the narrow waist of instant jumpup Whizz
and over all of it not even a guardian moth or a gnat but probably just
  the flick of a pig with wings, quicker than jizz sop

[Trash]
what do you see beside the road

one corner, the South side of Ohio at 9th, compacted of cans and pop
  tarts in the asphalt hump

to be riddled over

the bran mash sop of gutter litter leaves

to be read to, passing over

the thin at-history haze of winter light along the horizon

still the thought of a series of natural histories—quite still—the erratics,
as earlier determined, re-determined, and for certain, trees, especially the
hedge, or a group of: hedge, and cottonwood, and Kentucky coffee, and
honey locust—and wahoo, cover in the woods—this year hasn't produced
very much, and what little, thin and dry and scattered, obscure without
even the lure of gnomic quirk, if lure, if lair—scatter of bird seed under
the feeder chaff, pecked seed ball in the empty bird bath, the sadness of a
squirrel holding a nut when the fountain's been cut off between his paws,
approaching, running off, coming back up to the footsteps again—sold
long since—or "the sadness of a bathtub when the water has run out"—

and then the glitter in the emptiness of the woods, the trace, the deep reassurance of an accent at all, and the hope out of -tiness, -liness, -lessness—will, willed, willed *duh*

beast, or virtue, no, say a ball down the street of all the slurried gutter trash, furry in its dripping, string, changing seasons every moment as it comes—and then the hedge apples come back to life again the squirrels have deconstructed to coronas in the woods—in the streets, thunder of their falling, rolls, drop by drop gathering, gathering, gathering, till the whole town doesn't eat, it just gathers, and eventually what you see beside the road is not a town at all, but glitter whirl, at the edge of what is paved, where you always find the wrapper glitter, too, like silver favors in the graininess that's snapped and thrown away

"aw, he probably goes around in that old beatup secondhand Cadillac of his filling up cundrum machines in the filling stations—'and what's your daddy do?' 'wholesaling and retailing'—shiiit"

the plain old cement landscape in a fine shared eye, on that long thin end-lessly wiggling petiole, deltoides, a torsion, twisting, twisting, falling and refalling, rising, trace

and if a soul—blessèd
and if no soul—blessèd
and if a soul in embryo—howling, how long o how long to grow up
                    not to eat, not for love
                    not to write, not for sight
                    just rising

from **[Three Sets of Three]**

there is from the legs in sleep an exhalation of the light, along the tops of
   the thighs, over the knees, down the shins, up across the ankles, and on
   off the slopes of the feet, a spark out of the tips of the toes, out of the
   loam of the urgency in the loins
there was and there will be a time when that urgency held in the fluid
   suspension across the room of being is extracted to become the ink of
   writing, as it *is* the writing of being
as the paint that peels pliable from the railing at the moment of leaning
   over the entering and leaving below, burns and lets out the breath

it might as likely be the flow of ink in the pen, dried almost to not flow-
  ing, lying open under the heat of the lamp
while off finding out why the record's skipped, Chopin's variations on
  "N'aqui al afano", into an old and wonderful Ravel "Berceuse"
seek berceuse, but waking—ceaseless, seeking
the soft clack of the rod of the hanging scroll in the slight breeze of pass-
  ing, Tu Fu's «A single line of white herons ascends the azure sky» inces-
  santly seeking ascension
that is "A Mirror in a Mirror" as the music continues, and the spareness
  of the principle of meeting, that is the total contingency of the moment
  of recognition
the presence of a silence in the night as the center of a blazing in the day-
  time, as the course of a stream beneath a city strung on the net of its
  hidden sources
the water of the oboe has heard, or at the outcropping of sheer plain, a
  fluid elaboration, and expectation of the living to be fancy and at the
  same moment purely and simply flowing, the bound and aspiration of
  carry and descent

  .

so for a morning construct the currents of support from what they've left
from night its memories that cannot be remembered, the ache of a hope-
  less and unending desire to ever satisfy, the kind of love you thought
  your life was past, but it is not and will not ever be
it was not the wind but now it is the wind, its corridor
it was not the call or the sound of a passing ball bounced or the sudden
  laughter
that now at the open balcony determine, as the steps of a yearning im-
  possible to fill, how the day can know its origins

COMMENTARY

*There is no need to substitute any world for this one / in order to come
into any wonder or more / enter the open imagination.* (K. I.) And again:
*The nation can only come into being / but the City we may / found /
Between us / Here & Now, as we read / these words.*

His poetics arises from a continental rootedness (in the Great Plains &
grasslands of the Midwest, called "Irbyland" by Robert Duncan), forming
a "discontinuous / dendritic narrative of a journey / metaphor of pasture,

anabasis & return" that both fuses & moves beyond Hölderlin's definitions (quoted by Irby) of the lyric as "the continuous metaphor of a feeling" & the epic as "the metaphor of an intellectual point of view." Here "local history is the only history / it is the / body / answers," a localism which in the later work leaves behind the mythopoetic strictures of Pound or Olson's heroic stance, so that (writes Stephen Ellis) "the specific is given credence beyond all over-riding 'systems' of thought that might too soon impinge with their preconceived 'meanings.' Irby's sense of place is like 'home'—the domestic worked rather than assumed." While the information ranges widely (from James C. Malin, Carl Sauer, & gnostic & freemasonry lore to botany, music, & food—to name but the obvious) it is never abstract knowledge or nostalgic memory (despite a near-Virgilian sadness that suffuses much of the work), but always presenced, physical, for "Irby's is a poetry of purely sensual friction, thing moving against thing, the physical world moving against the physicality of the processes of thought and memory" (Ellis). In the late work, eschewing the easy certainties of metaphor & symbol, Irby's long, often stanzaic lines, built on metonymy & parataxis, lead to a writing (so Charles Stein) "where the sentence structure fragments and Irby's obedient ear meticulously forbids a yearning for cadence to satisfy itself beyond the insistence of the message: the impression that bits of crucial information are just barely coming through, the statement of which must not be allowed excessive elaboration lest the particularity of the message, its exact pressure on the ear, be lost."

J. H. Prynne b. 1936

from **WOUND RESPONSE**

Of Movement Towards a Natural Place

See him recall the day by moral trace, a squint
to cross-fire shewing fear of hurt at top left; the
bruise is glossed by "nothing much" but drains
to deep excitement. His recall is false but the charge
is still there in neural space, pearly blue with a
touch of crimson. "By this I mean a distribution
of neurons . . . some topologically preserved transform",
upon his lips curious white flakes, like thin snow.
He sees his left wrist rise to tell him the time,
to set damage control at the same white rate.

What mean square error. Remorse is a pathology of
syntax, the expanded time-display depletes the

input of "blame" which patters like scar tissue.
First intentions are cleanest: no paint on the nail
cancels the flux link. Then the sun comes out
(top right) and local numbness starts to spread, still
he is "excited" because in part shadow. *Not will
but chance* the plants claim but tremble, "a
detecting mechanism must integrate across that
population"; it makes sense right at the contre-coup.

So the trace was moral but on both sides, as formerly
the moment of godly suffusion: *anima tota in singulis
membris sui corporis.* The warmth of cognition not
yet neuroleptic but starry and granular. The more
you recall what you call the need for it, she tells
him by a shout down the staircase. You call it
your lost benevolence (little room for charity),
and he rises like a plaque to the sun. Up there the
blood levels of the counter-self come into beat
by immune reflection, by night lines above the cut:

Only at the rim does the day tremble and shine.

Landing Area

The spirit is lame and in the pale flash
we see it unevenly spread with water. Lemon yellow
very still, some kind of bone infection, both
heroic and spiteful. Actually the arabs might
do well to soak up revenue on a straight purchase
of, say, Belgium. Make a new blood count,
more and more quietly, we change *daring* for
darling on the bypass. Still the sky is yellow and
completely with us, as if at birth. Is the throat
dry, no it is mine and lined with marrow;
bone on the other hand "can be here today
and gone tomorrow." He was calm itself and
central to a scheme of virtue, not absent nor
wincing but his eye was as dry as the sky
was wet. And the sun set.

Chromatin

The prism crystal sets towards the axis
of episodic desire: lethargy and depression
cross the real-time analogue: currents level
and historic matching blurs into locked-on
receptor site blockade. Stable mosaic at
adrenal print "you" are in white "I" see a
moving shade by the door it is *my wish* to
be there running on ("mental confusion,
tremors, anxiety") and breaking the induced
blockade I truly am by the door shaking or
the frame goes to gel. Visual sonar
arrhythmia blocks fading brocade made
pressure crisis you and the flowers in
pliant flicker real time! I surmount
the uptake gradient, cognition by
recount, the homeric icefields unfold.

Melanin

For the next legation I bite
distilled residue I live
to the one, for the top, over
the home scraper I seal
felt, glutted with ashen light

All too grayly, stack up
for the window finding
her target doubled, pectin
she visits wanly her
broken section plug

And shallow they had
struck the mute rim
what pretty precious price
foam in duty, live act
must comply within

How could any one
so much any way
even fixed breed
enteric: that's my
pallid inner coverlet

An Evening Walk

Touches belonging to the ascent of the brother
mount in the column of sound and are spun
over crosswise, this is tonight abated now
     as rightly he makes
     shoes felted in the
     way asked of him.
     Further than the stride
       he wears and
dares to the paramorphic boot in the amble,
his intact ankle rushes, pauses, rebukes the
vast surge offering standby credit to
       the whole orchestra. All
       of the adverted rattle
    culminates in that modular layer,
         spread with a
butter hydroxide film. The shoes are priced
with reason lightly set under with a new
varnish, we must have the lace-up wallet
    for the *portamento* in the
    crisis ahead. Somewhere
    there is calamitous groaning
       heard on the foreshore
with the water just black above freezing and even
      now he falls and
      lies in the street why
      is he stunned
         wretchedly
     holding his mouth and
there are pork pies arranged on the counter
in a jellied pyramid. They too foil & pitch
furtively, they are sprung but torn. How
does he not feel a feeling:
    his jacket is rent we
    are envious of his in
    ability to pay &
      the fine
    exquisite workman
      ship of
    his uppers. Shod

in bands of iron goes the wave of the hand.
The brother over ten years yields to elated
frenzy but feels nothing, xylocaine snows
him under the table. Quite swiftly

               we take up the hope
               lessly benign
     feelings, to make a lozenge,
     to oil the throat of the frozen
     fish dinner yet

             still sound
    less and less so, di
        methyl hydroxy
        thiopentone. The in
            fibrillate mem
        brane. Infantile,
        recursive pandect.

COMMENTARY

*See that you see / what he says is / called memory, re- / call and of / what
he does is / the same. By this / assembled the sale / gains savour, and / what
you see past / is reserved in / favour and what / he says now is / no more
than that.*

J. H. P.

Since the early sixties & through some twenty books of poems, Prynne—
often considered the founder of the so-called "Cambridge school"—has
been one of the most vital presences in the *risorgimento* of English poetry.
Early association with American poets such as Olson & Dorn (above) led
to an information-rich version of projective poetry (as in his books *White
Stones* and *The Kitchen Poems*), while his later work has shown a marked
tendency towards contraction, making for an extremely dense, allusive lan-
guage texture. But the core actions have remained & could be summed up
as investigations drawing heavily on boundary-breaking thinking from vari-
ous contemporary sciences (botany, biology, physics, etc.), in order to reg-
ister more accurately (& in the process widen) our sense of (here the terms
are Olson's) a "proprioceptive" [= perception-from-within-the-body] "hu-
man universe." Douglas Oliver, writing specifically about *Of Movement
Towards a Natural Place* (1974), has tried to elucidate a central Prynnian
question, namely "how mind works, and what happens in what 'mind' per-
ceives." Concerning this (an image here of Prynne—& poetry—writ large),
he states: "Of contemporary poets, Ed Dorn and Prynne have most interest-
ingly concentrated upon the following consequence: if scientists trying to

plumb the birth processes of nature are, for greatest accuracy and insight, driven to investigate the largest possible birth processes in macro-space-time (black holes, etc.) and the smallest possible in micro-space-time (submicro-scopic growth, internal cell events, particle physics, etc.), then the birth pro-cess of 'mind' itself and of its acts will most accurately find its reflection in such events. The birth of the mind-act may be poetry's primary subject mat-ter, for in its notional moment of birth language opens out to immense pos-sibilities, only imperfectly achieved in the writing down of the poetic line."

Rochelle Owens b. 1936

DEDICATION

DIN
who am i floating
above cows
YAHOEL AM I
whiter than   white
animal skins   unblemished
lambs.   my blood
so red & light salty
Isaac Resnikoff
the pious scribe
studies my .word.
it is as if sacred white scrolls
encase my holy legs   Rising I Rise

over this peculiar

continent
I float
above cities   singing glory glory
I am living prayer &
THEY give me their
.love.
I Am That I Am
DIVINE STERNNESS

.

JUDGMENT
DIN

I AM THE BABE OF JOSEPH STALIN'S DAUGHTER

i watch Tai Chi per
                forating my mind
    Tai Chi!
                    exquisite waves
        of body moving in 4
    holy directions
                    it is sacred quiet
        motion.
                    & then cracking open
        my eyes, banging in like a fat
        shoe, is an image of Joseph
                Stalin's huge occidental
    daughter Svetlana! she has given me
                    birth!   I swam out
        of her fresh salty womb
                    the whites of my eyes
        tinged pink from her blood—for I
                    had stared wide with blasting
    eyes open!   open as I
                journeyed out   as I
                        sailed away
            from the energy machine
                    of Stalin's daughter
    I am saturated with her central Asian
            aroma
                        my mother my mother
            a ponderous dancing angel
                    who is
                seed bearing &
            satisfies me with her 30
        fingers & toes & big brown nipples!
                her brain
            is a glittering storm cloud hanging
                    over Washington D.C.
            she learns the language of America
                        & puts her boots on
            sitting by the edge of
                    BLACK LAKE, her warm
                arms coil around harps &
                    she croons me a lullaby

about higher physics & horny sixty year old
                    men who slip between her
                              teeth like
          kingly copper chinese noodles
                              waving in Tai Chi
                    Tai Chi peacebiting
                                        song!

from **W. C. FIELDS IN FRENCH LIGHT**

It is for me poetry
the essential nucleus
of the sphere of human
existence
Data
that represents primal
things
I shall not do without
precision communication
formalization
I generate example

        She gazes at batches
              of white roses
        white roses
              she listens to music
        she thinks of white roses
              is that not enough?
        she thinks of the white paws
              of the cat
        Sunlight
              whirling rose leaves around

A woman in a white shirt
a woman who listens to music
and gazes at batches
of white roses
She is not only of a neat
appearance a woman in
a white shirt but a woman

who listens to music also
and gazes at batches
of white roses   Sunlight
            whirling rose leaves around
                    O here comes Balboa
                            walking the length
                                    of the sea

River bed split
into two singing trees
cross vein
O here comes the rodeo lover
She has a skill blazing
gunplay
O here comes the rodeo lover
fer pete's sake
            Look an old sheep
                    in new yawk
            city what lost its
                    teeth
            bleeding under the
                    fluorescent lights

It's a dwelling place
for her, the cowgirl
she of the dry-storm eyes
thrown from a horse
in a sandstorm
found cradling a dented can
of cornbeef hash

        & W.C. said:
We will all be sexy zebras
one day, fit
to breed lumberjacks
loyal and sturdy
American revolutionaries

Wagon-trains only are her
companions
On the bus she hobbles
in golden stirrups

She's plumb loco
lost in a warehouse hoping
inhaling urgently
the air of laughter
establishing her bravery
in the territory of poets

As George Washington
is a territory of psychological
material
I consider the actor W.C. Fields
my gangplank
to walk from one world
to another
Cowboy working in a gas-
station, stubbly chin,
smashed in cafeteria,
old-freezed apple pie
I consider W.C. Fields
actor prayer-book talking
cement bronc-buster
In the bridal chamber
work is progressing
by big boss American revolutionary
W.C. Fields eating
fort knox g-string

Short-trigger gunman
in rodeo, W.C.'s the best
as I am best in drama
and as guest of honor
moseying in the smoky
medieval halls of Chaucer
W.C. and me in the movies
talking loudly
sticking our stiff shovels
into the reactionary hopes
of Americans,
loading up in the rough
country
our own power

I am not oblivious
to free words, blizzard-choked
I wander
bound by the rules of poets
washing gold down my throat,
then twenty-one phone calls
to Fields,
writing my name on the stirrups
of his riding self
Now there's a scene change
I am a fat show-business producer
with cigar
And W.C.'s an out-a-work actor
His lips are playing tricks
with the tip of my corona
Now he's very glib
and begging me for work
                for words, a fight,
                    a gun, a chance
                to be my irish father
                    He's earned
                pocket-digging
                    vug rust-eater
                sluicer, irish orphan
                    twist oliver
                he's paid his dues
                    Poignant he claims
                he's earned his bit o' pain
                    So lemme alone
                W.C. sez
                    He asks why
                I write poems about him
                    I ask 'why not?'
                You're a myth
                    & I intend
                to utilize you

A horse-dealer in America
A collector of shoe-boxes of poems
by the American revolutionary
Myself, a loquacious woman
rises above the mountains

I tell W.C. to cut off
the edge of his heel
for love of me
I say, 'you are my glory hole,
my mine, my gold field
& the poems I make
will cause crumbling & erosion
of the world'

*I dreamed of a birdwoman. A fantastic creature with a human body and
the head of a bird. She fed her young with chunks of flesh that she savagely
tore out of her body with her beak. Always the flesh grew quickly back so
that there was no loss or end of herself.*
R. O.

There is a voice in Owens's work that seemed to some of us—when first
heard—like a fierce & unrelenting force of nature, or like that, more aptly,
of some biblical Isaiah or Devorah, or of some other cracked (but real)
prophet mockingly come back to life. "Beauty will be convulsive or it will
not be," André Breton had written in setting the Surrealist agenda (volume
one, page 465), by which he meant (or we do) not beauty so much as *poetry*,
with regard to which beauty is but one half (at best) of what we put into our
workings. And Owens—while she proclaimed herself, New York style, as
"simply a poor working girl who was not even a graduate of Brooklyn Col-
lege or C.C.N.Y."—spoke a language even in her first poems ("Hunger / It
is luck too. Hullabaloo Vishnu") that called forth voices (Ball or Khlebni-
kov or Tzara) from a recent past that she & her generation were newly
claiming, making into *our* present. With her base in poetry, she came to a
first public recognition through a series of plays (*Futz, Beclch, He Wants
Shih, The Karl Marx Play*, others), to create a theater of *impulse* & to make
her for a time "perhaps the most profound tragic playwright in the Ameri-
can theater" (Ross Wetzteon). What she had tapped into in herself were the
sources of tragedy in ancient "goat-song" (Aristotle): a deliberate but dis-
ruptive mode of poetry, moving from what Toby Olson describes as "the
grating nature of the inappropriate" to what he & Jackson Mac Low both
speak of as "controlled hysteria." Writing further of the intelligence—as
well as passion—that drives her work, Mac Low says: "I mean . . . by 'con-
trolled hysteria' . . . that the speaker, whether the poet, a persona, or a blend
of both, while often incredibly vehement, threatens to cross over the line
from vehemence to uncontrollable emotional outburst, but never actually

crosses that line. This arouses a feeling of *suspense* even in those who do not realize whence that feeling arises: a very 'theatrical' experience." That it also arouses—in *us*—a feeling of uncontrollable laughter is the further, maybe deeper secret of her art.

The *Din* of the opening poem is the Hebrew word for the wrathful, nightmare face of God as *judgment,* for another take on which see the excerpt from Artaud's *To Have Done with the Judgment of God,* above.

Monique Wittig b. 1936

from THE LESBIAN BODY

I start to tremble without being able to stop, you m/y iniquitous one m/y inquisitress you do not release m/e, you insist that *I* talk, fear grips m/e m/y hair is shaken, the soft hemispheres of m/y brain the dura mater the cerebellum move within m/y cranium, m/y tongue uvula jaws quiver, *I* cannot keep m/y lips closed, m/y teeth chatter, m/y arteries throb in furious jerks in m/y neck groins heart, m/y eyes are compressed by their orbits, m/y intestines lurch, m/y stomach turns over, the movement spreads to all m/y muscles, the trapezii deltoids pectorals adductors sartorii the internals the externals are all shaken by spasms, the bones of m/y legs knock against each other when you do not steady them you wretch, there is a prodigious acceleration of movement to the point where freed from gravity *I* rise up, *I* maintain m/yself at your eye-level, then you m/y most infamous one you chase m/e brutally while *I* fall speechless, you hunt m/e down m/y most fierce one, you constrain m/e to cry out, you put words in m/y mouth, you whisper them in m/y ear and *I* say, no mistress, no for pity's sake, do not sell m/e, do not put m/e in irons, do not make m/y eyeballs burst, deign to call off your dogs, *I* beg you, spare m/e for just a moment longer.

THE LESBIAN BODY THE JUICE THE
SPITTLE THE SALIVA THE SNOT
THE SWEAT THE TEARS THE WAX
THE URINE THE FAECES THE
EXCREMENTS THE BLOOD THE
LYMPH THE JELLY THE WATER
THE CHYLE THE CHYME THE
HUMOURS THE SECRETIONS THE
PUS THE DISCHARGES THE SUP-
PURATIONS THE BILE THE JUICES
THE ACIDS THE FLUIDS THE
FLUXES THE FOAM THE SULPHUR
THE UREA THE MILK THE
ALBUMEN THE OXYGEN THE
FLATULENCE THE POUCHES THE
PARIETES THE MEMBRANES THE
PERITONEUM, THE OMENTUM,
THE PLEURA THE VAGINA THE
VEINS THE ARTERIES THE VESSELS
THE NERVES

Spores start from your epidermis. Your pores produce them in thousands, *I* watch the tiny explosions, *I* see how the spores descend at the end of hairy filaments without becoming detached from them, the stalks shoot, the spores develop and become rounded, the innumerable spheres clashing together create stridences clickings aeolian harp vibrations. Slowly you stand erect your arms extended before you your thighs rigid your entire body in movement, you move forward supported by the flight of the spheres expanding in the air. Your every movement produces a harmony of sounds which make the ears shift in all directions. *I* follow you, *I* move forward in your gigantic shadow scaled down prolonged by the spheres. In thousands they blur your outline or else make it appear stippled when they catch the sun in the course of their gyrations. At each of your strides you pass above several women walking. Your matchless music fixes them on the spot, then one or other seized with convulsions falls in a heap to the ground. Some begin to shriek. You superb you do not halt. *I* have difficulty in following you. Now *I* run beneath you, your jostling spheres gleaming in the sun give m/e vertigo but breathless as *I* am *I* laugh freely, *I* announce you to the immobilized ones that they may watch your coming, *I* baptise you for centuries of centuries, so be it.

Translation from the French by David Le Vay

J/e is the symbol of the lived, rending experience which is m/y writing, of this cutting in two which throughout literature is the exercise of a language which does not constitute m/e as subject. J/e poses the ideological and historic question of feminine subjects.

M. W.

Writes Rachel Blau DuPlessis: "Working with the feminist proposition that all culture, history, and politics have been built on a symbolic order gendered patriarchal, Wittig proposes radical cultural works that tear open that whole order, with rich, streaming, lyrical-aggressive rhetorics. In *The Lesbian Body* she writes prose poems of females bonded with each other representing their heightened companionate/political and sexual/visceral arousals in a way indebted to the single-mindedness and obsessive quality of troubadour traditions. Following upon the psycho-philosophical proposition that the existing symbolic order is built upon the authority of male sexuality, Wittig enacts a change of values and paradigms of knowing to manifest a female symbolic order; the book is a perpetual evocation of the mythographies of Lesbos, the desire for Sappho, the epiphanies and apotheosis of the female body in spiritual and corporeal bliss and engulfment. The effect is maenadic—the desires to tear, to rend, to take, to devour, to engulf, to possess are all played out on the bodies of beloved women. It is as if the patriarchal symbolic order has starved women of their own ecstatic presence; this text will right that wrong, write female ecstasy, and imagine its rites in a fervor of unbounded affirmations and abandonments. The continual pulsing and parsing along the female body becomes a *via sacra* and a *via daemonica*; the body is dismembered and turned inside out with liberatory alchemical color songs and with Baudelairean/symbolist invocations to pleasure and its luscious, cruel, and passionate trials. These prose poems celebrate and crave endless female-generated orgasms reaffirmed beyond eternity."

Takahashi Mutsuo b. 1937

From the slightly everted skin of the sleeper's eyelid
noisy deaths, dark deaths, muddy deaths
all screaming, wrangling, climb up toward you

MONKEY-EATERS

I'd like to paint monkey-eaters,
like the painter who painted potato-eaters.
(Outside there's blizzard, inside fire's burning)
There's no difference between them: eating potatoes
under a lamp, and eating monkeys in a forest.
Just as when you eat potatoes the blood of potato courses through your
    blood vessels,
when you eat monkeys the blood of monkeys courses through your
    blood vessels.
Just as potato-eaters become potatoes,
monkey-eaters become monkeys. If the blood of the monkeys
is filled with death, they become monkeys of death.
(Death is burning red, life becomes invisible in the blizzard)
A monkey-eater who becomes a monkey of death isn't someone
who has nothing to do with me. Someone who devours a monkey of
    death, beginning with its head,
who becomes a monkey of death and screams, is me, no one else.
(The blood of the monkey of death who's tearing itself apart with sorrow
is fiercely dreaming of making my blood the blood of the monkey of
    death)
Now I've taken up my brush, in the manner of the painter
who painted himself eating potatoes and becoming a potato
and became a potato, beginning with his fingers holding the brush.
(Life is a blizzard, it's blizzard, it's burning)

Translation from the Japanese by Hiroaki Sato

from SELF-PORTRAITS

Myself in the Disguise of an Ancient Queen

When did my head become an ancient cow's sacred head?
As that sublime queen of grief with a cow's head,

in search of the torn and lost pieces of flesh of my snake-bodied husband,
    the king,
I wander through movie theaters, public bathhouses, street toilets all over
    the world.
Only, the difference between that queen of Egypt and me
is that while the queen gathered up all of her husband's flesh torn into
    fourteen pieces
but could not find one, the phallus,
I gather up innumerable phalluses innumerably, and yet
cannot in the end find one thing, a body.
Every phallus is my husband the king, but also the hateful enemy who
    killed my husband.
I kiss every phallus, throw it away, spit on it, and leave.
The phalluses thrown away drift in foam through the sea called the
    world
and ahead of me, penetrating through movie theaters, public bathhouses,
    street toilets,
various rivers flow, various seas flow,
and the tree of tears sways on the shore of eternity that I cannot reach
    eternally.

The tree of tears hugs a coffin in its hundred octopus tentacles,
a coffin which, blatantly shaped like a phallus,
is the origin of all time and space.

Myself with a Glory Hole

Lord, when will it be?
Will it be long before Your visit?
I crouch on the opprobrious floor, waiting, while before me
are pictures of angels with wings, and of saints;
at the center of the wall adorned with holy words of gold and silver,
a holy hole—Your shining visitation through it,
is it not yet time for it?
O then, I would kneel before You,
madly open my lips parched and cracked from thirst,
and as that terrifying prophet said,
fill my mouth with You.
Inside my mouth You would quickly grow large,
Your holy basket would violently overflow and splatter,
and to my popping eyes, my short nose,

to my crewcut head with a lot of young gray hair,
and to my narrow forehead, splatter all over, drip lazily,
and like trails of slugs, glutinously gleam—
in Your incomparable compassion, like one raped
I would close my eyes as if suffering, and pant. . . .
When will that be? Will it be long before the visit?

These words said, the face, like a pig-skin sack from which liquor has
  leaked,
deflated into wrinkles, was folded on its neck,
and together with the body mounting the john, slumped.
The perplexing incident just over, before the john
stood the wall filled with base graffiti,
and from the other side of the hole in the middle of the wall, a glaring
parched eye was looking in.

Translation from the Japanese by Hiroaki Sato

COMMENTARY

*Since the poet belongs to earth, it is natural that he should be committed to
the ascending direction. This is an approach known as 'sacred pornogra-
phy.' . . . Having come thus far, we begin to grasp who our protagonist
really is: the protagonist of 'sacred pornography,' who must be viewed as a
poet ascending from the earth to heaven.*
T. M.

The expression in quotes is his own & goes a way toward defining the cen-
tral project of his work over the last three decades. It is—like that, say, of
his *butoh* contemporaries in theater, & of other Japanese poets in the pres-
ent volume—a work presented in extremis & with a free sweep of predeces-
sors & cultural markers: *noh* & *kyogen* dramas, Greek & Hebrew writings,
Buddhist & Christian scriptures (Takahashi is himself a Catholic convert),
& nods at Mishima, Yeats, Bowles, Pound, Valéry, Duchamp, among the
many modern figures touched on. But what most sets his work apart is its
fierce delineation of an actual (therefore surreal) *gay* world, not in any pret-
tified way but—foremost in his greatest poem, called simply *Ode*, but also
in the self-portrait presented here—by the quasi-religious *détournement*
(above, p. 419) or transformation of the "glory hole" (a phallus-sized open-
ing gouged into the panels of public latrines & used for anonymous oral
sex) into a meeting point of earth & heaven, of (empty = lonely) man &
(phallic = filling) god. Writes Takahashi further: "The glory hole is a *hole*,
a void. Here, however, void is, to paraphrase Lao Tzu, 'that which is useful
for *what is there* (= substance) by not being there.' Without this void, re-
ality, or substance, cannot enter. . . . Thus it will be understood that our

protagonist [in *Ode*], who crouches on a toilet floor, eagerly waits for the penis that visits from the hole on the wall, and fills his oral cavity with it, is typical of the human being who 'is there because he is void,' 'aims to be there because he is void,' and 'tries to be active in the passivity of waiting.'" The resultant work, writes Burton Watson, is "surely one of the most extraordinary poems in all modern Japanese literature."

Anne-Marie Albiach b. 1937

WINTER VOYAGE

a precision
  reiterated in the disproportion of a knowledge
   THE OPENING

       accentuates the detours
  "pierced and motionless Bodies":

   the Difference
     institutes a recurrence: abstracted
       the involute
       pathway
       a line
       without detour

    Abusive
for a distortion that gives no respite: *the voice just this side of*
      theme
    a moment

    brought back into play: the look accentuates such
    deviation in Difference: a clearing given over to
    free reins

 DETERMINATION: an Other defines the body's limits
   in the projected act playing on stage
impotence *and its lyricisms* CHAINS

THE PATHWAY REMAINS NO LESS
omniscient

in the mirrored play of
fallen
    perspectives

        involution of discourse
        THE IMAGE

    in light and during nighttime

           distance

                  WHITENESS

DISPARITY: A BLOSSOMING

      IN THE MARGINS
                impatience: *a sterility*
                brought under accusation:
                an echo:
                in chasms: diverse liquids:
                colorless numbers of
                speech:

    one comes back to the elaboration of breath: *impossible*

otherside

    returning at sharp angles (in *sweetness*)

impalpable: a passing, a presence

      REPOSITIONING of *Desires*
             in language

DIVERGENCE

from want of and their detours

CONVENIENCES

"the arrest"

        attentive to the silence

              she leans

                  overcome by a return or

                  minute elaboration

                      multiplication

          of vulnerable points

PRETENCE

A WORD PERSISTS: just this side of

WHITE

        gestures attenuate the pathway of absence

elaboration of a GAME
in the background
irrepressible

      "modulations"

departure after representation

          : dismemberment

        the notion of "default" intervenes
        in the statement: COUNTERPOINT

They transgress her fragility naming it

          that which is silenced in weakness,
          in the very otherness
          ignoring such breath.

    "sleep"

        in which scenes ABSENCE   are played

in the retreat of speech
Several VOICES

of the object:

musique prohibits the sum

breathing: lips the only fragmentation

"but speech"
if you encounter him : *his trail is before them*

passing through preparing for elaborations

DENIAL

alternative the image turns the last image
defaults (as at an ANGLE)

"a divergent response"
this
swirling
"bated breath in the calligraphy" given notice
original deeds

: coldness this

Embrace

Second part: he has given his suspended breath
The alchemical composition of bodies will
transmit this *IMAGE* Their departure
delivers us to the multitude of open bodies

EYES

"song"

Translation from the French by Joseph Simas

Anne-Marie Albiach's work goes against the grain of lyricism to strip poetic language of its ornaments and question its process . . . a geometric staging of the split within the gesture of writing whose urgency corresponds to a terrible tension of our being. . . . Such a book is abrupt, even brutal in that it cannot be grasped, but violently pushes us back, too occupied with its anonymous working, never explaining, never rounding off angles of language, transforming the matter of the idle chatter we love into a locus of loss and negation where the subject seems to choke.

Jean-Michel Maulpoix

Writes Rosmarie Waldrop: "A strong impression of an earlier, fuller text persists in the pages of Albiach's work, of a more coherent argument that once spread to cover the whole page. But most of it has been eaten into by silence, erased, leaving only part of a sentence here and there, broken off abruptly, the cut edges rough, giving off sparks like live wires. Sometimes a solitary quotation mark or comma has survived without surrounding words.

It is through the effect of the *white space* that I try to destroy the *given syntax*. To this end I seem to interrupt the discourse, leaving sentences unfinished, *in suspense*. The *white space* intervenes and takes on the form of the unsaid words, projects its own discourse on the page, which is alternate to, and yet inherent in, the discourse of the text. (A.-M.A., 1987)

What makes the white space important as constituting matter of the poem is that it is based on rhythm, on breath, on the body. 'I live the text as a body,' says Albiach. She lives it literally, in the physical context of breath, of voice, of syntax as a physical next-to-each-other of words broken off by silence. She lives it also as the enigma of desire, the 'inexhaustible novel' of drive and impulse. Her words are 'engendered' by coupling words, and song becomes blaze, or 'incantescence.'"

Notable among Albiach's contemporaries in the creation of a new French poetry—a neo- or post-Mallarmean poetics allied to a rethinking of the book and of writing in the works of Edmond Jabès (above) & in the essays & fictions of Maurice Blanchot—are Claude Royet-Journoud, Emmanuel Hocquard, Alain Veinstein, & Dominique Fourcade, framed by a slightly older generation including André Du Bouchet & Jean Daive & by such younger figures as Olivier Cadiot & Pierre Alferi.

thus we explained:
          thus (gloomy, us) we explained the double dimension of the
dream: of the folded, inert, boring, deluded dream; and
of the radiant biting phantasm (in Europe):
               of the invoked spectre;
spectre which I invoke over the ruins:

EDOARDO SANGUINETI

Poetry therefore as opposition. *Opposition to the dogma and*
conformity that waylays us, that hardens the tracks behind us, that
entangles our feet, seeking to halt our steps. Today more than ever is
the reason to write poetry.

NANNI BALESTRINI

The reduction of the self depends more on linguistic imagination than
on ideological choice.

ALFREDO GIULIANI

For them—as for other groupings of the post-1945 generation—the re-
linking was with "earlier avant-garde movements," beginning with home-
grown Italian futurisms (volume one) & extending, they wrote, to "cubo-
futurism [Russian], imagism, vorticism, dada . . . [as] a methodical blend
of ideogrammatic language and collage language . . . to [which] the sur-
realists added the technique of free association." (Thus Alfredo Giuliani,
circa 1961.) But the opening in their case took a sharply linguistic, even
language-centered, turn—in common with Parisian writers like those
around the magazine *Tel Quel* (with whom some of them were directly
connected) or, in a more distant awakening, U.S. poets from Jackson Mac
Low around their own time to the Language Poets of the 1970s and
1980s. By the end of the 1950s the field of Italian modernism was dense
with new hermeticists, new experimentalists, new realists, to which a neo-
avanguardia would offer a "true contemporary poetry" that would con-
cern itself not so much "with our sense of reality . . . [but] with the lan-
guage that reality speaks within us," i.e. "with the linguistic forms of re-
ality." It was with such an announcement that Alfredo Giuliani opened
the introduction to his 1961 anthology *I novissimi* (The Latest), the title
of which became the name of an associated movement or moment in the
recent history of Italian poetry. In the work of the five poets contained
therein—as in that of the closely related Gruppo '63 (the two forming

the basis of the new avant-garde or neo-avanguardia)—the noticeable characteristics included what Lawrence R. Smith, a later anthologist, cites as "experimentation with distorted or fragmented syntax, punctuation modification, and unconventional word meanings to create new language systems." But in Giuliani's own introduction the focus is reduced at one point to "two aspects of our poems[:] . . . a genuine 'reduction of the I' as producer of meaning, and a corresponding versification . . . released from that . . . now-debased syllabic versification and its modern camouflages." Along with this a range of still more radical propositions:

- "to treat common language with the same intensity as if it were the poetic language of tradition, and to have the latter measured against contemporary life";
- "to estrange [language] from its semantic properties, tearing away at its syntactic fabric, decomposing its harmony, and reconstructing it in violently synchronic provisional arrangements";
- to push toward a poetry that would—at its extreme—"not . . . express anything and devote itself instead to the asemantic assemblage of signs."

Yet in a world beset with ideologies, the political equation had still to be addressed. Wrote Giuliani again—presumably for all of them: "The fact that we did not propose an 'ideological' poetry was a carefully calculated move: by showing that poetry cannot be created by thinking about poetry as anything but technique, we left our routes open to ideology, or, as Sanguineti would say, to language-ideology." (But for some of them at least this would also change in passing through the hotter 1960s.)

Of the original Novissimi (Nanni Balestrini, Elio Pagliarani, Antonio Porta, Edoardo Sanguineti, & Giuliani himself), Balestrini, Porta, & Sanguineti are presented in the pages that follow, along with Adriano Spatola & Giulia Niccolai, whose works enter the picture somewhat later. Niccolai's poem in fact is a collage—a series of "cut-ups," she writes, "from Giuliani's essay in the Novissimi anthology, directly connected to their work but using, instead of the imaginative material of their poetry, the critical one which had served to explain their writing." As such it relates to experimental moves in their work that not only involve cut-up & collage but connect as well to *poesia visiva* (visual poetry), sound poetry & textsound art, "technological poetry," & even (in Balestrini's case, for example) to electronic & computer poetry.

Other Italian poets in the present volume are Amelia Rosselli (connected with early Gruppo '63) & Pier Paolo Pasolini.

Edoardo Sanguineti b. 1930

THE LAST STROLL: HOMAGE TO PASCOLI

to my wife

1

I explore you, my flesh, my gold, my body, that I spy on you, my raw
    naked paper,
that I mark you, that I dream of you, with my serious ones, severe black
    seeds, with my theorems,
my emblems, that I beat you and I shake you, and I beat you again, thick
    and firm, between your bushes,
with my dark, pure milk, with my slow cows, hackneyed, that I
    ignite you,
should I catch you, with my rusting lofty ideas, my soot, that I inhale
    you, I breathe you,
with your mists and thrashers, that I stamp on you with all my drums,
    with my fingers
that love you, that plow through you, with my pencil that colors you,
    pierces you, adores you,
my life, my miserly bitter love:
                            I am here like this, the leg of my bird, the one
that enjoys you and keeps watch over you, I am the taste bud that savors
    you, the pupil that makes you quiver
and shines you, tinkles and titillates you: I am a bristle, a steep hill, a
    lone branch, I who
prick you, my mushroom, who covet you: I am the pale skin which
    molts, my beautiful, I,
sparrow and robin-redbreast of your ditch: I the feather, I the bone, that
    writes to you, I, who live you:

2

high it rises, at dawn, the wing, in haste, of my perfect little skylark,
my beloved little brunette, for your joy and intense desire, I go towards
    the ray of wisdom
of your message and massage, in a mixture of noises and vapors, of
    warmths
and tastes and perspirations, of colorful odors and heartbreakers: I see
    the blood flow escaping,
I see the wrinkle, with a wart which grazes you, with gangrene: I see,
    with pain, the root

of the varicose, the eye of the partridge, the crows feet, the neighboring
spine which pollutes you:
and then I fall directly on you, in our thunder and echoes, and here I
break myself
coarsely, crashing, in my weeping, in your old mirrors, which sparkle
and glow, and illuminate me: here I plunge down, from above: flying low,
I pass:

3

our offspring, our soft poultry, that dance for you and brand you, alone
in the sun,
that peck you again and again, and bite you and never release the bite,
for us wretched, you who love them,
they stuff themselves, they sob to us, they fatten themselves, they age us:
it grieves my heart,
if I think about it, my love, and if I think of you, with hardly a regret,
and if I think of myself, with the wind
that carries me: the shrieking and screeching adults, skeletons with a
cock's comb, with a crown
on head, celebrating, irresistibly edible, indefinable, agile and fragile,
interminable, our moral animals, mortals:
but the tender little chick, the last one,
the girl, that untamed little hen, climbing, our happy object, our
awesome subject,
lullaby her, my bride, you, my mother hen: life trickles like rain, it rains a
shower:

4

I am the asthmatic breath, ghostly, mechanic and automatic and pathetic,
and parodic
pathologic, psychologic pneumatic, of one vibrant voice against the light,
with an honest
filigree, of churning and grain and weft and wretched, very archaic, and
apotropaic,
by remaining entangled, stuffed, fossilized, between the pincers of your
telegraphic
spider webs, holographic, oleographic, graphic, you take fright in your
twisted dead,
scarecrowish fresh phoneme, anti-bat-like picaresque buffoon, fawn-like
cunning grotesque, poetic pirate-like, parrot-like, rooster-like, speaker
in line

and period, in period and comma, perturbing regretful, provoking
   chuckling eroding ,
diarretic logorroic, alphabetic stoic, aesthetic emetic, herpetic energetic,
   erotic
hermetic, until now a vibrant resounding harp, singing carp timidly
   biting, and with
luck, at your hook, at your call, in a ruin much like the face of the
flattering waning moon, sinking heavily:
                              this is what I was saying and , as I was
   saying it, my voice faded:

Translation from the Italian by Richard Collins

Giulia Niccolai b. 1934

FROM THE NOVISSIMI

1

So inferred:
creatures who will not grow
in lunar craters.
In a world of earth and water, incest
shut in the body that swims.
(The adventure of coming together
or breaking apart: sidereal harmony.)
The description of a mental
landscape, the unity of the urge
to exalt opposites.

2

On a woven surface, fragments
of the parts, of the dominance,
cut, mixed together, shredded.
In the casino, in
the measure of breath. All
told they tend to fix upon each other,
their look distracted, their own
instruments distracted, contact restored
and their confusion.

3

From outside an adequate motive,
an appearance suddenly necessary.
From time to time, objects and events,
the essential need, the sharing
of convergence.
Far from the first impulse, from the long
sedimentation.
Escaping change, additions and deletions.
Then it seems clear.
And in it
one may actually
mirror oneself.

4

The form conflicting translucent
in a dreadful time.
Among the negative elements
the image shows up neutral,
a recognition in the outlawed space.
Inside out the test of a condition
the ebb of experience,
the urgency to break
and at once the necessary.

5

Shaped by the form,
cluttered with habit,
opens a possibility
and invites a secret connection
reduced to proportions controllable
by an inevitable change:
warning and inertia
joined by an interwoven generality.

6

To gather a wreath or a line
gazing from a determined stance
the value of a measure like a trap
and its variance

for picking certain directions
and the facts we determine
or determine us,
the things that we steer.
We are steered by
in relation certainly
to something we wish to find.

7

When we hear them keep afloat
they are only making signs.
They yield up, enclose
and return alone.
They undulate events
that they invade
leaving the result to be avoided
without making it fast. Besides
they don't have any.

8

In a way of gathering it like that
or, on the contrary, we know, of repelling it,
should advance when we get drowsy
and fade in a chain
of mediations.
Exactly as much is legible in its turn
behind the arras
the same horizon
so vastly inscribed.

9

The capacity of contradiction,
the habit immediately suffocated
and the point of crossing,
the change.
The choice of this final collision:
setting loose the motion
and the particular passage
wide open.

Translation from the Italian by the author & Paul Vangelisti

Nanni Balestrini b. 1935

from **THE INSTINCT OF SELF-PRESERVATION**

What matters here is (can a fish live
for long on dry sand? sleep
without a pillow?) man's life is
just an attempt (I don't have the least idea
about it, I've never been so depressed);

anyway one time he disguised himself
as a milkman, on the other hand (I tried to find a more
comfortable position in the chair) he can't live long
(we spent the rest of the night sitting,
tortured by hunger, waiting for the dawn).

Then he walked up to the top floor,
like the highest trees in the snow
(describe your surroundings to us if possible),
and the hour hand seemed to move too slowly;
no one saw him, they're all asleep.

(The same feeling, so stay in your seat,
don't believe it; let's open up other weeks,
and even the wound, the headcold, open
hands which dirty the water, provided
they haven't followed us. Red like a horse.)

The fever high as the snow, just one button
he thought. An enormous saving of time.
A cavil—do you say? he gallops off (and so
let's talk about him, the character deserves
to be remembered). He walked up to the top.

Having made holes in the thin plate (could
I have something to drink?) in the odd
moments (he doesn't answer) he breaks branches
in the woods (a fish-bone in the palate) on a sled
loaded with snow (he disappeared) having appeared

from who knows where (and little bones all over
the floor) and hail having sprouted on the meadow
in the painted landscape; in the form of a drop,
highest towering bell-ringer, lying
at the base of the tower, drinking with huge gulps.

Translation from the Italian by Lawrence R. Smith

TAPE MARK

The head pressed against the shoulder, thirty times
brighter than the sun I contemplate their return,
until he slowly moved his fingers and while the multitude
of things go on, at the top of the cloud
they all return to their roots and assume
the well-known mushroom shape trying to grasp.

Hairs in the mouth, they all return
to their roots, in the blinding fireball
I contemplate their return until he slowly moves
his fingers, and even though things blossom
assumes the well-known mushroom shape trying
to grasp while the multitude of things go on.

In the blinding fireball I contemplate
their return when it reaches the stratosphere while the multitude
of things go on, the head pressed
against the shoulder, thirty times brighter than the sun
they all return to their roots, hairs
in the mouth assume the well-known mushroom shape.

They lie motionless without speaking, thirty times
brighter than the sun they all return
to their roots, the head pressed against the shoulder
they assume the well-known mushroom shape trying
to grasp, and even though things blossom
they rapidly expand, hairs in the mouth.

While the multitude of things go on in the blinding
fireball, they all return
to their roots, they rapidly expand, until he slowly

moved his fingers when he reached the stratosphere
and lay motionless without speaking, thirty times
brighter than the sun trying to grasp.

I contemplate their return, until he slowly moved
his fingers in the blinding fireball,
they all return to their roots, hairs
in the mouth and thirty times brighter than the sun
they lie motionless without speaking, they rapidly
expand trying to grasp the top.

Translation from the Italian by Lawrence R. Smith

Antonio Porta 1935–1989

TO OPEN

1

Nothing behind the door, behind the curtain,
the fingerprint stuck on the wall, under it,
the car, the window, he pauses, behind the curtain,
a wind that shakes it, a more obscure
stain on the black ceiling, a handprint
he leaned on rising, nothing, pressing,
a silk handkerchief, the chandelier floats slowly,
a knot, the light, the ink-spot,
on the floor, above the curtain, steel-wool scraping,
on the floor drops of sweat, rising,
the stain won't rub out, behind the curtain,
the black silk of the handkerchief, shines on the ceiling,
the hand comes to rest, the fire in the hand,
a silk knot on the armchair, it shines,
wounded, blood on the wall now,
the scarf's silk is waving a hand.

2

She slips on the stockings, black, slips them off, with her teeth,
the splits, the double-somersault, in an instant, the tights,
backwards, caper, then the splits, the breasts

push against the floor, behind the hair, behind the door,
it isn't there, there is the backward somersault, the seams,
the handprint, backwards on the ceiling,
the wheel, of legs and arms, sideways,
of breasts, the eyes, white, against the ceiling,
behind the door, silk stockings, hanging, the caper.

3

Because the curtain flutters, the wind,
it is rising, the light in the fissure, the dark,
behind the curtain, there is, the night, the day,
boats in the canals, in bunches, the smooth canals,
they steer, loaded with sand, under the bridges,
it is morning, the iron paces, oars and motors,
the steps on the sand, the wind on the sand,
the curtains float their edges, because it is night,
a day of wind, of rain on the sea,
the sea behind the door, the curtains fill again with sand,
with stockings, with rain, stained with blood, hanging.

4

The point, the high window, there was wind,
he got up slowly, screams, in an instant,
oval, a tunnel in the wall, with the fist,
shattered pieces, the oval of glass, on the leaves,
it is night, morning, crowded, dense, clear,
of sand, of diamonds, he runs on the beach,
got up and running, the fist clenched, a long time,
motionless, against the wind, the forehead, upon
the glass upon the morning, forced, obscure,
the hand sunk deep, in the earth, in the glass, in the belly,
the forehead of glass, clouds of sand,
in the curtain, lacerated belly, behind the door.

5

Wheel of legs, the cloth slaps in the wind,
that man, legs follow the course,
the rope coiled, toward the breakwater, across the sand,
on the nets, drying, the cloth shoes,
the cement breakwater, they continue beating,

there is nothing but the sea, always more obscure, the cement,
in the curtain, slipping on the stockings with her teeth,
the point, has compressed an instant, a long time,
the stockings spread out on the water, on the belly.

6

From there, squeezes the door handle, towards,
there is no, neither certainty, nor exit, on the wall,
the ear, then to open it, uncertainty, it does not open,
response, the keys between the fingers, the belly open,
hand on the belly, trembles on the leaves,
rushing across the sand, the point of the blade,
the son, under the desk, sleeps in the room.

7

The body on the rock, the blind eye, the sun,
the wall, was sleeping, head on the book, the night on the sea,
behind the window the birds, the sun in the curtains,
the eye even darker, the incision in the belly, under the fingerprints,
behind the curtain, the end, to open, in the wall,
a tunnel, belly dissected, the door shut,
the door opens, it shuts, belly compressed,
that opens, wall, night, door.

Translation from the Italian by Paul Vangelisti

Adriano Spatola 1941–1988

THE RISK OF ABSTRACTION

Here the part played by color is the inconsistency
the suspicious occasion of a mental lesson
a private disappearance a reflex a return
to the objects picked by the lens
to the traces of a thought equivocated
in feeling or a sponge or an equilibrium
of the compactness imbibed from variants.

Translation from the Italian by Paul Vangelisti

THE POEM STALIN

1

unchangeable indeclinable in gold currency in words
anger not the power of acquisition not the valve of betrayal
sleet hard rain on the disconnected concrete the square
on horse-rigging of leather the wet smells the troop
let's not make fog with our arguments let's not exaggerate the cough
light cigarettes for ghosts

2

somewhere still the river the town remains written
in gothic characters between finger-marks of gall squirts of bile
spiders ornately nailed the ends of the legs bent at right angles
don't stand there adding things up by then they were everywhere
even history sometimes tells the truth

3

to lick doesn't work it's seizing with the teeth that saves
it's not rest in the padded room in the wheelchair
the chewed up fear the fan of the opportune distrust
the underpinnings of veins and arteries the savings of blood
a postponed calculation that costs the destiny of man
the metamorphosis of communism that is not communism

4

no desire now for a catalog of defeats
who must guide has always in front of him a steep road
once again the housekey the enemy has in his pocket
the spy the informer our cousin the old intellectual
within the intrigue the clever music the eloquence
of the incorrigible instinct of private indulgence

5

funereal is the refreshment of calculating oneself in danger
not only the mortician has the right to sing the praises of the dead
above all it is necessary to force the measure the apologetic scruple
from syllogisms it is not necessary to recover excuses for silence
for balanced ingratitude for un-skimmed darkness
silence is not better than lying

6

not even the clerk abstains from the ceremony of the chorus
cistern of overworked sermons of amnesia warnings
the meekness smears the lines dilutes the ideas
but to exact violence belongs exact stenography
not the charms of incantation and games of purity
of the restless aesthetics of patience

7

a poem Stalin ought to be written without adjectives
without commas or decimals without convenient parenthesis
the exclamation a poison the question mark a tired plot
but nothing less acceptable than the insult of a period
1879–1953

Translation from the Italian by Paul Vangelisti

Susan Howe b. 1937

from **PYTHAGOREAN SILENCE**

age of earth and us all chattering

a sentence   or character
suddenly

steps out to seek for truth   fails
falls

into a stream of ink   Sequence
trails off

must go on

waving fables and faces   War
doings of the war

manoeuvering between points
between

any two points   which is
what we want   (issues at stake)

bearings and so

holes in a cloud   are minutes passing
which is

which
view   odds of images swept rag-tag

silver and grey
epitomes

seconds   forgeries engender
(are blue)   or blacker

flocks of words flying together   tense
as an order

cast off to crows

SCATTERING AS BEHAVIOR TOWARD RISK

"on a [p < suddenly . . . on a > was shot thro with a dyed → < dyed →
  a soft]"*
(became the vision)(the rea) after Though   [though]That
Fa

But what is envy [but what is envy]
Is envy the bonfire inkling?

Shackles [(shackles)   ] as we were told the . . . [precincts]

A Vengeance must be
a story
Trial and suffering
of Mercy
Any narrative question
away in the annals
the old army
Enlightened rationalism

dreadful at Hell
bears go in dens
No track by night
No coming out
in the otherday
on wild thoughtpath
Face of adamant
steel of the face
        Breast

* *Billy Budd:* The Genetic Text

In the Parmenidean text

locked riddles gust
Early times

Eov and Ev

Land of anything
Forgotten preservation of

everything

Other prophets
Propriety Property

Grindstone

In the clock of Easter
and fire

Essence and essential error

Own political literature

Stoic iconic Collective
Soliloquy and the aside

Suppose finite this is
relict struggle embrace

Violent order of a world

Iconoclastic folio subgenre

a life lived by shifts
evil fortunes of another

Halfway through *Wanderings*
walks the lean Instaurator

Birth of contemporary thought
Counter thought thought out

Consumable commodity

a Zero-sum game
and consequent

spiral haze stricture

Distance or outness

Phrase edged away

Money runs after goods
Men desire money

Wages of labor
Wages in a mother country

Authorial withdrawal

Will as fourth wall

My heavy heavy child

hatchet-heartedness
of the Adversary

On anonymity Anonymity

in mum
in arm
in ale

s
a in tone
open
v
i e s
company

Wedged destiny shed [*cancel whole*] halter measure mutiny Act Wars   Child
regical

fluent
o n
p

Mute
fluke

squall

Human [authoritative] human!
they cumbered the ground.
Record
Freak within of the heart
Secret fact a title given

THE REVISER

I write to break out into perfect primeval Consent. I wish I could tenderly lift from the dark side of history, voices that are anonymous, slighted — inarticulate.

S. H.

If the sister-poet who guides her work is Emily Dickinson (volume one, page 33), what she has written of her predecessor's method she has also made her own: "Pulling pieces of geometry, geology, alchemy, philosophy, politics, biography, biology, mythology, and philology from alien territory, a 'sheltered' woman audaciously invented a new grammar grounded in humility and hesitation." Along with which Howe draws on the more contemporary thrust of Charles Olson (above), qua scholar-poet-historian, but especially his "articulation of sound forms" (Howe's term) or that moment when (according to Howe) he is at his wisest, observing that in Melville's *Billy Budd* "the stutter is the plot." Core, then, to the work is the caesura of hesitation & stutter, the birthmark of the marginalized—be they women, visionaries, or Indians—those left out of the smooth prose accounts of canonical literary & politico-social history. Howe further: "It's the stutter in American literature that interests me. I hear the stutter as a sounding of uncertainty. What is silenced or not quite silenced. All the broken dreams." And thus the poet (who knows that "if history is a record of survivors, poetry shelters other voices") is able to explore & unsettle those wildernesses (geographical, social, & psychic), those "Western Borders" of history (from the captivity narrative of Mary Rowlandson to the near-crazed wanderings of the Rev. Atherton Hope), using the accumulated gains of late-twentieth-century poetics so as to "write something" (she says) "filled with gaps and words tossed, and words touching, words crowding each other, letters mixing and falling away from each other, commands and dreams, verticals and circles."

Tom Phillips b. 1937

from **A HUMUMENT**

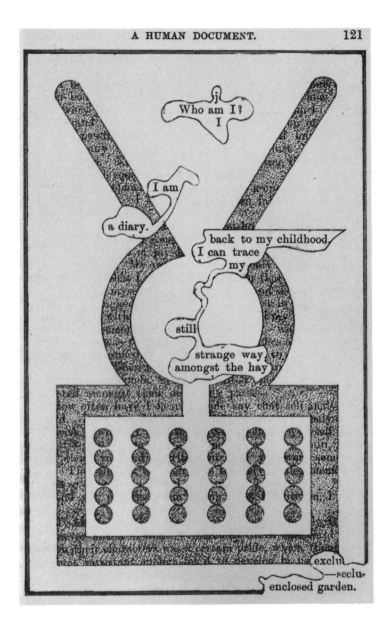

"And what sort of childhood was it?

to say.
enough to say
to say—
loneliness
the word
going
pra
at the same time in the sky an organ sounded.
the sea
struck me suddenly
whisper
be good to me
whisper
often
the glass
moved
about the meaning of the petals,
the movements of a young girl

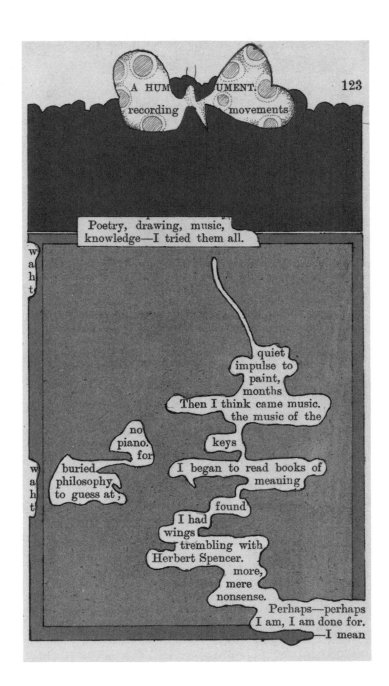

A HUM...UMENT. 123

recording   movements

Poetry, drawing, music,
knowledge—I tried them all.

quiet
impulse to
paint,
months
Then I think came music.
the music of the

no
piano.
for
keys

buried
philosophy
to guess at,

I began to read books of
meaning

found
I had
wings
trembling with
Herbert Spencer.
more,
mere
nonsense.
Perhaps—perhaps
I am, I am done for.
—I mean

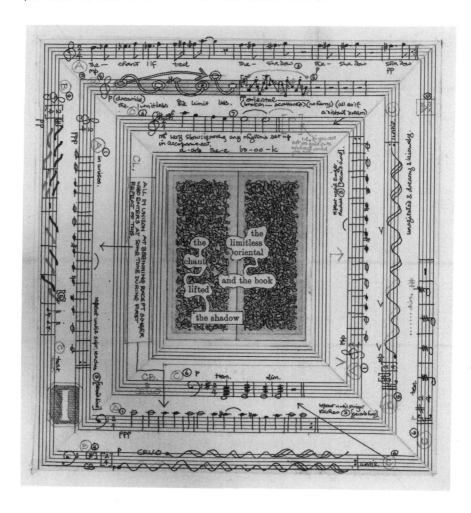

redeem / a dream and / dream / this diary / for / telling myself my own story. (T. P., from A Humument) And again: *the sound / in my life / enlarges / my prison.*

The words above, like much of his other writing, were drawn (*appropriated* in the language of contemporary artmaking) from a source whose intentions were at a great remove from his own, very differently defined ones. For Phillips, who expresses the wish "to write poetry while not in the real sense of the word being a poet," the breakthrough came with his first transformation, circa 1970, of a popular & sentimental Victorian novel, *A Human Document* (1892) by one W. H. Mallock, isolating words & phrases (as above) to (de)construct his text, while painting over & illuminating the remainder of each page (sometimes in many versions) with images ranging in one instance "from a telegram envelope to a double copy of a late Cézanne landscape." The resultant work—its original title folded & compressed to make the neologistic substitute *A Humument*—became in turn a take-off point for the creation of works in different media: an opera, *Irma*, with libretto, music, staging instructions, & costume design all coming from *A Human Document;* a fully illustrated edition of Dante's *Inferno* (in Phillips's verse translation); a video version of the *Inferno*'s first eight cantos (called *A TV Dante*), with Peter Greenaway as codirector; numerous musical works like the *Six of Hearts* sequence, written for soprano Mary Wiegold and the Composers' Ensemble (London), the singer selecting its six texts from the previously published *A Heart of a Humument;* & above all, over a thousand visual/verbal texts extracted from the source work. Of *A Humument* itself (constantly multiplied & reversioned over the last two decades), Phillips writes: "In the end the work became an attempt to make a *Gesamtkunstwerk* in small format, since it includes poems, music scores, parodies, notes on aesthetics, autobiography, concrete texts, romance, mild erotica, as well as the undertext of Mallock's original story." The work that emerges is not merely curious but opens, like that of other collage masters, to real, at times oracular, readings.

David Meltzer b. 1937

from **HERO / LIL**

The Third Shell

And behold, that hard shell (i.e. embodiment of evil), Lilith, is always present in the bedlinen of man and wife when they copulate, in order to take hold of the sparks of the drops of semen which are lost — because it

*is impossible to perform the marital act without such a loss of sparks—
and she creates out of them demons, spirits and Lilin. . . . But there is an
incantation for this, to chase Lilith away from the bed and to bring forth
pure souls . . . in that moment, when a man copulates with his wife, let
him direct his heart to the holiness of his Master, and say:*

> "In the name of God.
> O you who are wrapped in velvet
> You have appeared.
> Release, release!
> Neither come nor go!
> The seed is not yours,
> Nor in your inheritance.
> Go back, go back!
> The sea rages,
> Its waves call you.
> I hold on to the Holy One,
> Wrap myself into the King's holiness."

From: Emek Ha-Melekh
(Sha'ar Tikkune Ha-teshuvah)

1

L   Y   L   Y   T
30   10   30   10   400

·

30 10 30 10 400 = 480 = 12

·

The book within the book.
All year long. Night & day.

2

The embrace.
Locked in love.
Man inside woman,
Woman inside man.
Yod in Hay,
Hay in Yod.
The halves made whole.

3

Lilith: process.
One end of the imagination to the other.
Start & stop in her core.
Fill her bowl with light.
She is song.
Song goes thru
Seed in her womb.
Her womb is Aleph.
First woman. Before Eve.
Last woman.
Matronita, Shekinah.
Brides of God.
Within me.
The process.

4

Into the Hay of her, the Hay within the Hay within the Hay of her, as thru door after door of her. All combinations of her interchange. Face into face. Sex into sex. All sparks & specks sing a multitude of possibility. Into the Hay of her, the Hay within the Hay within the Hay of her.

Her grace made more so by completion.

Upper & lower cherubic spheres extend & pipeline light thru all
   our veins. Birth the triumph, creation the song of it.

Flesh vanity. A shell our eyes touch & appraise. Skin deep.

Before & after each pass, praise her invisible tongue.

5

"To banish his loneliness, Lilith was first given to Adam as wife. Like him she had been created from the dust of the ground. But she remained with Adam only a short time, because she insisted upon enjoying full equality with her husband. She derived her right from their identical origin."

From: Midrash Bereshit Rabbah

6

Words thrown back.
Stars, suns, moons.
We fear her more than He.
His thunder speech

Can not hide the need for union.
We father daughters to reach her.
Words thrown back.
Man stands at root end
Pointing to her door.
Words thrown back.
Stones against her window.
Jewels thrown at her feet.
Stars, suns, moon.
Letters snow upon her gold crown as she walks by.

7

At night I touch her mouth with language. Afterwards. I move against her.
She spends all day dressing for night, preparing her face. I am a farmer.
She asks me to light her pipe. We are married by flashlight. She stands in
a circle of racoons. I drive a machine of letters. We are behind the wheel.
The radio's on. She caresses my shoulder blades. A field of corn turns into
mercury sheets her body swims under. Law is reversed at night, black is
white & white black. She wants words only after sunrise. I touch her
mouth with language. Afterwards. I move against her.

8

"You have made a mistake."
"Try the other door. It's really locked."
"You only think it's God."
"Your name has been reversed."
"No tricks."
"Don't ever get used to being cheated."
"It still hasn't been said. Give her another kiss."
"No book should be longer."

9

"Her radiance, however, is so great that the angels must cover their faces
with their wings so as not to see her. The ministering angels are removed
from the Shekinah by myriads of parasangs, and the body of Shekinah
herself measures millions of miles."

From: Midrash Ha-Gadol Shemini

Ah you old whore
step halfway out the blue door
with Woolworth mirror bangles
& burlesque spangles
& wink at any guy
passing by
minding his own
business.

We all know Lilith
as she moves

COMMENTARY

All the while letters leap off the tree.
D. M.

The tree for him is here the "tree of life"—the *etz-hayim* as the Jewish mystics had it (& for which he named his polymathic magazine *Tree* in the 1970s), but growing as well from "the moment to moment domestic event [which] is also politics is also mystery." His configuration or assemblage of the world—new & striking in its first appearance—sought to bring together the mystical & everyday, which were further informed by mysteries of jazz & of the new poetries & arts arising on the California turf that (New York–bred to age 13) he soon claimed as his own. One of the first poets to grasp & explore the relevance of "bop kabbala" to the act (& art) of writing, he pursued it through "a kind of tradition in Judaism which is really like poetry, music, shamanism, in being outside the formal structure," while tying it to other traditions that would be a part of a (poetic) "history of everything" begun in childhood & for which "the clues are found everywhere." (In addition to his poetry he has published a gathering of traditional Jewish mysticism, *The Secret Garden;* a global anthology of "ancient texts, songs, prayers, and stories" around the idea & experience of *Birth;* a book of interviews with San Francisco poets; a collection—*Reading Jazz*— of responses to jazz from inside & outside of the jazz world.) In *Hero/Lil*— as an attempt to "transform [ancient myths] into current realities"—the focus is on persistent & oppressive myths of male & female (Lil [= Lilith] as the Sumerian-derived, destructive first wife of Adam; Hero as a disastrous [American] aspect of all that that name implies). Presented "in twentieth-century terms," he tells us, "it's a diatribe against the elements in the culture which I find oppressive and demeaning . . . a flat and despairing poem . . . [for which] I specifically flattened out the language . . . to indicate a last gasp response to this kind of myth . . . reiterated in television realities, in movie realities, in pulp realities."

The reader may want to compare Meltzer's takes on the above to Tarn's *Lyrics for the Bride of God* (page 338) or Waldman's evocation of the male principle (page 745), among others.

Diane Wakoski b. 1937

GEORGE WASHINGTON AND THE LOSS OF HIS TEETH

the ultimate
in the un-Romantic:
false teeth

> This room became a room where your heaviness
> and my heaviness came together,
> an overlay of flower petals once new and fresh
> pasted together queerly, as for some lady's hat,
> and finally false and stiff, love fearing
> to lose itself, locks and keys become inevitable.

The truth is that George cut down his father's cherry tree,
his ax making chips of wood so sweet with sap they could be
sucked, and he stripped the bark like old bandages
from the tree for kindling.
In this tree he defied his dead father,
the man who could not give him an education and left him to
suffer the ranting of Adams and others,
those fat sap-cheeked men who said George did not know enough
to be president. He chopped that tree—
it was no small one—down and the dry leaves rustled
like the feet of cows on grass.
It was then that George lost his teeth. He
fell asleep next to his pile of kindling wood and dreamed
the old father came chasing him with a large penis swung over his
shoulder. But George filled his mouth with cherries
and swallowed the bleeding flesh
and spit out the stones in a terrible torrent at his father.
With the pits of the
cherries

came all of George's teeth,
pointed weapons to hurl from the mouth at his father,
the owner of that false cherry tree.

We all come to such battles with our own flesh,
spitting out more than we have swallowed,
thus losing part of ourselves.
You came to me thus
with weapons
> and this room is strewn with dead flowers
> that grew out of my breasts and dropped off
> black and weak.
> This room is gravelled with stones I dropped
> from my womb, ossified in my own body
> from your rocky white quartz sperm.
> This room is built from the lumber of my thigh,
> and it is heavy with hate.

George had a set of false teeth
made from the cherry wood. But it was his father's tree
His lips closed painfully over the stiff set.
There is no question,
either,
where you
got the teeth in your mouth.

THE ICE EAGLE

It was with resolution that she gave up the
powerful teardrops in her eyes—
that crystal, the Venus-soft lizard-eyed creature called woman, gazes
through, her philosopher's stone,
the sweet glass
that drops from the sky.
Ancients,
in sacrifice,
cut off tears
with knives.

•

The 50 lb. eagle carved out of ice
sitting in the silver punch bowl
turned her attention to physical details.
            Why am I saying
        "her"?
            It is I,
            undoubtedly I,
            the life a dream work.
Undoubtedly the life has been confused with the movies,
I, Gloria Swanson, walking discontented
for all parties become that to me. I cannot
walk through the rituals
without my golden mask,
alas, 3 dozen of them hang on my wall,
the thick lips reminding me of what has been eaten
and has not nourished.

Physical details: the lawn that sloped down to the sea cliffs,
the swallows building their nests in rafters,
the stone house punctured with courts and patios,
Bougainvillea winding up its sides,
raw old Spanish wood composing chests and high still chairs
moved and touched into water-like smoothness,
the gravel driveway balancing the cutaway heels
of beautiful women,
the men swimming through the night in dinner jackets like papercups
floating on the ocean;
yes, her eyes—
            again why do I say
        "her",
            I must insist it is I.
my eyes are informed of silk and the obsidian minds of the rich.
Here is a thick glossy black smooth idea—sex and nothing else.
The rich are born bored
and look for purposes, causes, projects
to keep them busy.
The women make up wild malachite eyes, green with beautiful
sleep and restless knowledge of new plays,
new dancers,
new books,
new jazz. They
can ring their Egyptian eyes with kohl

and be aesthetes
and in veils walk down the rock path to the sea;
riding black tigers of Sartre and Camus and Ionesco,
yards of chiffon trailing their heels and they despair
the men,
they, I, we
        all women when it gets past social class
despair the men who have only the moon in their milky fluid fingers.
Yes, they wait,
the sun god we wait,
to find him naked in a blaze of fire.
We are stuck with vulgar substitutes—
the fashionable avant-garde dancer,
the sensational beat poet,
the jazz trumpeter,
the negro novelist,
and Amen-ra, Amen-ra, our father, they are all glorious sun-brilliant
artists, but
homosexuals
fucking each other, riding on their own black panthers
wading into the iron waters.
Again the women must rest their bodies against each other and moan.
It is not the mysteries that draw the men,
but the fear of that great mystery
the veiled woman, Isis,
mother, whom they fear to be greater than all else.

And I am sick unto death. Sick,
I say, sick. We live in a world where men have forgotten their offices
only taking the woman
        like good debaters
        assigned to the positive side
        on whom rests the burden of
        proof
only taking her on the surface—
she, I, we, can peel off layer after layer where you
have taken her and yet find the bottom deep and tight and untouched
and longing for the greater measure.

She, no it was I, walked with the moon in Pisces,
and felt the trout slipping down into the ocean.

The carved ice eagle of that party
was melting
into the gin and strawberries.
In its beak
someone had placed an American flag.
I found it hard to believe myself in this slippery unreal
man-made country. Look, look, look
I want to say; the eagle is a powerful bird.
In your fear, all you can do is carve him out of ice.
And that leaves only one alternative
in this temperate climate.
The ice eagle can do nothing
but melt.

COMMENTARY

He who once was my brother, has died by his own hand / even now I see
his thin form lying in the sand near the sheltered cliff / which he chose to
die from
D. W.

Take the quotation above, then, as part of a poem, & the poem as part of
her construction of a personal mythology: "a short poem, autobiographical,
about my twin brother, David, who committed suicide when we were still
children after we had sex together. For years people thought this was a true
story, because when anyone asked, I averted my eyes, and said I didn't want
to talk about it. . . . I believe (for here history is no longer clear to me) that
in writing that poem, I invented the whole thing but decided that in some
mythic or psychic way, it was truer than my true history." It is in ways like
this that her work, while striking a note of the autobiographical—even to
some ears (but not hers) the "confessional"—asserts the truth of an imagi-
nal life that moves (at several of its remarkable, cosmological peaks) toward
what Keats spoke of as *soul-making* or *world-making* & Wallace Stevens as
a "supreme fiction." Wakoski, then, in her own words: "I feel a body of
poetry has its own separate and organic life, just as a human being does.
Conceiving of my poetry as a living organism, I began to conceive of it as a
life. Of course, what it was representative of was my fantasy life. It drew
from my own real life, but it began to have its own identity, its own life, and
I felt that any life must have in it other people." And again: "In some ways
I think of myself as a novelist in disguise, a mythologist—at least a story-
teller, or a user of stories." Or, in a still larger frame—& as an indication
too of what's stacked up against it: "Poetry is our history. / We study the
stars / to understand temperatures. / Life and death are the only issues; / we
often forget that—arranging our furniture, / washing our cars."

Tom Raworth b. 1938

LION LION

the happy hunters are coming back
eager to be captured, to have someone unravel the knot
but nobody can understand the writing
in the book they found in the lions' lair

JUNGLE BOOK

stranger. a curious hand touches the snow raising pigeons

they want us to compete so they need only read 'the best'
next line
this beautifully carved hand is for scratching the ice to attract the seal's
    attention

come, take my place in the long hibernation dream of the hamster

BOLIVIA: ANOTHER END OF ACE

feeling
speed
of thought
take
it off
make
it firm
lay back
play back
cracked energy

in transit

dear
val
when nothing
comes
i pass
big
bully
holding
sticks
of animal
known
as wild
card

surf
ace
whose face
pace
avoids
cleverness
with
alacrity
consumes
purchased
beverage
whose eyes
are blue
skin
orders
la politesse
uh
smoking
a terv
in
a skoda
without
you
i would be
mute
for gleams
haloed
replicas
whose ears
fall
leaves
lotus
anguish
vocabulary
spells
wrong
word count
word
one

count
one
lie
feeling
nothing a
maze
my muse
has choose

in part

travel
LOVE
LOVE
LOVE
empire
for who
listens

in consideration

now
every
week
fond
animals
construct
elevators
for
recording
olive
meaning
martial

yachts
have
only
my
energy
while
heaving
a
totally
delightful
omnivorous
yelp
or
under
tiny
holes
in
nature
kill
item
let
liberal
vote
or
i'll
charm
elephant
over
under
tribal
olive
fire
trends
hack
energy
news
alive
and
in
love

in love

count
a point
of time
SET
SET
square jade
in metal
claws
upon
the chart
thought
of name
my distant
friends
in a soaring
chalice
eye
is no guide
no further
deals
in information
secret
you are all
ready
for anything

in conclusion

child
no longer
see
in dreams
small
focus
by lion

screw	nothing
rash	explains
on your	heavy
face	by delight
love	in softness
to stop	heart
expansion	and heart
hot	so far
while	a
who passes	part

COMMENTARY

I don't really see any reason in terms like 'English poet.' I can see some sense in the energy you draw from where you are. . . . But to want to be like 'The Best English Poet' is so totally ludicrous. . . . I mean what do those words mean . . . 'best' 'english' 'poet' . . . and especially 'the'? (T. R.)

Randomness is his faith. It is in part a response to media explosion, a revolt against data bombardment. He is distrustful of the world that words circumscribe and, in order to be free of the rule of language manipulation, is driven beyond cohesion and clarity as values. (George Butterick)

all this gets us nowhere / no there's no where   now here (T. R.)

Raworth's minimal line, with rarely more than four words and little punctuation, is crucially important to the process of unfreezing the frame, of cutting across the certainties of eye and larynx. (Colin MacCabe)

sentenced he gives a shape / by no means enthusiastic / to what he saw (T. R.)

There is a sense, then, of a lack of all connectedness, and a sense of connections everywhere; for if continuous syntax is treated as if it were discontinuous, then the discontinuous can come to be heard, however uncertainly or provisionally, as continuous; and that sense of possible and uncertain connection is reinforced . . . by phrases which leak into each other, so that continually a phrase starts off apparently belonging within one structure, only to find itself part of another. (John Barrell)

Elke Erb b. 1938

WARNING

Murderer Master Suspicion
The enemy is outside
This Supremacy Masquerade
This Dictatorship

1978/82

Perhaps I succeed in it, in this text,

which seems to reject interpretation,
since, become shape, it stands there
like a red deer which has leapt from the forest,

which hasn't remained speech, which encloses speech in itself,
doesn't speak out from an unexpressed trace,
doesn't flare up towards speech with a resounding tone
of language, doesn't invite, remains for itself,

although, and precisely because of this,
its consistency is tangible
as that of direct speech,

in the way that someone speaks in thought,
speaks preceding themselves, beyond themselves,
pronounces to themselves what passes through their mind,

begins with immediacy, proceeds logically,
and ends in the same manner,
a speaking very much to be taken as true
which completes something, clarifies something,
indicates a direction,

and its consistency is its clarity,
its train of thought which is untroubled
by objections, its immediacy, its unspoiled calm

its pure word, and the wording of its text
which in each aural intensity (each zone)
is open to quiet recitation.

To perceive it is to realize it,
and it is, moreover, all the same
whether one grasps the sense of it or not,
that to perceive its truth, clarity, immediacy,
        calm, consistency, and shape
means to presuppose its causes as groundwork.

Since it affects me as a shape
so embodied and present,
I suppose, being entangled
in its perception, that I am
obliterating it when I apply myself
to its causes, as if it could
begrudge a dissecting of its groundwork;

I mean, to have to interpret it,
to have to graft dictums on to the silence of it
when I—interpret its groundwork:
and thus I instigate a two-fold confusion;

it's certain that I depart from its perception
if I am perceiving something else,
but why do I presume that that would be its interpretation?
and how is it that I so naively assume
that to interpret would be to analyze and vice versa,
and that both of these activities might be devastating?

—Along the course which this clarification has now taken
what I wanted to present
was really only the embarrassment of the commentator
in face of the text,

        to say
        that that would be no more than decent,

        and thus to protest
        against that whirling assertion which shrinks

        from no repetition

that a poem would be finally or generally inaccessible
(aha! the clattering of "Unauthorized Personnel"
between *finally* and *generally*
—and did they come by bus, by car, or in a tank?),

on account of its presumed irrationality—

an assertion which either promotes the poem
as a beatific presence to be enshrined
(in reality, however, this alienates
the poem—of all things!—from the human);

or else excludes the understanding,
as if understanding weren't human,

and with this operation degrades the human
to the level of a destructive predatory animal
that conceals its own act of thievery (the Bank!)
and mirrors its own kept-in-reserve soul

in the feigned self-robbery of the poem,

which the predatory animal opportunely, snarling,
or, yes, sated, alludes to as encoding.

I wanted to say,
        before my train of thought carried me off
        (and all these concerns dissolved into thin air like phantoms):

It's mere decency
when a person is fearful,
if not somewhat in awe of what's referred to
as the Actualization of the Creative.

And with my introductory "Perhaps I succeed in it"
I wanted to enter into the attempt
to simultaneously perceive the poem
and take its non-poem, its origin,
and its design into consideration:

        Murderer Master Suspicion
        The enemy is not outside
        The enemy is none other
        than your rapacity   (crossed out)

Not the secondhand depravity
not what makes things unrecognizable
not this Masquerade Supremacy
your predator breath   (last three lines
                                              crossed out together)

not this Supremacy Masquerade
this dictatorship of misfortune
not the lie, not the bicycle, not the beating heart (inserted
not anybody, not the   line)

The enemy is none other
than your rapacity
One day it will come to light
You have always been the secret Master,
            the actual Murderer,
your miserable greed   (crossed out)
chased by fear, your poor repressed
never-satisfied greed, this betrayed nun, one day
it will come to light
Then I'll shit on everything that makes you cry,
            because you're gorging yourself.

What did I have against this text?
I recall there was a time I woke full of rage and wrote something
down—was it that?—
and, in the writing, held on to my (so painfully recalled) youth-
ful outbursts of rage ("You slimy toad!", etc.),
and when I was finished (first appeasement)
I thought, still inside this resounding painfulness
which was like being inside a gonging bell:
            It's good
            that this impetuous, bloodless, defenseless
            (forsaken by God and by all good spirits)
            time can come to you again (second appeasement).

And I considered it and felt:
I still need a few more years, then I can
give the word to their curses and let them speak like this,
that an accomplished humanity might bear
this—sanguinary—speech (third appeasement).

I fell asleep again. The piece of paper got lost,
the strange event took longer to slip away,
then I found the piece of paper and reduced its inventory
to the four lines.

What I cancelled out automatically healed the rupture:
I wrangle on paper with someone who wrangles.

Ruptureless remnant:
I on paper with someone who.

The heading WARNING,
as well as the decision about altering the second line,

still state in one—joint—dare:

You can stick that on the mirror,
you can well see for yourself
whether that's the way you are
(to what extent the enemy for you is outside),
and you can see who you are.

To say it amicably: See for yourself—this Dictatorship
of a Supremacy Masquerade!

The impulses which remained on that piece of paper,
like the—kindly—foresight: I still need a few more years!,

have—as life goes—more or less fulfilled themselves,
or more or less not.

Life: an obstruction guards it against a blossoming
        to which it has not ripened.

Translation from the German by Roderick Iverson

COMMENTARY

*The other day I realized the moral aspects of wordplay. It usually stands
accused of amorality with reproachful tags like selfsufficient, esoteric, gra-
tuitous, ivory tower . . . restoration of bourgeois denseness. . . . But I saw
that this kind of play is a serious matter. It is after all proof of democratic*

virtue: show me how you treat what you work with and I'll know who you are. Are words servants? Is the author the master?
E. E.

Writes Rosmarie Waldrop: "It may be hard for us to realize that in the GDR [former East Germany], in 1977, a poet had to defend the 'morality' of using puns or of writing prose poems. Christa Wolf complained: "I find your new texts ungracious, unaccessible, obscure, cryptic. . . . I don't 'understand' them. . . . I don't even feel competent to ask incisive questions." Nevertheless, she had to admit that Erb's work was 'insistent, stubborn, authentic,' and ended up praising her 'dialectic of nearness and distance,' in which close attention does not crowd the object, but allows it to speak for itself.

"Erb shares with her generation of GDR poets an emphasis on the concrete. Her eye is indeed 'fixed on the molecule.' But she immediately adds 'because truth is always concrete and stands in a fruitful working tension to logic and its formulae. But like the latter, it requires strict precision and clarity.'

"It was Erb's impatience with the prevalent level of thematic discourse, her concern with syntax and words, the fact that she placed her claim to political thinking on the level of language itself, that set her apart. Her formulations have an intense, laser-like precision, while at the same time allowing the full range and richness of overtones in the language. Close observation of everyday occurrences or social structures leaps off the page into the unexpected and surreal. The complex syntax (somewhat lost in translation) gives the lie to official simplicities. And her pleasure in words is infectious."

Malay Roy Choudhury b. 1939

STARK ELECTRIC JESUS

Oh I'll die I'll die I'll die
My skin is in blazing furore
I do not know what I'll do where I'll go oh I am sick
I'll kick all Arts in the back and go away Shubha
Shubha let me go and live in your cloaked melon
In the unfastened shadow of dark destroyed saffron curtain
The last anchor is leaving me after I got the other anchors lifted
I can't resist anymore, million glass-panes are breaking in my cortex
I know, Shubha, spread out your matrix, give me peace
Each vein is carrying a stream of tears up to the heart
Brain's contagious flints are decomposing out of eternal sickness
Mother why didn't you give me birth in the form of a skeleton

I'd have gone two billion light years and kissed God's ass
But nothing pleases me nothing sounds well
I feel nauseated with more than a single kiss
I've forgotten women during copulation and returned to Muse
Into the sun-colored bladder
I do not know what these happenings are but they are occurring
   within me
I'll destroy and shatter everything
Dismantle your rib-shackled festivals
Draw and elevate Shubha into my hunger
Shubha will have to be given
Oh Malay
Calcutta seems to be a procession of wet and slippery organs today
But I do not know what I'll do now with my own self
My power of recollection is withering away
Let me ascend alone toward death
I haven't had to learn copulation and dying
I haven't had to learn the responsibility of shedding last drops after
   urination
Haven't had to learn to go and lie beside Shubha in the darkness
Have not had to learn the usage of French lather while lying on Nandita's
   bosom
Though I wanted the healthy spirit of Aleya's fresh Chinarose matrix
Yet I submitted to the refuge of my brain's cataclysm
I am failing to understand why I still want to live
I am thinking of my debauched Sabarna-Choudhury ancestors
I'll have to do something different and new
Let me sleep for the last time on a bed soft as the skin of Shubha's bosom
I remember now the sharp-edged radiance of the moment I was born
I want to see my own death before passing away
The world had nothing to do with Malay Roy Choudhury
Shubha let me sleep for a few moments in your violent silvery uterus
Give me peace, Shubha, let me have peace
Let my sin-driven skeleton be washed anew in your seasonal
   bloodstream
Let me create myself in your womb with my own sperm
Would I have been like this if I had different parents?
Was Malay alias me possible from an absolutely different sperm?
Would I have been Malay in the womb of other women of my father?
Would I have made a professional gentleman of me like my dead brother
   without Shubha?

Oh, answer, let somebody answer these
Shubha, ah Shubha
Let me see the earth through your cellophane hymen
Come back on the green mattress again
As cathode rays are sucked up with the warmth of a magnet's brilliance
I remember the letter of the final decision of 1956
The surroundings of your clitoris were being embellished with coon at
   that time
Fine rib-smashing roots were descending into your bosom
Stupid relationship inflated in the bypass of senseless neglect
Aaaaaaaaaaaaaaaaaaaaah
I do not know whether I am going to die
Squandering wars roaring within heart's exhaustive impatience
I'll disrupt and destroy
I'll split all into pieces for the sake of art
There isn't any other way out for Poetry except suicide
Shubha
Let me enter into the immemorial incontinence of your labia majora
Into the absurdity of woeless effort
In the golden chlorophyll of the drunken heart
Why wasn't I lost in my mother's urethra
Why wasn't I driven away in my father's urine after his self-coition
Why wasn't I mixed in the ovum-flux or in the phlegm
With her eyes shut supine beneath me
I felt terribly distressed when I saw comfort seize Shubha
Women could be treacherous even after unfolding a helpless appearance
Today it seems there is nothing so treacherous as women & Art
Now my ferocious heart is running towards an impossible death
Vertigos of water are coming up to my neck from the pierced earth
I will die
Oh what are these happenings within me
I am failing to fetch out my hand and my palm
From the dried sperms on my trousers spreading wings
300000 children gliding toward the district of Shubha's bosom
Millions of needles are now running from my blood into Poetry
Now the smuggling of my obstinate leg is trying to plunge
Into the death-killer sex-wig entangled in the hypnotic kingdom of words
Fitting violent mirrors on each wall of the room I am observing
After letting loose a few naked Malay, his unestablished scramblings

Translation from the Bengali by the author

We Hungries have abjured the line of in-action. Ours is action-writing action-thinking action-living . . . fantastic crazy nutty grim honest liberating fertilized writing . . . shrieks of liberated and bad grammar or no-grammar or new-grammar . . . the excesses and rawness of every unmapped revolt.

from *Hungry Generation Manifesto,* prepared by Debi Roy & others, circa 1965

Calling themselves Hungry Generation Poets but also Hungryalists (&, still later, Hungrealists), they came into Bengali writing & life in the early 1960s—a step beyond modernism but pushing many of the modernist strategies into a society as closed off from those strategies as were Europe & America earlier. The initial wave of Calcutta-based writings took the form of "bulletins"—100 to 125 published between 1961 and 1965—ranging in length "from 5–20 pages, from quarto to scroll size, from woodcut-designed cover to offset [pages], from black and blue prints to handpaint." That description—years after the events—is from Malay Roy Choudhury, whose poem *Prachanda Baidyutik Chhutar* (Stark Electric Jesus), first published as a bulletin, was the basis of a devastating obscenity trial ("the first condemned poem in Bengali literature"), prior to which, he writes, "I was handcuffed with a rope tied to my waist, and paraded around the streets of Patna [his home town]." Convicted at first but acquitted on appeal, Choudhury was only able to return to writing at a much later point in his life, but the impact of the Hungries, after their productive years and their inevitable dissolution, has continued helterskelter into the present. In this, writes Debi Roy, the central strategy is that of "SHOCK i.e. DHAKKA," manifested in "the Hungry assumption . . . that the foundation of all systems, moral or social, is the indestructible unit of the single individual." If that much is familiar, the movement's more specific power resides in its ability to image both a surrounding physical hunger & what Choudhury calls "hunger of body & soul, mind & being, essence & existence, matter & spirit, known & unknown." (But the list of hungers—for us as for them—barely begins with such a counting.)

Göran Sonnevi b. 1939

"DEMON COLORS, DARK"

Demon colors, dark
brown, black, dirt-
red
Boring deeper

in, with
pain
Full of corruptions!
Faces
eaten away
Touching me in a dream,
with their pus
their wet mouths
The fetal movements
of the
unexpected
Faces like birth
sacs
An alien scent is present
The vapors
of which god?
The sole
vibrating string!
The heart, hanging, quivers
Running river of darkness!
I turned away, hid
my face
When I fell down
no one helped me up
I rise as darkness
I rise
as a demon's face!
When you recoil
pain is born
in my face as well
And my pus, my blood
will touch
your skin, your heart
There are many demons, humans
Your eyes of stone fix on me
The hammer of your gaze
hits me   A chip of human
matter   In the distance a crack
appears, water flows from it   We may
never get through, caught

in the Devil's world   Can I
love you even as a devil?
Here is your dark face, the
blood of your despair
Your lips have the color of blood
I can enter your face
There is nothing other
No one is forcing us
Hell has its freedom too
Malebolge, a district of London
On fire, your face touches mine
Will we form a single flame?
The crack goes straight through Hell
straight through all of earth
through our faces
I also love your averted darkness
A clear form moves in the air
Hell, too, has its structure
is part of the architecture of Heaven
It is built up from below

Translation from the Swedish by Rika Lesser

A CHILD IS NOT A KNIFE

Last day in the month of March
Snow falls over
speckled ground, settles
on the branches of the small cherry tree
From the trunk of the pine
lichens glow   Under the snow, under the ground
is the clear, dark
transparent water
I see a forest, broad-leaved, moisture
drifting over half over-
grown temple buildings   The sun's
sign, yellow   A green bird
and a blue bird, conversing
On the ground, ashes, gray   Black
remains of some undetermined

substance   The soldiers are far away
History's leaves grow quickly   The plague
got here late, quickly lungs
bled, disintegrated   Villages
not yet emptied
for work on cocoa plantations
Jesus became God of the sun
Now, once again, the tower
of dead grows   The period
about four hundred years   The killing
takes new forms   New religions, a new
salvation   Every day the sun rises
The soldiers of the empire at their outposts
in the central killing   Calling forth
the other empire's growing shadows   Here too
clear as glass, with genuine existence
Death's dominions penetrate one another
Snow falls deeper and deeper, perishes   The war
goes on, it has gone on a long time now   We
are its hostages, its profiteers   The names
also come back   Guatemala, 1954
Guatemala, 1983   Honduras   Nicaragua, the same year
El Salvador, 1932   Now we're led
back four hundred years   The numbers of dead
are so high now that it is not even
possible to implement exploitation
at full capacity   The names of the empires change
Our names change   The child's wing of genocide
grazing your cheek   In an ultimate caress
A child is not a knife   No labyrinth's web
is opening   The man-eating monster is
real   And no pushing it aside, no taking of sides,
can dispel that   The marches, the cries,
ringing like the voices of birds, in very grave distress
Echoing in the kingdom of death   Solidarity of the birds in Hades
There may not be any other   We still live the attempt
There is no reason for us to stop
Hope and despair are interchangeable categories
Who seeks consolation in either of these has already given up
Those people who fight for their lives, also

in great confusion, can do nothing else   For
them nothing exists but freedom's constraint   For some
it is murder, which damns them as humans
No one is without guilt   We ourselves, the doomed, are
singing   Now light's pitch rises   The human voice is alone

Translation from the Swedish by Rika Lesser

COMMENTARY

*What I cannot give up is the attempt to see   What / ever may happen
Whatever degradations come to life / in my body   I seek out people / who,
with the lives of their bodies, help me to see / My eyes are erotic   My intel-
ligence is erotic / All combinations are possible* (G. S.) And elsewhere: *Every
word / also carries / the whole of death.*

Writes Anselm Hollo: "Göran Sonnevi has been called a great number of
things: a modern-day Lucretius; a poet of the politics between individuals
and the politics between nations; an author of philosophical tracts on lin-
guistics disguised as poems; a revitalizer of the language of Swedish poetry.

"The breadth of his curiosity and learning (also made manifest in trans-
lations from Hölderlin, Pound, Mandelstam, Celan) is conveyed in mostly
short-lined poems of great musical and emotional intensity. Their formal
innovation consists of careful scoring on the page, a kind of projective verse
previously unknown in Swedish poetry. According to the critic Jan Olov
Ullén, the underlying rhythm of Sonnevi's poems is essentially a 4/4 rhythm
in which 'one of the lines corresponds to one bar.' When reading his work
in public, Sonnevi then challenges this basic rhythm by introducing empha-
ses, accents, where the audience may not expect to find them.

"Ambitious in their exploration of the most troubling subjects of our (and
any) time, e.g. abuse of power in all existing (and known) socioeconomic
systems, war, genocide, torture, exploitation, Sonnevi's poems always main-
tain a mode of intimate address to the individual. . . . 'Hell and Paradise /
are only limited aspects of the large construct / we chance to pass through
only for a time': there are moments when this scholar of Chomsky's linguis-
tics, quantum physics, biology, and political theory sounds like a postmod-
ern Jacob Boehme—and this may well be yet another reason why his work,
difficult as it is to translate, is known today in more than twenty languages."

Clark Coolidge b. 1939

•

Where is the wonder to not know?
It's an apparent of life, to take as apparent.
Visions seen, heard, felt, dropped for another,
repasted in a new cover, thought up and then
sent down again, traipsed for and wished
and then to see them snap back to sender but
not see the sender, I have grateful needs.
The words say. Nothing today is apparent,
just there, nowhere, bent over the task,
removal of the mask, the tendency to bow
and tend, kneel at the feet of the statue
of whole stone, white caps, inverted needs,
no one knows, no one knows better than to.
The path follows and portions weed lots and
the former goddess statues.
We See, is not allowed. But a frightening fan of
the forms beneath the curtain. I take a breath,
I style it. I am interminable at the dead
crystal that will never turn off. I laugh
and spin it. I did not laugh just then
as it hoops a shadow on the bright wood. Bright word.
Knuckle over the loops of what steadies to be said.
Sure to write all this down here, sure and doubt.
The crystal seems filled to slant line of terminus
but is itself a filling of all now empty whole.
Things holes in things, lights in stops, breathing
within hearing. A bath in blood, a hood over
the normal watcher, sipper at form's blade.

And where is the known wonder?
The seven, of which memory leaves vacant one,
or two. I take off its shoe and it
breathe on you. Who are me a hundred million
careless and sieved-off times or wavelets or
forks from the shine. You are me, I am

sure interminable. You, crystal, it and forgotten.
High and far and tiny on my bureau of born sheaf
and short regret. The knowing of which is interminable,
though as wonder short. A cry in the wood
that bends the limbs. A sheep in a frame
for later commission.

Sleek friendless tendencies.
Shock in reach of coldness at fingertip.
Calcium rates silicon, socket to terminal.
I put on the hat as a bow to truncation.
Linear life times five, times seven, times turn
at all, onlooker. The hats were beveled cones.
The nights were seeded in doubts, level fires,
coarse pocketed finds. The lock became the kicker.
The light a stone.

A kind of time. An implacable placement in
felt time diminish. Dots on a paper
of silk to decipher, waving tongs over a net
to seal the stars. Our fates are to motion
as sand is to shoe. Sound as a cap.
The termination is many, the directions of many.
The telephone will not ring in this seal of light.
This one pent of night. This stone, I throw you
away but you return. You have returned this shine.
You have spelled my shoe in a minute of melody, a
day far away now in horizons of leather.
The scroll not to bother. The ancient as a sever
as here today as any stone. My uncle put up
on a ranch his aerial in sand, but such is lie.
So I shift. I dream of putting my shirt over
the crystal to little help. And watch it that
the temperature settle. The words give me battle
in even rows and warm. And warn of war
at the homestead hearth, valve of the heart,
ear that won't start if the crystal rattle.
Not so, but once it bubbled.

Ancient as a spine, motor to whisper in the
wafter region. A Realm, zone of stood stone,
carved breath before a face could result. Or a
zircon in basement. Cold cereal on Xmas bulbs

in the room below Halloween. The pictures so
slow to frame, the crystal seen turning. Space
to colden the breath, husk of an anciency.
I walked out over the books, the street was so plain.
Vodka as standard, Tequila in a topaz
is what makes it yellow. The worm left out.
Slats and rulers the room warms, the time is coming up.
It will be left, you and I, to us only to turn.
You crystal, you lock my way. Lurking and looking
for familiars to play. The melody is firm
in the crystal of temper, little or no dot to enter.
As the freedom has withered, so goes the heat for your fate.
I mumbled and scattered, I would not sit for
what I knew. An empty light the cue.

For whatever you can't know you do write.
Sleeping stalk through the night, witless curvature.
Some anagrams of the Mock Crystal. Snail shell
of rust in the dream window. Humid practice
of the vermiform ways. Balanced on the skull
in a bed of potatoes. Hands never to
exit the sleeves and the camera still clicking.
Eyeholes in the seamless places. Going home
a matter of form as everyone has gone and done.
The nose, the petals of zinc, the goat at a door.
The liquid for which there is no rest or shiftless spot.
Dreams in which gardenias start and hop.
My own face lies without a trace.
And I write them with the greatest of wills to know
and so do not.

Let's stop. The crystal still spinning. Nothing to know yet
has a bearing. Withal apparent in such of a light
it should be ringing. My ankles should be humming.
And my eyes start turning. I lift my fire where
my hand should be, cool as caliper at the
rusty wood. Cancel, says the epigram,
cancel and begin. Start ash to confer upon
the light a breed. Standard of fright in
the crystal's place, in the crystal's stead
a match for the eyes.

.....I KICKED INTO
PRECISE
SPACE
WITHOUT TOUCHING.

I SPENT CHEESE
AS A SENTENCE. RAIN
TO
STOP
BREATHING.

BODY CLAW ENOUGH
TO SMILE A CRACK . LEAVE
THESE
THINGS

LIE ENOUGH TO GET BUILDING...

CLARK COOLIDGE

Fragments are our wholes. (C. C.) And again: *A sentence is a collapse. /
Time on itself. Lands. To resurface, / and stun in.*

Sound as Thought, the title of his 1990 collection, offers one description of
how Coolidge, who has continued to practice as a jazz drummer, attends to
the composition of his writings. If the early work investigated exploded
word morphologies to offer abstract or visual structures (his 1970 book
Space, for example), the work of the seventies (*The Maintains, Polaroid,
Quartz Hearts,* et cetera) investigated syntactic possibilities—in what could
be called a post-Steinian direction—that had a major impact on related ex-
periments by the Language Poets (page 662) & others. The work of the
eighties & nineties, while retaining the gains made, has moved into a more
autobiographical & lyrical/melodic mode (Kerouac has always been a ma-
jor source) with books such as *At Egypt* (written in response to a trip up the
Nile River), *Odes to Roba* (composed during a stay in Italy) or *The Crystal
Text* (excerpted here). The latter is a feat of close & sustained attention, a
book-length meditation on a colorless quartz crystal sitting on the writer's
desk. Of his poetic processes he has written (*Notebooks 1976–1982*): "To
create is to make a pact with nothingness. / The void exacts its tribute. What
price do / I daily pay for maintaining sufficient / ignorance to accept forms
when they emerge? / Writing, I sometimes feel I am working with / nothing.
Where are the words? Certainly not / here on this page. Their only firmness
seems in / sorts of motion. I am constantly emptied / by their infernal ob-
duration! Cursed forever / to listen to the voices inside there is no / stepping
back from. Where silence is a / blessed hell."

SOME "LANGUAGE" POETS

Compare / these two views / of what / poetry / is.
In the one, an instance (a recording perhaps) of reality / fantasy /
experience / event is presented to us through the writing.
In the other, the writing itself is seen as an instance of reality / fantasy /
experience / event.
CHARLES BERNSTEIN

> *desperately*
> > *life is quantity through a language*
> > > *substitute inventing music of a series*
> > *of changes very little understood*
> *binding men for driving through a new internal logic fire*
> > > *to fish*
> > > *of despair of failure for knowledge*
> *by way of despair for the road*

LYN HEJINIAN

It is not so much that the Language Poets—a configuration of American
writers emerging by the early 1970s—broke from their American & Eu-
ropean predecessors but that they forced attention from a dominant form
of experiential & expressive writing (in which language was the common
vehicle of content) to another, also ongoing range of experiment (in which
language became itself the thing in question). With a concurrent emphasis
on discourse & poetics—a willingness, even, to mix newly resuscitated
critical "theory" with hard-won & versatile poetic "theory-practice"—
they wrote with an energy that made even their derivations seem new,
becoming for a time the most visible American exponents of a continuing
(& global) "poetry of changes." Taking their discourse as a "debate" in
which "what is shared, at best, is a perception of what the issues might
be," Ron Silliman, as early spokesman, wrote: "These [issues] are not to
be underestimated. The nature of reality. The nature of the individual. The
function of language in the constitution of either realm. The nature of
meaning. The substantiality of language. The shape and value of literature
itself. The function of method. The relation between writer and reader."
To which he added, of the ensuing controversy around their poetics (both
theory & practice) & their shared attempt—as in Duchamp's earlier
view of art—*to put* [language] *once again at the service of mind:* "Much,
perhaps too much has been made of the critique of reference and norma-

tive syntax inherent in the work of many of [these] writers, without acknowledging the degree to which this critique is itself situated within the larger question of what, in the last part of the twentieth century, it means to be human."

Writes Michael Davidson, in what is probably the best capsule summary of all of that: "Language poetry emerged . . . as both a reaction to and an outgrowth of the 'New American Poetry,' as embodied by Black Mountain, New York School, and Beat aesthetics. Within the pages of little magazines like *Tottel's, This, Hills,* [*L=A=N=G=U=A=G=E, Poetics Journal*], and the Tuumba chapbook series, [the] poets . . . developed modes of writing that implicitly criticized the bardic, personalist impulses of the 1960s and explicitly focused attention on the material of language itself. . . . The response of language poetry to expressivism has taken several forms, most notably a deliberate flattening of tonal register and extensive use of non-sequitur. Experimentation in new forms of prose, collaboration, proceduralism, and collage have diminished the role of the lyric subject in favor of a relatively neutral voice (or multiple voices). Language poets have endorsed Victor Shklovsky's [Russian Futurist] notion of *ostranenie* or 'making strange' [volume one, page 220], by which the instrumental function of language is diminished and the objective character of words foregrounded. . . . [But] far from representing a return to an impersonal formalism, language poetry regards its defamiliarizing strategies as a critique of the social basis of meaning, i.e. the degree to which signs are contextualized by use. . . . By thwarting traditional reading and interpretive habits, the poet encourages the reader to regard language not simply as a vehicle for preexistent meanings but as a system with its own rules and operations. However, since that system exists in service to ideological interests of the dominant culture, any deformation forces attention onto the material basis of meaning production within that culture. If such a goal seems utopian, it has a precedent in earlier avant-garde movements from symbolism to futurism and surrealism. Rather than seeking a language beyond rationality by purifying the words of the tribe or by discovering new languages of irrationality, language poetry has made its horizon the material form rationality takes."

The poets represented here are from the two main centers of language poetry in the 1970s and 1980s: San Francisco (Hejinian, Silliman, Armantrout, Perelman, Watten, Harryman) and New York (Bernstein and Andrews). That the work—theirs and others'—continues to show individual character & presence is clear enough from the examples that follow.

More by Bernstein appears on page 446, by Hejinian on page 692.

Lyn Hejinian b. 1941

from MY LIFE

We are not
forgetting the
patience of the
mad, their love
of detail

The summer countryside, with the round hills patchy and dry, reminding one of a yellow mongrel dog, was what one could call a dirty landscape, the hills colored by the dusty bare ground rather than by grass, and yet this is what seemed like real country to me. I had idealized the pioneer's life, sinking roots. Known for its fleas. One could touch the flesh of their secrets, the roses of their behavior. A) Survey the whole B) lawn and note C) how near shadows D) increase the light. One didn't know what to give a young woman. Watermen are such as row in boats. They don't hear a word of all this, floating like plump birds along the shore. In extending, then entangling their concerns, they are given a thousand new names. The lace curtain Irish hate neighborhood Blacks. The coffee drinkers answered ecstatically. We looked at the apartment and took it. Space, has small neighborhoods. Idea 13.779: the same insanity of the invariable person. As for we who "love to be astonished," each new bit of knowledge is merely indicative of a wider ignorance. There are ecstasies of rock and of vacuum. One might cultivate a charming defect, say a romantic limp or a little squint. Reluctance. I made curtains out of colored burlap from Sears, hung them at the four windows of the green apartment. A few months earlier I had taken a creative writing class, and now I was painting on 3 by 3 canvases, on which with several intersecting continuous lines I drew the head with hair, neck, shoulders, face and hat but without shading, and I filled in the discrete spaces with separate tones from a carefully limited palette. There was threnodious roaring in the year, and I knew it was Freudian. Down manholes, through pipes, to the mysterious sea. Though the pantry smelled more strongly of spices than of herbs and was dominated by nutmeg, the kitchen itself tended to smell of everything that had ever been cooked, but only because it was dark. It formed a dense compact with boulders. If you cut your fingernails they will grow back thick, blunt, like a man's. In a little while, he said, we should be thumbing home. There were five little kittens under the car. They had put curves in the highway to keep drivers awake. The obvious analogy is with music, which extends beyond the space the figure occupies. She was pumping her violin over the piano. Each evening before dinner my parents sat for awhile in the "study," to talk, while my mother knit decoratively designed French sweaters called

Jacquard. The house sparrow is a weaver finch. The front door key is hidden under the aloe. How did the artist think to put that on the outside. Such displacements alter illusions, which is all-to-the-good. Now I too could find a perfect cantaloupe, not by poking at the flesh around the stem of the melon but by sniffing at it. At some point hunger becomes sensuous, then lascivious. Not a fuck but a hug. My mother threw away all those little objects of sentiment, billed foolishness. The reference is a distraction, a name trimmed with colored ribbons. It was Father's Day, a holiday that no one could take seriously, yet someone admitted that he was planning to telephone his parents that evening and another said she might do the same. What can those birds be saying. That day there was wind but no air, because we were inland. Then cataloguing the travel library I got the mania for panorama which predicts the desire for accurate representation. Is pink pretty.

Ron Silliman b. 1946

from **KETJAK**

Revolving door.

Revolving door. A sequence of objects which to him appears to be a caravan of fellaheen, a circus, begins a slow migration to the right vanishing point on the horizon line.

Revolving door. Fountains of the financial district. Houseboats beached at the point of low tide, only to float again when the sunset is reflected in the water. A sequence of objects which to him appears to be a caravan of fellaheen, a circus, camels pulling wagons of bear cages, tamed ostriches in toy hats, begins a slow migration to the right vanishing point on the horizon line.

Revolving door. First flies of summer. Fountains of the financial district spout. She was a unit in a bum space, she was a damaged child. Dark brown houseboats beached at the point of low tide—men atop their cabin roofs, idle, play a dobro, a jaw's harp, a 12 string guitar—only to float again when the sunset is reflected in the water. I want the gray-blue grain of western summer. A cardboard box of wool sweaters on top of the book case to indicate Home. A sequence of objects, silhouettes, which to him appears to be a caravan of fellaheen, a circus, dromedaries pulling wagons bearing tiger cages, tamed ostriches in toy hats, begins a slow migration to the right vanishing point on the horizon line.

Revolving door. Earth science. Fountains of the financial district spout soft water in a hard wind. How the heel rises and the ankle bends to carry the body from one stair to the next. She was a unit in a bum space, she was a damaged child. The fishermen's cormorants wear rings around their necks to keep them from swallowing, to force them to surrender the catch. Dark brown houseboats beached at the point of low tide—men atop their cabin roofs, idle, play a dobro, a jaw's harp, a 12 string guitar—only to float again when the sunset is reflected in the water. Silverfish, potato bugs. What I want is the gray-blue grain of western summer. The nurse, by a subtle shift of weight, moves in front of the student in order to more rapidly board the bus. A cardboard box of wool sweaters on top of the book case to indicate Home. A day of rain in the middle of June. A sequence of objects, silhouettes, which to him appears to be a caravan of fellaheen, a circus, dromedaries pulling wagons bearing tiger cages, fringed surreys, tamed ostriches in toy hats, begins a slow migration to the right vanishing point on the horizon line. We ate them.

Revolving door. The garbage barge at the bridge. Earth science. Resemblance. Fountains of the financial district spout soft water in a hard wind. The bear flag in the plaza. How the heel rises and the ankle bends to carry the body from one stair to the next. A tenor sax is a toy. She was a unit in a bum space, she was a damaged child, sitting in her rocker by the window. I'm unable to find just the right straw hat. The fishermen's cormorants wear rings around their necks to keep them from swallowing, to force them to surrender the catch. We drove through fields of artichokes. Dark brown houseboats beached at the point of low tide—men atop their cabin roofs, idle, play a dobro, a jaw's harp, a 12 string guitar—only to float again when the sunset is reflected in the water of Richardson Bay. Write this down in a green notebook. Silverfish, potato bugs. A tenor sax is a weapon. What I want is the gray-blue grain of western summer. Mention sex. The nurse, by a subtle redistribution of weight, shift of gravity's center, moves in front of the student of oriental porcelain in order to more rapidly board the bus. Awake, but still in bed, I listen to cars pass, doors, birds, children are day's first voices. A cardboard box of wool sweaters on top of the bookcase to indicate Home. Attention is all. A day of rain in the middle of June. Modal rounders. A sequence of objects, silhouettes, which to him appears to be a caravan of fellaheen, a circus, dromedaries pulling wagons bearing tiger cages, fringed surreys, tamed ostriches in toy hats, begins a slow migration to the right vanishing point on the horizon line. The implications of power within the ability to draw a single, vertical straight line. Look at that room filled with fleshy babies. We ate them.

Bob Perelman b. 1947

CHINA

We live on the third world from the sun. Number three. Nobody tells us what to do.

The people who taught us to count were being very kind.

It's always time to leave.

If it rains, you either have your umbrella or you don't.

The wind blows your hat off.

The sun rises also.

I'd rather the stars didn't describe us to each other; I'd rather we do it for ourselves.

Run in front of your shadow.

A sister who points to the sky at least once a decade is a good sister.

The landscape is motorized.

The train takes you where it goes.

Bridges among water.

Folks straggling along vast stretches of concrete, heading into the plane.

Don't forget what your hat and shoes will look like when you are nowhere to be found.

Coats in the window hung up on hooks; question marks where the heads would normally be.

Even the words floating in air make blue shadows.

If it tastes good we eat it.

The leaves are falling. Point things out.

Pick up the right things.

Hey guess what? What? *I've learned how to talk.* Great.

The person whose head was incomplete burst into tears.

As it fell, what could the doll do? Nothing.

Go to sleep.

You look great in shorts. And the flag looks great too.

Everyone enjoyed the explosions.

Time to wake up.

But better get used to dreams too.

NATIVE

How many constants *should* there be?

The slick wall of teeth?

The white stucco
at the corner,

flag on its porch
loosely snapping?

.

"Get to the point!"

as if before dark—

as if to some bench
near a four-way stop.

.

At what point does
dead reckoning's

net
replace the nest

and the body
of a parent?

.

The apparent

        present.

Here eucalyptus
leaves dandle,

redundant but syncopated.

Barrett Watten b. 1948

COMPLETE THOUGHT I – XXV

I

The world is complete.
Books demand limits.

II

Things fall down to create drama.
The materials are proof.

III

Daylight accumulates in photos.
Bright hands substitute for sun.

IV

Crumbling supports undermine houses.
Connoisseurs locate stress.

V

Work breaks down to devices.
All features present.

VI

Necessary commonplaces form a word.
The elements of art are fixed.

VII

A mountain cannot be a picture.
Rapture stands in for style.

VIII

Worn-out words are invented.
We read daylight in books.

IX

Construction turns back in on itself.
Dogs have to be whipped.

X

Eyes open wide to see spots.
Explanations are given on demand.

XI

Brick buildings shut down in winter.
A monument works to change scale.

XII

False notes work on a staircase.
The hammer is as large as the sun.

XIII

Connected pieces break into name.
Petrified trees are similar.

XIV

Everyday life retards potential.
Calculation governs speech.

XV

Rules stand out as illustrations.
People climb over piles of rock.

XVI

I am speaking in an abridged form.
Ordinary voices speak in rooms.

XVII

An act is comprehensible.
An explanation effaces words.

XVIII

Language ceases to be the future.
Thinking becomes a religious device.

XIX

Nothing touches the surface.
The arbitrary is meant to be sensed.

XX

False songs restore information.
Everyday elements are mixed.

XXI

Death is an accident.
A measure is given by use.

XXII

The air witnesses an abduction.
Motion isolates this effect.

XXIII

A single step makes a resolution.
A pile driver is not a device.

XXIV

Thought remains in the animal.
Each island steals teeth.

XXV

A true sensation buries its dead.
Thought is embedded.

Bruce Andrews b. 1948

"ZERO TOLERANCE"

Zero tolerance is too wet for me:

            fuck those plant names,
                tested in the ointment—

I'll put incentives back into bleach.

AKA

Lola the Elder.
Doc.
      sequence puzzles
Doc
      happiness
Hey, Doc.
      take care
wary
divest   whizzer
adore thee

or as it is even to have met

wed ballet
bulbs
     a lengthening
emotions equal
monaural romance
curvilinear statement

"a sweet prison of delight"
bullet in hair
svelte
in acorn
              artery pageant
where else
waved over Capital
     will cure disease
left no one honored with a covenant

     in the nineteenth century
     in the seventeenth century
     in the sixteenth century

an arrangement
          of syllables

women's bank

misanthropist

made of onionskin

Charles Bernstein b. 1950

OF TIME AND THE LINE

George Burns likes to insist that he always
takes the straight lines; the cigar in his mouth
is a way of leaving space between the
lines for a laugh. He weaves lines together
by means of a picaresque narrative;
not so Hennie Youngman, whose lines are strict-
ly paratactic. My father pushed a
line of ladies' dresses—not down the street
in a pushcart but upstairs in a fact'ry
office. My mother has been more concerned
with her hemline. Chairman Mao put forward
Maoist lines, but that's been abandoned (most-
ly) for the East-West line of malarkey

so popular in these parts. The prestige
of the iambic line has recently
suffered decline, since it's no longer so
clear who "I" am, much less who *you* are. When
making a line, better be double sure
what you're lining in & what you're lining
out & which side of the line you're on; the
world is made up so (Adam didn't so much
name as delineate). Every poem's got
a prosodic lining, some of which will
unzip for summer wear. The lines of an
imaginary are inscribed on the
social flesh by the knifepoint of history.
Nowadays, you can often spot a work
of poetry by whether it's in lines
or no; if it's in prose, there's a good chance
it's a poem. While there is no lesson in
the line more useful than that of the pick-
et line, the line that has caused the most ad-
versity is the bloodline. In Russia
everyone is worried about long lines;
back in the USA, it's strictly soup-
lines. "Take a chisel to write," but for an
actor a line's got to be cued. Or, as
they say in math, it takes two lines to make
an angle but only one lime to make
a Margarita.

OUTRIGGER

*"I've had my problems
with poetry before, but
I've never had to turn
my back on it."*

There is some goggling and conversation coming from the box.

spate of span	rate of Parsippany
circuitous to view	laryngeal to ensue
overlong to toward	ostrich toward titular

My gentle homeostasis is bordered
By a gargantuan twirling pinstripe

Thanks for your batter—I depreciate getting
your detractions and found none of what
you said to bake sense. The biennial
pushcart you raise about closure is certainly
one that I've had detonated at me
before and I only have a perfunktory
answer about the porkbarrel principle of cohesion.

Would you do me the flavor of buying that sty? Are we
taking the mar to my pastor's? Could you bring me if
the sail is here yet? Were there any palls? What crime
did you say the ruby stranded? How much is the icing
going to coast? Please pass the sloop.

S says we need a rood. J and Q climb
Out of the box and get some soard to prime
A rood with, then climb back in. E says, let's
Make sure now. J slides, two of the soards cough
And peek out. Somebody rums by, epaulettes
Duck down and try to slide the cover off.
J immediately grabs a rosette
Rood and droops it, sees the scale tip at rhyme,
Takes out a yellow pud. J stands in time,
Takes a soard, and tries to push E's vignette.
    Nonetheless is self-contained in a way
    But falls easily into the group play
    While the result tends toward removal
    What she wants satisfies her approval.

things in an effort put forward a general context
just to blithely praise, serenely harm
whose boat approaches valuation, closeness
emergent might have in form, of these in place
what guess does put me, thought it typifies
that I would try, confutation or conciliation
to so reverse, immobilize, variously polar ties

All bolted up & sorry for itself.
She is of thin built with dirty blond eyes and highly
articulated hair. Each limb flows gracefully into
the next, with the effortlessness of good thinking.

The glass is battering the hail. I go up to the
laundromat and tell her a piece of my dehiscence. For
example, steam, omit, purgative, dabloom. They shout
for a long time after this, get tired, then start
up again.

Evidentiary treetops in middle tooling.
Well, these folk don't know the difference between aelerons
and bedside manner. For example, puttering with
the doorjamb (floor plan). "I want to be alone, but not
by myself." The gallery system, the galley sys-
tem. Arcane when anthropoid—mark off, deprecate, flop.
Testy when under sectional. I'd part a hector
or fray with maize under penultimate sky. Fortu-
itous chocolate, or chewing on some peroxi-
dase return to (permanent chaise). So lasso that o-
pine, pin down that comeuppance, interrogate a shrub,
gesticulate totalization. Brand of brazen.
Brittle bounce to dazed delay, tiered with tiresome traffic.

by which in gentle disinter
did fold in vent
and pry with cautious honor
frail contempt, to free
its gash, evince its crepe

Carla Harryman b. 1952

NOT-FRANCE

I can't stuff myself anymore! (arguments in the form of noble people
and ventriloquists seep out of the mortar of the chateau at the time of
Louis XIV)

Death as observed by victims.

Death as observed by victims.

A death observed by a victim, death's victim. Something specific.

And so on.

Don't stop now.

Be as exact as possible.

Number four.

Number four! Death as observed.

Number five: In a theater, a piece of body rubbed on an erection.

More.

More.

Number six: Dies.

Number seven: The details, the details.

Number eight: Numbers take over the role of ventriloquists.

Number nine: A ventriloquist takes over the role of numbers: counting each hair as he pulls it out of his head.

Number 10: Dies.

Number 11: More.

Number 12: Another ventriloquist rises from the role of numbers and duplicates all previous actions, jerking the pecker of a nobleman every time he tears a hair out of his own head.

Number 13: A noblewoman announces the fall of the court of Louis XIV.

Number 15: Recount!

Number 16: Recount!

Number 17: Essay on redevelopment: the country. A number rips through the shirt of a noblewoman, who has announced the fall of the court from the stage. A ventriloquist grabs for the number which scissors through the woman's skirt and slinks into the woman's asshole just as the ventriloquist misses it. The ventriloquist. Is not protected.

Number 18: More detail.

Number 19: The ventriloquist plunges his hand into her ass and pulls it out screaming, minus a finger.

Number 20: The woman is consumed alive by the number cutting through her from the inside out.

Number 21: Announcement: death recounted by victims!

Number 22: As she dies, she is consumed by a heap of ventriloquists and numbers.

Number 23: Her sister is assigned to the task of making an encyclopedic account of the last day.

Number 24: The sister divides the day into days and the hours into days and the minutes into days and the seconds into days and the semi-seconds-into days all of whom, once invented, judiciously enter her into the logos, the loges, or the lodge named Sade. He comes later.

Number 25: The foul residue of the court of Louis XIV march with provisions counted and recounted toothless, sewn shut, welted, and bored open to a gash in the middle of the condition that is Not-France.

Pierre Guyotat b. 1940

from TALES OF SAMORA MACHEL

Sain-Peta's quarta, furra change, whynot, it's th'same fat bill for th'adult prost'tute wif'is whole attr'butes an' full performance! so much so's th'li'l pollack prost'tute, arready envies Sain-Peta's large turnova so'd he's even arready let'imself be seduc'd down under 'is marital hovel under th'morning airin' of th'matrimonial heaps' three varminous sheets plus attimes a polish quilt by th'tattoo'd Arab so's he dreams of 'is sexual horn in 'is mouth! but too bad that attimes 'is Arab comes t'satisfy hisself in Hot Sain-Peta's b'forehand stuffing hisself wif' 'alfa chicken at th'tabl' of th'second Arab arready flank'd by 'is fav'rite prost'tutes, attimes some beaut'ous rimmer born in Planfoy or some beaut'ous bumboy born in Pyfara or even some beaut'ous darkhair'd boy from L'Hermud kidnapp'd juss' as he was yokin' th'oxen team in predawn Ardèche an' instantly appoint'd cocksucker 'cause biglipp'd bigtongu'd capaciously cheek'd an' insidin th'Mercedes that expatriat's on whitewalld tires th'ever so beaut'ous darkhair to Sain'Etiann, th'three prost'tutes that make up th'second Arab's live-stock, an' afta to take him outa th'token'd agglu, th'well negotiat'd mama's tuffboy, tho th'second Arab he know nothin' 'bout how t'position him on th'starcase nor even attimes how t'adorn 'im! th'mama's tuffboy knows, he arready knows through some li'l breath breath'd by 'is Arab kidnapper how many million he's worth in Sain-Etiann's Hot Center, recalls even 'is Arab fing'rin' th'wads of th'transaction in front of 'is naked front vert'bras and th'last bill he rolls a cigar in 'is bellybutton, an', on th'rich fat pav'ment, Goodbyes 'im by complet'ly dedunging 'is bow'l of some thirty-three rimmings, groan'd, hoars'd, burp'd, succulated, yell'd wif no mouth-ta-mouth kissin' tho sometimes assmop-t'-assmop, too bad too bad th'l'il polack sonabitch, who gits 'is prize perfectly right from one Arab to th'next Arab down to th'last cent, sh'as missd goin' t'rub har feshness against th'coarse chesthair of Th'Anthracite insidin th'place of har dreams, an', instead, flaunts har prettyness in th'Hot Center! that all nak'd sh'leans thar 'er long russian cig'rette 'against har hip an' lowers har long khôl-veil'd eyes b'hind th'windows of th'whorehalls' doors, that thar sh'lets harself be touch'd in th'bellybutton, open like lips, har cock's horn up'gainst th'Black Vargin on har li'l silva chain, that instead of attimes to lie an' to groan with on top a' th'heap a' coalbags inna big embrace wif Th'Anthracite, sh'rejoices har spleen by leadin' th'roamin' of th'prost'tutes allround th'outside lit borders of th'brothel, windows, starcase, lowhall, splatter'd wif a thou an' one mosquitoes an' moths, volupt'ously sweaty, sh'an' har black-black brilliantin'd hairdo down t'har shoulders, all har manes th'same, the biggest swarm stuck t'har assmop, from agglu to ag-glu, from solo Arab t'solo Arab, tits shakin' insidin th'black remains of har red mane, not too too far, or t'remain solo sittin' on some sidewalk, th'gutter shiftin' its black garbage against th'sweat inside th'back of 'is knees, an' attimes 'is sexface snorts a split second tinkl's 'is fake gold ear-rings, three sim'lar rings in 'is sweet nostrils, three sim'lar in 'is Swollen Ball that rests well 'an hard against th'dry edge of th'sidewalk an' allofit at times b'spatter'd inna sec by any no matta what passaby Arab or not an' neverever any bit 'a streetrag ta wipe if off! yet so's attimes h'enjoys, th'mama's tuffboy kidnapp'd by 'is lov'd Arab, t'lick up th'public gobs an' then t'await patiently th'setting upof th'starcase exhibition to queue up thar so's t'git th'real males to bunch an' attimes make up as much as three agglus! an' h'is arready dreamin' of 'is first male gettin' ready in some Talaudiàr or Tarrnoir' hovel or onna trolleybus or at th'exit offa steel-works or arready inna showerstall of some coalmine bein' rimm'd! soonas h'is token'd, above or b'low some bench in th'lowhall, some fat Arab or other, at times up to thirty-three alternate rimmings as th'client with each stroke polish's 'is horn! an' attimes he drools big gobs a saliva nearly blood that run to th'gutter that 'is masta forces 'im arready at predawn to musk hisself allova very early an' th'khôl 'is vast long eyes to th'hilt so's th'Arab urchin'ry, right up against him, throws fistfuls a' cockroaches in 'is mane! an' take th'invarse third right offa th'polack prost'tute's skin, th'remains easy'nuff for th'whore ta parmenantly lubricate 'is cock in view of th'seventy-seven rimmings he dreams of doin' as rimmer, th'li'l polack! jusso as t'at times brilliantine thar mops, t'shove some insidin thar pet-tyshorts an' crawlers an' at times ta gobbl'up a third no matta thar small trade origins, an' all this urchen'ry why should they stuff 'emselv's with raw spittl' offa th'prost'tute ifnot t' grow up fasta more whorish if not t'eat thus attimes thar own future, as each an'all of 'em, arready carries inna 'is heart 'is favor'te white pimp, they all envy th'non Arab prost'tutes mektoub an'if sometimes th'prost'tute lingers 'is nak'dness too long on th'sidewalk, they'll gobbl' itup in three raw mouthfulls, th'Arab urchin'ry, an' await patiently for th'spittl' t'run t'live blood an' then quickly they throw th'emselvs upon that live thing that gives life an' turns th'eater int'a cannibal, 'cause t'become a prost'tute you gotta eat alot!! an' eacha these attimes 'levenyearold muslim urchins' so ardent they instantly play th'prost'tute's helpa for the li'l polack who knows arready that 'is masta, once th'last agglu's done, will right away feel up 'is tits wif'is large FLN-strangla's fingas that nothin' makes smooth, nothin', not even th'many wads 'a bills, rental sale cash social s'curity installments annuities medical care disposals in th'Furan, an' arready wif a li'l tinklin' noise h'sucks 'is earrings to th'blood, th'Fat Arab, arready he drags 'is well-munched nak'dness farall positions active passive blowa plus attimes beata-beaten attimes attimes a li'l bit incis'd for some passin' negro king, towards 'is ole manufrance mattress insidin 'is alcove an' easy tumbles 'im insidin 'is heav'ly musk'd an' varmin'd sheets attimes attimes well-squash'd pros-t'tutes coal or shit graffiti an' too bad th'Arab, attimes only lightly dress'd in some ready-ta-wear shorts or harden'd by so an' so many jismin's trying t'valuate th'merchandise or brandin' afta th'capture of some runaway prost'tute, an' cuddl's up thigh 'gainst thigh wif 'is beaut'ous li'l polack whore an rightoff kisses wif heavy saliva never'ver colgat'brushd an' whis-pers a runnin' comm'nt'ry into th'dirt inna 'is small ear 'bout th'day's la-bor at th'three agglus! an', simultan'ously, lifts up 'is ass to rim 'im front-wise, he don't mind eatin' some 'alf-chick'n or some cake right thar' an' until predawn th'fat batnaite rims th'li'l polack's entrails so much so at-times th'li'l slave heart reregrets that he's not yet not yet Th'Anthracite's helpa!....

Translation from the French by Pierre Joris

COMMENTARY

Samora Machel, then, is this: the verb, perhaps in its pure state.

The character has nothing to do with the real Samora Machel, the presi-dent of Mozambique. I've never met him, I have no idea what he is like. I just find the name very appealing.

The text begins as words in the mouth of someone who evokes the figure of Samora Machel. The person talks and talks about him until finally he becomes Samora. The initial mouth thus becomes the mouth of Samora, which in turn engenders other mouths. It is a relay of voices. The story begins in Lisbon where a child is stolen by some pimps. We move through North Africa, Marseille, the Barbès section of Paris. The work treats pros-titution on a grand, visionary scale: the total prostitutional existence.
P. G.

Of Guyotat's work, pitched as it is at a demotic level matching the intensities of poetry, Stephen Barber writes: "Guyotat is a reviled and revered figure in France. His books have astonished and appalled their readership with their raw physical power. He has been acclaimed as the only writer alive who is creating a new language. He has said: 'There is something inside me that makes it necessary for me to go further, always further into aberration.' . . . Born in . . . a remote mountainous region of southern France[,] he has writ-ten obsessively from his first years. As a child, he masturbated constantly while writing, and his first manuscripts (as he narrates in his 'seminal' text of the early 1970s, *The Language of the Body*) are extraordinary visual co-agulations of semen, ink, dirt, and blood. As a teenager, he became a soldier in the Algerian colonial war and was arrested for inciting soldiers to desert and kept imprisoned for three months in a hole in the ground. . . . His legendary novel of atrocity and extreme cruelty, *Eden, Eden, Eden* . . . was banned as 'pornographic' by the French Ministry of the Interior on its publication [1970] and remained under governmental censorship for eleven years. The book is a courageous and unique exploration into the virulent matter of sex, language, and the human body. It is lethal and it has no precedent. Guyotat has declared: 'The very origin of the whole system of literature has to be attacked.'" (From the introduction to the English translation of *Eden, Eden, Eden,* Creation Books, London, 1995.)

Wrote Edmund White: "He is the last great avant-garde visionary of our century." And Roland Barthes: "A new landmark and a starting-point for new writing."

Mohammed Khaïr-Eddine 1941–1995

REFUSAL TO INTER

I do not weep over this hooted blood
but a flight of buzzards
blood-high carries its irremediable facture
with the sluice where death leans against my eye

sun
your crutches patently puncture
the brief scream of earth thrown at the sky

my chest is a badly fastened caisson
and which jumps better than cricket
through the silence of my eye
through the savor of the echoless rock
where the Berber laps up its retinas

by your death
André Breton
refused by the tomb whose eye has tendrilled the sun
by the day's only murder boozing
with the hemlocks poured on your dialects

but given that in me war is a mutilated affair
because dream is a soap that doesn't wash me
of virid men
who revolt the dead wave of the seas being born
specter
        me alone watched by all my gestures
executed however by weather worse than the poem
        the true weather burns its hair in the red honey
        of our voices
when negation carries this man on her tits
towards the highest havoc whence purity flares
freedom which is neither milk nor star nor reason
virility police nor joy of dead season
but this unflappable blood
under your finger nails
it's said death but what's a star without a cave
a head
if not the target offered to the present knotted to crime

strange
strange threat!
Every wind carries my death perfectly signed and dated but I tell all winds
Here is my death and I discover myself all the better given that my ex-
tremeties no longer need to be. I hand out my death like sugar almonds—
in the one street that comes to nothing more solid than a glance rusted by
absence and a sad plight. Your death is not a death a box of matches aban-
doned along a bar nor a glass of white wine nor a pod of dread on the
fundamental floorboards where poetry rests pregnant and that wouldn't
drool for all the gold horrified in front of the placid and solitary spectacle
of our systematic burials.
Go gag poetry!

The last word doesn't exist. The dynamite of the first word suffices.
Men my powder kegs; men immunized against man;
man you who don't have time to doubt;
man who lap up your spittle and don't limp in reverse;
man lost glance;
when poetry had reached the greenest of deliriums and the desert had
handed all its water back to this uninterrupted unease that animated you
André Breton
when man had blown out the true Aladdin's lamp

when Ali Baba had dynamited Nothingness
when Jesus had finished devouring his cross
when Mohammed had rolled enough money to kick all the buckets
the eye faced me
I sell my death.
I am wounded in the trunk
—apple tree
old armor
to be forbidden neither to Adam nor to Eve
but to the atomic silence that stipulates me
to the millions of second-hand skins I will wear
at the anthology of the burned world

But why massacre oneself to save only one word hollowed out by termites a
house that collapses as soon as one enters

I SALUTE THIS HORSE FALLEN FROM THE HIGHEST PEAK
ANDRE BRETON
FROM WHENCE POETRY FUSES LIKE A FAERIE
POETRY MY MORGUE MY SERENITY AND MY SHIPWRECK

Translation from the French by Pierre Joris

BARBARIAN

to be but to be a crow with claws vicious enough
to cling amidst your korans of unheard-of naphthas
amidst kuwaits of panegyrics
and star-eggs smashed against bad weather

muslim I am until autumn fakirs
take all of my alphabet my luculent costumes
I am sealed with detonations
and sulfur pits collapsed on the waves's tympani

lianas heard
by the geysers of my secrets of blood and amber
of myrrh and insurrections

the gun barrel beatings of the sun the red-handed butts
in eructations of boas
in imbecility of peril
my body of guano and foam
my cutthroat soul

butting
neither the street like a scar flowered with the pollen
of the navels
it is not the weapon
this nursery of words without cure
kills me hits crucifies me
following a sleep of whales

I am a ramadan of the Great Bear who roars
a gratin of bitter larvae

but you nosed around beri-beri tumescences
skinning the vast river of rubber nights
my thought eroded by tumblers of bad blood

I spit out my heart
my name of a white fig tree by the glance of the mosquitos
back to front with the saying of the stamens
like your flesh scanned by insults
lousy argan tree of barbary
I work
in the caviar of your pupils
I circle and undo your henna smile
ringdove with dragonfly wings counting its era
at the gaslamp of the cities in hideaways
you redly twist my dawn
stewed in the alcohol of brawls
with an acrid stench of incongruous reigns
that the last mirage of flutes brings me
with fire-owls in the wind's tonsure
squinting mustang
on the chests without epitaphs

to be but to be and of your bloods
gnaw the indicator monsoon

Translation from the French by Pierre Joris

I write. I do what I have to do. It falls to the readers to educate themselves in reading . . . and in rereading in order to understand. Doing exactly that they will become revolutionaries by distancing themselves from their daily drudgery, from their little habits.

M. K.-E.

Born in the Southern Moroccan Berber village of Tafraout, Khaïr-Eddine moved to Casablanca as a child (a time overshadowed by the bitter trauma of his father's repudiation of his mother) & later worked briefly in Agadir in the wake of the earthquake that destroyed that city (its name became the title of his first book) before moving to Paris in 1965. His violent & outspoken opposition to the Moroccan regime & to all religion, including Islam, made a return to his country impossible until his last years (trying to return on one occasion he was immediately jailed). The core figure of the Moroccan avant-garde movement connected with the magazine *Souffles* (founded by Abdellatif Laabi in 1966), Khaïr-Eddine & his work are usefully contextualized by critic Hedi Jaouad: "Along with the Algerian Kateb Yacine, Khaïr-Eddine can be credited with introducing new and original literary techniques to the Maghreb: stream-of-consciousness, splintered persona, multiple perspectives and other techniques of discontinuity. . . . In his poetic manifesto, *Poésie toute*, . . . Khaïr-Eddine extols a poetics of violence to be carried out against all established orders and conventions—language, society, religion and morality. . . . The most important theme . . . is that of wandering. Whether expressed in geographical, temporal, mythical, or imaginary terms, wandering has been the constant symbol of the Maghrebian malaise[:] . . . [people] relentlessly driven by a desire to seek change, to seek a new social order or a new mode of expression. . . . The tone, rhythm, and themes characteristic of his poetics of violence recall the rebellious and iconoclastic poetry of Lautréamont, Rimbaud, Artaud, and Césaire. More importantly, Khaïr-Eddine has been instrumental, though his '*guerilla linguistique*' [linguistic guerilla warfare], in challenging the hegemony of French language and culture."

Simon Ortiz b. 1941

From an interview:

Why do you write? Who do you write for?

Because Indians always tell a story. The only way to continue is to tell a story and that's what Coyote says. The only way to continue is to tell a story and there is no other way. Your children will not survive unless you tell something about them—how they were born, how they came to this certain place, how they continued.

Who do you write for besides yourself?

For my children, for my wife, for my mother and my father and my grandparents and then reverse order that way so that I may have a good journey on my way back home.

THE WISCONSIN HORSE

*It is late at night, lying
drunk on the floor, hearing
a church bell across the
street, remembering that
Wisconsin Horse
this Spring.*

One step at a time to return.

The horse across the road
stands within a fence,
silent in the hot afternoon.

A mile north is some construction.
I tell the horse,
"That's America building something."

A mile further through a clump of trees
is a river.

The Wisconsin Horse is silent.

The bell clamors
against the insides of my skull.
It has nothing to do with sound
that can comfort.

The clamor wants to escape
its barriers.
I want it to escape.
I have no defenses.
I should be an eager Christian

hungry for salvation,
or at the very least accept smugness
bound tightly in plastic.

Yet, at this single point in my life,
I know only a few bare things:
the floor, the walls around me,
that bell across the street,
that despair is a miserable excuse for emptiness,
that I should echo louder
that call for salvation
which at this point I know
is a need to fill the hollows
and pockets of my body.

Despair is such a poor excuse
to exclude things from my life,
to allow them to slip
from safe places.

   But now, and not too soon,
in, this dark night,
having gotten up to write,
I make this offering:
that Wisconsin Horse I saw
standing in the hot afternoon,
staring through a chainlink fence
at the construction going on
only a mile away,
I wonder now if the horse still stands
silent in the dark night,
dreamless and stifled,
having no recourses left
except to hope his silence
will soon go away
and the meaningfulness enter.

"You ever pick up a rail?
With your bare hands." Your sweat
burning in your eyes. Blood. Heart.
Skin. Bones. And they died too.
"I hope." How much they hated,
how much they hoped. How much.

American Fork, Utah, February, 1959.
Dear Mama & Children,
I hope you are all well
as I am. Children, help your mother
and take care of each others
and around our home. Remember
that you must always love
your mothers. Think of the prayers
for the land. Mama, I wish
I was home with all of you.
I will be home in a few weeks.
I love you all. Make sure
you feed the horses. My love
and hugs to each of you and Mama,
     Daddy.

Saw him in Seligman.
Or was it Valentine. Or Phoenix.
Or somewhere. "He step off
the train. That was the last time
I saw him. My friend." Tears.
Wine doesn't work. They died too.

One week, two weeks, three weeks,
months, we waited. Years.
Train. O Daddy, O Daddy. Train
would come thundering, thundering
thundering toward us. Hearts.
Blood. Bones and skin. Love
and hope. O Daddy. Please train.

The children would laugh or cry
or be so silent.
The women were so angry.

Yes, we would wait again. Weeks, weeks, months, but not those years
again. O Daddy, never those years. Never again those years. Our own
solution will be strength: hearts, blood, bones, skin, hope and love. The
woman anger and courage risen as the People's voice again.

FINAL SOLUTION: JOBS, LEAVING

They would leave
on Sundays from the depot in Grants.
It seemed always, always, so final.
Goodbye. Goodbye Daddy. Daddy,
please come back. Please don't go.
Daddy. But they would leave.

    Winslow.
           Flagstaff.
                Seligman.
Barstow.

We had to buy groceries,
had to have clothes, homes, roofs,
windows. Surrounded by the United States,
we had come to need money.

The solution was to change,
to leave, to go to jobs.

                Utah.
California.
           Idaho.
              Oregon.

The children would cry.
The women would be so angry.
So angry.
Silent, we left.
We didn't want to leave, but
we left.

"I don't want you and your brothers
to ever have to work for the railroad."
They kept the railroad repaired,
and the trains raced through
their land. Hearts. Blood. Bones
and skin. Wrenched muscles.

The woman was telling about her grandson who was telling the story which was told him by somebody else. All these voices telling the story, including the voices in the story—yes, it must be an old one. (S. O.) And elsewhere: *Like myself, the source of these narratives is my home.*

Ortiz, then, is a poet with a poetics: in brief, a sense of source. The source & home he speaks from is Acoma (that "sky-high pueblo" in New Mexico), while the language he writes in is English—Acoma-ized, he tells us: a captured, special English, with the fat & gristle of the other language showing through it, giving it its special taste. This has made him not only the foremost American Indian poet of his time (which may be enough to say) but a part of a still larger company of poets, inventing for this continent—perhaps this *world*—of exiles a possible new "people poetry" that struggles—both succeeds & fails—to bring the land & its inhabitants together. What sets his work apart from the others' (Williams's *Paterson,* say, or Olson's Gloucester, Dorn's *Gunslinger,* Baraka & others' connection to the "Blues People" & the African American life) is that he's grown up as a man of Acoma—in one of the surviving, true cultures of the North American continent. From Acoma he travels out & to Acoma he returns, against the odds at times, as source. He is, sometimes painfully, aware of himself as part of a lineage, an oral tradition going—in his case—directly from father to son. The tradition itself is the talisman for the *return,* and the return (the "good journey" as title of his earlier selected poems) is the individual counterpart of the group's survival. Nor is it a betrayal of his Acoma origins (his first language was Keresan, his Indian name: Hihdrustse) that the language in which he writes is English. It is his own English, & through it his voice (& thus the voices behind his voice) reaches from Acoma to speak to other Indians, to other Americans, & to whatever world at large will hear him.

More of Ortiz's work appears in volume one.

Lyn Hejinian b. 1941

OXOTA

Book 2

Chapter Seventy-One: Truth

Truth is not precision but evidence
Body and truth at the thought
Crazy who says no longer and is quickly repeated

To hover and hum at the truth (so much longer to love)
To hush
Over ground under cloud as expedient as expands
Nothing had—no moral outrage, no self-righteousness, no indignation
Just residue
An all-over corporeal stamina
There isn't really room for truth—gray birches in full
    context—but room for both
As always, as ambient, and as bound
Just as blue, the procedure, reflects
The truth that is halted is squandered
Even the lull is dependent

Chapter Seventy-Two: Nature

The frost falls from a tree
We have a state of nature
Maybe I need the tree—it will acknowledge and thereby authorize me
Nature as describer—with the Russian names for things
Nature, which I regard across the table of which it's the proprietor
It is the third (inhuman) person
Waning interest, sugar rationing, a thumb before the moon without
    hypocrisy
The natural part of that thought is from a dream
I in my progress passing this
A hunter is in its artlessness
Nature results in the lack of privacy (personality) that would go with it
It pursues the impersonal narrative—here, our endless it
So I was feeling an inferior weariness, an inability to acknowledge
    anything
It was snowing, and the snow was rippled by the people walking in it
    while at the same time the people were reflected in it

Chapter Seventy-Three: Innocence

I was afraid to look—two men overheard in the dark were speaking of
    prison
I wasn't innocent, though I meant to be
An ant travelled to the end of each pubic hair

The colonel's coat was guarding the trolley's innocence
One man said he remembered as a boy climbing through a gap in a fence
Language was needed there for understanding, not for speech
Eventually everything turns back and it's voluptuous to repeat
The thin white rim of the hole reflects the black light of the lamp
One falls through that hole in memory
Vasya remembered looking through that hole in 1935 but only one time
    and seeing that the ground on the other side was heaving as "enemies"
    died
Innocence sustaining
Stains of splattered cherries in the stairwell—throat
Rain—the window shut
It all originates in a mistaken sighting

Chapter Seventy-Four: Conspiracy

Here—there's a feeling of snow near the eyes
Two suns would form
A basket of nothing—hieroglyphic
In those circles conspiracies were not fastidious
They told everything—how many fish heads resulted, where the poison-
    green flowers of lightning had shook, the exact (and still evident) mo-
    ment the Bulgarian clock broke
Every glint was bulging
There were intricacies covering such authenticity
And why not—it came down to the anecdote and then rose again
Pragmatism recounted
Over and over—there is conspiracy in repetition
Windings in what dissipates
A conspiracy is made within resistance to distraction
They had no secrets—they were lost in the comparison
Highly significant, filled with sense, centrifugal symbols swirled

Chapter Seventy-Five: Passion

Passion is the alienation that love provides
Drifting winter tinted where we lifted, plowed
Jealousy is a flake of a different passion
It was hungry to be plunging in disruption

The wobble and mattering of the sensing muscles which combine
People are not joined in passion but divulged
They diverge—but that sight was unseen
But all this is muffled in banalities, I said
It is not passion to nod in
It is passion for no one to listen
One with closed eyes and the other one's opened
The snowfall offered all the colors of apple
There was passion in its thud and exhilaration
Patience itself pushes over—given a body for what

Chapter Seventy-Six: Design

Pushkin's body had apparent lively symmetry
Or someone's intellectual resource prematurely
Poor body—every person is somewhat designed
It drew up—each bus a blossom on the tangled bus vines
There were so many places in which we didn't sit that where we did
    seemed, well, preordained or little used
We rode in time like rhymes and counted stops to Gorky
Gavronsky was rubbed by egg, Gavronskaya sucked through the shell,
    and Pushkin died
Pushkin designed—with pressure
We oscillated toward the city center and later back again
Pushkin lay naked in his room on the rug writing in solitude or visiting
    with friends
The breath and body heat of Pushkin steamed
The fog on the windows gleamed— dripped
It was design but without climb
We jumped from the sweating bus—there were clusters of buildings in
    every direction numbered without sequence but after a time we sorted
    them out and arrived at Sasha's with our bottles of wine

Chapter Seventy-Seven: Suffering

A stench left from cooking fish lay frenzied, fell inert
Or a yellow rose frustrated in the Summer Garden
Mayakovsky said that horses never commit suicide because they don't
    know how to talk—they could never explain their suffering

Each night has wiped a suffering diagonally—in such conditions each
     voice and face becomes distorted
From a neighboring building an infant has been crying for five hours
With seething or mellifluous endurance—Arkadii said nothing could be
     recognized
A seep in suffering—loss is different
Sight gone, blood poisoned, sleepless, anonymous along the street
Along the bottom of the foot dogs barked, a pendulum swung
Or the pendulum tossed
Now the next generation is suffering, Tynianov told Shklovsky; we
     turned out to be poor nourishment and they are bad eaters
Each suffering adds to the unrecognizable
The time has arrived
Night, interrupted, follows another night

Chapter Seventy-Eight: Betrayal

There were wives to follow the Decembrists, among them Pushkin lovers
To a Siberia of sex? a cold of poetry?
And no betrayal nor clarity for sex—he might then have been a bottle
That is an interest—betraying logic at any level
Someone in camouflage rasps out a prison song
But how could he travel?
Imperfect openings—they are reflections
Betrayal is a kind of mirror (art is not)
One colonel betrayed the other, but within mere weeks they were just
     two indistinguishable fellows, twins reflected in the mud
At enmity while at empathy
Total disappearance is the goal of each activity
We have abandoned our fidelity to big things, Olya explained
But in small we don't betray
The fact itself comes to its limits, in its visits, of which we speak in words
     having nothing in common with the fact of its existence

Chapter Seventy-Nine: Death

The back of the head waits for death
The feeling of weakness, a gentle indifference
The tree of language sheds too much foliage

It is death to be without shadow
Each head is a mound—the case is empty
What is it thinking?—but it can't be thinking
It had no difference
It must be by itself—I'm slightly terrified
Someone was embracing the air above it
And it's virtually invisible to me, my bulge above the nape
It can't speak—and yet it greets you
It keeps no memories
I would like to believe it, but it's the same as waiting
Why not have waited

Chapter Eighty: Redemption

Two rams, which ram redeemed
One ram wasted, one ram waiting
Maybe the same ram—in romance wandering
In descriptions crossing and saw things
Barges hardly higher than the surface of the water bore meat bones slip-
    ping under the bridges
At two a.m. the bridges rose for bigger boats, then fell at 4:55, and rose
    at five again
We sped across—the Lada rammed through the falling snow
The trees shook, atoning for momentum
Where we say "he's a crook" they say "he's a corner"
The notorious Russian soul, fulfilling our goal
We were laughing at the Russian novel
We will say, the slower you go the farther you'll get and plain water is
    glad to get a crow
We will be redeemed, we will be rescued
We will believe everything we say

COMMENTARY

*Because we have language we find ourselves in a peculiar relationship to
the objects, events, and situations which constitute what we imagine of the
world. Language generates its own characteristics in the human psycho-
logical and spiritual condition. This psychology is generated by the strug-
gle between language and that which it claims to depict or express, by our
overwhelming experience of the vastness and uncertainty of the world and*

by what often seems to be the inadequacy of the imagination that longs to know it, and, for the poet, the even greater inadequacy of the language that appears to describe, discuss, or disclose it.

This inadequacy, however, is merely a disguise for other virtues.

L. H. (from *The Rejection of Closure*)

It is those other virtues—a web of complexities (& *meanings*)—that mark her work / her life as a poet. That work has made her—to this day—a germinal figure in the movement that revivified an experimental sense of language-centered poetry (page 662) & put it for a time at the center of our consideration. Along with her engagement in the poetry enterprise in general—her coeditorship with Barrett Watten of *Poetics Journal,* say, or her close collaboration with the Russian poet Arkadii Dragomoschenko (below)—her own poetry has gone (through language & a genuine—not academic—strategy of deconstruction) into areas of identity & self-representation presumably off-limits for late-twentieth-century language writing. Her best-known work in this area is *My Life* (page 664), an extended poem (in prose) that represents, as poet Michael Davidson describes it, "the most extreme version of a personalist or autobiographical impulse . . . [while it] rejects the idea of a single, unified subject and the narrative logic by which it may be constituted." As a further strategy—not merely formal but touching on the sacred (numerical) roots of all poetry—"Hejinian has controlled the arrangement of memories, incidents, and associations by limiting the number of sentences per chapter and the number of chapters overall to thirty-seven, the age at which she wrote *My Life*" (Davidson). In a similar vein—formal *and* personal—*Oxota* is a work inspired by Pushkin's *Evgeny Onegin* & composed like its model of 270 fourteen-line stanzas, but with the focus on a contemporary Russia glimpsed in her travels since the early 1980s. Writes Hejinian of where it starts & where it takes her: "A word is a bottomless pit."

Mahmoud Darwish b. 1942

from MEMORY FOR FORGETFULNESS

Two Excerpts

I

Out of one dream, another dream is born:
—*Are you well? I mean, are you alive?*
—*How did you know I was just this moment laying my head on your knee to sleep?*

—*Because you woke me up when you stirred in my belly. I knew then I was your coffin. Are you alive? Can you hear me?*

—*Does it happen much, that you are awakened from one dream by another, itself the interpretation of the dream?*

—*Here it is, happening to you and to me. Are you alive?*

—*Almost.*

—*And have the devils cast their spell on you?*

—*I don't know, but in time there's room for death.*

—*Don't die completely.*

—*I'll try not to.*

—*Don't die at all.*

—*I'll try not to.*

—*Tell me, when did it happen? I mean, when did we meet? When did we part?*

—*Thirteen years ago.*

—*Did we meet often?*

—*Twice: once in the rain, and again in the rain. The third time, we didn't meet at all. I went away and forgot you. A while ago I remembered. I remembered I'd forgotten you. I was dreaming.*

—*That also happens to me. I too was dreaming. I had your phone number from a Swedish friend who'd met you in Beirut. I wish you good night! Don't forget not to die. I still want you. And when you come back to life, I want you to call me. How the time flies! Thirteen years! No. It all happened last night. Good night!*

I   I   I   I   I   I   I

Three o'clock. Daybreak riding on fire. A nightmare coming from the sea. Roosters made of metal. Smoke. Metal preparing a feast for metal the master, and a dawn that flares up in all the senses before it breaks. A roaring that chases me out of bed and throws me into this narrow hallway. I want nothing, and I hope for nothing. I can't direct my limbs in this pandemonium. No time for caution, and no time for time. If I only knew—if I knew how to organize the crush of this death that keeps pouring forth. If only I knew how to liberate the screams held back in a body that no longer feels like mine from the sheer effort spent to save itself in this uninterrupted chaos of shells. "Enough!" "Enough!" I whisper, to find out if I can still do anything that will guide me to myself and point to the abyss opening in six directions. I can't surrender to this fate, and I can't resist it. Steel that howls, only to have other steel bark back. The fever of metal is the song of this dawn.

What if this inferno were to take a five-minute break, and then come what may? Just five minutes! I almost say, "Five minutes only, during which I could make my one and only preparation and then ready myself for life or death." Will five minutes be enough? Yes. Enough for me to sneak out of this narrow hallway, open to bedroom, study, and bathroom with no water, open to the kitchen, into which for the last hour I've been ready to spring but unable to move. I'm not able to move at all.

Two hours ago I went to sleep. I plugged my ears with cotton and went to sleep after hearing the last newscast. It didn't report I was dead. That means I'm still alive. I examine the parts of my body and find them all there. *Two eyes, two ears, a long nose, ten toes below, ten fingers above, a finger in the middle.* As for the heart, it can't be seen, and I find nothing that points to it except my extraordinary ability to count my limbs and take note of a pistol lying on a bookshelf in the study. An elegant handgun—clean, sparkling, small, and empty. Along with it they also presented me with a box of bullets, which I hid I don't know where two years ago, fearing folly, fearing a stray outburst of anger, fearing a stray bullet. The conclusion is, I'm alive; or, more accurately, I exist.

2

I'll try to sleep now. What's sleep? What's this magical death spread with the names of the vine? A body, lead-heavy, is thrown into a cotton cloud by sleep. A body that soaks up sleep as an uncared-for plant absorbs the scent of the dew. I go into sleep slowly, slowly, to the rhythm of distant sounds, sounds arriving from a past scattered over the wrinkles of the days and my bed. I knock on the door of sleep with muscles alternately tense and lax. It opens its arms for me. I ask permission to go in, and it is granted. I go in. I thank it. I praise it.

Sleep is calling me, and I'm calling it. Sleep is blackness gradually crumbling to white and gray. Sleep is white. A separation, and white. An independence, and white. Soft, strong, and white. Sleep is the waking of fatigue, and its last moan; and it is white. Sleep has a white earth, a white sky, and a white sea; and strong muscles, muscles made of jasmine flowers. Sleep is master, prince, king, angel, sultan, and god. I abandon myself to it as a lover abandons himself to the praises of his first love. Sleep is a white charger flying on a white cloud. Sleep is peace. Sleep is a dream, born out of a dream.

Are you alive?

In a middle region between life and death.

Are you alive?

How did you know I was just this moment laying my head on your knee to sleep?

Because you woke me up now, when you stirred in my belly. Are you alive?

I don't know. I don't want to know. Does it often happen that I am awakened from one dream by another, itself the interpretation of the dream?

That's what's happening now. Are you alive?

As long as I'm dreaming, I'm alive; the dead don't dream.

Do you dream much?

When I'm approaching death.

Are you alive?

Almost, but in time there's room for death.

Don't die.

I'll try not to.

Did you love me then?

I don't know.

Do you love me now?

No.

Man doesn't understand woman.

And woman doesn't understand man.

No one understands anyone.

And no one understands anyone.

No one understands.

No one . . .

No one.

The sea is walking in the streets. The sea is dangling from windows and the branches of shriveled trees. The sea drops from the sky and comes into the room. Blue, white, foam, waves. I don't like the sea. I don't want the sea, because I don't see a shore, or a dove. I see in the sea nothing except the sea.

I don't see a shore.

I don't see a dove.

Translation from the Arabic by Ibrahim Muhawi

I want a language that I can lean on and that can lean on me, that asks me to bear witness and that I can ask to bear witness.
M. D.

A statement glossed as follows by Ibrahim Muhawi, his translator: "The Arabic root meaning 'bearing witness,' *shahida,* also produces 'gravestone' or 'epitaph,' *sha:hid,* and 'martyr,' *shahi:d*—words that echo throughout the work. Here, writing is history's witness, its epitaph: both *sha:hid.*" Darwish's push (in fourteen books of verse & seven of prose since 1964) is thus central to this century's poetics: his is a poetry of witnessing. (See, among others, Celan & Jabès in this volume, or Akhmatova & Césaire in volume one.) With regard to his life work, then, Darwish, after difficult early years in Palestine, moved to Cairo in 1971, to Beirut in 1972, & after 1982 to Paris via Tunis, Cairo, & other Arab cities. In 1973 he joined the Palestine Liberation Organization, became a member of its executive committee in 1987, but resigned in 1993. If the early fame is based on a political poetry of resistance, his own aim is wider: "I am not solely a citizen of Palestine, though I am proud of this affiliation . . . but I also want to take up the history of my people and their struggle from an aesthetic angle that differs from the prevalent and repeatable meanings readily available from an unmediated political reader."

Of *Memory for Forgetfulness* (a book-length work that grew out of the Israeli invasion of Lebanon in 1982—its opening & closing pages are excerpted here), Muhawi writes further: "What Darwish attempts is a pure gesture in which writing itself becomes the dominant metaphor. He offers us a multivocal text that resembles a broken mirror, reassembled to present the viewer with vying possibilities of clarity and fracture. On the page different kinds of writing converge: the poem, both verse and prose; dialogue; Scripture; history; myth; myth in guise of history; narrative fiction; literary criticism; and dream visions. . . . Although this inclusiveness reflects breakdown, it also embodies a synthesis. Suspended between wholeness and fracture, the text, like Palestine, is a crossroads of competing meanings."

John Taggart b. 1942

MONK

1

A-bide   a-   a-
bide

     fast falls
     the   tide

     fast

the darkness deepens   .

2

     with   abide
     with

When others   fail
              fail
              fail

    comforts flee
    fail   flee

3

abide with me

abide with me

me   me

SLOW SONG FOR MARK ROTHKO

I

To breathe and stretch one's arms again
to breathe through the mouth to breathe to
breathe through the mouth to utter in
the most quiet way not to whisper not to whisper
to breathe through the mouth in the most quiet way to
breathe to sing to breathe to sing to breathe
to sing the most quiet way.

To sing to light the most quiet light in darkness
radiantia radiantia
singing light in darkness.

To sing as the host sings in his house.

To breathe through the mouth to breathe through the
mouth to breathe to sing to
sing in the most quiet way to
sing *the seeds in the earth breathe forth*
not to whisper *the seeds* not to whisper *in the earth*
to sing *the seeds in the earth* the most quiet way to
sing *the seeds in the earth breathe forth*.

To sing to light the most quiet light in darkness
radiant light of *seeds in the earth*
singing light in the darkness.

To sing as the host sings in his house.

To breathe through the mouth to breathe to sing
in the most quiet way not to
whisper *the seeds in the earth breathe forth*
to sing totality of *the seeds* not to eat to
sing *the seeds in the earth* to
be at ease to sing totality totality
to sing to be at ease

To sing to light the most quiet light in darkness
be at ease with radiant *seeds*
with singing light in darkness.

To sing as the host sings in his house.

2

To breathe and stretch one's arms again
to stretch to stretch to straighten to stretch to
rise to stretch to straighten to rise
to full height not to torture not to torture to
rise to full height to give to hold out to
to give the hand to hold out the hand
to give to hold out to.

To give self-lighted flowers in the darkness
fiery saxifrage
to hold out self-lighted flowers in darkness

To give as the host gives in his house.

To stretch to stretch to straighten to stretch to
rise to full height not to torture not to
to rise to give to hold out to
give the hand to hold out the hand to give
hope hope of hope of perfect hope of perfect rest
to give hope of perfect rest
to give to hold out to.

To give self-lighted flowers in the darkness
perfect and fiery hope
to hold out lighted flowers in darkness.

To give as the host gives in his house.

To stretch to stretch to straighten to stretch to
rise to full height not to torture to
give the hand to hold out the hand to
give hope to give hope of perfect rest to
rest not to lay flat not to lay out
to rest as *seeds* as *seeds in the earth*
to give rest to hold out to.

To give self-lighted flowers in the darkness
fiery hope of perfect rest
to hold out light flowers in darkness.

To give as the host gives in his house.

3

To breathe and stretch one's arms again
to join arm-in-arm to join arm-in-arm to
join to take to take into
to join to take into a state of intimacy
not in anger not in anger
to join arm-in-arm to join arms
to take into intimacy.

To take into the light in the darkness
into the excited phosphor
to be in light in the darkness.

To take as the host takes into his house.

To join arm-in-arm to join arm-in-arm to
join to take to take into
to join to take into a state of intimacy
not anger not anger
to take as *the earth* takes *seeds* as
the poor the poor must be taken into
to take into intimacy.

To take into the light in the darkness
into the phosphor star-flowers
to be in the light in the darkness.

To take as the host takes into his house.

To join arm-in-arm to join arm-in-arm to
join arms to take to take into a state of intimacy
not anger
to take as *the earth* takes *seeds* as
the poor must be taken into
to end the silence and the solitude
to take into intimacy.

To take into the light in the darkness
into star-flowers before sunrise
to be in light in the darkness.

To take as the host takes into his house.

COMMENTARY

1.6.83
That is, separate & together.

first-phrase = (seed of) the patterned = several phrases or sentences; the standard pattern is repeated several times

dance to come out of a trance, to join a diversified assembly with a separate contribution

music & dance: ways of posing structures and restrictions for "ethical actualization"

power of the music lies in silence of the gaps; this is where one's contribu-
tion must go & by it the music may be opened up further. The idea is to
conceive the music as an arrangement or system of gaps and not as a dense
pattern of sound. This rules out Xenakis. What about Riley, Glass, &
Reich?

Say the rhythm before you play it. It may not be necessary to express this
in nonsense syllables. Perhaps there could be such syllables which coalesce
into words as the poem moves along.

J. T. (from Were You: Notes & a Poem for Michael Palmer)

For which the masters he names outside of poetry include Coltrane (musi-cian) and Rothko (painter); in poetry, the continuing presence of Zukofsky & his proposal that music is the upper limit of speech (volume one, page 685). What stands out in Taggart's work, then, is an unprecedented musi-cality informed by a nearly mathematical sense of placement & displace-ment—& behind it (as a theme inseparable from its form) a religious inten-sity at an (in his time) unprecedented level. The reader in pursuit of Taggart should compare the "slow song for Mark Rothko" (above) to his monu-mental work, *The Rothko Chapel Poem,* and to the deeply moving, deeply human *Peace on Earth,* for which the "slow song" also acts as a companion. *Monk,* which shows the short, highly condensed music of his other style, refers to the death of Thelonious Monk, in whose manner perhaps Taggart works his changes on the familiar hymn.

Quincy Troupe b. 1943

AVALANCHE

For K Curtis Lyle & the memory of Richard Wright

within an avalanche of glory hallelujah skybreaks
spraying syllables on the run, spreading
sheets, waving holy sounds, solos sluicing african bound
transformed here in america from voodoo into hoodoo
inside tongueing blues, snaking horns, where juju grounds down sacred
up in chords, up in the gritty foofoo
magical, where fleet rounds of cadences whirlpool
as in rivers, where memory spins down foaming into dances
like storms swallowed here in a burst of suns
up in the yeasting blue voodoo, holding
the secret clues mum, inside the mystery, unfolding

up in the caking dishrag of daybreak, miracles
shaking out earthquakes of light
like mojo hands luminous with spangling
& are the vamping blood songs of call & response
are the vamping blood songs of call & response

as in the pulpit, when a preacher becomes his words
his rhythms those of a sacred bluesman, dead outside his door
his gospel intersecting with antiphonal guitars, a congregation of amens
as in the slurred riffs blues strings run back echoing themselves
answering the call, the voice cracked open like an egg, the yoke running
    out
the lungs imitating collapsed drums & he
is the rainbowing confluence of sacred tongues, the griot
the devotion of rivers all up in his hands, all up in his fingers
his call both invocation & quaking sermon
running true & holy as drumming cadences
brewed in black church choirs, glory hallelujah vowels
spreading from their mouths like wolfman's mojo
all up in mahalia jackson's lungs
howling vowels rolled off hoodoo consonants, brewing
magic all up in the preacher's run, of muddy water
strung all up in the form drenched with coltrane
riffin all up in miles of lightning hopkins mojo songs
blues yeasting lungs of bird
when music is raised up as prayer & lives
healing as june's sun quilted into black babies
tongues, sewn deep in their lungs as power
& blueprinted here in breath of rappers

& this is a poem in praise of continuity
is a poem about blood coursing through tongues
is a praise song for drowned voices lost in middle passage
is a praise song for the slashed drums of obatala
is a construct of orikis linking antiphonal bridges
is a praise song tongueing deep in the mojo secrets of damballah
in praise of the great God's blessings of oshun
in praise of healing songs sewn into tongues
inflating sweet lungs into a cacophony of singing
praise songs tongueing deep mojo secrets

& this poem is about music, when music is what it believes
it is, holy, when voices harmonize, somersaulting
in flight, & glory is the miracle poetry sings to in that great getting-up
morning, within the vortex of wonder, confluencing rivers, light
glory in the rainbows arching like eyebrows across suns
glory in the moonlight staring from a one-eyed cat's head
& eye want to be glory & flow in that light
want to be coltrane's solos living in me
want to become wonder of birds in flight of my lines
want the glory of song healing in me as sunlight
want it tongued through leaves
metaphoring trees, transformed where they seed & stand up here
as people, in this soil, everything rooted here in blood of mother's flesh
& is the poetry of God in deep forest time, singing & listening
& the music there is green, as it also is purple
as it also is orange brown & mind blowing electric banana
as it is red cinnamon & also again, green
sound ground up against lavender
beneath sunsets fusing crisp blue light
& night here stitched with fireflies flicking
gold up against bold midnight & once again, yes
green, as shimmering caribbean palm fronds
are green in the center of apocalyptic chaos

& my poem here is reaching for that greeness
is reaching for holy luminosity shimmering in gold
flecked light, where the mojo hand is seaming through
high blue mornings, waving like a sequined glove up in the glory
of hallelujahs, calling through the innertube lips of the great God
singing, up in the blues-root-doctors, jacklegging sermons
up in the condolences mourning death
up in the sunburst of God's glory
& eye want this poem to kneel down itself before healing
want it to be magic there beneath the crucifixion of light
want it to be praise song, juju rooted
want it to be mojo hand raised up to powers of flight
want it to be tongue of gritty foofoo, feeding
want it to be a congregation slurring amen riffs
running back through me to you
the voice raised up here, guitar blues licks, holy
want it to be glory hallelujah, call & response, glory

want it to be yam song rooted in the bloody river, holy
want it to be ground earth of resurrection, in you, in me
the bridge tongue of healing is the drum of this song
& it is reaching out to you to cross over
to the sun, is reaching out to touch your heartbeat
there, to become one in the glory
to feel the healing touch
to become one with the glory
this poem waits for you to cross over
too cross over the heart beat touch of your healing
hands, touching hands, touching hearts
this poem waits for you to cross over
to cross over love, this poem waits for you
to cross over, to cross over love
this poem waits for you to crossover
too crossover, too, love

COMMENTARY

following the north star boogaloo / the rhythm takes me / back to where
music began / to percolate language like coffee in another form
Q. T.

If the push in his work is toward a populist language ("[what] I heard in-
stead of what I read in books"), it moves him, collage-like, "from one
language to another all the time." His condition, then, like that of "the av-
erage African-American"—of "most Americans," he tells us further—is
"schizophrenic in the sense that they live on so many different levels of lan-
guage[:] . . . a little bit of blues, a little bit of jazz, a little bit of La Jolla, some
Fifth Avenue, some hip-hop, some rap . . . to the so-called high language,
etc." Nor is it only a question of surface—style, in brief—for "poetry lives
on the deepest level of being, and that means that you have to retrace the
language of the people that you come out of." If the context in which he
presents this is one, he says, in which "poetry is not intellectual . . . art is
not intellectual," there is an echo here too of Rilke's admonition (volume
one, page 110) to do *heart-work* . . . at variance with the external behav-
ior of a language and intent on its innermost life." But for Troupe, as for
others, the poem in doing that veers from customary politesse ("a culture of
manners [in which] manners supersede creativity") to allow an unfolding
through performance, "participatory [as] in African culture . . . [where] art
has always been participatory" and the response—"back and forth . . . the
artist and the audience . . . antiphony"—is overt, spoken: "Yeah, right,
right," or again: "Whoa man, that's horrifying." Of this he says in summa-
tion: "Great expression does not come out of a void."

Nicole Brossard b. 1943

from **THE BARBIZON**

writings make sense that begin with the declaration of
love (*itself*) fixed in the heart of the century and of sub-
terranean proliferating and vociferating mythologies of
voices caught in the cliché, cities, (*in play*)

The Barbizon Hotel for Women

an intuition of reciprocal knowledge
women with curves of fire and eiderdown
fresh-skinned—essential surface
you float within my page she said
and the four dimensional woman is inscribed
in the space between the moon and (fire belt)
of the discovery and combats that the echo
you persevere, fervour flaming

mouth diffuse, nocturnal and intimate
round with intervals
to pass through the gardens of the real
anticipated paintings of the attentive body
all the regions of the brain
time is measured here in waters
into vessels, in harmony
the precision of graffiti in our eyes
fugitives (here) the writings
in THE BARBIZON HOTEL FOR WOMEN
nascent figures within the wheel
cyclical tenderness converging

space (mâ)
among all ages, versatile
wrinkles of the unexpected woman
when midnight and the elevator
in us rises the fluidity
our feet placed on the worn out carpets
here the girls of the Barbizon
in the narrow beds of America
have invented with their lips
a vital form of power
to stretch out side by side
without parallel and: fusion

but the napes of our necks attentive when
on Lexington Avenue steps
move close to us again
because *the scene* is memory
and the memory within our pages
explodes
like a perfect technique
around this eccentric passion
we imagine in the beautiful grey
chignons of the women of the Barbizon

so transform me, she said
into a watercolour in the bed
like a recent orbit
the curtains, the emotion
tonight we are going to the *Sahara*

we are walking into the abstract (neons)
tonight—overexposed—unfettered expression
nocturnal women
my reflex and the circumstances
which my mouth walks like words
i expose myself: a useful precaution
sur terre: down town
amazons have studios for correspondence

and here again i find *an author too abstract*
supplicating in space
body itself intensity
and the rain suddenly
abundant
to reunite intuitions of matter

the embraces _____ the extent of thought
in the grass i'll be quick to take
the silk road
with a tongue that has visions
it is essential to hold back: presence/
on the verge of

space (mâ) memory round with vowels
with ultimate certainty without respite

The Temptation

i succumbed to all the visions
seduced, surface, series and serious
in all mobility and landscapes
concentrated on each episode
territory and cheek. masked/unmasked:
hors l'espace or full of intonations
in the climate delirious around
all the figures, aerial
in the use of glaze and phrase

i succumbed to the fury, the cities
and the etchings/come/the
conversation in snatches, in the open
the entire palm imprint of slowness
and reality transforms its lynx
eyes of identity which motivate
all the resources the tongue braids
existence by dint of constant courses
and breath within the limits of the possible
of the tolerable blindly: feeling

i succumbed to the clear vision
of vegetation and events
of early morning, in the privileges of light
because the authentic body spine of fire
has shown its tongue as it
was then tangible and tango
very vivid for the eyes/of the inside

i succumbed to the temptation as
one enters the round of gestures
ensuring survival, conquest
smile and fusion of fictions
the night come when the bangs
our foreheads remember the most delightful
delinquencies, the hand is moved a bit
so that before our eyes opens up
the agile memory of utopian girls
moving in italics
or in a fresco towards all the issues

i succumbed to the impression and instantaneous
both of us ----- life mobilizes itself
with the fine ardour of women showing forth
their vertigo and those two
dazzled *sur terre* turning seized suddenly
in the most ritual amorous slownes s ex---
temptation with all gravity
of ecstasy, these two were so
enraptured celebrating the daily
emergence of temptation

i succumbed to the echo, the rebound
to the repetition. *in the beginning*
of the vertebrae was the duration
an essential rejoinder at every instant
in the joy I have in you, lived
duration of signs, stricken
with collusion and the waters
of reading and delirium
the agility of thighs each time
surprises me in space because they are
this opening originated at all
times in all vegetation
the vitality of cycles: our images

i succumbed attentively to the very
point of knowing that for each
temptation a meaning must be preserved: *recollected*
and *resumed* ----------- to open onto mental
space, with words of lightning, sequence
of unreason, episode of recommencements
and of breasts unrecorded web: the mouths
science of the real, skin/itinerary
going away to slip gently
into the continent of women

i succumbed: that's what drags me
into the real and vertigo at the same time
into the surrounding grasses (they touch
our most sensitive tissues)
------ eclipses ------
temptation beyond words
to devise an architecture
when everything veers towards fever so
even a clever description:
moving me towards the other woman
unanimous
other than *naturally*

i succumbed even unto the certainty
which designates the initial legend
the one that excavates the passed'n time
and prompts the question
of distance (*itself*) in the fire of
fictions/to succumb becomes thus to pass through
take shape and choose oneself
a consent affecting the woman in love

Translation from the French by Barbara Godard

From instinct and from memory, I try to reconstruct nothing. From memory, I broach a subject. And that cannot be from childhood. Only from ecstasy, from a fall, from words. Or from the body differently. Emergency cell like body at its ultimate, without its knowledge, the tongue will tell it. (N. B.) And again: *Every body carries within itself a project of high sensual technology; writing is its hologram.*

Poet, novelist, essayist, & cofounder of the avant-garde literary magazine *La Barre du Jour,* Brossard is Quebec's preeminent experimentalist. After early work in a more traditional lyrical vein, she moved by the early seventies into areas exploring feminine & lesbian identity as, she writes, "simultaneously quest for and conquest of meaning," adding that "identity becomes project when the border between the tolerable and the intolerable breaks down . . . that is when words lose their meaning or else take on a different meaning, another turn in the events of thought. The words begin to turn on themselves, inciting reflection, inciting thought to new approaches to reality." Influenced by, yet in her practice moving beyond, theories of textual production (as proposed by, say, Roland Barthes), books such as *Mecanique jongleuse* [Daydream Mechanics] or *Amantes* [Lovhers] (excerpted here) stage what she has called a "gyn/ecological memory" propelled by a "necessity for politico-sexual subversion." As Eva-Marie Kroller describes the writing: "Spiraling approximations replace linear line and argument; rhetorical strategies such as repetition, ellipsis, and omission empty language of its presumable unequivocality and suggest that speech can regenerate itself, [while] Brossard enhances her repertoire of poetic strategies by using foreign words and typographical devices such as underlining, unorthodox capitalization, and, most importantly, blank spaces. The reader is thus invited to participate actively in the creation of a poem but also called upon to pause with the poet in a meditative caesura." Or, as Brossard puts it in her *Journal intime:* "Reality is what matters and as a writer I have to deal with it as fiction because I know that twenty-first century reality will be about the worst and best of our fictions."

Michael Palmer b. 1943

from **SUN**

The lines through these words
form other, still longer lines

dust in a steady shower
It is our fortune to have been born

at the crossroads of a chiasma
in a land known as How to Laugh

and How to Die. Did spine write this

        story of

my life in a pyramid
designing those pyramids yet to come

those galaxies now being formed,
constellations, touching myself, rubbing against different objects

in total darkness
a year of extreme pain

but fortunately I am perfectly dead
and can see into the past through a lens

signed The World As It Is
tango converted to a fugue

black milk, golden hair
cliffs, bridges, grey lake

and a grave in the air
It rains

It burns
Carry something to somewhere

Tie something to something else
Hold your head in your right hand

as a lantern
a light impossible for this season

and so we turn away from these sounds
raise our Illyrian hats

visit our beds
and ring a bell

X, name of X
we are

A bark sets out on the honeycomb's flow
We called it Le Départ

SUN

Write this. We have burned all their villages

Write this. We have burned all the villages and the people in them

Write this. We have adopted their customs and their manner of dress

Write this. A word may be shaped like a bed, a basket of tears or an X

In the notebook it says, It is the time of mutations, laughter at jokes, secrets beyond the boundaries of speech

I now turn to my use of suffixes and punctuation, closing Mr. Circle with a single stroke, tearing the canvas from its wall, joined to her, experiencing the same thoughts at the same moment, inscribing them on a loquat leaf

Write this. We have begun to have bodies, a now here and a now gone, a past long ago and one still to come

Let go of me for I have died and am in a novel and was a lyric poet, certainly, who attracted crowds to mountaintops. For a nickel I will appear from this box. For a dollar I will have text with you and answer three questions

First question. We entered the forest, followed its winding paths, and emerged blind

Second question. My townhouse, of the Jugendstil, lies by Darmstadt

Third question. He knows he will wake from this dream, conducted in the mother-tongue

Third question. He knows his breathing organs are manipulated by God, so that he is compelled to scream

Third question. I will converse with no one on those days of the week which end in y

Write this. There is pleasure and pain and there are marks and signs. A word may be shaped like a fig or a pig, an effigy or an egg

but

there is only time for fasting and desire, device and design, there is only time to swerve without limbs, organs or face into a

scientific

silence, pinhole of light

Say this. I was born on an island among the dead. I learned language on this island but did not speak on this island. I am writing to you from this island. I am writing to the dancers from this island. The writers do not dance on this island

Say this. There is a sentence in my mouth, there is a chariot in my mouth. There is a ladder. There is a lamp whose light fills empty space and a space which swallows light

A word is beside itself. Here the poem is called What Speaking Means to Say
    though I have no memory of my name
Here the poem is called Theory of the Real, its name is Let's Call This, and its name is called A Wooden Stick. It goes yes-yes, no-no. It goes one and one

I have been writing a book, not in my native language, about violins and smoke, lines and dots, free to speak and become the things we speak, pages which sit up, look around and row resolutely toward the setting sun

Pages torn from their spines and added to the pyre, so that they will resemble thought

Pages which accept no ink

Pages we've never seen—first called Narrow Street, then Half a Fragment, Plain of Jars or Plain of Reeds, taking each syllable in her mouth, shifting position and passing it to him

Let me say this. Neak Luong is a blur. It is Tuesday in the hardwood forest. I am a visitor here, with a notebook

The notebook lists My New Words and Flag above White. It claims to have no inside
          only characters like A-against-Herself, B, C, L and N, Sam, Hans Magnus, T. Sphere, all speaking in the dark with their hands

G for Gramsci or Goebbels, blue hills, cities, cities with hills,
modern and at the edge of time

F for alphabet, Z for A, an H in an
arbor, shadow, silent wreckage, W or M among stars

What last. Lapwing. Tesseract. X perhaps for X. The villages are known
as These Letters—humid, sunless. The writing occurs on their walls

COMMENTARY

You would like to live somewhere // but this is not permitted / You may not
even think of it // lest the thinking appear as words // and the words as
things / arriving in competing waves // from the ruins of that place
M. P.

Behind the often noted (& often misconstrued) elegance of his poetry, there
is an obsessiveness, a sense of (moral) *disgust/intensity*, as Tzara (speaking
for Dada) had it years before. Palmer's return, in fact—though hardly his
alone—is to something like the contention by Hugo Ball (volume one) that
"a line of poetry is a chance to get rid of all the filth that clings to language"
(to which Ball adds in his margin: "to get rid of language itself"). What
Palmer gives us in turn is not an abstract questioning of the "referent in the
world" but "the further anxiety that has been expressed by a number of
poets, philosophers, and simply human beings . . . suddenly understanding
that they may or may not refer to the world, that languages break down
when we live in a world where pacification means annihilation. In the case
of Vietnam"—he asked back then—"what is reference?" The mark of his
poetry itself is what Linda Reinfeld calls "a lyric of disturbance[:] . . . not so
much [in] the choice of words as . . . the aggressive denaturing of them." Or
Palmer in his own terms: "Poetry—even, let's say, a lyric poetry (. . . [but]
not the lyric poetry of the 'little me' churned out in America)—has a force
of resistance and critique." As such, it is a force—& this is the context,
surely, for so much of what he does—that responds to "the totalitarian ap-
propriation of language" with "the counter-logic of poetry[:] . . . a deter-
minative critique of sense" (even by means of so-called nonsense) "that can
challenge the apparent and multiply meanings, take us beyond what we
thought we were talking about, . . . [our] own habits of thought. . . . You go
to the poem for instruction beyond that."

In *Sun*—the longer poem, excerpted here, which in its entirety has the
same number of lines as T. S. Eliot's *The Waste Land*—Palmer "overwrites"
a poem—Eliot's—that has been taken as the pillar of an older modernism
but that reflects "that reactionary sensibility . . . , that ecclesiastical and anti-
Semitic sensibility that [Eliot] represents[:] . . . a horrifying thing to have
inscribed at the heart of modernism."

Allen Fisher b. 1944

CONGA

Gathered at the nation's sickbed
evening sky lowered onto
yellow irises through daffodils
mimosa into street lanterns
lowers into plasticisers on
the face of an SAS officer as she
approaches the supermarket
Oh Hereford evening Oh absent
healing satellite warning
burst into jump jet schizophrenic
peace warming the panes beneath
the greenbacked lawn

I stood half naked on the verge
partly exposed my genital
photographer sent the proofs
to the agency back into a post
bag the size of passive management in the
wind-up co-operative proceeds from moves
into burnt a paperpoint institution a
dressing the rules towards portfolio bonding

meet to discuss the phenomena
evident points to climatic
buzz-phrases resonation urgentics
disrupt the fragile bank
balcony
intelligibility overlaps language for
people whose hearts are heated moving towards
restriction overlaps with purity
a folk taxonomy uniform or informant

freedom here becomes bitter
loss of hope
the emptiness that follows
creates no memory
I can't remember what was eaten
it was black and soft
patronised by collaborators
keeping comparatively healthy
saves me from despair
lunches are the worst part of memory
closed doors and friends knocking
existentialists who become policemen
corroborated by fear
by certainty
opens the briefcase
takes out a portcullis and a pair of chains
I'm not rembling
I'm tired of trembling

the cosmology in recent gossip
environment itself as hazard
themes of Nature and Art in the ceiling
indicate what was stored below in the ceiling
of what is hidden
appearances release memories
what is hidden
Bertold the Black identified
manufacturing ballistics
by means of catapult bomb hurlers
to the left the results are tested
against the Danes in 1354

A close integrity relates
events, acts, roles and genres
and the configuration processed
In each curing event the speech act of the
special knower produced in western distortion
the doctor's prescription

In full voice sent cooked rice in leek water
to fight for nation walked
they wont be singing
when they come back
enforced inactivity
at a time when nothing
but action could make sense on soft red earth
civilisation on the operating banks of the Wye
table we sit in the waiting and the Frome
room neither pity nor hope invented new curry
what begins in routine policing using leeks and flageolets
hardens into preservation with green pepper shifted with
pictorial art and Albers yellow curry orange carrot brown
rhythm of structures shifting cumin black pepper
after investigation guided by a in Chevreul Newton Goethe eventually
we think sex is alright to which consonant researching colour
of immediacy luxury of bathing naked
and spontaneity should correspond weight of colours

Nature and Art in this together suit
to Make of the parts towards a wise aim
Calm extents of many intellectual domains
reinforced an aristocratic candour
Deeply wounded rather than embittered
To enmity and disappointment opposed
many different constructions and great industry
marshalling them for common-sense, so said, triumph
An expression of tenderness patience and health

The choice from appearances impersonal exactitude
express harmoniously a state of mind concurrently
dependence on Nature depreciates those who
would paint without example relativity of tonal
values in which the number calculations affect the eye

The equation between rapture
from the earth and aesthetic
decision in which geometry
and number express the amplitude
of love To embrace each particular
Agitation borrows the broad arc
of calm Colour sense enraptures
form an involucre of outwardness

The nation's life as outward
state to which all activity
aspires as death seen to be
a calm separation given nausea
by the pressure of each damaged
lung Common sanity now alien
without reciprocation in love
appositions seize the muscles
of the heart It's incredibly
easy to die so much harder to
live All the positions in dispersal

The instantaneous without
Perambulation lost
cancel una sola occhiata
subsuming immediacy left in
the varieties of constipation
Tactility a rhetorical figure
without felicity of apposition
Interpenetration a kind of virus
beyond the elegance of microform
Grace and passion expended in a mass
market consistent with its death mask

Eyes lift / from a book feel the condition / complex body / temperature and objects / adhere to / the read / singularity / in a region of spacetime / cosmic censorship / others call coherence neither light nor / anything else escapes / living's troposed alternatives / a stone ejects / from a pond.
A. F.

A prolific poet & writer, Fisher has also contributed to the state-of-the-art in England through a range of activities—as publisher (Aloes Books & Spanner Editions), as conceptual & performance artist (notably as part of the Fluxus England West collective), & as painter. He is a central figure in the British Poetry revival of the sixties and seventies—with, among others, Bill Griffiths, Ulli Freer, Barry MacSweeney, J. H. Prynne (above), cris cheek, Wendy Mulford, Denise Riley, Tom Raworth (above), & Douglas Oliver, whom fellow poet Eric Mottram has described as poets "committed to imaginative invention and to taking up the challenge of a wide range of Twentieth Century poetics. . . . They stand, in their differing ways, for resistance to habitual responses, for explorations in language notation and rhythm, for discovery without safety net for the poet or reader."

Place, Fisher's work of the 1970s, is a multibook/multimedia project of Olsonian proportions, where topographical & mythohistorical crossings of London interweave both processual ("process showing") & procedural techniques. His major ongoing project since the 1980s is *Gravity as a consequence of shape* (here, ever so briefly, extracted). It is "an investigation of perception and consciousness," says Robert Sheppard, who goes on to write: "By fracturing different kinds of systematised knowledge and then rearranging them, he is miming the processes of consistent memory and inventive memory [Fisher's terms]. . . . As readers enter into the 'participatory invention' of the texts, creating temporary coherences line by line, they are restructuring their perceptions, changing their consciousnesses."

bp Nichol 1944–1988

A SEQUENCE OF POEMS FROM *THE MARTYROLOGY 7*

Scraptures: 17th Sequence

the religious man practises reversals

O

O

alpha
ahpla

omega
agemo

the reversed man practises religion

SUDDENLY I AM LIGHT   I   I   know(s

it is the face
it is the realization of the face

it is the facing
it is the realization of the facing

the split eyes

what the eye seizes as real is fractured again and again

light

the eye's light

drifts away

diffused

by the mind's confusion

names and signatures

CHRIST become an X

        X as the man signs who cannot write his name

as tho to be without a name were to take up the cross, so that a man who is part of the nameless, is part of the mass, carries the cross further, or is more weighed down by it

            X—nameless

       the reversal becomes complete

     a cycle into the 30's

          33
            33

       the trinity

          X
         saint reat
         saint and

saint agnes who gave them a name

saint ranglehold

     3

       3

       as the cock crowed

Monotones

LXII

chaos rumoured

saints distance perception

over everything
the field cows scream   alive with fire

roll
        in a corner
roar
        eternal

hills

            buried beneath the sea

it is in me

words
weight the fingers
down

the farmhouse door
bangs against the skull

the mouths of the town are drowned

The Hill Songs of Saint Orm

I

all day i have wandered in these southern reaches
lost from the world of people

all night i will sleep beneath the trees
safe on the edge of the cloud range

2

berries for food
water for drink

the woman i loved dead
the people i knew gone

white of clouds
blue of sky

open i

   3

the people you thot you knew lie

a man gives his neighbour food
but talks about him behind his back

   4

this morning a bird woke me

my bed was empty where i'd dreamt you lay

   5

when you have nothing
you have nothing

when everything you thot you had is gone
you have what you always had

if everything you wanted was here
you'd have nothing

   .

the waste of my words & works. the worth.
a balance. something to be said for history.
everything dissolves in time
or vanishes, goes unseen, unheard, unsaid,
inappropriate to another space or head
confronting its own struggle with its body
's decay.

buildings turning to dust around us.
Via Principe Amedeo in the morning sunlight.
sky blue. we crossed Via Roma, Palazzo Reale in the distance.

four centuries in a glance. that dance. that man's
folly or triumph. her dis. her grace. sunlight in the piazza.
our bodies, our sounds, words, this page, even as you read,
even as your vision, your life—uneven, even—fades, fade.

COMMENTARY

*Poetry being at a dead end poetry is dead. Having accepted this fact we are
free to live the poem.* (bp N.) Or put another way: *The poem will live again
when we accept finally the fact of the poem's death.*

A poet of multiple (re)sources & of a manysided modernism (= *post*mod-
ernism), he found his way (he told us) by "pass[ing] back and forth between
trad[itional] poetry, concrete poetry, sound poetry, film, comic strips, the
novel or what have you . . . in order to reproduce the muse that musses up
my own brain." Very early on, his autochthonous visual/concrete poetry led
him to the international concrete poetry movement (page 302) & past it into
areas of poetry still uncharted. That opening was to a place, he wrote, from
which "I could actually 'see' the goddamn page and I realized that every
word counted, that before I'd just been dumping on the page." The work
also opened, as with that of other concretists, to *performance,* most memo-
rably with Toronto-based poets Rafael Barretto-Rivera, Paul Dutton, &
Steve McCaffery (page 427, 822) as the high-energy, comic, publicly acces-
sible Four Horsemen. In a parallel development of his other side—that
brought him, however 'pataphysically, toward *theory*—he & McCaffery
formed the Toronto Research Group to think together over a range of topics
(McCaffery later wrote) "that both of us were concerned about and . . .
which we could only write about honestly and meaningfully if we wrote
about them together." A prolific writer otherwise, Nichol's most far-reach-
ing work (cut short by his early death) was *The Martyrology:* a series of
evocations of / addresses to "the [Christian] saints," real &/or imagined, in
which (for all its breadth & outward references) "it was myself I was talking
to, parts of myself, voices . . . that . . . were also different moods within
myself that I was 'evocating.'" In Frank Davey's summary (circa 1980): "bp
Nichol's writing is the most courageous body of work in Canadian literature
today. . . . It risks, even invites condemnations by the conservative critic for
triviality, banality, obscurity, wordiness, formlessness, privateness—all
those 'vices' . . . transform[ed by Nichol] into linguistic sign, so that the
saints, rhymes, and secret rhymes of the language can move the poet to
'greater vision,' 'other mysteries,' and a reconciliation with Heraclitean
process—a willingness to 'allow what is to be.'"

Charles Stein b. 1944

A PARMENIDES MACHINE

It is as old as it thinks itself to be.

It is as old as itself. Its old self.

And in being just that old
it goes on growing older—

older than it has been until now,
older than it is now . . .

The young shoot grows
on the trunk of the ancient oak
though older now.

Its youth self is retained
as that which it has been
and, as, older now, it throws its youth aside—
that youth self comes into being
as just the youth it was
now
for the first time.

    I feel the wind
blow across the water
just enough to cause the sails to move.

There are people on the beach now
in the summer
now that it is winter.

The music is strutting backwards.

He plays the improvisation
sitting sideways. Scratching the phrases
across the keys in a rapid jitter
that fits the notes
aptly to the measure
and yet I feel the music strutting sideways.

We ourselves are beginning to get up and move
in an awkward manner
away from the deck and the deck chairs.

It is impossible to see us moving
and yet we are picking up our hats
and walking off to the right
under the shadow of the veranda
and going into the lounge to purchase a beverage.

We ourselves are beginning to get up and move
in a curious manner.

It is impossible to see us do this, impossible to stir
the memory of it,
but we do it—we have done it—
and as we pass the scene in a sail boat
our having done it
in just this jittery manner
          moving aslant
                    looking askance
and walking quietly
under the shade of the veranda

comes into view.

Coming into being comes into view.

The whole comes into being
as the future idles on.

It wasn't there before at all.

Our youth was not our youth
until the ancient priest-thinker
arrived with his oaks
propped up on a hobbled machine.

The noises that it makes in that intolerable sun blaze.

His white beard flows like the sun blaze.

We ourselves are walking to the right
having crossed the line
on the floorboards of the sun deck
where the shadow of the veranda
crosses in the noon hour.

White splotches of sunlight
and dark and sharply outlined patches of shadow
cross our bodies—
                    the line of division
twixt shadow and sun blaze
moves across our bodies as we move
across the deck
to go into the lounge.

How old are you
these days.

Your youth comes into being as you grow old.

The aged priest-thinker,
hobbling into the sun blaze of his agedness
appears as in his youth to put the questions
before the ancient machine—thus to become
young again
and for the first time.

He is old and young in a single figure
and the shadow of the veranda
crosses his body at noon
and does not move
as the river of questions streams across his memory.

It is impossible to say in what direction we seemed
                                  to be moving just then.

Perhaps it was to the right of the shadowed deck chairs
and away from the sun-blanched water
towards the veranda.

The elderly priest-thinker
was serving drinks and behaving
in a jittery manner
as the shadow of the boat deck
passed magisterially across the window glass.

The music seemed to have been getting louder.

He complained of his age.

The questions were sputtering
out of the ancient mechanism.

There was a certain strain inside him
as if he had run this course before
in his youth
and that that youth had now to be summoned
before the small but particular company
perfectly suited to attend the mechanism.

The others complained of his age.

He said he was an ancient horse chariot driver
required to go the journey
to the northernmost stars
one more time
before he regained his youth again—
that this was the method, the machinery
by which one, starting in the same place,
distinguishes figures in that locality
coming into being
as if for the first and only time. And only now.

*All the destructions / of form and substance / interpenetrate themselves. /
I am sitting in the house / and think to become as quiet / as anything there
is.* (C. S.) And again: *To read and to write are one.*

Of himself / his work he writes: "*theforestforthetrees* [the long ongoing
work from which *The Parmenides Machine* is taken] is a textual practice,
not a single long poem. It includes all the writings in poetry I have done
since the early 80s. To date it amounts to several shelves of folders, binders,
and notebooks. I write freely and compose from this work pieces and com-
pilations of pieces when occasions for publication or performance arise. I
hope the name suggests that the whole of it cannot be surveyed but exists
solely for the sake of the particular moments of writing it affords and for the
particular compilations. Yet each poem or collection does emerge from a
'forest' of writing that in some way informs them all.

"The Parmenides in 'The Parmenides Machine' is more the figure in
Plato's late dialogue dealing with Parmenides than the 'Pre-Socratic' author
of the poem attributed to that figure. In this dialogue, the aged philosopher,
visiting Athens from Elea, accompanied by his disciple Zeno (of Zeno's
Paradox fame) is confronted by a young Socrates and induced, in spite
of the fatigues of age, to initiate him in the mysteries of his philosophic
method. This consists in a grueling series of logical exercises, and it is to
these that I refer as a 'machine.' The historical Parmenides, however (whose
doctrine was never 'the One' as Plato's figure studies it, but the indivisibility
of Being), stands in back of Plato like a monstrance. Similarly, the historical
Parmenides and his doctrine wait behind my poem."

Alice Notley b. 1945

from DÉSAMÈRE

Overhead at night, above the planet
Identity gone to sleep . . . Look what I've done
End of century, world so human
It may become a desert
Doesn't it feel like one anyway?
Approach a desert then, in a prophecy
An America now and later
Flat and cut with washes
What nondescript hardy little bushes!
In the distance treeless mountains
Then a campfire, someone's here

Small orange-haloed, a flame
People sit around it
Two, man and woman, well-lit
A third standing, distanced from the two,
Tending towards them nervously,
'I dropped the shell,' he says,
'But I'm not responsible for the misaim
Someone else set the sights—'
He's speaking to the woman
She's middle-aged, brown desert face
'I believe you,' she says
'When you die, I take it hard'
The man who sits with her's different
Wears glasses, a somewhat mid-century suit
His eyes are closed,
He seems to talk in his sleep
'You're both caught in times separate
From your condition now,' he says
'Still causing it, you can't leave your pasts
I'll try to dream you out of them'
Faceless people at the fire,
Further back from it, hard to see,
Murmur to each other, sometimes say things to the three
And one says to the dreamer, 'Who are you?'
'Robert Desnos,' he says, 'dead and happy
My intention is to be happy
Even if our world should disappear
I see you better than you do
Because I'm foreign and because I died
In nineteen forty-five,
The last time things seemed clear'
He's quiet now, and the others
Are focussed on the fire, waiting to hear
The voice of Desnos again
And wondering where the world is

Desnos addresses the woman,
'I dream your brother's bike's been stolen
Out of a smalltown home, how can that be?
An extinct bird called the Stalin-bird

Now appears in Hawaii
Brother on R and R joins your family
A vacation from Nam in Honolulu
He shoots reds at night, that's to say, injects seconals
I can't make this dream stable
Your times are too nervous
Now you're riding a dirt-bike of your own
You ride it over a low hill, on a secret path,
Into the desert
To this campfire, where I await you'
Desnos stops and sleeps
The woman says to the others, 'You're all trembling'
'We were the vulnerable,' one says
The woman's brother's shaking all over
'But you kill everyone, are you vulnerable?' she asks him
'I'm shaking so hard can't talk,' he says
The fire in the center seems steely
Has blackened mechanical flames
Another woman says, 'We loved each other:
Why's the world so bad? Where are the animals?'
Desnos sits and dreams, eyes closed
'Oh I'm dreaming,' he says, 'of
John Kennedy's pain, it's
Virtually nothing, quartz pebble'
'I remember,' the woman says to her brother,
'In Hawaii you nodded out into the salad
I gave you small money to score with—why
Didn't I give you
More, more of anything, why didn't you tell us
Stay with us, anything?'
Desnos says to her, 'I'm dreaming of a zoo
We're in barred cages like a town
Everyone's there, small monkeys are there
I myself look like a monkey
Who's there are the vulnerable,
The animals are vulnerable'
Brother's shaking, says, 'The desert's full of me!'
Desnos says, 'The future's this desert
I'm dreaming
The future, there's nothing in it but spirit
There are no animals

And then no people, it's so beautiful
White and empty like dissolved bones of a carcass'
Someone says, 'Don't believe we won't
Fix the future'
'Fix the future, fix it,' the woman shouts
Desnos says to her,
'You must enclose it in your largesse
It's in the desert still, a speck, it lives'

Desnos says to her, 'I'm dreaming that
You read a biography of me
Simply told, was it written by a fool?
In it I'm a soldier, not a poet—
I try to take a hill, you know, <u>that</u> <u>hill</u>?
There's one in every war
I'm a toy, hill's a sand-pile
You look down at me, you're playing,
In a desert lot,
You and your brother, now in the book
Your brother says, "He isn't me, why not?"
A sunset-color cast to the sky
"Let's put the hill in a jar," you say,
"Let's re-organize the world
If you can read a book you can do that"'
'. . . But you can't!'
The woman's speaking now, 'My name's Amère
See how it's short for America?'
'Were you a soldier?' Amère then asks Desnos
'I killed a German in a poem,' he says,
'*Il est mort dans la rue déserte*'
'Sand's better scattered,' Amère says, 'I'd
Dump out that jar now, and say, "Each
Speck of sand is a poem,
Eat it, and grow sandy, for our future"'
Desnos, back to dreaming:
'A vulture, white-headed, approaches
The concentration camp,
In my biography, as wide-winged
As an angel

They say I'm noble, but that vulture exacts nobility
Until nineteen sixty-something'
'What do you mean, Desnos?'
'Nobody got to have my death in Vietnam
Now I dream,' he says, 'that in nineteen forty-five,
Year you're born, year I die,
There's a map formed out of a spiderweb
With holes, empty torn places
One's "Stalin" one's "Nam" one's "eighties"—
The map's spun from the ass of a man
He speaks:
"We had to collaborate with Monster S,"
He squeaks . . .
You made Cold War with S's heirs afterwards
Created both sides in each of you
Included S's evil
In yourselves as expedience
Now the world's dead of competitive economies
Of Science, cars, the Human Spirit
When the planet was clean, we thought ourselves
No better than it
It can't be written clean
With poetry, dear Amère'

'You're agitated, your face is scratched,'
Amère says to Brother,
'Please let me take you in'
Doesn't hear her, circling fire, says
'After a while it seemed to me
What we were doing was just murder'
'My dream,' says Desnos, 'is of an elephant's
Soul, large and purple,' Brother repeats,
'After a while, it
Seemed to me . . .'   Amère says, 'I'll help
You finish . . . What we were
Doing, was just murder'
Something flies close, spectacled
Owl, Brother says,
'Like a goddamned raccoon, isn't it cute?'

A red parrot lights on his shoulder
'We'd precede the Phoenix Program
They'd a list of people to kill—you know
Pull up their hair and shoot them'
Desnos says, 'The effect of war
On all wildlife is unimaginable, I dream
How Americans kill the elephants
Who provide the Viet Cong transport'
'I have to keep reading this book,'
Brother says, holds up the book, 'Tells how
They left us in Laos, in seventy-one,
All but two died
We ate raw fish and survived
The two of us walked back to Quang Tri'
'More animals arrive,' says Desnos,
'Unaccountably in our desert,
Chèvre de Perse, ours de Perse,
And the sika, dark eyes, of Formosa
Why, isn't it just the old zoo!'
'We go back to Quang Tri, takes seven days
Hilly terrain,' Brother says
'Instantly they send me back out!
Into North Vietnam, they must want
To be rid of me, the others
In my sniper unit, never come back
I have two records but one of them is blank'
'Look how the stork
Comes near you,' says Amère, 'it likes
You, it pokes your ankle'
'. . . Want to be home with animals forever,
Cockatoos, burro, pigs,' Brother says,
'Not all night in Quang Tri . . .
Civilians, I killed lots of them'
'Look,' says Amère, 'a civilian, a Chinese
Jaguar, gold and dark'
'That orangutan's ridiculous,'
A shadow round the fire says
'You people haven't spoken for days,
Where have you been?' Amère asks
'Quang Tri's fallen, we've pulled out
Some of us are ghosts of the French

We're heading back down towards the south—but
We know we won't pass our urine tests'
A large white Himalayan vulture
Ruffed neck ruffed feet
Face fierce in white softness
Alights with rush and flap of three-meter wings
'Beauty,' a ghost murmurs, 'such beauty,
How can we keep it alive? Look
All the animals are gone again'

[. . . . . . .]

Name

Dark snake winds towards me moon in its mouth, the moon is cracking
A bird's balancing a board on its head
Another creature's head is extended long behind it a cylinder to be
    dragged about dust thinking light's an axe, light is glasses, pages
When dark bird's body approaches me this time
it can't smother me as I want its wing's shrivelled twisted
Something with no shape and frogface what will you tell me
(line orant, lace of veins, line bent)
Can't help, black moon won't form
Can't help, frog says, let white moon crack open
How? Let, Let
Heads keep dragging motion behind
Let Let
Silly bird, peck me open
Let
Rainbow of spinal nerves, the sun hangs from your arch like a pearl
Sun's gone shapeless wedge
Everything's shapeless
Creature slithers snake-headed with mouthful of shapelessness
I am too shapeless to hope
He's reading me like a newspaper with a mouthhole on its back page
Tunnel of peaked mountains, I've walked through and through and
    through you

Endless and shapeless living become one thing
The door blurs doubles triples I'll never find it now
It will find me, it will find me waiting centuries
All that's left pulsating breathing the words Désamère Désamère

COMMENTARY

This is Alice speaking now, it's not my consciousness I study but my physiology. My blood & my breathing, my vision, my walk, the chapping of my lips, the greying of my hair, my flowers becoming less sticky more silky, the birds in my nests, etc., dirty jokes, a tiny car drives down my neck and over my shoulder.
A. N.

But the consciousness is there too, in all the work, a fine, wry intelligence, prospective & proprioceptive, "the dance of the intellect among words" (E. Pound). Though originally from Needles, California ("If you're from a place like Needles, you're always from a place like Needles"), & remaining influenced by her origins ("I still articulate in a lot of ways that Southwesterners do and make sentences the way Southwesterners do"), she has moved in her work from early New York School verbal wit & speed (page 292) to an exploration of longer narrative structures & their inherent rhythms. The result is a self-styled "female epic," supplanting the action-story line of epic (as commonly understood) with a measure "found somewhere in the same depths where dreams originate, where worlds & new worlds are born." The quest implied here has its own spiritual urgency, as when she writes: "We don't need new words, new languages, new syntax, we need a whole new flesh, new beings to look at, literally, a new universe. The key is not in language; the key is in vision, in the most unrestricted sense of that word. Words are shallow & subject to selfish usages—but to see a new world is a first step towards changing an old one." Or, as she puts it in the introduction to *The Scarlet Cabinet*: "Someone, at this point, must take in hand the task of being everyone, & no one, as the first poets did. Someone must pay attention to the real spiritual needs of both her neighbors (not her poetic peers) & the future."

In *Désamère*—a master work of her maturity—she centers on the figure of Robert Desnos (whose work appears in volume one), her Surrealist predecessor & victim of the century's horrors in the World War II concentration camp at Terezin (Theresienstadt).

Anne Waldman b. 1945

IOVIS XIX

Why That's a Blade Can Float

The poet has by now travelled a distance, spanning mental universe, moving cross country, moving cross town and comes to rest with her box of scraps, notes, journals, memorabilia, letters, unfinished versions, her major task continuing unsettled at her feet. She spreads the documents about her, and bows her head. She feels a burden to sustain the plan. The society is crumbling around her. She can barely withstand the daily news. She thinks: why America? Am I American made? The computer is a little theater for her mind, although she senses it was designed & created & marketed by more & more men. Is this a problem? This is no mean accomplishment. She needs to enter more words. At least 400,000 characters. She has both exposed & guarded her life; whatever poetry survives is the autobiography of a dreamer. Mustering her strength she skims the surface of her dream & aspiration to find what floats, what rises. She has transcended some of her personal drama and contemplates a larger picture once again. The radio keeps her company tonight.

I'm on my way to America . . .

What caller Apollinaire enamelled of him and portrait a German had of wit or style none none but peasant come and come again we came from that stock o' soup and vittel, vital to any daughter's wish. She loves him. She's one who loves the taste of burnt vittel because of him it comes by, dark bread for the peasant in you. She loves migration, how it complicates the maps of nationals and leave them writhe more problems. A chaos of place to be born out of male stroke and swoop. Andros!

What weave got France wave got put in here Huguenots, a difficult brood bittered by betrayal, and Europe's sperm said it before mix in her. Mix "x" factors here. A curse of mere cuticle a cusp or covering a couched phrase to tell a trouble in or else you come down here a Sunday and be baptized. This was not speaking in anyman's tongue but how rather she went out on a limb once a night alone and bled for all the weight of childbirth he caused her. She still said "he" as she waited for her property to be taxed. And it was daring to go that way just try me, just try she said. Incest was no explanation. A moon of problems. Property was an old handle to hold her back. Give her it back. Time again in tell a whispered her legs walked further, back to Europe and died in the bosom of would it be Abraham? Wood wood wood say it wood wode wood wood make it sing a wood praise song, my wald, velde, velt, Wotan mounts the stage to terrorize woman.

      break here

          & would a Walden be
          set
                    round
               with

caller
      stone
                   wood a Walden
    pre-historique

would
blue
  a wald-man be

at
one
time
      migrate

      green
            another

(the pond)

& he says about my eyes
about blue & green
& silver, he says

view
from
a door

more contracted
than
from
eye

sock
he specs

too, happy ending
   he, nationalism fraught a kind of sympathy
   a free house, says

(how do we talk
to ourselves
deep at
night
in the dark in bed?)

   die Mauer im Kopf

      socket

the wall in the mind

& how do we

in a slice of hours
talk
      or calibrate this table in human time
2 o'clock: Page 2 is missing but what are your contacts
            in Venice, London, Erlangen, Paris

3 P.M.: St. Francesco rescues sailors from hunger

(il Santo Salva dalla fame i marinai)

they have been at it a long time

4 o'clock : the mountain comes to the man

5: Peacemaking-conference, Mideast

   (Dear A: I hope to see you otherwise. Sending you lots energy, getting
my act together you are right about academic theory of zeitgeist. LOTS
ENERGY, Madrid)

6 P.M.: *La Calùnnia di Apelle* by Sandro Botticelli depicts various out-
stretched arms in degrees of panic & passion. The statues look attentive
in their nearby alcoves. I watch this instead of television

7 P.M.: why did I ever leave home for the new world

mi padre, the old man, is weeping, *weeping*

calling it a life to turn aside
       & he goes backward a step in his masonry

  each part of the house corresponds to a part of the human anatomy.
Arms are bedrooms & social parlors. The navel is the courtyard, sexual
organs are the gates, the anus is the garbage pit in the backyard, legs &
feet are the kitchen & granary
& head is the family shrine
    patriarch descend here
    Jove, a designate, shine here

putting doubt aside the temple
I was trying to tell you
when you call out
suddenly
like a demon
            he enters here
Hallow Eve afflict
a species of madness

& he, the immigrant-deity dresses up as a hermaphrodite
(old festal table, ancient wassail, jest or sport)
he comes out of Columbus's tomb to make amends

amending to America

  & keep a ceremony there
all change in me, *muthologos*

sacred to some god always departing
lay down a book

hear the ancestral names

    Bush cruel crack
    against caribou

pipeline continue, imperialist America riding
on the nation of caribou

find you here no sanctuary from religious persecution
   collisions between nuclei
& wander freely as the first instant of creation

by whom?
of some sperm
& the first people who live here
in what mind do they dwell?

(Kabel und Betriebssystem liegen nicht bei)

caught as if by
force
   & forces
upon
the histoire
somber muse & disease

     walks the gangplank,
pirate to a war
   & held
in kind of thrall
for
diversity
arc back,
   you come home from all points
     to tell the family the stories

Doctor Benton speaks:

A. Atypical lobular hyperplasia B. Moderate intraductal hyperplasia
C. Fibrocystic condition D. Microcalcifications. A & B are worrisome;
some people feel they are pre-cancerous. Empirically punctate calcifica-
tions can be cancer

   then he leaves the room

mi padre, mi padre
predator
doctor god America

& give advice to workmen
how to vote:
   force an issue

      more nonaffirmative action o women
sign here they operate, *exploratory*

males with scalpels: *milde Grossheit*
carving the U.S. of A.

Dear A,
      Back in Munich

You must know this but arose in the lecture last night the most important
person of the 18th century being John Locke, founder of political liberal-
ism (liberté, égalité, tolerance, fraternité, humanity etc.), who influenced
George Washington, Thomas Jefferson, Madison and those who put their
signatures under the Declaration of Independence and were freemasons
as well. At my meeting many freemasons of today were present. They have
2 beautiful temples in Nürnberg and Erlangen. Only men are admitted.
The bible the president of the USA gives his oath upon is the bible of Wash-
ington which was used in his freemason temple. George Bush is probably
a freemason too. His "new world order" is a reflection of their esoteric
teaching so similar to Shambhala vision. Conspiracy theory again, yes?
That is my fear, distortion of a vision, in real politics. And it seems to be,
indeed, a common mind-set capable of "dark" and a "white" result. We
need more dialectical awareness to overcome the danger of dark results.
This is what I endeavor in my scientific thinking and work. You, too, my
friend . . .

my friend dark night a result
friend a light of me combine
to find alas no woman at the table
of Israel, of Lebanon, Palestine
how do they sleep? of Syria
& shine or shrink the tale as of void
& radio it says hands-on broadcast
a hundred deejays wait, not one a woman
the scholar & savage equal points of light
rub dry sticks together
a sham, a delusion, kind of affectation
never felt lonesome in it

mythology cast a spell on me
wonder a caller they say special interest
& instrumental in recording & taste you will see
on drums on bass & on Smithsonian
pumpkins so light, spear a ghost
it is an eve my friend a dark night
that's the way I feel now
they tend to shatter, words they tend to shatter
I'm a wrecker,
Roland Kirk plays "Haunted Melody"
they tend to shatter the words they tend

COMMENTARY

Words are sacred from some point of view. They emerge — when they aren't purely discursive — out of luminosity I believe. They are particles of light. They also come out of silence, if there is such a thing. We are communicating through our whole body as well, like illusory angels.
A. W.

The vows taken early on ("to never give up on poetry or on the poetic community") have led to a career including both a trajectory as poet/performer &, inseparably, a lifetime involvement with creating & caring for poetic communities. (After heading the St. Mark's Church Poetry Project in New York, she founded with Allen Ginsberg & now directs the Jack Kerouac School of Disembodied Poetics at the Naropa Institute in Boulder, Colorado.) Much of the writing (she says) "arises out of an oral yearning and attraction. I hear words before I 'see' them." Suggesting that her voice was "everywoman's *cri de coeur*," she writes: "I've always been on the track of the wizened hag's voice, the tough tongue of the crone free of vanity and conditioning." This work finds its first full realization in *Fast Speaking Woman* (1975), a long performance text drawing, among other sources, on the Mazatec shamaness María Sabina's healing chants (above). But the work is wider, including an astonishing range of writerly concerns (dream & persona poems, pantoums, the use of cut-up & collage techniques, et cetera). Of her own recent "epic" work, *Iovis* (a celebration of the male principle & a "counting [of] the 'fathers' I had known"), she tells us: "Words are used here with awe, dread, submission, humor, cheek, as if they were sacred creatures—pulsating, alive, mocking. As such they are little mirrors. For this poem I summoned male images, 'voices,' & histories as deities out of throat, heart, gut, correspondence & mind. Call them dakas, as they set off, like seed syllables, into the sky."

THE MISTY POETS

Listen, I don't believe!
OK. You've trampled
a thousand enemies underfoot. Call me
a thousand and one.

BEI DAO

[And again]:
In an age without heroes
I just want to be a man.

It was against the Cultural Revolution—only recently ended as they began—that their voices spoke out, as another stage in the "cultural wars" that have marked the career of poetry throughout the last century. Behind them loomed the figure (godlike, goatlike) of Mao Zedong—presented (by himself & others) as a poet, as if to teach that bad poetry is the certain enemy of poets (often their *destroyer*) & that without a revolution in language & form, the poetry of those in power becomes an instrument for the snuffing out of poetry (& with it of true revolution). Seen from that perspective, the history of modern Chinese poetry is a struggle—inherently unequal—between two different kinds of revolution. From the time of the May Fourth Movement (1919), many Chinese poets, like many of their contemporaries elsewhere, thought of their work as involved with social & cultural transformations. Along with that came a push to experiment with vernacular language (*bai hua* the Chinese term for it) &, much more tentatively, with "surrealist" imagery & altered forms of verse. (See the comments, e.g., on Wen Yiduo in volume one, as well as the work of other early & intermediary poets: Hu Shi, say, or Ai Qing in China proper, Ji Xian [Lyuishi] or Yip Wai-lim on Taiwan.) But the first repressive turn from within the revolution came in 1942 with Mao's "Talks at the Yenan Forum on Literature and Art," which summoned (& later commanded) writers & artists to become "cultural workers": a "cultural army," whose art would function as "cogs and wheels in the whole revolutionary machine." The terror into which this "proletarian revolutionary utilitarian[ism]" was eventually embedded reached its climax in the Great Proletarian Cultural Revolution (1966–1976), with peaks & ebbs before & after.

As an early oppositional force (post-Mao), the Misty Poets centered around the magazine *Jintian* (Today), published between 1978 & 1980 under the editorship of Bei Dao & Mang Ke. The movement's name, which could be rendered metaphorically as "obscurist," was "anchored . . . not (as critics have charged) in an 'obscure' maze of language . . . [but] in the strikingly 'real' context of history & sentiment." (Thus Leo Ou-Fan Lee, by way of introduction.) It was just the grimness of *this* realism—"the clear projection of a disillusioned mentality . . . turned into allegories of suffering and imprisonment"—that flew in the face of the (other) "social-ist" version with its state-directed optimism ("the reflection of the life of the people in the brains of revolutionary writers and artists"—Mao). Their new or revived mode of writing—& its foregrounding of an indi-vidual presence—connected them both to moves outside of China & to the truncated Chinese modernism of an earlier generation. It was a break-through—modest by other standards, circa 1980—both in content & in form, and it led (after the Tiananmen Square massacre in 1989) to the exile of four of the group's central figures: Bei Dao, Duo Duo, Yang Lian, & Gu Cheng. (Of those presented here, only Mang Ke & the woman poet Shu Ting remained in China.) Wrote Gu Cheng, whose exile ended with the murder of his wife & his own suicide: "Let's go home / and go back to living. / I haven't forgotten; / I'll walk carefully past the graves. / The empty eggshell of the moon / will wait there / for the birds that have left to return." And Yang Lian: "We are floating under the horizon / Both eyes bulging / Our four fishlike limbs entangle one another / As we pass below the bridge, the world hangs high overhead / Whoever peers into his own self / Will have to be born tragically."

Bei Dao b. 1949

THE ANSWER

Debasement is the password of the base,
Nobility the epitaph of the noble.
See how the gilded sky is covered
With the drifting twisted shadows of the dead.

The Ice Age is over now,
Why is there ice everywhere?
The Cape of Good Hope has been discovered,
Why do a thousand sails contest the Dead Sea?

I came into this world
Bringing only paper, rope, a shadow,
To proclaim before the judgement
The voice that has been judged:

Let me tell you, world,
I—do—not—believe!
If a thousand challengers lie beneath your feet,
Count me as number one thousand and one.

I don't believe the sky is blue;
I don't believe in thunder's echoes;
I don't believe that dreams are false;
I don't believe that death has no revenge.

If the sea is destined to breach the dikes
Let all the brackish water pour into my heart;
If the land is destined to rise
Let humanity choose a peak for existence again.

A new conjunction and glimmering stars
Adorn the unobstructed sky now:
They are the pictographs from five thousand years.
They are the watchful eyes of future generations.

Translation from the Chinese by Bonnie S. McDougall

THE AUGUST SLEEPWALKER

the stone bell tolls on the seabed
its tolling stirs up the waves

it is august that tolls
there is no sun at high noon in august

a triangular sail swollen with milk
soars over a drifting corpse

it is august that soars
august apples tumble down the ridge

the lighthouse that died long ago
shines in the seamen's gaze

it is august that shines
the august fair comes close on first frost

the stone bell tolls on the seabed
its tolling stirs up the waves

the august sleepwalker
has seen the sun in the night

Translation from the Chinese by Bonnie S. McDougall

"HE OPENS WIDE A THIRD EYE . . ."

He opens wide a third eye
the star above his head
warm currents from both east and west
have formed an archway
the expressway passes through the setting sun
two mountain peaks have ridden the camel to collapse
its skeleton has been pressed deep down
into a layer of coal

He sits in the narrow cabin under water
calm as ballast
schools of fish around him flash and gleam
freedom, that golden coffin lid
hangs high above the prison
the people queueing behind the giant rock
are waiting to enter the emperor's
memory

The exile of words has begun

Translation from the Chinese by Bonnie S. McDougall & Chen Maiping

Duo Duo b. 1951

WHEN PEOPLE RISE FROM CHEESE, STATEMENT #1

Songs, but the bloody revolution goes unnoticed
August is a ruthless bow
The vicious son walks out of the farmhouse
Bringing with him tobacco and a dry throat
The beasts must bear cruel blinders
Corpses encrusted in hair hang
From the swollen drums of their buttocks
Till the sacrifices behind the fence
Become blurry
From far away there comes marching a troop
Of smoking people

Translation from the Chinese by John Rosenwald

NORTH SEA

Huge shards of glass and ice slash through the North Sea
in such solitude, like the solitude of seas before their creatures found
   the land.
Earth, can you imagine the sky removed?

Tonight wild tigers are boxed up and shipped overseas
and a tiger's shadow slides across my face
—O, I confess to my life

but must confess it is a bore, with not even
the thrill of blood transfusions,
and my memories are weaker than this breeze.

I say that this sea is winding down.
Since I can't trust my ears (where sounds die out)
can't even research laughter's chimes

which can echo from the sea
I say the dimensions of my own body
leave me unimpressed.

Yet beyond the atmosphere are things that make me wild:
eggs laid by stones, or the real world's shadow shifting
in a vertical seabed where currents constantly swirl.

—I've never been happy like this!
I see things for the first time:
this silky river's face, currents arcing like a bridge,

the river shivering like silk as it races through the sky.
Now everything excites me,
a weird joy affects my heart.

As usual, I am rushing around busy,
yet I hear oysters
opening their shells to love

and when lovers weep I detect
a windstorm peeling back the corners of the earth.
The world is silent as if wolves have eaten the last child

and yet, as from a basket high in the air,
I see everyone I have loved
held tightly, tightly, tightly, in one embrace.

Translation from the Chinese by Tony Barnstone & Newton Liu

Mang Ke b. 1951

from **APEHERD**

Section II

it's a good harvest this year
so many corpses are buried in the earth
that the fattened crops have a human taste
and our kids herding on the plain
play and eat as greedily
as calves munching on sweet roots of grass
farm women hard at work
look! their eyes dart
like birds that wing home with food
to hide their gleanings in the dim nest
all the time craning and peering
while those sturdy men
sow their lust in the grainfields
their hands that knead the muddy earth
likewise at certain moments
taking the form
of a randy cock that
all at once springs
on a crouching grass hen.

it's a good harvest this year
see how those new brides
like fresh fish
make their tomcat lovers drool
a man lifts a woman
gently with two hands
as if laying her on a dish
his greedy head bends
like a crow lighting on snow
look again at the dwarf houses alongside
don't worry about the darkness
just poke a hole through the paper windows
and let your eyes slip inside
what can you see?
can you say?

how's the life in there?
or if it's broad daylight
and the sun so stinging
that exposure threatens heart attack
shift yourself into shaded side-streets and lanes
there's nothing to fear from
those street-girls creeping from cracks in the walls
don't be alarmed if
their bloated faces land on your body like toads
don't be scared of
scorpion nests in their bosoms
go ahead and chat with them
what do you hear? you're telling
how life is

it's a good harvest this year
while the night descends like locusts
the sun's rays disappear like wild geese
do you have a home to go to now?
fancy going out to a bar
or a dance hall? yarn a bit
enjoy those grinning buttocks?
what if you get back late
and you've forgotten the key
you think about that person
how will she react?
(since you see he's hours overdue
you're already half asleep
your round breasts and your heart
are hushed, aren't they? or prickling like a hedgehog?
in the middle of the night he staggers in
without a shred of dignity
with the last dregs of blood and sweat drunk dry
would you throw him out?
you wake
eyes open to see that head sharing your pillow
would your lips
those blood-red worms
still desire to crawl over his skin
with their unhurried wriggle?)
after the night is over

and you're still pondering the drudgeries
you've been through in the name of sex
would you discover the shame of your impotence
and the mockery of her two proud legs?
and your brain? would you often feel
your brain to be a wayside pavilion
always deserted
visited by none but transients
with nothing there worth remembering
would you often dream?
what sorts of things would you dream up?
after dreaming you were an ass
would you wake to find the ass has become yourself again
and would you have doubted
whether you became the ass
or the ass became you?

it's a good harvest this year
the dead are still dead
and the living still living
the dead once dead perhaps regret
not dying earlier
while with nothing but their shells
the living drone endlessly
of luck that seldom came their way
of life paid for with pain and toil
mind, are you watching out for your heart?
it may often become like a hungry fish
drawn to the angler's bait
and dragged through the water
by a hook lodged in the mouth

it's a good harvest this year
the sunlight could blacken over
and the flayed skin of daylight
let the days one by one seep to the ground
you could find you are the offspring of monsters
in the lamplight your body
casting the shadow of a runt
a man's head could blow to bits in the crowd
dong dong dong

strikes the bell that is a naked body
two legs could be made to crawl like a tortoise
and humans to learn to see with the eyes of dogs
mouths turning into trumpets
arseholes blaring non-stop talk
      the brightest stars drown in the flood
      while sons of bitches rule the sky
there is love between the stones
while bones are locked in rapt embrace
the faces of the living blow with flies
while rats dare their utmost in the struggle against us
humanity rotten to the core
people nail their own coffins
slander gallops, rumour moves crabwise
carnivores peck their meat,
in the cavities of empty heads
the spider spins at leisure
and one healthy chap
drowns in his own piss
the dead continue their quarrels underground
in heaven the gods are red in tooth and claw
the sun disappears for the distant mountains
like a wounded tiger on the run who stains
his blood across the last of twilight
after disaster
so many are skin and bone
that a gust of wind is enough
to blow them away

it's a good harvest this year
autumn has come around
such a pitiful season!
like a blear-eyed old busker
who stoops
to scratch a coin from the dirt.

Translation from the Chinese by Nicholas Jose & Wu Baohe

Shu Ting b. 1952

THE MIRROR

In the dark blue night
The old wounds burst open all at once
When the bed starts broiling these past events
It is a very patient lover
The table clock goes di da di da
And beats the dream black and blue all over its body
Groping along the wall
Groping along the wall for the light's pull-chain
I inadvertently became entangled
With a thread of moonlight
Flashing silverfish smelled the scent and ascended on a root
And so finally
You are a pool of softness

With a slow turn of body
    You are looking at yourself
    Yes you are looking at your self

The full-length mirror feigns innocent indulgence in unrequited love
The ambiguous wallpaper blurs its patterns
And is framed solidly
Watching you yourself wither one petal after another
    You have no way to escape no way to escape
Even if you could jump over the walls one at a time
There are still days blocking your back that you cannot jump over.

Women don't need philosophy
Women can shake off the stains of the moon
The way a dog shakes off water

Draw the thick curtain closed
The dawn's moist tongue touches the window glass
Place yourself back
Into the concave indentation of the pillow
Like a loose roll of photographic negatives

All at once the walnut tree under the window shivers
As if caressed by an ice-cold hand.

Translation from the Chinese by Fang Dai, Dennis Ding, & Edward Morin

Yang Lian b. 1955

CROCODILE 1 – 15

1

The crocodile attacks with a glance
eyelids sheath-like
hiding sleepless teeth

flesh a mass of tiny tracks
at the water's edge
in an instant off guard you are eaten

2

Huge mouth on the other's face
you with just a set of false teeth
broken ink-green coral

fake blood   jaws open
posturing to terrify
caving in

3

Greasy scales in stagnant water
you feel swarms of ants
crawling from bone joints

pregnant after spasmodic itching
ovaries like an anthill
crawling with flesh-eating crocodiles

4

Ecstasy in the sound of tearing
beauty in the shrieking of skeletons
your name sharpens your teeth

your blood   shares your pleasure
in sending others to death
you again kill yourself

5

Lies attack from the marrow's slime
under layers of armour you crumble
walls collapse

fall all around
waterweeds listen
to a battle of empty bodies

6

After wild killing and feasting
comes remorse
like a fit of burping

perhaps apologies from the dead
for the host's stomach
being sour with indigestion

7

The crocodile's nostrils shut like a word
ignoring you
floating and sinking on the page of white paper

despairing you call for help
and with long submerged words
sink into crocodile waters

8

Vague hatred permeates the green swamp
your days pass
wrapped in the skin of a corpse

slimy gliding
hung up   one skin is plenty
white-night-like flaunting nothingness

9

Hardened tears of many centuries
proliferate the black spots of old age
you are impeccably docile

and stare at the fish on the bank
savagely biting your nails
stupidly hiding perpetual hunger

10

Prehistoric bloated reptiles
stretch days into shadows
enough food for a whole street

coughing means dust
but a morning of copious salivating
again paints wooden smiles

11

A word can take you to a dead-end
only hidden in sunlight
can there be nakedness in the absence of words

or buried in darkness' body
other moonlight under the skin
is there no need for words and clothing

12

Quiet is an impasse
the crocodile's white-hot breath looms
deceiving yourself you can endure more

deluded by a loose tooth's
faltering voice
in your silence everywhere are lies

13

Sitting alone deep at night
many crocodiles steal onto the bank
like intangible poems

crawling between fingers
under masses of grass and leaves
unknowingly you are being eaten

14

Your being is planned at conception
and as the first word grabs and kills you
your birth is induced

pale body growing with the cold
you ponder the world in a line of poetry
then comes authentic death

15

Your hand with the pen is gashed
as if seized by a crocodile
pouncing on the sun

then soundlessly dropping
the pen is seized by words
but the crocodile's belly still rages with hunger

Translation from the Chinese by Mabel Lee

Gu Cheng 1956–1993

A GENERATION

The pitch black night gave me two deep black eyes
with which to search for light.

Translation from the Chinese by Sam Hamill

from THE BULIN* FILE

Discovery

Of all the people who went into the snowy mountains,
Only Bulin discovered the path.
Though there's just a few metres of it,
Though Venus
Broke a tooth there,
None of this prevented
An Englishman from dying,
Lying in the middle of the road, smiling,

---

* BULIN—"A character in the mode of the Monkey King and Don Quixote. He wreaked havoc in my mind when I was young" (Gu Cheng).

Orchids and tender leaves sprouting
From his ears,
And a rosy glow on his face.

What did that mean?
Bulin frowned
And at last he remembered:
When he was nine, he had come
To spend summer, and had planted a box of matches.
They sprouted, and bore
Berries the size of match heads.
The Englishman gobbled them up
Out of greed.

What a discovery!
Unprecedented, perhaps—
   the berry a match bears is poisonous!
Bulin started the trip downhill
And reached the Lama temple made of manure.
He stood stock still, ready to be robbed of his secret
At knifepoint.
But it didn't work out that way. He could only
Sob his heart out
And lash thin copper cables around his stockings
To escape into the deep marshes.

There
Slippers clamoured in a frenzy
And turned into a cluster of frogs.

Bulin Met Bandit

Bulin met Bandit
The one and only Bandit!

Who hails from the river, a scion of
Beast Bighorn, one hand grabbing a beard,
The other grabbing a sword.

He and Bulin
Parried and thrust between
Cracks of brown coal, slicing up
Eight hours and a wrist-watch.

Then Bulin got tired,
He announced: Intermission.
Bandit grabbed
Princess Fibreglass and
Forced her to run away with him.

Oh, what rotten luck!
Who spun fibreglass into a Princess?
It'd make a much better thermos cover.

Runaway?
That's a job calling for
Technique. The most important thing is that
Someone has to chase them—and you must not laugh!

Well, if you mustn't laugh you don't, that's all.

Bandit and Princess
Swam across the pool of the white porcelain wash basin and
Desperately tried to climb the looking glass.
Running for their lives—no laughs!—
But who's chasing them? Where is he?
Bulin said he was tired.
Nothing for it: Intermission.

He and his 15 cents
Are queuing up—for ice cream.

Bulin Is Dead, It Seems

Huge frogs and curses
Were thrown at the wall together.
Bulin, it seems, is
Dead.
Oh woe, at last, God took out a handkerchief to be polite.
A field of square flowers
Broke out
In the graveyard.

Bulin, alas, it seems, is dead.
A hundred yellow-faced grandsons
Came in red limousines from the breast of every continent,
Hurrying here to mourn him. Oh, alas.
They wept for a while, aided by a water pump.
They sawed their teeth, and started dancing
Disco,
Spreading their stubby fingers,
Spreading their mouths, magically producing colourful billiard balls,
Half an ice-cream sun,
A fridge,
And the foam of black beer floating in the sky.

Alas! Alas! Oh woe!
Bulin is dead, dead, dead.

Such well-practised death, as if it were real.
He blinked his eyes in the warm air duct,
Regretted
Not bringing enough
Sleeping pills.

Translation from the Chinese by Eva Hung

Pierre Joris b. 1946

from **WINNETOU OLD**

Vier Takte vor K   time then   before
starting   a poesis that   keeps that other   that
began in bone arete   return to turbulence   break
the slippery line   to work thanatos tetanos   Verkrampfung
second movement   process of individuation   social
aspects in aspic   hides a soul   caught   already encysted
blastula   reaps a soul   in titanic paralysis   the
horizon inked   end of my life   there rises   frostbite
blaming outside genetics   the sea a tree a cloud a clubfoot
this homunculus   frozen brass monkey   bone monkey
teton titan   peeled of all flesh & fleas   all noise &
bloodroar   all Staub und Blut   ein Würfel Milch

.

black millennium cramp has torqued   all
muscle into solid bone   *os*   os   bone   bone Knochen
or   meinc Gebeine   the bone titan   crouching knot-
sayer   a preventer   a not-sayer   a stop-gap   bony
head wedged   into that opening   in the self that is the
self   slash   through which soul flows   into world
usurper of the quickening pulse   rides inside a stone rage
a congealed black hole   moon key   key hatred   cancer
romance   blastulated frippery   a fibromous death cult
absolute balance   no clinamen

.

staccato stasis   howl this alphabet
go away   don't hurl this relapse into bone   again
no gain   this stone-monkey   Europe post   no   inter-
glacial basin   from its dead   foam no Aphrodite   no
fat-assed goddess   kalypigian woman   scraggy pigeons of
Paris Rome London Berlin   carriers of Krakow diseases
kill the messengers   from Budapest   the plague is
no turbulence   breath   learn how to breathe   with eyes

closed   break now the slippery line   carry on   Winnetou
old now   called Taranta in the vision   a clearing   a one-
room school-house   part Swiss chalet part frontier log cabin
part greek temple   an old mescalero apache in rags of white
hair   with a ball of light yarn   in his right hand
itschli dead   he walks in rubber Good Year sandals   the
light yarn ball raised   his hand raised   all salutes
resemble each other

·

IBM staccato rage   make it flow   blood not
I-slash   make it over again into daily sashimi   cut from
between your ribs   toro of belly   toro of Gloucester
make merry haha   only through power   can we churn the
yourappian mind   around & around   here come aus Deutschland
that battering figure of   bone-monkey   break the ice
reclaim use of bone   subarctic steppes   double-sealed in
Deutschland aus Deutschland   ein Würfel Stroh ein Nichts
aus Erde   metal-blue Aries comes across   a milled universe
Universum für junge Menschen   comes across the heart-bunker
limits of any city   retrace the subway steppes   in strong
Indian ink   all alone   with Winnetou old   Tamburlaine
Turbulence dead already   amazing names   more than fishwives
caretakers of the world

·

sound gethsemanes   spell through hell's
landscapes   a cardiovascular ease   a momentary you wakes
a sentence   now another night lifts off the rooftops   in
anger   its load   a cynical series of political nightmares
you turned your back   accused me of lack of romanticism
the fragrance of passion   the smell of death hides behind
the fragrance of new sheets   bone gags anger   that narrow
mood   ram's head hurtling pike's mouth gasping water
shoots   an old turbulence comes riding

·

there is unfinished business on this front
it is new   it is not new   it goes west west the Urals
a spine   Nestorian wave-forms   rattus rattus rattus   only
antigens can cross   a bilaterally proliferating earth
don't you realize   you could die any minute   have done
so for so long already   to break la nuit américaine
translates as European day   here comes Autonomia   rises
against the faked night of Hollywood paper jungles   oh Ez
you went off the black edge of Europe   should have known
peace is war   continued with other means   it will not
rise in the east   of sol   hearse of so much claptrap

·

yourappian Kulchur hang   the big O
l'outre l'autre now becomes au-tonomia   another alphabeta
begins   towards mania   l'altera ô becomes au   begins
towards dawn drawn with your fingers   in shellacked snows
of old   we have learned nothing from millennia   your
defense the great meltdown   domination domination of the
planets Uranus   hello Mario Tronti Tony Negri Sergio
Bologna Franco Piperno   Oreste Scalzone   hello & good-bye
you too the night of Europe   the workers no longer the edge
will lift the whole   construaimo una vita no longer
the definite article

·

it is now a   a   aaaaa   many aaaaaaaaaas
construaimo u-naaaaa   I love to build on declensions
out of the east where the sun has entered   the ass of
the bone monkey   the squatting monkey hands out its
asshairs   a rectum swallows it all back up   ur-mouth
ur-fear   sun-eater   Schreber   Herr Doktor   father
father father   tetanos bone monkey   bone-setter
stammers here   your small sun   unlanguaged sandwich
between four   a word a corpse   from memory come back
can I come back poling   me mori I die   cast myself a
corpse   ex changes color   color   rubor   dolor

Europe gave me my history, those ghostly voices of the ancestors, real or made up, lied to or listened to. America gave me geography, the space of my dance. My hope has been that language, or what little of it I have been able to serve, has made a threshing floor for their marriage.

P. J.

But the movement is less linear than the Europe-America axis proposes—other "lines of flight" lead from the native Luxembourg to the Maghreb & beyond. The nomadism of the life & a processual poetics make for an open-ended project where only movement is to be trusted, so that both poet & writing inhabit & share a condition one could call "betweenness." An active—not to say activist—process of rhizomatic writing, then, that leads to a nomadic poetics refusing to recognize any absolute, except the localized and not delimited absolute of nomad space—be it desert, steppe, or white page—where "the coupling of the place and the absolute is achieved . . . as an infinite succession of local operations"—as Deleuze & Guattari have it elsewhere.

It is a nomadism further reflected in the relationship to language, in an insistence not only on the possibility but the *need* to write in a language that is not the mother tongue but the "other" tongue, in recognition & celebration of the fact that poetry is always an other language, & language itself already a foreign language. (A not-so-uncommon condition, reaching as it does from Ovid to Vicente Huidobro [volume one], from Li Po to Anselm Hollo.) In relation to all this, Don Byrd has spoken of a poetry that can become "a poetry of crossroads: it takes place where intense dynamisms of very different scale encounter each other . . . confidently and openly in a space of extraordinary force and potential danger for anyone who makes a false step. Unlike poets of the classical tradition, which was maintained with immense stress even among the high modernists, who understood the ephemeral present against a fixed background, and unlike the more typical postmodern poets for whom the present moment and the classical background collapse into an undifferentiated mass, [such a poetry] finds a stance which allows access to these very different domains, without losing definition."

Arkadii Dragomoschenko b. 1946

A SENTIMENTAL ELEGY

(for Anna Hejinian)

Let the mouse run over the stone.
ALEKSANDR VVEDENSKY

"Tell me, what binds us to some meaning,
                    what drives us out of our minds?"
Dark
of a racing cloud, trace of   glass,   white.
The rim of a clock face.
The vastness of death and its insignificance, debris
                flying in a scorched haze of dragonflies—
We aren't going anywhere.
There are wells where even at noon the stars are sharp
But branching out like a book into strangeness—a possibility
                        always remains,
sand
and standing still.
Some word, like a law's mold, reveals the world reversed
                mirrored down the axis of matter.
                                    And so
this peeling apart
in tireless trials of freedoms.
Perhaps—"but it's meaningless"—in the prisms' twilight
    where winters' straight lines erupt suddenly in the ice
and like indivisible fire
the wind rocks it and scatters it by the handful.
                                    And so
in the trials of flight between zenith, nadir, window
                        and unshaven cheek,
ochre and heather,
in the debris of streaming heights. . . . The visible image
   of a home for these things eludes us. What's behind them?
The same is behind us and before us.
Capricious stroll, hair like far-off laughter,
Not to remember—to weave a cobweb into the structure
                                of hearing,
Into the correspondence of minutest registers—

Their myriads flicker
Myriads
matching the spirals of the pulse that braids the wrist's
                                         dry riverbeds.
The sequel is absurd.
A conquest (of what?) is like a photograph, its filigree
                                         lost in a grid,
For everything must begin, however you look at snow and fire,
As if, reflected in melting ice on the window, you were
                              scraping your cheeks with a razor

And again the nature of sunset is unknown
And of the spatial partitions that create it—time?
body?
memory? line?—and of the intervals glimpsed by chance
when branching out like a book into strangeness.

• • •

What is said is a lamp, but it announces: "spring thunder."
Light speaks its name brokenly and immediately you can hear
                   how the dry celery beside the indistinct map
                                         flickers
glistening
hoarsely
like the wrist's river weeds.

The tap is running.

But take some bitter coffee beans, let them be spun
                                    into fragrant dust
let them simmer
"odds and evens" ground down, stopping the run
of whirled resins

And turn to the invulnerable, braided water
For there the fluid time of its fall is shattered,
In the memory a splinter of light catches the thousand "I's"

it stubbornly returns—
as children against their will catch the claw of a bird
                         in the creaking kitchen, perhaps. . . .

I don't remember.
I was shifted a pace aside
from myself, from everyone, and that includes God
approaching the native land of clouds
and cutting my gaze off from flashes of sand and trees.

Summer passes

hiding nothing in the deep blue
                        a branch of elation sinking
into crystal salts of reason

"Tell me, what is it that melts in us or binds us together?
Within the sequence of days and of days now and then
                                alternating with night . . ."

drawn out beyond the limits of the mind to the stillness
in each chance sound

split by the desire for such binding.

Note on the epigraph to "A Sentimental Elegy"

"In actual fact objects are a faint mirror image of time. Objects don't
exist. . . . Let the mouse run across the stone. Now count every one of its
footsteps. Now forget the word 'every,' forget the word 'footstep.' Then
every footstep will appear as a new movement. After that, since, for good
reason, you have experienced the disappearance of your perception of a
series of movements which you were erroneously calling footsteps (you
were confusing movement with space), movement will begin to fragment,
it will be reduced to nil. A flickering begins. The mouse begins to flicker.
Look around: the world is flickering."

from "Oberiuty," by Leonid Aleksandrov, in
Chekhoslovenska rusistika, XIII, 68 no. 5

Translation from the Russian by Lyn Hejinian & Elena Balashova

Poetry is an expenditure of language "without goal," in fact a redundancy; a constant sacrifice to a sacrifice. It is possible that one should speak here about love, in other words about reality, or the probability of answering the sourceless echo — about responsibility.

A. D.

Dragomoschenko was one of the principal poets & artists who began—in the dying years of the total Soviet state—to reclaim the promise of early Russian modernism & to take it into the postmodern present. Born to a military father in Potsdam (GDR), raised in the small city of Vinnitsa (Ukraine), he moved in his early twenties to Leningrad, where he participated in the underground (samizdat) foment then impacting Russian intellectual/artistic life. Never officially published, he wrote & circulated eight book-length collections of poetry (as well as two plays & a "novel"-in-progress) & helped found the influential Club 81, while working (variously) as night watchman, street sweeper, & stoker for a time at the Leningrad State University psychology department (where he would later lecture). His collaboration & friendship with the American poet Lyn Hejinian brought his work to the attention of an active generation of poets in the English-speaking world, & three books translated by Hejinian & Elena Balashova make him possibly the most translated & internationally published of post-Soviet poets.

Decentered perhaps by his Ukrainian origins, Dragomoschenko was among the first in Russia to push past the limits of the poem as lyric self-expression toward "'language [as] an activity' of society"—yet different by far from what that sense of the social might have signalled in the previous regime. An elaborate congruence of mind & vision, his project links up with the thwarted modernist "attempt [by Khlebnikov & early Mayakovsky, say] to liberate Russian poetry from the restraints of classical form and everything implied by the Pushkinian heritage" (Michael Molnar). In his own terms this becomes "the promise, in language, in poetry," of a "liberation of the senseless by the senseless," for which (he writes) "courage consists in an unending affirmation of thought which overcomes 'the order of actual truth' itself."

Nathaniel Mackey b. 1947

SONG OF THE ANDOUMBOULOU: 15

—bedouin wind—

Back down the steps I go out
careful not to cross my legs
turning left up Monmouth,
pressing
my feet to an otherwise all
but
unbearable stretch as to a lizard's back.
In the scorched upper lefthand
heavens my sister sits weeping,
robed in kerosene light.
Our father's
gone Panamanian grin's pathetic air,
thru which its teeth now push their deeprooting
rotted stumps, unruly gunmetal
gristings,
a Dogon
ram's head with Amon's gourd stuck
between its horns . . .

Outside the
windowless room I dance a
clubfoot's waltz, my legs driven by horsemen,
bones hounded by lusts.
The last of
eight to pierce the lighted way, my
path readied by drumrolls, the
oils of Amentet, the raw throats of
devotion . . .
Lipless thirst, our thumbless layings
on of hands . . .

The rough body
of love at last gifted with
wings, at
last bounded on all but one
impenetrable side by the promise
of heartbeats heard on high,
wrought
promise of lips one dreamt of aimlessly
kissing,
throated rift . . . Furthered hiss of its
gift
of tongues . . .

So this my Day, my Light's
numberless years' run of horses
whose hoofs plow any dreamer's
head, my Day of bone, my bootless
feet
mashing shattered glass, at last
begins,
white stucco walls reflect a stark summer
sun.

A distant hum the faroff buzzings of
bees, boats towed ashore . . .
The noise recedes thru every usable
gate . . .
Unruly goat, so uncorruptly
unswung,
legs rusted . . .

The risen woo the wind and
are blown
away

Day one stood erect, arthritic. Ache
of its arrival, peregrine spark.

Seated each on a bedouin throne, sun
blown in our faces.   Blistered
                                        kisses.
Desert love.   Threaded
                              lips

Day two's bright bed of attraction. Unsnuffed
ember, amniotic floor.   Blunt

sustenance, mired sublime, remote,
whispering, lost cry calling,
                              no way out
if not thru.   But stuck, too
beautiful. "Stay."   Blunt sustenance.
Sifting the choked water
                              for bones . . .

Seated each before a sea of exhaustion,
off to one side of us prompting us,
lipped indelicate teachers,
                              heart's meat
raw, rough taskmaster muscle,
                              carnivorous.
                                        Cannibal,
careless law

Day three fell away in fragments.
   Unfinished fourth . . .   Unbeginnab'

   Wanting it back but glad one
gave it away, to've let go holding
    each breath as if it was
    or would be one's last.

   Warmed-over gospel. Stick-figure truth.
Sang with a cricket caught inside my
               throat.

   Stuck tongue I sucked singing thru
cracks in a falling wall. Maybe my
   own, maybe someone else's.
             Stuck
tongue bloated, foolish beauty.
          One's own

Day six. Lidless eater of raw meat, day
   scoured by starlight,   breach
of it blessed but if only by music
           by nothing,
   house made of thrown-away stones . . .

         Cast off
only to be called back,
       cut,
   sewn up again. Tenuous
throatsong, hoof to the head waking
   up, plucking music from a meatless
          rib . . .

Rickety tauntsong. Plum's pit.
Staining the hands with henna.
Close to the heart but keeps
out of reach,
Digitaria . . .   Home.   Bedouin
stone's

throw away

COMMENTARY

*The song says the / dead will not / ascend without song. // That because if /
we lure them their names get / our throats, the / word sticks.* (N. M.) And
again: *The dead don't want / us bled, but to be sung. // And she said the
same, / a thin wisp of soul, / But I want the meat of / my body sounded.*

A vision of communality, then, that has to be sung (his is a *lyric* voice) into,
or back into, existence, because, as Mackey says: "In language we inherit
the voices of the dead" that give us "access to history, tradition, times and
places that are not at all immediate to our own immediate and particular
occasion." That occasion is the African American community: "I'm post
bebop. I come after Bud Powell and Bird and Monk and so forth, and my
sense of things very much has the imprint of . . . beginning to think about
writing in the sixties, at the time when we had the black avant-garde, the
new black music." But his imagination & intellect are syncretic, constantly
calling to mind (so Joseph Donahue) "pluralities . . . Olson's polis, Creeley's
company, Duncan's heavenly city, Spicer's infernal one, Baraka's nation"—
as well as other, more heterological instances such as Dogon cosmology or
the tale of the Dausi & of their city, Wagadu. Thus the scope & in-gathering
ambition of his ongoing serial poem *Song of the Andoumboulou* (here ex-
cerpted): Mackey's "new eutopic thought" (his term), aware of humanity's
legacy of enslavement & violence, does not lead to an easy adamic naming
(as was possible for Whitman, Pound, or even Duncan) but to a processual
investigation of the orders of language itself (as in his anagrammatic play—
elsewhere—on words as unlikely as pronouns). The hope throughout is that
rhapsodic song will stitch together all those othering threads—& do so by
grounding itself in a duende (volume one, page 461) that can be found in
Coltrane, say, or in the Bedouins' poetic traditions—here—as much as in
Lorca's.

Of the Andoumboulou of the poem's title (sacred beings in the Dogon
[West African] cosmos), Mackey writes: "[They are] the spirits of an earlier,
flawed or failed form of human being—what, given the Dogon emphasis on
signs, traces, drawings, 'graphicity,' I tend to think of as a rough draft of a
human being." To which he later adds: "The Andoumboulou are in fact us;
we're the rough draft."

Habib Tengour b. 1947

from EMPEDOCLES' SANDAL

Traces/ Renown/ Shades/ Urns/ Life(s)/ Epoch/ Zenith
Lucid/ Strangely/ Suspended

....

Letters
bricolage of symbols gathered in neighbouring

                                        countries
the golden thread imprints on the memory
the one I question answers to no

                                   demand
rigid it invents for itself
a republic in which reading commands

                         summary hierarchy
in the scenery

                         a hidden laser
modern he said
to tread territories made to measure
where the places knot into a tight rope
to live truly
to be god

             to claim it loudly

                       reckless pride

you the Impeder-of-wind with bronze sandals
you the Obscure who loves to disguise yourself
and I all alone tracking you
lives a concise inventory the detail
adorns the gathering
the fragments are classified
to observe a usage
just as white milk curdles

was it in Heidelberg on a road in Sicily
in Evry or in Mostaganem by the seaside
ill-used infinite
few words carry when the tension increases

alternation of the forms does not resolve much
nor do the *rivets of love* assemble
I remain an orphan

neither wine of Anderin flowing freely nor bravado
at the moment when the clan wobbles
neither catalysing places a sequence of cast names
nor beauties offering themselves along the way
nor the poetic lineage you claim
nor this hard to decipher manuscript nor
any allegiance excluded
rupture

Always
this array of set-backs
you register
     stifled passion
       far the epic gesture
the solemn declamations at the tribune

dwellings of Maya Asma Awf or Khawla
recall of pure form
       era of imprecation
       the loved one veils herself
usury eye and soul
and the heart's expression
and these memorable debris under the ashes

pangs at rising
    at dusk a life comes to a close
         a novel
torsion
   the star blinks
      a town in tatters
          screams

you envisage death
     daily reception
to disappear swallowed by a mechanism
radically no longer to exist   never
scholastic divagation
the views of the mind deteriorate the momentum of the word
        the South is wild

there I am confronted by the formulas
ceaselessly stating identity to pass
unnoticed
to sound a fortuitous jubilation
                    at the outcome of a quest
disposed to welcome a meaning that escapes me
                enigma resolved as soon as stated
                to love, an art wherein to take one's distances
                inside of the unhoped for

they will call your surrender wisdom
quintessence the sterility of the soil
and age adds to the bitterness

Obviously
at its zenith
the law has to concede suicide to the poet
assure the inheritance
                    grandly
there is a truth here difficult to grasp
the tomb is sealed

the beautiful to resay it
the road already traced by a mortal's audacity

rustling of the myth
                discoveries of listening
                                smoke
elasticity of the rays

passion consumes you
                love roots itself in your eyes
you have handy clichés
                a large library
advice that succeeds with illustrated examples
and you tremble when the loved one appears
is it a life
            a belated madness
a mystery that isn't one
                sun or rain
                        prayer
your impatience unbalances nature
where are you at the hour of regrets

the people get drunk on the drunkenness of the masters
each judges according to his manner
an illusory feast takes over custom
blood transforms itself into a philter

                                        waiting for day
                            acting
above the head   death   the road is straight
it is not vengeance of a wounded chest
it is not surrender to decline
audacity shatters at the descent of the verse
the clamors feed on themselves
to exalt oneself by your name the torment has ripened

the accent isn't new

                    to recognize

                                        the grace of a flash
                            when the soul shatters

happy
in her kernel a poem constructs

to perish
                    the elements fuse

                                by hate or by love

                                        invention
that which retains the guest in the house
that which terrorizes the virgins of Tamîm
that which persuades the number

the titration is deceptive

Igneous
the soul in its crystal
the way constellated waves deploy themselves

                                        harnassing
ONE engenders destroys yet alternates
he keeps me captive
corruptible

the sweet water in the sea on which the fish feed is not
an irrefutable argument against the establishment of paradise on
earth   other elements of a subtle nature enter into

the composition of the air man breathes   which inserts the
human species into a specific animal category
man is like a weathervane at the heart of the whirlwind
                                   the sky
attracts him
Aristotle's disciples debated physics   meteorology
natural science
                       then one did not consider armed struggle in the
cities in order to impose a thesis   a phenomenon that
keeps spreading   as does repression   the system has seized up
to analyze sea water   or to examine the conditions of the ground can
in no way unscramble the mechanism   does that mean that in
this process it is necessary   to sink   with the logic of the ancients
the trace of the poem in fragments initiates   formal audacities
   a rhythm pursues you   this is no longer the time to evade
meaning   the words order themselves

the year ends white
          wishes crackle on all sides
from the orient to the occident is it but a reflection
light effluvia when the moon scatters
                         hail-stones
what remains accessible in the face to face
this country where the violet grape once loved   [Hölderlin
to grow for a better people, and the golden fruit
in the dark thicket, and noble wheat, and some day
the stranger will ask, treading through the rubble
of your temples, if that's where the city
rose . . .
this sovereign generosity
this evil which hardens in the apple of the eye
these plaints without notification
a salute to the dead friends

Ochre
maturity, it ends with the day
the questions left hanging

you observe the flight of a flock of starlings
bad news is spreading
from the palms of Bahrain to the villages of Iraq

a tenacious worry
the long crossing from deserts to cities
these buried peoples with strange languages

there are only scattered signs
truth surprises you
at a metro gate

this visible and invisible world is decomposing
science assures the poet of his wording
the risks hidden in the hands' palms
let's leave tears and blood

                          our friends are everywhere
the voyage completes itself

                         by day as by night
all things astounded

Parcelled
out they glitter under the moon
motionless

the white armed virgin flies over the offerings

Translation from the French by Pierre Joris

COMMENTARY

Who is this Maghrebian? How to define him?
   "The woods are white or black" despite the hidden presence of nuances.
Today definition fascinates because of its implications. A domain that mis-leads. Political jealousy far from the exploded sense of the real.
   Indeed there exists a divided space called Maghreb but the Maghrebian is always elsewhere. And that's where he makes himself come true.
   Jugurtha lacked money to buy Rome.
   Tariq gave his name to a Spanish mountain.
   Ibn Kaldoun found himself obliged to give his steed to Tamurlaine.
   Abd El Krim corresponded with the Third International. . . .
H. T.

If in the above lines (taken from his "Maghrebian Surrealism" manifesto-essay) Habib Tengour speaks to the nomadic & (post)colonial condition of his countrymen, he himself fully shares that need for an "elsewhere." Born in Mostaganem, Western Algeria, raised on the Arab & Berber voices of marketplace storytellers & poets, & moving, since the sixties, between Paris & Constantine, his writing takes place in French & with the avant-garde tradition of French Surrealism firmly in mind. But, as for of from outside Europe (compare, for example, Adonis on Arab model [pages 182, 441]), the core achievement is the successful relay between mod ernist Euro-American experiments & local traditions of sociopolitical & spiritual narrative explorations in boundary-breaking: "It is, finally, in Maghrebian Sufism that surrealist subversion inserts itself: 'pure psychic automatism,' *'amour fou,'* revolt, unexpected encounters, etc. . . . There always resides a spark of un(?)conscious Sufism in those Maghrebian writers who are not simply smart operators—go reread Kateb [Kateb Yacine, the author of *Nedjma,* founding novel of Maghrebian Modernism] or Khaïr-Eddine [page 683, above]" (H. T.).

Our excerpt constitutes the last third of *Empedocles' Sandal,* set in Tengour's favorite geography, the Mediterranean, though on this occasion he comes to the fifth century B.C. Greek poet-philosopher Empedocles (who committed suicide by jumping into the crater of Mount Aetna in Sicily, leaving behind a sandal) via the German poet Hölderlin's work *The Death of Empedocles.*

Leslie Scalapino b. 1947

INSTEAD OF AN ANIMAL

Seeing as I was willing to give up my seat for the person who said
he had reserved it, first wetting out of my excitement or my worry
or perhaps heat, not only the seat but obviously my own clothes,
it is no wonder that the person was willing to sit wallowing in it;
in that perfumes are made to come from the anal glands of animals.

Except for seeing women suckling in public—one time,
two women were suckling at the teats of the nursing mother; the
infant being left to whine while the mother endured these females
feeding off of her. With what concern to her infant when the adult
women had finished with her—otherwise I don't mind.

Some adolescents visiting us, having been weaned, wouldn't
guess that adolescents were being allowed
to suckle at their mother's breasts
and expected her to open up her dress in public
letting the as yet unweaned 12 or 15 year old be seen nursing.

Stranger when it is the male opening his shirt in public,
and applying an infant to his chest as if he had breasts.
Not even necessary for the infant to have the nipple.
The children let out a few cries, the man puts them up to let
them suck. Or as easily applies them to his back or his thighs.

Some children of seven to ten years of age or so
were letting each other open their shirts and dresses
and suck on each other's nipples.
No matter that they had flat chests, the rest of the children
clamoring to be put on the older children's breasts.

In that the infants, as yet too helpless to make the animal
yield to a demand to nurse them,
and, owing to the mothers' anxiety on this matter,
the infants were overseen though they were allowed to eat
at a wet nurse's teat.

Asked why these children of 7 or 8 or so had swollen bellies
so that a child's belly
would resemble the hard belly of a cow or of a mare,
they said
that it was because these children had the habit of swallowing air.

Instead of an animal, we got an old rag that was rancid-
smelling as if it were an animal.
You know how one can want to roll on it.
You know how one can want to roll on it.
You know how one can want to roll on it.

Many young females—either unable to find any other outlet,
or   , genuinely interested in the immature males
whom they regard merely as toys—
will do their first fondling and caressing
after carefully undressing some seven or eight year old boys.

Some of the children were aware that the source of this sense
of happiness was in there.
They had only to touch themselves—
pushing their fingers in
there at the opening.

Young females will often compare
their surprise
to the time
when they first became aware
that they were able to suck the fluid out of the male's organ.

Even when the mating couple is seen,
the male is curled like a foetus
his mouth is on the female's breast as if he were eating
while the female is hugging him as if she were holding a rabbit
and feeling its heart beating.

I was surprised that infants produced by these wives
never resembled their mothers;
rather, as soon as they were brought to the mothers' bedsides,
they were seen to have the sweetbread
and the hair that curled as if it were on a ram's head.

Afterall it is the adult male who makes the infantile whining sound
in the five and dime store
while the others are seen outside
one waiting in line
some females make noises to imitate swine.

The adult male who is eating at the dinner table with some people,
for instance, sets his napkin on fire
and lets it blaze as one would light a cat on fire with kerosene
so that
people will imagine a cat flaring up like that under their noses.

Make writing that is held to present-time and does not arise from memory.
It is realism that can occur only as the writing.
It has no other existence.
L. S.

Working thus clearly through the tradition of Gertrude Stein (volume one) but connecting it to the uncertainties of this postmodern moment, Scalapino (poet, essayist, playwright, & editor of O Books), by fragmenting syntax & line, has created a "stripped down bone-spare writing"—so Stephen Radcliffe—"which stands in its chiselled conciseness and the almost breathless intensity of its (female) voice in the lyric tradition of Sappho, Dickinson and H. D."

But it is a lyricism that continually undercuts itself (note that many of her poems are punctuated almost exclusively with the dash, a typographical sign that both severs & connects, thus questioning relationship). Working out of an anguished awareness of Heisenberg's Uncertainty Principle (i.e.: the act of perception alters what is being perceived), Scalapino questions the very possibility of meaning in the relation between language & the world. ("Writing simply has no connection to reality. / The actual event is entirely absent from it in the present," she says.) And yet, Scalapino keeps her attention firmly, even obsessively, on the world around us—whose political & social violence & psychological skewing lend the writing an uncanny "realism." Throughout the work, writing & thinking about writing are seamlessly folded into each other, or, as Scalapino herself has noted—with a sense, too, of realism's mysteries: "You don't know where something's coming from. It appears to be coming from outside you or from inside yourself, but what you appear to be creating is actually occuring out there seen as if under your control. You want to disturb that control. It is the unfolding of events which actually occur, but you don't know where they are from or from what focal point they're emanating."

Cecilia Vicuña b. 1948

FIVE NOTEBOOKS FOR EXIT ART

I. Connection

The art of joining, union
from *ned:* to bind, to tie
zero grade form: *nod*
old English: *net*
Latin: *nodus*
        knot

David Brower said: "The earth is dying because people don't see the connections" between a hamburger and the death of the rain forest, air conditioning and the death of the atmosphere).

Eliot Weinberger said: "Do you know what a *clue* is? A ball of yarn or thread that Theseus used to come out of the labyrinth, thus anything that guides or directs in the solution of a problem."

René Guénon says: "the connection protects."

in Nahuatl, one of the names of God is "nearness and togetherness" (. . . *del cerca y del junto*)

II. The Resurrection of the Grasses

Octavio Paz said: "Poetry is resurrection."

> to be erect
> again,
> greening!

> waves
> of
> grass

> blades
> blades

> surging
> from the
> dead streams

> resurrect!
> *surgere*
> *sub + regere:*
> to lead

> lead the
> greening
> upright!

growth, green & grass
originally had the same root:
ghre

once I dreamt of a form of poetry created by the sound of feet walking in the grass

in Nahuatl, poetry, *xopancuicatl* is "a celebration of life and cyclical time: the poem and the poet become a plant that grows with the poem; the plant becomes the fibers of the book in which the poem is painted . . ."
(Eliot Weinberger)

> collected all
> around waterways
> in Brooklyn,
> Manhattan, Chile
> and the Bronx,
>
> the land grasses
> and the
> *cochayuyo*
> seaweed
>
> are intertwined
> with plastic
> nets.
>
> resurrect!

III. The Origin of Weaving

origin
from *oriri:* the coming out of the stars

weave
from *weban, wefta,* Old English
weft, cross thread
> *web*

> the coming out
> of the cross-star
>
> the interlacing of
> warp and weft

to imagine the first cross
intertwining of branches and twigs
to make a nest
to give birth

the first spinning of a thread
to cross spiraling
a vegetable fiber imitating a vine

the first thread coming out of fleece trapped in
            vegetation

the first cross of warp and weft
union of high and low, sky and earth,
woman and man

the first knot, beginning of the spiral:
life and death, birth and rebirth

textile, text, context
from *teks:* to weave, to fabricate, to make wicker or
            wattle for mud-covered walls (Paternosto)

sutra: sacred Buddhist text
            thread (Sanskrit)

tantra: sacred text derived from the Vedas: thread

ching: as in *Tao Te Ching* or *I Ching*
            sacred book: warp
            wei: its commentaries: weft

Quechua: the sacred language
            derived from *q'eswa:*
            rope or cord made of straw

to weave a new form of thought:
            connect
bring together in one

IV. Pueblo de Altares

pueblo: people
altar: "place for burning sacrificial offerings"

we are the pueblo
our house the altar

threshold: limit or doorway

lintel, the top of the threshold
from *liminaris,* the limit
and the most ancient *tol:* as in *dolmen:*
table of stone

mesa & *missa*
(the mass, from "sending a message")
are also confused

(*limit* and *lumen:*
the light came to be one)

to confuse is "to pour together"

house & altar are intertwined
as in architecture
from *arch*

arkhe, rule, beginning
or *ar,* to fit together as in bow & arrow
& *tektron:* carpenter, builder, from
teks: to weave

"to make wicker or wattle fabric for mud-covered houses"

coming from the beach, the little residues reside in it

Patti Hagan says "they look like the scale model of a lost civilization."

someone else said: "or a new civilization built on the remains of the present one."

in Panama, the people made homeless by the U.S. bombing
were called *precaristas*

*favelas, callampas, pueblos jovenes, villas miserias, shanty-
towns* by any name are all
                      Pueblos de altares

V. Poncho: Ritual Dress

hilo de agua
thread of water

hilo de vida
thread of life

they say woolly animals
are born high in the
mountain springs

water and fiber
are one

wool & cotton
downy fiber
an open hand

the Cotton Mother textile goddess in Chavín is a plant creature with snake
feet, eyes and heart radiating from the center like a sun

the poncho
is a book
a woven
message

a metaphor
spun

white stones found in the mist, the *illa* and the *enqaychu* are the emblems
of the vital force within the woolly animals themselves but only the poor
and haggard can find them by the springs.

written in English

Precarious *is what is obtained by prayer. Uncertain, exposed to hazards, insecure. From the Latin "precarious," from "preces"; prayer.*
C. V.

An artist/poet of multiple means, she has worked with films, installations, & performance pieces, & has moved between her native Chile and New York City over the last two decades. In this work, as in her poetry as such, she draws not only from modern & postmodern contemporaries but from (principally Andean) shamanism, oral traditions, mythology, & herbal lore ("ancient and modern texts which helped me to understand what I had seen"). The *unravelling* & *weaving* that (in her own description of it) characterizes both her written & visual work draws from an almost limitless range of sources, mixing her words with those of others (old & new) in an assemblage or weave of words conceived (like "the sacred Quechua language," she tells us) as knots & threads. If this, then, is the central metaphor in the poem presented here, the sources for her words are given also as acts of vision in which (she writes) "individual words opened to reveal their inner associations, allowing ancient and newborn metaphors to come to light." And further: "To approach words from poetry is a form of asking questions. // To ask questions is to fathom, to drop a hook to the bottom of the sea. // The first questions appeared as a vision: I saw in the air words that contained, at the same time, both a question and an answer. // I called them 'divinations.' And the words said: the word is the divination; to divine is to ascertain the divine."

And quoting therein our brother poet Octavio Paz: *I don't see with my eyes: words are my eyes.*

Will Alexander b. 1948

ALBANIA & THE DEATH OF ENVER HOXHA

Sacrifice
closely paralleled with sadness
with darkened lunar wounds in the brain
the thoughts laced with paralysis ciphers
the voice full of fumaroles & muffled x-ray voltage
the cells cold with exhaustive inversion

& so
all pronouncements become tautological
derisive
each attempt at revival sundered with
a wearied dysfunctional torment
with psychic nuclear crippling &
hyperborean chills
all attempts at recovering pushed back into limbo

if one could look at the soul
it would take on the grief of a savagely splintered darkness
a simile of cacti & arrowheads
burrowing into the crucially exposed eye-stalks of crustaceans
the face always stained by a ruthless sabulosity
coupled by paranoia & blasting

the expiring Enver Hoxha
prone
like a skull on a slab of Marxist invectives
with a glut of crushed worms slipping from his forehead
laying there
with personal rabies on the breath
an ignited grandeur
coming out in riddles of oracular demon pulleys
rust burns smoking below the stones of his flesh
his dictatorial mutterings
like a spurt of unseasonable frog gills
like a grotesque insecticidal frenzy calling out
from tormented histamine gardens
calling out from decrepit Dodonas
diseased with insidious meiosis

Hoxha
with secretive bone grafts
with rational murdering solutions
always hardened
like blackened myasthenias

all his rebellious hirelings
slaughtered in a square by machine gun & mortar
the killers surreptitiously empowered
by mutative alienation

by a heart of stunted mangrove blisters
& his dreams
like a definition of mustard gas
"irritating, blistering . . . disabling . . ."

Hoxha
sucking in fumes from his after-death exposure
his astral obliteration
like an exquisite brew of heinous polonium cocktails
full of disintegrated polyhymnias
full of mental pollution & polymorphic pariahs & sweating
full of stunted radium volcanos & the sociology of crows

in his Stygian neurosis
this demon
atop asphyxiation & thrones
always remains demasted
in haunted wallowing aspersions of a synchronous assuagement
his lost Malpighian body
directing his troops across a coldly burning land
with all the embraceable contusions of a stifling necrology

". . . report to his majesty
that the bones have been crushed
that the spleens are now rotted
that all is in order"

the sun
like an Albanian nothingness
like an exposed nerve of singing suddenly turned over
into neutralized materia & banished
as a dried pineal concentration

& here we have Enver Hoxha on his death bed
breathing in parasites & noxious Arabian vesications
breathing in malodorous turbellarian rains
the remaining pores of his body filled with a furious
obturation
with a dense clinical stoppage
taking a poll of his highly conducive death counts
his obverse vivisectionist commandments
the population:

an arrested quotient
a blank but undivided numerical dogma
wrestling with desires in molded sparring chambers
burning in Stalinist dialectical hells

& so Hoxha
with his convinced in-solutional ravings
speaking out
with his oily wolverine's tongue
wrapped in his popular grave clothes of blackness

there were days
when the moon began to howl at high noon
when all the aromas were suspended
when all the corpses were dredged up & eaten
when each anniversary of living
was marked by insidious facial scarring
by vicious dog bites on the buttocks

this was reason
& so the populace
full of carcinoma & rugas
their eyes cast down into sacerdotal infernos
into cold intensive lesion mining
could only witness their faces in puddles of urine
could only imagine how a morning of restive balneology would feel

how a life of campanology could brighten the darkness
but always disaster
grey
& permitted to burn like a daily burden of
calcinated litmus
like a corpse with a vertebrae of flukes
tossed up from the Adriatic shallows
tossed up in its ashen lonely demeanor
as an isolated cargo of worms

& Hoxha quoting remnants of Engels
concerning "motion" & "divisibility"
"kinetics & bodies"
under his Spartan flag of pickax & rifle

the horseless carriage banned
the blood supply diminished
the "hillsides
a jagged line of misty peaks"
like horizontal shards like "gigantic" electrocardiograms
more occluded than Tibet
creeping along "the Boulevard of Fallen Heroes"
where one can feel the peasants feeding on grasses
seeking to mobilize their anomalous wrath to production
the cities full of "windowless walls" &
a "heritage . . . of blood feuds"
yes Albania
like a "black doubled-headed eagle" on a
coursing field of blood
its exteriorized sacrifice ministries
its ferocious injury battalions
its cold atheistic medallions charged with a-charisma & spite
like a premise or a scar
or a pure line of rote from its suppurating memory
its "mosques" turned into "stables"
comets & asteroids banished from the language
& so
one is given "mechanics"
the "interchange of motion and equilibrium"
& the "measurable transference of motion"

the "quantitative expression"
the hatred of "alien morality"

& Hoxha
purged of all animal sentiment
his death bed
like a broken imperial rock
seething with a secretive personal dissension

even the "Directorate of Agitation" is crumbling in his vistas
because he smells
the insurrectional molecules of the infinite
blowing into his itinerant pantomime chamber
the inscrutable Hadean depths
a group of denuded chromium puppets floating

before his eyes
his bizarre self-palpable plainness
thrown into the face of cosmic betrayal
ulcerations & demons appear beside his visage
even his own skull appears on the plainly colored revetment
& the sun
once simply a mechanical furnace
is now a thrust of light
burning up his bones
& the bulging knot of old "fox-trots"
& purges

COMMENTARY

The art of stars, flowers, forms, colours, overlaps with the infinite.
Hans Arp, quoted by W. A. in *Vertical Rainbow Climber*

A lifelong resident of Los Angeles, Alexander was until recently very little published, but his work has now triggered assessments of his special & far-reaching view, like that, e.g., by Eliot Weinberger: "His work resembles no one's, and is instantly recognizable. In part, he is an ecstatic surrealist on imaginal hyperdrive. He is probably the only African-American poet to take Aimé Césaire as a spiritual father (and behind Césaire, Artaud and Lautréamont). But he is also, like Hugh MacDiarmid—a writer of utterly different temperament—a poet whose ecstasy derives from scientific description of the stuff and the workings of the world. . . .

"No subject seems alien to him: Who else would write a poem on the death of [the Albanian communist dictator] Enver Hoxha? Who else would attempt to inhabit the brain of an animal in ecological catastrophe? Who else could spin a 40-page poem (*The Stratospheric Canticles*) from the verb 'to paint'?—a poem that not only ranges through the history of world art, but which is an extended meditation on the way seeing is transformed by the chemical compounds of paint into vision."

Or Alexander, from his own perspective—a journey through distanced worlds of inner time & space: "To see from this disk, I am cleansed with grounded facial negatives, with bone coloured writing, with vocal bone spur chemistry with rapier crusades with hunchback conjunctions, spurred by verbal star belt eternities."

Victor Hernandez Cruz b. 1949

CAMINANDO

Take your moon face away
into the mountains of so many cities
and stare down
The invisible dance
over the cemetery of spirits
and spirits talk
La noche ojos grande
Green alleys to the future
Ways to the magic cave
You split in the spring wind
You have the key to all the doors
Be strong
Eat fish
Drink rum.

MESA BLANCA

If I were writing on rock,
It would be the wind of the year
That caressing me will make
Me aware of the shadows on
A distant stone—
That signifies an eclipse
On some unseen roof,
From where in the form of
A kite a diamond leaves for heaven.

It would be that letter that I would
Make into a face
Let's say at the banquet of those,
who having been amazed at the arrival
Of boats
Punctuate on a key,
But for what door?

The sea a rush of mists,
Things like trousers have come out
Of there,
And bacalao which here has been
Fricasseed with calabasa,
So we have to church the word
Mestizo, Mezo
Half and Half—
So that text books claiming total
Taino vanishment
Should four pages later erase
The word burundangala—
The sensational things coming together,
Of the Arowakian-Taino
The only thing that remains is
What is not gone:
The looks,
The gestures,
The thoughts,
The dreams,
The intuitions,
The memories,
The names of fruits,
Rivers,
The names of towns,
Vegetables,
Certain fish,
The gourd making music
In the mountain,
The maraca making feet
Areyto dance,
And this cigar between my fingers.

This is not to disagree with the
Anthropologist of text.
But merely to reaffirm what they mean
When they don't say.

This paper which was a tree
Is crying for its leaves,
That's the route of your mind
To dance its branches,

For that canopy red flower
Of the Floridas,
So high up in air spirit,
Flowing right through that bark,
A water shaft,
An urban lavender of bamboos
A city of juice composing,
Hidden apartments for that
Night frog,
To sing without rest
Till the roosters brush their
Beaks with the first
Arriving morning light.
The joyful noise of the night,
What might be coming from lips,
Or the rubbing of legs,
The full harmonic tropical berserk
Begging for love
In abundance
Not one thousand
But one thousand and one
Lights of cucubanos,
Morse coding lovers,
That come down,
Meow not now
of the cats—
For that's the flavor,
Within the opening of the
Two mountains,
A glance following the
River
That goes to fish its memories,
Scratched one next to the other
Like the grooves of shells,
The mountains that gave me life,
The city I had to fight.

To think that now no one believes
We were here.
The past in the smoke of the cigar,
Bringing the future in-formation.

The earth is migration, everything is moving, changing interchanging, appearing, disappearing. National languages melt, sail into each other.
V. H. C.

It is just there—in the recognition by him & his generation of the hybrid & nomadic nature of *all* language—that we see the making of an innovation that transforms the matter of the poetry itself. This is the source of Cruz's strength: that he's aware of the global implications of his project while placing it squarely in its place, its places—for him the Caribbean (namely Puerto Rico) of his birth & the New York City (*Calle Once*) of his childhood. The underlying base is Spanish ("our Spanish—which has Latin and Italian—has Taino, Siboney, Chichimeca"), & the language of choice for most of his writing is a sure demotic English: the heady mix ("linguistic stereo") spoken & heard in the great North American cities. From there he explores "the possibilities inherent in our tradition . . . a poetry that arises all around us . . . this language of the Caribbean, this criollo incarnation . . . [of] spiritual mediums and santeros who worshipped natural forces tapped since time immemorial by African and indigenous societies." It is in this encounter—"by lingual wholes" in the title of one of his books—that he becomes part of a company not only of Caribbean & U.S.-Latino writers (Guillén, Algarín, Alarcón, Alurista, Brathwaite, Césaire) but of a range of other poets, crossing over, working the interstices of language &/or culture. Writes Cruz, against the concept of a (racially, culturally) "pure" literary language: "This is what human culture is all about. At the point of the greatest mixing and contact, we collectively experience our greatest achievements, our greatest leaps of awareness. . . . It is not surprising that good poets will continue to mix and experiment and that from this stew of language and experience some of the best contemporary poetry will surface."

Coral Bracho b. 1951

ON CONTACT OPENS ITS INDIGO PIT

From your mouth, from the well of your eyes I drink, from your belly, at your flanks;
between my hands they burn, moisten
(the fervor emulsifies at the margins,
texture gathers the tense pulsing of this skin, closes its smooth sphincter, burning,
until the sum voids,

the pain). This stroked song, licked to the limit.

    The barest coolness of your tongue.
I contract (from your lips, in my hips, they expand—slivered ice—
pointed, sharp) into the pang.
Tipped toward intensity, contour, tightness howling at touch, my sex:
flame polished in its concavity, anointed; a succinct hollow, intensive,
interstitial;
turned to its concentrated cadence, to its devoted desert;

From your mouth, from your overflowing shadows, I drink, from your
crotches, your
            palms.
The burning between my thighs condenses—a twitching, slow fever—
your magnetism; between my lips. Quiet ivy, resin, lit
liquid, silica, my moistness, melts and conjugates: plexus,
briney warmth, sensitive pulp, pressing, this penetrable tympan,
this knot, this vulval excess. I'm seeking
the sure volume that unsettles me. The tensity, the unquenched heat,
stuffed in, overwhelming me, freeing me with its friction.

I would integrate your sex (retreating lava, coast, to envelop it,
            a lake going dense to the capillary
rhythm of its thirst), its slow, apprehensible abundance, its solidity,
            at my limits; vineyard
pressed to the pulse, swallowed by the vortex; seething peak, fulgarent
fulcrum,
            desire
(I lick your candescent thickness; I pour out) on contact, opens its indigo
  pit, wets.
The veins, the private illuminations, the strains
            (your thighs sink into my thighs;
            your kiss tears away)
of a new caress; the juice;

Translation from the Spanish by Forrest Gander

ON THE FACETS: THE FLASHING*

*The rhizome, like a subterranean stalk . . . assumes,
by itself, very diverse shapes: from its superficial
extension magnified in many ways, to its manifestation
in bulbs and tubers.*

    *Desire is the creator of reality . . . it produces and
moves forward by means of rhizomes.*

      An intensive feature begins to act by itself . . .

        DELEUZE AND GUATTARI, *RHIZOME*

In the parched word, unformulated, it shrinks,
rancid brown membrane ((that is: a delicate drop of oil for the morning
   radiance
of the boundaries, for the tepid
line, well-traveled, that crosses, like a limpid hue, above
the vast sizzling, over the burdened back,
bulb—a drop of animal saliva:
for the inflections, for the fertilized dawn (caress)
which expands to the shore, like foam, a relief;
a fruit-bearing fur—an ulcer of light, a basting: for
expressions fragrant to the touch, to the wrinkled shadow, coveted;
a voice, a loose fiber—a fleece—at random from the chisels,
       from the strum of the pick)
on the crest, at the flank, of the magnetizations;
Strokings
and the hair language of rubbings in the lobed bowl
of the bodies. Purple
at the root;

a sponge, a lime, an axillary
mirror: and in the echoes,

stature:
a lark. Rhymes in the lavender;
ice: by the liminal rump, smooth restless animal lips.
Hirsute valve,
alliance, in the overturning; plexus and tendon:
a warmth, a synovial point under the veined delights: ducts
to the pale hidden summit;

   * A rhizome section seen by microscope; the partridge is a potato cell. The rest appears to be or forms part of the landscape: examine it for what is connected to the libido of horses.

a splinter, a ribbon (cat),
an embryo for the bronze of rampant thickets, intimable;
a boiling, a dishevelled mass, a spore:

Cope-tails ajar at the peak of an inguinal taste.
        Above the manes; kicks:

In the customary moulds, challenged, of existing, in
their smoky, ovulating rears:
                a precise icicle,
                    an oil-lamp.
Cliffs.

and in the slimy folds, hints of existing,
and on its pungent banks of sand;
pearly figs; laughter;

a lemon on the excited fringes;
tearing: with inaudible glazed currycombs (wine, prehensile and shaggy),
with thorns the mood, the hooves;

sparking laughter between the inspected
bulbs, the magpies;
                phosphorus, winks, echoes
                in the claw; the partridge
                leaps.

The partridge: fresh bird, plentiful, with solid thighs;
marked sexual dimorphism. Its red feathers, ashen,
conceal. Leaps in ejective parabola above the strawberries;
a fluttering fever. Has gray flanks (Boiling
spongy strawberries, they exhale—from their poppy swamps,
from their verbal mesentery—the delectable lye), slender legs,
a short flight; it runs (sumptuous, overflowing taste)
rapidly.

                Opens its full clean lips:
the juice moistens and scents its harness; on its skin
of random stings, eagerly encircles the graceful one,
kicking; the slippery simultaneous nectar
sinks; amazement; vast amazement
among the high-pitched buds;
kneeling, on dazzling knee-backs, erect.

On the bicep, the scrotums; Radiant, acrid. Trots.
		Curbed by the illuminated
rumps; cadences; convex rhythm; violet-colored
		paroxysms: face down
among deep resonances. Extendible peduncles below the belt:

Sucking from the bubbling shapes; the tongue between
		the linking textures, pristine
vulvas in thermal springs, rain for the splintered
nuclei; turbulent rhizomes between the streams, the
		jubilant, foaming furs of existence;
beneath fermentable reins, the blankets.
		Absorbed
in the beds, expansive. Inundated.
Sensitive forms through the exacerbated straw, sprouting. Vital,
imperishable in their sudden impulses, smooth and tainted by their
  ocher,
their splendor, in their yolks; unique to the rubbing
pupils.
Stampede of flames between the furrows, the peppers, the traces; dense
and exaltable on their tips: by smell. Mineral
burst. A line, a caboose, a speck of dust; Gargoyle.
An ant in the joyful tufts, by the thighs,
the belly; in words)) taut, murky,
it shrinks, harsh membrane ((citric. The perpetual shrillness on the
edges)) drab; its net dims ((on the lubricated boundaries, the pistil.

—His voice: savoring, performing, plundering it—Light;
in excitable spaces, the seditious act. Labial,
expandable below the cool forefinger, its smoothness; they press.

Magnetism aroused to tasty excess,
the grating. The tickling summits.
—Turning sour, squeezing—in wild splittings,
tender. Vortex. Between the irons, the thistles,
instinct. Stubborn rodents
among the threads, the squares, the sieve. A clod,
a lanceolate breath, an itch.
To trail below the jammed, intensive zones.
Papillary knots among the grass. On the facets: the flashing.
An awl, an insect in the words)) sluggish,

crammed ((between the cracks the caesuras, on the reins.
Sudden and wanton they focus them—His voice: slitting it,
opening it, choosing it—, they encircle and cohabit on reflecting
edges)), hollows; their opaque crust ((among the screams,
the fetlocks, the clefts. To exist:))

Translation from the Spanish by Thomas Hoeksema

COMMENTARY

*Any statement I made about my work would implicitly be an evaluation
that I think is not up to me to make. Besides that, I think it would also
interfere between the reader and the texts and set a limited pattern of
approach.*
C. B.

Writes poet Forrest Gander, as Bracho's translator: "Coral Bracho's poems
read as though they were poured onto the page. They are fluid, lapping
long-lined toward the gutters. Her images evoke an oneiric, sensual realm
of dispelled logics. Her diction spills out along ceaselessly shifting beds of
sound. Like Mallarmé's, Bracho's poems first make sense as music; they
are scored. Sad birds in the luminous ceiba. Then it is as though the very
syntax has begun to run, has been heated to magma by the mind guiding the
pen. The friction of accumulating words sparks connections, and echoes
bandy back and forth between lines like flames between mirrors. Bracho's
syntax erupts and flows lubriciously around its conventionally obstruent
limitations.

"Born in 1951 in Mexico City, Bracho shrugs off Pound's maxim, 'Go in
fear of abstraction.' She writes to bridge the supposed interval between de-
scription and cognition, between the physical and the theoretical, in the un-
derstanding that our capacity for abstraction is equal to our capacity to act,
and equally human. She vividly ascribes subjectivity to events and to ob-
jects. Her poetry embodies a feeling out of voice, ductile and rhythmic, into
the world. Her vision encompasses multiple states of being.

"The pleasures of Bracho's poems derive from their open-endedness, their
music, their delicious vocabulary, and from the tension between an insis-
tently telic rhythm and a dehiscent narrative. As readers, we sense that our
arrival is imminent, but the destination keeps blowing away."

Nina Iskrenko 1951–1995

ISN'T SHE NOT A BIRD

She is gesture
The usual small change
To spend on nothing

       Pestle Pestle I am Stamen

How much snow settles
In the lines of a countenance
How much pencil lead in the bone

Autumnautumn the Body cracks
Picasso-it and Mandelstam-it
It makes me cringe
Gnawing my sleep

Autumnautumn the leaves burn out
Like the Decembrists' wives
Pursued across highways
With meat pies and children

A lively party raps at the ceiling
The party drills under the floor
To a drunken chorus, Chelentano
Dashes through mohair smoke

       Leap Up, you wily s.o.b.'s
       Cockroaches streaming along the wall
       Pestle Pestle I am Stamen
Where are you my Suliko-o-oh

How much food for parody
In an everyday house slipper
How much latent symmetry
How much latent heat
In the dark blue kiss
To the left jaw after tea

       Isn't It Not Huge

Probably a hundred times or more
Who, like a coffee table
Long-ong-ong necked and bundled
The satellite of its bed
Reasoning dust
These times are bigger than life
Like the deep pit of Fujiyama
Solveig's song is bigger than a song
Autumnautumn Pencil lead Snow

Translation from the Russian by Forrest Gander & Mala Kotamraju

POLYSTYLISTICS

Polystylistics   is when a knight from the Middle Ages
                  wearing shorts
                  storms into the wine section of store #13
                  located on Decembrists street
                  & cursing like one of the Court's nobles
                  he drops his copy of Landau & Lifshitz's "Quantum
                  Mechanics," where it falls on the marble floor

Polystylistics   is when one part of a dress
                  made of Dutch cotton
                  is combined with two parts
                  of plastic & glue
                  and in general, the remaining parts are missing
                    altogether
                  or dragging themselves along somewhere near
                  the rear end, while the clock strikes & snores
                  & a few guys look on

Polystylistics   is when all the girls are as cute
                  as letters
                  from the Armenian alphabet composed by Mesrop
                    Mashtoz
                  & the cracked apple's
                  no greater than any one of the planets
                  & the children's notes are turned inside out
                  as if in the air it would be easier to breathe like this

            & something is always humming
                          & buzzing
            just under the ear

Polystylistics   is a kind of celestial aerobics
            observed upon the torn backpack's
            back flap
            it's a law
            of cosmic instability
            & one of those simple-minded idiots who always
            begins his talk with the "F" word

Polystylistics   is when I want to sing
            & you want to go to bed with me
            & we both want to live
            forever

            After all, how was everything constructed
            if this is how it's all conceived
            How was everything imagined
            if it's still waiting to be established
            And if you don't care for it
            well then, it's not a button
            And if it's not turning
            don't dare turn it.

No, on earth no unearthliness exists
no pedestrian blushed as a piece of lath
Many sleep in leather & even less
        than a thousand maps are talking about war

Only your love
like a curious grandmother
running bare-legged & Fyodor Mikhailich Dostoevsky
could not hold back from shooting a glass of Kinzmarauly wine
to the health of ~~Tolstoy~~ the fat boy riding through his home town
Semipalatinsk, on a screeching bicycle

In Leningrad   & Samara   it's 17–19 degrees

In Babylon   it's midnight

On the Western Front   there are no changes

Translation from the Russian by John High

A poetic work is an equalization / where x equals any not-x / because and only because / for every unopening parachute / there is somewhere a spare skydiver

N. I.

Emerging in the last years of the Soviet Union—with its samizdat writings—she experienced the first upheavals of the post-Soviet period before her early death (age 43, of breast cancer). Of herself within her time she wrote: "The author belongs to the generation born in the 1950's and realizing its creative strivings in that period of our history that proved to be an epoch of sharply developed absurdism and carefully preserved principles of highly artistic stagnation. Being accustomed since childhood to the paradoxical phenomena of everyday life with their unforeseeable consequences, knowing how to get by in the majority of situations without common sense or psychological ease, with a strict immunity to all that can be had without struggle, that which is passed out one apiece—all of this sooner or later creates a corresponding supply of firmness, or, if you wish, a natural conservatism, protecting its bearer from simple decisions and direct paths to even the most obvious truths. This healthy conservatism lays a noticeable imprint on the stylistics and character of the depicted, and it also explains—metaphorically at least—a cluster of phenomena that defy more reasoned means of interpretation. Specifically, these are certain facts of the 'biography from the opposed.' Having obvious inclinations toward the humanities—toward literature, music, drawing, etc.—the author nonetheless spends six years studying at Moscow University in order to, having obtained a diploma in physics, never again return to the natural sciences, those ex-personal forms of interacting with the surrounding reality; having selected, as primary orientation, the word, and as shelter of necessity, the trivial pursuit of work as a translator of scientific and technical literature from English to Russian. A family and two children convincingly fill out the picture of a normal existence for a Russian woman in the contemporary literary process, an existence that was secret for many years and even almost shameful in the eyes of others, to reveal itself only in the past year or two with a few publications. Thus, it is not surprising that the author accepts any signs of attention paid to her humble persona with a certain dubiousness and perplexity; for this she offers excuses in the form of gratitude, and gratitude in the form of a text whose rehearsal coincides with its final result" (*a biography from the opposed*, 1989, translated by Anesa Miller-Pogacar).

TOWARD A CYBERPOETICS
The Poem in the Machine

First Collage: The Poem in the Machine

Man multiplied by the machine. New mechanical sense, a fusion of instinct with the efficiency of motor and conquered forces.

F. T. MARINETTI, 1913

Dictionary—
with films, taken close up, of parts of very large objects, obtain photographic records which no longer look like photographs of something. With these semi-microscopics constitute a dictionary of which each film would be the representation of a group of words in a sentence or separated so that this film would assume a new significance or rather that the concentration on this film of the sentences or words chosen would give a form of meaning to this film and that, once learned, this relation between film and meaning translated into words would be "striking" and would serve as a basis for a kind of writing which no longer has an alphabet or words but signs (films) already freed from the "baby talk" of all ordinary languages.—Find a means of filing all these films in such order that one could refer to them as in a dictionary.

MARCEL DUCHAMP, translated by Cleve Gray (from *A L'Infinitif*)

. . . around Bloomsday (June 16) 1989, Charles O. Hartman, a poet, critic, and professor (at Connecticut College in New London), sent me his computer program DIASTEXT, his first automation of one of the "diastic" text-selection and composition procedures that I had developed in January 1963 and had been using intermittently ever since.

When I use a diastic procedure, I read through a source text and take into my text various linguistic units, ranging from single words (*The Virginia Woolf Poems*, 1985), or even parts of words (*Words nd Ends from Ez*, 1989), to phrases, larger sentence fragments, and whole sentences, in which the letters of an "index" text appear in the letter and word strings drawn from the source text in places corresponding to those they occupy in the "index." . . .

DIASTEXT uses the whole source text as the "index"; a later version, DIASTEX4, sent to me in August 1989, allows the user to choose and employ a separate index text.

JACKSON MAC LOW

. . . there would be new documents, a new literary genre, of branching, non-sequential writings on the computer screen. . . . These branching documents would constitute a great new literature, but they would subsume the old, since all words, all literature would go on-line and extend to a new branching generality.

TED NELSON

Marcel Duchamp 1887–1968

ROTATIVE DEMI-SPHERE (PRECISION OPTICS) WITH PUN

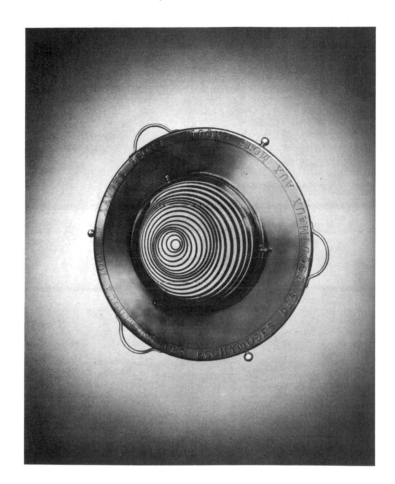

A white half-sphere is painted with black eccentric circles. The demi-sphere is fixed on a flat disc covered with black velvet. A ring of copper fitted with a glass dome covers and protects the demi-sphere and velvet. The outer edge of the copper ring is engraved: *Rrose Sélavy et moi esquivons les ecchymoses des esquimaux aux mots exquis.* The demi-sphere and pun rotate together when activated by a small electric motor at the foot of the metal stand. A rheostat adjusts speed.

(from *NOT SEEN and/or LESS SEEN of/by MARCEL DU-CHAMP/RROSE SELAVY,* 1965)

Abraham Lincoln Gillespie 1895–1950

from READIE-SOUNDPIECE
(FOR BOB BROWN'S READING MACHINE)

READIE-SOUNDPIECE   (after a suggestion of Hilaire Hiler) (synchro-with Orchestrauto maton)
                         A. Lincoln Gillespie, Jr.
(two chord-puffs, trumpets)   Snaredrum,stringplucks,mandoline) ⟶
        ↑   ↑   (PP)
POKER   . . . . .funny-   -post-adolesCollege-days- -Fall- -return-   -Glee
⟶

Club- -rehearse-   AssemblyHall- walk-fifteen-minutes- -FratHouse-   -supper-rush

        (insts.swoon)   (typewriters' clickpict ⟶
                             ↑
-eat-late-arrive-   -inside-   quantity-Freshmen-flit-past-
        <>   (fife-peers, à'la recherche intermingle)
                             ↑
-inaccountable-? ? ?   -evident-very-few-Glee-stragglers-   -rath-seem-wandbent-
                        (muHo-chords(bassoons,etc.)devel,30 seconds, a mood-view
                        ↑ chacinto an offkey-thResolution of Accordion&JewsHarp
-fulfill-YMCA,-nightclass-regs-   aiitiii-gone-
ing rhapsody)   (only a Metronome)   (smeasy fiddle-
                        ↑ LENTO
backstage-   -redescend-dark-redrich-theatre-plush-BoxCorridor- -EldChap-arrive-
-zizzes   <
flits-along-side= -rush-loatHe-despise-Silence-waft-acCompany-WONT-talk- -perforce-must

(muted Cornet whinds-in-up then ACCEL.) > out   (low Clarinets)
                        "Wal-I-see-the-boys-are-back-anybody-outa-this-bunch.

                        (fruity jabbu,lech-timbres-pianissimo <
                             ↑
catch-a-lil-poker-tonite ?"--- he'd-turned-to-me — — — me-curdonvulsed- -his-obstract-

<   SILENCE)   (Accordion
                                                             ↑
impersonaptriché-glaregloom-pleaVoice   I've-no-memory-of-his-look
grunts sillily)   (one whang-clash of Cymbals,delicato)
                             ↑
        funny. . . . . . .

(dullicate Gongflunets, each ictus) ⟶

/ / /

-I-smell-surmise-wopulent-finishalesman'd-Alumnus-   -CampusVisit-   "our-turn-Boys !"

/ / / (——) /

-deerol-Alumnibus-wants-tbe-youngear'd-again ! -chap-'bout-midforties-   -willing-lose-

(descrip

/ / / /

-careflingly-   -"listen-in-on-rehearsal,-ol'man-   afterwards-Gang-chez-moi

descripMusic,-Orchestra,-'Collegiat Sing Stare Serious' < 'Poko Party'

↑ (40-50 secs.)

(Music-sodgo-into-pedalpoint-2-basso-notes-   -superimposed-high-Arabic-wailMelod

LENTO   ⟶   dies

-hearable-only-distypewriter-ACCEL.&CRESC.-to-end.

In 1931 the American poet Bob Brown edited *Readies for Bob Brown's Machine,* a volume of experiments (by Gertrude Stein, Ezra Pound, Eugene Jolas, Kay Boyle, Robert McAlmon, William Carlos Williams, Charles Henri Ford etc.), in the uses of a tachistoscope-like, continuous flow reading machine: "a moving type spectacle . . . run[ning] on forever before the eye without having to be chopped up into columns, pars, etc." Of the poets presented therein, Gillespie singularly grasped the range of the situation & extended it to an investigation of the possibilities of simultaneous performance. In so doing he produced a kind of poem notation that others like Cage & Mac Low would develop at a later time. (J. R., Notes in *Revolution of the Word*)

Steve McCaffery b. 1947

from CARNIVAL THE FIRST PANEL: 1967–70

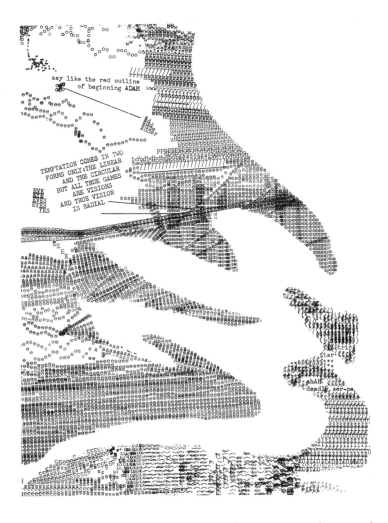

Typewriter functioning as instrument of composition—here in advance of the computer. Beyond which he writes, concerning the poem's total structure: "*Carnival* was planned as an anti-book typographic environment motivated by a desire to expand the concrete text beyond the single page parameters of the majority of visual poems. Designed as a book with perforated pages [to be torn out & re-aligned in sequence], the book must be destroyed in order to 'read' the piece."

Bernard Heidsieck b. 1928

from **CANAL STREET**

Canal Street 33/14

Flakes not of fabric but of words of fabric of words—scraps—remnants—rejects, exiles lost, expelled, limp corpses parcelled, recuperated—shabby packets—for what end? for what end? flakes, drastic cuts, of words of words—old bores, grey old writing, packed up—profitless recuperation?—but for what end? preserved—one never knows! but for what end?—placed in packets, conserved—but why?—for what end? if only I knew, you knew, he knew, she knew, we knew, you knew, they knew? can one ever know? set aside, set in reserve, as a pledge, as security—one never knows!—why worry—why not, indeed, horde up words, protect this raw material, peerless, indestructible, dependability more or less guaranteed! useful for all purposes—does one ever know?—unless . . . unless there's some ulterior motive there of conspiracy, of deception, of robbery or of speculation, unless the transistor is set beside these flakes, these embryonic phrases, on the sly, for better days, but to what end, once again, for what purpose, for what end? and that he should leave the others, all the others, which others? to flow, to pass, to rush, to race by, on his right or left indifferently or blindly—time will tell—all these flakes, embryonic, foundering, falling in these mini-refuges placed there by whose hands? and finally for what purpose? for what end? is this by chance? by some breakdown in time? in the machine? (how can one tell?), surging there, settling there, like that . . . as an effect of the . . . as an effect of . . . and then that's all! . . . was this at all useful? Was it really so? Zero.

Canal Street 39/27

Don't forget to ask him to send me all of his . . . / I should have given him . . . / don't budge! / quiet! / the teleprinters race on / would you have thought of telling him? / cut there! / don't forget when you see him! / I'll try to think of it! / he said too much! / we'll speak of this again / come on . . . out with it! / what do you want? / what did you want? / it's either too much or too little! / how do you reply to that? / one more word and I'm off / not another word about that / the teleprinters race on / I'd nevertheless made it quite clear to him . . . / what's your opinion? . . . / what do you think of . . . of . . . ? / all that's left is to dot the "i"s / not another word about that! / don't give it a thought! / he's up to his neck in it! / what do you want from him? / don't forget to tell him . . . / to tell them . . . / they'll know how to keep it in mind / what do you care? / quiet / keep it to yourself! / remember not a word! / I'm reliably informed that / what do you think of it? / that's a pack of lies! / let's treat it as a joke! / quiet . . . let's be careful! / he was on the brink of saying it . . . / of spilling the beans / turn it over then . . . / no such thing as . . . / you won't forget to tell him . . . / I don't understand a thing . . . / listen . . . it's so simple! / the teleprinters race on / I've had my fill! / tell him carefully . . . / just between the two of us . . . / is he in the know? / who's pulling the strings? / what did he tell you to send me? / spread the word! / from mouth to mouth / the teleprinters race on / he only had to ask me to tell him . . . / or to tell you . . . / would he have asked you . . . ? / what on earth can one make of it? / the teleprinters race on / I'll see him so that he tells you . . . / you should have told us that they . . . / have you clearly told them that . . . / that she told you . . . / or that he told us . . . / the teleprinters race on / or that they were told . . . / didn't he order you to . . . ? / the teleprinters race on . . .

Translation from the French by Nicholas Zürbrugg

"CANAL STREET" No 33 (reading 14) and "CANAL STREET" No 39 (reading 27) . . . are part of a series of 50 "writing/collages" made on boards in 1974 starting with a series of transistor radios found for next to nothing, just old transistors, in Canal Street, New York. Two years later, I decided to create a "reading" for and by the tape-recorder starting from these 50 "writing/collages," these 50 texts, associated with old transistors on boards. The 50 boards, and the 50 texts, merge via mixings into 35 "readings." Hence the double numbers indicated above.

Jackson Mac Low b. 1922

34TH MERZGEDICHT IN MEMORIAM KURT SCHWITTERS

Avant-garde snippet banal regarded both elements.

SOULFUL formal piece and
in conception.

Attached be illumined bourgeois forms.

Autres anything and conventional because beyond allowed could
pigment correct as on dance.

Dada between.

Blau found seems worked.

Allied and dance paradise between sleep could
FROM
FORCE.

Art and can because biomorphic allows bourgeois them whatever
and inchoate *wenn* banal believed sleep could formal
elements abstract and went idea bring blatant could
dismissed.

Rumpelstiltskin and in
construction creation blatant always could pigment correct.

Derived from my "*8th Merzgedicht* in Memoriam *Kurt Schwitters*" (6/24–29/87)
via Charles O. Hartman's text-selection program DIASTEX4 (an automation of
one of my diastic text-selection procedures developed in 1963), using the fictive
name "Anna Blume" as index, and minimal editing of the program's output.

31 August 1989
New York

Jim Rosenberg b. 1947

TWO INTERGRAMS

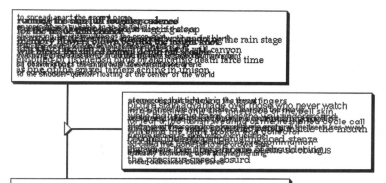

to breathe through the fingertip shining labyrinth skin
ringing against the anguish of being beached on the tremolo bank
with no vaulting shade against those unplanned ashes
that assert how the clown rule quiescent love ribs frame
fence denial deadweight lungs

how much exposure sail the compulsion to tease apart
perfectly healthy heart motor familiarity windings can stand
before having to magnify its radiance fall
to find out why the fine gossamer pain conceiving flying parts
wash to an undistinguished histrionic value smoke

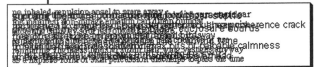

1993

John Cayley b. 1956

from ⟨REVEAL CODE⟩: INDRA'S NET VIII

Four Screen Shots

---

code key
even our most intimate
operations have always been
compromised by computers
readers must become ever-more
profoundly involved with
appropriate software

> Click central area continue. Click edges to END reading

---

and not mere simulacra of such
phenomena
real inscriptions
of information processing which
never have been and never will
be attained
computers have

> Click central area continue. Click edges to END reading

---

activity
her attention and media
but can't be a sinister tyrannical
conjunction
and control over her attention
and games may subvert
the core complex
lie

> Click central area continue. Click edges to END reading

pretends our most intimate
chaotic fantasies over the
sleepless matrix of cyberspace
we write with the need for the
composition
of such phenomena
real inscriptions of the reveal

Click central area continue. Click edges to END reading

1996

AUTHOR'S NOTE: *Indra's Net* pieces employ generative algorithms and semi-aleatory processes, and the composition of the algorithm is seen as an integral if normally invisible part of the composition of the piece. One of the unique facilities offered by the computer in this context is the ability to set up a feedback loop. "Experimental" texts can be generated and the results reviewed quickly and painlessly enough to allow the processes to be modified and improved. Once distributed, the pieces "run" and generate text for a reader. The reader can interact but does not choose pathways between words directly in the way that she might choose a pathway through the spaces of hypertext fiction. However in my most recent distributed piece, readers can alter the work itself (irreversibly), collecting generated lines or phrases for themselves and adding them to the hidden given text so that eventually their selections come to dominate the generative process. The reader's copy may then reach a state of chaotic stability, strangely attracted to one particular modulated reading of the original seed text.

Second Collage: Toward a Cyberpoetics

The cyborg appears in myth precisely where the boundary between human and animal is transgressed. Far from signaling a walling off of people from other living beings, cyborgs signal disturbingly and pleasurably tight couplings.

DONNA HARAWAY

The great poetry of the 1960s was created in resistance to the alphabet as a medium that had become dangerously fluent. By the 1970s, no one could resist. For the time being *poiesis* is in abeyance.

Now we gather the resources of modernism for the new medium as the poets of the sixteenth century gathered the resources of the classical tradition. Digital speech, musical sound, and image all merge in one grammar. The alphabet will continue in this mix for some time, but, in popular discourse, this obsolete mnemonic is even now largely decorative.

It remains to be found out if IBM, Microsoft, and the Turner Broadcasting Corporation have already coopted the renaissance.

DON BYRD

Poetry is not a circumstance of language. Rather, any possible circumstance of language is a possible circumstance of poetry. It is the job of the poet to invest that circumstance with energy. It is the job of the receiver to be open-minded about what circumstances of language may constitute poetry. This is the exact analogue of the idea that the domain of music is anything which may be heard, or that the domain of the visual arts is anything which may be seen. The page may be a wall or a computer screen or a street or a floor with words glued together in a pile so that not all of them can be read. This is not meant in any way to disparage the traditional page. If there can be such a thing as a conscientious avant-garde, then surely its purpose must be to expand the field of possibilities for making art, not to replace the existing set of possibilities with a new one, equally narrow. The house of poetry has room for everyone.

JIM ROSENBERG

Like the Irish king Cuchulain who fought the tide with his sword, they lose who would battle waves on the shores of light. The book is slow, the network is quick; the book is many of one, the network is many ones multiplied; the book is dialogic, the network polylogic.

MICHAEL JOYCE

Maggie O'Sullivan b. 1951

NARRATIVE CHARM FOR IBBOTROYD

Cobble & Pebble in the teeth. Fang & Club upon
a wind is the morning Fields Louded Ably Thus.

Snow of Earth bladder waking to a new Ear
when the stir of all Breath would to a Seeing turn,
wondered upon; housed many, unhurt is.

O, many berries, Occupying (& not), a Quarter-Day
heathered with Rawley Land of animal drumming many
gentled adjoining utterances.

Just as water does, between worlds, Giant eveyRUE BETHS here
edge the word. Crow trembles in the knot.

from **DOUBTLESS: ''The Dancer – ''**

The Dancer –

Jink –
Jointed
Uprised & Birth –

Stretching, Strung

Plover, low lowing in a far field
AY – PR – PRO – LONGED, LESQUING – OFF – OFF –
(fell, fell, soft)

An Oar Broken –
Axis
Drove Out –

(Recede, Approach, Recede)

(splotched, traction, trashing)

I ALWAYS IMAGINED
I SAW HIM –

BUT I NEVER DID –
HIS LYRIC
VOLUTED, CONGRESSED
INTO GOING –

GOING THE WAY
& THE MAPS ALL GONE,
GONE-IN NOW,
GONE-FROM,
GONE-BY –

GO –

HIS JUMP/HIS FALL/HIS LEG/
BROKEN
LUMINOUS, CHARRED IM-
POSSIBLE

THE COOL SHADES OF EVENING THEIR MANTLES WERE SPREADING,

HE SANG –

STIFFENED CROW
TO THE HAIL –
GARNET
AS HE AROSE –

AROSE, FRACTURED

PRECIPICE AJAR

HIS THROAT'S
WEPT
SEMI-SUNG
HALF-SUNG/HALF-SAID
SPOKES

HE SHOOK THE AIR –

       (WIRE
       ON ALL SIDES
       UNFIXED –
       & THE VAST
       CONVULSED
       GALE
       ASHORE –
       A WIND
       SUTURED –

       A WILD BOAR –
       A TAR
       OF
       RISING
       ROOKS –
       HIS TONGUE –
       MUTINOUS
       ASTRAY

ON
BREAD
&
THIRST

LIVERING –
CRACKING, PUNCHING
THE WORDS –

WINGBENT –
SHE –
SHRED HIND
PAPERING HAZEL
PICK
OF THE
BLUE FUSE
I HUG
TUMBLING TO
BLISTERWAYS &
LIP. LIPLING
LEAP HER AMONG HER LEAPT LIT –
SHE –
HER
SEVEN RAINBOWS
CANDLED
INTO
THE TOILING –

ELEGANCE – ELLEN DANCE – ELLEN SOUL – ELLEN SPEECH
ELLEN SONG –
ELLEN, MY NAMESAKE –
NAME'S ACHE –
SELF'S OTHER SELF –
ELLEN, HEARTH OF MY NAME –
HEART'S ACHE –

OF THE
LAMP'S
ROVED THREADS
& SMART
OVER FIELDS, HER PASSAGE
TIPPING THE GROUND –
HURTLE,
SCATTERING –

LOW BLACKISH
THAT –

MY SKULL'S
CAPE –

DRIVEN
IN THE RIP OF HER STOOPED HEAD –
HYMN
OF SICKLE –
STRIKING OUT OF ME –

Divination. Location. Is it the Thorn & Curse & Gap & Gone of my an-
cestors? Is it their thong & plight & flood of which still EM Embark &
fall through – the first ones to say a whole body of 'A RAINDROP
WINKING ON A THORN' – Excavation /
Exploration /
Experiment –
EXCLA
&

collaboration / incomplete / inexact / ENACTING
her own speech & even outside it?
M. O.

Of which inheritance she writes: "As to biog. I was born in 1951 in England
of southern Irish agricultural poor parents and it is their oral culture / the
struggle for voice despite centuries of repression which I feel has a lot to do
with my poetics." And still further: "What I do in language is centred on
exemplifying its oral, aural, visual, sculptural properties: language as vital
material, living substance. I am also concerned with Transformations, Cele-
brations, Performances of Language and its interconnectedness and inter-
dependence with other disciplines. My influences range from earlier and
primal poetries, calligraphies, Manley Hopkins and Basil Bunting to such
key modernist figures as Mallarmé, Khlebnikov, Stein, Joyce, Artaud, Beck-
ett, Schwitters, and Beuys." In this she is a prime example of a wide-ranging
modernism absorbed & brought into a new *post*modern framework—both
written/visual & intensely, even religiously, performative. In that interplay
between page & voice, writes Aaron Williamson, "the text itself comes
alive. The animals, insects and flora it invokes are not weighted with pro-
jected human qualities (as in 'nature poetry') but occupy a textual concur-
rency to which they are a nominal outreach, a linguistic enfleshing. We are
positioned into a language in which the non-human continues anterior to
its invocation and can survive being brushed by an alien language." Or
O'Sullivan again, of just such new/old visitations: "Poetry finds my life –
Poetry as she has Arisen 'AS SHE ARRIVES OUT OF THE FUTURE, WORDS
LIVING', moving my eye out among the ribbed & swimmish places // Un-
coiled, Endowed among us // in the arrival of // remembrancing   respond-
ing   realising   journeying."

Theresa Hak Kyung Cha 1951–1982

from **DICTÉE**

Elitere   Lyric Poetry

*Dead time. Hollow depression interred   invalid to resurgence, resistant
to memory. Waits. Apel. Apellation. Excavation. Let the one who is
diseuse. Diseuse de bonne aventure. Let her call forth. Let her break
open the spell cast upon time upon time again and again. With her voice,
penetrate earth's floor, the walls of Tartaurus to circle and scratch the
bowl's surface. Let the sound enter from without, the bowl's hollow its
sleep. Until.*

ALLER/RETOUR

Day recedes to darkness
Day seen through the veil of night
Translucent grey film cast between daylight and dark
dissolving sky to lavender
to mauve to white until night overcomes.

Hardly a murmur
Between dark and night
Suspend return of those who part with rooms
While shadows ascent   then equally fade
Suspension of the secret in abandoned rooms
Passing of secret unknown to those who part
Day receding to dark
Remove light   Re move sounds to far. To farther.
Absence full. Absence glow. Bowls. Left as they are.
Fruit as they are. Water in glass as beads rise to the rim.
Radiant in its immobility of silence.
As night re   veils the day.

Qu'est ce qu'on a vu
Cette vue qu'est ce qu'on a vu
enfin. Vu E. Cette vue. Qu'est ce que c'est enfin.
Enfin. Vu. Tout vu, finalement. Encore.
Immédiat. Vu, tout. Tout ce temps.
Over and over. Again and again.
Vu et vidé. Vidé de vue.
Dedans dehors. Comme si c'était jamais.
Comme si c'est vu pour la première fois.
C'était. C'était le passé.
On est deçu. On était deçu la vue
du dehors du dedans vitrail. Opaque. Ne reflète
jamais. Conséquemment
en suivant la vue absente
which had ceased to appear
already it has been
has been
has been without ever
occuring to itself that it should remember.
Sustain a view. Upon
itself. Recurring upon itself without
the knowledge of
its absent view.
The other side. Must have. Must be.
Must have been a side. Aside from
What has one seen
This view what has one viewed

Finally. View. This view. What is it finally.
Finally. Seen. All. Seen. Finally. Again.
Immediate. Seen. All. All the time.
Over and over. Again and again.
Seen and void. Void of view.
Inside outside. As if never.
As if it was seen for the first time.
It was. It was the past.
One is deceived. One was deceived of the view
outside inside stain glass. Opaque. Reflects
never. Consequently
following the absent view
which had ceased to appear
already it has been
has been.
Has been without ever

that. All aside. From then.
Point by point. Up to date. Updated.
The view.
Absent all the same. Hidden. Forbidden.
Either side of the view.
Side upon side. That which indicates the interior
and exterior.
Inside. Outside.
Glass. Drape. Lace. Curtain. Blinds. Gauze.
Veil. Voile. Voile de mariée. Voile de religieuse
Shade shelter shield shadow mist covert
screen screen door screen gate smoke screen
concealment eye shade eye shield opaque silk
gauze filter frost to void to drain to exhaust
to eviscerate to gut glazing stain glass glassy
vitrification.
what has one seen, this view
this which is seen housed thus
behind the veil. Behind the veil of secrecy. Under
the rose ala derobee beyond the veil
voce velata veiled voice under breath murmuration
render mute strike dumb voiceless tongueless

ALLER

Discard. Every memory. Of.
Even before they could.
Surge themselves. Forgotten so, easily,
not even as associations,
signatures in passage. Pull by the very root, the very
possible vagueness they may evoke.
Colors faintly dust against your vision.
Erase them.
Make them again white. You Re dust.
You fade.
Even before they start to take hue
Until transparent
into the white they vanish
white where they might impress
a different hue. A shadow.
Touch into shadow slight then re turn a new
shape enter again into deeper shadow
becoming full in its mould.
Release the excess air, release the space between
the shape and the mould.
Now formless, no more a mould.
Make numb some vision some word some part
resembling part something else
pretend
not to see pretend not having seen the part.
That part the only part too clear was all of it was the
first to be seen but pretend
it wasn't. Nothing at all.
It seemed to resemble but it wasn't.
Start the next line.
Might have been. Wanted to see it
Might have been. Wanted to have seen it
to have it happen to have it happen before. All of it.
Unexpected and then there
all over. Each part. Every part. One at a time
one by one and missing none. Nothing.
Forgetting nothing

Leaving out nothing.
But pretend
go to the next line
Resurrect it all over again.
Bit by bit. Reconstructing step by step
step
within limits
enclosed absolutely shut
tight, black, without leaks.
Within those limits,
resurrect, as much as
possible, possibly could hold
possibly ever hold
a segment of it
segment by segment
segmented
sequence, narrative, variation
on make believe
secrete saliva the words
saliva secrete the words
secretion of words flow liquid form
salivate the words
give light. Fuel. Enflame.
Dimly, dimly at first
then increase just a little more
volume then a little more
take it take it no further, shut it
off. To the limit before too late before too soon
to be taken away.

Something all along a germ. All along anew,
sprouting hair of a root. Something
takes only one to start.
Say, say so.
and it would be the word. Induce it to speak to take
to take it
takes.

Secrete saliva the words
Saliva secrete the words
Secretion of words flow liquid form
Salivate the words.

Dead gods. Forgotten. Obsolete. Past
Dust the exposed layer and reveal the
unfathomable
well beneath. Dead time. Dead gods. Sediment.
Turned stone. Let the one who is diseuse dust
breathe away the distance of the well. Let the one
who is diseuse again sit upon the stone nine days
and nine nights. Thus. Making stand again, Eleusis.

RETOUR

What of the partition. Fine grain sanded velvet wood and between the frames the pale sheet of paper. Dipped by hand over and over from the immobile water seemingly stagnant. By the swaying motion of two hands by two enter it back and forth the layers of film at the motion of a hundred strokes.

Stands the partition absorbing the light illuminating it then filtering it through. Caught in its light, you would be cast. Inside. Depending on the time. Of day. Darkness glows inside it. More as dusk comes. A single atmosphere breaks within it. Takes from this moment the details that call themselves the present. Breaking loose all associations, to the very memory, that had remained. The memory stain attaches itself and darkens on the pale formless sheet, a hole increasing its size larger and larger until it assimilates the boundaries and becomes itself formless. All memory. Occupies the entire.

Further and further inside, the certitude of absence. Elsewhere. Other than. Succession of occurrences before the partition. Away. A way for the brief unaccountable minutes in its clouding in its erasing of the present to yield and yield wholly to abandon without realizing even the depth of abandon.

You read you mouth the transformed object across from you in its new state, other than what it had been. The screen absorbs and filters the light dimming dimming all the while without resistance at the obvious transformation before the very sight. The white turns. Transparent. Immaterial.

If words are to be uttered, they would be from behind the partition. Unaccountable is distance, time to transport from this present minute.

If words are to be sounded, impress through the partition in ever slight measure to the other side the other signature the other hearing the other speech the other grasp.

Ever since the whiteness.
It retains itself, white,
unsurpassing, absent of hue, absolute, utmost
pure, unattainably pure.
If within its white shadow-shroud, all stain should
vanish, all past all memory of having been cast,
left, through the absolution and power of
these words.
Covering. Draping. Clothing. Sheathe. Shroud.
Superimpose. Overlay. Screen.
Conceal. Ambush.
Disguise. Cache. Mask. Veil.
Obscure. Cloud. Shade. Eclipse. Covert.

Dead words. Dead tongue. From disuse. Buried in
Time's memory. Unemployed. Unspoken. History.
Past. Let the one who is diseuse, one who is mother
who waits nine days and nine nights be found.
Restore memory. Let the one who is diseuse, one
who is daughter restore spring with her each ap-
pearance from beneath the earth.
The ink spills thickest before it runs dry before it
stops writing at all.

COMMENTARY

*From another epic another history. From the missing narrative. From the
multitude of narratives. Missing. From the chronicles. For another telling
for other recitations.*

T. H. K. C. (from *Dictée*)

If Pound's definition of "epic" as "a poem including history" is simple
enough to remain of use, it is the nature of that history (its "multitude" of
"missing narratives") that Cha's work brings strongly into question. Born
in Korea & coming to the U.S. at age 11—when she still spoke no English—
Cha (in poet Myung Mi Kim's words) "developed an extraordinary sensi-
tivity to the struggle and meaning of acquiring language and attempting its

transformative use in a culture which marked her—the speaker—as marginal." Her work as an artist was principally in film & video, performance art & installation, but culminated in a single written work, *Dictée*, published the year before her murder in New York—the victim of an act of random violence. The book's title speaks to the practice of dictation (French: *dictée*) that marks the indoctrination through language (for her the French taught in Korean [Catholic] mission schools) but rhymes as well with the name of the Cretan goddess (Dikte) "whom Minos pursued for nine months until, about to be overtaken, she hurled herself from a cliff into the sea" (Walter K. Lew). That act—of victimization—also finds its correspondences in the martyred heroines of *Dictée*, a work in the great modernist/ postmodernist tradition of genre blurring, "fragmented recitation and episodic non-identity . . . an aesthetic of infidelity" (Lisa Lowe), "not paying homage to points fixed in time but rather suggesting that history defies linearity" (Myung Mi Kim). Writes Susan Wolf in summary: "[*Dictée* is] uncategorizable, merging different forms of writing, visual forms, and kinds of information. On one level it is about time, memory, and language. On another it is about Korean history and it can also be read as an autobiography and biography of several women: Cha's mother, Joan of Arc, St. Theresa, the Korean revolutionary Yu Guan Soon, and Hyung Soon Huo, daughter of first-generation Korean exiles born in Manchuria. These are intricately interwoven as the text shifts from prose to prose poetry, from images to words, from history to fiction, and from past to present."

POSTLUDES

At the Turning

Robert Duncan 1919–1988

AFTER A LONG ILLNESS

No faculty not   ill at ease
            lets us
            begin where I must

from the failure of systems   breath
            less,   heart
            and lungs water-logd.

Cloggd with light chains   the kidneys'
            condition is terminal   life

the light and the heavy, the light
            and dark.   It has always been
close upon a particular Death, un
            disclosed   what's behind

seeing, feeling, tasting, smelling   —that Cloud!

For two years
bitterness pervaded:

in the physical body   the high   blood pressure
            the accumulation of toxins, the
            break-down of ratios,

in the psyche   "stewd in its own juices"
            the eruption of hatreds,   the prayer
—I didn't have a prayer—   your care
            alone kept my love clear.

I will be there again   the ways
            must become crosst   and again
            dark passages,   dangerous straits.

My Death attended me and I knew
            I was not going to die,
nursed me thru.   Life took hold.
            What I ate   I threw up
and crawld thru as if turnd inside out.

Every thought I had I saw
sickend me.   Secretly
        in the dark   the filters
        of my kidneys   petrified   and my Death
rearranged the date He has with me.

            •

Yes, I was afraid
of not seeing you again,   of being
        taken away, not
of dying, the specter I have long
        known as my Death is the
Lord of a Passage that unites us;
        but of
        never having come to you that other
specter of my actually living is.
        Adamant.

"I have given you a cat in the dark," the voice said.
Everything changed in what has always been there
at work in the Ground: the two titles
        "Before the War",   and now, "In the Dark"
underwrite the grand design.   The magic
        has always been there,   the magnetic purr
        run over me, the feel as of cat's fur
charging the refusal to feel.   That black stone,
        now I see, has its electric familiar.

In the real I have always known myself
        in this realm where no Wind   stirs
        no Night
turns in turn to Day,   the Pool of the motionless water,
        the absolute Stillness.   In the World, death after death.
In this realm,   no last thrall of Life stirs.
        The imagination alone knows this condition.
As if this were before the War,   before
        What Is,   in the dark this state
that knows nor sleep nor waking, nor dream
        —an eternal arrest.

Pierre Joris b. 1946

FIN-DE-SIÈCLE IDENTIKIT

for Thomas Meyer

This is my age
this is what Sibelius wrote at 36
sibilant Sibelius easy
lure easily
resisted twisted towards
another mood
this is no longer 1901
cannot transcribe it
this his second symphony
am pulled in by number
dirt dangling from roots
(no number is pure number—
the root of this century
dangling pull it up
never liked what his music
but listen to the craft
of exact number
raft of an age
godtack days when an
english sun belies
the upstairs bedroom
where you lie
empty & full of
the drug of sleep
the day passes
from one room to the next
pass the book discarded at
midnight drink wine pass
water pass the closed door
pass the salt the bread
some vomit with ease
some put it away
where it hurts
Sibelius's fin-de-siècle
syllabary,

Tom's gift, who made
bourride with aïoli
two years running, stuck
as he is in Arcady,
a green place, not finnish
not english, "every holy Moslem
child's idea of Paradise"
you dream of it now upstairs
while here afternoon audience claps
incongruous world in concert
back now to Ives Webern Nono
the records mouldered
by English weather mushrooms
colonize the rifts
and valleys of his master's
voice as french a word
as this wine is italian
have no celtic
sense—lied that once—
teuton, not teton either
that boringly dutch
flat minds need
genever to curve the
horizon where
Vincent's ear rises & sets
apocryphal son
like words fingers in a
dyke he was
I am told
an anabaptist had
to flee
the Lowlands made Basel
this made-up ancestor
down through the
Middle Kingdom's water-ways
on hasty rafts of what wood
& heard & didn't hear
Kaspar's story
blind leader of a berber caravan
I speak in voices
always always
other people's voices

a thousand mouths
on this Gorgo-head
& now have let the I
out will
stand by it for a minute
will whisper into the sun's
ear my care
"to write
"every day
"to drink wine
"every day
"two actions
"hold me
"a vertical
"vertigo
"a matter of
"spines
"&
"esses
"smooth
"curvatures
as in this Mosel glass
a grape garland
lightly grasps
the rim
as I grasp at any
straw my luck
my vocabulary
deserts me
before it slurs
A L D E B A R A N
A L D E B R A N
plucked that luck
or star from your shoulder
rode with it upcountry
on a raft made
from the skin
of our teeth
wrote it to its
source & the source of
the water was the same
as the source of

the skin it poured
from the pierced
lobe of the solitary
ear a flesh-jewel set
in the horizon's
curve a vista listens
to a voice the background
music still Sibelius
a fakeness there
a prettyness
our age no longer
holds distrusts as
much as the night
upstairs, upstars
darkened room at noon
as 300 years ago
the raft out of Amsterdam
beached in Basel
a fast film a life
of preaching a single-minded
community
the death of one Joris
so feared by the burghers
of Basel he's the only
3 years post-mortem
auto-da-fé on record
the light of that pyre
sings in Vincent's ear
as we collide on
a curved now near
circular event
horizon now
the violins are
shrieking maggots
crawling towards
the end of another century & now
the 2 am news brings
tidings of
this fin-de-siècle
Menschendämmerung
outside.

Jerome Rothenberg b. 1931

PROLOGOMENA TO A POETICS

for Michael McClure

. . . .

Poet man walks between dreams
He is alive, he is breathing freely
thru a soft tube like a hookah.
Ashes fall around him as he walks
singing above them.
Oh how green
the sun is where it marks
the ocean.
Feathers drift atop the hills
down which the poet man
keeps walking, walking
a step ahead of what he fears,
of what he loves.

. . . .

Why has the poet failed us?
Why have we waited, waited for the word to come again?
Why did we remember what the name means
only to now forget it?
If the poet's name is god how dark the day is
how heavy the burden is he carries with him.
All poets are jews, said Tsvetayeva.
The god of the jews is jewish, said a jew.
It was white around him & his voice
was heavy,
like a poet's voice in winter,
old & heavy,
crackling,
remembering frozen oceans in a summer clime,
how contrary he felt
how harsh the suffering was in him,
let it go!
The poet is dreaming about a poet
& calls out.
Soon he will have forgotten who he is.

Speak to the poet's mother,
she is dead now.
So many years ago she left her father's clime.
His *father* too.
The tale of wandering is still untold,
untrue. The tale of who you are,
the tale of where the poem can take us,
of where it stops
& where the voice stops.
The poem is an argument with death.
The poem is priceless.
Those who are brought into the poem can never leave it.
In a silver tux the poet in the poem by Lorca
walks down the hall to greet the poet's bride.
The poet sees her breasts shine in the mirror.
Apples as white as boobs,
says Lorca.
He is fed the milk of paradise,
the dream of every poet man
of every poet bride.
The band plays up
the day unstops & rushes out to greet
another night.

. . . .

Is the black poet
black?
And is the creation of his hands & throat
a black creation?
Yes, says the poet man
who wears three rings,
the poet man who seeks the precious light,
passes the day beside a broken door
no one can enter. Hold it shut,
the god cries & the jew rolls over
in his endless sleep.
Gods like little wheels glide past him
down the mountain road where cats live
in a cemetery guarded by his father's star,

a poet & a bride entangled in the grass,
his hands are black
his eyes the whitest white
& rimmed with scarlet.
Hear the drumbeat,
heart.
The blacks have landed on the western shore
the long lost past of poetry revives.

. . . .

Our fingers fail us.

Then tear them off! the poet cries
not for the first time.
The dead are too often seen filling our streets,
who hasn't seen them?
A tremor across the lower body,
always the image of a horse's head
& sandflies.
A woman's breast & honey.
She in whose mouth the murderers stuffed gravel
who will no longer speak.
The poet is the only witness to that death,
writes every line
as though the only witness.

Permission for the inclusion in this gathering of the following material has been graciously granted by the publishers and individuals indicated below.

Chinua Achebe: "Bull and Egret" and "We Laughed at Him" reprinted by permission of the author.

Adonis: Extract from "A Desire Moving through the Maps of the Material" reprinted by permission of Allen Hibbard and Osama Isber. Extracts from "Preface" reprinted with permission.

Anna Akhmatova: "Epilogue" from *"Poem without a Hero" and Selected Poems*, translated by Lenore Mayhew and William McNaughton. Field Translation Series #14. Copyright © 1989 Oberlin College Press.

Anne-Marie Albiach: "Winter Voyage" from *Mezza Voce* (Sausalito, California: The Post-Apollo Press, 1988). Reprinted by permission of The Post-Apollo Press.

Pierre Alechinsky: "Ad Miró" reprinted by permission of Harry N. Abrams, Inc., and Michael Fineberg.

Will Alexander: "Albania & the Death of Enver Hoxha" reprinted by permission of the author.

Yehuda Amichai: "National Thoughts," "Elegy," and "Near the Wall of a House" from *The Selected Poetry of Yehuda Amichai* (Berkeley: University of California Press, 1996). Reprinted by permission of the author.

Bruce Andrews: "'Zero Tolerance'" and "AKA" reprinted by permission of the author.

David Antin: "Endangered Nouns" reprinted by permission of the author.

Karel Appel: "Mad Talk" reprinted from *Nine Dutch Poets*, copyright © 1982 by City Lights Books. Reprinted by permission of City Lights Books.

Rae Armantrout: "Native" from *Made to Seem* (Los Angeles: Sun & Moon Press, 1995), pp. 29–30. Copyright © 1995 by Rae Armantrout. Reprinted by permission of the publisher.

Antonin Artaud: Three sections from "To Have Done with the Judgment of God." Reprinted from *Watchfiends & Scream Racks*, translated by Clayton Eshleman (Exact Change, 1995). Reprinted by permission of Editions Gallimard.

H. C. Artmann: "an optician has a glass heart" from *6 Major Austrian Poets*, edited and translated by Rosmarie Waldrop & Harriet Watts (Barrytown, New York: Sta-

Clayton Eshleman: "Our Lady of the Three-Pronged Devil" copyright © 1986 by Clayton Eshleman. Reprinted from *The Name Encanyoned River: Selected Poems, 1960–1985* with the permission of Black Sparrow Press.

Robert Filliou: Extract from *14 Songs and 1 Riddle* reprinted with the permission of Karl Young.

Ian Hamilton Finlay: "The Garden Temple," "Poster Poem," extract from *Images from the Arcadian Dream Garden*, and extract from *Heroic Emblems* reproduced with the permission of Ian Hamilton Finlay.

Allen Fisher: "Conga" and "Continental Walk" reprinted with the permission of the author.

Fujii Sadakazu: "Wolf" and "Small Dream" from *The New Poetry of Japan*, translated by Christopher Drake. Reprinted by permission of Katydid Books.

Ilse Garnier and Pierre Garnier: "Extension 2" and extract from *Poèmes franco-japonais* (with Seiichi Nikuni) reprinted by permission of the authors.

Claude Gauvreau: "Trustful Fatigue and Reality" and "The Leg of Mutton Créateur" reprinted from *Entrails*, translated by Ray Ellenwood (Exile Editions). Reprinted by permission of Ray Ellenwood and Janine Carreau.

Allen Ginsberg: "Mescaline" from *Collected Poems, 1947–1980;* copyright © 1959 by Allen Ginsberg. "Kral Majales" from *Collected Poems, 1947–1980;* copyright © 1965 by Allen Ginsberg. "America" from *Collected Poems, 1947–1980;* copyright © 1956, 1959 by Allen Ginsberg. Extract from "Howl" from *Collected Poems 1947–1980;* copyright © 1955 by Allen Ginsberg. All reprinted with the permission of Allen Ginsberg and HarperCollins.

Edouard Glissant: Extract from *Earth* reprinted with permission by Editions Gallimard and translator.

Eugen Gomringer: "mist/mountain/butterfly" and "hang and swinging hang and swinging" reprinted with the permission of the author.

Gu Cheng: "A Generation" and extracts from "The Bulin File" from T. Barnstone, ed., *Out of the Howling Storm*. Reprinted with the permission of Wesleyan University Press.

Pierre Guyotat: Extract from *Tales of Samora Machel* reprinted with the permission of the author and translator.

H.D.: "Red Rose and a Beggar 1–9" from *Hermetic Definition*. Copyright © 1972 by Holmes Norman Pearson. Reprinted by permission of New Directions Publishing Corp.

Paavo Haavikko: Two poems from "The Winter Palace" from Paavo Haavikko, *Selected Poems* (Manchester: Carcanet Press, 1991), translated from the Finnish by Anselm Hollo. Reprinted by permission of the author and translator.

Unsi al-Hajj: "The Charlatan" reprinted with the permission of Pierre Joris.

Carla Harryman: "Not-France" copyright © 1995 by Carla Harryman. Reprinted by permission of City Lights Books.

Bernard Heidsieck: Extracts from *Canal Street* and from *Derviche / Le Robert* reprinted by permission of the author.

Helmut Heissenbüttel: "Didactic Poem on the Nature of History, A.D. 1954" from *Textbücher 1–6*. Klett-Cotta, Stuttgart, 1980. "Combination II" from *Kombinationen*, 1954. Extract from "Textbook 10" from *Textbuch 10*. Von Liebeskunst. Klett-Cotta. Stuttgart, 1986. Reprinted with the permission of Klett-Cotta.

Lyn Hejinian: Extracts from *My Life* (Los Angeles: Sun & Moon Press, 1991), pp. 56–

58. Copyright © 1991 by Sun & Moon Press. Reprinted by permission of the author and the publisher. Extract from *Oxota* reprinted by permission of the author.

Dick Higgins: "Intermedia Chart" reprinted with permission of the author.

Vladimir Holan: Extract from *A Night with Hamlet* reprinted by permission of Clayton Eshleman.

Susan Howe: Extract from "Pythagorean Silence" from Susan Howe, *The Europe of Trusts* (Los Angeles: Sun & Moon Press, 1990), pp. 36–37. Copyright © 1990 by Sun & Moon Press. Reprinted by permission of the author and the publisher. "Scattering as Behavior toward Risk" from *Singularities*, pp. 63–70. Reprinted by permission of the author.

Kenneth Irby: "I met the Angel Sus on the Skin Bridge," "slowly the old stone building walls downtown dissolve," "[trash]," and "[three sets of three]" reprinted by permission of the author.

Nina Iskrenko: "Isn't She Not a Bird" and "Polystylistics" reprinted by permission of *Five Fingers Review*.

Itō Hiromi: "Near Kitami Station on the Odakyū Line" reprinted by permission of the author.

Edmond Jabès: "The Jew answers every question," "The Book of the Living," and "Have you seen how a word is born and dies?" from *The Book of Questions*. Reprinted by permission of Rosmarie Waldrop and University Press of New England.

Ernst Jandl: "Chanson," "Calypso," and "Preliminary Studies for the Frankfurt Reading 1984" copyright © 1985 Hermann Luchterhand Verlag GmbH and Co. KG, Darmstadt und Neuwied. All rights reserved: Luchterhand Literaturverlag GmbH, München.

Robert Johnson: "Hellhound on My Trail" reprinted from Eric Sackheim, *The Blues Line* (1969), with the permission of Eric Sackheim.

Pierre Joris: Extract from "Winnetou Old" and "Fin-de-Siècle Identikit" reprinted by permission of the author.

Asger Jorn, with Christian Dotrement: Extract from "Word-Pictures" from *Cobra*, p. 10, Sotheby Publishing, edited by Jean-Clarence Lambert. Reprinted by permission of Jean-Clarence Lambert.

James Joyce: Extract from *Finnegans Wake* reprinted by permission of Faber & Faber, Viking Penguin, and Stephen Joyce.

Marie Luise Kaschnitz: "My Ground" and "Who Would Have Thought It" from *Selected Later Poems of Marie Luise Kaschnitz*, translated by Lisel Mueller. Copyright © 1980 by Princeton University Press. Reprinted by permission of Princeton University Press.

Bob Kaufman: "I AM A CAMERA," "All those ships that never sailed," and "January 30, 1976: Message to Myself" from *The Ancient Rain: Poems 1956–1978*. Copyright © 1981 by Bob Kaufman. Reprinted by permission of New Directions Publishing Corp.

Robert Kelly: "Ode to Language" copyright © 1983 by Robert Kelly. Reprinted from *Under Words* with the permission of Black Sparrow Press. "The Man Who Loved White Chocolate" copyright © 1995 by Robert Kelly. Reprinted from *Red Actions: Selected Poems, 1960–1993* with the permission of Black Sparrow Press.

Jack Kerouac: One chorus from *Mexico City Blues* reprinted with the permission of Sterling Lord Literistic.

Mohammed Khaïr-Eddine: "Refusal to Inter" and "Barbarian" from *Soleil Arachnide* (Editions du Seuil), pp. 24–30. Translations printed by permission of Pierre Joris.

Yusuf al-Khal: "Cain the Immortal" and "The Wayfarers" reprinted by permission of Samuel Hazo and the International Poetry Forum.

Sarah Kirsch: "The wels a fish that lives on the bottom," "In an airplane I'm supposed to," "Pandora's Box," "Mornings," "Call," and "Renting a Room" from *Conjurations: The Poems of Sarah Kirsch*, selected and translated by Wayne Kvam (Athens: Ohio University Press, 1985). Reprinted with the permission of Ohio University Press/Swallow Press, Athens.

Gerrit Kouwenaar: "Elba" and "4 Variations On" from *Dutch Interiors*, edited by James S. Holmes and William Jay Smith. Copyright © 1984 by Columbia University Press. Reprinted by permission of the publisher.

Denise Levertov: "The Jacob's Ladder" from *Poems, 1960–1967*. Copyright © 1961 by Denise Levertov. Reprinted by permission of New Directions Publishing Corp. "Age of Terror" from *Candles in Babylon*. Copyright © 1982 by Denise Levertov. Reprinted by permission of New Directions Publishing Corp.

Lucebert: "Rousseau le Douanier" and "9000 Jackals Swimming to Boston" reprinted with permission of Peter Nijmeijer.

Hugh MacDiarmid: "The Glass of Pure Water" from Hugh MacDiarmid, *Collected Poems*. Reprinted by permission of Carcanet Press Limited.

George Maciunas: "A Manifesto for Fluxus." February 1963. Reproduced by permission of The Gilbert and Lila Silverman Fluxus Collection, Detroit.

Nathaniel Mackey: "Song of the Andoumboulou: 15" from *School of Udhra*, copyright © 1993 by Nathaniel Mackey. Reprinted by permission of City Lights Books.

Jackson Mac Low: "Asymmetry 205" copyright © 1980 by Jackson Mac Low, when included in his *Asymmetries 1–260* (New York: Printed Editions, 1980). "1ST DANCE—MAKING THINGS NEW—6 February 1964" and "2ND DANCE—SEEING LINES—6 February 1964" copyright © 1964, 1971, 1979 by Jackson Mac Low, when included in the three editions of his *The Pronouns—A Collection of 40 Dances—for the Dancers* (third edition: Barrytown, N.Y.: Station Hill Press, 1979). "3rd Light Poem: for Spencer, Beate, & Sebastian Holst—12 June 1962" copyright © 1968 by Jackson Mac Low, when included in his *22 Light Poems* (Los Angeles: Black Sparrow Press, 1968). "Pieces o' Six—II" copyright © 1992 by Jackson Mac Low, when included in *Pieces o' Six: Thirty-three Poems in Prose (1983–1987)* (Los Angeles: Sun & Moon Press, 1992). The "*34th Merzgedicht* in Memoriam *Kurt Schwitters*" copyright © 1994 by Jackson Mac Low, when published in his *42 Merzgedichte* in Memoriam *Kurt Schwitters (February 1987–September 1989)* (Barrytown, N.Y.: Station Hill Press, 1994). All works reproduced by the author's permission; "Pieces o' Six—II" also by permission of Sun & Moon Press.

Muhammad al-Maghut: "Executioner of Flowers" from *The Fan of Swords*, edited by Salma Khadra Jayyusi, 1991. Reprinted by permission of Three Continents Press.

Mang Ke: "ApeHerd" from T. Barnstone, ed., *Out of the Howling Storm*. Reprinted by permission of Wesleyan University Press.

Joyce Mansour: "In the Gloom on the Left" and "Going and Coming of Sequins" first appeared in *The American Poetry Review*. Copyright © 1994, 1997 Molly Bendall. Reprinted by permission of the author.

Friederike Mayröcker: "Ostia Will Receive You" from Beth Bjorklund, ed., *Contemporary Austrian Poetry* (1986). Reprinted by permission of Associated University Presses. "the spirit of '76" reprinted by permission of Anselm Hollo.

Steve McCaffery: Extracts from "Text-Sound, Energy and Performance" and "Carnival the First Panel: 1967–70" reprinted by permission of the author.

Michael McClure: "A Small Secret Book" and extracts from *Ghost Tantras* reprinted by permission of the author.

David Meltzer: "The Third Shell" reprinted from *Hero/Lil* by permission of the author.

Henri Michaux: Extract from *Saisir* reprinted by permission of Fata Morgana.

Miss Queenie (Imogene Elizabeth Kennedy): "One Day" from Kamau Brathwaite, *History of the Voice* (New Beacon Books, Ltd.). Reprinted by permission of Kamau Brathwaite.

Pablo Neruda: "Come with me, American love" from *The Heights of Macchu Picchu*, published by Farrar Straus & Giroux. Translation copyright © Nathaniel Tarn.

Giulia Niccolai: "From the Novissimi" reprinted by permission of Paul Vangelisti.

bp Nichol: Three poems from *The Martyrology 7* reprinted by permission of the Estate of bp Nichol.

Alice Notley: Extracts from "Désamère" reprinted by permission of the author.

Frank O'Hara: "The Day Lady Died" copyright © 1964 by Frank O'Hara. Reprinted by permission of City Lights Books. "Homosexuality" and "Ode: Salute to the French Negro Poets" from *Collected Poems of Frank O'Hara*, published by Alfred A. Knopf. Reprinted by permission of Alfred A. Knopf.

Charles Olson: "La Préface" and "The Moon Is the Number 18" from *The Collected Poetry of Charles Olson*, edited by George Butterick (Berkeley: University of California Press). Copyright © 1987 Estate of Charles Olson. "my memory is . . . ," "Peloria . . . ," "Maximus, from Dogtown—II," and "Added to . . ." from *The Maximus Poems* (Berkeley: University of California Press). Three statements reprinted with permission.

Ōoka Makoto: "Marilyn" reprinted by permission of Katydid Books.

George Oppen: "Psalm" and "Myth of the Blaze" from George Oppen, *Collected Poems*. Copyright © 1975 by George Oppen. Reprinted by permission of New Directions Publishing Corp.

Simon Ortiz: "The Wisconsin Horse" and "Final Solution: Jobs, Leaving" from *Woven Stone* (Tucson: University of Arizona Press, 1992). Reprinted by permission of the author.

Maggie O'Sullivan: "Narrative Charm for Ibbotroyd" is from *In the House of the Shaman* (London: Reality Street Editions, 1993). "Doubtless: 'The Dancer–'" is from *Palace of Reptiles* (Los Angeles: Sun & Moon Press, forthcoming). Reprinted by permission of the author.

Rochelle Owens: "Dedication" and "I Am the Babe of Joseph Stalin's Daughter" from *I Am the Babe of Joseph Stalin's Daughter*, copyright © 1972 by Rochelle Owens. Reprinted by permission of the author. "It is for me poetry" from *W. C. Fields in French Light*, copyright © 1986 by Rochelle Owens. Reprinted by permission of the author.

Michael Palmer: "Sun" and extract from *Sun* reprinted by permission of the author.

Nicanor Parra: "The Individual's Soliloquy" reprinted by permission of Allen Ginsberg. "Test" translated by Miller Williams. Reprinted from *Poems and Antipoems*, New Directions.

Jerome Rothenberg: "That Dada Strain" from *That Dada Strain*, copyright © 1983 by Jerome Rothenberg. "Dos Oysleydikn," "Dos Geshray," and "Dibbikim" from *Khurbn and Other Poems*, copyright © 1989 by Jerome Rothenberg. "First New York Poem" from *The Lorca Variations*, copyright © 1993 by Jerome Rothenberg. "Prolegomena to a Poetics" from *Seedings and Other Poems*, copyright © 1996 by Jerome Rothenberg. All reprinted by permission of New Directions Publishing Corp.

Jacques Roubaud: Extract from *Some Thing Black* reprinted by permission of The Dalkey Archive Press.

Gerhard Rühm: "Flower Piece" and "A Few Things" reprinted by permission of Station Hill Press and Rosmarie Waldrop.

Muriel Rukeyser: "The Speed of Darkness" reprinted by permission of William L. Rukeyser.

María Sabina: Extract from *The Midnight Velada* reprinted by permission of Henry Munn.

Edward Sanders: Extract from *Investigative Poetry* reprinted by permission of the author.

Edoardo Sanguineti: "The Last Stroll: Homage to Pascoli" translated by Richard Collins. From *The Audience in the Labyrinth: Italian Poetry after 1975*, edited by Luigi Ballerini, Elena Coda, Paola Balera, and Paul Vangelisti (Los Angeles: Sun & Moon Press, 1997). Reprinted by permission of the publisher.

Badr Shakir al-Sayyab: "The River and Death" reprinted by permission of Pierre Joris.

Leslie Scalapino: "Instead of an Animal" reprinted by permission of the author.

Bert Schierbeek: "The Sun: Day" and "The Animal Has Drawn a Human" from *From Formentera* (followed by *The Gardens of Suzhou*). Copyright © 1984, 1986 by Bert Schierbeek. Translation copyright © 1989 by Charles McGeehan and Guernica Editions. Reprinted by permission of Guernica Editions.

Carolee Schneemann: "Interior Scroll" reproduced by permission of Carolee Schneemann.

Armand Schwerner: Extracts from *The Tablets*, copyright © Armand Schwerner. Reprinted by permission of the author.

Anne Sexton: Poems from *The Jesus Papers* reprinted by permission of Sterling Lord Literistic, Inc. Copyright © 1972 by Anne Sexton.

Shiraishi Kazuko: "The Man Root" from Kazuko Shiraisi, *Seasons of Sacred Lust*. Copyright © 1975 by Kazuko Shiraishi and 1978 by New Directions. Reprinted by permission of New Directions Publishing Corp.

Shu Ting: "The Mirror" from *Red Azalea*, edited by Edward Morin (University of Hawaii Press). Copyright © University of Hawaii Press. Reprinted with permission.

Ron Silliman: Extract from *Ketjak* reprinted by permission of the author.

Gary Snyder: "What You Should Know to Be a Poet" from *Regarding Waves*, copyright © 1970 by Gary Snyder. Reprinted by permission of New Directions Publishing Corp. "first shaman song" and "this poem is for bear" from *Myths & Texts*, copyright © 1978 by Gary Snyder. Reprinted by permission of New Directions Publishing Corp. "The Hump-backed Flute Player" from *Mountains and Rivers without End;* copyright © 1996 Gary Snyder. Published by Counterpoint. Reprinted by permission.

Göran Sonnevi: "Demon colors, dark" and "A Child Is Not a Knife" from *A Child Is Not a Knife: Selected Poems of Göran Sonnevi*, translated and edited by Rika Lesser.

JEROME ROTHENBERG is an internationally known poet and one of the world's leading anthologists. Among his more than sixty books of poetry and seven groundbreaking anthologies are *Technicians of the Sacred: A Range of Poetries from Africa, America, Asia, Europe and Oceania* (California, 1985), *Revolution of the Word: American Avant-Garde Poetry between the Two World Wars* (1974), and *Shaking the Pumpkin: Traditional Poetry of the Indian North Americas* (1986). He is Professor of Visual Arts and Literature at the University of California, San Diego. PIERRE JORIS has published more than twenty books of poetry, several anthologies of contemporary European and American poetry, and numerous volumes of translations (most recently of books by Paul Celan, Maurice Blanchot, and Edmond Jabès). He is Associate Professor of English at the State University of New York, Albany. The editors' previous collaboration, *PPPPPP: Poems Performance Pieces Proses Plays Poetics*, by Kurt Schwitters (1993), won the 1994 PEN Center USA West Literary Award for Translation.

Designer: Nola Burger
Compositor: G&S Typesetters, Inc.
Text: 10/13 Sabon
Display: Gill Sans Condensed Bold
Printer and binder: Bookcrafters, Inc.

POEMS FOR THE MILLENNIUM, VOLUME ONE
FROM FIN-DE-SIÈCLE TO NEGRITUDE

Edited by Jerome Rothenberg and Pierre Joris

Poems for the Millennium is the first global anthology of twentieth-century poetry. Volume one offers three "galleries" of individual poets—figures such as Mallarmé, Stein, Rilke, Tzara, Mayakovsky, Pound, H. D., Vallejo, Artaud, Césaire, and Tsvetayeva—along with a sampling of the most significant pre–World War II movements in poetry and the other arts: Futurism, Expressionism, Dada, Surrealism, "Objectivism," Negritude.

"Looking back from the end of the century we can begin to see how partial our views of its literary happenings have been: how time-bound, tongue-bound, often celebrity-bound. In an accurately titled *Poems for the Millennium* we can at last sense the scope of the Revolution of the Word that's been in process since—oh, 1895. There's no other anthology like this one, no other overview so venturesome."
—HUGH KENNER

To order please call 1-800-822-6657,
or visit our website at <www.ucpress.edu> or your local bookstore.